THE ESSAY CONNECTION

Readings for Writers

EIGHTH EDITION

Lynn Z. Bloom
The University of Connecticut

Houghton Mifflin Company
Boston   New York

Editor-in-Chief: Suzanne Phelps Weir
Development Manager: Sarah Helyar Chester
Assistant Editor: Anne Leung
Editorial Associate: John McHugh
Senior Project Editor: Rosemary R. Jaffe
Editorial Assistant: Deborah Berkman
Senior Art and Design Coordinator: Jill Haber
Senior Photo Editor: Jennifer Meyer Dare
Composition Buyer: Chuck Dutton
Senior Manufacturing Coordinator: Renée K. Ostrowski
Senior Marketing Manager: Cindy Graff Cohen

Cover image: Walkway and Steps on Huangshan Mountains at Dawn, Anhui
Province, China. Copyright © Daryl Benson/Masterfile

Credits for texts, graphic essays, photographs, and illustrations appear on pages
650–653, which constitute a continuation of the copyright page.

Printed in the U.S.A.

Library of Congress Control Number: 2005934806

Instructor's exam copy
ISBN 13: 978-0-618-73120-6
ISBN 10: 0-618-73120-2

For orders, use student text ISBNs:
ISBN 13: 978-0-618-64365-3
ISBN 10: 0-618-64365-6

123456789-EB-09 08 07 06 05

CONTENTS

❈ *Student writings.*

PHOTO ESSAY: WAR AND PEACE
IMAGES, IMPRESSIONS, INTERPRETATIONS

Topical Table of Contents

❖ *Student writings.*

3 Families/Heritage

6 Science and Technology

9 Society and Community

10 Turning Points/Watershed Experiences

11 Language, Literature, and the Arts

12 Humor and Satire

13 Creative Writing

Creative Nonfiction

Fiction

Graphic Essay

Poetry

PREFACE
Transforming a Textbook for a Transformed World

Like the symbolic bridge on the cover of this book, *The Essay Connection* attempts to span the distance between reading and writing and bring the two activities closer together. To read, to write is to be human, to find the voice, the power, and the authority to communicate. As we become immersed in a new century, the importance of communication—clear, elegant, to the point—has never been more important.

"Writing," observes Toni Morrison, "is discovery; it's talking deep within myself." In *The Essay Connection* the voices in this conversation are many and varied—professional writers, experts in a variety of fields, and students with their own abilities and experiences, side by side. Their good writing is good reading in itself, provocative, elegant, engaging, sometimes incendiary. This writing is also a stimulus to critical thinking, ethical reflection, social and political analysis, humorous commentary—and decision-making, on how to live in the present and to make meaningful contributions to life in the newly uncertain future. These are among the many possibilities when students write essays of their own.

The attack on the twin towers of the World Trade Center and on the Pentagon on September 11, 2001, changed our world. America's complacency, security, and relation to nations and peoples throughout the world all continue to change even as *The Essay Connection* goes to press. This eighth edition is designed not only to keep up with major changes, but also to anticipate them.

What's Familiar, What's New

In the spirit of renovating an elegant building, the changes made to this edition of *The Essay Connection* retain the fundamental character of its distinguished architecture while bringing the work fully into the twenty-first century.

Reading Pictures

A decade ago, we could not have anticipated the effect of the Internet on the nature of reading and writing. While it's still comfortable—and comforting—to curl up with a good book, the alternative electronic options are so common that they need no identification here. Every author, every topic is accessible by Internet search. Sherry Turkle, in fact, addresses many of the issues in "How

Computers Change the Way We Think"; among the primary changes is our extensive engagement with visual elements. For instance, we expect to see things listed on the page or the screen—as in PowerPoint presentations—and the format influences the way we think about the subject. Photographs, illustrations, cartoons, designer graphics often travel in the company of words, and so they do in the revised *Essay Connection,* holding up their share of the dialogue.

Graphic essays   Graphic essays—whether this is a new and fancy name for comic books is up to readers to decide—are demanding and often more complicated than they appear to be at first glance. They tell a story, make a point—or more stories with more points—sometimes with no words at all, as in the cartoon narratives of Lynda Barry's "Common Scents," Art Spiegelman's "Mein Kampf," and Linda Villarosa's diagram "How Much of the Body Is Replaceable?"

Photo essay   Eliza Griswold's poem, "Buying Rations in Kabul" argues that "any peace/that must be kept by force/contains another name. It's war"—a commentary on the intimate relations between war and peace that the seven photographs in this full-color section address, both openly and by implication. There are several iconic photographs: raising the American flag on Iwo Jima, February 25, 1945; raising the American flag in the wreckage of the World Trade Center after the terrorist attack on September 11, 2001; the barn roof being painted with the American flag. Images of wars, past and present, reverberate in the other illustrations, as well: Fritz Scholder's Indian, sardonically wrapped in the flag; children playing in war-ravaged areas of Afghanistan and Iraq; the beautiful baby and baby tender in the now-peaceful landscape of Vietnam.

Abundant photographs   To reinforce—and enliven—the sense of what is both contemporary and timeless, the essays in this edition of *The Essay Connection* are now supplemented by forty-eight photographs and eight cartoons. These range from depictions of historical events (President Abraham Lincoln arriving at Gettysburg to deliver his address); to the timeless (families eating, working, playing together); to the contemporary (the precariously poised skeleton of the World Trade Center). Many of the photographs show people engaging in familiar activities—studying, reading, writing, fishing, working, learning, arguing, loving. Just as there is no one right way to read a text, for much of the meaning resides in the reader and in the context in which any given work is read, there is no single way to look at, to "read" a photograph. Thus these pictures can be interpreted literally, and metaphorically as well; the added layers of meaning are enriched by juxtaposition.

Creative Nonfiction

The label *creative nonfiction* makes explicit in this edition of *The Essay Connection* what real writers have known all along, that many writers use the techniques of fiction to tell true stories. As two distinguished pieces, student Amanda N. Cagle's "On the Banks of the Bogue Chitto" and Meredith Hall's "Killing Chickens" reveal, these techniques include a narrator or narrative voice, plot, characters, dialogue, and setting. Other autobiographical essays use these techniques to provide social commentary and critique with a human face, a human voice—Richard Rodriguez's "Family Values," Scott Russell Sanders's "Under the Influence: Paying the Price of My Father's Booze," and Dr. Martin Luther King, Jr.'s "Letter from Birmingham Jail."

Fiction

Two works of fiction new to this edition of *The Essay Connection* resonate with the creative nonfiction and many other essays as well: Elizabeth Tallent's "No One's a Mystery" and Tim O'Brien's "How to Tell a True War Story," a chapter of his Vietnam War novel *The Things They Carried.* Readers believe "Killing Chickens" and "On the Banks of the Bogue Chitto" are true because the authors say so, even though these works read like stories. Fiction writers send the same signals: they use character, plot, dialogue, settings, and symbols to explore multiple themes in works we are not expected to regard as literally true, even though we have met characters like Tallent's nameless romantic teenage girl, and joyriding Jack, her transient lover. Yet even while O'Brien is giving us advice on "How to Tell a True War Story" that promotes the truth, he is pointing out the ambiguity of the truth, the blurred line between truth and fiction, which concurrently compel our belief—and call it into question.

Poetry

There are eight new poems in this new edition of *The Essay Connection.* In addition to Seamus Heaney's powerful "Horace and Thunder," Eliza Griswold's "Buying Rations in Kabul" and Walt Whitman's "A Noiseless Patient Spider" also comment on matters of war and peace. The other poems, engaging in themselves, reflect the rhetorical theme of the chapters they begin, and also serve as commentaries on the topics of the essays.

Whole Essays

To maintain the integrity of the authors' style and structure as well as their arguments, most of these essays are printed in their entirety, averaging three to eight pages; a number are chapters or self-contained sections of books. Footnotes are the authors' own.

Readings

The Essay Connection includes ninety-six readings: lively, varied, timely, provocative—and of high literary quality. Here you will find sixty-one favorite essays, modern classics and contemporary works, and thirty-five new selections, including nine poems, by a wide range of writers, discussed in later sections of this Preface. The first three chapters address aspects of the writing process—Finding the Words, Getting Started, Writing, and Revising. The next nine chapters are organized according to familiar rhetorical principles—Narration, Process Analysis, Cause and Effect, Description, Division and Classification,

Definition, Comparison and Contrast, Deductive and Inductive Arguments, and Emotional and Ethical Appeals. The last two chapters comprise an argument casebook on terrorism and peace.

Familiar Essays

Sixty-one favorite essays have been retained from the previous edition, by authors such as Frederick Douglass, Stephen Jay Gould, Martin Luther King, Jr., Maxine Hong Kingston, Anne Lamott, Richard Rodriguez, Scott Russell Sanders, E. B. White, and Elie Wiesel. Amy Tan's "Mother Tongue" opens the readings, a happy balance to the concluding discussions of terrorism and peace, which are themselves affirmations of the essential values of civilization, and of life itself. Although humorous works by authors such as Mark Twain, Ntozake Shange, and David Sedaris signal the book's upbeat tone, they do not diminish the seriousness of its essential concerns or its underlying ethical stance.

New Authors

Among the essays new to this edition of *The Essay Connection* are those by Sherman Alexie, Lynda Barry, Chang-rae Lee, Bill McKibben, Richard Rodriguez, David Sedaris, Peter Singer, Sherry Turkle, and Mark Twain. Representations of women, cultures, and writers who address issues of class, race, ethnicity, and disabilities have been maintained in this edition, as in its predecessors.

Student Authors

Fourteen essays are by students, although a total of twenty-seven pieces of student work appear because an additional thirteen excerpts from student notebooks are combined in one selection. Although all the works were written when the students were enrolled in American universities, these students have come from places throughout the United States—from Connecticut to Pennsylvania to Minnesota to Utah to Hawaii—and all over the world, from Jamaica to England to Pakistan to the People's Republic of China.

These distinguished student writings discuss a variety of compelling subjects: coming to terms with oneself; with one's parents—whether known or unknown, living, or dead—with one's ethnic, political, or religious background— African-American, Asian, Chinese, Jewish, Muslim, Native American—and with one's social and economic class. All provide examples of excellent writing that other students should find meaningful as models in form, technique, and substance.

Varied Subjects, Varied Disciplines

The essays in this edition are drawn from many sources, mostly engaging and distinguished contemporary writing on varied subjects, as indicated in the Topical Table of Contents, with a leavening of classics by such authors as Swift, Lincoln, and Darwin. The exception is the collection of excerpts from the speeches of recent winners of the Nobel Peace Prize—the point here is to emphasize the common elements of their values and work, rather than to address the political conditions in their respective countries and cultures that triggered their activism, imprisonment, or exile. *The Essay Connection* includes, not surprisingly, the work of professional writers distinguished in a variety of genres: *essayists*—classical and newly canonical—Anne Fadiman, Linda Hogan, Scott Russell Sanders, and E. B. White; *creative non-fiction* writers Anne Lamott, William Least Heat-Moon, and David Sedaris; *autobiographers* Frederick Douglass and Richard Rodriguez; *novelists* Stephen King, Maxine Hong Kingston, and Amy Tan; *journalists* Gelareh Asayesh, Anna Quindlen, and Charles M. Young; *satirists* Sherman Alexie and Jonathan Swift; *playwright* Ntozake Shange; and *composition scholars* Donald Murray and John Trimbur.

Other fine essayists are specialists in other professions: *physicians* (Atul Gawande, Abraham Verghese); *scientists and science writers* (Natalie Angier, Isaac Asimov, Charles Darwin, Stephen Jay Gould, Bill McKibben); *religious leaders* (the Dalai Lama, Martin Luther King, Jr.); *political leaders* (Kofi Annan, Jimmy Carter, Frederik Willem de Klerk, Thomas Jefferson, Aung San Suu Kyi, Abraham Lincoln, Nelson Mandela, Yitzak Rabin); *political activists* (Rigoberta Menchú Tum, Betty Williams); *artist* (Laurie Fendrich); *political scientist* (Mark Juergensmeyer); *cartoonists* (Lynda Barry, Art Spiegelman); *linguist* (Deborah Tannen); *psychologist* (Howard Gardner); *economist* (Robert Reich); *computer scientist* (Sherry Turkle); and *sociologist* (Stephanie Coontz).

Critical Thinking, Reading, and Writing

Many readings are clustered thematically to encourage dialogue and debate among authors, and among student readers and writers. For example, the chapter *Narration* emphasizes the significance of family, race, and class; and the development of new insight into people (including oneself) and places revisited as one comes into maturity. The chapter *Process Analysis* clusters essays on processes involved in science and technology, and includes two on processes reflecting racial and family heritage in connection with processes of harvesting. We tend to think of *Description* as pertaining to a *physical place:* Mark Twain's uncle's Arkansas farm, Linda Hogan's Zia pueblo terrain, Asiya S. Tschannerl's China. Yet many descriptions pertain to *processes* (in "Killing Chickens," killing the birds parallels the destruction of a marriage) and to *character analysis.* Thus in addition to the physical description of bodies—Villarosa's diagram—there is an autobiographical portrait of Scott Russell Sanders's alcoholic father and his abstemious son, and Britt's character analysis of fat (and thin) people. The chapter on *Definition* includes several types of definition: *relational* (Spinner on twinhood, in poetry and prose), *analytic* and *operational* (Innerarity on "Code Blue"), and *narrative* (Verghese's "Code Blue"). The *scientific definitions* of intelligence (*evolutionary* by Darwin, and *operational* by Gardner) refract with Gould's argument on evolution in the chapter *Comparison and Contrast.*

Blended Types

In difficulty the essays range from the easily accessible to the more complicated. They have been chosen to represent the common essay types indicated by the chapter divisions, from narration and definition through argumentation and analysis of contemporary social and political phenomena. Nevertheless, because these are real essays by real writers, who use whatever writing techniques suit their purpose, there are very few "pure" types. Thus in the *descriptive essay* "Under the Influence: Paying the Price of My Father's Booze," Scott Russell Sanders begins with *descriptions* of his alcoholic father's behavior, including dialogue, actions; *statistics; linguistics; cartoons;* and *explanation* and *analysis* of "the family secret"; and an extended *narrative* of life with an alcoholic father. Consequently, although the introduction to each essay and the study questions following it often encourage the reader to view the work through the lens of its designated category in the Table of Contents, the reader should be aware that the category represents only one segment of a broad spectrum of possible readings.

Mini-Casebook: *Controversy in Context: Implications of World Terrorism and World Peace*

Controversy in Context: Implications of World Terrorism and World Peace was added after September 11, 2001, and is updated here. Eighteen core readings and a photo essay help students find a foothold and a focus on the most significant issues of our still-young century: war—of a kind scarcely imaginable to most of us before September 11, 2001—and, as the antithesis of international terrorism, world peace. As is true of any earth-shaking event, we looked at our world one way before the attacks on the World Trade Center and the Pentagon, and afterward have come to see it another way—in fact, many other ways. Has the world changed? Or have we? Words and images alike address profound issues, such as whether our sojourn involves nation with (or against) nation; culture with (or against) culture; technology, economy, or ideology with (or against) its counterpart.

"We tell ourselves stories in order to live," says Joan Didion; these readings incorporate true stories by eyewitnesses and those more distant, and analyses from a wide range of literary, philosophical, historical, political, and economic perspectives. The readings on international terrorism by poet Seamus Heaney, artist Laurie Fendrich, historian Bernard Lewis, and political scientist Mark Juergensmeyer provide a starting point from which students can begin to find their way through the tangle of evidence and interpretations—the messiness of life into which reflective writing can hope to bring some order.

It would be inappropriate to allow this book to end on the shrill note of sirens, falling planes, and terror in the skies, on the streets, in our hearts. Indeed, the creative writings, Tim O'Brien's "How to Tell a True War Story" and Kandi Tayebi's "Warring Memories," could serve as commentaries on peace as well as war; they integrate the perspectives of both chapters. Thus, in this Casebook section it is fitting to balance terrorism against tranquillity, war against peace, national interests against global, humanitarian concerns. Consequently, the "World Peace" chapter consists of excerpts from Nobel Peace Prize acceptance speeches by men and women of global distinction who form an international spectrum of the brave, the bold, the morally beautiful. Goodness, selflessness, and adherence to high moral principles, as the lives and works of the Nobel Peace Prize winners reveal, can emerge even in times of trauma—often in response to the challenges of trauma itself. Their talks, like their works, are beacons of faith, hope, goodwill, and moral courage.

Conceptual Context of the Book

The Essay Connection is informed conceptually by extensive classroom testing of the essays and writing assignments included here. The book is likewise informed by contemporary scholarship in the dynamic fields of composition, literary and rhetorical theory, autobiography, creative nonfiction, and the teaching of writing. The language of *The Essay Connection* intentionally remains clear and reader-friendly.

Apparatus

The essays are placed in a context of materials designed to encourage reading, critical thinking, and good writing. The following materials reinforce *The Essay Connection*'s pervasive emphasis on the process(es) of writing.

- **Tables of Contents.** The main Table of Contents reflects the book's organization, by types of writing. The Topical Table of Contents offers an alternative organization by subject to provide many alternative possibilities for discussion and writing.
- **Chapter introductions.** These define the particular type of writing in the chapter and identify its purposes (descriptions, process analysis, etc.), uses, and typical forms. They also discuss the rhetorical strategies authors typically use in that type of writing (for instance, how to structure an argument to engage a hostile audience), illustrated with reference to essays in the chapter, summarized in a concluding checklist.
- **Biographical introductions to each author.** These capsule biographies are intended to transform the writers from names into real people, focusing on how and why the authors write to identify their audience.
- **Study questions.** These follow most of the essays, and are intended to encourage thoughtful discussion and writing about Content, rhetorical Strategies/Structures/Language, and larger concerns. Note that throughout the book, whatever is said or implied about writing processes may be adapted to accommodate either individual or collaborative writing.
- **Suggestions for Writing.** Each set of study questions ends with suggestions For Writing pertinent to a given work. Most chapters end with a longer list of Additional Topics for Writing that encourage dialogue and debate about essays related in theme, technique, or mode. Often these incorporate strategic suggestions for writing particular papers and for avoiding potential pitfalls.
- **Multiple strategies for writing in a given mode** are identified at the beginning of the list of topics that concludes each chapter. Thus, for example, *Multiple Strategies for Writing Process Analysis* includes *definitions,*

explanations of terms, equipment involved; a *narrative* of how the process proceeds, from start to finish; *illustrations, examples, diagrams;* discussion of *cause and effect, comparison and contrast,* and consideration of *short term and long term consequences* of a particular process.

- **Glossary.** The Glossary defines terms useful in discussing writing (analogy, argument, voice) with illustrations from the essays.

Acknowledgments

The Essay Connection has, in some ways, been in the making for the past forty years, and I am particularly indebted to the candid commentaries of multitudes of writing teachers and students over the years whose preferences and perplexities have so significantly influenced both the shape and emphasis of this volume, and the process-oriented style of teaching that it reflects.

I am also indebted to the reviewers who contributed to the development of the eighth edition of *The Essay Connection:* Martha R. Bachman, Camden County College; Christopher Baker, Armstrong Atlantic State University; Richard Baker, Adams State College; Jessica Bryant, Eastern Kentucky University; Samuel J. Goldstein, Daytona Beach Community College; Betty L. Hart, University of Southern Indiana; Linda Cooper Knight, College of the Albemarle; Helene Seltzer Krauthamer, University of the District of Columbia; Valerie M. Smith, Quinnipiac University; Jenny Spinner, St. Joseph's University; Margaret Whitt, University of Denver; and Rosemary Winslow, The Catholic University of America.

Their work has been supplemented by a series of superb research assistants: Kathrine Aydelott; Sarah Aguiar; Matthew Simpson, co-author of the Instructor's Guide; Laura Tharp; Ning Yu; and Valerie M. Smith. Lori Corsini-Nelson, office manager, cheerfully handled the paper flow. Houghton Mifflin editors Suzanne Phelps Weir, Anne Leung, and Rosemary R. Jaffe have been enthusiastic supporters of the current edition; they have aided the production from start to finish with goodwill, good humor, and good sense.

When the first edition of *The Essay Connection* was in process, my sons, Laird and Bard, were in high school. Over the intervening years they've earned doctorates (in biology and computer science), have married inspiring women, Sara (a U.S. attorney) and Vicki (a food scientist), and parented joyous children, Paul, Beth, and Rhys. An ever-active participant in the protracted process of making *The Essay Connection* more friendly to readers has been my writer-friendly husband, Martin Bloom, social psychologist, professor, world traveler, and fellow author. He has provided a retentive memory for titles and key words that I've called out from an adjacent lane during our daily lap swims, homemade apple pies at bedtime, and all the comforts in between. My whole family keeps me cheerful; every day is a gift.

Lynn Z. Bloom

Part 1

ON WRITING

Writers in Process—
Finding the Words,
the Forms, and the
Reasons to Write

On Reading

As the photograph on page 1 implies, writing is a complicated process that involves reading—immersing oneself in others' ideas—whether you're reading a hardcopy book or a computer screen; whether you're looking at words or visual images: photographs, cartoons, graphic novels. Part of this intellectual context of reading involves evoking what you already know about the subject—from firsthand experience, hearsay, media presentations, or other reading. Reading also involves immersing yourself in the conventions of the genre: we read poetry, short stories, and creative nonfiction somewhat differently from the way we read essays, as will be discussed on pages 2–12.

Who Is the Author?

- When did the author live? Where? Is the author's class, ethnic origin, gender or sexual preference, or regional or national background relevant to understanding this essay?
- What is the author's educational background? Job experience? Do these or other significant life experiences make him or her an authority on the subject of the essay?
- Does the author have political, religious, economic, cultural, or other biases that affect the essay's treatment of the subject? The author's credibility? The author's choice of language?

What Are the Context and Audience of the Essay?

- When was the essay first published? Is it dated, or is it still relevant?
- Where (in what magazine, professional journal, book, or website, if at all) was the essay first published?
- For what audience was the essay originally intended? How much did the author expect the original readers to know about the subject? To what extent did the author expect the original readers to share his or her point of view? To resist that view?
- Why would the original audience have read this essay? What ideas on the subject were current at the time?
- What similarities and differences exist between the essay's original audience and the student audience now reading it?
- What am I as a student reader expected to bring to my reading of this essay? My own or others' beliefs, values, past history, personal experience? Other reading? My own writing, previous or in an essay I will write in response to the essay(s) I am reading?

What Are the Purposes of the Essay?

- Why did the author write the essay? To inform, entertain, describe, define, explain, argue, or for some other reason or combination of reasons?
- Is the purpose explicitly stated anywhere in the essay? If so, where? Is this the thesis of the essay? Or is the thesis different?
- If the purpose is not stated explicitly, how can I tell what the purpose is? Through examples? Emphasis? Tone? Other means?
- Does the form of the essay suit the purpose? Would other forms or combinations of forms have been more appropriate?

What Are the Strategies of the Essay?

- What does the author do to make the essay interesting? Is he or she successful?
- What organizational pattern (and subpatterns, if any) does the author use? How do these patterns fit the subject? The author's purpose?
- What emphasis do the organization and proportioning provide to reinforce the author's purpose?
- What evidence, arguments, and illustrations, verbal or graphic, does the author employ to illustrate or demonstrate the thesis?
- On what level of language (formal, informal, slangy) and in what tone (serious, satiric, sincere, etc.) does the author write?
- Have I enjoyed the essay or found it stimulating or otherwise provocative? Why or why not?
- If I disagree with the author's thesis or am not convinced by or attracted to the author's evidence, illustrations, or use of language, am I nevertheless impelled to continue reading? If so, why? If not, why not?

The ways we read and write, and how we think about the ways we read and write, have been dramatically altered in the past thirty years. The New Critics, whose views dominated the teaching of reading and writing during the early and mid-twentieth century, promoted a sense of the text as a static, often enigmatic entity, whose sleeping secrets awaited a master critic or brilliant teacher to arrive, like Prince Charming on a white horse, and awaken their meaning. The numerous courses and textbooks encouraging students to read for experience, information, ideas, understanding, and appreciation reflect that view.

Yet contemporary literary theory encourages the sense of collaboration among author, text, and readers to make meaning. How we interpret any written material, whether a recipe, computer manual, love letter, or Martin Luther King, Jr.'s "Letter from Birmingham Jail" (444–57) depends, in part, on our prior knowledge of the subject, our opinion of the author, our experience with other works of the genre under consideration (what other recipes, or love letters, have we known?), and the context in which we're reading. We read Dr. King's "Letter" differently today than when he wrote it, jailed in Birmingham in 1963 for civil rights protests; liberals read it differently than conservatives; African-Americans may read it differently than whites, Southern or Northern. Where readers encounter a piece of writing greatly influences their interpretation, as well. Readers might read Dr. King's "Letter" as a document of news, history, social protest, argument, literary style—or some combination of these—depending on whether they encounter it in a newspaper of the time, in a history of the United States or of the civil rights movement, or in *The Essay Connection.*

A variety of critical theories reinforce the view that a work invites multiple readings, claiming that strong readers indeed bring powerful meanings to the texts they read. The selections in *The Essay Connection,* supplemented by photographs, cartoons, and visual essays by Art Spiegelman (116–17), Linda Villarosa (246–47), and Lynda Barry (354–63), open up a world of possibilities in interpreting not only what's on the page, but also what is *not* on the page. What's there for the writer, as for the reader, is not just another story but an assemblage of stories, all that has occurred in one's life and thought, waiting to bleed through and into the paper on which these stories, in all their variations, will be told. Readers and writers alike are always in process, always in flux, no matter what their sources of inspiration or places to think.

There are many ways to learn a language and to learn to read, determined by age, culture, and physical and intellectual circumstances. In "Living Without/With Words" (19–21), B. K. Loren, an aphasic for a decade, writes of the difficulties in finding the words themselves. Amy Tan's mother ("Mother Tongue" 13–18), Ning Yu ("Red and Black, or One English Major's Beginning" 173–82), and David Sedaris ("Make That a Double" 306–8) deal with issues and difficulties of learning to speak a new language and learning to "read" the culture embodied in that language. Sherman Alexie, in "What Sacagawea Means to Me" (93–95), like Tan and Sedaris and a host of other writers throughout *The Essay Connection,* demonstrates the influences of our cultural heritage on providing not only the words, but our understanding—of both the language and its cultural connotations. Writers, in any language, any culture are looking for ideal readers, people who share the author's attitude toward the subject and love the style, readers who, as Eudora Welty says of her mother, "read Dickens in the spirit in which she would have eloped with him." Yet most writers can't count on such automatic adoration or agreement. So they load their work with information, evidence, appeals to ethics, the senses, the imagination (see Chapters 11 and 12) to win readers to their point of view.

Working with the conventions of a genre will soon become as automatic for experienced readers as working with the conventions of reading are for new readers. In English, these familiar conventions include reading from left to right, with pauses dictated, in part, by punctuation: short ones for commas, slightly longer ones for periods, perhaps a bit more time out at the end of the paragraph.

When several (or more) readers share a background, common values, and a common language, they may be considered a *discourse community*. In "Mother Tongue" (13–18), Amy Tan explores how her writing reflects her Chinese-American discourse community. She understands, and uses, "all the Englishes I grew up with"—one for formal writing, another for intimate conversation with Chinese family members, and a combination of public and private languages for storytelling. Tan also understands, very well, the conventions of a professional American discourse community. When she speaks to her mother's stockbroker (¶s 10–12) or hospital personnel (¶ 14), she knows that her impeccable standard English will get the respect—and results—that prejudice denies to her mother's Chinese-accented English.

What Is an Essay?

What do we talk about when we talk about essays? Just what are we reading and writing? As a rule, in both college and high school, we're writing either literary nonfiction or a more academic essay. Both do the following.

- Essays are *prose*—they may lack poetic meter and usually don't rhyme, but the sentences, paragraphs, and whole work flow from beginning to end.
- Essays usually focus on a central *theme* or *subject*.
- Essays are *short*, ranging from a single paragraph to a book chapter.
- Essays are *true*—hence the term "nonfiction." Essayists claim and readers believe that what they're reading is the truth.
- Thus essays *present evidence from real life or research* that either the author or the readers can verify.
- Essays are *organized into recognizable patterns,* such as definition, comparison and contrast, argument; *most of the time these patterns appear in combination and serve multiple purposes.* Thus Suzanne Britt's "That Lean and Hungry Look" (261–63) *describes* thin and fat people through *comparison and contrast,* thereby *defining* each type as a way to *argue* that the fat are decidedly superior to the thin.
- The *essay's author has a point of view,* either expressed or implied, even if the author is unobtrusive or not identifiable as a character in the work (known as an authorial persona). This viewpoint governs the choice of evidence (and counterevidence), organization, and language. In general, the author is asking the reader to, in the words of Joan Didion, *"Listen to me, see it my way, change your mind."*

As later chapters will illustrate, much of your writing in college will be articles in the language and conventions of the particular subjects you study—critical interpretations of literature, position papers in philosophy or political science, interpretive presentations of information in history, case histories in psychology or business or law, explanations of processes in computer science or auto mechanics. For instance, in the course of explaining what's "Inside the Engine" (142–46), master mechanics Tom and Ray Magliozzi tell readers how and why motor oil keeps the engine humming smoothly. Dr. Martin Luther King, Jr., in "Letter from Birmingham Jail" (444–57) uses evidence from world religions, his own life experience and that of numerous other African-Americans, theology, history, and the law to make the case for civil disobedience. And in "Blaming the Family for Economic Decline" (213–16), Stephanie Coontz interprets American public policy as it affects the way the American public conceives of the relationship between family stability and economic status—a confusion, she contends, between cause and effect.

Articles such as these do not have to be dry or devoid of a point of view. For instance, the science writings of Isaac Asimov (132–40), Atul Gawande (218–23), Natalie Angier (291–94), Sherry Turkle (397–402), and Bill McKibben (413–23) are known for their reader-friendly clarity as well as their absolute accuracy. We can count on them to have a point of view— Angier invariably favors what is moderate and healthful. Even academic essays don't have to be deadly serious (or dull), plodding along under the weight of obscure jargon, as all of these essays indicate.

Why a person writes often determines his or her point of view on a particular subject. George Orwell claims that people write for four main reasons: "sheer egoism," "esthetic enthusiasm," "historical impulse," and— his primary motive—"political purpose, the desire to push the world in a certain direction."

In "Why I Write" (29), student Matt Nocton identifies the reasons many of us write: to dispel lies, to seek the truth, to discover new things about one's self and one's life, to express oneself, or to wage war with written words "while eluding enemy fire, at least temporarily."

In "Why I Write: Making No Become Yes" (23–27), Elie Wiesel interprets *"see it my way"* as the role of the writer as witness. The survivor of imprisonment in several Nazi concentration camps, Wiesel explains, "I was duty-bound to give meaning to my survival, to justify each moment of my life. . . . Not to transmit an experience is to betray it." In this eloquent essay Wiesel, winner of the 1986 Nobel Peace Prize, demonstrates his continuing commitment to make survivors, the entire world, continually remember the meaning of the Holocaust: "Why do I write? To wrench those victims from oblivion. To help the dead vanquish death"— a purpose also served by the museum at the Dachau concentration camp (see photo page 24).

In addition to articles, *The Essay Connection* includes many types of essays that include elements of creative nonfiction. These include *memoir* and *partial autobiography,* such as Scott Russell Sanders's "The Inheritance of Tools" (148–54); *character sketches,* like Chang-rae Lee's "Coming Home Again" (156–64); *descriptions of a place,* as in Linda Hogan's "Dwellings" (273–76), or of *an experience,* such as the excerpts from Zitkala-Sa's *The School Days of an Indian Girl* (196–202); *narratives of events,* including Frederick Douglass's account of how he stood up to his cruel overseer ("You have seen how a man was made a slave; you shall see how a slave was made a man.") (109–13); *interpretations of phenomena,* such as Scott Russell Sanders's "Under the Influence: Paying the Price of My Father's Booze" (249–59); and *social commentary,* such as Jonathan Kozol's "The Human Cost of an Illiterate Society" (204–11).

Creative Nonfiction

Creative nonfiction (sometimes called literary nonfiction) does everything that essays in general do, but in ways that make the writing look like fiction. Creative nonfiction speaks through a human face, a human voice, and has the following characteristics.

- A conspicuous, individual recognizable *voice*—usually the voice of the *narrator or the central character,* who is often a conspicuous commentator or actor in the narrative. Sometimes more than one voice speaks—for example, when there are several characters or the narrator is at different stages of life, as in autobiographies.
- A *plot,* a causal relationship among events that tells a story, usually with a beginning; a middle that may lead to a climax in the action or a profound (or less earthshaking) understanding of events or phenomena; and an ending.
- *Dialogue.* Sometimes, not always.
- *Shifting time,* departures from logical or chronological order; events may be narrated through flashback or flash forward.
- *Setting*—usually a place or combination of places, or an interior, a mental landscape.
- *Symbolism*—any character and anything in the environment may stand for something larger than itself, as well as for its intrinsic qualities.
- An *argument that is implied,* rather than stated explicitly, if in fact an argument is presented at all. This is made more often through indirect or emotional means than through evidence from research or scientific investigation. "Show, don't tell" is the advice that creative writers follow.

Each of these characteristics may appear in more academic essays. Anthropologist Clifford Geertz refers to "blurred genres," in which documentaries "read like true confessions," and scientific discussions contain novelistic elements. Every writer in *The Essay Connection,* for instance, has a distinctive voice, a recognizable style. But not every essayist combines most of these techniques in a single work unless he or she is writing creative nonfiction. *The Essay Connection* highlights two creative nonfiction essays. In "On the Banks of the Bogue Chitto" (191–95), student Amanda Cagle presents an evocative portrait of her beloved Choctaw father, his many strengths ultimately unable to overcome the difficulties of poverty and racism in Louisiana bayou country. In "Killing Chickens" (242–45), Meredith Hall tells the story of the day when paradise is lost, as the inevitability of divorce snaps into sharp focus for a young mother and her two children. The experience of reading—and writing—a piece of creative nonfiction is very much like that of reading a short story: we respond to the characters in the narrative as we would to people we know; we may identify with them or be repelled by their fully human experiences. But because we believe in the truth of the creative nonfiction, if the tale is well told, we will not only care deeply about the characters, but we will want to know how their fate extends beyond the narrative.

Creative Nonfiction and Short Stories

The main difference between reading and writing creative nonfiction, as opposed to a short story, is the unspoken pact between writer and reader.

- In creative nonfiction, the writer claims to be telling a true story, whether literally or psychologically true, or both.
- The reader accepts the work as true and responds to it as to other real-world events as capable of external verification.

Fiction—including the short stories in *The Essay Connection*—employs the same techniques as creative nonfiction: characters, narrative voice(s), plot, dialogue, shifts of time, settings, symbols, and implied argument or message. But these are the main difference between creative nonfiction and fiction, whether short story or novel.

- Fiction is not expected to be true. The narrator, even one who claims to be telling a true story—as does Robinson Crusoe or Ishmael, the narrator of *Moby Dick*—is conceived of as the author's invented creation. Most authors and readers agree on this point.
- Thus events, even true ones, like the Vietnam War, can be altered to make a point or a "good story" in fiction. They do not require external corroboration, though internal consistency provides a coherence that helps readers' interpretations.

Readers of stories (and novels) accept their characters and events as fictional, even if they seem to be slightly changed versions of reality. The reader of fiction exercises a "willing suspension of disbelief," plunges into the story, and—if it's a good one—for the duration of its reading, enters the world of the narrative—down the rabbit hole of *Alice in Wonderland,* up in the hot air balloon of *Around the World in 80 Days,* cast away on Robinson Crusoe's desert island. The title of Elizabeth Tallent's "No One's A Mystery" (388–90) comes from the lyrics of a Rosanne Cash song and conveys to readers country music's eternal theme of love, betrayal, and heartbreak. We are not surprised to learn—in two brief pages of dialogue—that the anonymous, eighteen-year-old narrator's view of her future differs considerably from that of her lover, an older man who is currently cheating on his wife as the couple speeds down the road at "eighty miles an hour" in a dirty pickup, smoking cigarettes and drinking tequila to the pulsating beat of country music on the radio. Whereas she creates a romantic scenario of her marriage ("grandmother's linen and her old silver") and two darling children born within three years, Jack predicts that "in two years you'll write, 'I wonder what that old guy's name was, the one with the curly hair and the filthy dirty pickup truck and time on his hands.'" Whether readers are world-weary cynics or not, we know whose version we'll believe—clued in by the story's first "fact": Jack's birthday gift of a "five-year diary" with a broken lock. It doesn't matter to us whether these specific characters ever existed in real life; what we see and hear and smell in that pickup (note the pun on the style of that truck) is enough.

Tim O'Brien's "How to Tell a True War Story" (from *The Things They Carried,* a collection of narratives about the Vietnam War) intermingles good advice on writing a war story that rings true with characters—soldiers in the Vietnam war—and events presented as fiction. Whether or not the characters are real people, or are even based on real people, or whether or not the events actually happened, they illustrate O'Brien's points about true war stories because the reader will check the truth of O'Brien's advice against his or her own understanding of reality: "In any [true] war story . . . it's difficult to separate what happened from what seemed to happen. What seems to happen becomes its own happening and has to be told that way. The angles of vision are skewed" (545). If we haven't been in a war—although the events of 9/11 brought war into our very homes—we can check its truth against what we already know is plausible in war and also against the fictional evidence O'Brien gives us: "And in the end, of course, a true war story is never about war. It's about sunlight. . . . It's about love and memory. It's about sorrow. It's about sisters who never write back and people who never listen" (550). In this work, which O'Brien calls fiction despite its compelling re-creation of characters in a grimly surreal Vietnam jungle setting, factual truth doesn't matter. But O'Brien's kind of truth matters greatly: "You can tell a true war story by the questions you ask. Somebody tells a story, let's say, and afterward you ask, 'Is it true?' and if the answer matters, you've got your answer" (548).

Poetry

Poetry has conventions of its own; its meaning is compact, compressed. Whether or not it rhymes—and lots of poems don't—a poem is held together by its metrical pattern (rhythm), sounds, and often a dominating image or emotion. The poems in *The Essay Connection* are short and sufficiently straightforward so readers can understand them without a lot of outside explanation. These poems usually depict a character (Penelope Pelizzon's "Clever and Poor"), relationship (Jenny Spinner's "Together in the Old Square Print, 1976"), emotion (Mary Oliver's "August"), event (Seamus Heaney's "Horace and Thunder"), experience (Marilyn Nelson's "Asparagus"), social principle (Martín Espada's "The Community College Revises its Curriculum in Response to Changing Demographics"), or world view (Walt Whitman's "A Noiseless Patient Spider").

Children who are reared on Dr. Seuss and nursery rhymes learn to love poetry at an early age. Too often, however, as they proceed through school, they learn to dislike it in formal contexts (say, textbooks) while nevertheless responding informally to the lyrics of rap, reggae, hip-hop, rhythm and blues, and rock music. Whereas memorizing and reciting poetry may become an embarrassment in the elementary grades, there are at least thirty-five high school Precision Poetry Drill Teams who compete and award school letters. In and out of college, poetry readings, poetry slams, and online poetry sources abound. A Google search for "poetry" on April 23, 2005 (Shakespeare's birthday!) listed 68,600,000 hits—a lively subject indeed. Thus one aspect of a college education is to reintroduce students as adults to poetry—in case you might have tuned out the more literary versions while tuning in on your iPod.

The Glossary contains terminology useful for discussing poetry: rhyme, meter, stanzaic form, imagery, and more (639). Some of your concerns as a reader surface whether you're reading any genre, in prose or in poetry.

- Who is the *author?* When did she or he write the poem?
- Who is the *speaker* in the poem? Unlike essays, where the speaker or narrative voice is usually the author, this is not necessarily the case in poetry.
- What is *the poem about?* What is its point? Try paraphrasing it, perhaps line by line or sentence by sentence. What evidence in the poem itself supports your interpretation? Does any evidence contradict your interpretation? If so, reread the poem to accommodate as much evidence as possible.
- What does the *title* signify?
- What is the prevailing *tone?* What does this tell you about the author's attitude toward the subject?

Because poetry is concentrated, often allusive, some additional considerations can help you as you read.

- Read the poem more than once, more than twice—give it a chance for the meaning to sink in.
- Read the poem aloud. Try this, listening to its sounds, and to the sounds of silence.
- Read the poem according to the punctuation, rather than according to the end of the line. Poetic sentences don't necessarily end at the line ends.
- Read the poem according to the meter but with gentle grace to convey its subtle heartbeat—though not the force of a heart attack.
- Many poems are full of ambiguity. If you've caught some of the meanings and have arrived at an interpretation that satisfies you, be prepared to enjoy what you've discovered—and to argue your case with people whose interpretations differ from your own.

Indeed, the best advice for all readers, and for all writers, is to enjoy yourself. As long as you're in the right ballpark, don't worry about touching all the bases. There's more than one way to play the game, more than one way to read the essays and the creative nonfiction, the stories and the poems. And don't forget the pictures, cartoons, and graphic essays.

Illustrations

"Reading" a photograph or cartoon involves many of the same considerations you bring to poetry. You look at it, once, twice, several times, sort of like watching a polaroid develop, and the meaning gradually becomes clear. In many cases, the longer you look or the more often you revisit the picture, multiple meanings emerge.

- *Subject.* What's in the picture? What's missing from it that the viewer would ordinarily expect to find and have to supply? In a joke, for instance, as in Istvan Banyai's "Inflation" (264) what changes—in the figure and in the cost of the postage stamp—occur in the successive panels?
- *Artist's attitude toward the subject.* What is the point? How do you know? Does the artist tell a story in a single illustration or in a sequence?
- If there are *captions* or *dialogue blocks*, what is the relation of these to the visual art? How can you tell when these are straightforward, as in Linda Villarosa's "How Much of the Body Is Replaceable?" (246–47) or satiric, as in Evan Eisenberg's "Dialogue Boxes You Should Have Read More Carefully" (469)?

- *Context.* If you can tell, where did the illustrations originally appear? How large were they? Full page? Small boxes? Are they free-standing or intended to accompany a written text? When there is a cartoon sequence, as in Lynda Barry's graphic narrative "Common Scents," what story do the pictures, speech balloons, and captions tell?
- *Design*—overall visual sense. How does the artist's use of color, light and dark, sunshine and shadows, balance, and general layout affect your interpretation?
- *Ambiguities, uncertainties.* How can you be certain that your interpretation of the figures, ground, context is accurate? Do you need any additional information to understand what you're seeing?

There is no single right way to view an illustration, just as there is no single way to write about it. Indeed, there are as many ways to write as there are writers, for style is as individual as a fingerprint, and just as distinctive, as we'll see in the chapters that follow.

AMY TAN

Tan was born in Oakland, California, in 1952. Fascinated with language, she earned a BA in English (1972) and an MA in linguistics (1973) from San Jose State University. As a language development specialist working with disabled children, Tan's sensitivity to languages both spoken (conversation) and unspoken (behavior) was translated into the stories of complex relationships between Chinese-born mothers and their American-born daughters that comprise *The Joy Luck Club,* whose publication in 1989 brought her immediate fame, fortune, and critical esteem.

Tan followed this book with the equally successful *The Kitchen God's Wife* (1991), a novel modeled on her mother's traumatic life in China before she emigrated to the United States after World War II; *The Hundred Secret Senses* (1995); and *The Bonesetter's Daughter* (2001). Indeed, as Tan explains in the essay "Mother Tongue," originally published in *Threepenny Review* in 1990, her ideal reader became her mother, "because these were stories about mothers." Tan wrote "using all the Englishes [she] grew up with"—the "simple" English she used when speaking to her mother, the "broken" English her mother used when speaking to her, her "watered down" translation of her mother's Chinese, and her mother's passionate, rhythmic "internal language." Her mother paid the book the ultimate compliment: "So easy to read." Hearing these multiple languages by reading the essay aloud weds the words and the music.

Mother Tongue

I am not a scholar of English or literature. I cannot give you much more than personal opinions on the English language and its variations in this country or others. 1

I am a writer. And by that definition, I am someone who has always loved language. I am fascinated by language in daily life. I spend a great deal of my time thinking about the power of language—the way it can evoke an emotion, a visual image, a complex idea, or a simple truth. Language is the tool of my trade. And I use them all—all the Englishes I grew up with. 2

Recently, I was made keenly aware of the different Englishes I do use. I was giving a talk to a large group of people, the same talk I had already given to half a dozen other groups. The nature of the talk was about my writing, my life, and my book, *The Joy Luck Club.* The talk was going along well enough, until I remembered one major difference that made the whole talk sound wrong. My mother was in the room. And it was perhaps the first time she had heard me give a lengthy speech, using 3 the kind of English I have never used with her. I was saying things like, "The intersection of memory upon imagination" and "There is an aspect of my fiction that relates to thus-and-thus"—a speech filled with carefully wrought grammatical phrases, burdened, it suddenly seemed to me, with nominalized forms, past perfect tenses, conditional phrases, all the forms of standard English that I had learned in school and through books, the forms of English I did not use at home with my mother.

4   Just last week, I was walking down the street with my mother, and I again found myself conscious of the English I was using, the English I do use with her. We were talking about the price of new and used furniture and I heard myself saying this: "Not waste money that way." My husband was with us as well, and he didn't notice any switch in my English. And then I realized why. It's because over the twenty years we've been together I've often used that same kind of English with him, and sometimes he even uses it with me. It has become our language of intimacy, a different sort of English that relates to family talk, the language I grew up with.

5   So you'll have some idea of what this family talk I heard sounds like, I'll quote what my mother said during a recent conversation which I videotaped and then transcribed. During this conversation, my mother was talking about a political gangster in Shanghai who had the same last name as her family's, Du, and how the gangster in his early years wanted to be adopted by her family, which was rich by comparison. Later, the gangster became more powerful, far richer than my mother's family, and one day showed up at my mother's wedding to pay his respects. Here's what she said in part:

6   "Du Yusong having business like fruit stand. Like off the street kind. He is Du like Du Zong—but not Tsung-ming Island people. The local people call putong, the river east side, he belong to that side local people. That man want to ask Du Zong father take him in like become own family. Du Zong father wasn't look down on him, but didn't take seriously, until that man big like become a mafia. Now important person, very hard to inviting him. Chinese way, came only to show respect, don't stay for dinner. Respect for making big celebration, he shows up. Mean give lots of respect. Chinese custom. Chinese social life that way. If too important won't have to stay too long. He come to my wedding. I didn't see, I heard it. I gone to boy's side, they have YMCA dinner. Chinese age I was nineteen."

7   You should know that my mother's expressive command of English belies how much she actually understands. She reads the *Forbes* report, listens to *Wall Street Week*, converses daily with her stockbroker, reads all of Shirley MacLaine's books with ease—all kinds of things I can't begin to understand. Yet some of my friends tell me they understand 50 percent of what my mother says. Some say they understand 80 to 90 percent. Some say they understand none of it, as if she were speaking pure Chinese. But to me, my mother's English is perfectly clear, perfectly natural. It's my mother tongue. Her language, as I hear it, is vivid, direct, full of observation and

imagery. That was the language that helped shape the way I saw things, expressed things, made sense of the world.

Lately, I've been giving more thought to the kind of English my mother   8
speaks. Like others, I have described it to people as "broken" or "fractured" English. But I wince when I say that. It has always bothered me that I can think of no way to describe it other than "broken," as if it were damaged and needed to be fixed, as if it lacked a certain wholeness and soundness. I've heard other terms used, "limited English," for example. But they seem just as bad, as if everything is limited, including people's perceptions of the limited English speaker.

I know this for a fact, because when I was growing up, my mother's   9
"limited" English limited *my* perception of her. I was ashamed of her English. I believed that her English reflected the quality of what she had to say. That is, because she expressed them imperfectly her thoughts were imperfect. And I had plenty of empirical evidence to support me: the fact that people in department stores, at banks, and at restaurants did not take her seriously, did not give her good service, pretended not to understand her, or even acted as if they did not hear her.

My mother has long realized the limitations of her English as well.   10
When I was fifteen, she used to have me call people on the phone to pretend I was she. In this guise, I was forced to ask for information or even to complain and yell at people who had been rude to her. One time it was a call to her stockbroker in New York. She had cashed out her small portfolio and it just happened we were going to go to New York the next week, our very first trip outside California. I had to get on the phone and say in an adolescent voice that was not very convincing, "This is Mrs. Tan."

And my mother was standing in the back whispering loudly, "Why   11
he don't send me check, already two weeks late. So mad he lie to me, losing me money."

And then I said in perfect English, "Yes, I'm getting rather concerned.   12
You had agreed to send the check two weeks ago, but it hasn't arrived."

Then she began to talk more loudly. "What he want, I come to New   13
York tell him front of his boss, you cheating me?" And I was trying to calm her down, make her be quiet, while telling the stockbroker, "I can't tolerate any more excuses. If I don't receive the check immediately, I am going to have to speak to your manager when I'm in New York next week." And sure enough, the following week there we were in front of this astonished stockbroker, and I was sitting there red-faced and quiet, and my mother, the real Mrs. Tan, was shouting at his boss in her impeccable broken English.

We used a similar routine just five days ago, for a situation that was   14
far less humorous. My mother had gone to the hospital for an appointment, to find out about a benign brain tumor a CAT scan had revealed a month ago. She said she had spoken very good English, her best English, no mistakes. Still, she said, the hospital did not apologize when they said

they had lost the CAT scan and she had come for nothing. She said they did not seem to have any sympathy when she told them she was anxious to know the exact diagnosis, since her husband and son had both died of brain tumors. She said they would not give her any more information until the next time and she would have to make another appointment for that. So she said she would not leave until the doctor called her daughter. She wouldn't budge. And when the doctor finally called her daughter, me, who spoke in perfect English—lo and behold—we had assurances the CAT scan would be found, promises that a conference call on Monday would be held, and apologies for any suffering my mother had gone through for a most regrettable mistake.

15   I think my mother's English almost had an effect on limiting my possibilities in life as well. Sociologists and linguists probably will tell you that a person's developing language skills are more influenced by peers. But I do think that the language spoken in the family, especially in immigrant families which are more insular, plays a large role in shaping the language of the child. And I believe that it affected my results on achievement tests, IQ tests, and the SAT. While my English skills were never judged as poor, compared to math, English could not be considered my strong suit. In grade school I did moderately well, getting perhaps B's, sometimes B-pluses, in English and scoring perhaps in the sixtieth or seventieth percentile on achievement tests. But those scores were not good enough to override the opinion that my true abilities lay in math and science, because in those areas I achieved A's and scored in the ninetieth percentile or higher.

16   This was understandable. Math is precise; there is only one correct answer. Whereas, for me at least, the answers on English tests were always a judgment call, a matter of opinion and personal experience. Those tests were constructed around items like fill-in-the-blank sentence completion, such as, "Even though Tom was _____, Mary thought he was _____." And the correct answer always seemed to be the most bland combinations of thoughts, for example "Even though Tom was shy, Mary thought he was charming," with the grammatical structure "even though" limiting the correct answer to some sort of semantic opposites, so you wouldn't get answers like, "Even though Tom was foolish, Mary thought he was ridiculous." Well, according to my mother, there were very few limitations as to what Tom could have been and what Mary might have thought of him. So I never did well on tests like that.

17   The same was true with word analogies, pairs of words in which you were supposed to find some sort of logical, semantic relationship—for example, "*Sunset* is to *nightfall* as _____ is to _____." And here you would be presented with a list of four possible pairs, one of which showed the same kind of relationship: *red* is to *spotlight, bus* is to *arrival, chills* is to *fever, yawn* is to *boring.* Well, I could never think that way. I knew what the tests were asking, but I could not block out of my mind the images already created by the first pair, "*sunset* is to *nightfall*"—and I would see a burst of colors against a darkening sky, the moon rising, the lowering of a curtain

of stars. And all the other pairs of words—red, bus, spotlight, boring—just threw up a mass of confusing images, making it impossible for me to sort out something as logical as saying: "A sunset precedes nightfall" is the same as "a chill precedes a fever." The only way I would have gotten that answer right would have been to imagine an associative situation, for example, my being disobedient and staying out past sunset, catching a chill at night, which turns into feverish pneumonia as punishment, which indeed did happen to me.

I have been thinking about all this lately, about my mother's English, about achievement tests. Because lately I've been asked as a writer, why there are not more Asian Americans represented in American literature. Why are there few Asian Americans enrolled in creative writing programs? Why do so many Chinese students go into engineering? Well, these are broad sociological questions I can't begin to answer. But I have noticed in surveys—in fact, just last week—that Asian students, as a whole, always do significantly better on math achievement tests than in English. And this makes me think that there are other Asian-American students whose English spoken in the home might also be described as "broken" or "limited." And perhaps they also have teachers who are steering them away from writing and into math and science, which is what happened to me. 18

Fortunately, I happen to be rebellious in nature and enjoy the challenge of disproving assumptions made about me. I became an English major my first year in college, after being enrolled as pre-med. I started writing nonfiction as a freelancer the week after I was told by my former boss that writing was my worst skill and I should hone my talents toward account management. 19

But it wasn't until 1985 that I finally began to write fiction. And at first I wrote using what I thought to be wittily crafted sentences, sentences that would finally prove I had mastery over the English language. Here's an example from the first draft of a story that later made its way into *The Joy Luck Club*, but without this line: "That was my mental quandary in its nascent state." A terrible line, which I can barely pronounce. 20

Fortunately, for reasons I won't get into today, I later decided I should envision a reader for the stories I would write. And the reader I decided upon was my mother, because these were stories about mothers. So with this reader in mind—and in fact she did read my early drafts—I began to write stories using all the Englishes I grew up with: the English I spoke to my mother, which for lack of a better term might be described as "simple"; the English she used with me, which for lack of a better term might be described as "broken"; my translation of her Chinese, which could certainly be described as "watered down"; and what I imagined to be her translation of her Chinese if she could speak in perfect English, her internal language, and for that I sought to preserve the essence, but neither an English nor a Chinese structure. I wanted to capture what language 21 ability tests can never reveal: her intent, her passion, her imagery, the rhythms of her speech and the nature of her thoughts.

22   Apart from what any critic had to say about my writing, I knew I had succeeded where it counted when my mother finished reading my book and gave me her verdict: "So easy to read."

Content

1. What connections does Tan make throughout the essay between speaking and writing? Why is it necessary for the writer to be "keenly aware of the different Englishes" she uses? In what English has Tan written "Mother Tongue"? Why?

2. What is Tan's relationship with her mother? How can you tell?

3. What problems does Mrs. Tan experience as a result of not speaking standard English? Are her problems typical of other speakers of "limited" English?

4. Do you agree with Tan that "math is precise" but that English is "always a judgment call, a matter of opinion and personal experience" (¶ 16)? Why or why not? If English is so subjective, how is it possible to write anything that is clear, "so easy to read" (¶ 22)?

Strategies/Structures/Language

5. Tan uses illustrative examples: a story told in her mother's speech (¶ 6), her mother's altercation with the stockbroker (¶s 10–13), her mother's encounter with rude and indifferent hospital workers who lost her CAT scan (¶ 14). What is the point of each example? Does Tan have to explain them? Why or why not?

6. How do the "Englishes" that Tan and her mother use convey their characters, personalities, intelligence? In what ways are mother and daughter similar? Different?

For Writing

7. How many Englishes did you grow up with? Explain, either in speaking or in writing, to someone who doesn't know you very well, two of the different languages—whether these are variations of English or another language—that you use and identify the circumstances under which you use each of them—perhaps at home, in conversation with friends, or in writing papers. Consider such features as vocabulary (and amount of slang or specialized words), sentence length, and simplicity or complexity of what you're trying to say. How much can you count on your readers to understand without elaborate explanation on your part? Do you write papers for English classes in a different language than papers for some of your other courses?

8. If you are trying to communicate with someone whose native language or dialect is different from yours, how do you do it? To what extent does this communication depend on words? Other means (such as gestures, tone of voice, pictures)? As Tan does, tell the story of such an experience (to a reader who wasn't there) in order to explain the nature of your communication. If there were any misunderstandings, what were they? How did they occur, and how did you resolve (or attempt to resolve) them? What advice would you offer to help others in similar situations to communicate clearly?

9. Present to an audience of college-educated readers an argument for or against the necessity of speaking in standard English for general, all-purpose communication. Are there any exceptions to your position?

 For comprehension, writing, and research activities and resources, please visit the companion website at <college.hmco.com/english>.

B. K. LOREN

Loren is a widely published essayist, journalist, and environmental activist. *The Way of the River: Adventures and Meditations of a Female Martial Artist* was published in 2001. She attended the University of Iowa Writers' Workshop, where she also taught workshops on editing and writing dialogue. Of "Learning to Write Great Dialogue," she comments, "I once earned my keep by transcribing, verbatim, conversations in psychoanalytic group therapy. I'm sworn to confidentiality, but I can tell you I learned how people talk. I also learned that 'real life' dialogue sometimes makes for bad fiction and nonfiction. There's a craft to writing dialogue that goes beyond words. Good dialogue moves the plot forward, develops character, creates voice and image, and in short, solidifies all the elements of descriptive prose, bringing the story to life. Bad dialogue often kills an otherwise great story." For a person such as Loren, who has "come into existence alongside words," when the words disappear, as they do in aphasia, or come out wrong, language "becomes holy."

Loren's Iowa Workshop descriptions reveal the concern for both silence and language apparent in "Living Without/With Words." This was initially published in *Parabola* and reprinted in *The Best American Spiritual Writing* of 2004. In re-creating the mental perspective of someone with aphasia, the fear and the frustration, she reminds us that to have the right words on hand and to be able to utter them is to live; to write is to live.

Living Without/With Words

Once, I became aphasic. "Synapses," my neurologist explained to me, "are an all or none proposition." Mine were none. 1

Fish: *Bagel.* 2

Lion: *Table.* 3

Pelican: *Funicular.* 4

This is the way I named things. *The funicular skimmed the surface of the* 5 *ocean searching for bagels.* Ocean was big enough, usually, to fit on my tongue and palate, to dance on my tongue and groove. The rest of the words I've filled in after the fact, like we usually do with memory (aphasic or not). We like to be understood. What I really might have said may have involved "funicular" and "bagel," but the words between would have been gibberish. My brain was an unplanned language poem and I a woman who tires easily of language poetry for its insistence upon intrinsic ambiguity. When you don't have it, language becomes unflinchingly precise.

6   Signifier: Signified: Bullshit.

7   Words carry on their backs their entire histories. This is what I learned the day they packed up and left me languageless. No forwarding address, no wish-you-were-here postcard.

8   Postcard: *Night Cream.*

9   Yard: *Breast.*

10   Water: *Orgasm.*

11   Holy shit. I was dead in the water without language.

12   As it is with any lover, I didn't see my words packing their bags to go. If I had, I'd have tried to stop them. I'd have begged, "Let's work this out, you and me. Let's find a middle ground."

13   I didn't see the verbs colluding with the nouns, the adverbs separating off, the adjectives running like lemmings to the cliff of my lips. I went to bed one night with a congregation gathering in my throat to sing me awake the next morn, and I woke with a stale mix of nonsense in my mouth, Fruit Loops instead of the promise of eggs hatching thoughts in my brain for breakfast.

14   My doctors were flummoxed.

15   A year into it, and I was depressed. I do not mean sad. I mean looking for the word *gun* daily, something to put in my mouth. I'd studied classics instead of writing in college. I couldn't stand to see words played with as they were in some writing workshops.

16   I needed to know the genetic origin of words. Their family tree. I mean, without that, all words are adopted. They grow up angry foster children wanting to burn things down. I wanted to know their mother and grandmother. I wanted to know their Adam, their Eve, their Eden, their original sin. Knowledge.

17   When you use the word *flummox,* for instance, your tongue rolls across the same territory of every person who has ever spoken that word. It carries every sentiment every flummoxed person has ever implied, plus your own.

18   Muriel Ruckeyser has said, "The world is made of stories, not atoms." They say that every third breath you breathe contains at least one of the same molecules Caesar exhaled as he was dying. Think of the words, then, the same words you breathe that have been inhaled and exhaled throughout history. If you're looking for a link, there it is. They are only shapes and noises formed into meaning. But how many shapes and sounds have crossed the tongues of those who have come before? And this exact shape and sound has crossed centuries to come to you, fully formed, Athene from Zeus's head (or so you believe as it transforms itself even as it leaves

your lips). Words say simultaneously too much and too little. This is why they are perfect for communication, most people's lives operating in the balance between too much and too little. Nothing more precise.

In those years without language, I was limbless. I had no way to reach   19
out. I had no way to touch others or myself. Water: *Orgasm.* My body had no reason to come or go anywhere.

Words are my nourishment. They are the molecules that seethe in   20
my veins. They are the light that filters through the rods and cones of my eyes to create color and dimension. They are my resting heart rate, my tulips, my knives, my forks, my spoons.

My art, to me, means food. Means sustenance. If I had another choice,   21
I tell you, I would make money. It's a catch-22. You must eat to live, must live to work. I eat my art for breakfast because I know what it is to go word-less, to be naked on the tongue and groping for a story that makes sense.

Towel: *Meridian.*   22
Apple: *Bird.*   23
Chalice: *Fly.*   24
Write: *Live.*   25
Silence: *Die.*   26

It's a cliché. But here's what I know. I have come into existence along-   27
side words. Others have come into existence alongside business or sculpture or music or humor or science. Words carry with them a unique challenge. We use them daily, whether we love them or not. And so, loving them is a fix. Unless you're stuck in a Hollywood musical, people do not usually sing to you as a form of communication. Unless you are Neanderthal, they do not usually draw. But people will talk to you with words even when you're a writer. They'll toss your medium around willy-nilly. They'll use it to bad ends. They'll use it to create wars, to manipulate leaders, to rape people, to sell.

You will be tempted to think your medium mundane, sometimes evil.   28
You will be forced to discipline yourself against this. It will make you poor.

Once, I was aphasic. The condition lasted, to some extent or another,   29
nearly ten years. When I came back to words I came back like a loser who'd had a mistaken affair. Once the damage is done, it's done. But there's a care-fulness that follows. You don't take things for granted. You speak from the soles of your feet, a current of meaning running through your body, each word carrying with it its history and the intimate mouths of your ancestors speaking it. Their lips touch yours as the word leaves you.

This is what connects you to who you are. What you love. What you   30
caress. Whatever it is that leaves you and in its absence makes you lonelier than God.

When it returns, it becomes holy. When it returns, you see the sacred   31
in the profane. You do not fall prostrate before it. You hold it close. You let it go. You live with it. You live.

ELIE WIESEL

Wiesel, a survivor of the Holocaust, explains, "For me, literature abolishes the gap between [childhood and death]. . . . Auschwitz marks the decisive, ultimate turning point . . . of the human adventure. Nothing will ever again be as it was. Thousands and thousands of deaths weigh upon every word. How speak of redemption after Treblinka? and how speak of anything else?" As a survivor, he became a writer in order to become a witness: "I believed that, having survived by chance, I was duty-bound to give meaning to my survival, to justify each moment of my life. I knew the story had to be told. Not to transmit an experience is to betray it." Wiesel has developed a literary style that reflects the distilled experience of concentration camps, in which "a sentence is worth a page, a word is worth a sentence. The unspoken weighs heavier than the spoken. . . . Say only the essential—say only what no other would say . . . a style sharp, hard, strong, in a word, pared. Suppress the imagination. And feeling, and philosophy. Speak as a witness on the stand speaks. With no indulgence to others or oneself."

In May 1944, when he was fifteen, Wiesel was forcibly removed from his native town of Sighet, Hungary ("which no longer exists," he says, "except in the memory of those it expelled"), to the first of several concentration camps. Although six million Jews died in the camps, including members of his family, Wiesel was liberated from Buchenwald in April 1945 and sent to Paris, where he studied philosophy. For twenty years he worked as a journalist for Jewish newspapers, but the turning point in his career as a writer came in 1954 when he met novelist François Mauriac, who urged him to speak on behalf of the children in concentration camps. This encouraged Wiesel (who has lived in New York since 1956) to write some forty books of fiction, nonfiction, poetry, and drama, starting in 1958 with *Night*, which opens, "In the beginning was faith, confidence, illusion." He published his memoirs *All the Rivers Run to the Sea* in 1996, and *And the Sea Is Never Full* in 1999. Wiesel, true citizen of the world, named Jewish "Humanitarian of the Century," received the Nobel Peace Prize in 1986 for his efforts epitomized in "Why I Write: Making No Become Yes," originally published in the *New York Times Book Review,* April 14, 1986.

Why I Write:
Making No Become Yes

W hy do I write?   1
    Perhaps in order not to go mad. Or, on the contrary, to touch the   2
bottom of madness. Like Samuel Beckett, the survivor expresses himself
"en désepoir de cause"—out of desperation.

Speaking of the solitude of the survivor, the great Yiddish and Hebrew   3
poet and thinker Aaron Zeitlin addresses those—his father, his brother,
his friends—who have died and left him: "You have abandoned me," he
says to them. "You are together, without me. I am here. Alone. And I make
words."

So do I, just like him. I also say words, write words, reluctantly.   4

There are easier occupations, far more pleasant ones. But for the   5
survivor, writing is not a profession, but an occupation, a duty. Camus
calls it "an honor." As he puts it: "I entered literature through worship."
Other writers have said they did so through anger, through love. Speaking for myself, I would say—through silence.

It was by seeking, by probing silence that I began to discover the   6
perils and power of the word. I never intended to be a philosopher, or a theo-
logian. The only role I sought was that of witness. I believed that, having
survived by chance, I was duty-bound to give meaning to my survival, to
justify each moment of my life. I knew the story had to be told. Not to transmit an experience is to betray it. This is what Jewish tradition teaches us.
But how to do this? "When Israel is in exile, so is the word," says the Zohar.
The word has deserted the meaning it was intended to convey—impossible
to make them coincide. The displacement, the shift, is irrevocable.

This was never more true than right after the upheaval. We all knew   7
that we could never, never say what had to be said, that we could never
express in words, coherent, intelligible words, our experience of madness
on an absolute scale. The walk through flaming night, the silence before
and after the selection, the monotonous praying of the condemned, the
Kaddish of the dying, the fear and hunger of the sick, the shame and suffering, the haunted eyes, the demented stares. I thought that I would never
be able to speak of them. All words seemed inadequate, worn, foolish,
lifeless, whereas I wanted them to be searing.

Where was I to discover a fresh vocabulary, a primeval language?   8
The language of night was not human, it was primitive, almost animal—
hoarse shouting, screams, muffled moaning, savage howling, the sound
of beating. A brute strikes out wildly, a body falls. An officer raises his arm
and a whole community walks toward a common grave. A soldier shrugs
his shoulders, and a thousand families are torn apart, to be reunited only
by death. This was the concentration camp language. It negated all other

The United States Holocaust Memorial Museum provides ongoing exhibits of "man's inhumanity to man" wherever, whenever it occurs in the world. These exhibits serve as witnesses to genocide, through photographs, sound and text, background information, and suggestions about how people worldwide can help the living victims, and "help the dead vanquish death," as Wiesel explains. Brian Steidle's photograph from the exhibit "In Darfur my camera was not nearly enough," shows the beginning of the burning of the village of Um Zeifa, Darfur, Sudan in 2004, after being looted and attacked by the Janjaweed. This government-supported militia, along with Sudanese government soldiers, has waged ethnic war, murdering tens of thousands of African ethnic groups, raping thousands of women, and has driven over 1.5 million civilians from their homes, torching their villages and looting their property. What is the point, the hope, the expectation of exposing audiences in America—including yourselves as students—to such pictures?

language and took its place. Rather than a link, it became a wall. Could it be surmounted? Could the reader be brought to the other side? I knew the answer was negative, and yet I knew that "no" had to become "yes." It was the last wish of the dead.

9   The fear of forgetting remains the main obsession of all those who have passed through the universe of the damned. The enemy counted on people's incredulity and forgetfulness. How could one foil this plot? And if memory grew hollow, empty of substance, what would happen to all we had accumulated along the way? Remember, said the father to his son, and the son to his friend. Gather the names, the faces, the tears. We had all taken an oath: "If, by some miracle, I emerge alive, I will devote my life

to testifying on behalf of those whose shadow will fall on mine forever and ever."

That is why I write certain things rather than others—to remain faithful.   10

Of course, there are times of doubt for the survivor, times when one gives in to weakness, or longs for comfort. I hear a voice within me telling me to stop mourning the past. I too want to sing of love and of its magic. I too want to celebrate the sun, and the dawn that heralds the sun. I would like to shout, and shout loudly: "Listen, listen well! I too am capable of victory, do you hear? I too am open to laughter and joy! I want to stride, head high, my face unguarded, without having to point to the ashes over there on the horizon, without having to tamper with facts to hide their tragic ugliness. For a man born blind, God himself is blind, but look, I see, I am not blind." One feels like shouting this, but the shout changes to a murmur. One must make a choice; one must remain faithful. A big word, I know. Nevertheless, I use it, it suits me. Having written the things I have written, I feel I can afford no longer to play with words. If I say that the writer in me wants to remain loyal, it is because it is true. This sentiment moves all survivors; they owe nothing to anyone, but everything to the dead.   11

I owe them my roots and my memory. I am duty-bound to serve as their emissary, transmitting the history of their disappearance, even if it disturbs, even if it brings pain. Not to do so would be to betray them, and thus myself. And since I am incapable of communicating their cry by shouting, I simply look at them. I see them and I write.   12

While writing, I question them as I question myself. I believe I have said it before, elsewhere. I write to understand as much as to be understood. Will I succeed one day? Wherever one starts, one reaches darkness. God? He remains the God of darkness. Man? The source of darkness. The killers' derision, their victims' tears, the onlookers' indifference, their complicity and complacency—the divine role in all that I do not understand. A million children massacred—I shall never understand.   13

Jewish children—they haunt my writings. I see them again and again. I shall always see them. Hounded, humiliated, bent like the old men who surround them as though to protect them, unable to do so. They are thirsty, the children, and there is no one to give them water. They are hungry, but there is no one to give them a crust of bread. They are afraid, and there is no one to reassure them.   14

They walk in the middle of the road, like vagabonds. They are on the way to the station, and they will never return. In sealed cars, without air or food, they travel toward another world. They guess where they are going, they know it, and they keep silent. Tense, thoughtful, they listen to the wind, the call of death in the distance.   15

All these children, these old people, I see them. I never stop seeing them. I belong to them.   16

17   But they, to whom do they belong?

18   People tend to think that a murderer weakens when facing a child. The child reawakens the killer's lost humanity. The killer can no longer kill the child before him, the child inside him.

19   But with us it happened differently. Our Jewish children had no effect upon the killers. Nor upon the world. Nor upon God.

20   I think of them, I think of their childhood. Their childhood is a small Jewish town, and this town is no more. They frighten me; they reflect an image of myself, one that I pursue and run from at the same time—the image of a Jewish adolescent who knew no fear, except the fear of God, whose faith was whole, comforting, and not marked by anxiety.

21   No, I do not understand. And if I write, it is to warn the reader that he will not understand either. "You will not understand, you will never understand," were the words heard everywhere during the reign of night. I can only echo them. You, who never lived under a sky of blood, will never know what it was like. Even if you read all the books ever written, even if you listen to all the testimonies ever given, you will remain on this side of the wall, you will view the agony and death of a people from afar, through the screen of a memory that is not your own.

22   An admission of impotence and guilt? I do not know. All I know is that Treblinka and Auschwitz cannot be told. And yet I have tried. God knows I have tried.

23   Have I attempted too much or not enough? Among some twenty-five volumes, only three or four penetrate the phantasmagoric realm of the dead. In my other books, through my other books, I have tried to follow other roads. For it is dangerous to linger among the dead, they hold on to you and you run the risk of speaking only to them. And so I have forced myself to turn away from them and study other periods, explore other destinies and teach other tales—the Bible and the Talmud, Hasidism and its fervor, the shtetl and its songs, Jerusalem and its echoes, the Russian Jews and their anguish, their awakening, their courage. At times, it has seemed to me that I was speaking of other things with the sole purpose of keeping the essential—the personal experience—unspoken. At times I have wondered: And what if I was wrong? Perhaps I should not have heeded my own advice and stayed in my own world with the dead.

24   But then, I have not forgotten the dead. They have their rightful place even in the works about the Hasidic capitals Ruzhany and Korets, and Jerusalem. Even in my biblical and Midrashic tales, I pursue their presence, mute and motionless. The presence of the dead then beckons in such tangible ways that it affects even the most removed characters. Thus they appear on Mount Moriah, where Abraham is about to sacrifice his son, a burnt offering to their common God. They appear on Mount Nebo, where Moses enters solitude and death. They appear in Hasidic and Talmudic legends in which victims forever need defending against forces that would crush them. Technically, so to speak, they are of course elsewhere, in time

and space, but on a deeper, truer plane, the dead are part of every story, of every scene.

"But what is the connection?" you will ask. Believe me, there is one. 25 After Auschwitz everything brings us back to Auschwitz. When I speak of Abraham, Isaac and Jacob, when I invoke Rabbi Yohanan ben Zakkai and Rabbi Akiba, it is the better to understand them in the light of Auschwitz. As for the Maggid of Mezeritch and his disciples, it is in order to encounter the followers of their followers that I reconstruct their spellbound, spellbinding universe. I like to imagine them alive, exuberant, celebrating life and hope. Their happiness is as necessary to me as it was once to themselves.

And yet—how did they manage to keep their faith intact? How did 26 they manage to sing as they went to meet the Angel of Death? I know Hasidim who never vacillated—I respect their strength. I know others who chose rebellion, protest, rage—I respect their courage. For there comes a time when only those who do not believe in God will not cry out to him in wrath and anguish.

Do not judge either group. Even the heroes perished as martyrs, even 27 the martyrs died as heroes. Who would dare oppose knives to prayers? The faith of some matters as much as the strength of others. It is not ours to judge, it is only ours to tell the tale.

But where is one to begin? Whom is one to include? One meets a 28 Hasid in all my novels. And a child. And an old man. And a beggar. And a madman. They are all part of my inner landscape. The reason why? Pursued and persecuted by the killers, I offer them shelter. The enemy wanted to create a society purged of their presence, and I have brought some of them back. The world denied them, repudiated them, so I let them live at least within the feverish dreams of my characters.

It is for them that I write, and yet the survivor may experience re- 29 morse. He has tried to bear witness; it was all in vain.

After the liberation, we had illusions. We were convinced that a new 30 world would be built upon the ruins of Europe. A new civilization would see the light. No more wars, no more hate, no more intolerance, no fanaticism. And all this because the witnesses would speak. And speak they did, to no avail.

They will continue, for they cannot do otherwise. When man, in his 31 grief, falls silent, Goethe says, then God gives him the strength to sing his sorrows. From that moment on, he may no longer choose not to sing, whether his song is heard or not. What matters is to struggle against silence with words, or through another form of silence. What matters is to gather a smile here and there, a tear here and there, a word here and there, and thus justify the faith placed in you, a long time ago, by so many victims.

Why do I write? To wrench those victims from oblivion. To help the 32 dead vanquish death.

(Translated from the French by Rosette C. Lamont)

Content

1. Wiesel says, "The only role I sought [as a writer] was that of witness" (¶ 6). What does he mean by "witness"? Find examples of this role throughout the essay.
2. What does Wiesel mean by "not to transmit an experience is to betray it" (¶ 6)? What experience does his writing transmit? Why is this important to Wiesel? To humanity? Does "Why I Write" fulfill Wiesel's commitment to "make no become yes" (¶ 8)? Explain.

Strategies/Structures/Language

3. Identify some of Wiesel's major ethical appeals in this essay. Does he want to move his readers to action as well as to thought?
4. Why would Wiesel use paradoxes in an effort to explain and clarify? Explain the meaning of the following paradoxes:

   a. "No, I do not understand. And if I write, it is to warn the reader that he will not understand either" (¶ 21).
   b. I write "to help the dead vanquish death" (¶ 32).

5. For what audience does Wiesel want to explain "Why I Write"? What understanding of Judaism does Wiesel expect his readers to have? Of World War II? Of the operation of concentration camps? Why does he expect his reasons to matter to these readers, whether or not they have extensive knowledge of any of them?
6. Does Wiesel's style here fulfill his goals of a style that is "sharp, hard, strong, pared"? Why is such a style appropriate to the subject?
7. Explain the meaning of "concentration camp language" (¶ 8). Why did it negate all other language and take its place (¶ 8)?

For Writing

8. Make two lists: (1) reasons to write and (2) reasons not to write. You could divide each list into categories: good reasons, real reasons, bad or irrelevant reasons. Which reasons appeal to you the most? Why?
9. Are there some occasions on which it's easier, and preferable, to write? Others in which it's impossible to write, or that you know in advance that the writing will be uninspired, off the mark? Discuss with friends, or classmates and a sympathetic teacher, ways to jump-start your writing. Here are some suggestions.

   a. Reading or watching something you enjoy.
   b. Listening to music. Is so, what kind?
   c. Eating. Exercising. Followed by a brief nap.
   d. Debating ideas with others.

 For comprehension, writing, and research activities and resources, please visit the companion website at <college.hmco.com/english>.

MATT NOCTON

Nocton (born 1975) has spent most of his life in the vicinity of his home-town, Simsbury, Connecticut, except for a year's sojourn in California—a cross-country trek that stimulated some of his best writing. An English major at the University of Connecticut (BA 2002), he now lives in western Massachusetts, selling online advertising.

❄ *Why I Write*

I write to dispel lies. I write because I seek the truth. Writing for me is a source of discovery. I write because I feel a sense of freedom and adventure in writing. To me writing is a place that I can return to again and again where the scenery of my life is always new and exciting. I write because I am always in the process of changing, and writing is a way to take a snapshot of who I am today. I want to rediscover myself and remind myself of who I was. I like to discover where I am going and where I am coming from. I write because I find it relaxing and it takes my mind off the dreadful events in the world today. I write to prove that I exist.

I write because I can express myself in ways I find impossible with spoken words. I write to prove a fact or sway an opinion. Through writing, I find that I can put things in perspective and see things differently, more clearly. I write to express my ideas or feelings. I write to emulate the styles of writers I admire. I write to delve into places that I have never been, and to explore new places within myself. I also write for others. I write to apologize and I write to forgive. I write to greet people and I write to amuse. I write to sustain my mind with the exercise and nourishment that it needs to stay healthy.

Being a quiet person, one thing I most enjoy about writing is the ability to avoid interruptions that occur in conversation. Arguing with words on paper can be an excellent method for waging war while eluding enemy fire, at least temporarily.

Getting Started

To expect some people to learn to write by showing them a published essay or book is like expecting novice bakers to learn to make a wedding cake from looking at the completed confection, resplendent with icing and decorations. Indeed, the completed product in each case offers a model of what the finished work of art should look like—in concept, organization, shape, and style. Careful examination of the text exposes the intricacies of the finished sentences, paragraphs, logic, illustrative examples, and nuances of style. The text likewise provides cues about the context (intellectual, political, aesthetic . . .) in which it originated, its purpose, and its intended audience. But no matter how hard you look, it's almost impossible to detect in a completed, professionally polished work much about the process by which it was composed—the numerous visions and revisions of ideas and expression; the effort, frustration, even exhilaration; whether the author was composing in bed (see the photo of Mark Twain above), at a desk, or at a computer terminal (see the photos on pages 1 and 56). Blood, sweat, and tears don't belong on the printed page any more than they belong in the gymnast's flawless public performance on the balance beam. The audience doesn't want to agonize over the production but to enjoy the result.

Becoming a Writer

For better and for worse, computers and other manifestations of electronic technology influence the ways we think, read, and write. (For more extensive analyses of their effects, see the essays by Deborah Tannen [391–95] and Sherry Turkle [397–402].) Growing up surrounded by sounds—from iPods, computers, and cell phones—may provide an electronic wall between the listener and the rest of the world, including other sounds natural and human. Confronting electronic screens—of computers, television, even automobile GPS day in and night out—imposes other people's configurations of reality on one's own view of the world, just as an orientation to books and newspapers did for earlier generations. Through the media and reading, we see the world through others' eyes; and the broader and more diverse these sources of vision, the more points of view the thoughtful person has available to ponder, accept, reject, ignore, or file away for future reference.

For college students, writing provides innumerable opportunities for both processing what you've already been exposed to and escaping from it. You can help yourself focus if you shut out the distractions—other people's words arriving by screen, headphones, or live conversation or music, and colors and images moving in and through your peripheral vision.

As you start to work, urges Stephen King in "A door . . . you are willing to shut" (35–37), find a private writing space, keeping people and other distractions out and yourself in. "The closed door is your way of telling the world and yourself that you mean business; you have made a serious commitment to write. . . ." King suggests you settle on a "daily writing goal" and get to work.

For many people, the most difficult part of writing is getting started. It's hard to begin if you don't know what to write about. In "Polaroids" (39–40) Anne Lamott illustrates a good way to find a subject, analogous to "watching a Polaroid develop. You can't," she says, "know exactly what the picture is going to look like until it has finished developing." Indeed, you're "not supposed to know" at the outset what you'll find when you begin to focus; the picture emerges as you immerse yourself in the subject and begin to identify themes, individuals, revealing details. And gradually the overall shape and structure appear. Aha!

Making "A List of Nothing in Particular" (42–45), as William Least Heat-Moon did when he drove his van through the "barren waste" of west Texas on a circuit of the country, can enable one to extract some meaning, some significance even out of a territory where " 'there's nothing out there.' " Least Heat-Moon's list has an eclectic span, seemingly random until it snaps into focus, ranging from "mockingbird" to "jackrabbit (chewed on cactus)" to "wind (always)." Talking with others, making an "idea tree," brainstorming, reading, thinking—even dreaming or daydreaming—all of these can provide you with something to write about, if you remain receptive to the possibilities.

You may end up writing a piece—preferably short—composed entirely of lists. Even if you simply go somewhere and take notes on what you see, once you've organized them into categories that make logical or artistic sense, you've got the start—if not the finish—of a paper.

Writers' Notebooks

Keeping a writer's diary or notebook, whether you do it with pencil, pen, word processor, or even cell phone, can be a good way to get started—and even to keep going. Writing regularly—and better yet, at a regular time of the day or week—in a notebook or its electronic equivalent, can give you a lot to think about while you're writing, and a lot to expand on later. You could keep an account of what you do every day (6:30–7:30, swimming laps, shower; 7:30–8:15, breakfast—toasted English muffin, orange juice, raspberry yogurt . . .), but if your life is routine, that might get monotonous.

The notebook entries included in this section were written in a variety of circumstances. "Selections from Student Writers' Notebooks" (47–54) met not only course requirements, but were also obviously outlets for many types of expressions and explorations, ranging from the meaning of education, race, and sexuality to the importance of family, music, an ordered environment, and writing.

A provocative and potentially useful writer's notebook might contain any or all of the following types of writing, and more:

- Reactions to one's reading: "I should pick up *Mansfield Park* again. Reading Austen or anyone that good reminds me of what I could be saying, and of the work that has to be put into it" (Loftus 47).
- Provocative quotations—invented, read, or overheard; appealing figures of speech; dialogue, dialect: "I hate the word *gay*. . . . I am happier with the less polite *queer*" (Rodriguez 310).
- Lists—including sights, sounds, scents: "On one wall [of the living room] was a dart board with no darts and the wall behind pocked with holes. The lining had been torn from the bottom of a yellow Chippendale sofa and stuffing poked through. . . . (K. King 51).
- Memorable details—of clothing, animals, objects, settings, phenomena, processes: "The camp seems loudest at night. A huge, dulled murmur flows up from the valleys with hacking, rattling coughs, unending moaning like mantras, mules braying, wails, and shrieks like a child stepped on a nail. Clank tap-tapping, metal pots clanking and wood chopping sounds but no sounds of laughter" (Ryan 54).
- Personal aspirations, fears, joy, anger: "My apartment is stark. I'm stark. . . . I want my masculine, minimal, logical, problem-solving self to dominate. I want that hard, durable exterior that is not unlike a wall. A cool marble wall that endures" (Yoritomo 50).

- Sketches of people, either intrinsically interesting or engaged in intriguing activities, whether novel or familiar: "A tall African American man with no front teeth . . . handed me a Polaroid someone had taken of him and his friends. . . . His two friends in the picture had Down's syndrome. . . . He pointed to his own image. 'That,' he said, 'is one cool man'" (Lamott 40).
- Analyses of friendships, family relationships: "My parents are getting divorced. . . . We did not put up a [Christmas] tree. . . . This year mom said we could eat when we wanted. But we never did. I ate a beans n franks dinner [by myself] later. My brother went to drink his gift certificate" (Weast 51).
- Commentary on notable events, current or past, national or more immediate: "In California thongs are still Nipper Flippers or Jap Slaps. . . . December seventh is the Ides of March. I'm asked how I can see, is my field of vision narrowed?" (Watanabe 53).
- Possibilities for adventure, exploration, conflict: "Today in class Dudley said he's 'tired of racial issues in class.' Well—if he's tired of them, how does he think I feel? For years I have been the only Black (or at most one of two or three) in class and I have had to deal with white negativism towards Blacks" (Coles 52).
- Jokes, anecdotes, and humorous situations, characters, comic mannerisms, punch lines, provocative settings: "two circling buzzards (not yet, boys)" (Least Heat-Moon 43).

You'll need to put enough explanatory details in your notebook to remind yourself three weeks—or three years—later what something meant when you wrote it down, as the notebook keepers here have done. As all of these notebook entries reveal, those of the student writers in particular, in a writer's notebook you can be most candid, most off guard, for there you're writing primarily for yourself. You're also writing for yourself when you're freewriting—writing rapidly, with or without a particular subject, without editing, while you're in the process of generating ideas. As you freewrite you can free-associate, thinking of connections among like and unlike things or ideas, exploring their implications. Anything goes into the notebook, but not everything stays in later drafts if you decide to turn some of your most focused discussion into an essay. If you get into the habit of writing regularly on paper, you may find that you're also hearing the "voices in your head" that professional writers often experience. As humorist James Thurber explained to an interviewer, "I never quite know when I'm not writing. Sometimes my wife comes up to me at a party and says, 'Dammit, Thurber, stop writing.' Or my daughter will look up from the dinner table and ask, 'Is he sick?' 'No,' my wife says, 'he's writing something.'"

Playing around with words and ideas in a notebook or in your head can also lead to an entire essay: a narrative, character sketch, reminiscence, discussion of how to do it, an argument, review, or some other form suitable for an extended piece of writing. After several drafts (76–82), Mary Ruffin's evocative portrait of her mother, who died when Mary was thirteen, emerged from fragments in her writer's notebook to become the polished "Mama's Smoke" (82–84), sophisticated in concept and techniques.

No matter what you write about, rereading a notebook entry or a freewriting can provide some material to start with. Ask yourself, "What do I want to write about?" "What makes me particularly happy—or angry?" Don't write about something that seems bland, like a cookie without sugar. If it doesn't appeal to you, it won't attract your readers either. As you write you will almost automatically be using description, narration, comparison and contrast, and other rhetorical techniques to express yourself, even if you don't attach labels to them. Enjoy.

STEPHEN KING

"People want to be scared," says Stephen King (a.k.a. Richard Bachman and John Swithen), but "beneath its fangs and fright wig," horror fiction is quite conservative, for readers understand that "the evildoers will almost certainly be punished." He was born in Portland, Maine, in 1947, and after working as a janitor, mill hand, and laundry laborer, he graduated from the University of Maine (BA, 1970) and taught high school English briefly while writing his enormously popular first novel, *Carrie* (1974). This inaugurated a career-long series of bestsellers, from *The Shining* (1977) to *From a Buick 8* (2002), as well as short stories, film, and video scripts characterized by a mix of horror, fantasy, science fiction, and humor. In June 1999 he was hit by a car while taking his habitual walk along a Maine highway. During his long recuperation from serious injuries he wrote *On Writing: A Memoir of the Craft* (2000), in which "A door . . . you are willing to shut" appears.

"Once I start to work on a project," explains King, "I don't stop and I don't slow down. . . . I write every day, workaholic dweeb or not. That includes Christmas, the Fourth [of July], and my birthday." Not working, he says, "is the real work. When I'm writing, it's all the playground, and the worst three hours I ever spent there were still pretty damn good." The work starts, he says, by finding "a door . . . you are willing to shut," avoiding distractions such as telephones and video games. "Put your desk in the corner, and every time you sit down there to write, remind yourself of why it isn't in the middle of the room. Life isn't a support-system for art. It's the other way around."

"A door . . . you are willing to shut"

Y ou can read anywhere, almost, but when it comes to writing, library   1
carrels, park benches, and rented flats should be courts of last resort—Truman Capote said he did his best work in motel rooms, but he is an exception; most of us do our best in a place of our own. Until you get one, you'll find your new resolution to write a lot hard to take seriously.

Your writing room doesn't have to sport a Playboy Philosophy decor,   2
and you don't need an Early American rolltop desk in which to house your writing implements. I wrote my first two published novels, *Carrie* and *'Salem's Lot,* in the laundry room of a doublewide trailer, pounding away on my wife's portable Olivetti typewriter and balancing a child's desk on my thighs; John Cheever reputedly wrote in the basement of his Park Avenue apartment building, near the furnace. The space can be humble (probably *should* be, as I think I have already suggested), and it really needs only one thing: a door which you are willing to shut. The closed door is

your way of telling the world and yourself that you mean business; you have made a serious commitment to write and intend to walk the walk as well as talk the talk.

3   By the time you step into your new writing space and close the door, you should have settled on a daily writing goal. As with physical exercise, it would be best to set this goal low at first, to avoid discouragement. I suggest a thousand words a day, and because I'm feeling magnanimous, I'll also suggest that you can take one day a week off, at least to begin with. No more; you'll lose the urgency and immediacy of your story if you do. With that goal set, resolve to yourself that the door stays closed until that goal is met. Get busy putting those thousand words on paper or on a floppy disk. In an early interview (this was to promote *Carrie*, I think), a radio talk-show host asked me how I wrote. My reply—"One word at a time"—seemingly left him without a reply. I think he was trying to decide whether or not I was joking. I wasn't. In the end, it's always that simple. Whether it's a vignette of a single page or an epic trilogy like *The Lord of the Rings*, the work is always accomplished one word at a time. The door closes the rest of the world out; it also serves to close you in and keep you focused on the job at hand.

4   If possible, there should be no telephone in your writing room, certainly no TV or videogames for you to fool around with. If there's a window, draw the curtains or pull down the shades unless it looks out at a blank wall. For any writer, but for the beginning writer in particular, it's wise to eliminate every possible distraction. If you continue to write, you will begin to filter out these distractions naturally, but at the start it's best to try and take care of them before you write. I work to loud music—hard-rock stuff like AC/DC, Guns 'n Roses, and Metallica have always been particular favorites—but for me the music is just another way of shutting the door. It surrounds me, keeps the mundane world out. When you write, you want to get rid of the world, do you not? Of course you do. When you're writing, you're creating your own worlds.

5   I think we're actually talking about creative sleep. Like your bedroom, your writing room should be private, a place where you go to dream. Your schedule—in at about the same time every day, out when your thousand words are on paper or disk—exists in order to habituate yourself, to make yourself ready to dream just as you make yourself ready to sleep by going to bed at roughly the same time each night and following the same ritual as you go. In both writing and sleeping, we learn to be physically still at the same time we are encouraging our minds to unlock from the humdrum rational thinking of our daytime lives. And as your mind and body grow accustomed to a certain amount of sleep each night—six hours, seven, maybe the recommended eight—so can you train your waking mind to sleep creatively and work out the vividly imagined waking dreams which are successful works of fiction.

But you need the room, you need the door, and you need the deter- ₆ mination to shut the door. You need a concrete goal, as well. The longer you keep to these basics, the easier the act of writing will become. Don't wait for the muse. As I've said, he's a hardheaded guy who's not susceptible to a lot of creative fluttering. This isn't the Ouija board or the spirit-world we're talking about here, but just another job like laying pipe or driving long-haul trucks. Your job is to make sure the muse knows where you're going to be every day from nine 'til noon or seven 'til three. If he does know, I assure you that sooner or later he'll start showing up, chomping his cigar and making his magic.

Content

1. Why are "the basics" King identifies—"the room," "the door," "the determination to shut the door," and "a concrete goal"—so important for writing? In your own experience, is each of equal importance? Do you share King's preference for writing with the shades drawn to "loud music—hard-rock stuff"? What is your ideal writing environment? How can you or do you control it?

2. If you've read any of King's fiction or seen his movies, how does this knowledge affect your receptiveness to his advice on writing? Does King's advice pertain to other types of writing in addition to the mixture of horror, fantasy, sci-fi, and humor that characterizes most of his work?

Strategies/Structures/Language

3. Advice givers often preach. And readers often resent being preached at. King delivers his advice very emphatically. Is he preaching? If he doesn't offend you, will you take his advice?

4. King alludes to the muse of creativity—traditionally considered a beautiful woman playing alluring music—as a male, "chomping his cigar and making his magic" (¶ 6). Why does King choose such a macho muse instead of a more traditional figure? How does this muse relate to King's writing—his subjects and his style?

5. "A door which you are willing to shut" (¶ 2) works on both the literal and metaphorical levels. Explain why this is a good way to get double mileage out of your language.

For Writing

6. Take King's advice and find a private writing space to which you can retreat daily. Make it your own by adapting the furniture and decoration (if possible), the temperature, ventilation, view (or no view), and sound (music? If so, what kind?) to your liking. Write one page (around 250 words) a day for a full week. As the week goes on, try changing some of the features in your environment (write at different times of the day or night, let people or pets in or keep them out, turn off the

music or TV), stop answering the telephone, and see what effect each of these changes has on the quantity and quality of your writing.

7. Write an essay that advises beginners about "the basics" of some activity that you love and know how to do well. What do they have to know first? What builds next on that? Then what? What is the desired result? Where can they go astray? Try presenting this information in a step-by-step fashion, and then write at least one step as a narrative (King's method) to see which works better. Have a novice try out your directions to see whether they are clear and produce the intended outcome. If not, ask your reader to help you figure out what needs to be added. More information? A diagram? Bulleted steps? Then, revise your directions and try again.

 For comprehension, writing, and research activities and resources, please visit the companion website at <college.hmco.com/english>.

ANNE LAMOTT

Lamott, born in San Francisco in 1954, dropped out of Goucher College after two years to return to Marin County, California and write fiction. Although she published four novels in the 1980s, *Hard Laughter, Rosie, Joe Jones,* and *All New People,* her nonfiction has drawn the most attention— and affection—for its author. *Operating Instructions: A Journal of My Son's First Year* (1993) is an ironically witty account of her first months as a single parent at age thirty-six, including sleep deprivation, financial anxieties, speculations on what she will tell Sam when he asks about his absent father, and her appreciation of the friends and relatives who constitute *family. Plan B: Further Thoughts on Faith* was published in 2005.

But the book from which serious writers take comfort, as well as good advice, is *Bird by Bird: Instructions on Writing and Life* (1994), of which "Polaroids" is an early chapter. Her explanation of the book's title serves also as an explanation of the metaphorical connection between the process of pictures emerging in Polaroid photographs and the way controlling ideas gradually emerge from a writer's experience and come into focus with slow precision. She says,

> Thirty years ago my older brother, who was ten years old at the time, was trying to get a report on birds written that he'd had three months to write. [It] was due the next day. We were out at our family cabin in Bolinas, and he was at the kitchen table close to tears, surrounded by binder paper and pencils and unopened books on birds, immobilized by the hugeness of the task ahead. Then my father sat down beside him, put his arm around my brother's shoulder, and said, "Bird by bird, buddy. Just take it bird by bird."

Polaroids

W riting a first draft is very much like watching a Polaroid develop.   1
You can't—and, in fact, you're not supposed to—know exactly
what the picture is going to look like until it has finished developing. First
you just point at what has your attention and take the picture. In the last
chapter, for instance, what had my attention were the contents of my lunch
bag. But as the picture developed, I found I had a really clear image of the
boy against the fence. Or maybe *your* Polaroid was supposed to be a picture of that boy against the fence, and you didn't notice until the last
minute that a family was standing a few feet away from him. Now, maybe
it's his family, or the family of one of the kids in his class, but at any rate
these people are going to be in the photograph, too. Then the film emerges
from the camera with a grayish green murkiness that gradually becomes
clearer and clearer, and finally you see the husband and wife holding their
baby with two children standing beside them. And at first it all seems very
sweet, but then the shadows begin to appear, and then you start to see the
animal tragedy, the baboons baring their teeth. And then you see a flash of
bright red flowers in the bottom left quadrant that you didn't even know
were in the picture when you took it, and these flowers evoke a time or a
memory that moves you mysteriously. And finally, as the portrait comes
into focus, you begin to notice all the props surrounding these people, and
you begin to understand how props define us and comfort us, and show
us what we value and what we need, and who we think we are.

You couldn't have had any way of knowing what this piece of work   2
would look like when you first started. You just knew that there was
something about these people that compelled you, and you stayed with
that something long enough for it to show you what it was about.

Watch this Polaroid develop: 3

Six or seven years ago I was asked to write an article on the Special   4
Olympics. I had been going to the local event for years, partly because a
couple of friends of mine compete. Also, I love sports, and I love to watch
athletes, special or otherwise. So I showed up this time with a great deal
of interest but no real sense of what the finished article might look like.

Things tend to go very, very slowly at the Special Olympics. It is not   5
like trying to cover the Preakness. Still, it has its own exhilaration, and I
cheered and took notes all morning.

The last track-and-field event before lunch was a twenty-five-yard   6
race run by some unusually handicapped runners and walkers, many of
whom seemed completely confused. They lumped and careened along,
one man making a snail-slow break for the stands, one heading out toward
the steps where the winners receive their medals; both of them were shep-
herded back. The race took just about forever. And here it was nearly noon
and we were all so hungry. Finally, though, everyone crossed over the line,

and those of us in the stands got up to go—when we noticed that way down the track, four or five yards from the starting line, was another runner.

7   She was a girl of about sixteen with a normal-looking face above a wracked and emaciated body. She was on metal crutches, and she was just plugging along, one tiny step after another, moving one crutch forward two or three inches, then moving a leg, then moving the other crutch two or three inches, then moving the other leg. It was just excruciating. Plus, I was starving to death. Inside I was going, Come on, come on, come on, swabbing at my forehead with anxiety, while she kept taking these two- or three-inch steps forward. What felt like four hours later, she crossed the finish line, and you could see that she was absolutely stoked, in a shy, girlish way.

8   A tall African American man with no front teeth fell into step with me as I left the bleachers to go look for some lunch. He tugged on the sleeve of my sweater, and I looked up at him, and he handed me a Polaroid someone had taken of him and his friends that day. "Look at us," he said. His speech was difficult to understand, thick and slow as a warped record. His two friends in the picture had Down's syndrome. All three of them looked extremely pleased with themselves. I admired the picture and then handed it back to him. He stopped, so I stopped, too. He pointed to his own image. "That," he said, "is one cool man."

9   And this was the image from which an article began forming, although I could not have told you exactly what the piece would end up being about. I just knew that something had started to emerge.

10   After lunch I wandered over to the auditorium, where it turned out a men's basketball game was in progress. The African American man with no front teeth was the star of the game. You could tell that he was because even though no one had made a basket yet, his teammates almost always passed him the ball. Even the people on the *other* team passed him the ball a lot. In lieu of any scoring, the men stampeded in slow motion up and down the court, dribbling the ball thunderously. I had never heard such a loud game. It was all sort of crazily beautiful. I imagined describing the game for my article and then for my students: the loudness, the joy. I kept replaying the scene of the girl on crutches making her way up the track to the finish line— and all of a sudden my article began to appear out of the grayish green murk. And I could see that it was about tragedy transformed over the years into joy. It was about the beauty of sheer effort. I could see it almost as clearly as I could the photograph of that one cool man and his two friends.

11   The auditorium bleachers were packed. Then a few minutes later, still with no score on the board, the tall black man dribbled slowly from one end of the court to the other, and heaved the ball up into the air, and it dropped into the basket. The crowd roared, and all the men on both teams looked up wide-eyed at the hoop, as if it had just burst into flames.

12   You would have loved it, I tell my students. You would have felt like you could write all day.

Content

1. In what ways is participating in the Special Olympics like finding one's way into writing about a particular topic? Is it possible to be both a spectator (appreciating what's going on, including the out-of-control parts, but sometimes getting frustrated by the slow pace [¶s 5–7]) and a participant concurrently?

2. What is Lamott's attitude toward the participants in the Special Olympics? How does she convey this? What clues does she give to indicate that she expects her readers to share her point of view? Would the families of Special Olympics participants have a similar point of view? Would the participants themselves?

3. In this essay about "the beauty of sheer effort" (¶ 10), intended as advice for beginning writers, why doesn't Lamott spend more time actually talking about writing?

Strategies/Structures/Language

4. Why does Lamott use the relation of the gradual development of a Polaroid picture (¶s 1–3) as a metaphor for the process of writing? How does this relate to the actual Polaroid photograph (¶ 8) that appears in the essay? Why is the first paragraph so much longer than those that immediately follow it?

5. Only paragraph 10 is of comparable length to the opening paragraph. Why is it located where it is? In it, Lamott uses two scenes, an enactment of a basketball game in action and her replay of "the scene of the girl on crutches making her way . . . to the finish line." How do these scenes contribute to the author's "Aha!" moment, her sudden insight as the meaning of the essay snaps into place?

6. Lamott's technique is to present a collage of many snapshots to illustrate her point. Identify some of these snapshots and explain how they reinforce her concept of "Polaroids."

7. Identify some of the ways in which Lamott conveys the slow pace of the Special Olympics and indicates her changing attitude toward this pace.

For Writing

8. Use an extended metaphor coupled with a series of illustrations to explain to newcomers how to perform a process (see the Magliozzis' "Inside the Engine" [142–46] for examples).

9. In many areas of academic research today, ethical questions are raised about who has the right to speak for whom. In "Polaroids," as in many other essays in this book (see those by Kozol [204–11] and Coontz [213–16]), the author speaks on behalf of people who can't always speak articulately for themselves. With other classmates, compose a set of guidelines for a writer's ethical behavior in representing such people, and include your rationale for these guidelines.

 For comprehension, writing, and research activities and resources, please visit the companion website at <college.hmco.com/english>.

WILLIAM LEAST HEAT-MOON

William Least Heat-Moon, as William Trogdon renamed himself to acknowledge his Osage Indian ancestry, was born in 1939 in Kansas City, Missouri. He earned four degrees from the University of Missouri–Columbia, including a BA in photojournalism (1978) and a PhD in literature (1973). His books include *PrairyErth* (1991) and *River-Horse* (1992). On one cold day in February 1979, "a day of canceled expectations," Least Heat-Moon lost both his wife ("the Cherokee") and his part-time job teaching English at a Missouri college.

True to the American tradition, to escape he took to the road, the "blue highways"—back roads on the old road maps—in the van that would be home as he circled the United States clockwise "in search of places where change did not mean ruin and where time and men and deeds connected." His account of his trip, *Blue Highways* (1982), is an intimate exploration of America's small towns, "Remote, Oregon; Simplicity, Virginia; New Freedom, Pennsylvania; New Hope, Tennessee; Why, Arizona; Whynot, Mississippi; Igo, California (just down the road from Ono). . . ." Though he tried to lose himself as a stranger in a strange land, as he came to know and appreciate the country through its back roads and small towns, Least Heat-Moon came inevitably to know and come to terms with himself. "The mere listing of details meaningless in themselves, at once provides them with significance which one denies in vain," says novelist Steven Millhauser. "The beauty of irrelevance fades away, accident darkens into design." Consequently, traveling—moving along a linear route—lends itself to list making, a good way to impose design on happenstance, to remember where you're going, where you've been, whom you've met, what you've seen or done.

A List of Nothing in Particular

1   Straight as a chief's countenance, the road lay ahead, curves so long and gradual as to be imperceptible except on the map. For nearly a hundred miles due west of Eldorado, not a single town. It was the Texas some people see as barren waste when they cross it, the part they later describe at the motel bar as "nothing." They say, "There's nothing out there."

2   Driving through the miles of nothing, I decided to test the hypothesis and stopped somewhere in western Crockett County on the top of a broad mesa, just off Texas 29. At a distance, the land looked so rocky and dry, a religious man could believe that the First Hand never got around to the creation in here. Still, somebody had decided to string barbed wire around it.

3   No plant grew higher than my head. For a while, I heard only miles of wind against the Ghost; but after the ringing in my ears stopped, I heard

myself breathing, then a bird note, an answering call, another kind of bird-song, and another: mockingbird, mourning dove, an enigma. I heard the high zizz of flies the color of gray flannel and the deep buzz of a blue bumblebee. I made a list of nothing in particular:

1. mockingbird
2. mourning dove
3. enigma bird (heard not saw)
4. gray flies
5. blue bumblebee
6. two circling buzzards (not yet, boys)
7. orange ants
8. black ants
9. orange-black ants (what's been going on?)
10. three species of spiders
11. opossum skull
12. jackrabbit (chewed on cactus)
13. deer (left scat)
14. coyote (left tracks)
15. small rodent (den full of seed hulls under rock)
16. snake (skin hooked on cactus spine)
17. prickly pear cactus (yellow blossoms)
18. hedgehog cactus (orange blossoms)
19. barrel cactus (red blossoms)
20. devil's pincushion (no blossoms)
21. catclaw (no better name)
22. two species of grass (neither green, both alive)
23. yellow flowers (blossoms smaller than peppercorns)
24. sage (indicates alkali-free soil)
25. mesquite (three-foot plants with eighty-foot roots to reach water that fell as rain two thousand years ago)
26. greasewood (oh, yes)
27. joint fir (steeped stems make Brigham Young tea)
28. earth
29. sky
30. wind (always)

That was all the nothing I could identify then, but had I waited until dark when the desert really comes to life, I could have done better. To say nothing is out here is incorrect; to say the desert is stingy with everything except space and light, stone and earth is closer to the truth.

I drove on. The low sun turned the mesa rimrock to silhouettes, an-⁴ gular and weird and unearthly; had someone said the far side of Saturn looked just like this, I would have believed him. The road dropped to the Pecos River, now dammed to such docility I couldn't imagine it formerly demarking the western edge of a rudimentary white civilization. Even the old wagonmen felt the unease of isolation when they crossed the Pecos, a small but once serious river that has had many names: Rio de las Vacas (River of Cows—perhaps a reference to bison), Rio Salado (Salty River), Rio Puerco (Dirty River).

5   West of the Pecos, a strangely truncated cone rose from the valley. In the oblique evening light, its silhouette looked like a Mayan temple, so perfect was its symmetry. I stopped again, started climbing, stirring a panic of lizards on the way up. From the top, the rubbled land below—veined with the highway and arroyos, topographical relief absorbed in the dusk—looked like a roadmap.

6   The desert, more than any other terrain, shows its age, shows time because so little vegetation covers the ancient erosions of wind and storm. What appears is tawny grit once stone and stone crumbling to grit. Everywhere rock, earth's oldest thing. Even desert creatures come from a time older than the woodland animals, and they, in answer to the arduousness, have retained prehistoric coverings of chitin and lapped scale and primitive defenses of spine and stinger, fang and poison, shell and claw.

7   The night, taking up the shadows and details, wiped the face of the desert into a simple, uncluttered blackness until there were only three things: land, wind, stars. I was there too, but my presence I felt more than saw. It was as if I had been reduced to mind, to an edge of consciousness. Men, ascetics, in all eras have gone into deserts to lose themselves—Jesus, Saint Anthony, Saint Basil, and numberless medicine men—maybe because such a losing happens almost as a matter of course here if you avail yourself. The Sioux once chanted, "All over the sky a sacred voice is calling."

8   Back to the highway, on with the headlamps, down Six Shooter Draw. In the darkness, deer, just shadows in the lights, began moving toward the desert willows in the wet bottoms. Stephen Vincent Benét:

> *When Daniel Boone goes by, at night,*
> *The phantom deer arise*
> *And all lost, wild America*
> *Is burning in their eyes.*

9   From the top of another high mesa: twelve miles west in the flat valley floor, the lights of Fort Stockton blinked white, blue, red, and yellow in the heat like a mirage. How is it that desert towns look so fine and big at night? It must be that little is hidden. The glistening ahead could have been a golden city of Cibola. But the reality of Fort Stockton was plywood and concrete block and the plastic signs of Holiday Inn and Mobil Oil.

10   The desert had given me an appetite that would have made carrion crow stuffed with saltbush taste good. I found a Mexican cafe of adobe, with a whitewashed log ceiling, creekstone fireplace, and jukebox pumping out mariachi music. It was like a bunk house. I ate burritos, chile rellenos, and pinto beans, all ladled over with a fine, incendiary sauce the color of

sludge from an old steel drum. At the next table sat three big, round men: an Indian wearing a silver headband, a Chicano in a droopy Pancho Villa mustache, and a Negro in faded overalls. I thought what a litany of grievances that table could recite. But the more I looked, the more I believed they were someone's vision of the West, maybe someone making ads for Levy's bread, the ads that used to begin "You don't have to be Jewish."

Content

1. What details of the desert landscape does Least Heat-Moon use to describe it? How clearly can you visualize this place? Although this desert can be precisely located on a highway map, do you need to know its exact location in order to imagine it? What does it have in common with other deserts? Does it have any particularly unique features?

2. Travel writer Paul Theroux says, "The journey, not the arrival, matters." Is that true for Least Heat-Moon? Explain your answer.

Strategies/Structures/Language

3. Least Heat-Moon structures this chapter from *Blue Highways* according to time (daylight to night) and distance. How does the structure relate to the subject matter?

4. What is the effect of ending this trip through the desert with the image of "three big, round men"—an Indian, a Chicano, and a black (¶ 10)? Does the reference to Levy's Jewish rye bread in the last sentence trivialize this example?

5. What kind of character does Least Heat-Moon play in his own narrative? Is this character identical to the author who is writing the essay?

6. Least Heat-Moon includes many place names. With what effect? Do you need to read the essay with a map in hand?

7. Why are the parentheses in the list? Why do they appear beside some items and not others?

For Writing

8. Make a list of "nothing in particular" that you observe in a place so familiar that you take its distinguishing features for granted: your yard, your refrigerator, your clothes closet, your desk, a supermarket or other store, a library, or any other ordinary place. Write down as many specific details as you can, in whatever order you see them. (Use parenthetical remarks, too, if you wish.) Then, organize them according to some logical or psychologically relevant pattern (such as closet to farthest away, most to least dominant impression, largest to smallest, whatever) and put them into a larger context. For instance, how does the closet or the refrigerator relate to the rest of your house? Does organizing the list stimulate you to include even more details? What can you do to keep your essay from sounding like a collection of miscellaneous trivia? Add drawings, photographs, or diagrams as desired.

9. Write an essay about some portion of a trip you have taken, where you have been a stranger in a strange land. Characterize yourself as a traveler, possibly an outsider, with a particular relationship to the place you're in (enjoyment, curiosity,

boredom, loneliness, fear, fatigue, a desire to move on, or any combination of emotions you want to acknowledge). Illustrate with maps, photographs, or travel documents, if you wish.

 For comprehension, writing, and research activities and resources, please visit the companion website at <college.hmco.com/english>.

❄ *Selections from Student Writers' Notebooks*

RICHARD LOFTUS, JILL WOOLLEY, ART GREENWOOD, BARBARA SCHOFIELD, SUSAN YORITOMO, BETTY J. WALKER, TAMMY WEAST, KRISTIN KING, ROSALIND BRADLEY COLES, CHERYL WATANABE, STEPHEN E. RYAN

The students who kept these writers' notebooks in courses at the University of Connecticut, Virginia Commonwealth University, and the College of William and Mary in recent years majored in a variety of subjects: King, Loftus, Ryan, and Watanabe, English; Woolley, archaeology; Greenwood, general studies; Schofield, education; Yoritomo, filmmaking; Walker, human resource management; Weast, mass communications; Coles, biology and creative writing. All share a love of the sounds as well as the sense of words, all like to play around with the language; some read omnivorously while others focus on visual images. All bring creativity to their work, which ranges from assisting on archaeological digs to personnel administration to pharmacological laboratory research to editing publications for a hospital and for the Wolf Trap music foundation.

The selections from their notebooks reflect a range of interests and moods as varied as the writers. Reactions to keeping a notebook ("It's better to do it than to talk about it"), a satiric recipe ("Oh, Mom, was there ever a worse cook than you?"), self-analysis ("I could get by, looking good"), an attempt at self-improvement ("I've been trying to put cigarettes down for six years now"), explorations of sound ("HE'LL BANG EM AND HIS CYMBALS CRASH AND HISS"), analysis of an apartment style that mirrors the writer's personal style ("My apartment is stark. I'm stark"), a humorous tirade against housework ("I hate it"), the devastating impact of a divorce on a family's Christmas ("My brother went to drink his gift certificate"), reactions to being black in a white world (Coles), homosexual in a straight world (Loftus), Asian in America (Watanabe). And a joyous reaction to the writer's first publication—"and not in the Letters to the Editor column, either."

These entries offer just a hint of the infinite potential of writers' notebooks.

Richard Loftus

I read something in some book from some new author in some bookshop   1
somewhere to the effect that writer's block is "reading old fat novels
instead of making new skinny ones." My secret is out.

• • •

I don't feel like writing now. I should pick up *Mansfield Park* again. Read-   2
ing Austen or anyone that good reminds me of what I could be saying,
and of the work that has to be put into it. How often have I begun a journal and stopped because two days later it didn't seem so good? I suppose
I saved myself from some self-flagellation, but also from a record of
growth. There are some people in the class who write often, and though
their perceptions are no more acute or their difficulties in writing no less
than my own, I feel that they're ahead. I must remember what Susan said
to me, that "It's better to do it than talk about it." This is doing it, huh?
This is getting it down on paper. Knowing that I have to keep this record
is the best part.

• • •

Green Bean Surprise Casserole

1 can green beans, drained
1 can cream of mushroom soup
1 box cheez-bits

Layer ingredients—beans, then soup and cheez-bits—in greased
casserole. Place casserole in preheated 350° oven. Bake forty-five
minutes. Serve.

I'm telling you something I've never told anyone. Never, through the   3
long years of dinners made possible by the invention of the electric can
opener and the publication of Peg Bracken's *The I Hate to Cook Cookbook*.
Never, though the mention of meatloaf still conjures images of a dark,
brick-like thing, ketchup glazed and gurgling angrily in a sea of orangish
drippings in a pyrex baking dish. Never, even when her mantra spun in
my brain like an old forty-five: "Some people live to eat, Richard (my name
spoken with accusative gravity), *I* eat to live." Oh, Mom, was there ever a
worse cook than you?

Jill Woolley

I don't want to be a scholar. I run on intuition. My pleasure is in creating.   4
. . . I hate collecting information and acting like I have something new and

exciting to say about any of it. I'm not an organizer. Maybe I'm not a syn-thesizer. I'm all talent and no discipline. I can get away with some sweat and inspiration. I can get by with bullshit because my bull is better than 85% of everybody else's hard work. But I know what's coming off the top of my head. I know I'm a phony. At least that's how I feel. No substance. I've disconnected my soul. I've sold myself out because I could get by, looking good.

• • •

5   I meant to throw these boots away. I had them in a box for the Salvation Army pick-up. Somehow they worked their way back on to my feet. It's the same with so many things—boots, men, cigarettes—you try to get them out of your life and they keep coming out on top.

6   I've been trying to put cigarettes down for six years now, on and off. Still, day after day, I pay my [money] for a pack of poison. Why is it easier to smoke than to not smoke? It certainly isn't easier to exercise than to not exercise. It isn't easier to work hard than to not work hard. So why is it easier to smoke?

7   I try all kinds of tricks. I count how many cigarettes I've smoked in a day. I wait until dark to light up. I brush my teeth after every cigarette. But these gimmicks soon fall away and again I'm chain smoking from the time I get up until I retire.

8   I guess I'll keep trying though. Tomorrow, the boots go back on the pile for the Salvation Army. It's a start.

Art Greenwood

9   I live in an apartment with two musicians. Stan is a black man with a deep voice and a mild relaxed demeanor, who plays the drums. Meloni is his complement, fair-skinned and youthful , she sings and she plays the guitar. The are both rock musicians, perhaps, but their types of music are very different. STANLEY—HE PLAYS HIS DRUMS, SOMETIMES, AND HE BANGS EM, HE BANGS EM AND HE BANGS EM, HE'LL ROLL EM, BACK AND FORTH AND BACK REAL QUICK WITH A BASE THUMP, AND HE'LL BANG EM AND HE'LL BANG EM AND HIS CYMBALS CRASH AND HISS WHILE HE BANGS EM AND THE BASE THUMPS. And when he does this it's loud, and the place gets filled, and it feels good, as if you were in your own heart while it was beating. Meloni's music, though, is as different from his as she is, physically, from him. The deep rhythm of his drums doesn't surface in the trickling stream of her singsong. He puts you in your heart, but she leads you through your head. When you listen to her it's like the breeze in the trees or butterflies in springtime: light, airy, and hopeful.

*In what ways does this group strike you as typical of
performing musicians? What do you imagine their music
sounds like? Are there any clues as to whether they are
amateur or professional? What analogies can you make
between performing music and writing in collaboration with
others (see Trimbur, 72–75)? Why aren't there any women in
this group? In what sorts of musical groups would women
appear more prominently? Choose three adjectives that best
characterize the performance you're watching here.*

Barbara Schofield

Sitting in class I realized that I would never be more naked than when I   10
shared my writing. It is painful; it is frightening, because you open your
very soul to acceptance or rejection by your peers. All this attempt to communicate with others is complicated by each individual's understanding
of language; we try to present ourselves to others with as much clarity
and understanding as is possible for another human being to comprehend
of another.

In my mind's eye, I see all my physical, and thus symbolically, men-   11
tal scars and deformities, and I wonder. Do my classmates see the moles
on my neck? Do they see the puffy rolls of my flesh, my stretch-marked
belly reminiscent of three pregnancies? Do they see the eight inch long scars
down the sides of each thigh that resemble railroad tracks? What about the

broken blood vessel at the back of my left knee that came with the stress of the second hip surgery? Do they see the peculiar scar on the first digit of my right hand, a constant reminder of the day I sliced a piece of me off with the salami onto the deli scale? If they do, do they recognize these things for what they are, representations of someone's life? Do they accept all this? Do they reject it? And if they do, does it really matter? Have they not come naked to this class also, and aren't their scars just as visible? Of course they are, or so I tell myself, but it barely soothes me enough to honestly write about who I am, and how I came to be the way I am, today.

Susan Yoritomo

12   I want to be safe, so I'll hide in my apartment. I'm always hiding in my apartment. I love my apartment. I can see the sunset from one window and sunrise from another. And it's not really hiding, there's no one after me. It's isolation. It's windows and doors and walls and floors and ceilings, the physical barriers I cherish. I have plants. I wonder and worry and care for them, but it's very technical. There's no love. I like them because they soften the sterile interior of my apartment. As a friend said, they are the "bare minimum" in the way of plants. I have to agree. They are the pointy, blade-like plants which are called tropical but are reminiscent of the desert. Stark. My apartment is stark. I'm stark. I strive for starkness. I hate those irresponsible, indulgent feminine traits that are me, the real me. I want my masculine, minimal, logical, problem-solving self to dominate. I want that hard, durable exterior that is not unlike a wall. A cool marble wall that endures.

Betty J. Walker

13   HOUSEWORK—Housework—I hate it. I have tried for the past 20 years to learn to like it but to no avail. It is so boring. It is repetitive and stagnates the mind. Anyone can do it; it requires no real talent except the willingness to do the same thing over and over again.

14   Now take dusting . . . an exercise in sheer futility. You take a cloth and spray some type of polish on it. You move it around on the surface of the table or chair or whatever and pick up the dust on the rag. You move around the room dusting whatever level surface there is available that does not move. You move on from room to room. After a lapsed period of perhaps 20 minutes, you return to the room you dusted first. What do you find there . . . dust!

15   How about dishwashing and cooking. Those two things will drive you crazy. The cooking goes on forever and you no sooner get one meal completed then it is time to begin another. . . . Over the years I have developed a standard menu of things I can prepare that I don't burn or cause people to be poisoned. My family has learned that if it's Tuesday, it must

be hamburgers. Or, if it's Friday, it must mean that we'll eat out. You see, I don't cook on Fridays. . . .

Lest you form the opinion that I am lazy, let me reassure you—I am. [16] I will work all day at something I enjoy doing. Writing or sewing or creating something keeps me interested and busy and I am never bored. But the repetitive things drive me up the walls. The trouble with housework is that once you have it all done and the house is all clean and shining, six months later you have to do it all over again.

Tammy Weast

What makes Christmas Christmas? It is not the carols, the decorations, nor [17] the cold weather. It is not even Santa Claus or turkey advertisements on TV. It must be something in the mind. That's it. Christmas is a state of mind.

My parents are getting divorced. This was the first Christmas my [18] mom, brother, and I have spent without my dad. We did not put up a tree. I got the decorations out of the attic though. The first box I opened contained dad's stocking. Mom cried so I put it all away.

December 25th was weird. I did not get up until 11 A.M. The whole [19] world had opened their presents while I slept. My brother gave me a leather briefcase. I gave him a $50 gift certificate from Darryl's restaurant. He goes there and drinks a lot lately.

Dinnertime has always been around 3 P.M. on holidays. That was be- [20] cause my dad liked to watch the football games. This year mom said we could eat when we wanted. But we never did. I ate a beans n franks dinner later. My brother went to drink his gift certificate.

I worked the day after Christmas. All the secretaries in my office had [21] new gold necklaces from men. They all cooed about what a wonderful holiday they had had. I got nauseous because everyone was asking me, "How was your holiday, Tammy?" or "What did Santa bring you?" or "How long will you be eating turkey leftovers?"

I went home early. Mom and my brother were all early too. We each [22] seemed to have upset stomachs. It must have been something we didn't eat. Or maybe it was just our state of mind.

Kristin King

They lived in a two-million-dollar house that looked like a sty. I remember [23] walking into the living room once and seeing the abuse. On one wall was a dart board with no darts and the wall behind pocked with holes. The lining had been torn from the bottom of a yellow Chippendale sofa and stuffing poked through where the buttons had been ripped off. In front of the sofa was a cherry table with a half-finished model spread out and a tube of glue dripping. There were several high-backed chairs in the room, one Windsor without an arm, another with a torn velvet cover. On the carpet in front of the chair was a bowl of milk with Cheerios floating. An empty pop bottle lay on the brick hearth. Someone had tossed a crumpled McDonald's bag on the ashes of last winter's fires. A Steinway stretched underneath a broad picture window. Water rings spoiled the finish and a tinker toy was wedged between two keys. The piano bench, loaded with *Sports Illustrated,* was pushed against the wall. A china bureau, filled with Wedgwood and Lenox, stood in the corner next to the door. A lacrosse stick was propped against one of its broken panes. A black woman in a blue housecoat was attempting to compensate for the absence of a cat's litter box by pushing a vacuum back and forth over the stained carpet.

Rosalind Bradley Coles

24   Today in class Dudley said he's "tired of racial issues in class." Well—if he's tired of them, how does he think I feel? For years I have been the only Black (or at most one of two or three) in class and I have had to deal with white negativism towards Blacks. . . . Every time I've taken writing classes I've had to deal with some white person who had to put a Black person in their story— unfortunately the Black person is never a professional or middle class person, but illiterate, poor, kitchen workers or country hicks or rapists. Even Dudley in his first essay continuously used the word nigger derogatorily (although that's the only way whites can use it). . . . In the same week Grace had a sentence in her essay about a rural man who "knew the difference between a nigger and a colored man." Buffy is writing a story about two Blacks (with college degrees) who interact with a white lawyer. She is trying to adopt a Black dialect for her characters that has rhythm. What she has produced are illiterate Blacks.

25   Sometimes I wonder if these stories are written simply because it was what the author wanted to tell, or if it is a personal attack against me (which really isn't fair to assume, but it has happened so often). It's easy for Dudley to be tired of racial issues when he's white and surrounded mostly by whites. But what about me? Dudley's tired of racial issues. Well, I'm tired of having to see only the negative side of my people portrayed by my peers.

Richard Loftus, again

26   Should I write about sex? Not to be sensational. That's purposeless. I don't think it would be wrong to write about sex, because sex is so personal a subject that to use it is akin to plowing up earth. In the wake of the plow you find things you would not have expected to find, fragments of bone, earthworms, snakes, an old boot, strange rocks, an old wristwatch. Talking about sex digs down and throws up old lies, new lies, guilt, excess, happy memories, all manner of self perceptions ranging from the most superficial to most basic. So sex becomes the catalyst towards some reaction.

I think I see my own sexuality—my homosexuality—as the thing ²⁷
that made me a better listener. Because it was at thirteen something unpleasant to own up to. Can you imagine having to admit to yourself that
you're black? Almost amusing, because I can remember little of my self-
consciousness of that particular time, but it was definitely the experience
of being the outsider, living through my friends' heterosexual fumblings,
being the uninvolved sexless sage. Later, having come out, an experience
that has now been appropriated by ostomites, alcoholics, barren parents
and anorexics, I was learning the joys of rhetoric. Gay politics is nothing if
not rich in rhetoric. The difference between homosexual and gay? Homosexual is what the *New York Times* calls you; gay is what you earn the right
to call yourself.

It was always surprising to listen to others, if somehow they were ²⁸
aware of my sexuality, if, somehow, the subject came up. Listening to them
as they revealed their positions, feigned acceptance, gushed too readily
their acceptance, or guarded their words, or condemned—it seemed always
to be an exercise in measuring and dissecting. They say this, they mean
that. It made me even more careful to choose words that expressed my own
individual sense and that told the truth. It also made me aware of how to
lie, without *really* lying (hah!). Through listening, nuance is learned.

Cheryl Watanabe

After the homes were lost, the businesses destroyed, after the furniture ²⁹
was sold or stolen, after the fathers were taken away and the rights of the
land-born children erased you come—to offer money and recognition.
Deeds not willing to be forgotten haunt you: Utah or California, horse
stalls for hotels, manure for freshener, the death of our sons in Italy whose
parents, buried deep in the desert, watered the brush with tears. But your
offer comes too late. The children have grown, the night classes paid for,
the businesses reestablished, and prominence regained. We have wealth
enough to forgive with charity. Just put it in the textbooks, you never put
it in the textbooks.

In California thongs are still Nipper Flippers or Jap Slaps. People im- ³⁰
itate Japanese (or is it Chinese?) when I walk by. December seventh is the
Ides of March. I'm asked how I can see, is my field of vision narrowed?
Would I like to go to Japan? Only after I've seen Europe and Israel. Do I
speak Japanese? No. How come? Do you, being fourth generation French,
Polish, Greek, speak French, Polish, or Greek? "I was hoping you'd be
Buddhist." "Say some Japanese for me." "Play for me, dance for me, sing
for me, cook for me—I love rice." Prejudice is the spear of Ignorance. "You
write English very well. Where are you going for vacation?" Back to California. "Have you ever been there?" Yes, I was born in San Mateo and
raised in San Jose.

Stephen E. Ryan

Refugee Camp 2
Turk/Iraqi Border
Company A, 2nd Battalion, 10th Special Forces Group (Airborne)

31   The camp seems loudest at night. A huge, dulled murmur flows up from the valleys with hacking, rattling coughs, unending moaning like mantras, mules braying, wails and shrieks like a child stepped on a nail. Clank tap-tapping, metal pots clanking and wood chopping sounds but no sounds of laughter. The footsteps and shifting of thousands make a pressure on the ear just below the level of a sound. And no strong wind whistles close distractions or carries the sound away. Rising to the hill in the middle of 85,000 Kurdish refugees, the sounds articulate our mission.

32   In the morning, A–10 jets fly across in a low, slow demonstration. The screaming whine of their turbofans demands acknowledgement of their habitual, matin visits. The men look up out of makeshift tents with squinted eyes in a fearful reflex drawn from the sound. They have been down south where the wells still burn. Former conscripts twice fleeing, they fled Coalition destruction and then fled Saddam's genocide. But they and we and the Iraqi division beneath the border know the jet's other sound; the harsh, ripping bellow of the main gun, the tank killer. Welcome, sweet, fearsome companion.

33   Under the wide, banking circles, the women walk the morning road carrying clutched bundles pressed close. The bundles are soft-wrapped like cocoons, the folds unlike the sharp creases in the strained faces of the mothers' dry, silent anguish carrying children to graves. Behind them, men carry angular, longer, wrapped burdens as the dust rises.

34   Above, a rhythmic, tympanic beat from the north begins the helos' arrivals. They approach the small landing pad at full power remonstrating loudly at their heavy loads in the thin, high altitude air. They settle in ungraceful bobs and tilts as wheels unevenly touch down and sag with rotor blade slowing, drooping, giving back their cargo's weight to the ground. Today's arrival of rations, medicine and plastic-bottled water is too late for some, desperate hope for many.

Betty J. Walker, again

35   GOOD NEWS. . . . When it first happened, I was so excited I wanted to just jump up and down and hug the world. I felt like a balloon being blown up and up and up until I was about ready to explode—a feeling of excitement and satisfaction, a pleased-with-myself feeling. I wanted to tell everyone, but at the same time I wanted to keep it as a delicious secret. . . . I am going to have something that I have written published in the newspaper, and not in the Letters to the Editor column, either.

Content

1. Compare your reading of diaries by people with well-known reputations with the way you read the student writers' notebooks. To what extent does external information, about the authors, their other work, or the conditions of their lives and writing, influence your reading of a particular diary segment—or other writing for that matter? What clues in the language can tell readers whether the writer meant to keep the work private or meant for other people to read it?

For Writing

2. Keep a diary, writer's notebook, or blog, writing three to four times a week for fifteen minutes at a time. Use it as a place to jot down ideas for present or future writing. These may include:

   a. Sketches of people you know well or whom you've recently met
   b. Minidramas of people in action, discussion, or conflict
   c. Reactions to news events or to your reading, other writing, media viewing, or Internet messages
   d. Thoughts you've had or decisions you're pondering
   e. Colorful or otherwise memorable language—read, overheard, seen in ads, on menus, on packages or elsewhere
   f. Events or issues that evoke a strong reaction from you, positive or negative—but not lukewarm
   g. Anything else you want

 For comprehension, writing, and research activities and resources, please visit the companion website at <college.hmco.com/english>.

Writing: Re-Vision and Revision

The pun is intentional. *Re-vision* and *revision* both mean, literally, "to see again." Revision is likewise implied by the photograph above, for what the writer begins in pen on notepad will be transferred to the waiting laptop before she leaves the shelter of the tree. The introduction to this book's first part, "Writers in Process," briefly identified some of the dramatic changes in the ways we currently think about reading and writing, our own and others' works (1–12).

The examples of revision by Donald Murray and student Mary Ruffin reveal the passionate commitment writers make to their work. Because they are fully invested in their writing, mind, heart, and spirit, they care enough about it to be willing to rewrite again and again and again until they get it right—in subject and substance, structure and style.

Of course, these examples are meant to inspire you, as well, to be willing "to see again." When you take a second, careful look at what you wrote as a freewriting or a first draft, chances are you'll decide to change it.

If and when you do, you're approaching the process that most professional writers use—and your own work will be one step closer to professional. As playwright Neil Simon says, "Rewriting is when writing really gets to be fun. . . . In baseball you only get three swings and you're out. In rewriting, you get almost as many swings as you want and you know, sooner or later, you'll hit the ball."

Some people think that revision means correcting the spelling and punctuation of a first—and only—draft. Writers who care about their work know that such changes, though necessary, are editorial matters remote from the heart of real revising. For to revise is to rewrite. And rewrite, though not in the spirit that Calvin tells Hobbes in the cartoon (70) that makes bad writing incomprehensible. Novelist Toni Morrison affirms, "The best part of all, the absolutely most delicious part, is finishing it and then doing it over. . . . I rewrite a lot, over and over again, so that it looks like I never did. I try to make it look like I never touched it, and that takes a lot of time and a lot of sweat."

When you rewrite, you're doing what computer language identifies as *insert, delete, cut and paste* (reorganize), and *edit.* The concept of "draft" may have become elusive for people writing on a computer; one part of a given document may have been revised extensively, other parts may be in various stages of development, while still others have yet to be written. For simplicity's sake, I'll use the term *draft* throughout *The Essay Connection* to refer to one particular version of a given essay (whether the writer considers it finished or not), as opposed to other versions of that same document. Even if you're only making a grocery list, you might add and subtract material, or change the organization. If your original list identified the items in the order they occurred to you, as lists often do, you could regroup them according to your route through the supermarket by categories of similar items: produce, staples, meat, dairy products, providing extra details when necessary—"a pound of Milagro super-hot green chilies" and "a half gallon of Death by Chocolate ice cream."

Some writers compose essentially in their minds.* They work through their first drafts in their heads, over and over, before putting much—if anything—down on paper. As Joyce Carol Oates says, "If you are a writer, you locate yourself behind a wall of silence and no matter what you are doing, driving a car or walking or doing housework . . . you can still be writing." There's a lot of revising going on, but it's mostly mental. What appears on the paper the first time is what stays on the paper, with occasional minor changes. This writing process appears to work best with short pieces that can easily be held in the mind—a poem, a writing with a fixed and conventional format (such as a lab report), a short essay with a single central

---

* Note: Some material on pages 56–59 is adapted from Lynn Z. Bloom, *Fact and Artifact: Writing Nonfiction,* 2nd ed. (Englewood Cliffs, N.J.: Blair Press [Prentice Hall], 1994), 51–53.

point, a narrative in which each point in the sequence reminds the writer of what comes next, logically, chronologically, psychologically. If you write that way, then what we say about revising on paper should apply to your mental revising, as well.

Other writers use a first draft, and sometimes a second, and a third, and more, to enable themselves to think on paper. Novelist E. M. Forster observed, "How do I know what I think until I see what I say?" How you wrote the first draft may provide cues about what will need special attention when you revise. If you use a first draft to generate ideas, in revising you'll want to prune and shape to arrive at a precise subject and focus and an organization that reinforces your emphasis, as Mary Ruffin did between the ninth draft and final version of "Mama's Smoke" (82–84). Or your first draft may be a sketch, little more than an outline in paragraph form, just to get down the basic ideas. In revising you'd aim to flesh out this bare-bones discussion by elaborating on these essential points, supplying illustrations, or consulting references that you didn't want to look up the first time around. On the other hand, you may typically write a great deal more than you need, just to be sure of capturing random and stray ideas that may prove useful. Your revising of such an ample draft might consist in part of deleting irrelevant ideas and redundant illustrations.

In *Write to Learn* (Fort Worth, Tex.: Harcourt, 1993), Donald Murray suggests a three-stage revising process that you might find helpful in general, whether or not you've settled on your own particular style of revising:

1. A quick first reading "to make sure that there is a single dominant meaning" and enough information to support that meaning.
2. A second quick reading, only slightly slower than the first, to focus on the overall structure and pace.
3. A third reading, "slow, careful, line-by-line editing of the text . . . here the reader cuts, adds, and reorders, paragraph by paragraph, sentence by sentence, word by word" (*Write to Learn*, 167).

First you look at the forest, then at the shape and pattern of the individual trees, then close up, at the branches and leaves. Although this may sound slow and cumbersome, if you try it, you'll find that it's actually faster and easier than trying to catch everything in one laborious reading, alternating between panoramic views and close-ups. Murray expands on these ideas in "The Maker's Eye" (63–71).

John Trimble, in *Writing with Style* (Englewood Cliffs, N.J.: Prentice Hall, 1975), offers a number of suggestions for writing in a very readable style that work equally well for first drafts as well as for revision. Trimble's cardinal principles are these: (1) Write as if your reader is a "companionable friend" who appreciates straightforwardness and has a sense of humor. (2) Write as if you were "talking to that friend," but had enough time to express your thoughts in a concise and interesting manner. He also suggests that if you've written three long sentences in a row, make the fourth sentence short. Even very short. Use contractions. Reinforce abstract discussions with "graphic illustrations, analogies, apt quotations, and concrete details." To achieve continuity, he advises, make sure each sentence is connected with those preceding and following it. And, most important: "Read your prose aloud. *Always* read your prose aloud. If it sounds as if it's come out of a machine or a social scientist's report . . . spare your reader and rewrite it" (82).

Maxine Hong Kingston's "On Discovery" (60–61) makes a metaphor literal to illustrate the dramatic effects of re-vision, re-seeing, reconfiguring one's subject. Here she shows how a man's perspective on the world becomes utterly transformed when Tang Ao, a traditional Chinese male, is obliged to live and act as a woman.

John Trimbur's "Guidelines for Collaborating in Groups" (72–75) illustrates the enrichment that a variety of perspectives can bring to the writing process when several people are involved, such as a group leader, mediator, notetaker, critic, timekeeper. The photograph on page 73, three generations of males fishing and transmitting knowledge, serves as a metaphor for the way a good collaboration can work.

Ernest Hemingway has said that he "rewrote the ending of *A Farewell to Arms,* the last page of it, thirty-nine times before I was satisfied"—which means a great deal of rewriting, even if you don't think he kept exact count.

"Was there some technical problem?" asked an interviewer. "What had you stumped?"

"Getting the words right," said Hemingway.

That is the essence of revision.

STRATEGIES FOR REVISING

1. Does my draft have a *thesis,* a focal point? Does the thesis cover the entire essay, and convey my attitude toward the subject?
2. Does my draft contain sufficient *information, evidence* to support that meaning? Is the writing developed sufficiently, or do I need to provide additional information, steps in an argument, illustrations, or analysis of what I've already said?
3. Who is my intended *audience*? Will they understand what I've said? Do I need to supply any background information? Will I meet my readers as friends, antagonists, or on neutral ground? How will this relationship determine what I say, the order in which I say it, and the language I use?
4. Do the *form* and *structure* of my writing suit the subject? (For instance, would a commentary on fast-food restaurants be more effective in an essay or description, comparison and contrast, analysis, some combination of the three—or as a narrative or satire?) Does the *proportioning* reinforce my emphasis (in other words, do the most important points get the most space)? Or do I need to expand some aspects and condense others?
5. Is the writing recognizably mine in *style, voice,* and *point of view*? Is the body of my prose like that of an experienced runner: tight and taut, vigorous, self-contained, and supple? Do I like what I've said? If not, am I willing to change it?

MAXINE HONG KINGSTON

Kingston's autobiographical writings are haunted by questions of gender and identity and belonging: what relation has she and the others she writes about to China, to other family members, to America, how much to herself alone? And what belongs to her? Kingston was born in Stockton, California, in 1940, to recent Chinese immigrants. At home she learned Chinese, her only language until she started first grade (which caused her to score "zero" on her first I.Q. test, in English), and Chinese customs from stories exchanged in her parents' laundry. She graduated from the University of California (Berkeley, 1962), taught school in Hawaii, and—after publishing her widely acclaimed autobiography, *The Woman Warrior: Memoirs of a Girlhood Among Ghosts* (1975), returned to Berkeley to write. Her other novels include *Tripmaster Monkey: His Fake Book* (1989) and a sequel, *The Fifth Book of Peace* (2005), totally rewritten after the original manuscript was burned up in a house fire.

China Men focuses primarily on the meaning of immigration, cultural displacement, and cultural assimilation for Chinese men who emigrated to America, the "Gold Mountain" of Chinese legend. Its opening section, "On Discovery," is a parable in which a traditional Chinese man arrives by accident in the Land of Women, where he is forced into looking and behaving like a woman through the painful processes of having his ears pierced, his foot bones broken and bound, his eyebrows plucked and face made up—much to his embarrassment and shame. This metaphorical definition of a Chinese woman implies an equation: Chinese women are to Chinese men as Chinese men are to Americans. And this equation defines China men (note the connotation of fragility) in America. Metaphors and parables are useful devices for making meaning—explaining, discovering, or inventing new significance.

On Discovery

1   Once upon a time, a man, named Tang Ao, looking for the Gold Mountain, crossed an ocean, and came upon the Land of Women. The women immediately captured him, not on guard against ladies. When they asked Tang Ao to come along, he followed; if he had had male companions, he would've winked over his shoulder.

2   "We have to prepare you to meet the queen," the women said. They locked him in a canopied apartment equipped with pots of makeup, mirrors, and a woman's clothes. "Let us help you off with your armor and boots," said the women. They slipped his coat off his shoulders, pulled it down his arms, and shackled his wrists behind him. The women who kneeled to take off his shoes chained his ankles together.

A door opened, and he expected to meet his match, but it was only two old women with sewing boxes in their hands. "The less you struggle, the less it'll hurt," one said, squinting a bright eye as she threaded her needle. Two captors sat on him while another held his head. He felt an old woman's dry fingers trace his ear; the long nail on her little finger scraped his neck. "What are you doing?" he asked. "Sewing your lips together," she joked, blackening needles in a candle flame. The ones who sat on him bounced with laughter. But the old women did not sew his lips together. They pulled his earlobes taut and jabbed a needle through each of them. They had to poke and probe before puncturing the layers of skin correctly, the hole in the front of the lobe in line with the one in back, the layers of skin sliding about so. They worked the needle through—a last jerk for the needle's wide eye ("needle's nose" in Chinese). They strung his raw flesh with silk threads; he could feel the fibers.

The women who sat on him turned to direct their attention to his feet. They bent his toes so far backward that his arched foot cracked. The old ladies squeezed each foot and broke many tiny bones along the sides. They gathered his toes, toes over and under one another like a knot of ginger root. Tang Ao wept with pain. As they wound the bandages tight and tighter around his feet, the women sang footbinding songs to distract him: "Use aloe for binding feet and not for scholars."

During the months of a season, they fed him on women's food: the tea was thick with white chrysanthemums and stirred the cool female winds inside his body; chicken wings made his hair shine; vinegar soup improved his womb. They drew the loops of thread through the scabs that grew daily over the holes in his earlobes. One day they inserted gold hoops. Every night they unbound his feet, but his veins had shrunk, and the blood pumping through them hurt so much, he begged to have his feet re-wrapped tight. They forced him to wash his used bandages, which were embroidered with flowers and smelled of rot and cheese. He hung the bandages up to dry, streamers that dropped and draped wall to wall. He felt embarrassed; the wrappings were like underwear, and they were his.

One day his attendants changed his gold hoops to jade studs and strapped his feet to shoes that curved like bridges. They plucked out each hair on his face, powdered him white, painted his eyebrows like a moth's wings, painted his cheeks and lips red. He served a meal at the queen's court. His hips swayed and his shoulders swiveled because of his shaped feet. "She's pretty, don't you agree?" the diners said, smacking their lips at his dainty feet as he bent to put dishes before them.

In the Women's Land there are no taxes and no wars. Some scholars say that the country was discovered during the reign of Empress Wu (A.D. 694–705), and some earlier than that, A.D. 441, and it was in North America.

DONALD M. MURRAY

Murray was a successful writer long before he began teaching others to write. Born in Boston in 1924, he was educated at the University of New Hampshire (BA, 1948) and Boston University. He wrote editorials for the *Boston Herald,* 1948–1954, for which he won a Pulitzer Prize in 1954; in retirement, he writes "Reflections," an award-winning column for the *Boston Globe.* During his quarter-century of teaching at the University of New Hampshire, Murray wrote poetry; a novel, *The Man Who Had Every-thing* (1964); and his most influential work, *A Writer Teaches Writing* (1964; rev. 1985). In this writer-friendly book, he explained how people really write—as opposed to how the rule books say they should—thereby persuading generations of writing teachers to focus on the process of writing, rather than on the finished product. More recent books include *The Craft of Revision* (1997) and *My Twice-Lived Life* (2001), a memoir.

Revision, in Murray's view, is central to the writing process: "Good writing is essentially rewriting," by making changes—in content, in form and in proportion, and finally in voice and word choice—that will substantially improve their work, even though "the words on a page are never finished." Indeed, Murray completely rewrote this essay twice before it was first published in *The Writer* in 1973. Then, for an anthology, Murray "re-edited, re-revised, re-read, re-re-edited" it again. A draft of the first twelve paragraphs of the "re-edited, revised" version, with numerous changes is reprinted below. As you examine both versions, note that many changes appear in the final ("re-re-edited") version that are not in the "revised" draft.

THE MAKER'S EYE: REVISING YOUR OWN
MANUSCRIPTS* by DONALD M. MURRAY

When ~~the beginning writer~~ a students completes ~~his~~ a first draft, ~~he~~ they 1
~~usually reads it through to correct typographical errors and~~
— and their teachers too often agree.
consider the job of writing done, When ~~the~~ professional
writers completed ~~his~~ the first draft, ~~he~~ they usually feel ~~he is~~ they are at
the start of the writing process. ~~Now that he has~~ when a draft,
~~he can begin~~ writing (is completed, the job of / can begin.

That difference in attitude is the difference between 2
amateur and professional, inexperience and experience,
journeyman and craftsman. Peter F. Druc̣ker, the prolific
business writer, for example, calls his first draft "the
zero draft"--after that he can start coun̯ting. Most
~~productive~~ writers share the feeling ~~that~~ the first draft,
and ~~most of those~~ all which follow are ~~is an~~ opportunities to discover
what they have to say and how they can best say it.

~~Detachment and caring~~

To produce a progression of drafts, each of which says 3
more and says it better, the writer has to develop a special
kind of ~~reading~~ skill. In school we are taught to ~~read~~ decode what ~~is~~ appears on
as finished writing.
the page, ~~We try to comprehend what the author has said,~~
~~what he meant and what are the implications of his words.~~

Writers, however, face a different category of possibility 4
and responsibility. To them, the words are never finished
on the page. Each can be changed, rearranged, set off
a chain reaction of confusion or clarified meaning.
This is a different kind of reading, possibly more
difficult and certainly more exciting.

---

* A different version of this article was published in *The Writer,* October 1973.

5   ~~The~~ writer~~s of such drafts~~ must [learn to] be ~~his~~ [their] own best enemy. ~~He~~ [Writers] must accept the criticism of others, [-- especially teachers --] and be suspicious of it; ~~he~~ [they] must accept the praise of others, [-- especially teachers --] and be even more suspicious of it. ~~He~~ [Writers] cannot depend on others. ~~He~~ [They] must detach ~~himself~~ [themselves] from ~~his~~ [their] own page[s] so that ~~he~~ [they] can apply both ~~his~~ [their] caring and ~~his~~ [their] craft to ~~his~~ [their] own work.

6   Detachment is not easy. Science fiction writer Ray Bradbury supposedly puts each manuscript away for a year and then rereads it as a stranger. Not many writers can afford the time to do this. We must read when our judgment may be at its worst, when we are close to the euphoric moment of creation. The writer "should be critical of everything that seems to him most delightful in his style," advises novelist Nancy Hale. "He should excise what he most admires, because he wouldn't thus admire it if he weren't . . . in a sense protecting it from criticism."

7   ~~The writer must learn to protect himself from his own ego, when it takes the form of uncritical pride or uncritical self-destruction.~~ As poet John Ciardi points out, ". . . the last act of the writing must be to become one's own reader. It is, I suppose, a schizophrenic process, to begin passionately and to end critically, to begin hot and to end cold; and, more important, to be passion-hot and critic-cold at the same time."

~~Just as~~ [unproductive] ~~dangerous as the protective writer is the despairing one, who thinks everything he does is terrible, dreadful, awful. If he is to publish, he must save what is effective on his page while he cuts away what doesn't work. The writer must hear and respect his own voice.~~

Remember ~~how each~~ how the craftsman you have seen--the carpenter 9

~~eyeing the level~~ looking at the lie of a shelf, the mechanic listening to the

motor--takes the instinctive step back. This is what ~~the~~

writer ~~has to~~ have to do when ~~he~~ they read~~s~~ ~~his~~ their own work. "The writer

must survey his work critically, coolly, and as though he

were a stranger to it," says children's book writer Eleanor

Estes. "He must be willing to prune, expertly and hard-

heartedly. At the end of each revision, a manuscript may

look like a battered old hive, worked over, torn apart,

pinned together, added to, deleted from, words changed and

words changed back. Yet the book must maintain its

original freshness and spontaneity."

¶ We are aware of ~~the~~ writers who think everything 8
they have written is literature but a more ~~serious~~
frequent and serious problem ~~is the are writers is~~ who
are ~~overly~~ overly critical of each page, tear~~s~~ up each
page and never complete~~s~~ a draft. The ~~cut~~ writer
must cut what is bad to ~~save~~ reveal what is good.

~~It is far easier for most~~ beginning writers to 10

~~understand the need for rereading and rewriting than it is to~~

~~understand how to go about it. The publishing writer doesn't~~

~~necessarily break down the various stages of rewriting and~~

~~editing; he just goes ahead and does it~~ ¶ ~~One of our most~~
in the English-speaking world,
prolific ~~fiction~~ writer~~s~~, Anthony Burgess, says, "I might

revise a page twenty times." Short story and children's

writer Roald Dahl states, "By the time I'm nearing the end

of a story, the first part will have been reread and altered

and corrected at least 150 times. . . . Good writing is

essentially rewriting. I am positive of this."

11   ~~There is nothing virtuous in~~ the rewriting process~~.~~ *itself about* *isn't virtuous* It is
simply an essential condition of life for most writers. There
are *a few* writers who do very little rewriting, mostly because they
have the capacity and experience to create and review a large
number of invisible drafts in their minds before they get to
the page. And ~~many~~ *some* writers *who slowly produce finished pages, performing* ~~perform~~ all ~~of~~ the tasks of revision
simultaneously, page by page, rather than draft by draft. But
it is still possible to break down the process of rereading
one's own work into the sequence most published writers follow
most of the time.
~~as he studies his own page.~~

~~Seven elements~~

12   Many writers ~~at first just~~ scan their manuscript, reading
as quickly as possible ~~for~~ *to catch the larger* problems of subject and form. *They take the* ~~In this
way, they stand back~~ *craftsman's step back* from the more ~~technical~~ *superficial* details of language
the larger problems in writing.
so they can spot ~~any weaknesses in content or in organization.~~
Then as they reread — and reread and ~~the reader~~ *reread — they*
~~When the writer reads his manuscript, he is usually looking~~
move in closer in a logical sequence which usually ~~must~~ *involves,*
~~for~~ *seven elements.*

13   The first is subject. *As a writer* ~~Do you have anything to say? If~~
Sometimes writers are lucky *they* *Writers look first to discover if they have* ~~you are lucky, you will find~~ ~~that~~ indeed ~~you do~~ have something to
that they ~~anything to say~~ *said*
say~~,~~ perhaps a little more than you expected. If the subject *anything*
writers know they can't write ~~nothing,~~
is not clear, or if it is not yet limited or defined enough
for you to handle, don't go on. What you have to say is *SAVE*
always more important than how you say it.

*Novelist Elizabeth Janeway says, "I think there's a nice
cooking word* ~~which~~ *that explains a little of what
happens while (the manuscript is) standing. It
clarifies, like a consommé perhaps."*

The Maker's Eye: Revising Your Own Manuscripts

W hen students complete a first draft, they consider the job of writing done—and their teachers too often agree. When professional writers complete the first draft, they usually feel they are at the start of the writing process. When a draft is completed, the job of writing can begin.

That difference in attitude is the difference between amateur and professional, inexperience and experience, journeyman and craftsman. Peter F. Drucker, the prolific business writer, calls his first draft "the zero draft"—after that he can start counting. Most writers share the feeling the first draft, and all which follow, are opportunities to discover what they have to say and how they can best say it.

To produce a progression of drafts, each of which says more and says it more clearly, the writer has to develop a special kind of reading skill. In school we are taught to decode what appears on the page as finished writing. Writers, however, face a different category of possibility and responsibility when they read their own drafts. To them the words on the page are never finished. Each can be changed and rearranged, can set off a chain reaction of confusion or clarified meaning. This is a different kind of reading which is possibly more difficult and certainly more exciting.

Writers must learn to be their own best enemy. They must accept the criticism of others and be suspicious of it; they must accept the praise of others and be even more suspicious of it. Writers cannot depend on others. They must detach themselves from their own pages so that they can apply both their caring and their craft to their own work.

Such detachment is not easy. Science fiction writer Ray Bradbury supposedly puts each manuscript away for a year to the day and then rereads it as a stranger. Not many writers have the discipline or the time to do this. We must read when our judgment may be at its worst, when we are close to the euphoric moment of creation.

Then the writer, counsels novelist Nancy Hale, "should be critical of everything that seems to him most delightful in his style. He should excise what he most admires, because he wouldn't thus admire it if he weren't . . . in a sense protecting it from criticism." John Ciardi, the poet, adds, "The last act of the writing must be to become one's own reader. It is, I suppose, a schizophrenic process, to begin passionately and to end critically, to begin hot and to end cold; and, more important, to be passion-hot and critic-cold at the same time."

Most people think that the principal problem is that writers are too proud of what they have written. Actually, a greater problem for most professional writers is one shared by the majority of students. They are overly critical, think everything is dreadful, tear up page after page, never complete a draft, see the task as hopeless.

8   The writer must learn to read critically but constructively, to cut what is bad, to reveal what is good. Eleanor Estes, the children's book author, explains: "The writer must survey his work critically, coolly, as though he were a stranger to it. He must be willing to prune, expertly and hardheartedly. At the end of each revision, a manuscript may look . . . worked over, torn apart, pinned together, added to, deleted from, words changed and words changed back. Yet the book must maintain its original freshness and spontaneity."

9   Most readers underestimate the amount of rewriting it usually takes to produce spontaneous reading. This is a great disadvantage to the student writer, who sees only a finished product and never watches the craftsman who takes the necessary step back, studies the work carefully, returns to the task, steps back, returns, steps back, again and again. Anthony Burgess, one of the most prolific writers in the English-speaking world, admits, "I might revise a page twenty times." Roald Dahl, the popular children's writer, states, "By the time I'm nearing the end of a story, the first part will have been reread and altered and corrected at least 150 times. . . . Good writing is essentially rewriting. I am positive of this."

10   Rewriting isn't virtuous. It isn't something that ought to be done. It is simply something that most writers find they have to do to discover what they have to say and how to say it. It is a condition of the writer's life.

11   There are, however, a few writers who do little formal rewriting, primarily because they have the capacity and experience to create and review a large number of invisible drafts in their minds before they approach the page. And some writers slowly produce finished pages, performing all the tasks of revision simultaneously, page by page, rather than draft by draft. But it is still possible to see the sequence followed by most writers most of the time in rereading their own work.

12   Most writers scan their drafts first, reading as quickly as possible to catch the larger problems of subject and form, then move in closer and closer as they read and write, reread and rewrite.

13   The first thing writers look for in their drafts is *information*. They know that a good piece of writing is built from specific, accurate, and interesting information. The writer must have an abundance of information from which to construct a readable piece of writing.

14   Next writers look for *meaning* in the information. The specifics must build to a pattern of significance. Each piece of specific information must carry the reader toward meaning.

15   Writers reading their own drafts are aware of *audience*. They put themselves in the reader's situation and make sure that they deliver information which a reader wants to know or needs to know in a manner which is easily digested. Writers try to be sure that they anticipate and answer the questions a critical reader will ask when reading the piece of writing.

16   Writers make sure that the *form* is appropriate to the subject and the audience. Form, or genre, is the vehicle which carries meaning to the

reader, but form cannot be selected until the writer has adequate information to discover its significance and an audience which needs or wants that meaning.

Once writers are sure the form is appropriate, they must then look at the *structure,* the order of what they have written. Good writing is built on a solid framework of logic, argument, narrative, or motivation which runs through the entire piece of writing and holds it together. This is the time when many writers find it most effective to outline as a way of visualizing the hidden spine by which the piece of writing is supported. 17

The element on which writers may spend a majority of their time is *development.* Each section of a piece of writing must be adequately developed. It must give readers enough information so that they are satisfied. How much information is enough? That's as difficult as asking how much garlic belongs in a salad. It must be done to taste, but most beginning writers underdevelop, underestimating the reader's hunger for information. 18

As writers solve development problems, they often have to consider questions of *dimension.* There must be a pleasing and effective proportion among all the parts of the piece of writing. There is a continual process of subtracting and adding to keep the piece of writing in balance. 19

Finally, writers have to listen to their own voices. *Voice* is the force which drives a piece of writing forward. It is an expression of the writer's authority and concern. It is what is between the words on the page, what glues the piece of writing together. A good piece of writing is always marked by a consistent, individual voice. 20

As writers read and reread, write and rewrite, they move closer and closer to the page until they are doing line-by-line editing. Writers read their own pages with infinite care. Each sentence, each line, each clause, each phrase, each word, each mark of punctuation, each section of white space between the type has to contribute to the clarification of meaning. 21

Slowly the writer moves from word to word, looking through language to see the subject. As a word is changed, cut, or added, as a construction is rearranged, all the words used before that moment and all those that follow that moment must be considered and reconsidered. 22

Writers often read aloud at this stage of the editing process, muttering or whispering to themselves, calling on the ear's experience with language. Does this sound right—or that? Writers edit, shifting back and forth from eye to page to ear to page. I find I must do this careful editing in short runs, no more than fifteen to twenty minutes at a stretch, or I become too kind with myself. I begin to see what I hope is on the page, not what actually is on the page. 23

This sounds tedious if you haven't done it, but actually it is fun. Making something right is immensely satisfying, for writers begin to learn what they are writing about by writing. Language leads them to meaning, and there is the joy of discovery, of understanding, of making meaning clear as the writer employs the technical skills of language. 24

"I used to hate writing assignments, but now I enjoy them," Calvin observes. "With a little practice, writing can be an intimidating and impenetrable fog." Are readers meant to take him seriously? How can you tell? Judging from the authors in this book, particularly the pieces on writing, what is the ideal style—or range of styles—of writing for college essays?

25   Words have double meanings, even triple and quadruple meanings. Each word has its own potential for connotation and denotation. And when writers rub one word against the other, they are often rewarded with a sudden insight, an unexpected clarification.

26   The maker's eye moves back and forth from word to phrase to sentence to paragraph to sentence to phrase to word. The maker's eye sees the need for variety and balance, for a firmer structure, for a more appropriate form. It peers into the interior of the paragraph, looking for coherence, unity, and emphasis, which make meaning clear.

27   I learned something about this process when my first bifocals were prescribed. I had ordered a larger section of the reading portion of the glass because of my work, but even so, I could not contain my eyes with this new limit of vision. And I still find myself taking off my glasses and bending my nose towards the page, for my eyes unconsciously flick back and forth across the page, back to another page, forward to still another, as I try to see each evolving line in relation to every other line.

28   When does this process end? Most writers agree with the great Russian writer Tolstoy, who said, "I scarcely ever reread my published writings, if by chance I come across a page, it always strikes me: all this must be rewritten; this is how I should have written it."

29   The maker's eye is never satisfied, for each word has the potential to ignite the new meaning. This article has been twice written all the way through the writing process, and it was published four years ago. Now it is to be republished in a book. The editors made a few small suggestions, and then I read it with my maker's eye. Now it has been re-edited, re-revised, re-read, re-re-edited, for each piece of writing to the writer is full of potential and alternatives.

30   A piece of writing is never finished. It is delivered to a deadline, torn out of the typewriter on demand, sent off with a sense of accomplishment

and shame and pride and frustration. If only there were a couple more days, time for just another run at it, perhaps then. . . .

Content

1. Why does Murray say that when a first "draft is completed, the job of writing can begin" (¶ 1)? If you thought before you read the essay that one draft was enough, has Murray's essay convinced you otherwise?

2. How does Murray explain John Ciardi's analysis of the "schizophrenic process" of becoming one's own reader, "to be passion-hot and critic-cold at the same time" (¶ 6)? Why is it important for writers to be both?

3. What are writers looking for when they revise? How can writers be sure that their "maker's eye" accurately sees in revision the "need for variety and balance, for a firmer structure, for a more appropriate form" and "for coherence, unity, and emphasis" (¶ 26)? How do you know whether your writing is good or not?

Strategies/Structures/Language

4. Murray revises for conciseness. For example, the first sentence of paragraph 11 initially read, "There is nothing virtuous in the rewriting process." Murray then revised it to "The rewriting process isn't virtuous." The published version says, "Rewriting isn't virtuous." What are the effects of these successive changes and of other comparable changes?

5. Compare and contrast the deleted paragraph 8 of the original version and the rewritten paragraphs 8 and 9 of the typescript with paragraphs 7 and 8 in the printed version. Why did Murray delete the original paragraph 8? Which ideas did he salvage? Why did he delete the first two sentences of the original paragraph 9? Are the longer paragraphs of the printed version preferable to the shorter paragraphs of the original?

6. In many places in the revision typescript (see ¶s 1, 5) Murray has changed masculine pronouns (he, his) to the plural (they, their). What is the effect of these changes? What occurred in America between 1973, when the essay was first written, and 1980, when it was again revised, to affect this usage?

7. In the typescript Murray has added references to students and teachers which were not in the original published version. For whom was the original version intended? What do the additions reveal about the intended readers of the revision?

For Writing

8. Prepare a checklist of the points Murray says that writers look for in revising a manuscript: information, meaning, audience, form, structure, development, dimension, voice (¶s 13–20). Add others appropriate to your writing, and use the checklist as a guide in revising your own papers.

 For comprehension, writing, and research activities and resources, please visit the companion website at <college.hmco.com/english>.

JOHN TRIMBUR

Trimbur, born in San Francisco in 1946, grew up in the San Joaquin Valley and earned a BA in history at Stanford, followed by a PhD in English at the State University of New York at Buffalo (1982). He currently directs the Technical, Scientific, and Professional Communication Program at Worcester Polytechnic Institute, where he is Distinguished Professor of Humanities. His professional papers and books focus on writing theory and cultural studies of literacy, as is clear in the co-edited, prize-winning *The Politics of Writing Instruction* (1993). "Guidelines for Collaborating in Groups" appears in his recent textbook, *The Call to Write* (2nd ed., 2002).

Trimbur explains his divergent views on writing alone and on collaborative writing, which he calls "co-writing." "I like to do both," he says, "in part because they're different. Co-writing gives me a lot of energy and accountability. There's less anxiety because you can pass a text back and forth, building and changing it along the way, believing that your team is eventually going to get it into a shape that everyone can live with." In contrast, he says, "when I'm writing by myself I sometimes wonder whether what I'm saying makes any sense or holds together in a public way. I keep wondering whether I'm adequate to the task, whereas in co-writing I'm confident we'll eventually get it right."

Guidelines for Collaborating in Groups

1   Any group of people working together on a project will face certain issues, and a group collaborating on a writing project is no exception. The following guidelines are meant to keep a group running smoothly and to forestall some common problems.

Recognize that Group Members Need to Get Acquainted and that Groups Take Time to Form

2   People entering new groups sometimes make snap judgments without getting to know the other people or giving the group time to form and develop. Initial impressions are rarely reliable indicators of how a group will be. Like individuals, groups have life histories, and one of the most awkward and difficult moments is getting started. Group members may be nervous, defensive, or overly assertive. It takes some time for people to get to know one another and to develop a sense of connectedness to the group.

What is the relationship among the people fishing here? In what ways are they collaborating? If not all participants can be expected to contribute equally in all circumstances, what should determine the extent and nature of the contribution of each? How can the principles underlying their collaborative behavior apply to other collaborative activities, including writing? If there are disagreements among the participants, on what grounds should they be resolved?

Clarify Group Purposes and Individual Roles

Much of people's initial discomfort and anxiety has to do with their uncertainty about what the purpose of the group is and what their role in the group will be. Group members need to define their collective task and develop a plan to do it. This way, members will know what to expect and how the group will operate.   3

Recognize that Members Bring Different Styles to the Group

. . . Individual styles of composing can vary considerably. The same is true of individuals' styles of working in groups. For example, individuals differ in the way they approach problems. Some people like to spend a lot of time formulating problems, exploring the complexities, contradictions, and nuances of a situation. Others want to define problems quickly and then spend their time figuring out how to solve them. By the same token people have different styles of interacting in groups. Some people like to develop their ideas by talking, while others prefer to decide what they think before   4 speaking. So successful groups learn to incorporate the strengths of all these styles, making sure that even the most reticent members participate.

Recognize that You May Not Play the Same Role in Every Group

5   In some instances you may be the group leader, but in other instances the role you'll need to play is that of the mediator, helping members negotiate their differences, or the critic, questioning the others' ideas, or the time-keeper, prompting the group to stick to deadlines. You may play different roles in the same group from meeting to meeting or even within a meeting. For a group to be successful, members must be willing and able to respond flexibly to the work at hand.

Monitor Group Progress and Reassess Goals and Procedures

6   It's helpful to step back periodically to take stock of what has been accomplished and what remains to be done. Groups also need to look at their own internal workings, to see if the procedures they have set up are effective and if everyone is participating.

Quickly Address Problems in Group Dynamics

7   Problems arise in group work. Some members may dominate and talk too much. Others may withdraw and not contribute. Still others may fail to carry out assigned tasks. If a group avoids confronting these problems, the problems will only get worse. Remember, the point of raising a problem is not to blame individuals but to promote an understanding about what's expected of each person and what the group can do to encourage everyone's participation.

Encourage Differences of Opinion

8   One of the things that makes groups productive is the different perspectives individual members bring to group work. In fact, groups of like-minded people who share basic assumptions are often not as creative as groups where there are differences among members. At the same time, group members may feel that there are ideas or feelings they can't bring up in the group because to do so would threaten group harmony. This feeling is understandable. Sometimes it's difficult to take a position that diverges from what other members of the group think and believe. But groups are not forms of social organization to enforce conformity; they are working bodies that need to consider all the available options and points of view. For this reason, groups need to encourage the discussion of differences and to look at conflicting viewpoints. . . .

Division of Labor or Integrated Team?

Some groups approach collaborative projects by developing a division of labor that assigns particular tasks to group members who complete them individually and then bring the results back to the group. This has been the traditional model for collaborative work in business, industry, and government. It is an efficient method of work, especially when groups are composed of highly skilled members. Its limitations are that weak group members can affect the quality of the overall work and that group members may lose sight of the overall project because they are so caught up in their own specialized work. 9

More recently, groups have begun to explore an integrated approach in which group members all work together through each stage of the project. An integrated-team approach involves members more fully in the work and helps them maintain an overall view of the project's goals and progress. But it also takes more time—time must be devoted to meetings and, often, to developing good working relations among members. 10

These two models of group work are not mutually exclusive. In fact many groups function along integrated-team lines when they are planning and reviewing work, but also farm out particular tasks to individuals or subgroups. So you need to discuss and develop some basic guidelines on group functioning. 11

Content

1. Why has Trimbur arranged the principles for collaborating in groups in the order in which they appear here?
2. In what ways can these principles be adapted to the interests and abilities of the group at hand? To what sorts of activities in addition to writing might these principles apply?
3. Discuss—preferably with a group—how Trimbur's principles might apply to writing a particular document—for instance, a report or other presentation of information.

For Writing

4. Form a group, draw up some principles of collaboration, and follow your group's guidelines to write a collaborative document. Then revise the principles to reflect your experience of collaborative writing and revise the document.

 For comprehension, writing, and research activities and resources, please visit the companion website at <college.hmco.com/english>.

MARY RUFFIN

Ruffin was born in Richmond, Virginia, in 1964, and she earned a BA in English and philosophy from Virginia Commonwealth University in 1984 and an MA in 1986. Her mother, an artist and aspiring writer, died when Ruffin was thirteen. As a college student, Ruffin attempted for several years in her writing to come to terms with the meaning of her mother's life and death. The nine notebook entries that follow show the genesis and evolution of "Mama's Smoke" over a two-month period. They include one freewriting (#1), three drafts of a poem (#2, 3, 7), a playful free association of words (#6), and the completed poem (#8)— with which she was "never happy." In retrospect, she found the poem's first draft "far better than [its] final draft . . . because the VOICE IS REAL! I killed it."

The three preliminary prose versions (#4, 5, 9) developed from the original freewriting. The ninth and tenth (final) versions both included the same topics and most of the same language. However, following classmates' recommendations, Ruffin revised the paper so that the opening paragraphs reinforced the essay's main theme, signaled in the title. In the process of discovering the version that best suited her and her subject, Ruffin tried dramatically different modes of writing— poetry, free association, and prose—much as Pelizzon did in writing "Clever and Poor" (91–92). "Mama's Smoke," the resulting combination of epitaph, eulogy, and portrait, is a tribute to the continuing complexity of the relationship between mother and daughter, the different aspects of it coalescing through the catalyst of good writing and the love it expresses.

❄ *Writer's Notebook Entries: The Evolution of "Mama's Smoke"*

2/23   #1
Freewriting

A freewrite is all I can do again because the page is glaring, more ominous even than its traditional blank stare.

The poetry won't come. I've killed it with the spearhead of desire to be Outstanding English Major.

The prose won't come because it can't break out of the stillborn poetry.

The academics won't come because they're forced into the name-dropping realm of pretension. . . . Plus, I hate traditional white male southern writers. With those accents that sound like my mother but aren't my mother at all. . . .

There must be a starting point somewhere—a thread to grasp.

Can't do it all. Must at least reach out to the part that reaches back.

Mama.

2/24   #2
Writer's Notebook, first poem draft

Mama had fierce green eyes and black hair
I know from the black and white pictures
forty years old and more
and the salt and pepper I remember
and the tired hazel that I ~~be~~ inherited
for she could have been my grandma.

Jet black hair so thick the sheen
Matched the fierceness of green eyes
That were my Mama I know cause I've
heard tell and seen the faded black and
white pictures stuffed in the cookie tin
she had for twenty some odd years
and I've kept for ten, and the memory
of the permed salt and pepper I played
in dangling my feet in mid air hung
over the chair back and the tired
hazel nestled in the hooded lids,
I inherited her eyes but without
the green snap

2/25   #3
Writer's Notebook, second poem draft

<u>Rites</u>

Back
~~When~~

~~Back~~ When
It was cool to smoke, she did, and was
I imagine, of course not able to remember,
the picture of glamourousness. It was
In the days before that surgeon general
Determined the hazardousness
~~immediately~~   is now as immediate as
that ~~to rings in my ears in unison~~
~~with~~ "once upon a time", ~~steeped in~~ possessing
The familiarity of ~~what raised~~ that with which
                    reared.'
Unfiltered   we were ~~raised. Or reared,~~ ~~She was never without~~
Camels in   An ivory holder I've heard tell
and seen the legendary
                              & fits
~~the~~ flash of her ^fierce green eyes
~~in the wrinkled~~   rusted   ~~yellowed~~
yellowing and wrinkled in the ~~cookie~~ tin of ^black and
              snapshots
white ~~photos~~ she hung onto for
twenty some odd years, and I now
for ten.   difficult
The lid is ~~not easy~~ to pry open.
~~She passed on a spark to me, hazel~~
~~eyes~~   miraculously
The spark ~~somehow~~ passed on,
Miscellaneous barely discernible in my hazel,
          mediated by ~~brown~~ and the bloodshot
              ^Gray chromosomes
~~irritant~~ of Menthol Virginia Slim^ultra Lights
~~itches, smolders and goes cold.~~ incessant.
itches ~~a dry itch, beyond my years.~~

2/27   #4
Writer's Notebook, first prose draft

She was a smoker, but that began in the days when it was cool to smoke. Long before that surgeon general determined the hazardousness of the habit, and the behaviorists blasted it as an infantile fixation, she was glamorous. It was unfiltered Camels in the beginning, though by the time I was around she had gone to Merits, clunky with thick filters wrapped in blotchy brown.

My mother was an artist. She used to paint, in a turquoise studio smock, portraits of everyone she knew. Though I don't remember her ever painting herself—that is except for the red polish on her toenails. Her fingernails stayed natural yellow, she said because of the turpentine, but I think nicotine contributed to the hue. I've heard that when she was young she was never without her ivory cigarette holder. She readily admitted to her vanity.

later, 2/27
Writer's Notebook, first prose draft, second installment (excerpt)

She comes to me in the middle of the night, or rather I come to her, chase her even, through strange landscapes and insidescapes. Sometimes she is an old crone, witch-like, her black hair full of salt and her green eyes bloodshot knifeslits. . . .

3/3/85   #5
Writer's Notebook, second prose draft

She can surface without warning, anytime, anyplace. Sometimes she comes and goes so quickly that I hardly notice her presence. The other day, for instance, I stood in the kitchen staring at the can of Crisco and a tattered, encrusted cookbook page. Spoon in hand, I wondered blankly for a moment how to measure solid shortening. When the idea of displacement struck me and I filled the cup half full with water, I thought it was the ghost of a physics text. By the time I realized that it had been her, she was long gone and I had to shake my head. That's the way it happens frequently.

She never answers to her name—she almost seems to run away when she comes to mind. She is called Peggy, the only nickname for Margaret she could ever tolerate. She told me once that was why I had such a simple name, something virtually unalterable, to have forever. I resemble Peggy slightly, but just like the futility of calling her, when I look for the resemblance in the mirror it isn't there—It's those other times, catching an unexpected glimpse of my reflection out of the corner of my eye, that she suddenly appears.

3/10   #6
Writer's Notebook, "playing" (free association)

Dragons

Cookie tin——shining armor——rusty knight
Desert——fire——camels——dragons
Green dragons
Slain dragons & fair maidens
Dark fair maidens——unfair damsels
Once upon atime hazardousness——dragon
Dragon——take a "drag on" a cigarette
Smoke——cool smoke——hot smoke——smoke breath
Dragon's lair——womb——cave
cookies & stories——yellowing green
eyes & hazel bloodshot
Grendel's mother
Damsel in distress
Legend——spark of the divine
Glamourousness——amourousness——clamourousness
Reptiles——evolution——snake——fake——fang
Red nails——red lips——glamour is dark——beauty light
Medieval——Middle Ages——
Middle age——
The Tale——the monomyth——hero's journey
Separation——Initiation——Return
Smoke——illusion
Birthrite——legacy——heir——air——smoke
Glamour as aloof passion——cool hotness——
artifice——surface image——imagination
hard——glamour = armor——defense mechanism
Smoking as oral fixation
Smoking as magic
Fairy tales——scales——fear in fairy tails——wicked
stepmother——poison

3/17   #7
Writer's Notebook, third poem draft (excerpt)

Rites

Back when it was cool to smoke, she did, and was
I imagine, of course not able to remember, the picture
of glamourousness. It was in the days before the surgeon
general determined the dreadful gnawing
hazardousness that is now as immediate as

once-upon-a-time, possessing the familiarity
of that with which we were reared. . . .

3/28/85   #8
Writer's Notebook, final poem

Once Upon a Time

Back when it was cool to smoke, she did, and was
I imagine, of course not able to remember, the picture
of glamourousness.
Chains of unfiltered Camels, never without the ivory
holder between blood-red nails, I've heard tell
and seen the legendary flash of her fierce green
eyes yellowing and wrinkled in the rusted
cookie tin filled to brimming with brittle
undated black and white snapshots she hung onto
for twenty-some-odd years, and I still keep.

It is difficult to pry open the lid.

Once I caught her in the mirror, her tears
a simple bewilderment to me then,
turning more complex. Now
I catch her only on the edges
of my own reflection. Her spark in my hazel,
barely discernable, bloodshot
itches, runs, waters, burns
incessant.

4/2   #9
Writer's Notebook, third prose draft
(excerpt of entire essay)

Mama's Smoke

"Not 'plain'! Pure and ageless, incorruptible! That's what your name
is. I always hated mine with a passion! When people called me 'Margaret'
I felt squeamish. And 'Maggie'—ugh—a literal punch in the stomach! But
it's awkward to go through life with a nickname. It makes you feel always
like you're not quite ever really yourself. I didn't want that for you."

Peggy wanted only the best for me, the best being an abstraction she
pondered incessantly. When I was little, I would sit on the ancient wobbly
wooden stool in the corner of the kitchen, rocking and squeaking, listening to her. I liked that spot because it was right over the heat duct in the
winter, and caught the breeze from the screen door in the utility room in

the summer. Evenings, I asked her all kinds of questions—never afraid to broach any subject—and her answers usually took off miraculously, soaring.

Sometimes I just listened to the rhythm of her plastic-soled slippers. . . .

4/23   Mama's Smoke #10
final prose version (whole essay, revised and completed)

Mama's Smoke

1   I never thought I would smoke. With her it was different—she started way back when it was cool to smoke—had been the very picture of glamour. But that was before the surgeon general determined the hazardousness that is as immediate in the origins of my consciousness as once-upon-a-time.

2   Myths are absorbing. I've been told of the chains of unfiltered Camels she used to smoke, never without the legendary ivory holder between fingers with blood-red nails. By the time I was around she had switched to Merits.

3   Peggy thrived on craving. She wanted only the best for me, the best being an abstraction she pondered incessantly. When I was little I would sit on the ancient wobbly wooden stool in the corner of the kitchen, rocking and squeaking, listening to her. I liked the spot because it was right over the heat duct in the winter, and caught the breeze through the screen door in the utility room in the summer. Evenings, I asked her all kinds of questions—never afraid to broach any subject—and her answers usually took off miraculously, soaring.

4   "Not 'plain'! Pure and ageless, incorruptible! That's what your name is. That's why I gave it to you. I always hated mine with a passion! When people called me 'Margaret' I felt squeamish. And 'Maggie'—ugh—a literal punch in the stomach! But it's awkward to go through life with a nickname. It makes you feel always like you're not quite ever really yourself. I didn't want that for you."

5   If I didn't understand the songs she sang, I knew the syllables by heart. Sometimes I would just listen to the rhythm of her plastic-soled slippers. I creaked my stool in time as her slippers slid on the red and white tiles, moving from one end of the long counter to the other and back, to the sink, ice box, sink again, stove, counter. There was a regularity to the irregularity that soothed me.

6   As I draw deeply on my menthol Virginia Slims Light, looking through the yellowing black and white snapshots in the rusty old cookie tin she held onto for twenty-some-odd years, I wonder what happened to make me start smoking. The lid is difficult to open. Inside there are faces, one face altered over and over, with fierce green eyes flashing, despite the brittle fadedness of the images. My hazel eyes have the spark, but only enough of a spark to torment me, to always make me seem not quite all

me. Peggy stays away when I look at the pictures of her—maybe she doesn't identify with them anymore herself. She certainly used to.

But she also used to answer me when I called, and she no longer does 7 that either. Often deep in my sleep I glimpse her and chase her through strange insidescapes, but she always refuses to recognize me. Once recently she consented to meet me in an abandoned ice rink. When I skated in late, she simply stared down my apologies. Suddenly busying herself with an old movie projector, her back to me, she became a flailing chaos of limbs in the darkness of the rink. I gave in to the oppression of futility and seated myself behind her. At first the picture jumped and lurched on the screen, out of focus, broke once, and then smoothed out. Peggy danced a vaudeville set in our old kitchen, twirling whisks and spatulas to the soundtrack of "Clementine." When the lights came on she had disappeared, and I was alone shivering, with the distorted tune ringing in my ears.

Usually she surfaces so briefly and unobtrusively that I'm not sure 8 she has been there until after she's gone. Sometimes she appears an old haggard crone, the salt in her hair so thick that the pepper looks like dirt streaks washing away. Other times she is vital, younger than I am, the sheen of her black hair almost blinding. In the buttered daylight of my kitchen, as I stand blankly staring at the can of Crisco and the Pyrex measuring cup, I guess it is the sudden memory of a physics lesson that makes me think of using water to measure the solid substance. Displacement. Only later, as I gently knead the biscuit dough, careful not to bruise it, I realize that she has been there. Her smirk of disgust at the soybean powder in the open cabinet gave her away—she couldn't resist a mild "eee-gad" under her breath.

Peggy is steeped in colloquialism, figures of speech that barely es- 9 cape the shallows of cliché. She wrote a novel once, some kind of sequel to *Gone With the Wind* and now she comes to me at the typewriter sometimes, though rarely at the notebook stage, and whispers more criticism than commentary. She burned it, burned it in a fit of rage. Justified, for they wouldn't make her known. One attempt, one refusal. The only grace is to make a clean break.

She is something like a sequel to herself, elliptical and confusing, out 10 of context. She speaks in fragments, interrupting in the middle of my own sentences, giving to others the illusion that I have spoken her words. But that's not exactly accurate either. The others don't know her, don't know her words from mine. The illusion is mine.

The hiss of the word "fixatif" on a spray can evokes a frustrated 11 whimper of reminiscence. The bite of turpentine and linseed oil draws her. She is a painter of portraits and has rendered a likeness of almost everyone she is close to at one time or another, I believe, with the exception of herself. When I pick up a piece of charcoal she jumps in and jerks my hand, refusing to let me catch an image clearly. I have forsaken our art and she will not let me be forgiven so easily. But when I settle back and contemplate my own regrets, she relents. I feel her take her dry brush in hand and trace my features, a delicious tickle I revered as a child.

12   The legacy of paint stains on her pale turquoise smock, like the rhythm of the shuffle of her slippers on the floor, is her highest art. She denies it, of course, as obstinately as she refuses to appear when I look for her in the mirror. But she proves it as she shows up at those moments when I catch my reflection unexpectedly out of the corner of my eye.

13   The conversations we have now in black coffee cups and clouds of smoke are the closest we come to shared sustenance. They are always late, the times when it's most conspicuous to be awake. We plan the colors for the drapes and the throw pillows to furnish some future studio. The studio gradually takes shape, perfect, and then shatters in a coughing fit. I hear her in another room, hacking, fading, and then she's gone.

14   Just as she never stays, she never stays away for long. She was beautiful in her day and she still preens, still believes underneath in the ultimate importance of surfaces.

15   At parties, her old acquaintances appear as her friends. They ask me if I'm in art school and the flinching negative reply is overridden by their awe at my study of "philosophy."

16   "So like her! Right down to the hair and eyes, though not quite so dark, not quite so green. But underneath, Peggy *was* a philosopher, she was, so wise. . . ."

17   And Peggy surfaces and "eee-gads" so loudly in my ear that the friends' politenesses go under and my own return politenesses are just-not-quite-right. I sip my wine and kick Peggy in the shin. The acquaintances wander off whispering, "Almost the spitting image, except not nearly so . . . *genuine*. . . . This new generation. . . ."

18   Later, Peggy and I have pillow fights. The pillows are wet. The stains in the morning are on my face in the angry mirror. My eyes are hazel, murky. Peggy's eyes are clear, stinging green. When the lids began to droop, right before they closed for good, she cried bitterly in the mirror. Then I felt simple bewilderment, turning more complex. She still will not understand that her spattered smock is finer than the portraits. We light up. We cough out our truce.

For Writing

These various drafts of notebook, poetry, freewriting, and prose demonstrate the evolution of Mary Ruffin's "Mama's Smoke." You can compare and analyze these for evidence of development of character, style, narrative persona, changes in organization, incorporation of poetic language into the prose versions, and control over tone and relationship between the mother and daughter. You might also want to try to write a poem as a preliminary draft of a prose paper. Just play around with words, ideas, images, and sounds until they coalesce.

 For comprehension, writing, and research activities and resources, please visit the companion website at <college.hmco.com/english>.

Part II

DETERMINING IDEAS IN A SEQUENCE

Narration

Western culture is embedded in narrative: what happened then, and then, and after that, with causation and consequences strung together like beads along a timeline necklace. Analyses of processes (Chapter 5) , cause-and-effect relationships (Chapter 6), some descriptions (Chapter 7), and many arguments (Chapters 11 and 12) are based on narrative, stated directly or implied. Research proposals in the social, physical, and natural sciences, in medicine and business, require narrative interpretations: if we do this, we expect these events or phenomena to follow and to yield the following results.

Most commonly, we think of narration as telling a story, true or invented, or containing some mixture of each. What story does the photograph on page 85 tell? Who are the two people? What is their relationship? Why do they have their arms around each other? What has happened? What is about to happen? Where are they—in the immediate setting? In what part of the world? Is enough information apparent in the picture to answer these questions? What do you have to infer from your own knowledge of people and the world? Might there be alternative ways of interpreting this photograph, leading to alternate stories? What story would make this an appropriate illustration for V. Penelope Pelizzon's poem, "Clever and Poor" (91–92)?

Narration is a particularly attractive mode of writing, and ours is a storytelling culture. It is as old as Indian legends, Br'er Rabbit, Grimm's fairy tales, and the stories of Edgar Allan Poe. It is as new as speakers' warm-up jokes ("A funny thing happened on my way to . . .") and anecdotal leads to otherwise impersonal news stories. Narration can be as profound as the story of a life, the chronicle of a discovery, the history of a nation, or the account of one single, intense moment. Don DeLillo begins a brief story.

> Ash was spattering the windows, Karen was half dressed, grabbing the kids and trying to put on some clothes and talking with her husband and scooping things to take out to the corridor, and they looked at her, twin girls, as if she had fourteen heads.
>
> They stayed in the corridor for a while, thinking there might be secondary explosions. They waited, and began to feel safer, and went back to the apartment.
>
> At the next impact, Marc knew in the sheerest second before the shock wave broadsided their building that it was a second plane, impossible, striking the second tower. Their building was two blocks away, and he'd thought the first crash was an accident.

This excerpt from DeLillo's essay "In the Ruins of the Future" (*Harper's*, December 2001, 33) contains the major elements of a narrative.

1. *Characters:* Karen, Marc (whom we later learn is DeLillo's nephew), their twin daughters, and unidentified antagonists who are crashing planes into the World Trade Center

2. *Setting:* an apartment two blocks away from the World Trade Center
3. *Conflict:* terrorists versus New York's peaceful civilian population
4. *Plot*—beginning to unfold: Will this family survive? Will more attacks occur? What will be the consequences?
5. *Motives:* although the attackers' are murky, the victims' motives are clear—safety for themselves and their children
6. *Point of view:* a third-person account by an omniscient narrator who understands what the characters are thinking

It is unnecessary to specify the date, indelibly engraved on the minds of the readers as well as the participants. Only *dialogue* is missing; actions and eloquent silence say what is necessary. All these features make the incident or any vivid narrative a particularly easy form of writing for readers to remember. As this narration reveals, a narrative does *not* necessarily have to be a personal essay.

Narratives can be whole novels, stories, creative nonfiction essays, poems, or segments of other types of writings. They can be as long and as complicated as Charles Dickens's novels or an account of the events leading up to 9/11 and its aftermath, including the war in Iraq and a host of unforeseen consequences (see Chapter 13). Or they can be short and to the point, as in V. Penelope Pelizzon's elliptical interpretation of her parents' courtship in "Clever and Poor" (91–92). This evocative poem (yes, poems can and do tell stories) offers revealing, snapshot-like glimpses of two people [*characters*], both clever and heartbreakingly poor—the woman "here off the Yugoslav train" [*setting*], arriving to meet the "newspaper-man who liked her in the picture." The primary *purpose* of the meeting is matrimony. But the woman's expectations of escaping poverty [the immediate *motivation* for her journey] are immediately undercut by "what is poor is what she sees" in the dispiriting station [*setting*] at which she arrives, with its cracked clock and girls selling "candle grease"—a poor offering indeed, reflected, perhaps literally, in the poverty of her husband-to-be, "his shined shoes tied with twine." How the *plot* will unfold is implied by the clever deceptions already accomplished by the cape "hiding her waist" as her presumably out-of-wedlock baby is "left with the nuns" and the valiant attempts of each of the characters to hide their poverty—a condition evident to the sympathetic narrator [*point of view*], the daughter who wrote the poem, and the readers, as well.

A narrative need not be fictional, as the above examples and the essays in this section indicate. When you're writing a narrative based on real people, actual incidents, you shape the material to emphasize the *point of view, sequence of action* (a chase, an exploration), a *theme* (greed, pleasure), a *particular relationship between characters* (love, antagonism), or the *personalities of the people involved* (vigorous, passive). This shaping—supplying information or other specific details where necessary, deleting trivial or irrelevant material—is essential in transforming skeletal notes or diary entries (see "Student Notebooks," 47–54) into three-dimensional configurations.

A narrative can *exist for its own sake,* as does "Clever and Poor." As sixteenth-century poet and courtier Sir Philip Sidney observed, such writing can attract "children from play and old men from the chimney corner." Through a narrative you can also *illustrate or explore a personality or an idea.* In the classic "Once More to the Lake" (97–103), E. B. White uses his own experiences on a timeless summer vacation to explore the continuity of generations of parents and children, embedding short narrative vignettes into the overarching narrative structure. The photographs of people fishing on pages 73 and 101 tell two different stories, perhaps more, despite their common elements.

In Chapter 5 "The Inheritance of Tools" (148–54) Scott Russell Sanders uses a comparable narrative technique to interpret the character of his father. As Sanders's essay becomes a tribute to his father, and to the extended family of which his father was a member, Sanders describes his legacy, the carpenters' tools ("the hammer [that] had belonged to him, and to his father before him") and the knowledge of how to use them, transmitted through years of patient teaching and an insistence on high-quality work, "making sure before I drove the first nail that every line was square and true." This type of description consists of stories embedded within stories: how Sanders's father taught him to use the hammer (¶s 6, 9), the saw (¶s 10, 12), the square (¶s 14–16). Still more stories incorporate the current use to which Sanders puts this knowledge (he's building a bedroom in the basement), the incident of the gerbil escaping behind the new bedroom wall (¶s 17, 22), learning of his father's death (¶s 26, 28)—all embedded in the matrix of the stories of four generations of the Sanders family.

If you wish to write a personal narrative you can *present a whole or partial biography or autobiography,* as does Frederick Douglass in "Resurrection" (109–13), an excerpt from his *Life and Times* that recounts a single narrative incident in the life of a slave. Here Douglass tells the story of how he defied—in a two-hour fistfight—a Simon Legree–like overseer who had determined to break his spirit through repeated beatings. This, explains Douglass, was "the turning-point in my career as a slave. . . . It recalled the departed self-confidence, and inspired me again with a determination to be free. . . . It was a glorious resurrection, from the tomb of slavery, to the heaven of freedom." The photograph on page 111 corroborates Douglass's story with a story of its own.

Through narration you can *impart information* or *an account of historical events,* from either an impartial or—more likely—an engaged eyewitness point of view. The resulting narrative is always an interpretation, whether of an individual, a group, or a historical or contemporary event. Jason Verge's "The Habs" presents a comical account of his lifelong love for his favorite hockey team, the Montreal Canadiens, as well as a facetious self-portrait: "If you had to give up either me or hockey, which would you choose?'" asks his girlfriend. If she has to ask, we know the answer. Self-mockery is a convincing stance for any sports fan to adopt, since not everyone reading the narrative is guaranteed to love the home team—whatever that team may be—as much as the author does. Verge writes to entertain readers, partly at his own expense.

At other times, the narrative point of view can be satiric and highly critical of causes, unfolding events, outcomes, or all three. Sherman Alexie's satiric "What Sacagawea Means to Me" (93–95) is a critical commentary on white America's appropriation and exploitation of the historical Sacagawea, transformed into an icon ("our mother") in the process. Alexie tells only fragments of Sacagawea's story—that she accompanied Lewis and Clark on their "immigrant" expedition to spread the colonizing virus amongst the Indians; that she carried her first child, baby "Jean-Baptiste," with her on the journey; that she "died of some mysterious illness when she was only in her twenties." Sacagawea's biography—whether actual or imaginative, literal or symbolic—is composed of many contradictions embedded in the question "Why wouldn't she ask her brother and her tribe to take revenge against the men who had enslaved her?" Indeed, they are asked by the narrator, a Native American who himself is "a contradiction; I am Sacagawea."

Art Spiegelman's "Mein Kampf," with its embedded story of the Nazi death camps of the Holocaust, signals satire in its very title—also the title of Adolf Hitler's autobiography. In a mere sixteen cartoon panels we are invited to "read" the author's multigenerational life story and to interpret this through the split perspective of his critical eyes and our own. Thus we understand the Cave of Memory to be full of the memories identified by the signs on the labeled doors—"repressed memories," memories erotic and neurotic, intrauterine memories and childhood memories. His childhood memories are augmented by two photographs: one of Spiegelman as a child in a Cisco Kid outfit and one of his small son, Dashiell, in a Superman costume—both prepared to hold their own, if not to conquer their own corners of the world. The antihero cartoonist renders his life, the memories of his parents who "survived Auschwitz," and the image of his own child to comment on the need for struggle and survival against evil.

Fables, parables, and other *morality* or *cautionary tales* are as old as Aesop, as familiar as the Old and New Testaments, as contemporary as Spiegelman's "Mein Kampf" and Anne Fadiman's "Under Water" (104–7), a cautionary tale whose sunny beginning belies its complex moral undertow, which the narrator does not fully acknowledge until the passage of slow time for reflection, twenty-seven years after she was eighteen and "wanted to hurry through life as fast as I could." Although Fadiman focuses on telling the story and what it means to her, she expects the readers to apply to their own lives the moral understanding gained from reading about her experience of pleasure transformed, over time, to shame. The photograph on page 105 captures the event, but does it convey the spirit and tone of Fadiman's essay?

Must a story have a happy ending? This is guaranteed only in some versions of some fairy tales, and then only after great suffering. Douglass's victory over the vicious slave overseer, Covey, strengthened him to defy other oppressors and eventually to escape to freedom, where he found life difficult as well. Fadiman survives her teenage companion's death by drowning, but lives for years with the guilt. Although the desperately hopeful couple in Pelizzon's poem may marry, their beginning does not augur well for their future. Even the most benign of narratives, "Once More to the Lake," ends with a reminder of "the chill of death."

To write a narrative you can ask, What do I want to demonstrate? Through what characters, performing what actions or thinking what thoughts? In what setting and time frame? From what point of view do I want to tell the tale? Do I want to use a first-person involved narrator who may also be a character in the story, as are the narrators of all the essays in this section? Or would a third-person narrator be more effective, either on the scene or depending on the reports of other people, as in the account of terrorism quoted on page 86? An easy way to remember these questions is to ask yourself

1. *Who* participated?
2. *What* happened?
3. *Why* did this event/these phenomena happen?
4. *When* did it (or they) happen?
5. *Where* did it (or they) happen?
6. *How* did it (or they) happen? Under what circumstances?
7. Was the outcome expected, unexpected? With what consequences, actual or potential?

Narratives have as many purposes, as many plots, as many characters as there are people to write them. You have but to examine your life, your thoughts, your experiences, to find an unwritten library of narratives yet to tell. Therein lie a thousand tales. Or a thousand and one. . . .

STRATEGIES FOR WRITING— NARRATION

1. You'll need to consider, "What is the purpose of my narrative?" Am I telling the tale for its own sake, or am I using it to make a larger point?
2. For what audience am I writing this? What will they have experienced or be able to understand, and what will I need to explain? How do I want my audience to react?
3. What is the focus, the conflict of my narrative? How will it begin? Gain momentum and develop to a climax? End? What emphasis will I give each part, or separate scenes or incidents within each part?
4. Will I write from a first- or third-person point of view? Will I be a major character in my narrative? As a participant or as an observer? Or both, if my present self is observing my past self?
5. What is my attitude toward my material? What tone do I want to use? Will it be consistent throughout, or will it change during the course of events?

V. PENELOPE PELIZZON

V. Penelope Pelizzon's first poetry collection, *Nostos* (Ohio University Press, 2000) won the Hollis Summers Prize and the Poetry Society of America's Norma Farber First Book Award. Her new poems, nonfiction essays, and critical writings on film have recently appeared in *The Hudson Review, Field, The Kenyon Review, The New England Review, 32Poems, Fourth Genre, The Yale Journal of Criticism, Post Script, American Studies,* and *Narrative.* Educated at the University of Massachusetts, Boston (BA, 1992), the University of California, Irvine (MFA, 1994), and the University of Missouri (PhD, 1998), in 2002 she joined the faculty at the University of Connecticut, where she directs the Creative Writing Program and teaches courses in literature and film.

She says, "'Clever and Poor' is one of a tiny clutch of poems that survived from my MFA days and actually made it, years later, into my first book. I think of it as the first *real* poem I ever wrote. By that I mean it was the first poem I wrote where the form was inevitable given the subject matter—the subject created the shaping device of the two framing adjectives. This story, an account of my parents' first meeting, was one I had tried to write, in every possible genre, for several years. The problem was that it was such a fantastically interesting series of events, this postwar precursor to match.com, rife with physical privations, social barriers, and gender taboos. Obviously, it was very emotionally loaded for me, too. Hence the challenges: how to create a portrait that was *not merely descriptive* but dramatic, what point of view to adopt that was intimate but not editorializing. Perhaps most difficult was deciding what information to leave out. So for years I struggled with this as a long narrative poem, a short story, a dialogue. Nothing worked. Then one morning I woke up early and realized—insert cartoon lightbulb over head—that I could tell the whole story quite simply using those two words as a sort of balancing gesture, almost like a game. I wrote for less than an hour, and the result was 'Clever and Poor.' The poem taught me to trust that a story will tell you its true form (which is not to say that you won't have to wrestle near to death with it until it speaks)."

Clever and Poor

She has always been clever and poor,
    especially here off the Yugoslav train

on a crowded platform of dust. Clever was
    her breakfast of nutmeg ground in water

in place of rationed tea. Poor was the cracked
    cup, the missing bread. Clever are the six   5

handkerchiefs stitched to the size of a scarf
    and knotted at her throat. Poor is the thin coat

patched with cloth from the pockets
10   she then sewed shut. Clever is the lipstick,

Petunia Pink, she rubbed with a rag on her nails.
        Poor nails, blue with the cold. Posed

in a cape to hide her waist, her photograph
        was clever. Poor then was what she called

15   the last bills twisted in her wallet. Letter
        after letter she was clever and more

clever, for months she wrote a newspaper man
        who liked her in the picture. The poor

saved spoons of sugar, she traded them
20   for stamps. He wanted a clever wife. She was poor

so he sent a ticket: now she could come to her wedding
        by train. Poor, the baby left with the nuns.

Because she is clever, on the platform to meet him
        she thinks *Be generous with your eyes.* What is poor

25   is what she sees. Cracks stop the station clock,
        girls with candle grease to sell. Clever, poor,

clever and poor, her husband, more nervous
        than his picture, his shined shoes tied with twine.

SHERMAN ALEXIE

Alexie (born 1966) is a Spokane/Coeur d'Alene Indian who grew up on
the Spokane Indian Reservation in Wellpinit, Washington. By the time he
earned his BA from the University of Washington (1995)—prognostic of his
literary future—he had already published five volumes of poetry, a collection of short stories, and a novel, *Reservation Blues*. Indeed, the novel's title
is the motif for much of Alexie's writing. His works, including films (*Smoke
Signals*, 1998; *The Business of Fancydancing*, 2002), present Alexie's characteristically ironic, humorous interpretations of three profound central questions: "What does it mean to live as an Indian in this time? As an Indian
man? On an Indian reservation?" Alexie's Indians, laid-back, casual, comic,
often drunk, are waging war on two fronts. They battle as colonized people
must on reservations—against alcoholism, poverty, and cultural destruction;
they can never be treated fairly—anywhere. They also battle the stereotyping of Indians, not only in the popular media (as in the iconic figures
of Tonto and Sacagawea), but also in the "Mother Earth Father Sky" clichés

promoted in the works of other Indians, such as N. Scott Momaday and Linda Hogan (see 273–76). Along with the publication of numerous books (sixteen to date, and counting) have come a host of awards for poetry, screenwriting, and Alexie's short story collection, *Ten Little Indians* (2003).

Alexie says, "I think humor is the most effective political tool out there, because people will listen to anything if they're laughing. . . . There's nothing worse than earnest emotion and I never want to be earnest. I always want to be on the edge of offending somebody. . . . Humor is really just about questioning the status quo." "What Sacagawea Means to Me," first published in *Time* (June 30, 2002), is written in the same satiric vein as, for instance, another essay whose title is self-evident: "I hated Tonto (still do)." Alexie offers a critique of the mythic, white version of the Lewis and Clark expedition, a "multicultural, trigenerational, bigendered, animal-friendly" exploration, through a counterinterpretation of their faithful companion and guide Sacagawea, the American Eve, "our mother," "a contradiction. . . ."

What Sacagawea Means to Me

I n the future, every U.S. citizen will get to be Sacagawea for fifteen min-   1
utes. For the low price of admission, every American, regardless of race, religion, gender, and age, will climb through the portal into Sacagawea's Shoshone Indian brain. In the multicultural theme park called Sacagawea Land, you will be kidnapped as a child by the Hidatsa tribe and sold to Toussaint Charbonneau, the French-Canadian trader who will take you as one of his wives and father two of your children. Your first child, Jean-Baptiste, will be only a few months old as you carry him during your long journey with Lewis and Clark. The two captains will lead the adventure, fighting rivers, animals, weather, and diseases for thousands of miles, and you will march right beside them. But you, the aboriginal multitasker, will also breastfeed. And at the end of your Sacagawea journey, you will be shown the exit and given a souvenir T-shirt that reads, IF THE U.S. IS EDEN, THEN SACAGAWEA IS EVE.

Sacagawea is our mother. She is the first gene pair of the American   2
DNA. In the beginning, she was the word, and the word was possibility. I revel in the wondrous possibilities of Sacagawea. It is good to be joyous in the presence of her spirit, because I hope she had moments of joy in what must have been a grueling life. This much is true: Sacagawea died of some mysterious illness when she was only in her twenties. Most illnesses were mysterious in the nineteenth century, but I suspect that Sacagawea's indigenous immune system was defenseless against an immigrant virus. Perhaps Lewis and Clark infected Sacagawea. If that is true, then

---

We often forget that many—perhaps most—professional quality photographs are staged. This photograph was staged by anthropologist Franz Boas (left) and photographer George Hunt (right) during a late-nineteenth-century expedition to study indigenous cultures of the Pacific Northwest, which were becoming increasingly infiltrated by western "civilization." The creation of an artificial backdrop enables the Kwakiutl woman weaving cedar bark to appear more "authentic" than she would have if posed against the picket and stockade fences, or the building with columns and Romanesque arches, behind her. How do you "read" the photograph in front of the blanket background? How does the presence of the actual background influence your reading? In what ways does this photograph metaphorically capture the essence of "What Sacagawea Means to Me"? In what ways can a photograph of one century be used to comment on an essay written a century later?

certain postcolonial historians would argue that she was murdered not by germs but by colonists who carried those germs. I don't know much about the science of disease and immunities, but I know enough poetry to recognize that individual human beings are invaded and colonized by foreign bodies, just as individual civilizations are invaded and colonized by foreign bodies. In that sense, colonization might be a natural process, tragic and violent to be sure, but predictable and ordinary as well, and possibly necessary for the advance, however constructive and destructive, of all civilizations.

3   After all, Lewis and Clark's story has never been just the triumphant tale of two white men, no matter what the white historians might need to believe. Sacagawea was not the primary hero of this story either, no matter

what the Native American historians and I might want to believe. The story of Lewis and Clark is also the story of the approximately forty-five nameless and faceless first- and second-generation European Americans who joined the journey, then left or completed it, often without monetary or historical compensation. Considering the time and place, I imagine those forty-five were illiterate, low-skilled laborers subject to managerial whims and nineteenth-century downsizing. And it is most certainly the story of the black slave York, who also cast votes during this allegedly democratic adventure. It's even the story of Seaman, the domesticated Newfoundland dog who must have been a welcome and friendly presence and who survived the risk of becoming supper during one lean time or another. The Lewis and Clark Expedition was exactly the kind of multicultural, trigenerational, bigendered, animal-friendly, government-supported, partly French-Canadian project that should rightly be celebrated by liberals and castigated by conservatives.

In the end, I wonder if colonization might somehow be magical. After 4 all, Miles Davis is the direct descendant of slaves and slave owners. Hank Williams is the direct descendant of poor whites and poorer Indians. In 1876 Emily Dickinson was writing her poems in an Amherst attic while Crazy Horse was killing Custer on the banks of the Little Big Horn. I remain stunned by these contradictions, by the successive generations of social, political, and artistic mutations that can be so beautiful and painful. How did we get from there to here? This country somehow gave life to Maria Tallchief and Ted Bundy, to Geronimo and Joe McCarthy, to Nathan Bedford Forrest and Toni Morrison, to the Declaration of Independence and Executive Order No. 1066, to Cesar Chavez and Richard Nixon, to theme parks and national parks, to smallpox and the vaccine for smallpox.

As a Native American, I want to hate this country and its contradic- 5 tions. I want to believe that Sacagawea hated this country and its contradictions. But this country exists, in whole and in part, because Sacagawea helped Lewis and Clark. In the land that came to be called Idaho, she acted as diplomat between her long-lost brother and the Lewis and Clark party. Why wouldn't she ask her brother and her tribe to take revenge against the men who had enslaved her? Sacagawea is a contradiction. Here in Seattle, I exist, in whole and in part, because a half-white man named James Cox fell in love with a Spokane Indian woman named Etta Adams and gave birth to my mother. I am a contradiction; I am Sacagawea.

Content

1. Alexie's short piece depends on readers to understand a host of common cultural references: Sacagawea as a cultural and historical figure; Lewis and Clark and the purpose(s) and nature of their expedition; other members of the expedition (including the Newfoundland dog); and all of the people and events referred to in ¶ 4: Miles Davis, Hank Williams, Emily Dickinson, Crazy Horse, and Custer. Do

you recognize most of them? If you don't, can you still understand Alexie's general point and the means by which he's making it? Or is he too allusive? Explain.

2. Identify and amplify from your own knowledge of history the various roles in American history that Alexie attributes to Sacagawea whether she actually played them or not: Indian icon who helped Lewis and Clark on their expedition (a fact so well-known that Alexie does not fully articulate it in this essay); child kidnap victim; wife of a French-Canadian trader; mother of infant Jean-Baptiste, who accompanied her on the journey. He also calls her the mother of our nation, an undeserving victim of "immigrant" viruses, diplomat between her "long-lost brother and the Lewis and Clark party," a "contradiction" who lives on in subsequent Indian generations. Do you disagree with any of his interpretations? If so, explain why.

3. Why does Alexie say "Sacagawea was not the primary hero of [the Lewis and Clark story], no matter what the Native American historians and I might want to believe" (¶ 3). Who is the hero, if not Lewis and Clark or Sacagawea?

Strategies/Structures/Language

4. Why does Alexie set up Sacagawea's brain as a "multicultural theme park called Sacagawea Land," into which readers go for a "low price of admission" to allegedly recreate the Indian's experiences? What are readers expected to learn as a consequence of all the roles they'll play therein (see question 1)?

5. At what point in the essay do you recognize that Alexie is being sarcastic? Why did he title the piece "What Sacagawea Means to Me"?

For Writing

6. Write a short "true" story of some historical event—particularly one involving oppression of other groups or cultures—that you thought you understood but that a new rendering (perhaps as a new story rather than just a collection of facts) or new information reveals a new concept to you and to your readers. How much information will you have to supply? How much can you expect your readers to understand? If you can write with a partner who represents the other culture you're examining, so much the better.

7. Compare the satiric politics of Alexie's writing (this essay or any other that strikes your fancy) with Fritz Scholder's paintings, such as an Indian with a quill in his hand and an American flag on his lap, evoking the Founding Fathers and Betsy Ross (see photo essay). What is Scholder trying to prove? How do you know?

 For comprehension, writing, and research activities and resources, please visit the companion website at <college.hmco.com/english>.

E. B. WHITE

Born in peaceful Mount Vernon, New York, in 1899, White was editor of the Cornell *Daily Sun* during his senior year in college. In 1927, he joined the staff of the year-old *New Yorker*, writing "Talk of the Town," "Notes and Comments" columns, and some 30,000 witty ripostes to stuffy or false writing and grammatical blunders that appeared in newspapers and in "Letters We Never Finished Reading." In 1957 the Whites moved to Allen Cove, Maine, where White wrote until his death in 1985. His distinguished works include the essays collected in *One Man's Meat* (1944), *The Second Tree from the Corner* (1954), and *The Points of My Compass* (1962); landmark advice on how to write clear, plain prose, *The Elements of Style* (rev. 1973), with his Cornell professor, William Strunk; and three classic children's books, *Stuart Little* (1945), *Charlotte's Web* (1952), and *The Trumpet of the Swan* (1970).

"Once More to the Lake," a narrative of father and son, timeless generations in the eternal Maine countryside, conveys significant intangibles (love—parental and filial; the importance of nature; the inevitability of growth, change, and death) through memorably specific details. White leads us to the lake itself ("cool and motionless"), down the path to yesteryear, where the continuity of generations intermingles past, present, and future until they become almost indistinguishable: "The years were a mirage and there had been no years. . . ." Everywhere White's son, thoroughly identified with his father, does the same things White had done at the same lake as a boy—putting about in the same boat, catching the same bass, enjoying the same ritualistic swim after the same summer thunderstorm (see also Scott Russell Sanders's "The Inheritance of Tools," 148–54). The benevolent mood that White recreates indelibly shifts, however, in the cosmic chill of the last sentence.

Once More to the Lake

One summer, along about 1904, my father rented a camp on a lake in Maine and took us all there for the month of August. We all got ringworm from some kittens and had to rub Pond's Extract on our arms and legs night and morning, and my father rolled over in a canoe with all his clothes on; but outside of that the vacation was a success and from then on none of us ever thought there was any place in the world like that lake in Maine. We returned summer after summer—always on August 1st for one month. I have since become a salt-water man, but sometimes in summer there are days when the restlessness of the tides and the fearful cold of the sea water and the incessant wind which blows across the afternoon and into the evening make me wish for the placidity of a lake in the woods. A few weeks ago this feeling got so strong I bought myself a couple of bass hooks and a spinner and returned to the lake where we used to go, for a week's fishing and to revisit old haunts.

2   I took along my son, who had never had any fresh water up his nose and who had seen lily pads only from train windows. On the journey over to the lake I began to wonder what it would be like. I wondered how time would have marred this unique, this holy spot—the coves and streams, the hills that the sun set behind, the camps and the paths behind the camps. I was sure the tarred road would have found it out and I wondered in what other ways it would be desolated. It is strange how much you can re-member about places like that once you allow your mind to return into the grooves which lead back. You remember one thing, and that suddenly reminds you of another thing. I guess I remembered clearest of all the early mornings, when the lake was cool and motionless, remembered how the bedroom smelled of the lumber it was made of and of the wet woods whose scent entered through the screen. The partitions in the camp were thin and did not extend clear to the top of the rooms, and as I was always the first up I would dress softly so as not to wake the others, and sneak out into the sweet outdoors and start out in the canoe, keeping close along the shore in the long shadows of the pines. I remembered being very careful never to rub my paddle against the gunwale for fear of disturbing the still-ness of the cathedral.

3   The lake had never been what you would call a wild lake. There were cottages sprinkled around the shores, and it was in farming country although the shores of the lake were quite heavily wooded. Some of the cottages were owned by nearby farmers, and you would live at the shore and eat your meals at the farmhouse. That's what our family did. But although it wasn't wild, it was a fairly large and undisturbed lake and there were places in it which, to a child at least, seemed infinitely remote and primeval.

4   I was right about the tar: it led to within half a mile of the shore. But when I got back there, with my boy, and we settled into a camp near a farmhouse and into the kind of summertime I had known, I could tell that it was going to be pretty much the same as it had been before—I knew it, lying in bed the first morning, smelling the bedroom, and hearing the boy sneak quietly out and go off along the shore in a boat. I began to sustain the illusion that he was I, and therefore by simple transposition, that I was my father. This sensation persisted, kept cropping up all the time we were there. It was not an entirely new feeling, but in this setting it grew much stronger. I seemed to be living a dual existence. I would be in the middle of some simple act, I would be picking up a bait box or laying down a table fork, or I would be saying something, and suddenly it would be not I but my father who was saying the words or making the gesture. It gave me a creepy sensation.

5   We went fishing the first morning. I felt the same damp moss cover-ing the worms in the bait can, and saw the dragonfly alight on the tip of my rod as it hovered a few inches from the surface of the water. It was the arrival of this fly that convinced me beyond any doubt that everything was

as it always had been, that the years were a mirage and there had been no years. The small waves were the same, chucking the rowboat under the chin as we fished at anchor, and the boat was the same boat, the same color green and the ribs broken in the same places, and under the floorboards the same fresh-water leavings and debris—the dead helgramite, the wisps of moss, the rusty discarded fishhook, the dried blood from yesterday's catch. We stared silently at the tips of our rods, at the dragonflies that came and went. I lowered the tip of mine into the water, tentatively, pensively dislodging the fly, which darted two feet away, poised, darted two feet back, and came to a rest again a little farther up the rod. There had been no years between the ducking of this dragonfly and the other one—the one that was part of memory. I looked at the boy, who was silently watching his fly, and it was my hands that held his rod, my eyes watching. I felt dizzy and didn't know which rod I was at the end of.

We caught two bass, hauling them in briskly as though they were 6 mackerel, pulling them over the side of the boat in a businesslike manner without any landing net, and stunning them with a blow on the back of the head. When we got back for a swim before lunch, the lake was exactly where we had left it, the same number of inches from the dock, and there was only the merest suggestion of a breeze. This seemed an utterly enchanted sea, this lake you could leave to its own devices for a few hours and come back to, and find that it had not stirred, this constant and trustworthy body of water. In the shallows, the dark, watersoaked sticks and twigs, smooth and old, were undulating in clusters on the bottom against the clean ribbed sand, and the track of the mussel was plain. A school of minnows swam by, each minnow with its small individual shadow, doubling the attendance, so clear and sharp in the sunlight. Some of the other campers were in swimming, along the shore, one of them with a cake of soap, and the water felt thin and clear and unsubstantial. Over the years there had been this person with the cake of soap, this cultist, and here he was. There had been no years.

Up to the farmhouse to dinner through the teeming, dusty field, the 7 road under our sneakers was only a two-track road. The middle track was missing, the one with the marks of the hooves and the splotches of dried, flaky manure. There had always been three tracks to choose from in choosing which track to walk in; now the choice was narrowed down to two. For a moment I missed terribly the middle alternative. But the way led past the tennis court, and something about the way it lay there in the sun reassured me; the tape had loosened along the backline, the alleys were green with plantains and other weeds, and the net (installed in June and removed in September) sagged in the dry noon, and the whole place steamed with midday heat and hunger and emptiness. There was a choice of pie for dessert, and one was blueberry and one was apple, and the waitresses were the same country girls, there having been no passage of time, only the illusion of it as in a dropped curtain—the waitresses were still fifteen; their hair had been washed, that was the only difference—they had been to the movies and seen the pretty girls with the clean hair.

8   Summertime, oh summertime, pattern of life indelible, the fade-proof lake, the wood unshatterable, the pasture with the sweetfern and the juniper forever and ever, summer without end; this was the background, and the life along the shore was the design, the cottages with their innocent and tranquil design, their tiny docks with the flagpole and the American flag floating against the white clouds in the blue sky, the little paths over the roots of the trees leading from camp to camp and the paths leading back to the outhouses and the can of lime for sprinkling, and at the souvenir counters at the store the miniature birchbark canoes and the postcards that showed things looking a little better than they looked. This was the American family at play, escaping the city heat, wondering whether the newcomers in the camp at the head of the cove were "common" or "nice," wondering whether it was true that the people who drove up for Sunday dinner at the farmhouse were turned away because there wasn't enough chicken.

9   It seemed to me, as I kept remembering all this, that those times and those summers had been infinitely precious and worth saving. There had been jollity and peace and goodness. The arriving (at the beginning of August) had been so big a business in itself, at the railway station the farm wagon drawn up, the first smell of the pine-laden air, the first glimpse of the smiling farmer, and the great importance of the trunks and your father's enormous authority in such matters, and the feel of the wagon under you for the long ten-mile haul, and at the top of the last long hill catching the first view of the lake after eleven months of not seeing this cherished body of water. The shouts and cries of the other campers when they saw you, and the trunks to be unpacked, to give up their rich burden. (Arriving was less exciting nowadays, when you sneaked up in your car and parked it under a tree near the camp and took out the bags and in five minutes it was all over, no fuss, no loud wonderful fuss about trunks.)

10   Peace and goodness and jollity. The only thing that was wrong now, really, was the sound of the place, an unfamiliar nervous sound of the outboard motors. This was the note that jarred, the one thing that would sometimes break the illusion and set the years moving. In those other summertimes all motors were inboard; and when they were at a little distance, the noise they made was a sedative, an ingredient of summer sleep. They were one-cylinder and two-cylinder engines, and some were make-and-break and some were jump-spark, but they all made a sleepy sound across the lake. The one-lungers throbbed and fluttered, and the twin-cylinder ones purred and purred, and that was a quiet sound too. But now the campers all had outboards. In the daytime, in the hot mornings, these motors made a petulant, irritable sound; at night, in the still evening when the afterglow lit the water, they whined about one's ears like mosquitoes. My boy loved our rented outboard, and his great desire was to

Who are the actors? What is the relationship between the man and the boy? What's the setting? The mood? What story or stories does this photograph tell—the overt action in progress? What—short and long term—has led up to this moment? What will happen after this event is over? Literally? In memory? How does your reading of E. B. White's "Once More to the Lake" affect your answers to these questions?

achieve singlehanded mastery over it, and authority, and he soon learned the trick of choking it a little (but not too much), and the adjustment of the needle valve. Watching him I would remember the things you could do with the old one-cylinder engine with the heavy flywheel, how you could have it eating out of your hand if you got really close to it spiritually. Motor boats in those days didn't have clutches, and you would make a landing by shutting off the motor at the proper time and coasting in with a dead rudder. But there was a way of reversing them, if you learned the trick, by cutting the switch and putting it on again exactly on the final dying revolution of the flywheel, so that it would kick back against compression and begin reversing. Approaching a dock in a strong following breeze, it was difficult to slow up sufficiently by the ordinary coasting method, and if a boy felt he had complete mastery over his motor, he was tempted to keep it running beyond its time and then reverse it a few feet from the dock. It took a cool nerve, because if you threw the switch a twentieth of a second too soon you would catch the flywheel when it still had speed enough to go up past center, and the boat would leap ahead, charging bull-fashion at the dock.

We had a good week at the camp. The bass were biting well and the sun shone endlessly, day after day. We would be tired at night and lie 11 down in the accumulated heat of the little bedrooms after the long hot day and the breeze would stir almost imperceptibly outside and the smell of the swamp drift in through the rusty screens. Sleep would come easily and in the morning the red squirrel would be on the roof, tapping out his gay routine. I kept remembering everything, lying in bed in the mornings— the small steamboat that had a long rounded stern like the lip of a Ubangi, and how quietly she ran on the moonlight sails, when the older boys played their mandolins and the girls sang and we ate doughnuts dipped in sugar, and how sweet the music was on the water in the shining night, and what it had felt like to think about girls then. After breakfast we would go up to the store and the things were in the same place—the min-nows in a bottle, the plugs and spinners, disarranged and pawed over by the youngsters from the boys' camp, the Fig Newtons and the Beeman's gum. Outside, the road was tarred and cars stood in front of the store. In-side, all was just as it had always been, except there was more Coca-Cola and not so much Moxie and root beer and birch beer and sarsaparilla. We would walk out with a bottle of pop apiece and sometimes the pop would backfire up our noses and hurt. We explored the streams, quietly, where the turtles slid off the sunny logs and dug their way into the soft bottom; and we lay on the town wharf and fed worms to the tame bass. Every-where we went I had trouble making out which was I, the one walking at my side, the one walking in my pants.

12   One afternoon while we were there at that lake a thunderstorm came up. It was like the revival of an old melodrama that I had seen long ago with childish awe. The second-act climax of the drama of the electri-cal disturbance over a lake in America had not changed in any important respect. This was the big scene, still the big scene. The whole thing was so familiar, the first feeling of oppression and heat and a general air around camp of not wanting to go very far away. In midafternoon (it was all the same) a curious darkening of the sky, and a lull in everything that had made life tick; and then the way the boats suddenly swung the other way at their moorings with the coming of a breeze out of the new quarter, and the premonitory rumble. Then the kettle drum, then the snare, then the bass drum and cymbals, then crackling light against the dark, and the gods grinning and licking their chops in the hills. Afterward the calm, the rain steadily rustling in the calm lake, the return of light and hope and spirits, and the campers running out in joy and relief to go swimming in the rain, their bright cries perpetuating the deathless joke about how they were getting simply drenched, and the children screaming with delight at the new sensation of bathing in the rain, and the joke about getting drenched linking the generations in a strong indestructible chain. And the comedian who waded in carrying an umbrella.

13   When the others went swimming my son said he was going in too. He pulled his dripping trunks from the line where they had hung all through the shower, and wrung them out. Languidly, and with no thought of going

in, I watching him, his hard little body, skinny and bare, saw him wince slightly as he pulled up around his vitals the small, soggy, icy garment. As he buckled the swollen belt suddenly my groin felt the chill of death.

Content

1. Characterize White's son. Why is he referred to as "my son" and "the boy" but never by name?

2. How do the ways in which the boy and his father relate to the lake environment emphasize their personal relationship? In which ways are these similar to the relationship between the narrator and his father, the boy's grandfather? Are there any significant differences, stated or implied?

3. White emphasizes the "peace and goodness and jollity" of the summers at the lake. What incidents and details reinforce this emphasis? Why, then, does White end with "As he buckled the swollen belt suddenly my groin felt the chill of death" (¶ 13)?

Strategies/Structures/Language

4. Many narratives proceed chronologically from the beginning to the end of the time period they cover, relating events in the sequence in which they occurred. Instead, White organizes this narrative topically. What are the major topics? Why do they come in the order they do, concluding with the thunderstorm and its aftermath?

5. What are the effects of White's frequent repetition of phrases ("there had been no years") and words ("same")? What details or incidents does he use to illustrate the cycle of time? What language does White use to sustain the essay's relaxed mood?

6. In *The Elements of Style* White advises writers of description to use few adjectives and adverbs—to put the weight on nouns and verbs instead. Does White himself do this? Consistently? Pick a paragraph and analyze it to illustrate your answer.

For Writing

7. Tell the story of a memorable experience in a particular place—school building, restaurant, vacation spot, hometown, place visited anywhere in the world—that emphasizes the influence of the place on the experience and on your understanding of it. Identify what makes it memorable, but do not describe it in the picture-pretty manner of a travel brochure.

8. Write a narrative detailing a significant relationship between yourself at a particular age and another family member of a different generation, either older or younger. Illustrate it with family photographs that reflect your interpretation. The specific aspects of your individual story will probably capture some of its common or universal elements, as well.

 For comprehension, writing, and research activities and resources, please visit the companion website at <college.hmco.com/english>.

ANNE FADIMAN

Fadiman was born (in 1953) to bookish parents, the noted writer and editor Clifton Fadiman and Annalee Fadiman, a writer. After graduating from Harvard (BA, 1975), Fadiman worked as an editor and staff writer for *Life* magazine, then as a columnist for *Civilization,* the now-defunct magazine of the Library of Congress. From 1998 to 2004 she was editor of *The American Scholar,* Phi Beta Kappa's national magazine, which published distinguished essays, including her award-winning commentary on "Mail," a learned romp that moves wittily from stagecoach delivery to e-mail. Her first book, *The Spirit Catches You and You Fall Down: A Hmong Child, Her American Doctors, and the Collision of Two Cultures* (1997), won a National Book Critics Circle Award for general nonfiction. Her second book, *Ex Libris: Confessions of a Common Reader* (1998), is a collection of personal essays about reading.

"Under Water" tells a very different story from White's "Once More to the Lake." It is the account of a happy summer wilderness expedition that turned into a tragedy. Although both stories focus on natural bodies of water, White's lake in Maine is tame and tranquil in contrast to the Green River, deceptively treacherous at flood stage. Both begin with the assumption of pleasure on the water, although only White's tale bears this out. Both incorporate precise details to evoke a powerful sense of place and its effect on the people present, and both recount a young person's summer experiences recollected years later from the perspective of a mature narrator, wiser and—in both instances—somehow sadder. Yet while White is contented, Fadiman is full of regret prompted by her inability not only to rescue her fellow student, but by her unworthy—though thoroughly human—thoughts during the futile rescue and ever since: "I find myself wanting to backferry, to hover midstream, suspended. I might then avoid many things: harsh words, foolish decisions, moments of inattention, regrets that wash over me, like water."

Under Water

1   When I was eighteen, I was a student on a month-long wilderness program in western Wyoming. On the third day, we went canoeing on the Green River, a tributary of the Colorado that begins in the glaciers of the Wind River Range and flows south across the sagebrush plains. Swollen by warm-weather runoff from an unusually deep snowpack, the Green was higher and swifter that month—June of 1972—than it had been in forty years. A river at flood stage can have strange currents. There is not enough room in the channel for the water to move downstream in an orderly way, so it collides with itself and forms whirlpools and boils and souse holes. Our instructors decided to stick to their itinerary nevertheless,

What has happened in this picture? What is about to happen? With what consequences? How does Fadiman's story in "Under Water" influence the ways you "read" this picture? Would you "read" it differently if you saw it as an ad for a wilderness travel company? An adventure film?

but they put in at a relatively easy section of the Green, one that the flood had merely upgraded, in the international system of white-water classification, from Class I to Class II. There are six levels of difficulty, and Class II was not an unreasonable challenge for novice paddlers.

The Green River did not seem dangerous to me. It seemed magnificently unobstructed. Impediments to progress—the rocks and stranded trees that under normal conditions would protrude above the surface—were mostly submerged. The river carried our aluminum canoe high and lightly, like a child on a broad pair of shoulders. We could rest our paddles on the gunwales and let the water do our work. The sun was bright and hot. Every few minutes, I dipped my bandanna in the river, draped it over my head, and let an ounce or two of melted glacier run down my neck.

I was in the bow of the third canoe. We rounded a bend and saw, fifty feet ahead, a standing wave in the wake of a large black boulder. The students in the lead canoe were backferrying, slipping crabwise across the current by angling their boat diagonally and stroking backward. Backferrying allows paddlers to hover midstream and carefully plan their course instead of surrendering to the water's pace. But if they lean upstream—a natural inclination, for few people choose to lean toward the difficulties that lie ahead—the current can overflow the lowered gunwale and flip the boat. And that is what happened to the lead canoe.

4   I wasn't worried when I saw it go over. Knowing that we might capsize in the fast water, our instructors had arranged to have our gear trucked to our next campsite. The packs were all safe. The water was little more than waist-deep, and the paddlers were both wearing life jackets. They would be fine. One was already scrambling onto the right-hand bank.

5   But where was the second paddler? Gary, a local boy from Rawlins, a year or two younger than I, seemed to be hung up on something. He was standing at a strange angle in the middle of the river, just downstream from the boulder. Gary was the only student on the course who had not brought sneakers, and one of his mountaineering boots had become wedged between two rocks. The other canoes would come around the bend in a moment, and the instructors would pluck him out.

6   But they didn't come. The second canoe pulled over to the bank and ours followed. Thirty seconds passed, maybe a minute. Then we saw the standing wave bend Gary's body forward at the waist, push his face underwater, stretch his arms in front of him, and slip his orange life jacket off his shoulders. The life jacket lingered for a moment at his wrists before it floated downstream, its long white straps twisting in the current. His shirtless torso was pale and undulating, and it changed shape as hills and valleys of water flowed over him, altering the curve of the liquid lens through which we watched him. I thought, He looks like the flayed skin of St. Bartholomew in the Sistine Chapel. As soon as I had the thought, I knew that it was dishonorable. To think about anything outside the moment, outside Gary, was a crime of inattention. I swallowed a small, sour piece of self-knowledge: I was the sort of person who, instead of weeping or shouting or praying during a crisis, thought about something from a textbook (H. W. Janson's *History of Art,* page 360).

7   Once the flayed man had come, I could not stop the stream of images: Gary looked like a piece of seaweed, Gary looked like a waving handkerchief, Gary looked like a hula dancer. Each simile was a way to avoid thinking about what Gary was, a drowning boy. To remember these things is dishonorable, too, for I have long since forgotten Gary's last name and the color of his hair and the sound of his voice.

8   I do not remember a single word that anyone said. Somehow, we got into one of the canoes, all five of us, and tried to ferry the twenty feet or so to the middle of the river. The current was so strong, and we were so incompetent, that we never got close. Then we tried it on foot, linking arms to form a chain. The water was so cold that it stung. And it was noisy— not the roar and crash of white water but a groan, a terrible bass grumble, from the stones that were rolling and leaping down the riverbed. When we got close to Gary, we couldn't see him; all we could see was the reflection of the sky. A couple of times, groping blindly, one of us touched him, but he was as slippery as soap. Then our knees buckled and our elbows unlocked,

and we rolled downstream, like the stones. The river's rocky load, moving invisibly beneath its smooth surface, pounded and scraped us. Eventually, the current heaved us, blue-lipped and panting, onto the bank. In that other world above the water, the only sounds were the buzzing of bees and flies. Our wet sneakers kicked up red dust. The air smelled of sage and rabbitbrush and sunbaked earth.

We tried again and again, back and forth between the worlds. Wet, 9 dry, cold, hot, turbulent, still.

At first, I assumed that we would save him. He would lie on the 10 bank and the sun would warm him while we administered mouth-to-mouth resuscitation. If we couldn't get him out, we would hold him upright in the river; and maybe he could still breathe. But the Green River was flowing at nearly three thousand cubic feet—about ninety tons—per second. At that rate, water can wrap a canoe around a boulder like tinfoil. Water can uproot a tree. Water can squeeze the air out of a boy's lungs, undo knots, drag off a life jacket, lever a boot so tightly into the riverbed that even if we had had ropes—the ropes that were in the packs that were in the trucks—we could never have budged him.

We kept going in, not because we had any hope of rescuing Gary after 11 the first ten minutes, but because we had to save face. It would have been humiliating if the instructors came around the bend and found us sitting in the sagebrush, a docile row of five with no hypothermia and no skinned knees. Eventually, they did come. The boats had been delayed because one had nearly capsized, and the instructors had made the other students stop and practice backferrying until they learned not to lean upstream. Even though Gary had already drowned, the instructors did all the same things we had done, more competently but no more effectively, because they, too, would have been humiliated if they hadn't skinned their knees. Men in wet suits, belayed with ropes, pried the body out the next morning.

When I was eighteen, I wanted to hurry through life as fast as I could. 12 Twenty-seven years have passed, and my life now seems too fast. I find myself wanting to backferry, to hover midstream, suspended. I might then avoid many things: harsh words, foolish decisions, moments of inattention, regrets that wash over me, like water.

Content

1. What is Anne Fadiman's purpose in writing this essay? Is she telling a tale for its own sake or is she using it to make a larger point? Could this be interpreted as a morality play? A cautionary tale? Explain your answer.

2. From what point of view does Anne Fadiman narrate the events that take place in "Under Water"? In what ways does Fadiman as author prepare her readers to interpret Fadiman as a character in this tale? How does she want the readers to react to the circumstances she describes and to the others on this trip, including the instructors?

3. Anne Fadiman's statement "The Green River did not seem dangerous to me. . . . Impediments to progress—the rocks and stranded trees that under normal conditions would protrude above the surface—were mostly submerged" (¶ 2) is meant to be read literally. Why can we also say it possesses another level of meaning that transcends the literal? How does this figurative meaning influence Fadiman's final paragraph?

Strategies/Structures/Language

4. Fadiman's tale unfolds chronologically, although she speaks in the present, merely remembering the past. How and why does she foreshadow the events that will occur with statements such as "Class II was not an unreasonable challenge for novice paddlers" (¶ 1)? At what point in the story is a reader likely to become aware of the inevitable outcome toward which the narrative is moving? Why not simply begin with the drowning of the young man?

5. Does Fadiman's tale contain all the major components of a narrative: characters, conflict, motives, plot, setting, point of view, and dialogue? Find examples from the text to illustrate which features are there. Since "Under Water" looks and reads like a short story, how do you know it's true?

6. Fadiman uses some extremely vivid description—for example, "Then we saw the standing wave bend Gary's body forward at the waist, push his face underwater, stretch his arms in front of him, and slip his orange life jacket off his shoulders" (¶ 6). What effect is such graphic representation likely to have on her readers?

For Writing

7. Write a narrative essay describing an incident you either witnessed or participated in that involved a serious error of judgment. This can be anything from a car accident to rejecting, insulting, discriminating against, or otherwise mistreating someone, to a benign event that turned serious and ugly. Then revise that essay so it is told from a different point of view. This should be a story with a moral point that is made indirectly, and it should provide implicit judgments of the major characters.

8. Write a true story in which the setting, preferably a natural one, plays a major role in relation to the human participants. This role may be benign or malevolent, active or passive, but it should be important (as it is in "Under Water" and "Once More to the Lake"), and the humans should be constantly aware of this role. Because you will need to pay close attention to the specific details of the setting, it should be a place you either know well or can revisit. Provide illustrations, drawings, photographs, or paintings that convey the prevailing mood.

 For comprehension, writing, and research activities and resources, please visit the companion website at <college.hmco.com/english>.

FREDERICK DOUGLASS

Douglass (1817–1895) was born a slave in Talbot County, Maryland. Unlike many slaves, he learned to read, and the power of this accomplishment coupled with an iron physique and the will to match, enabled him to escape to New York in 1838. For the next twenty-five years he toured the country as a powerful spokesperson for the abolitionist movement, serving as an adviser to Harriet Beecher Stowe, author of *Uncle Tom's Cabin,* and to President Lincoln, among others. After the war he campaigned for civil rights for African-Americans and women. In 1890 his political significance was acknowledged in his appointment as minister to Haiti.

Slave narratives, written or dictated by the hundreds in the nineteenth century, provided memorable accounts of the physical, geographical, and psychological movement from captivity to freedom. Douglass's autobiography, an abolitionist document like many other slave narratives, is exceptional in its forthright language and absence of stereotyping of either white or black people; his people are multidimensional. Crisis points, and the insights and opportunities they provide, are natural topics for personal narratives. This episode, taken from the first version (of four) of *The Narrative of the Life of Frederick Douglass, an American Slave* (1845), explains the incident that was "the turning point in my career as a slave," for it enabled him to make the transformation from slave to independent human being.

Resurrection

I have already intimated that my condition was much worse, during the first six months of my stay at Mr. Covey's, than in the last six. The circumstances leading to the change in Mr. Covey's course toward me form an epoch in my humble history. You have seen how a man was made a slave; you shall see how a slave was made a man. On one of the hottest days of the month of August, 1833, Bill Smith, William Hughes, a slave named Eli, and myself, were engaged in fanning wheat. Hughes was clearing the fanned wheat from before the fan. Eli was turning, Smith was feeding, and I was carrying wheat to the fan. The work was simple, requiring strength rather than intellect; yet, to one entirely unused to such work, it came very hard. About three o'clock of that day, I broke down; my strength failed me; I was seized with a violent aching of the head, attended with extreme dizziness; I trembled in every limb. Finding what was coming, I nerved myself up, feeling it would never do to stop work. I stood as long as I could stagger to the hopper with grain. When I could stand no longer, I fell, and felt as if held down by an immense weight. The fan of course stopped; every one had his own work to do; and no one could do the work of the other, and have his own go on at the same time.

2   Mr. Covey was at the house, about one hundred yards from the treading-yard where we were fanning. On hearing the fan stop, he left immediately, and came to the spot where we were. He hastily inquired what the matter was. Bill answered that I was sick, and there was no one to bring wheat to the fan. I had by this time crawled away under the side of the post and rail-fence by which the yard was enclosed, hoping to find relief by getting out of the sun. He then asked where I was. He was told by one of the hands. He came to the spot, and, after looking at me awhile, asked me what was the matter. I told him as well as I could, for I scarce had strength to speak. He then gave me a savage kick in the side, and told me to get up. I tried to do so, but fell back in the attempt. He gave me another kick, and again told me to rise. I again tried, and succeeded in gaining my feet; but, stooping to get the tub with which I was feeding the fan, I again staggered and fell. While down in this situation, Mr. Covey took up the hickory slat with which Hughes had been striking off the half-bushel measure, and with it gave me a heavy blow upon the head, making a large wound, and the blood ran freely; and with this again told me to get up. I made no effort to comply, having now made up my mind to let him do his worst. In a short time after receiving this blow, my head grew better. Mr. Covey had now left me to my fate. At this moment I resolved, for the first time, to go to my master, enter a complaint, and ask his protection. In order to do this, I must that afternoon walk seven miles; and this, under the circumstances, was truly a severe undertaking. I was exceedingly feeble; made so as much by the kicks and blows which I received, as by the severe fit of sickness to which I had been subjected. I, however, watched my chance, while Covey was looking in an opposite direction, and started for St. Michael's: I succeeded in getting a considerable distance on my way to the woods, when Covey discovered me, and called after me to come back, threatening what he would do if I did not come. I disregarded both his calls and his threats, and made my way to the woods as fast as my feeble state would allow; and thinking I might be overhauled by him if I kept to the road, I walked through the woods, keeping far enough from the road to avoid detection, and near enough to prevent losing my way. I had not gone far before my little strength again failed me. I could go no farther. I fell down, and lay for a considerable time. The blood was yet oozing from the wound on my head. For a time I thought I should bleed to death; and think now that I should have done so, but that the blood so matted my hair as to stop the wound. After lying there about three quarters of an hour, I nerved myself up again, and started on my way, through bogs and briers, barefooted and bareheaded, tearing my feet sometimes at nearly every step; and after a journey of about seven miles, occupying some five hours to perform it, I arrived at master's store. I then presented an appearance enough to affect

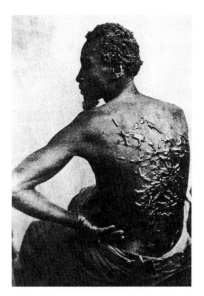

Interpret the pattern on the slave's back. What stories does this tell? Is there any ambiguity or uncertainty about their meaning? Do you need to know that this is a photograph of a slave to be able to understand the picture? Does it matter whether this picture was taken in the United States or somewhere else? What reactions did the photographer wish to elicit from the viewers?

any but a heart of iron. From the crown of my head to my feet, I was covered with blood. My hair was all clotted with dust and blood; my shirt was stiff with blood. My legs and feet were torn in sundry places with briers and thorns, and were also covered in blood. I suppose I looked like a man who had escaped a den of wild beasts, and barely escaped them. In this state I appeared before my master, humbly entreating him to interpose his authority for my protection. I told him all the circumstances as well as I could, and it seemed, as I spoke, at times to affect him. He would then walk the floor, and seek to justify Covey by saying he expected I deserved it. He asked me what I wanted. I told him, to let me get a new home; that as sure as I lived with Mr. Covey again, I should live with but to die with him; that Covey would surely kill me; he was in a fair way for it. Master Thomas ridiculed the idea that there was any danger of Mr. Covey's killing me, and said that he knew Mr. Covey, that he was a good man, and that he could not think of taking me from him; that, should he do so, he would lose the whole year's wages; that I belonged to Mr. Covey for one year, and that I must go back to him, come what might; and that I must not trouble him with any more stories, or that he would himself *get hold of me.* After threatening me thus, he gave me a very large dose of salts, telling me that I might remain in St. Michael's that night, (it being quite late,) but that I must be off back to Mr. Covey's early in the morning; and that if I did not, he would *get hold of me,* which meant that he would whip me. I remained all night, and, according to his orders, I started off to Covey's in the morning, (Saturday morning,) wearied in body and broken in spirit. I got no supper that night, or breakfast that morning. I reached Covey's about nine o'clock; and just as I was getting over the fence that divided Mrs. Kemp's fields from ours, out ran Covey with his cowskin, to give me another whipping. Before he could reach me, I succeeded in getting to the corn-field; and as the corn was very high, it afforded me the means of hiding. He seemed very angry, and searched for me a long time. My behavior was altogether unaccountable. He finally gave up the chase, thinking, I suppose, that I must come home for something to eat; he would give himself no further trouble in looking for me. I spent that day mostly in the woods, having the alternative before me—to go home and be whipped to death, or stay in the woods and be starved to death. That night, I fell in with Sandy Jenkins, a slave with whom I was somewhat acquainted. Sandy had a free wife who lived about four miles from Mr. Covey's; and it being Saturday, he was on his way to see her. I told him my circumstances, and he very kindly invited me to go home with him. I went home with him, and talked this whole matter over, and got his advice as to what course it was best for me to pursue. I found Sandy an old adviser. He told me, with great solemnity, I must go back to Covey; but that before I went, I must go with him into another part of the woods, where there was a certain *root*, which, if I would take some of it with me, carrying it *always on my right side,* would render it impossible for Mr. Covey, or any other white man, to whip me. He said he had carried it for years; and since he had done so, he had never received a blow, and never expected to while he carried it. I at first rejected the idea, that the simple carrying of a root in my pocket would have any such effect as he had said, and was not disposed to take it; but Sandy impressed the necessity with much earnestness, telling me it could do no harm, if it did no good. To please him, I at length took the root, and, according to his direction, carried it upon my right side. This was Sunday morning. I immediately started for home; and upon entering the yard gate, out came Mr. Covey on his way to meeting. He spoke to me very kindly, bade me drive the pigs from a lot near by, and passed on towards the church. Now, this singular conduct of Mr. Covey really made me begin to think that there was something in the *root* which Sandy had given me; and had it been on any other day than Sunday, I could have attributed the conduct to no other cause than the influence of that root; and as it was, I was half inclined to think the *root* to be something more than I at first had taken it to be. All went well till Monday morning. On this morning, the virtue of the *root* was fully tested. Long before daylight, I was called to go and rub, curry, and feed, the horses. I obeyed, and was glad to obey. But whilst thus engaged, whilst in the act of throwing down some blades from the loft, Mr. Covey entered the stable with a long rope; and just as I was half out of the loft, he caught hold of my legs, and was about tying me. As soon as I found what he was up to, I gave a sudden spring, and as I did so, he holding to my legs, I was brought sprawling on the stable floor. Mr. Covey seemed now to think he had me, and could do what he pleased; but at this moment—from whence came the spirit I don't know—I resolved to fight; and, suiting my action to the resolution, I seized Covey hard by the throat; and as I did so, I rose. He held on to me, and I to him. My resistance was so entirely unexpected, that Covey seemed taken all aback. He trembled like a leaf. This gave me assurance, and I held him uneasy, causing the blood to run where I touched him with the ends of my fingers. Mr. Covey soon called out to Hughes for help. Hughes came, and while Covey held me, attempted to tie my right hand. While he was in the act of doing so, I watched my chance, and gave him a heavy kick close under the ribs. This kick fairly sickened Hughes, so that he left me in the hands of Mr. Covey. This kick had the effect of not only weakening Hughes, but Covey also. When he saw Hughes bending over with pain, his courage quailed. He asked me if I meant to persist in my resistance. I told him I did, come what might; that he had used me like a brute for six months, and that I was determined to be used so no longer. With that, he strove to drag me to a stick that was lying just out of the stable door. He meant to knock me down. But just as he was leaning over to get the stick, I seized him with both hands by his collar, and brought him by a sudden snatch to the ground. By this time, Bill came. Covey called upon him for assistance. Bill wanted to know what he could do. Covey said, "Take hold of him, take hold of him!" Bill said his master hired him out to work, and not to help whip me; so he left Covey and myself to fight our own battle out. We were at it for nearly two hours. Covey at length let me go, puffing and blowing at a great rate, saying that if I had not resisted, he would not have whipped me half so much. The truth was, that he had not whipped me at all. I considered him as getting entirely the worst end of the bargain; for he had drawn no blood from me, but I had from him. The whole six months afterwards, that I spent with Mr. Covey, he never laid the weight of his finger upon me in anger. He would occasionally say, he didn't want to get hold of me again. "No," thought I, "you need not; for you will come off worse than you did before."

This battle with Mr. Covey was the turning-point in my career as a   ₃ slave. It rekindled the few expiring embers of freedom, and revived within me a sense of my own manhood. It recalled the departed self-confidence, and inspired me again with a determination to be free. The gratification afforded by the triumph was a full compensation for whatever else might follow, even death itself. He only can understand the deep satisfaction which I experienced, who has himself repelled by force the bloody arm of slavery. I felt as I never felt before. It was a glorious resurrection, from the tomb of slavery, to the heaven of freedom. My long-crushed spirit rose, cowardice departed, bold defiance took its place; and I now resolved that, however long I might remain a slave in form, the day had passed forever when I could be a slave in fact. I did not hesitate to let it be known of me, that the white man who expected to succeed in whipping, must also succeed in killing me.

Content

1. Twelve years after he successfully defied Mr. Covey, Douglass identified this incident as "the turning-point in my career as a slave" (¶ 3). Why? Would Douglass have been able to recognize its significance at the time or only in retrospect?

2. Would slave owners have been likely to read Douglass's autobiography? Why or why not? Would Douglass's emphasis have been likely to change for an audience of Northern post–Civil War blacks? Southern antebellum whites? What, if anything, does Douglass expect his audience—mostly white Northerners—to do about slavery, as a consequence of having read his narrative?

Strategies/Structures/Language

3. Douglass's account begins with Friday afternoon and ends with Monday morning, but some events receive considerable emphasis while others are scarcely mentioned. Which ones does he focus on? Why?

4. Why is paragraph 2 so long? Should it have been divided into shorter units, or is the longer unit preferable? Justify your answer.

5. Douglass provides considerable details about his appearance after his first beating by Covey (¶ 2), but scarcely any about the appearance of either Covey or Master Thomas. Why?

6. How sophisticated is Douglass's level of diction? Is it appropriate for the narrative he tells? How is this related to his self-characterization?

For Writing

7. Write a narrative in which you recount and explain the significance of an event in which you participated that provided you with an important change of status in the eyes of others. (See Yu's "Red and Black," 173–82.) Provide enough specific details so readers unfamiliar with either you or the situation can experience it as you did. Be sure to depict the personalities of the central characters; their physical appearance may not be nearly as significant.

8. Recount an incident expressing the difficulties of a minority or oppressed person or group. (See essays by Rodriguez, Yu, and Nocton.). Use the table to inspire your readers to take action concerning the problem. Try to move them by example rather than through preaching or an excess of emotion. Understatement is usually more appealing than overstatement.

 For comprehension, writing, and research activities and resources, please visit the companion website at <college.hmco.com/english>.

ART SPIEGELMAN

Art Spiegelman's innovative work *Maus, A Survivor's Tale* (two volumes: 1986 and 1992), a classic of Holocaust literature, is a sequentially illustrated narrative of genocide, survival, and family history. The idea of depicting Jews as mice and Nazis as persecutory cats came to Spiegelman when his college film professor compared cartoon cat-and-mouse chases to racist film stereotypes. Born to Holocaust survivors in Stockholm, Sweden (1948), Spiegelman grew up in Queens, New York City, in a neighborhood with many Jewish families. Influenced by popular cartoons and *Mad Magazine*, he made drawings for his junior high school newspaper, attended the famous public High School of Art and Design, and made it through three years at Harpur College in upstate New York before personal and family crises intervened. Spiegelman suffered a nervous breakdown and shortly afterward his mother committed suicide, partly out of depression after the loss of her brother in a car accident. In 1971 Spiegelman moved to San Francisco, where he joined the dynamic underground comic book scene and taught at the San Francisco Academy of Art. Returning to New York (1975), Spiegelman married, taught at the School of Visual Arts, and began researching *Maus* by journeying to Auschwitz in 1978 and again in 1986. His recent work includes *In the Shadow of No Towers* (2004), about the September 11 attacks seen from his perspective as a downtown New Yorker—and the geopolitical aftermath.

"Mein Kampf (My Struggle)," taken from the *New York Times Magazine* (1996), ironically bears the same title as Adolf Hitler's autobiography and manifesto of Nazi ideology. Spiegelman's struggle, however, concerns his artistic vision—specifically, how to find a new topic when a "5,000-pound mouse" is breathing down his neck.

Mein Kampf (My Struggle)

Content

1. As "Mein Kampf" begins, we learn that Spiegelman's previous artistic creation, *Maus,* is overpowering and intimidating him; the rest of the narrative unfolds from that premise. What other problems is Spiegelman facing, and how does he attempt to solve them?

2. What is the message of the last few panels, in which the artist's son appears? What is resolved by the ending, or in what way is the reader perhaps left hanging? Explain why this ending is either effective or ineffective.

Strategies/Structures/Language

3. For some readers, comics are mainly associated with humor; yet in "Mein Kampf" Spiegelman uses the comic book form to handle serious themes such as his troubled past, his artistic self-doubts, and his lack of appropriate memories. In what ways do his comic book techniques especially reinforce his themes?

4. What is the irony in Spiegelman showing himself being chased by a gigantic mouse, given what you know about his two-volume series *Maus* (see the headnote for information). What are some of the other ways that "Mein Kampf" uses visual or verbal humor? For what purposes?

5. To tell his story, Spiegelman uses a very distinctive color scheme (not visible in this black and white reprint), line, texture, frame-to-frame pacing, and approach to the human figure. How do these techniques help to create a visual narrative? For example, is it appropriate to set the action in the "murky caverns" of his memory? In what other ways do the visuals support the topics and themes of "Mein Kampf"?

6. For many readers, comics—or "sequential art"—have an instant attraction. Why do you suppose this is so? What are your favorite comic strips or works of sequential art, and why do you enjoy them?

For Writing

7. Write a panel-by-panel analysis of *how* "Mein Kampf" works as a narrative. What does the progression from one part of the sequence to the next tell you, aside from the information you get in the dialogue balloons? (See questions 3, 4, and 5 for ideas.) Consider details, such as the labels on the doors of Spiegelman's memories, as well as larger factors, such as his movements and facial expressions. Or compare Spiegelman's "Mein Kampf" with Lynda Barry's "Common Scents" (354–63). What does the graphic form enable these artists to do that sticking strictly to print would inhibit?

8. If you had the talents of a comic strip artist, what story would you tell? Would you base your work on your life experience, or would you create fiction and fantasy? What characters would you create? What color themes and visual effects would you use? Write a proposal for a work of sequential art, including a description of your topic, characters, and a sample story or episode. Explain what your artistic and literary goals are, and how the piece would achieve them.

 For comprehension, writing, and research activities and resources, please visit the companion website at <college.hmco.com/english>.

JASON VERGE

A Canadian who was born in Ottawa (1982) and grew up in Montreal, Verge's first language was French. His earliest passion was for the Montreal Canadiens, "The Habs," whose example encouraged him to play hockey as an adolescent. Then he "did what any die-hard hockey fan would do after graduating high school": he decided to attend college in Hawaii, where because of the time difference, he had to watch the games live at 9 A.M. Transferring to Marymount University, he completed his BA in English in 2005. Verge says he is "currently putting the finishing touches" on his first novel. Although he once owned a recording company, he decided he wasn't suited for the business world when he "accepted an 8-bit Nintendo in lieu of cash payment." He has now returned to writing.

He says of "The Habs," "my friends were tired of hearing me talk incessantly about hockey, so I decided to get it down on paper. It's a love letter to the sport and to the team, for the Habs are inextricably linked with the identities of myself and my family. I wanted the piece to be humorous without losing its honesty."

❄ *The Habs*

G ame seven: the deciding game of the Stanley Cup finals. I was six, captured in old home movies running and screaming "By the power of Greyskull!" at the top of my lungs. It was the only phrase I knew how to say in English, learned from episodes of *He-man*. Earlier that night, my family had been embroiled in a heated political argument, as was the custom when we got together. Watching the Montreal Canadiens play hockey was the only viable reason to put political arguments on hiatus, and so we had. With the game on, the light conflict in the air turned to a deep sense of unity. My grandfather—usually a calm man—cheered like a rabid child during the games. For the length of three periods, all worries went away; there were no financial worries, there were no disagreements. The only thing that seemed to matter in the entire universe was the Montreal Canadiens, or "the Habs," as we called them. The Habs were in our blood.

Calling the team "Habs" started in the 1920s as a joke. The Canadiens logo has an "H" in the center of the "C," which initially stood for "Hockey" in "Club de hockey Canadien." Tex Rickard, an Anglophone from the Toronto Maple Leafs, asked a Montreal coach what it stood for, and the coach said "Habitants" to mess with him. ("Club de hockey Canadien" was plastered everywhere when Tex asked.) Somehow, the name stuck. The story is mostly ignored these days because it's completely inexplicable—to most people—why the guy lied and said "Habitants" instead of the plain truth. A Montreal fan, however, instantly knows why the coach lied: because the team and the city's culture are inextricably linked and because no Toronto Maple Leafs Fan is deserving of a straight answer.

3   The Island of Montreal in Quebec is an oddity of sorts; the population is bilingual, whereas the rest of Quebec is devoutly French. Quebec has always been the proverbial stepchild of Canada; they have a different culture than the rest of Canada and never quite fit in. Quebec is a province divided between those who wish to secede from Canada (the devout French) and those who wish to remain a part of the country. Referendums occur where they actually vote on this issue; the last decided by 1 percent to stay. Whereas Americans determined divisive issues through a bloody civil war, Canadians prefer to vote incessantly on something until people lose their passion. It's too cold outside to fight. The votes from Montreal always swing the decision toward staying a part of the country. Somewhere down the line, the Habs became intertwined with the political debate. Habs fans are loyal to Canada. When the Habs played the Quebec Nordiques, people would come out in full force, the Habs fans being loyalists and the Nordiques fans being separatists. A win on the ice was a political victory of sorts, a justification for a person's given side of the political debate. Not only is hockey a way of life in Canada, it's also used to make important political decisions. (A little known fact: Canada entered World War I because the Habs won the night the decision was made.)

4   I was too big for the team jerseys when I started playing hockey in a league. The jerseys they handed out were made for the typical twelve-year-old, and I was anything but. I was already well over six feet by that time. I tried to stuff myself into the assigned jersey and ended up looking like a giant marshmallow. Instead, they let me wear my bright red Canadiens jersey. I'd imagine myself playing for the Habs, my family proudly watching me on TV (I'd reserve my tickets to the game for groupies).

5   Since the leagues were organized by age, I ended up playing with people I towered over. Years later, my dad would tell me that a lot of the parents were upset that a kid my height was allowed to play in the league. My dad tells me that that kind of made him proud. I was a goaltender, so it's not as if my physical play was a big factor—though I'm pretty sure I still hold the record for most penalty minutes by a goaltender. I wasn't a mean kid; in fact, most of the penalty minutes were justified. The only female player in the league was on my team, and I didn't take too kindly to watching her get roughed up. I was a big brother to her; if someone hurt her, I'd politely snatch their legs with my stick and trip them. It was nothing personal; it was all part of the game. Yep, I was a true gentleman.

6   Jacques Plante was the goalie for the Habs in the sixties. He was the first goalie to wear a mask during play, but only after years of pucks hitting him in the face. He had a reputation of being fearless on the ice and a true gentleman off it. In one game a puck hit him in the face and tore it open; he went back to the trainers, received over thirty stitches near his eye, and was back on the ice the next period. He didn't complain to anyone. The

cut was so bad that the swelling and blood almost completely blinded him, yet the tough bastard continued to play despite not being able to see. The coach eventually figured out that Plante couldn't see; when the coach asked him why he didn't say something, Plante said he didn't want to bother anyone. Jacques Plante was a true gentleman.

I did what any die-hard hockey fan would do after graduating high school: I decided to attend university in Hawaii. Apparently I was too busy thinking about doing homework on a beach to think of the ramifications it would have on my hockey viewing. Fortunately, I brought a few hockey videos, which I rationed with more intensity than the people in the movie *Alive* rationed peanuts. 7

However, my roommate from France was able to get a constant flow of soccer on the TV, feeding his addiction. His happiness made me sick. The soccer players, with the little shin guards and floppy hair, made me sick. Soccer was the bizzaro hockey; soccer blazed at the equivalent speed of a physics lecture. I began to lose my mind. 8

Luckily, salvation came in the form of the occasional game on ESPN 43. Since Hawaii had a six-hour time difference, it meant watching hockey at an ungodly early hour, or watching the replay. Since I enjoyed the consumption of beer during a game, I opted for the replay. Getting drunk at noon didn't quite appeal to me. I was so excited for that first game that I shook. The puck dropped and a giant grin appeared on my face. Not two minutes into the first period, the sports ticker on the bottom of the screen revealed the final score of the very game I was watching. I'm pretty sure I snapped something internally. I wanted the world to feel my wrath; I wanted to stand outside the movie theater and tell everyone how their movie would end. 9

Two weeks later, I would get my second chance. I slapped duct tape across the bottom of the screen so I wouldn't be able to see the ticker. During intermission, the nice people at ESPN told me the final score of the game once again. I screamed in such agony that Janine, a girl across the hall, came to see what was wrong. She got my mind off of the game with tales of her sexual exploits. I told her that I was a writer, and she responded by letting me read her diary. Based on what I read, I vowed never to touch Janine. 10

When my third attempt came around, I was emaciated and pale, despite the Hawaiian sun. Hadn't shaved. I was all set to turn off the TV when intermission began. I made it to the second period, and then I heard a knock on the door. It was Janine. I decided her tales of sexual exploits could wait: "Go away!" I yelled. 11

"What's wrong?" 12

"I'm not talking to anyone until the game's over." 13

"Your door's locked." 14

"Go away." 15

"Let me in, I saw the score and they lost." 16

17   From that point on, I disliked Janine. I began to wonder if I could get televised hockey in the mountains of Tibet. I also vowed to watch the next game live at—cringe—nine in the morning.

18   It took college to make me realize how counterproductive getting drunk at nine in the morning is. You'd think they'd cover it in high school, in health class or something. I found a friend who shared my enthusiasm for the sport, at least, so he claimed. I had a sneaking suspicion all he really wanted was an excuse to drink at nine in the morning. Through that experience, I learned that beer is not a proper substitute for milk in cereal (foams too much when you chew). Tuition put to good use.

19   After the first two meetings of the nine A.M. drinkers club, we disbanded. I was content simply watching hockey. The whole experience made me grateful for every minute of hockey I'd get to see.

20   Maurice "The Rocket" Richard played for the Habs back around the time my father was a kid. I see a twinkle in my dad's eye when he says Richard's name—I get the same twinkle these days. "The Rocket" was a quiet, humble man. In a way, I like to think of myself as having the same demeanor. On the ice, Richard became the most clutch player of all time. He received a concussion in a deciding playoff game against the Leafs one year and had to be carried off—he wobbled back on and scored the game-winning goal. When the reporters asked him about it later, he had no recollection. The following year, against the same team, he was evicted from the game and suspended for fighting back. After the announcer reported his fate, riots started. Police flooded the Montreal forum. The riots leaked out onto the street; the city shut down. Richard stood quiet despite the passion of his fans; he always felt weird talking about himself to the press. Despite his taciturn demeanor, he became a deity in Montreal. At his funeral, a decade ago, decades after he stopped playing, two hundred thousand people showed up.

21   I watched all but three of the eighty-two regular season Montreal games last year. My girlfriend at the time asked me, "If you had to give up either me or hockey, which would you choose?" I may be a man, but I'm not stupid. I told her I'd give up hockey. Then I told her never to ask me that question again—ever. After years of philosophy and ethics courses, I still have yet to encounter a bigger dilemma. After she left the room, I rubbed my jersey on my face and assured it that I would never give it up.

22   I have spent so many years devoted to my Habs that it has become a religion to me. I've spent a small fortune on a piece of cardboard with a Habs player on it. I've missed a final because it clashed with a playoff game. How could I not love a sport that combines the gracefulness of ice skating and the brutality of football? It is a paradox; it is beautiful yet violent. I am a Canadian; I come from a culture where aggressions are played out on the ice and not off it. Hockey is the opiate of my people.

I call my dad during intermissions to talk about the game, much as 23
he'd call his dad when he was younger. I once told my mom that I wanted
my ashes dumped in the arena the Canadiens play in. She didn't like
the idea.

(*Update: Due to arbitration, the 2004 hockey season was officially canceled until* 24
further notice. The author is currently seeking out a local mental institution that
will willingly let him pretend it is 1993, the last year the Canadiens won the
Stanley Cup.)

Content

1. If you're an American reader, what do you find in "The Habs" that makes it
distinctively Canadian? (If possible, discuss your views with a Canadian reader.)
At the editor's suggestion, Verge added paragraph 2, explaining the origin of the
term "the Habs." Would you have understood the meaning of the term without
this explanation?

2. Are rabid hockey fans any different from enthusiasts of any other sport?

3. If Verge is such a proud Canadian citizen and "die-hard" Habs fan, why would
he choose to go to college in Hawaii? Are his reasons self-evident, or don't they
matter?

Strategies/Structures/Language

4. Why is this piece funny? Do readers need to know much—or anything—about
hockey to appreciate the humor?

5. Like many comic writers, Verge characterizes himself in a variety of self-
deprecations. Identify some. Are readers expected to take him at his word—that
is, is he an utterly reliable narrator? Why or why not?

For Writing

6. Write an essay explaining your lifelong love for an activity (such as reading,
cooking, driving, painting, playing or listening to music, shopping), a sport—an
individual (running, fishing, boating) or team sport, or participation in a worthy
cause whose purpose is to benefit others rather than yourself. At the outset, try
writing comic and serious versions of the same subject until you find a mode and
vocabulary that does justice to both the topic and your attitude toward it. Try out
alternative versions on a reader to see how he or she reacts.

 For comprehension, writing, and research activities and resources, please visit
the companion website at <college.hmco.com/english>.

Additional Topics for Writing Narration

(For strategies for writing narration, see 90)

MULTIPLE STRATEGIES FOR WRITING NARRATION

In writing on any of the narrative topics below, you'll find it useful to draw on a variety of strategies to help tell your story.

You may choose to write your narrative using elements of *creative nonfiction,* and thus to tell the story through:

- a *narrator* in the role of either a storyteller or a character or both
- *dialogue*
- a *time sequence,* either in chronological order or with flashbacks or flashforwards, which, in combination, will provide a *plot,* with beginning, middle, and end
- *setting(s)*
- *symbolism,* through characters, objects, events
- an *implied*—rather than an overt—point or argument

Through the preceding techniques, or in a more conventional essay form, narratives can employ:

- *character sketches: who* was involved
- *illustrations* and *examples: what* happened and *when*
- *process analysis: how* it happened
- *cause* and *effect: why* it happened, with *what consequences*

Feel free to experiment, to use what works and discard what doesn't—but save the rejects in a separate file; you may be able to use them somewhere else.

1. Write two versions of the earliest experience you can remember that involved some fright, danger, discovery, or excitement. Write the first version as the experience appeared to you at the time it happened. Then, write another version interpreting how the experience appears to you now.

2. Write a narrative of an experience you had that taught you a difficult lesson (see Fadiman, "Under Water," 104–7; and Ning Yu, "Red and Black, or One English Major's Beginning," 173–82). You can either make explicit the point of the lesson or imply it through your reactions to the experience.

3. Sometimes a meaningful incident or significant relationship with someone can help us to mature, easily or painfully. Tell the story of such an incident or relationship in your own life or in the life of someone you know well. Douglass addresses this in "Resurrection" (109–13), Cagle in "On the Banks of the Bogue Chitto" (191–95), Sanders in "The Inheritance of Tools" (148–54) and "Under the Influence: Paying the Price of My Father's Booze" (249–59), and McGuire in "Wake Up Call" (225–31).

4. Have you ever witnessed an event important to history, sports, science, or some other field of endeavor? If so, tell the story either as an eyewitness or from the point of view of someone looking back on it and more aware now of its true meaning.

5. If you have ever been to a place that is particularly significant to you, narrate an incident to show its significance through specified details. (See White, "Once More to the Lake," 97–103; Fadiman, "Under Water," 104–7; Mark Twain, "Uncle John's Farm," 265–71; and Tschannerl, "One Remembers Most What One Loves," 278–81.)

6. Have you ever worshiped someone as a hero or heroine or modeled yourself after someone? Or have you ever been treated as someone's particular favorite (or nemesis)? Tell the story of this special relationship you have (or had) with a parent or grandparent, brother or sister, friend or antagonist, spouse, employer, teacher. Through narrating one or two typical incidents to convey its essence, show why this relationship has been beneficial, harmful, or otherwise significant to you. Control your language carefully to control the mood and tone. (In addition to the essays identified in question 3, see also Ruffin, "Mama's Smoke," 82–84; and Lee, "Coming Home Again," 156–64.)

7. If you have had a "watershed experience"—made an important discovery, survived a major traumatic event, such as an automobile accident, a natural disaster, a flood, or a family breakup; met a person who has changed your life—that has changed your life or your thinking about life significantly, narrate the experience and analyze its effects, short- or long-term. You will need to explain or imply enough of what you were like beforehand so readers can recognize the effects of the experience. (See Douglass, "Resurrection," 109–13; Hall, "Killing Chickens," 242–45; Fendrich, "History Overcomes Stories," 551–53; or Tayebi, "Warring Memories," 554–58.)

8. Explain what it's like to be a typical student or employee (on an assembly line, in a restaurant or store, or elsewhere) through an account of "A Day in the Life of. . . ." If you find that life to be boring or demeaning, your narrative might be an implied protest or an argument for change. (See Barry, "Common Scents," 354–63; and Nocton, "Harvest of Shame," 527–31.)

9. Write a fairy tale or fable, a story with a moral, or some other cautionary tale. Make it suitable for children (but don't talk down to them) or for people of your own age. (See Lamott, "Polaroids," 39–40; Kingston, "On Discovery," 60–61; and Tallent, "No One's a Mystery," 388–90.)

10. Write a pseudo-diary, an imaginary account of how you would lead a day in your life if all your wishes were fulfilled—or if all your worst fears were realized.

11. Imagine that you're telling a major news event of the day (or of your lifetime) to someone fifty years from now. What details will you have to include and explain to make sure your reader understands it? (See O'Brien, "How to Tell a True War Story," 543–53; and other essays in Chapters 13 and 14.)

12. Using your own experiences or those of someone you know well, write an essay showing the truth or falsity of an adage about human nature, such as

   a. Quitters never win. Or do they?
   b. Try hard and you'll succeed. Or will you?
   c. It doesn't matter whether you win or lose, it's how you play the game.
   d. Absence makes the heart grow fonder, or Out of sight, out of mind.

Process Analysis

Analysis involves dividing something into its component parts and explaining what they are, on the assumption that it is easier to consider and to understand the subject in smaller segments than in a large, complicated whole (see the chapter "Division and Classification," [285–327]). To analyze the human body, you could divide it into systems—skeletal, circulatory, respiratory, digestive, neurological—before identifying and defining the components of each. Of the digestive system, for instance, you would discuss the mouth, pharynx, esophagus, stomach, and large and small intestines.

You can analyze a process in the same way, focusing on *how* rather than *what*, that will lead to a particular consequence, product, or result.

A *directive process analysis* identifies the steps in how to make or do something: how to sail a catamaran; how to get to Kuala Lumpur; how to make brownies; how to collaborate in a writing group "to keep a group running smoothly and to forestall some common problems," as John Trimbur advises in "Guidelines for Collaborating in Groups" (72–73). The Introduction to Chapter 1 (2–12), for instance, explains the general processes embedded in reading and writing essays, poetry, stories, and creative nonfiction. One of the differences between an art and a science is that in the arts even those who follow a similar process will end up with qualitatively different results. For example, an accomplished singer's or writer's style is so markedly different from that of any other singer or writer that the individual performer is immediately recognized.

An *informative process analysis* can identify the stages by which something is created or formed, or how something is done. In "Those Crazy Ideas" (132–40), Isaac Asimov analyzes two "styles" of scientific investigation by comparing and contrasting the ways in which Charles Darwin (see 335–40) and Alfred Russel Wallace arrived "independently and simultaneously" at the theory of evolution. A process analysis can also explain how something functions or works, as Tom and Ray Magliozzi do in "Inside the Engine" (142–46): "Overfilling [your car oil] is just as bad as underfilling. . . . If you're a quart and a half . . . overfilled, you could have so much oil in the crankcase that the spinning crankshaft is going to hit the oil and turn it into suds. It's impossible for the pump to pump suds, so you'll ruin the motor. It's kind of like a front-loading washing machine that goes berserk and spills suds all over the floor when you put too much detergent in." Or a process analysis can explain the meanings and implications of a concept, system, or mechanism as the basis for a philosophy that incorporates the process in question. Thus in the process of explaining the medical processes involved in a "Code Blue" alert (365–69), Jasmine Innerarity offers not only a philosophy of lifesaving, but a philosophy of life.

A process analysis can incorporate an explanation and appreciation of a way of life, as implied in the photograph of the Mennonite carpenter (126), taken in 1999, but in many respects timeless. Ntozake Shange does this in "What Is It We Really Harvestin' Here?" (166–71). Shange explains how to grow potatoes, mustard greens, and watermelon, and how to cook "Mama's rice"; in the process, she offers a joyous interpretation not only of "'colored' cuisine," but of the people who cultivate, prepare, and eat this nourishment for the soul as well as the body. An analysis can also incorporate a critique of a process, sometimes as a way to advocate an alternative, as Scott Russell Sanders does in showing the deleterious effects of alcoholism on alcoholics' families in "Under the Influence: Paying the Price of My Father's Booze" (249–59). Matt Nocton's "Harvest of Gold, Harvest of Shame" (527–31) provides both an overt explanation of a process—how tobacco is harvested—and an implied critique of the exploitation of the migrant workers who do the backbreaking labor. Each worker must "must tie [a burlap sack] around his waist as a source of protection against the dirt and rocks that he will be dragging himself through for the next eight hours."

A process analysis can also embed a critique of the process it discusses. Ning Yu's "Red and Black, or One English Major's Beginning" (173–82) is an explanation of how he learned English from two sources: his father, a sophisticated professor of Chinese language and literature, and the anti-intellectual members of the People's Liberation Army, who expelled (and imprisoned) the intellectuals and took over the schools. Ning analyzes how the Reds taught: by lecturing and having the middle school pupils memorize verbal "hand grenades"—"Drop your guns! Down with U.S. Imperialism!"— which they didn't understand. Here Ning criticizes the teachers, the process, and the results: "books were dangerous," and ignorance prevailed. In contrast, Dr. Yu does it right, beginning with the alphabet, then on to the basics of grammar, and then the reading of short sentences and learning vocabulary, to provide his son with an adequate foundation for genuine reading and understanding—a particularly important heritage while Dr. Yu is imprisoned.

The following suggestions for writing an essay of process analysis are in themselves—you guessed it—a process analysis.

To write about a process, for whatever audience, you first have to *make sure you understand it yourself.* If it's a process you can perform, such as parallel parking or hitting a good tennis forehand, try it out before you begin to write, and note the steps and possible variations from start to finish.

Early on you'll need to *identify the purpose or function of the process and its likely outcome:* "How to lose twenty pounds in ten weeks." Then the steps or stages in the process occur in a given sequence; it's helpful to *list them in their logical or natural order* and to *provide time markers* so your readers will know what comes first, second, and thereafter. "First, have a physical exam. Next, work out a sensible diet, under medical supervision. Then. . . ."

If the process involves many simultaneous operations, for clarity you may need to *classify all aspects of the process and discuss each one separately,* as you might in explaining the photograph of what the Chinese boy is doing in order to learn to read and write his native language (176). For instance, since playing the violin requires bowing with the right hand and fingering with the left, it makes sense to consider each by itself. After you've done this, however, be sure to *indicate how all of the separate elements of the process fit together.* To play the violin successfully, the right hand does indeed have to know what the left hand is doing. If the process you're discussing is cyclic or circular—as in the life cycle of a plant, or the water cycle, involving evaporation, condensation, and precipitation—start with whatever seems to you most logical or most familiar to your readers.

If you're using specialized or technical language, *define your terms* unless you're writing for an audience of experts. You'll also need to *identify specialized equipment* and *be explicit about whatever techniques and measurements your readers need to know.* For example, an essay on how to throw a pot would need to tell a reader who had never potted what the proper consistency of the clay should be before one begins to wedge it or how to tell when all the air bubbles have been wedged out. But how complicated should an explanation be? The more your reader knows about your subject, the more sophisticated your analysis can be, with less emphasis, if any, on the basics. How thin can the pot's walls be without collapsing? Does the type of clay (white, red, with or without grog) make any difference? The reverse is true if you're writing for novices—keep it simple to start with.

If subprocesses are involved in the larger process, you can either *explain these where they would logically come in the sequence* or *consider them in footnotes or an appendix.* You don't want to sidetrack your reader from the main thrust. For instance, if you were to explain the process of Prank Day, an annual ritual at Cal Tech, you might begin with the time by which all seniors have to be out of their residence halls for the day: 8 a.m. You might then follow a typical prank from beginning to end: the selection of a senior's parked car to disassemble; the transportation of its parts to the victim's dorm room; the reassembling of the vehicle; the victim's consternation when he encounters it in his room with the motor running. If the focus is on the process of playing the prank, you probably wouldn't want to give directions on how to disassemble and reassemble the car; to do so would require a hefty manual. But you might want to supplement your discussion with helpful hints on how to pay (or avoid paying) for the damage.

After you've finished your essay, if it explains how to perform a process, ask a friend, preferably one who's unfamiliar with the subject, to try it out. (Even people who know how to tie shoelaces can get all tangled up in murky directions.) She can tell you what's unclear, what needs to be explained more fully—and even point out where you're belaboring the obvious. Ask your reader to tell you how well she understands what you've said. If, by the end, she's still asking you what the fundamental concept is, you'll know you've got to run the paper through your typewriter or computer once again.

Process analysis can serve as a vehicle for explaining personal relationships, as Marilyn Nelson does in the flirtatious poem, "Asparagus" (131). For example, an analysis of the sequential process of performing some activity can serve as the framework for explaining a complicated relationship among the people involved in performing the same process or an analogous one. In such essays the relationship among the participants or the character of the person performing the process is more important than the process itself; whether or not the explanation is sufficient to enable the readers to actually perform the process is beside the point.

Scott Russell Sanders's "The Inheritance of Tools" (148–54) is typical of such writing. Although his father is showing Sanders, as a young child, how to pound nails and to saw, the information is not sufficient in the text, even for such a simple process, to provide clear directions of how to do it. The real point of Sanders's commentary is not instructions in how to use tools, but in the relationship between the tender father and his admiring son. This is analogous to the relationship between Chang-rae Lee and his mother in "Coming Home Again" (156–64), expressed through the processes of playing basketball (his mother was a championship player in Taiwan) and cooking, at which his mother was also an expert. Although their relationship was a powerful force when he was growing up, it intensified during the last year of his mother's life, after Chang-rae had graduated from college and was living at home, trying to master the cooking as if his mother's life—and his—depended on it. In contrast, even though Ntozake Shange's "What Is It We Really Harvestin' Here?" (166–71) is not intended as a cookbook, her freewheeling recipes offer enough directions on how to prepare the food.

Writing parodies of processes, particularly those that are complicated, mysterious, or done badly—may be the ideal revenge of the novice learner or the person obsessed with or defeated by a process. Parodies such as these may include a critique of the process, a satire of the novice or victim (often the author), or both.

STRATEGIES FOR WRITING— PROCESS ANALYSIS

1. Is the purpose of my essay to provide directions—a step-by-step explanation of how to do or make something? Or is the essay's purpose informative—to explain how something happens or works? Do I know my subject well enough to explain it clearly and accurately?
2. If I'm providing directions, how much does my audience already know about performing the process? Should I start with definitions of basic terms ("sauté," "dado") and explanations of subprocesses, or can I focus on the main process at hand? Should I simplify the process for a naive audience, or are my readers sophisticated enough to understand its complexities? Likewise, if I'm providing an informative explanation, where will I start? How complicated will my explanation become? The assumed expertise of my audience will help determine my answers.
3. Have I presented the process in logical or chronological sequence (first, second, third . . .)? Have I furnished an overview so that my readers will have the outcome (or desired results) and major aspects of the process in mind before they immerse themselves in the particulars of the individual steps?
4. Does my language fit both the subject, however general or technical, and the audience? Do I use technical terms when necessary? Which of these do I need to define or explain for my intended readers?
5. What tone will I use in my essay? A serious or matter-of-fact tone will indicate that I'm treating my subject "straight." An ironic, exaggerated, or understated tone will indicate that I'm treating it humorously.

MARILYN NELSON

Nelson, daughter of an Air Force pilot and a teacher, was born in Cleveland in 1946. Brought up on different military bases, Nelson started writing while still in elementary school. Her college degrees are from the University of California, Davis BA, 1968), the University of Pennsylvania (MA, 1970), and the University of Minnesota (PhD, 1979). She is a widely published poet (as Marilyn Waniek before 1995) whose academic career has been primarily at the University of Connecticut. Recipient of numerous honors and fellowships (including a Guggenheim), in 2002 she was chosen as Connecticut Poet Laureate. *The Homeplace* (1990) honors her family, from Rufus Atwood (slave name "Pomp"), c. 1845–1915, to her father and his dashing, heroic group of black World War II aviators, the Tuskegee Airmen.

> Suddenly when I hear airplanes overhead—
> big, silver ones
> whose muscles fill the sky—
> I listen: That sounds like
> someone I know.
> And the sky looks much closer.

Nelson's numerous award-winning books include *The Fields of Praise,* which was a National Book Award finalist and recipient of the 1999 Poets' Prize, and *Carver: A Life in Poems,* which was both a Newbery Honor Book and a Coretta Scott King Honor book. Her work ranges widely, from a rendition of Euripides' play *Hecuba* to several books for children, including *Fortune's Bones: The Manumission Requiem* and *A Wreath for Emmett Till,* both published in 2005. In 2004 she opened her home, Soul Mountain, as a writers' retreat. "When I have time and energy, I make quilts," she says. "'Asparagus' is part of a 'bad marriage' sonnet sequence, influenced by George Meredith's 'Modern Love.'"

Asparagus

He taught me how to slurp asparagus:
You hold it in your fingers, eat the stem
by inches to the tender terminus,
then close your eyes and suck in the sweet gem.
First, cook it in its own delicious steam,   5
sauté breadcrumbs in butter separately,
combine, eat slowly. As he ate, a gleam
in his eyes twinkled with such *jeu d'esprit,*
it made me drunk with longing. In my chair
amid our laughing, slurping dinner guests,   10
I felt as smug as a new billionaire,

> not jealous, not rejected, not depressed,
> as almost obscene, almost a debauché,
> he slurped asparagus, and winked at me.

from *Rattapallax*

ISAAC ASIMOV

Asimov (1920–1992) said that his talent lay in his ability to "read a dozen dull books and make one interesting book out of them." He amplified, "I'm on fire to explain, and happiest when it's something reasonably intricate which I can make clear step by step." From these motives, Asimov wrote nearly five hundred books, averaging one every six weeks for over thirty-five years. Although Asimov held a doctorate in chemistry from Columbia University (1948), his subjects ranged from astronomy, biology, biochemistry, mathematics, and physics, to history, literature, the Bible, limericks, and a two-volume autobiography. Nevertheless, he is probably best known for his science fiction—stories and novels; "Nightfall" has been called "the best science fiction work of all time." In 1973 he won both the Hugo and Nebula Awards.

Even before the advent of word processors, Asimov wrote ninety words a minute, up to twelve hours a day, a superhuman pace. His demanding schedule allowed two—and only two—drafts of everything, the first on a typewriter, and in his final years, the second on a computer. He said, "But I have a completely unadorned style. I aim to be accurate and clear—whether for an audience of sci-fi fans or general readers, including children." Asimov has been praised for being "encyclopedic, witty, with a gift for colorful and illuminating examples and explanations"—qualities apparent in "Those Crazy Ideas." There he explains the creative processes by which two scientists, Charles Darwin and Alfred Russel Wallace, arrived independently at the theory of evolution. Then he analyzes how they worked to illustrate the common characteristics of the creative process, a combination of education, intelligence, intuition, courage—and luck.

Those Crazy Ideas

1 Time and time again I have been asked (and I'm sure others who have, in their time, written science fiction have been asked too): "Where do you get your crazy ideas?"

2 Over the years, my answers have sunk from flattered confusion to a shrug and a feeble smile. Actually, I don't really know, and the lack of knowledge doesn't really worry me, either, as long as the ideas keep coming.

But then some time ago, a consultant firm in Boston, engaged in a sophisticated space-age project for the government, got in touch with me.

What they needed, it seemed, to bring their project to a successful conclusion were novel suggestions, startling new principles, conceptual breakthroughs. To put it into the nutshell of a well-turned phrase, they needed "crazy ideas."

Unfortunately, they didn't know how to go about getting crazy ideas, but some among them had read my science fiction, so they looked me up in the phone book and called me to ask (in essence), "Dr. Asimov, where do you get your crazy ideas?"

Alas, I still didn't know, but as speculation is my profession, I am perfectly willing to think about the matter and share my thoughts with you.

The question before the house, then, is: How does one go about creating or inventing or dreaming up or stumbling over a new and revolutionary scientific principle?

For instance—to take a deliberately chosen example—how did Darwin come to think of evolution?

To begin with, in 1831, when Charles Darwin was twenty-two, he joined the crew of a ship called the *Beagle*. This ship was making a five-year voyage about the world to explore various coast lines and to increase man's geographical knowledge. Darwin went along as ship's naturalist, to study the forms of life in far-off places.

This he did extensively and well, and upon the return of the *Beagle* Darwin wrote a book about his experiences (published in 1840) which made him famous. In the course of this voyage, numerous observations led him to the conclusion that species of living creatures changed and developed slowly with time; that new species descended from old. This, in itself, was not a new idea. Ancient Greeks had had glimmerings of evolutionary notions. Many scientists before Darwin, including Darwin's own grandfather, had theories of evolution.

The trouble, however, was that no scientist could evolve an explanation for the *why* of evolution. A French naturalist, Jean Baptiste de Lamarck, had suggested in the early 1800s that it came about by a kind of conscious effort or inner drive. A tree-grazing animal, attempting to reach leaves, stretched its neck over the years and transmitted a longer neck to its descendants. The process was repeated with each generation until a giraffe in full glory was formed.

The only trouble was that acquired characteristics are not inherited and this was easily proved. The Lamarckian explanation did not carry conviction.

Charles Darwin, however, had nothing better to suggest after several years of thinking about the problem.

But in 1798, eleven years before Darwin's birth, an English clergyman named Thomas Robert Malthus had written a book entitled *An Essay on the Principle of Population*. In this book Malthus suggested that the human population always increased faster than the food supply and that the population had to be cut down by either starvation, disease, or war; that these evils were therefore unavoidable.

15   In 1838 Darwin, still puzzling over the problem of the development of species, read Malthus's book. It is hackneyed to say "in a flash" but that, apparently, is how it happened. In a flash, it was clear to Darwin. Not only human beings increased faster than the food supply; all species of living things did. In every case, the surplus population had to be cut down by starvation, by predators, or by disease. Now no two members of any species are exactly alike; each has slight individual variations from the norm. Accepting this fact, which part of the population was cut down?

16   Why—and this was Darwin's breakthrough—those members of the species who were less efficient in the race for food, less adept at fighting off or escaping from predators, less equipped to resist disease, went down.

17   The survivors, generation after generation, were better adapted, on the average, to their environment. The slow changes toward a better fit with the environment accumulated until a new (and more adapted) species had replaced the old. Darwin thus postulated the reason for evolution as being the action of *natural selection*. In fact, the full title of his book is *On the Origin of Species by Means of Natural Selection, or the Preservation of Favoured Races in the Struggle for Life*. We just call it *The Origin of Species* and miss the full flavor of what it was he did.

18   It was in 1838 that Darwin received this flash and in 1844 that he began writing his book, but he worked on for fourteen years gathering evidence to back up his thesis. He was a methodical perfectionist and no amount of evidence seemed to satisfy him. He always wanted more. His friends read his preliminary manuscripts and urged him to publish. In particular, Charles Lyell (whose book *Principles of Geology,* published in 1830–1833, first convinced scientists of the great age of the earth and thus first showed there was *time* for the slow progress of evolution to take place) warned Darwin that someone would beat him to the punch.

19   While Darwin was working, another and younger English naturalist, Alfred Russel Wallace, was traveling in distant lands. He too found copious evidence to show that evolution took place and he too wanted to find a reason. He did not know that Darwin had already solved the problem.

20   He spent three years puzzling, and then in 1858, he too came across Malthus's book and read it. I am embarrassed to have to become hackneyed again, but in a flash he saw the answer. Unlike Darwin, however, he did not settle down to fourteen years of gathering and arranging evidence.

21   Instead, he grabbed pen and paper and at once wrote up his theory. He finished this in two days.

22   Naturally, he didn't want to rush into print without having his notions checked by competent colleagues, so he decided to send it to some well-known naturalist. To whom? Why, to Charles Darwin. To whom else?

I have often tried to picture Darwin's feeling as he read Wallace's 23 essay which, he afterward stated, expressed matters in almost his own words. He wrote to Lyell that he had been forestalled "with a vengeance."

Darwin might easily have retained full credit. He was well-known 24 and there were many witnesses to the fact that he had been working on his project for a decade and a half. Darwin, however, was a man of the highest integrity. He made no attempt to suppress Wallace. On the contrary, he passed on the essay to others and arranged to have it published along with a similar essay of his own. The year after, Darwin published his book.

Now the reason I chose this case was that here we have two men making 25 one of the greatest discoveries in the history of science independently and simultaneously and under precisely the same stimulus. Does that mean *anyone* could have worked out the theory of natural selection if they had but made a sea voyage and combined that with reading Malthus?

Well, let's see. Here's where the speculation starts. 26

To begin with, both Darwin and Wallace were thoroughly grounded 27 in natural history. Each had accumulated a vast collection of facts in the field in which they were to make their breakthrough. Surely this is significant.

Now every man in his lifetime collects facts, individual pieces of data, 28 items of information. Let's call these "bits" (as they do, I think, in information theory). The "bits" can be of all varieties: personal memories, girls' phone numbers, baseball players' batting averages, yesterday's weather, the atomic weights of the chemical elements.

Naturally, different men gather different numbers of different varieties 29 of "bits." A person who has collected a larger number than usual of those varieties that are held to be particularly difficult to obtain—say, those involving the sciences and the liberal arts—is considered "educated."

There are two broad ways in which the "bits" can be accumulated. 30 The more common way, nowadays, is to find people who already possess many "bits" and have them transfer those "bits" to your mind in good order and in predigested fashion. Our schools specialize in this transfer of "bits" and those of us who take advantage of them receive a "formal education."

The less common way is to collect "bits" with a minimum amount of 31 live help. They can be obtained from books or out of personal experience. In that case you are "self-educated." (It often happens that "self-educated" is confused with "uneducated." This is an error to be avoided.)

In actual practice, scientific breakthroughs have been initiated by 32 those who were formally educated, as for instance by Nicolaus Copernicus, and by those who were self-educated, as for instance by Michael Faraday.

To be sure, the structure of science has grown more complex over the 33 years and the absorption of the necessary number of "bits" has become more and more difficult without the guidance of someone who has already absorbed them. The self-educated genius is therefore becoming rarer, though he has still not vanished.

34   However, without drawing any distinction according to the manner in which "bits" have been accumulated, let's set up the first criterion for scientific creativity:

35   1) The creative person must possess as many "bits" of information as possible; i.e., he must be educated.

36   Of course, the accumulation of "bits" is not enough in itself. We have probably all met people who are intensely educated, but who manage to be abysmally stupid, nevertheless. They have the "bits," but the "bits" just lie there.

37   But what is there one can do with "bits"?

38   Well, one can combine them into groups of two or more. Everyone does that; it is the principle of the string on the finger. You tell yourself to remember *a* (to buy bread) when you observe *b* (the string). You enforce a combination that will not let you forget *a* because *b* is so noticeable.

39   That, of course, is a conscious and artificial combination of "bits." It is my feeling that every mind is, more or less unconsciously, continually making all sorts of combinations and permutations of "bits," probably at random.

40   Some minds do this with greater facility than others; some minds have greater capacity for dredging the combinations out of the unconscious and becoming consciously aware of them. This results in "new ideas," in "novel outlooks."

41   The ability to combine "bits" with facility and to grow consciously aware of the new combinations is, I would like to suggest, the measure of what we call "intelligence." In this view, it is quite possible to be educated and yet not intelligent.

42   Obviously, the creative scientist must not only have his "bits" on hand but he must be able to combine them readily and more or less consciously. Darwin not only observed data, he also made deductions—clever and far-reaching deductions—from what he observed. That is, he combined the "bits" in interesting ways and drew important conclusions.

43   So the second criterion of creativity is:

44   2) The creative person must be able to combine "bits" with facility and recognize the combinations he has formed; i.e., he must be intelligent.

45   Even forming and recognizing new combinations is insufficient in itself. Some combinations are important and some are trivial. How do you tell which are which? There is no question but that a person who cannot tell them apart must labor under a terrible disadvantage. As he plods after each possible new idea, he loses time and his life passes uselessly.

46   There is also no question but that there are people who somehow have the gift of seeing the consequences "in a flash" as Darwin and Wallace did; of feeling what the end must be without consciously going through every step of the reasoning. This, I suggest, is the measure of what we call "intuition."

47   Intuition plays more of a role in some branches of scientific knowledge than others. Mathematics, for instance, is a deductive science in which, once certain basic principles are learned, a large number of items of information

become "obvious" as merely consequences of those principles. Most of us, to be sure, lack the intuitive powers to see the "obvious."

To the truly intuitive mind, however, the combination of the few necessary "bits" is at once extraordinarily rich in consequences. Without too much trouble they see them all, including some that have not been seen by their predecessors.[1]

It is perhaps for this reason that mathematics and mathematical physics has seen repeated cases of first-rank breakthroughs by youngsters. Evariste Galois evolved group theory at twenty-one. Isaac Newton worked out calculus at twenty-three. Albert Einstein presented the theory of relativity at twenty-six, and so on.

In those branches of science which are more inductive and require larger numbers of "bits" to begin with, the average age of the scientists at the time of the breakthrough is greater. Darwin was twenty-nine at the time of his flash, Wallace was thirty-five.

But in any science, however inductive, intuition is necessary for creativity. So:

3) The creative person must be able to see, with as little delay as possible, the consequences of the new combinations of "bits" which he has formed; i.e., he must be intuitive.

But now let's look at this business of combining "bits" in a little more detail. "Bits" are at varying distances from each other. The more closely related two "bits" are, the more apt one is to be reminded of one by the other and to make the combination. Consequently, a new idea that arises from such a combination is made quickly. It is a "natural consequence" of an older idea, a "corollary." It "obviously follows."

The combination of less related "bits" results in a more startling idea; if for no other reason than that it takes longer for such a combination to be made, so that the new idea is therefore less "obvious." For a scientific breakthrough of the first rank, there must be a combination of "bits" so widely spaced that the random chance of the combination being made is small indeed. (Otherwise, it will be made quickly and be considered but a corollary of some previous idea which will then be considered the "breakthrough.")

But then, it can easily happen that two "bits" sufficiently widely spaced to make a breakthrough by their combination are not present in the same mind. Neither Darwin nor Wallace, for all their education, intelligence, and intuition, possessed the key "bits" necessary to work out the theory of evolution by natural selection. Those "bits" were lying in Malthus's book, and both Darwin and Wallace had to find them there.

To do this, however, they had to read, understand, and appreciate the book. In short, they had to be ready to incorporate other people's "bits" and treat them with all the ease with which they treated their own.

---

[1] The Swiss mathematician, Leonhard Euler, said that to the true mathematician, it is at once obvious that $e^{\pi i} = -1$.

57   It would hamper creativity, in other words, to emphasize intensity of education at the expense of broadness. It is bad enough to limit the nature of the "bits" to the point where the necessary two would not be in the same mind. It would be fatal to mold a mind to the point where it was incapable of accepting "foreign bits."

58   I think we ought to revise the first criterion of creativity, then, to read:

59   1) The creative person must possess as many "bits" as possible, falling into as wide a variety of types as possible; i.e., he must be broadly educated.

60   As the total amount of "bits" to be accumulated increases with the advance of science, it is becoming more and more difficult to gather enough "bits" in a wide enough area. Therefore, the practice of "brain-busting" is coming into popularity; the notion of collecting thinkers into groups and hoping that they will cross-fertilize one another into startling new breakthroughs.

61   Under what circumstances could this conceivably work? (After all, anything that will stimulate creativity is of first importance to humanity.)

62   Well, to begin with, a group of people will have more "bits" on hand than any member of the group singly since each man is likely to have some "bits" the others do not possess.

63   However, the increase in "bits" is not in direct proportion to the number of men, because there is bound to be considerable overlapping. As the group increases, the smaller and smaller addition of completely new "bits" introduced by each additional member is quickly outweighed by the added tensions involved in greater numbers; the longer wait to speak, the greater likelihood of being interrupted, and so on. It is my (intuitive) guess that five is as large a number as one can stand in such a conference.

64   Now of the three criteria mentioned so far, I feel (intuitively) that intuition is the least common. It is more likely that none of the group will be intuitive than that none will be intelligent or none educated. If no individual in the group is intuitive, the group as a whole will not be intuitive. You cannot add non-intuition and form intuition.

65   If one of the group is intuitive, he is almost certain to be intelligent and educated as well, or he would not have been asked to join the group in the first place. In short, for a brain-busting group to be creative, it must be quite small and it must possess at least one creative individual. But in that case, does that one individual need the group? Well, I'll get back to that later.

66   Why did Darwin work fourteen years gathering evidence for a theory he himself must have been convinced was correct from the beginning? Why did Wallace send his manuscript to Darwin first instead of offering it for publication at once?

67   To me it seems that they must have realized that any new idea is met by resistance from the general population who, after all, are not creative. The more radical the new idea, the greater the dislike and distrust it arouses. The dislike and distrust aroused by a first-class breakthrough are so great that the author must be prepared for unpleasant consequences (sometimes

for expulsion from the respect of the scientific community; sometimes, in some societies, for death).

Darwin was trying to gather enough evidence to protect himself by 68 convincing others through a sheer flood of reasoning. Wallace wanted to have Darwin on his side before proceeding.

It takes courage to announce the results of your creativity. The greater 69 the creativity, the greater the necessary courage in much more than direct proportion. After all, consider that the more profound the breakthrough, the more solidified the previous opinions; the more "against reason" the new discovery seems, the more against cherished authority.

Usually a man who possesses enough courage to be a scientific genius 70 seems odd. After all, a man who has sufficient courage or irreverence to fly in the face of reason or authority must be odd, if you define "odd" as "being not like most people." And if he is courageous and irreverent in such a colossally big thing, he will certainly be courageous and irreverent in many small things so that being odd in one way, he is apt to be odd in others. In short, he will seem to the non-creative, conforming people about him to be a "crackpot."

So we have the fourth criterion: 71

4) The creative person must possess courage (and to the general 72 public may, in consequence, seem a crackpot).

As it happens, it is the crackpottery that is most often most noticeable 73 about the creative individual. The eccentric and absent-minded professor is a stock character in fiction; and the phrase "mad scientist" is almost a cliché.

(And be it noted that I am never asked where I get my interesting or 74 effective or clever or fascinating ideas. I am invariably asked where I get my *crazy* ideas.)

Of course, it does not follow that because the creative individual is 75 usually a crackpot, that any crackpot is automatically an unrecognized genius. The chances are low indeed, and failure to recognize that the proposition cannot be so reversed is the cause of a great deal of trouble.

Then, since I believe that combinations of "bits" take place quite at 76 random in the unconscious mind, it follows that it is quite possible that a person may possess all four of the criteria I have mentioned in super-abundance and yet may never happen to make the necessary combination. After all, suppose Darwin had never read Malthus. Would he ever have thought of natural selection? What made him pick up the copy? What if someone had come in at the crucial time and interrupted him?

So there is a fifth criterion which I am at a loss to phrase in any other 77 way than this:

5) A creative person must be lucky. 78

To summarize: 79

A creative person must be 1) broadly educated, 2) intelligent, 3) intui- 80 tive, 4) courageous, and 5) lucky.

81   How, then, does one go about encouraging scientific creativity? For now, more than ever before in man's history, we must; and the need will grow constantly in the future.

82   Only, it seems to me, by increasing the incidence of the various criteria among the general population.

83   Of the five criteria, number 5 (luck) is out of our hands. We can only hope; although we must also remember Louis Pasteur's famous statement that "Luck favors the prepared mind." Presumably, if we have enough of the four other criteria, we shall find enough of number five as well.

84   Criterion 1 (broad education) is in the hands of our school system. Many educators are working hard to find ways of increasing the quality of education among the public. They should be encouraged to continue doing so.

85   Criterion 2 (intelligence) and 3 (intuition) are inborn and their incidence cannot be increased in the ordinary way. However, they can be more efficiently recognized and utilized. I would like to see methods devised for spotting the intelligent and intuitive (particularly the latter) early in life and treating them with special care. This, too, educators are concerned with.

86   To me, though, it seems that it is criterion 4 (courage) that receives the least concern, and it is just the one we may most easily be able to handle. Perhaps it is difficult to make a person more courageous than he is, but that is not necessary. It would be equally effective to make it sufficient to be less courageous; to adopt an attitude that creativity is a permissible activity.

87   Does this mean changing society or changing human nature? I don't think so. I think there are ways of achieving the end that do not involve massive change of anything, and it is here that brainbusting has its greatest chance of significance.

88   Suppose we have a group of five that includes one creative individual. Let's ask again what that individual can receive from the non-creative four.

89   The answer to me, seems to be just this: Permission!

90   They must permit him to create. They must tell him to go ahead and be a crackpot.[2]

91   How is this permission to be granted? Can four essentially non-creative people find it within themselves to grant such permission? Can the one creative person find it within himself to accept it?

92   I don't know. Here, it seems to me, is where we need experimentation and perhaps a kind of creative breakthrough about creativity. Once we learn enough about the whole matter, who knows—I may even find out where I get those crazy ideas.

---

[2] AUTHOR'S NOTE: Always with the provision, of course, that the crackpot creation that results survives the test of hard inspection. Though many of the products of genius seem crackpot at first, very few of the creations that seem crackpot turn out, after all, to be products of genius.

Content

1. How does Asimov define "crazy ideas"? Is he using "crazy idea" as a synonym for a "new and revolutionary scientific principle"? How would Asimov (or you) distinguish between a "crazy idea" and a "crackpot" idea? Or the notion of a "mad scientist"?

2. Compare and contrast the creative processes by which Charles Darwin and Alfred Russel Wallace arrived independently at the theory of evolution. How appropriate is it for Asimov to generalize about scientific creativity on the basis of two examples from a particular field?

3. Identify the five qualities Asimov says are necessary for the creative process to operate. Has he covered all the essentials? How important is "luck" (¶ 78)? Is the creative process the same in all fields of the arts and sciences? To what extent must the "climate be right" for the creative process to function effectively? What becomes of "crazy ideas" too advanced for their time?

Strategies/Structures/Language

4. Show how Asimov's essay is an example of inductive reasoning—beginning with evidence, assessing that evidence, and drawing conclusions from it.

5. Asimov uses a conversational tone and vocabulary, as well as two extended narrative examples (of Darwin and Wallace). Would you expect to find such literary techniques in scientific writing? If so, for what kind of audience? (Compare Darwin, "Understanding Natural Selection" [335–40] and Gould, "Evolution as Fact and Theory" [404–11].)

6. Asimov always identifies the scientists to whom he is referring when he first introduces them (Lamarck, ¶ 11; Malthus, ¶ 14; Lyell, ¶ 18). What does this practice reveal about the amount of scientific knowledge Asimov expects his readers to have?

For Writing

7. What does it take to be successful? Identify and define the essential criteria (four or five items) for an outstanding performance in one of the fields or roles below. Illustrate your definition with a detailed example or two from the lives of successful people in that field or role, perhaps people you know:

   a. Parent or grandparent
   b. Medicine (doctor, nurse, social worker, medical researcher, therapist)
   c. Politics, military, and the law (police or military officer, lawyer, elected official, bureaucrat, judge)
   d. Athletics (player of team or individual sports, coach, referee)
   e. Education (student, teacher, or administrator)
   f. The fine arts (painter, sculptor, photographer, musician, dancer, writer, actor, filmmaker)
   g. Business (self-made man or woman, salesperson, manager, executive, accountant, broker)
   h. Another profession or occupation of your choice

 For comprehension, writing, and research activities and resources, please visit the companion website at <college.hmco.com/english>.

TOM AND RAY MAGLIOZZI

Tom (born 1938) and Ray (born 1947) Magliozzi were born in East Cambridge, Massachusetts, and educated at the Massachusetts Institute of Technology. Tom worked in marketing; Ray was a VISTA volunteer and taught junior high school. In 1973 the brothers opened the Good News garage in Cambridge, which Ray continues to operate while Tom teaches business at Suffolk University. Three years later their career as Click and Clack, the Tappet Brothers, began with a local call-in radio show on car repair, "Car Talk," which has become a favorite on National Public Radio since 1987.

Speaking, as one commentator has observed, "pure Bostonese that sounds a lot like a truck running over vowels," and with considerable humor, including unrestrained (some say "maniacal") laughter at their own jokes, the brothers dispense realistic, easy-to-understand advice about how cars work and what to do when they don't, on the radio; a host of CDs, such as *Maternal Combustion* (2005); and in their book *Car Talk* (1991), in which the following explanation of "Inside the Engine" appears.

Inside the Engine

1   A customer of ours had an old Thunderbird that he used to drive back and forth to New York to see a girlfriend every other weekend. And every time he made the trip he'd be in the shop the following Monday needing to get something fixed because the car was such a hopeless piece of trash. One Monday he failed to show up and Tom said, "Gee, that's kind of unusual." I said jokingly, "Maybe he blew the car up."

2   Well, what happened was that he was on the Merritt Parkway in Connecticut when he noticed that he had to keep the gas pedal all the way to the floor just to go 30 m.p.h., with this big V-8 engine, and he figured something was awry.

3   So he pulled into one of those filling stations where they sell gasoline and chocolate-chip cookies and milk. And he asked the attendant to look at the engine and, of course, the guy said, "I can't help you. All I know is cookies and milk." But the guy agreed to look anyway since our friend was really desperate. His girlfriend was waiting for him and he needed to know if he was going to make it. Anyway, the guy threw open the hood and jumped back in terror. The engine was glowing red. Somewhere along the line, probably around Hartford, he must have lost all of his motor oil. The engine kept getting hotter and hotter, but like a lot of other things in the car that didn't work, neither did his oil pressure warning light. As a result, the engine got so heated up that it fused itself together. All the pistons melted, and the cylinder heads deformed, and the pistons fused to the cylinder walls, and the bearings welded themselves to the crankshaft—oh,

it was a terrible sight! When he tried to restart the engine, he just heard a *click, click, click* since the whole thing was seized up tighter than a drum.

That's what can happen in a case of extreme engine neglect. Most of 4 us wouldn't do that, or at least wouldn't do it knowingly. Our friend didn't do it knowingly either, but he learned a valuable lesson. He learned that his girlfriend wouldn't come and get him if his car broke down. Even if he offered her cookies and milk.

The oil is critical to keeping things running since it not only acts as a lubri- 5 cant, but it also helps to keep the engine cool. What happens is that the oil pump sucks the oil out of what's called the sump (or the crankcase or the oil pan), and it pushes that oil, under pressure, up to all of the parts that need lubrication.

The way the oil works is that it acts as a cushion. The molecules of 6 oil actually separate the moving metal parts from one another so that they don't directly touch; the crankshaft *journals,* or the hard parts of the crankshaft, never touch the soft connecting-rod *bearings* because there's a film of oil between them, forced in there under pressure. From the pump.

It's pretty high pressure too. When the engine is running at highway 7 speed, the oil, at 50 or 60 pounds or more per square inch (or about 4 bars, if you're of the metric persuasion—but let's leave religion out of this), is coursing through the veins of the engine and keeping all these parts at safe, albeit microscopic, distances from each other.

But if there's a lot of dirt in the oil, the dirt particles get embedded in 8 these metal surfaces and gradually the dirt acts as an abrasive and wears away these metal surfaces. And pretty soon the engine is junk.

It's also important that the motor oil be present in sufficient quantity. 9 In nontechnical terms, that means there's got to be enough of it in there. If you have too little oil in your engine, there's not going to be enough of it to go around, and it will get very hot, because four quarts will be doing the work of five, and so forth. When that happens, the oil gets overheated and begins to burn up at a greater than normal rate. Pretty soon, instead of having four quarts, you have three and a half quarts, then three quarts doing the work of five. And then, next thing you know, you're down to two quarts and your engine is glowing red, just like that guy driving to New York, and it's chocolate-chip cookie time.

In order to avoid this, some cars have gauges and some have warn- 10 ing lights; some people call them "idiot lights." Actually, we prefer to reverse it and call them "idiot gauges." I think gauges are bad. When you drive a car—maybe I'm weird about this—I think it's a good idea to look at the road most of the time. And you can't look at the road if you're busy looking at a bunch of gauges. It's the same objection we have to these stupid radios today that have so damn many buttons and slides and digital scanners and so forth that you need a copilot to change stations. Remember when you just turned a knob?

11   Not that gauges are bad in and of themselves. I think if you have your choice, what you want is idiot lights—or what we call "genius lights"—and gauges too. It's nice to have a gauge that you can kind of keep an eye on for an overview of what's going on. For example, if you know that your engine typically runs at 215 degrees and on this particular day, which is not abnormally hot, it's running at 220 or 225, you might suspect that something is wrong and get it looked at before your radiator boils over.

12   On the other hand, if that gauge was the only thing you had to rely on and you didn't have a light to alert you when something was going wrong, then you'd look at the thing all the time, especially if your engine had melted on you once. In that case, why don't you take the bus? Because you're not going to be a very good driver, spending most of your time looking at the gauges.

13   Incidentally, if that oil warning light ever comes on, shut the engine off! We don't mean that you should shut it off in rush-hour traffic when you're in the passing lane. Use all necessary caution and get the thing over to the breakdown lane. But don't think you can limp to the next exit, because you can't. Spend the money to get towed and you may save the engine.

14   It's a little-known fact that the oil light does *not* signify whether or not you have oil in the engine. The oil warning light is really monitoring the oil *pressure*. Of course, if you have no oil, you'll have no oil pressure, so the light will be on. But it's also possible to have plenty of oil and an oil pump that's not working for one reason or another. In this event, a new pump would fix the problem, but if you were to drive the car (saying, "It must be a bad light, I just checked the oil!") you'd melt the motor.

15   So if the oil warning light comes on, even if you just had an oil change and the oil is right up to the full mark on the dipstick and is nice and clean—don't drive the car!

16   Here's another piece of useful info. When you turn the key to the "on" position, all the little warning lights *should light up*: the temperature light, the oil light, whatever other lights you may have. Because that is the *test mode* for these lights. If those lights *don't* light up when you turn the key to the "on" position (just before you turn it all the way to start the car), does that mean you're out of oil? No. It means that something is wrong with the warning light itself. If the light doesn't work then, it's not going to work at all. Like when you need it, for example.

17   One more thing about oil: overfilling is just as bad as underfilling. Can you really have too much of a good thing? you ask. Yes. If you're half a quart or even a quart overfilled, it's not a big deal, and I wouldn't be afraid to drive the car under those circumstances. But if you're a quart and a half or two quarts or more overfilled, you could have so much oil in the crankcase that the spinning crankshaft is going to hit the oil and turn it into suds. It's impossible for the pump to pump suds, so you'll ruin the

motor. It's kind of like a front-loading washing machine that goes berserk and spills suds all over the floor when you put too much detergent in. That's what happens to your motor oil when you overfill it.

With all this talk about things that can go wrong, let's not forget that   18
modern engines are pretty incredible. People always say, "You know, the cars of yesteryear were wonderful. They built cars rough and tough and durable in those days."

Horsefeathers.   19

The cars of yesteryear were nicer to look at because they were very   20
individualistic. They were all different, and some were even beautiful. In fact, when I was a kid, you could tell the year, make, and model of a car from a hundred paces just by looking at the taillights or the grille.

Nowadays, they all look the same. They're like jellybeans on wheels.   21
You can't tell one from the other. But the truth is, they've never made engines as good as they make them today. Think of the abuse they take! None of the cars of yesteryear was capable of going 60 or 70 miles per hour all day long and taking it for 100,000 miles.

Engines of today—and by today I mean from the late '60s on up—   22
are far superior. What makes them superior is not only the design and the metallurgy, but the lubricants. The oil they had thirty years ago was lousy compared to what we have today. There are magic additives and detergents and long-chain polymers and what-have-you that make them able to hold dirt in suspension and to neutralize acids and to lubricate better than oils of the old days.

There aren't too many things that will go wrong, because the engines   23
are made so well and the tolerances are closer. And aside from doing stupid things like running out of oil or failing to heed the warning lights or overfilling the thing, you shouldn't worry.

But here's one word of caution about cars that have timing belts: 24
Lots of cars these days are made with overhead camshafts. The camshaft, which opens the valves, is turned by a gear and gets its power from the crankshaft. Many cars today use a notched rubber *timing belt* to connect the two shafts instead of a chain because it's cheaper and easy to change. And here's the caveat: *if you don't change it and the belt breaks, it can mean swift ruin to the engine.* The pistons can hit the valves and you'll have bent valves and possibly broken pistons.

So you can do many hundreds of dollars' worth of damage by failing   25
to heed the manufacturer's warning about changing the timing belt in a timely manner. No pun intended. For most cars, the timing belt replacement is somewhere between $100 and $200. It's not a big deal.

I might add that there are many cars that have rubber timing belts   26
that will *not* cause damage to the engine when they break. But even if you have one of those cars, make sure that you get the belt changed, at the very least, when the manufacturer suggests it. If there's no specific recommendation and you have a car with a rubber belt, we would recommend that

you change it at 60,000 miles. Because even if you don't do damage to the motor when the belt breaks, you're still going to be stuck somewhere, maybe somewhere unpleasant. Maybe even Cleveland! So you want to make sure that you don't fall into that situation.

27   Many engines that have rubber timing belts also use the belt to drive the water pump. On these, don't forget to change the water pump when you change the timing belt, because the leading cause of premature belt failure is that the water pump seizes. So if you have a timing belt that drives the water pump, get the water pump out of there at the same time. You don't want to put a belt in and then have the water pump go a month later, because it'll break the new belt and wreck the engine.

28   The best way to protect all the other pieces that you can't get to without spending a lot of money is through frequent oil changes. The manufacturers recommend oil changes somewhere between seven and ten thousand miles, depending upon the car. We've always recommended that you change your oil at 3,000 miles. We realize for some people that's a bit of an inconvenience, but look at it as cheap insurance. And change the filter every time too.

29   And last but not least, I want to repeat this because it's important: Make sure your warning lights work. The oil pressure and engine temperature warning lights are your engine's lifeline. Check them every day. You should make it as routine as checking to see if your zipper's up. You guys should do it at the same time.

30   What you do is, you get into the car, check to see that your zipper's up, and then turn the key on and check to see if your oil pressure and temperature warning lights come on.

31   I don't know what women do.

Content

1. Does the Magliozzi brothers' explanation of how a car engine works contain sufficient information that readers can understand it? Why or why not? Do the analogies ("veins," ¶ 7; "suds," ¶ 17) help? Would a diagram or diagrams be useful? If so, what should they include?

2. What assumptions do the authors make about their readers' technical knowledge? Why do they provide basic information (such as how oil works in an engine, ¶s 5–9)? How are they able to do this without either offending their readers' intelligence or boring them?

Strategies/Structures/Language

3. Why do the authors begin their explanation of a process with a story—in this case, a cautionary tale of the guy whose beat-up old Thunderbird had a meltdown on the Merritt Parkway?

4. When writing about science and technology, why is it important to define fundamental terms, even terms readers have heard—and used—many times, such as *motor oil* (¶s 5–9), *gauges* (or *idiot gauges,* ¶s 10–12), and *oil warning light* (¶s 13–15)?

5. Does the authors' humor help you to understand how an engine works? Most science and technical writing isn't funny. Can you trust the authority of a humorist in general and these humorists in particular?

6. The authors give commands, such as "Don't drive the car!" when the oil warning light is on (¶ 15), and "Make sure your warning lights work" (¶ 29). Why can they expect readers to react to such commands without being offended?

For Writing

7. Write an essay for a nonspecialized audience explaining how a tool, mechanical object, or more abstract process (about which you know a great deal) works and how to get maximum performance from it. Possible topics include a specific brand and model of car; a piece of exercise equipment; a kitchen implement or power tool; a particular computer, PDA, MP3 player, cell phone, or other common electronic equipment. Use illustrations or diagrams as appropriate, and refer to them in the text of your essay.

8. Authors in the physical or social sciences customarily work in teams, reporting on their collaborative research. In this spirit of this model, pick a topic on which you are an expert (perhaps a sport or game; cooking; working as a waiter, staff member, lifeguard, teacher's aide, or camp counselor). Collaborate with another equally knowledgeable person or team to explain a technical aspect of the topic—a process, strategy, fundamental decision—to a specialized audience in the same field to (1) show them how to do it and (2) convince them to do it according to your instructions. Use appropriate illustrations or diagrams as necessary.

 For comprehension, writing, and research activities and resources, please visit the companion website at <college.hmco.com/english>.

SCOTT RUSSELL SANDERS

Sanders (born 1945) grew up in Ohio, earned a PhD in English from Cambridge University in 1971, and has taught ever since at Indiana University. His twenty-five books include fiction, a biography of Audubon, and several essay collections. Among them, *In Limestone Country* (1985), *Staying Put* (1993), *Writing from the Center* (1995), and *Hunting for Hope* (1998) focus on living and writing in the Midwest. "My writing . . . is bound together by a web of questions" concerning "the ways in which human beings come to terms with the practical problems of living on a small planet, in nature . . . and families and towns. . . ."

The elegiac "The Inheritance of Tools" appeared in the award-winning *The Paradise of Bombs* (1987), personal essays mainly about the American culture of violence. This essay reveals Sanders's concerns, as a writer and as a son, husband, and father, with the inheritance of skills and values through the generations. Here narration is explanation. Sanders shows how tools become not just extensions of the hand and brain, but of the human heart, as the knowledge of how to use and care for them is transmitted from grandfather to father to son to grandchildren. The ways in which people think about tools and use and care for them reflect their values and personalities; "each hammer and level and saw is wrapped in a cloud of knowing."

The Inheritance of Tools

1   At just about the hour when my father died, soon after dawn one February morning when ice coated the windows like cataracts, I banged my thumb with a hammer. Naturally I swore at the hammer, the reckless thing, and in the moment of swearing I thought of what my father would say: "If you'd try hitting the nail it would go in a whole lot faster. Don't you know your thumb's not as hard as that hammer?" We both were doing carpentry that day, but far apart. He was building cupboards at my brother's place in Oklahoma; I was at home in Indiana, putting up a wall in the basement to make a bedroom for my daughter. By the time my mother called with news of his death—the long distance wires whittling her voice until it seemed too thin to bear the weight of what she had to say—my thumb was swollen. A week or so later a white scar in the shape of a crescent moon began to show above the cuticle and month by month it rose across the pink sky of my thumbnail. It took the better part of a year for the scar to disappear, and every time I noticed it I thought of my father.

2   The hammer had belonged to him, and to his father before him. The three of us have used it to build houses and barns and chicken coops, to upholster chairs and crack walnuts, to make doll furniture and bookshelves and jewelry boxes. The head is scratched and pockmarked, like an old plowshare that has been working rocky fields, and it gives off the sort of dull sheen you see on fast creek water in the shade. It is a finishing hammer, about the weight of a bread loaf, too light, really, for framing walls, too heavy for cabinet work, with a curved claw for pulling nails, a rounded head for pounding, a fluted neck for looks, and a hickory handle for strength.

3   The present handle is my third one, bought from a lumberyard in Tennessee, down the road from where my brother and I were helping my father build his retirement house. I broke the previous one by trying to pull sixteen-penny nails out of floor joists—a foolish thing to do with a finishing hammer, as my father pointed out. "You ever hear of a crowbar?" he said. No telling how many handles he and my grandfather had gone through before me. My grandfather used to cut down hickory trees on his farm, saw them into slabs, cure the planks in his hayloft, and carve

handles with a drawknife. The grain in hickory is crooked and knotty, and therefore tough, hard to split, like the grain in the two men who owned this hammer before me.

After proposing marriage to a neighbor girl, my grandfather used 4 this hammer to build a house for his bride on a stretch of river bottom in northern Mississippi. The lumber for the place, like the hickory for the handle, was cut on his own land. By the day of the wedding he had not quite finished the house, and so right after the ceremony he took his wife home and put her to work. My grandmother had worn her Sunday dress for the wedding, with a fringe of lace tacked on around the hem in honor of the occasion. She removed this lace and folded it away before going out to help my grandfather nail siding on the house. "There she was in her good dress," he told me some fifty-odd years after that wedding day, "holding up them long pieces of clapboard while I hammered, and together we got the place covered up before dark." As the family grew to four, six, eight, and eventually thirteen, my grandfather used this hammer to enlarge his house room by room, like a chambered nautilus expanding its shell.

By and by the hammer was passed along to my father. One day he 5 was up on the roof of our pony barn nailing shingles with it, when I stepped out the kitchen door to call him for supper. Before I could yell, something about the sight of him straddling the spine of that roof and swinging the hammer caught my eye and made me hold my tongue. I was five or six years old, and the world's commonplaces were still news to me. He would pull a nail from the pouch at his waist, bring the hammer down, and a moment later the *thunk* of the blow would reach my ears. And that is what had stopped me in my tracks and stilled my tongue, that momentary gap between seeing and hearing the blow. Instead of yelling from the kitchen door, I ran to the barn and climbed two rungs up the ladder—as far as I was allowed to go—and spoke quietly to my father. On our walk to the house he explained that sound takes time to make its way through air. Suddenly the world seemed larger, the air more dense, if sound could be held back like any ordinary traveler.

By the time I started using this hammer, at about the age when I dis- 6 covered the speed of sound, it already contained houses and mysteries for me. The smooth handle was one my grandfather had made. In those days I needed both hands to swing it. My father would start a nail in a scrap of wood, and I would pound away until I bent it over.

"Looks like you got ahold of some of those rubber nails," he would 7 tell me. "Here, let me see if I can find you some stiff ones." And he would rummage in a drawer until he came up with a fistful of more cooperative nails. "Look at the head," he would tell me. "Don't look at your hands, don't look at the hammer. Just look at the head of that nail and pretty soon you'll learn to hit it square."

Pretty soon I did learn. While he worked in the garage cutting dove- 8 tail joints for a drawer or skinning a deer or tuning an engine, I would hammer nails. I made innocent blocks of wood look like porcupines. He did not talk much in the midst of his tools, but he kept up a nearly ceaseless humming, slipping in and out of a dozen tunes in an afternoon, often running back over the same stretch of melody again and again, as if searching for a way out. When the humming did cease, I knew he was faced with a task requiring great delicacy or concentration, and I took care not to distract him.

9   He kept scraps of wood in a cardboard box—the ends of two-by-fours, slabs of shelving and plywood, odd pieces of molding—and everything in it was fair game. I nailed scraps together to fashion what I called boats or houses, but the results usually bore only faint resemblance to the visions I carried in my head. I would hold up these constructions to show my father, and he would turn them over in his hands admiringly, speculating about what they might be. My cobbled-together guitars might have been alien spaceships, my barns might have been models of Aztec temples, each wooden contraption might have been anything but what I had set out to make.

10   Now and again I would feel the need to have a chunk of wood shaped or shortened before I riddled it with nails, and I would clamp it in a vise and scrape at it with a handsaw. My father would let me lacerate the board until my arm gave out, and then he would wrap his hand around mine and help me finish the cut, showing me how to use my thumb to guide the blade, how to pull back on the saw to keep it from binding, how to let my shoulder do the work.

11   "Don't force it," he would say, "just drag it easy and give the teeth a chance to bite."

12   As the saw teeth bit down, the wood released its smell, each kind with its own fragrance, oak or walnut or cherry or pine—usually pine because it was the softest, easiest for a child to work. No matter how weathered and gray the board, no matter how warped and cracked, inside there was this smell waiting, as of something freshly baked. I gathered every smidgen of sawdust and stored it away in coffee cans, which I kept in a drawer of the workbench. When I did not feel like hammering nails, I would dump my sawdust on the concrete floor of the garage and landscape it into highways and farms and towns, running miniature cars and trucks along miniature roads. Looming as huge as a colossus, my father worked over and around me, now and again bending down to inspect my work, careful not to trample my creations. It was a landscape that smelled dizzyingly of wood. Even after a bath my skin would carry the smell, and so would my father's hair, when he lifted me for a bedtime hug.

13   I tell these things not only from memory but also from recent observation, because my own son now turns blocks of wood into nailed porcupines, dumps cans full of sawdust at my feet and sculpts highways on the floor. He learns how to swing a hammer from the elbow instead of the wrist, how

to lay his thumb beside the blade to guide a saw, how to tap a chisel with a wooden mallet, how to mark a hole with an awl before starting a drill bit. My daughter did the same before him, and even now, on the brink of teenage aloofness, she will occasionally drag out my box of wood scraps and carpenter something. So I have seen my apprenticeship to wood and tools reenacted in each of my children, as my father saw his own apprenticeship renewed in me.

The saw I use belonged to him, as did my level and both of my   14
squares, and all four tools had belonged to his father. The blade of the saw is the bluish color of gun barrels, and the maple handle, dark from the sweat of hands, is inscribed with curving leaf designs. The level is a shaft of walnut two feet long, edged with brass and pierced by three round windows in which air bubbles float in oil-filled tubes of glass. The middle window serves for testing if a surface is horizontal, the others for testing if a surface is plumb or vertical. My grandfather used to carry this level on the gun rack behind the seat in his pickup, and when I rode with him I would turn around to watch the bubbles dance. The larger of the two squares is called a framing square, a flat steel elbow, so beat up and tarnished you can barely make out the rows of numbers that show how to figure the cuts on rafters. The smaller one is called a try square, for marking right angles, with a blued steel blade for the shank and a brass-faced block of cherry for the head.

I was taught early on that a saw is not to be used apart from a square: 15
"If you're going to cut a piece of wood," my father insisted, "you owe it to the tree to cut it straight."

Long before studying geometry, I learned there is a mystical virtue in   16
right angles. There is an unspoken morality in seeking the level and the plumb. A house will stand, a table will bear weight, the sides of a box will hold together, only if the joints are square and the members upright. When the bubble is lined up between two marks etched in the glass tube of a level, you have aligned yourself with the forces that hold the universe together. When you miter the corners of a picture frame each angle must be exactly forty-five degrees, as they are in the perfect triangles of Pythagoras, not a degree more or less. Otherwise the frame will hang crookedly, as if ashamed of itself and of its maker. No matter if the joints you are cutting do not show. Even if you are butting two pieces of wood together inside a cabinet, where no one except a wrecking crew will ever see them, you must take pains to ensure that the ends are square and the studs are plumb.

I took pains over the wall I was building on the day my father died.   17
Not long after that wall was finished—paneled with tongue-and-groove boards of yellow pine, the nail holes filled with putty and the wood all stained and sealed—I came close to wrecking it one afternoon when my daughter ran howling up the stairs to announce that her gerbils had escaped from their cage and were hiding in my brand new wall. She could hear them scratching and squeaking behind her bed. Impossible! I said. How on earth

could they get inside my drum-tight wall? Through the heating vent, she answered. I went downstairs, pressed my ear to the honey-colored wood, and heard the *scritch scritch* of tiny feet.

18   "What can we do?" my daughter wailed. "They'll starve to death, they'll die of thirst, they'll suffocate."

19   "Hold on," I soothed. "I'll think of something."

20   While I thought and she fretted, the radio on her bedside table delivered us the headlines: Several thousand people had died in a city in India from a poisonous cloud that had leaked overnight from a chemical plant. A nuclear-powered submarine had been launched. Rioting continued in South Africa. An airplane had been hijacked in the Mediterranean. Authorities calculated that several thousand homeless people slept on the streets within sight of the Washington Monument. I felt my usual helplessness in the face of all these calamities. But here was my daughter, weeping because her gerbils were holed up in a wall. This calamity I could handle.

21   "Don't worry," I told her. "We'll set food and water by the heating vent and lure them out. And if that doesn't do the trick, I'll tear the wall apart until we find them."

22   She stopped crying and gazed at me. "You'd really tear it apart? Just for my gerbils? The *wall?*" Astonishment slowed her down only for a second, however, before she ran to the workbench and began tugging at drawers, saying, "Let's see, what'll we need? Crowbar. Hammer. Chisels. I hope we don't have to use them—but just in case."

23   We didn't need the wrecking tools. I never had to assault my handsome wall, because the gerbils eventually came out to nibble at a dish of popcorn. But for several hours I studied the tongue-and-groove skin I had nailed up on the day of my father's death, considering where to begin prying. There were no gaps in that wall, no crooked joints.

24   I had botched a great many pieces of wood before I mastered the right angle with a saw, botched even more before I learned to miter a joint. The knowledge of these things resides in my hands and eyes and the webwork of muscles, not in the tools. There are machines for sale—powered miter boxes and radial-arm saws, for instance—that will enable any casual soul to cut proper angles in boards. The skill is invested in the gadget instead of the person who uses it, and this is what distinguishes a machine from a tool. If I had to earn my keep by making furniture or building houses, I suppose I would buy powered saws and pneumatic nailers; the need for speed would drive me to it. But since I carpenter only for my own pleasure or to help neighbors or to remake the house around the ears of my family, I stick with hand tools. Most of the ones I own were given to me by my father, who also taught me how to wield them. The tools in my workbench are a double inheritance, for each hammer and level and saw is wrapped in a cloud of knowing.

25   All of these tools are a pleasure to look at and to hold. Merchants would never paste NEW NEW NEW! signs on them in stores. Their designs

are old because they work, because they serve their purpose well. Like folk songs and aphorisms and the grainy bits of language, these tools have been pared down to essentials. I look at my claw hammer, the distillation of a hundred generations of carpenters, and consider that it holds up well beside those other classics—Greek vases, Gregorian chants, *Don Quixote*, barbed fish hooks, candles, spoons. Knowledge of hammering stretches back to the earliest humans who squatted beside fires, chipping flints. Anthropologists have a lovely name for those unworked rocks that served as the earliest hammers. "Dawn stones," they are called. Their only qualification for the work, aside from hardness, is that they fit the hand. Our ancestors used them for grinding corn, tapping awls, smashing bones. From dawn stones to this claw hammer is a great leap in time, but no great distance in design or imagination.

On that iced-over February morning when I smashed my thumb with the   26
hammer, I was down in the basement framing the wall that my daughter's gerbils would later hide in. I was thinking of my father, as I always did whenever I built anything, thinking how he would have gone about the work, hearing in memory what he would have said about the wisdom of hitting the nail instead of my thumb. I had the studs and plates nailed together all square and trim, and was lifting the wall into place when the phone rang upstairs. My wife answered, and in a moment she came to the basement door and called down softly to me. The stillness in her voice made me drop the framed wall and hurry upstairs. She told me my father was dead. Then I heard the details over the phone from my mother. Building a set of cupboards for my brother in Oklahoma, he had knocked off work early the previous afternoon because of cramps in his stomach. Early this morning, on his way into the kitchen of my brother's trailer, maybe going for a glass of water, so early that no one else was awake, he slumped down on the linoleum and his heart quit.

    For several hours I paced around inside my house, upstairs and   27
down, in and out of every room, looking for the right door to open and knowing there was no such door. My wife and children followed me and wrapped me in arms and backed away again, circling and staring as if I were on fire. Where was the door, the door, the door? I kept wondering. My smashed thumb turned purple and throbbed, making me furious. I wanted to cut it off and rush outside and scrape away at the snow and hack a hole in the frozen earth and bury the shameful thing.

    I went down into the basement, opened a drawer in my workbench,   28
and stared at the ranks of chisels and knives. Oiled and sharp, as my father would have kept them, they gleamed at me like teeth. I took up a clasp knife, pried out the longest blade, and tested the edge on the hair of my forearm. A tuft came away cleanly, and I saw my father testing the sharpness of tools on his own skin, the blades of axes and knives and gouges and hoes, saw the red hair shaved off in patches from his arms and

the backs of his hands. "That will cut bear," he would say. He never cut a bear with his blades, now my blades, but he cut deer, dirt, wood. I closed the knife and put it away. Then I took up the hammer and went back to work on my daughter's wall, snugging the bottom plate against a chalk line on the floor, shimming the top plate against the joists overhead, plumbing the studs with my level, making sure before I drove the first nail that every line was square and true.

Content

1. Sanders characterizes his father, and grandfather, and himself by showing how they used tools and transmitted this knowledge to their children. What characteristics do they have in common? Why does he omit any differences they might have, focusing on their similarities?

2. Sanders distinguishes between a machine and a tool, saying "The skill is invested in the gadget instead of the person who uses it" (¶ 24). Why does he favor tools over machines? Do you agree with his definition? With his preference?

Strategies/Structures/Language

3. What is the point of this essay? Why does Sanders begin and end with the relation between banging his thumb with a hammer and his father's death?

4. Why does Sanders include the vignette of his daughter and her gerbils, which escaped inside the "drum-tight wall" he had just built (¶s 17–23)? Would he really have wrecked the wall to get the gerbils out?

5. For what audience is Sanders writing? Does it matter whether or not his readers know how to use tools?

6. Show, through specific examples, how Sanders's language and quotations of his father's advice fits his subject, tools, and the people who use them. Consider phrases such as "ice coated the windows like cataracts" (¶ 1) and "making sure before I drove the first nail that every line was square and true" (¶ 28).

For Writing

7. Sanders defines the "inheritance" of tools as, "So I have seen my apprenticeship to wood and tools reenacted in each of my children, as my father saw his own apprenticeship renewed in me" (¶ 13). Tell the story of your own apprenticeship with a tool or collection of tools (kitchen utensils, art supplies, a sewing machine, computer, skis, or other equipment). The explanation of your increasing skill in learning to use it should be intertwined with your relationship with the person who taught you how to use it (not necessarily a family member) and the manner of the teaching— and of the learning. How many generations of teachers and learners does your inheritance involve? If you have taught others how to use it, incorporate this as well.

8. Sanders's father is the central figure in two essays in *The Essay Connection*, "The Inheritance of Tools" and "Under the Influence: Paying the Price of My Father's Booze" (249–59). Each uses a series of stories, narratives, to characterize this significant figure in Sanders's life, yet the father of "Inheritance" is a very different character

from the father in "Under the Influence." Write an essay in which you compare and contrast Sanders's portraits of his father to show the different ways of presenting the same person. Or—for an audience who doesn't know your subject—write a portrait of someone you know well, or of a public figure you know a great deal about. Use stories to present two or more significant—perhaps contradictory— sides of the same person.

  For comprehension, writing, and research activities and resources, please visit the companion website at <college.hmco.com/english>.

CHANG-RAE LEE

Lee was born in Seoul, South Korea, in 1965 and emigrated to the United States when he was three with his physician father and his mother, who— as "Coming Home Again" reveals—had been a championship basketball player in Korea. After leaving home in Syracuse, New York, to attend Phillips Exeter Academy, he attended Yale (BA 1987) and earned an MFA in creative writing from the University of Oregon (1993), where he taught before becoming affiliated with Hunter College and the Humanities Council and creative writing program at Princeton University (2002–). His first novel, *Native Speaker* (1995), received numerous awards. Its arresting beginning signals many of the motifs of Lee's work about "the plasticity of identity." As the novel opens, the central character's wife has decided to leave the marriage and as she goes calls her husband a "surreptitious/B+ student of life . . . /illegal alien/emotional alien/genre bug/Yellow peril: neo-American . . . stranger/follower/traitor/spy." As fellow author Jeff Yang explains, "All Asian-American stories, ultimately, are biocryptography—not fiction, not nonfiction, but *un*-fiction, coded answers to the question, 'Who am I?'" Lee has also published two other highly praised novels. *A Gesture Life* (1999) is derived from his research on the grim lives of Korean "comfort women," who were forced to supply sex to Japanese soldiers during World War II. In a departure from Lee's earlier Asian and Asian-American focus, the central character of *Aloft* (2004) is a middle-aged Italian-American Long Island retiree.

"Coming Home Again," originally published in *The New Yorker* (1996), describes a number of processes in action: the processes of cooking and eating delicious Korean foods, the gradual process of immigrant assimilation into American culture and Lee's own assimilation into his new school, the son's maturation process in contrast to his mother's gradual deterioration from illness, and the process of the father's and son's grief after his mother's death. As a consequence of examining all these processes, "Coming Home Again" provides a poignant and memorable definition of what it means to be a family, of any ethnicity, any place, any time.

Coming Home Again

1   When my mother began using the electronic pump that fed her liquids and medication, we moved her to the family room. The bedroom she shared with my father was upstairs, and it was impossible to carry the machine up and down all day and night. The pump itself was attached to a metal stand on casters, and she pulled it along wherever she went. From anywhere in the house, you could hear the sound of the wheels clicking out a steady time over the grout lines of the slate-tiled foyer, her main thoroughfare to the bathroom and the kitchen. Sometimes you would hear her halt after only a few steps, to catch her breath or steady her balance, and whatever you were doing was instantly suspended by a pall of silence.

2   I was usually in the kitchen, preparing lunch or dinner, poised over the butcher block with her favorite chef's knife in my hand and her old yellow apron slung around my neck. I'd be breathless in the sudden quiet, and, having ceased my mincing and chopping, would stare blankly at the brushed sheen of the blade. Eventually, she would clear her throat or call out to say she was fine, then begin to move again, starting her rhythmic *ka-jug;* and only then could I go on with my cooking, the world of our house turning once more, wheeling through the black.

3   I wasn't cooking for my mother but for the rest of us. When she first moved downstairs she was still eating, though scantily, more just to taste what we were having than from any genuine desire for food. The point was simply to sit together at the kitchen table and array ourselves like a family again. My mother would gently set herself down in her customary chair near the stove. I sat across from her, my father and sister to my left and right, and crammed in the center was all the food I had made—a spicy codfish stew, say, or a casserole of gingery beef, dishes that in my youth she had prepared for us a hundred times.

4   It had been ten years since we'd all lived together in the house, which at fifteen I had left to attend boarding school in New Hampshire. My mother would sometimes point this out, by speaking of our present time as being "just like before Exeter," which surprised me, given how proud she always was that I was a graduate of the school.

5   My going to such a place was part of my mother's not so secret plan to change my character, which she worried was becoming too much like hers. I was clever and able enough, but without outside pressure I was readily given to sloth and vanity. The famous school—which none of us knew the first thing about—would prove my mettle. She was right, of course, and while I was there I would falter more than a few times, academically and otherwise. But I never thought that my leaving home then would ever be a problem for her, a private quarrel she would have even as her life waned.

6   Now her house was full again. My sister had just resigned from her job in New York City, and my father, who typically saw his psychiatric patients

What is the relationship among the people in this picture? What clues tell you this is a family? Why do you assume they're eating at home? Do you assume they all live together? What clues are there concerning where this family lives? What indications of their social or economic status are present? To what ethnic or national group do they belong? In what ways would this photograph be a good illustration of Chang-rae Lee's "Coming Home Again"? If you were writing a story about this family, what would its plot be?

until eight or nine in the evening, was appearing in the driveway at four-thirty. I had been living at home for nearly a year and was in the final push of work on what would prove a dismal failure of a novel. When I wasn't struggling over my prose, I kept occupied with the things she usually did—the daily errands, the grocery shopping, the vacuuming and the cleaning, and, of course, all the cooking.

When I was six or seven years old, I used to watch my mother as she 7 prepared our favorite meals. It was one of my daily pleasures. She shooed me away in the beginning, telling me that the kitchen wasn't my place, and adding, in her half-proud, half-deprecating way, that her kind of work would only serve to weaken me. "Go out and play with your friends," she'd snap in Korean, "or better yet, do your reading and homework." She knew that I had already done both, and that as the evening approached there was no place to go save her small and tidy kitchen, from which the clatter of her mixing bowls and pans would ring through the house.

I would enter the kitchen quietly and stand beside her, my chin lodg- 8 ing upon the point of her hip. Peering through the crook of her arm, I beheld the movements of her hands. For *kalbi*, she would take up a butchered short rib in her narrow hand, the flinty bone shaped like a section of an airplane wing and deeply embedded in gristle and flesh, and with the point of her knife cut so that the bone fell away, though not completely, leaving it connected to the meat by the barest opaque layer of tendon. Then she methodically butterflied the flesh, cutting and unfolding, repeating the action until the meat lay out on her board, glistening and ready for seasoning. She scored it diagonally, then sifted sugar into the crevices with her pinched fingers, gently rubbing in the crystals. The sugar would tenderize as well as sweeten the meat. She did this with each rib, and then set them all aside in a large shallow bowl. She minced a half-dozen cloves of garlic, a stub of gingerroot, sliced up a few scallions, and spread it all over the meat. She wiped her hands and took out a bottle of sesame oil, and, after pausing for a moment, streamed the dark oil in two swift circles around the bowl. After adding a few splashes of soy sauce, she thrust her hands in and kneaded the flesh, careful not to dislodge the bones. I asked her why it mattered that they remain connected. "The meat needs the bone nearby," she said, "to borrow its richness." She wiped her hands clean of the marinade, except for her little finger, which she would flick with her tongue from time to time, because she knew that the flavor of a good dish developed not at once but in stages.

9   Whenever I cook, I find myself working just as she would, readying the ingredients—a mash of garlic, a julienne of red peppers, fantails of shrimp—and piling them in little mounds about the cutting surface. My mother never left me any recipes, but this is how I learned to make her food, each dish coming not from a list or a card but from the aromatic spread of a board.

10   I've always thought it was particularly cruel that the cancer was in her stomach, and that for a long time at the end she couldn't eat. The last meal I made for her was on New Year's Eve, 1990. My sister suggested that instead of a rib roast or a bird, or the usual overflow of Korean food, we make all sorts of finger dishes that our mother might fancy and pick at.

11   We set the meal out on the glass coffee table in the family room. I prepared a tray of smoked-salmon canapés, fried some Korean bean cakes, and made a few other dishes I thought she might enjoy. My sister supervised me, arranging the platters, and then with some pomp carried each dish in to our parents. Finally, I brought out a bottle of champagne in a bucket of ice. My mother had moved to the sofa and was sitting up, surveying the low table. "It looks pretty nice," she said. "I think I'm feeling hungry."

12   This made us all feel good, especially me, for I couldn't remember the last time she had felt any hunger or had eaten something I cooked. We began to eat. My mother picked up a piece of salmon toast and took a tiny corner in her mouth. She rolled it around for a moment and then pushed it out with the tip of her tongue, letting it fall back onto her plate. She swallowed hard, as if to quell a gag, then glanced up to see if we had noticed. Of course we all had. She attempted a bean cake, some cheese, and then a slice of fruit, but nothing was any use.

She nodded at me anyway, and said, "Oh, it's very good." But I was 13
already feeling lost and I put down my plate abruptly, nearly shattering it
on the thick glass. There was an ugly pause before my father asked me in
a weary, gentle voice if anything was wrong, and I answered that it was
nothing, it was the last night of a long year, and we were together, and I
was simply relieved. At midnight, I poured out glasses of champagne, even
one for my mother, who took a deep sip. Her manner grew playful and
light, and I helped her shuffle to her mattress, and she lay down in the
place where in a brief week she was dead.

My mother could whip up most anything, but during our first years of liv- 14
ing in this country we ate only Korean foods. At my harangue-like behest,
my mother set herself to learning how to cook exotic American dishes.
Luckily, a kind neighbor, Mrs. Churchill, a tall florid young woman with
flaxen hair, taught my mother her most trusted recipes. Mrs. Churchill's
two young sons, palish, weepy boys with identical crew cuts, always accompanied her, and though I liked them well enough, I would slip away
from them after a few minutes, for I knew that the real action would be in
the kitchen, where their mother was playing guide. Mrs. Churchill hailed
from the state of Maine, where the finest Swedish meatballs and tuna
casserole and angel food cake in America are made. She readily demonstrated certain techniques—how to layer wet sheets of pasta for a lasagna
or whisk up a simple roux, for example. She often brought gift shoeboxes
containing curious ingredients like dried oregano, instant yeast, and cream
of mushroom soup. The two women, though at ease and jolly with each
other, had difficulty communicating, and this was made worse by the often
confusing terminology of Western cuisine ("corned beef," "deviled eggs").
Although I was just learning the language myself, I'd gladly play the inter-
locutor, jumping back and forth between their places at the counter, dip-
ping my fingers into whatever sauce lay about.

I was an insistent child, and, being my mother's firstborn, much too 15
prized. My mother could say no to me, and did often enough, but anyone
who knew us—particularly my father and sister—could tell how much
the denying pained her. And if I was overconscious of her indulgence
even then, and suffered the rushing pangs of guilt that she could inflict
upon me with the slightest wounded turn of her lip, I was too happily ob-
tuse and venal to let her cease. She reminded me daily that I was her sole
son, her reason for living, and that if she were to lose me, in either body
or spirit, she wished that God would mercifully smite her, strike her down
like a weak branch.

In the traditional fashion, she was the house accountant, the maid, 16
the launderer, the disciplinarian, the driver, the secretary, and, of course, the
cook. She was also my first basketball coach. In South Korea, where girls'
high school basketball is a popular spectator sport, she had been a star, the
point guard for the national high school team that once won the all-Asia

championships. I learned this one Saturday during the summer, when I asked my father if he would go down to the schoolyard and shoot some baskets with me. I had just finished the fifth grade, and wanted desperately to make the middle school team the coming fall. He called for my mother and sister to come along. When we arrived, my sister immediately ran off to the swings, and I recall being annoyed that my mother wasn't following her. I dribbled clumsily around the key, on the verge of losing control of the ball, and flung a flat shot that caromed wildly off the rim. The ball bounced to my father, who took a few not so graceful dribbles and made an easy layup. He dribbled out and then drove to the hoop for a layup on the other side. He rebounded his shot and passed the ball to my mother, who had been watching us from the foul line. She turned from the basket and began heading the other way.

17   "*Um-mah,*" I cried at her, my exasperation already bubbling over, "the basket's over *here!*"

18   After a few steps she turned around, and from where the professional three-point line must be now, she effortlessly flipped the ball up in a two-handed set shot, its flight truer and higher than I'd witnessed from any boy or man. The ball arced cleanly into the hoop, stiffly popping the chain-link net. All afternoon, she rained in shot after shot, as my father and I scrambled after her.

19   When we got home from the playground, my mother showed me the photograph album of her team's championship run. For years I kept it in my room, on the same shelf that housed the scrapbooks I made of basketball stars, with magazine clippings of slick players like Bubbles Hawkins and Pistol Pete and George (the Iceman) Gervin.

20   It puzzled me how much she considered her own history to be immaterial, and if she never patently diminished herself, she was able to finesse a kind of self-removal by speaking of my father whenever she could. She zealously recounted his excellence as a student in medical school and reminded me, each night before I started my homework, of how hard he drove himself in his work to make a life for us. She said that because of his Asian face and imperfect English, he was "working two times the American doctors." I knew that she was building him up, buttressing him with both genuine admiration and her own brand of anxious braggadocio, and that her overarching concern was that I might fail to see him as she wished me to—in the most dawning light, his pose steadfast and solitary.

21   In the years before I left for Exeter, I became weary of her oft-repeated accounts of my father's success. I was a teenager, and so ever inclined to be dismissive and bitter toward anything that had to do with family and home. Often enough, my mother was the object of my derision. Suddenly, her life seemed so small to me. She was there, and sometimes, I thought, *always* there, as if she were confined to the four walls of our house. I would even complain about her cooking. Mostly, though, I was getting more and more impatient with the difficulty she encountered in doing everyday things. I was afraid for her. One day, we got into a terrible argument when

she asked me to call the bank, to question a discrepancy she had discovered in the monthly statement. I asked her why she couldn't call herself. I was stupid and brutal, and I knew exactly how to wound her.

"Whom do I talk to?" she said. She would mostly speak to me in 22 Korean, and I would answer in English.

"The bank manager, who else?" 23

"What do I say?" 24

"Whatever you want to say." 25

"Don't speak to me like that!" she cried. 26

"It's just that you should be able to do it yourself," I said. 27

"You know how I feel about this!" 28

"Well, maybe then you should consider it *practice*," I answered lightly, 29 using the Korean word to make sure she understood.

Her face blanched, and her neck suddenly became rigid, as if I were 30 throttling her. She nearly struck me right then, but instead she bit her lip and ran upstairs. I followed her, pleading for forgiveness at her door. But it was the one time in our life that I couldn't convince her, melt her resolve with the blandishments of a spoiled son.

When my mother was feeling strong enough, or was in particularly good 31 spirits, she would roll her machine into the kitchen and sit at the table and watch me work. She wore pajamas day and night, mostly old pairs of mine.

She said, "I can't tell, what are you making?" 32

"*Mahn-doo* filling." 33

"You didn't salt the cabbage and squash." 34

"Was I supposed to?" 35

"Of course. Look, it's too wet. Now the skins will get soggy before 36 you can fry them."

"What should I do?" 37

"It's too late. Maybe it'll be OK if you work quickly. Why didn't you 38 ask me?"

"You were finally sleeping." 39

"You should have woken me." 40

"No way." 41

She sighed, as deeply as her weary lungs would allow. 42

"I don't know how you were going to make it without me." 43

"I don't know, either. I'll remember the salt next time." 44

"You better. And not too much." 45

We often talked like this, our tone decidedly matter-of-fact, chin up, 46 just this side of being able to bear it. Once, while inspecting a potato fritter batter I was making, she asked me if she had ever done anything that I wished she hadn't done. I thought for a moment, and told her no. In the next breath, she wondered aloud if it was right of her to have let me go to Exeter, to live away from the house while I was so young. She tested the batter's thickness with her finger and called for more flour. Then she asked if, given a choice, I would go to Exeter again.

47   I wasn't sure what she was getting at, and I told her that I couldn't be certain, but probably yes, I would. She snorted at this and said it was my leaving home that had once so troubled our relationship. "Remember how I had so much difficulty talking to you? Remember?"

48   She believed back then that I had found her more and more ignorant each time I came home. She said she never blamed me, for this was the way she knew it would be with my wonderful new education. Nothing I could say seemed to quell the notion. But I knew that the problem wasn't simply the *education;* the first time I saw her again after starting school, barely six weeks later, when she and my father visited me on Parents Day, she had already grown nervous and distant. After the usual campus events, we had gone to the motel where they were staying in a nearby town and sat on the beds in our room. She seemed to sneak looks at me, as though I might discover a horrible new truth if our eyes should meet.

49   My own secret feeling was that I had missed my parents greatly, my mother especially, and much more than I had anticipated. I couldn't tell them that these first weeks were a mere blur to me, that I felt completely overwhelmed by all the studies and my much brighter friends and the thousand irritating details of living alone, and that I had really learned nothing, save perhaps how to put on a necktie while sprinting to class. I felt as if I had plunged too deep into the world, which, to my great horror, was much larger than I had ever imagined.

50   I welcomed the lull of the motel room. My father and I had nearly dozed off when my mother jumped up excitedly, murmured how stupid she was, and hurried to the closet by the door. She pulled out our old metal cooler and dragged it between the beds. She lifted the top and began un-packing plastic containers, and I thought she would never stop. One after the other they came out, each with a dish that traveled well—a salted stewed meat, rolls of Korean-style sushi. I opened a container of radish kimchi and suddenly the room bloomed with its odor, and I reveled in the very peculiar sensation (which perhaps only true kimchi lovers know) of simultaneously drooling and gagging as I breathed it all in. For the next few minutes, they watched me eat. I'm not certain that I was even hungry. But after weeks of pork parmigiana and chicken patties and wax beans, I suddenly realized that I had lost all the savor in my life. And it seemed I couldn't get enough of it back. I ate and I ate, so much and so fast that I actually went to the bathroom and vomited. I came out dizzy and sated with the phantom warmth of my binge.

51   And beneath the face of her worry, I thought, my mother was smiling.

52   From that day, my mother prepared a certain meal to welcome me home. It was always the same. Even as I rode the school's shuttle bus from Exeter to Logan airport, I could already see the exact arrangement of my mother's table.

53   I knew that we would eat in the kitchen, the table brimming with plates. There was the *kalbi,* of course, broiled or grilled depending on the

season. Leaf lettuce, to wrap the meat with. Bowls of garlicky clam broth with miso and tofu and fresh spinach. Shavings of cod dusted in flour and then dipped in egg wash and fried. Glass noodles with onions and shiitake. Scallion-and-hot-pepper pancakes. Chilled steamed shrimp. Seasoned salads of bean spouts, spinach, and white radish. Crispy squares of seaweed. Steamed rice with barley and red beans. Homemade kimchi. It was all there—the old flavors I knew, the beautiful salt, the sweet, the excellent taste.

After the meal, my father and I talked about school, but I could never 54 say enough for it to make any sense. My father would often recall his high school principal, who had gone to England to study the methods and traditions of the public schools, and regaled students with stories of the great Eton man. My mother sat with us, paring fruit, not saying a word but taking everything in. When it was time to go to bed, my father said good night first. I usually watched television until the early morning. My mother would sit with me for an hour or two, perhaps until she was accustomed to me again, and only then would she kiss me and head upstairs to sleep.

During the following days, it was always the cooking that started our 55 conversations. She'd hold an inquest over the cold leftovers we ate at lunch, discussing each dish in terms of its balance of flavors or what might have been prepared differently. But mostly I begged her to leave the dishes alone. I wish I had paid more attention. After her death, when my father and I were the only ones left in the house, drifting through the rooms like ghosts, I sometimes tried to make that meal for him. Though it was too much for two, I made each dish anyway, taking as much care as I could. But nothing turned out quite right—not the color, not the smell. At the table, neither of us said much of anything. And we had to eat the food for days.

I remember washing rice in the kitchen one day and my mother's 56 saying in English, from her usual seat, "I made a big mistake."

"About Exeter?" 57

"Yes. I made a big mistake. You should be with us for that time. I 58 should never let you go there."

"So why did you?" I said. 59

"Because I didn't know I was going to die." 60

I let her words pass. For the first time in her life, she was letting herself speak her full mind, so what else could I do? 61

"But you know what?" she spoke up. "It was better for you. If you 62 stayed home, you would not like me so much now."

I suggested that maybe I would like her even more. 63

She shook her head. "Impossible." 64

Sometimes I still think about what she said, about having made a mistake. I would have left home for college, that was never in doubt, but those years I was away at boarding school grew more precious to her as her illness progressed. After many months of exhaustion and pain and the haze of the drugs, I thought that her mind was beginning to fade, for more and more it 65 seemed that she was seeing me again as her fifteen-year-old boy, the one she had dropped off in New Hampshire on a cloudy September afternoon.

66   I remember the first person I met, another new student, named Zack, who walked to the welcome picnic with me. I had planned to eat with my parents—my mother had brought a coolerful of food even that first day—but I learned of the cookout and told her that I should probably go. I wanted to go, of course. I was excited, and no doubt fearful and nervous, and I must have thought I was only thinking ahead. She agreed whole-heartedly, saying I certainly should. I walked them to the car, and perhaps I hugged them, before saying goodbye. One day, after she died, my father told me what happened on the long drive home to Syracuse.

67   He was driving the car, looking straight ahead. Traffic was light on the Massachusetts Turnpike, and the sky was nearly dark. They had driven for more than two hours and had not yet spoken a word. He then heard a strange sound from her, a kind of muffled chewing noise, as if something inside her were grinding its way out.

68   "So, what's the matter?" he said, trying to keep an edge to his voice.

69   She looked at him with her ashen face and she burst into tears. He began to cry himself, and pulled the car over onto the narrow shoulder of the turnpike, where they stayed for the next half hour or so, the blank-faced cars droning by them in the cold, onrushing night.

70   Every once in a while, when I think of her, I'm driving alone some-where on the highway. In the twilight, I see their car off to the side, a blue Olds coupe with a landau top, and as I pass them by I look back in the mirror and I see them again, the two figures huddling together in the front seat. Are they sleeping? Or kissing? Are they all right?

Content

1. Explain the significance of the title, "Coming Home Again," as it pertains to father, mother, and son at various stages of their relationship. How does coming home again affect the son's maturation in contrast to his mother's gradual deterioration from illness?

2. Show the important ways in which Korean food, in preparation and consumption, is a prominent and integrating feature of this narrative. Must readers have eaten these foods—or at least know what they are—to understand the narrative? Explain. Why does Lee devote so much space to cooking and occasions for eating (see, for example, ¶s 7–9; ¶s 31–46; ¶s 50–53)?

Strategies/Structures/Language

3. There are two significant flashbacks in this tale: Lee's mother's effortless display of her expertise as a basketball player (¶s 16–19) and Lee's arrival at boarding school (¶s 66–69). Both demonstrate new aspects of the principal characters and their re-lationships. Explain.

4. What is the significance, symbolic and literal, of when people eat or can't eat or won't eat (¶s 9, 12–13, 55, 66)? Explore some of the significant connections between preparing and eating food and expressing love.

For Writing

5. Write a paper on significant aspects of "coming home again." What are your cultural expectations of when it is appropriate for children to move out of their parents' house and start living on their own? Under what circumstances is it appropriate for a grown child—living in America—to move back home with his or her parents? Have you—or someone close to you—ever done this? For what reasons? With what expectations? Consequences? Is this seen to be a temporary (and for how long a period) or a permanent condition? If you wish, you could write this with a partner whose experiences or views on the subject differ significantly from your own.

6. Explore some of the significant connections between preparing and eating food and expressing love (see also Britt, 261–63). Under what conditions can this be healthful? Potentially or actually destructive? Examine the relationship between using "Coming Home Again" as the starting point for your thinking.

7. In "Coming Home Again" the process of Lee's mother's gradual death is juxtaposed with the processes of Lee's own cooking, and family meals. Using this as a model, analyze one process to illuminate another. For instance, in going to college to master a field of knowledge, one is preparing for a professional career in many ways and at the same time (we hope) maturing as a human being in ways related to and independent of that career. Analyze these strands of maturation to show how they reinforce—and perhaps contradict—one another.

 For comprehension, writing, and research activities and resources, please visit the companion website at <college.hmco.com/english>.

NTOZAKE SHANGE

In 1971, the year after she graduated from Barnard with a BA in American Studies, Paulette Williams, daughter of a noted St. Louis surgeon and a social worker, adopted the Zulu name Ntozake Shange (en-toh-ZAH-kee SHAHN-gay), Ntozake meaning "she who comes with her own things" and Shange, "who walks like a lion." Within three years of earning an MA from the University of Southern California (1973), her first and most memorable play had been produced, *for colored girls who have considered suicide/when the rainbow is enuf.* It received an Obie award for the best play of 1977 and Tony and Grammy award nominations, and it established Shange as a writer as well as a dancer and an actress who performed in her own work.

Shange's works include over a dozen other plays and dramatic adaptations, ranging from *Boogie Woogie Landscapes* (1978) to an Obie award-winning adaptation of Bertolt Brecht's *Mother Courage and Her Children* (1981). She has written novels, including *Liliane: Resurrection of the Daughter* (1994);

poetry, of which *Nappy Edges* (1978) is the best known; children's books, including *Ellington Was Not a Street* (2003); and numerous short stories and essays. "What Is It We Really Harvestin' Here?" published in *Creative Nonfiction* in 1998, is characteristic of Shange's free-flowing form and fast-paced conversational style, simultaneously lyrical, comical, and satiric. In the process of explaining how to garden, Shange incorporates African-American history, social commentary, autobiography, and recipes—American studies with attitude.

What Is It We Really Harvestin' Here?

1   We got a sayin', "The blacker the berry, the sweeter the juice," which is usually meant as a compliment. To my mind, it also refers to the delectable treats we as a people harvested for our owners and for our own selves all these many years, slave or free. In fact, we knew something about the land, sensuality, rhythm and ourselves that has continued to elude our captors—puttin' aside all our treasures in the basement of the British Museum, or the Met, for that matter. What am I talkin' about? A different approach to the force of gravity, to our bodies, and what we produce: a reverence for the efforts of the group and the intimate couple. Harvest time and Christmas were prime occasions for courtin'. A famine, a drought, a flood or Lent do not serve as inspiration for couplin', you see.

2   The Juba, a dance of courtin' known in slave quarters of North America and the Caribbean, is a phenomenon that stayed with us through the jitterbug, the wobble, the butterfly, as a means of courtin' that's apparently very colored, and very "African." In fact we still have it and we've never been so "integrated"—the *Soul Train* dancers aren't all black anymore, but the dynamic certainly is. A visitor to Cuba in Lynne Fauley Emery's "Dance Horizon Book" described the Juba as a series of challenges.

> A woman advances and commencing a slow dance, made up of shuffling of the feet and various contortions of the body, thus challenges a rival from among the men. One of these, bolder than the rest, after a while steps out, and the two then strive which shall tire the other; the woman performing many feats which the man attempts to rival, often excelling them, amid the shouts of the rest. A woman will sometimes drive two or three successive beaux from the ring, yielding her place at length to some impatient belle.

3   John Henry went up against a locomotive, but decades before we simply were up against ourselves and the elements. And so we are performers in the fields, in the kitchens, by kilns, and for one another. Sterling Stuckey points out, in "Slave Culture," however, that by 1794 "it was illegal

to allow slaves to dance and drink on the premises . . . without the written consent of their owners," the exceptions being Christmas and the burials, which are communal experiences. And what shall we plant and harvest, so that we might "Hab big times duh fus hahves, and duh fus ting wut growed we take tuh duh church so as ebrybody could hab a pieces ub it. We pray over it and shout. Wen we hab a dance, we use tuh shout in a rinig. We ain't have wutyuh call a propuh dance tuday."

Say we've gone about our owners' business. Planted and harvested 4 his crop of sugar cane, remembering that the "ratio of slaves/sugar was ten times that of slaves/tobacco and slaves/cotton." That to plant a sugar crop we have to dig a pit 3 feet square and a few inches deep into which one young plant is set. Then, of course, the thing has to grow. A mature sugar-cane plant is 3–9 feet tall. That's got to be cut at exactly the right point. Then we've got to crush it, boil it, refine it, from thick black syrup to fine white sugar, to make sure, as they say in Virginia, that we "got the niggah out." Now it's time to tend to our own gardens. Let's grow some sweet potatoes to "keep the niggah alive."

Sweet Potatoes

Like everything else, we have to start with something. Now we need a small piece 5 *of potato with at least one of those scraggly roots hanging about for this native Central American tuber. This vegetable will stand more heat than almost any other grown in the United States. It does not take to cool weather, and any kind of frost early or seasonal will kill the leaves, and if your soil gets cold the tubers themselves will not look very good. Get your soil ready at least two weeks before planting, weeding, turning, and generally disrupting the congealed and solid mass we refer to as dirt, so that your hands and the tubers may move easily through the soil, as will water and other nutrients.*

Once the soil is free of winter, two weeks after the last frost, plant the potato 6 *slips in 6–12 inch ridges, 3–4.5 feet apart. Separate the plants by 9–12 inches. If we space the plants more than that, our tubers may be grand, but way too big to make good use of in the kitchen. We should harvest our sweet potatoes when the tubers are not quite ripe, but of good size, or we can wait until the vines turn yellow. Don't handle our potatoes too roughly, which could lead to bruising and decay. If a frost comes upon us unexpectedly, take those potatoes out the ground right away. Our potatoes will show marked improvement during storage, which allows the starch in them to turn to sugar. Nevertheless let them lie out in the open for 2 to 3 hours to fully dry. Then move them to a moist and warm storage space. The growing time for our crop'll vary from 95 to 125 days.*

The easiest thing to do with a sweet potato is to bake it. In its skin. I coat the 7 *thing with olive oil, or butter in a pinch. Wrap it in some aluminum foil, set it in the oven at 400 degrees. Wait till I hear sizzling, anywhere from 45 minutes to an hour after, in a very hot oven. I can eat it with my supper at that point or I can let it cool off for later. (One of the sexiest dates I ever went on was to the movies to see*

"El Mariachi." My date brought along chilled baked sweet potatoes and ginger beer. Much nicer than canola-sprayed "buttered" popcorn with too syrupy Coca-Cola, wouldn't you say?)

Mustard Greens

8   No, they are not the same as collards. We could say they, with their frilly edges and sinuous shapes, have more character, are more flirtatious, than collards. This green can be planted in the spring or the fall, so long as the soil is workable (not cold). It's not a hot weather plant, preferring short days and temperate climates. We can use the same techniques for mustard greens that we use for lettuce. Sowing the seeds in rows 12–18 inches apart, seedlings 4–8 inches apart. These plants should get lots of fertilizer to end up tender, lots of water, too. They should be harvested before they are fully mature. Now, you've got to be alert, because mustard greens grow fast, 25–40 days from the time you set them in the soil to harvest. When it comes time to reap what you've sown, gather the outer leaves when they are 3–4 inches long, tender enough; let the inner leaves then develop more or wait till it's hot and harvest the whole plant.

9   Now we cook the mustard greens just like the collards, or we don't have to cook it at all. This vegetable is fine in salads or on sandwiches and soups. If you shy away from pungent tastes, mix these greens with some collards, kale, or beet greens. That should take some of the kick out of them. I still like my peppers and vinegar, though. If we go back, pre-Columbus, the Caribs did, too. According to Spanish travelers, the Caribs, who fancied vegetables, added strong peppers called aji-aji to just about everything. We can still find aji-aji on some sauces from Spanish-speaking countries if we read the labels carefully. Like "La Morena." So appropriate.

Watermelon

10   The watermelon is an integral part of our actual life as much as it is a feature of our stereotypical lives in the movies, posters, racial jokes, toys, and early American portraits of the "happy darky." We could just as easily been eatin' watermelon in D. W. Griffith's "Birth of a Nation" as chicken legs. The implications are the same. Like the watermelon, we were a throwback of "African" pre-history, which isn't too off, since Lucy, the oldest Homo sapiens currently known is from Africa, too.

11   But I remember being instructed not to order watermelon in restaurants or to eat watermelon in any public places because it makes white people think poorly of us. They already did that, so I don't see what the watermelon was going to pre-cipitate. Europeans brought watermelon with them from Africa anyway. In Massa-chusetts by 1629 it was recorded as "abounding." In my rebelliousness as a child, I got so angry about the status of the watermelon, I tried to grow some in the flower box on our front porch in Missouri. My harvest was minimal to say the least.

12   Here's how you can really grow you some watermelon. They like summer heat, particularly sultry, damp nights. If we can grow watermelons, we can grow ourselves almost any other kind of melon. The treatment is the same. Now, these need some space, if we're looking for a refrigerator-sized melon or one ranging

from 25–30 pounds. Let them have a foot between plants in between rows 4–6 feet apart. They need a lot of fertilizer, especially if the soil is heavy and doesn't drain well. When the runners (vines) are a foot to a foot-and-a-half long, fertilize again about 8 inches from the plant itself. Put some more fertilizer when the first melons appear. Watermelons come in different varieties, but I'm telling you about the red kind. I have no primal response to a golden or blanched fleshed melon. Once your melons set on the vines and start to really take up some space, be sure not to forget to water the vines during the ripening process.

When is your watermelon ripe? You can't tell by thumping it nor by the 13 *curly tail at the point where the melon is still on the vine. The best way to know if your melon is ready is by looking at the bottom. The center turns from a light yellow to deep amber. Your melon'll have a powdery or mushy tasteless sorta taste if you let it ripen too long.*

Surely you've seen enough pictures or been to enough picnics to know how 14 *to eat a watermelon, so I won't insult you with that information. However, there is a fractious continuing debate about whether to sprinkle sugar or salt on your watermelon slice. I am not going to take sides in this matter.*

Some of us were carried to the New World specifically because we knew 15 'bout certain crops, know 'bout the groomin' and harvestin' of rice, for instance.

> Plantation owners were perfectly aware of the superiority . . . of African slaves from rice country. Littlefield (journalist) writes that "as early as 1700 ships from Carolina were reported in the Gambia River." . . . In a letter dated 1756, Henry Laurens, a Charleston merchant, wrote, "The slaves from the River Gambia are prefer'd to all others with us save the Gold Coast." The previous year he had written: "Gold Coast or Gambias are best; next to them the Windward Coast are prefer'd to Angolas."

These bits of information throw an entirely different, more dignified 16 light on "colored" cuisine, for me. Particularly since I was raised on rice and my mother's people on both sides are indefatigable Carolinians, South, to be exact, South Carolinians. To some, our "phrenologically immature brains" didn't have consequence until our mastery of the cultivation of "cargo," "patna," "joponica," and finally Carolina rice, "small-grained, rather long and wiry, and remarkably white" was transferred to the books and records of our owners. Nevertheless, our penchant for rice was not dampened by its relationship to our bondage. Whether through force or will, we held on to our rice-eatin' heritage. I repeat, I was raised on rice. If I was Joe Williams, insteada singin' "Every day, every day, I sing the blues," I'd be sayin', "Oh, every day, almost any kinda way, I get my rice."

My poor mother, Eloise, Ellie, for short, made the mistake of marry- 17 ing a man who was raised by a woman from Canada. So every day, he wanted a potato, some kinda potato, mashed, boiled, baked, scalloped, fried, just a potato. Yet my mother was raising a sixth generation of Carolinians, which meant we had to eat some kinda rice. Thus, Ellie was busy fixing potato for one and rice for all the rest every day, until I finally learnt how to do one or the other and gave her a break. I asked Ellie Williams how her mother, Viola, went about preparing the rice for her "chirren"—a Low-country linguistic lapse referring to off-spring like me. Anyway, this is what Mama said.

Mama's Rice

18 *"We'd buy some rice in a brown paper bag (this is in The Bronx). Soak it in a bit of water. Rinse it off and cook it the same way we do now." "How is that, Ma?" I asked. "Well, you boil a certain amount of water. Let it boil good. Add your rice and let it boil till tender. Stirring every so often because you want the water to evaporate. You lift your pot. You can tell if your rice is okay because there's no water there. Then you fluff it with a fork. You want every kind, extra, extra, what you call it. No ordinary olive oil will do.*

19 *"Heat this up. Just a little bit of it. You don't want no greasy rice, do you? Heat this until, oh, it is so hot that the smoke is coming quick. Throw in 3–4 cloves garlic, maybe 1 cup chopped onion too, I forgot. Let that sizzle and soften with ½ cup each cilantro, pimiento, and everything. But don't let this get burned, no. So add your 4 cups water and 2 cups rice. Turn up the heat some more till there's a great boiling of rice, water, seasonings. The whole thing. Then leave it alone for a while with the cover on so all the rice cooks even. Now, when you check and see there's only a small bit of water left in the bottom of the pot, stir it all up. Turn the heat up again and wait. When there's no water left at all, at all. Just watch the steam coming up. Of course you should have a good pegau by now, but the whole pot of your rice should be delicioso, ready even for my table. If you do as I say."*

20 For North Americans, a pot with burnt rice on the bottom is a scary concept. But all over the Caribbean, it's a different story entirely. In order to avoid making *asopao*—a rice moist and heavy with the sofrito or tomato-achiote mixture, almost like a thick soup where the rice becomes one mass instead of standing, each grain on its own—it is necessary to let the rice on the bottom of the pot get a crustlike bottom, assuring that all moisture has evaporated. My poor North American mother, Ellie, chastises me frequently for "ruining" good rice with all this spice. Then I remind her that outside North America we Africans were left to cook in ways that reminded us of our mother's cooking, not Jane Austen's characters. The rice tastes different, too. But sometimes I cheat and simply use Goya's Sazon—after all, I'm a modern woman. I shouldn't say that too loudly, though. Mathilde can hear all the way from her front porch any blasphemous notion I have about good cooking. No, it is her good cooking that I am to learn. I think it is more than appropriate that we know something about some of the crops that led to most of us African descendants of the Diaspora, being here, to eat anything at all.

But rather than end on a sour note, I am thinking of my classes with 21
the great Brazilian dancer, choreographer and teacher Mercedes Baptista
at the now legendary Clark Center. We learned a harvest dance, for there
are many, but the movements of this celebratory ritual were lyrical and
delicate, far from the tortured recounts of EuroAmericans to our "jiga-
boo" gatherings; no gyrations, repetitive shuffling that held no interest.
Indeed, the simple movement of the arms, which we worked on for days
until we got it, resembled a tropical port-à-bras worthy of any ballerina.
Our hip movements, ever so subtle, with four switches to the left, then
four to the right, all the while turning and covering space. The head leaning in the direction of the hips, the arms moving against it, till the next hip
demanded counterpoint.

A healthy respect for the land, for what we produce for the blessing 22
of a harvest begot dances of communal joy. On New Year's Eve in the late
fifties, we danced the Madison; today it's a burning rendition of "The
Electric Slide." Eighty-years-olds jammin' with toddlers after the weddin'
toast. No, we haven't changed so much.

Content

1. What's the point of Shange's title? What *is* it "we really harvestin'"?
2. Shange gives directions on how to grow, prepare, and eat several foods—
sweet potatoes, mustard greens, watermelon—and how to cook "Mama's Rice."
Like many other directions written by experts, these seem easy to follow and the
results seem assured. Why are most directions written so simply and positively?
3. "What Is It We Really Harvestin' Here?" was published in *Creative Nonfiction*,
a publication usually read by creative writers, not in a home or cooking magazine.
Why might this piece appeal to readers who are writers? Or to any readers who
don't garden? Or cook? Or eat much "'colored' cusine"?

Strategies/Structures/Language

4. Shange's planting instructions are presented in a matrix of African-American
political and social history (¶s 1–4), family history (¶s 16–17), and autobiography
(¶s 20–22). How do these elements make the reading different from the usual
instructions on how to perform a process, such as following a recipe or planting
a garden?
5. Whom does Shange include in *we?* Is the *we* of the title and "We got a sayin'"
(¶ 1, sentence 1), the same as the *we* of "*we* as a people" (¶ 1, sentence 2)? The same
as the *we* of "And so we are performers in the fields" (¶ 3, sentence 2)? Why does
it matter, to writer and readers, who *we* are?
6. How does Shange's style suit her subject? In this essay that is largely written
in standard English, what are the effects of using dialect spelling (as in *chirren* [¶ 7]),
or omitting the -*g* at the end of *ing* words, as in *puttin'* (¶ 1)? Why does Shange quote
entire sentences in dialect: "Wen we hab a dance . . ." (¶ 3)? Why does Shange use
dialect much more extensively in the first four paragraphs of the essay than later on?

For Writing

7. If you're a competent cook, write out a favorite recipe so others less experienced than you can prepare it. Identify unusual ingredients, the major steps to follow, and also any subprocesses that need to be done to prepare the dish. Have someone read (better yet, try out) your recipe. What questions do they ask? Incorporate the information from your answers into the recipe as you revise it.

8. Explain how to do or make something that's integral to your cultural background(s) (such as how to interpret or perform a particular religious ritual, celebrate a particular holiday, do a particular dance step, play a particular game, perform a specific athletic activity, engage in a flirtation or courtship). Embed your instructions, as Shange does, in a matrix of cultural, family, or personal history—tell some true stories to provide a context for the instructions that will help to explain why certain things are done in a certain way, as well as how. If diagrams or photographs would clarify, add them as appropriate.

For comprehension, writing, and research activities and resources, please visit the companion website at <college.hmco.com/english>.

NING YU

Ning Yu was born in 1955 in Beijing, People's Republic of China, and came to the United States in 1986 for graduate study. He earned a PhD in English from the University of Connecticut in 1993 and is now a professor of English and Chinese literature at Western Washington University.

Ning Yu recounts some of the significant events of his youth in the following prize-winning essay, "Red and Black, or One English Major's Beginning." When he was in fourth grade, his school was closed down as a consequence of the "Great Proletarian Cultural Revolution," which overturned the existing social order. The intellectual class (the "blacks," in Yu's classification scheme) to which Yu's family belonged because his father was a professor of Chinese language and literature, were replaced on their jobs by members of the People's Liberation Army, "the reds," whose status—as we can see from Ning Yu's teachers—was determined by their political loyalty rather than their academic training. So Ning Yu learned one kind of English at school, the rote memorization of political slogans: "Long live Chairman Mao! Down with the Soviet Neo-Czarists!" He explains that the Cultural Revolution stifled originality of language, as well as of thought. "Consequently," he says, "I used the clichés deliberately to create a realistic atmosphere for my story, and also ironically to attack the decade of clichés."

Ning Yu learned another kind of English, the rich, imaginative language of high-culture literature, from his father. On the verge of his fourth imprisonment as an intellectual (and therefore by definition subversive), Dr. Yu taught his teenage son the alphabet and some basic grammar. He gave his son a copy of Jane Austen's *Pride and Prejudice* and an old English-Chinese dictionary and told him to translate the novel—which Ning Yu "struggled through from cover to cover" during the nineteen months of his father's incarceration. Ning Yu's essay makes clear the relations among politics, social class, and education under the Maoist regime.

❄ *Red and Black, or One English Major's Beginning*

I have always told my friends that my first English teacher was my father. That is the truth, but not the whole truth. It was a freezing morning more than twenty years ago, we, some fifty-odd boys and girls, were shivering in a poorly heated classroom when the door was pushed open and in came a gust of wind and Comrade Chang Hong-gen, our young teacher. Wrapped in an elegant army overcoat, Comrade Chang strode in front of the blackboard and began to address us in outrageous gibberish. His gestures, his facial expressions, and his loud voice unmistakably communicated that he was lecturing us as a People's Liberation Army captain would address his soldiers before a battle—in revolutionary war movies, that is. Of course we didn't understand a word of the speech until he translated it into Chinese later:

> Comrades, red-guards, and revolutionary pupils:
> The Great Revolutionary Teacher Marx teaches us: "A foreign language is an important weapon in the struggle of human life." Our Great Leader, Great Teacher, Great Supreme-Commander, and Great Helmsman, Chairman Mao, has also taught us that it is not too difficult to learn a foreign language. "Nothing in the world is too difficult if you are willing to tackle it with the same spirit in which we conquered this mountain."
> Now, as you know, the Soviet Social Imperialists and the U.S. Imperialists have agreed on a venomous scheme to enslave China. For years the U.S. Imperialists have brought war and disaster to Vietnam; and you must have heard that the Soviet troops invaded our Jewel Island in Heilongjiang Province last month. Their evil purpose is obvious—to invade China, the Soviets from the north and the Americans from the south through Vietnam.
> We are not afraid of them, because we have the leadership of Chairman Mao, the invincible Mao Zedong Thought, and seven hundred million people. But we need to be prepared. As intellectual youth, you must not only prepare to sacrifice your lives for the Party and the Motherland, but also learn to stir up our people's patriotic zeal and to shatter the morale of the enemy troops. To

encourage our own people, you must study Chairman Mao's works very hard and learn your lessons well with your teacher of Chinese; to crush the enemy, you must learn your English lessons well with me.

2   Then Comrade Chang paused, his face red and sweat beading on the tip of his nose. Though nonplussed, we could see that he was genuinely excited, but we were not sure whether his excitement was induced by "patriotic zeal" or the pleasure of hearing grandiose sounds issued from his own lips. For my part, I suspected that verbal intoxication caused his excitement. Scanning the classroom, he seemed to bask in our admiration rather than to urge us to sacrifice our lives for the Party. He then translated the speech into Chinese and gave us another dose of eloquence:

> From now on, you are not pupils anymore, but soldiers—young, intellectual soldiers fighting at a special front. Neither is each English word you learn a mere word anymore. Each new word is a bullet shot at the enemy's chest, and each sentence a hand grenade.

3   Comrade Chang was from a "red" family. His name *hong* means red in Chinese, and *gen* means root, so literally, he was "Chang of Red Root." Students said that his father was a major in the People's Liberation Army, and his grandfather a general, and that both the father and the grandfather had "contributed a great deal to the Party, the Motherland, and the Chinese working people." When the "Great Proletarian Cultural Revolution" started, Mr. Chang had just graduated from the Beijing Foreign Languages Institute, a prestigious university in the capital where some thirty languages were taught to people "of red roots." Red youngsters were trained there to serve in the Foreign Ministry, mostly in Chinese embassies and consulates in foreign countries. We understood that Comrade Chang would work only for a token period in our ghetto middle school. At the time, the Foreign Ministry was too busy with the Cultural Revolution to hire new translators, but as soon as the "Movement" was over and everything back to normal, Comrade Chang, we knew, would leave us and begin his diplomatic career.

4   In the late 1960s the Revolution defined "intellectual" as "subversive." So my father, a university professor educated in a British missionary school in Tianjin, was regarded as a "black" element, an enemy of the people. In 1967, our family was driven out of our university faculty apartment, and I found myself in a ghetto middle school, an undeserving pupil of the red expert Comrade Chang.

5   In a shabby and ill-heated schoolroom I began my first English lesson, not "from the very beginning" by studying the alphabet, but with some powerful "hand grenades":

> Give up; no harm!
> Drop your guns!
> Down with the Soviet Neo-Czarists!

Down with U.S. Imperialism!
Long live Chairman Mao!
We wish Chairman Mao a long, long life!
Victory belongs to our people!

These sentences turned out to be almost more difficult and more ⁶
dangerous to handle than real grenades, for soon the words became mixed
up in our heads. So much so that not a few "revolutionary pupils" reconstructed the slogans to the hearty satisfactions of themselves but to the
horror of Comrade Chang:

Long live the Soviet Neo-Czarists!
Victory belongs to your guns!

Upon hearing this, Comrade Chang turned pale and shouted at us, "You
idiots! Had you uttered anything like that in Chinese, young as you are,
you could have been thrown into jail for years. Probably me too! Now you
follow me closely: Long live Chairman Mao!"

"Long live Chairman Mao!" we shouted back.   ⁷
"Long live Chairman Mao!"   ⁸
"Long live Chairman Mao!"   ⁹
"Down with the Soviet Neo-Czarists!"   ¹⁰
"Down with the Soviet Neo-Czarists!"   ¹¹
Comrade Chang decided that those two sentences were enough for ¹²
idiots to learn in one lesson, and he told us to forget the other sentences
for the moment. Then he wrote the two sentences on the chalkboard and
asked us to copy them in our English exercise books. Alas, how could anybody in our school know what that was!

I wrote the two sentences on my left palm and avoided putting my left ¹³
hand in my pocket or mitten for the rest of the day. I also remembered what
Comrade Chang said about being thrown into jail, for as the son of a "black,
stinking bourgeois intellectual," I grasped the truth in his warning. The two
English sentences were a long series of meaningless, unutterable sounds.
Comrade Chang had the power to impose some Chinese meaning on
my mind. So, before I forgot or confused the sounds, I invented a makeshift transliteration in Chinese for the phonetically difficult and politically
dangerous parts of the sentences. I put the Chinese words *qui, mian,* and
mao (cut, noodle, hair) under "Chairman Mao," and *niu za sui* (beef organ
meat) under "Neo-Czarists." "Down with" were bad words applied to the
enemies; "long live" were good words reserved for the great leader. These
were easy to remember. So I went home with a sense of security, thinking
the device helped me distinguish the Great Leader from the enemy.

The next morning, Comrade "Red Roots" asked us to try our weapons ¹⁴
before the blackboard. Nobody volunteered. Then Comrade Chang began
calling us by name. My friend "Calf" was the first to stand up. He did not
remember anything. He didn't try to learn the words, and he told me to
"forget it" when I was trying to memorize the weird sounds. In fact, none
of my classmates remembered the sentences.

What does it mean to become literate? Are there significant differences in this process among cultures, nationalities? Compare your own experience of learning to read and write English or another language with the processes of language learning that Ning Yu describes in "Red and Black."

15   My fellow pupils were all "red" theoretically. But they were not Comrade Chang's type of red. Their parents were coolies, candy-peddlers, or bricklayers. Poor and illiterate. Before the 1949 revolution, these people led miserable lives. Even the revolution didn't improve their lives much, and parents preferred their children to do chores at home rather than fool around with books, especially after the "Great Proletarian Cultural Revolution" started in 1966. Books were dangerous. Those who read books often ran into trouble for having ideas the Party didn't want them to have. "Look at the intellectuals," they said. "They suffer even more than us illiterates." They also knew that their children could not become "red experts" like Comrade Chang, because they themselves were working people who didn't contribute to the Party, the Motherland—or to the liberation of the working people themselves.

16   Thus my friends didn't waste time in remembering nonsense. Still Comrade Chang's questions had to be answered. Since I was the only one in class not from a red family, my opinion was always the last asked, if asked at all. I stood up when Comrade Chang called my name. I had forgotten the English sounds too, for I took Calf's advice. But before I repeated the apology already repeated fifty times by my friends, I glanced at my left palm and inspiration lit up my mind. "Long live *qie mian mao!* Down with *niu za sui!*" My friends stared, and Comrade Chang glared at

me. He couldn't believe his ears. "Say that again." I did. This time my classmates burst into a roar of laughter. "Cut noodle hair! Beef organ meat!" they shouted again and again.

"Shut up!" Comrade Chang yelled, trembling with anger and pointing at me with his right index finger. "What do you mean by 'cut noodle hair'? That insults our great leader Chairman Mao." Hearing that, the class suddenly became silent. The sons and daughters of the "Chinese working people" knew how serious an accusation that could be. But Calf stood up and said: "Comrade Teacher, it is truly a bad thing that Ning Yu should associate Chairman Mao with such nonsense as 'cut noodle hair.' But he didn't mean any harm. He was trying to throw a hand grenade at the enemy. He also called the Soviets 'beef organ meat.' He said one bad thing (not enough respect for Chairman Mao) but then said a good thing (condemning the Soviets). One take away one is zero. So he didn't really do anything wrong, right?"

Again the room shook with laughter.

Now Comrade Chang flew into a rage and began to lecture us about how class enemies often say good things to cover up evil intentions. Calf, Chang said, was a red boy and should draw a line between himself and me, the black boy. He also threatened to report my "evil words" to the revolutionary committee of the middle school. He said that in the "urgent state of war" what I said could not be forgiven or overlooked. He told me to examine my mind and conduct severe self-criticism before being punished. "The great proletarian dictatorship," he said, "is all-powerful. All good will be rewarded and all evil punished when the right time comes." He left the classroom in anger without giving us any new hand grenades.

I felt ruined. Destroyed. Undone. I could feel icy steel handcuffs closing around my wrists. I could hear the revolutionary slogans that the mobs would shout at me when I was dragged off by the iron hand of the Proletarian Dictatorship. My legs almost failed me on my way home.

Calf knew better. "You have nothing to worry about, Third Ass."

I am the third child in my family, and it is a tradition of old Beijing to call a boy by number. So usually my family called me Thirdy. But in my ghetto, when the kids wanted to be really friendly, they added the word "ass" to your number or name. This address upset me when I first moved into the neighborhood. I was never comfortable with that affix during the years I lived there, but at that moment I appreciated Calf's kindness in using that affix. Words are empty shells. It's the feeling that people attach to a word that counts.

"I'll be crushed like a rotten egg by the iron fist of the Great Proletarian Dictatorship," I said.

"No way. Red Rooty is not going to tell on you. Don't you know he was more scared than you? He was responsible. How could you say such things if he had not taught you? You get it? You relax. *Qie mian mao!* You know, you really sounded like Rooty." Calf grinned.

25   Although Calf's wisdom helped me to "get it," relax I could not. My legs were as stiff as sticks and my heart beat against my chest so hard that I could hardly breathe. For many years I had tried to get rid of my "blackness" by hard work and good manners. But I could not succeed. No matter how hard I tried I could not change the fact that I was not "red." The Party denied the existence of intermediate colors. If you were not red, logically you could only be black. What Chang said proved what I guessed. But, when cornered, even a rabbit may bite. Comrade Chang, I silently imagined, if I have to be crushed, you can forget about your diplomatic career. I created a drama in which Comrade Chang, the red root, and I, the black root, were crushed into such fine powder that one could hardly tell the red from the black. All one could see was a dark, devilish purple.

26   The next morning, I went to school with a faltering heart, expecting to be called out of the classroom and cuffed. Nothing happened. Comrade Chang seemed to have forgotten my transgression and gave us three handfuls of new "bullets." He slowed down too, placing more emphasis on pronunciation. He cast the "bullets" into hand grenades only after he was sure that we could shoot the "bullets" with certainty.

27   Nothing happened to me that day, or the next day, or the week after. Calf was right. As weeks passed, my dislike of Chang dwindled and I began to feel something akin to gratitude to him. Before learning his English tongue twisters, we only recited Chairman Mao's thirty-six poems. We did that for so long that I memorized the annotations together with the text. I also memorized how many copies were produced for the first, the second, and the third printing. I was bored, and Teacher Chang's tongue twisters brought me relief. Granted they were only old slogans in new sounds. But the mere sounds and the new way of recording the sounds challenged me. Still, as an old Chinese saying goes, good luck never lasts long.

28   Forty hand grenades were as many as the Party thought proper for us to hold. Before I mastered the fortieth tongue twister—"Revolutionary committees are fine"—our "fine" revolutionary committee ordered Comrade Chang to stop English lessons and to make us dig holes for air raid shelters. Comrade Chang approached this new task with just as much "patriotic zeal" as he taught English. In truth he seemed content to let our "bullets" and "hand grenades" rust in the bottom of the holes we dug. But I was not willing to let my only fun slip away easily. When digging the holes I repeated the forty slogans silently. I even said them at home in bed. One night I uttered a sentence as I climbed onto my top bunk. Reading in the bottom bunk, my father heard me and was surprised. He asked where I had learned the words. Then for the first time I told him about Comrade Chang's English lessons.

29   Now it may seem strange for a middle school boy not to turn to his family during a "political crisis." But at that time, it was not strange at all. By then my mother, my sister, and my brother had already been sent to the

countryside in two different remote provinces. Getting help from them was almost impossible, for they had enough pressing problems themselves. Help from my father was even more impractical: he was already "an enemy of the people," and therefore whatever he said or did for me could only complicate my problems rather than resolve them. So I kept him in the dark. Since we had only each other in the huge city of eight million people, we shared many things, but not political problems.

Our home in the working class neighborhood was a single seventeen-square-meter room. Kitchen, bathroom, sitting room, study, bedroom, all in one. There was no ceiling, so we could see the black beams and rafters when we lay in bed. The floor was a damp and sticky dirt, which defied attempts at sweeping and mopping. The walls were yellow and were as damp as the dirt floor. To partition the room was out of the question. Actually my parents had sold their king-sized bed and our single beds, and bought two bunk beds in their stead. My mother and sister each occupied a top bunk, my father slept in one bottom bunk, and my brother and I shared the other. Red Guards had confiscated and burned almost all of my father's Chinese books, but miraculously they left his English books intact. The English books were stuffed under the beds on the dirt floor. We lived in this manner for more than a year till the family members were scattered all over China, first my siblings to a province in the northwest, and then my mother to southern China. They were a thousand miles from us and fifteen hundred miles from each other. After they left, I moved to the top bunk over my father, and we piled the books on the other bed. Thanks to the hard covers, only the bottom two layers of the books had begun to mold.

That evening, after hearing me murmuring in English, my father gestured for me to sit down on his bunk. He asked me whether I knew any sentences other than the one he had heard. I jumped at the opportunity to go through the inventory of my English arsenal. After listening to my forty slogans my father said: "You have a very good English teacher. He has an excellent pronunciation, standard Oxford pronunciation. But the sentences are not likely to be found in any books written by native English speakers. Did he teach you how to read?"

"I can read all those sentences if you write them out."

"If *I* write them? But can't *you* write them by yourself?"

"No."

"Did he teach you grammar?"

"No."

"Did he teach you the alphabet?"

"No."

My father looked amused. Slowly he shook his head, and then asked: "Can you recognize the words, the separate words, when they appear in different contexts?"

"I think so, but I'm not sure."

41   He re-opened the book that he was reading and turned to the first page and pointed with his index finger at the first word in the first sentence, signaling me to identify it.

42   I shook my head.

43   He moved the finger to the next word. I didn't know that either. Nor did I know the third word, the shortest word in the line, the word made up of a single letter. My father traced the whole sentence slowly, hoping that I could identify some words. I recognized the bullet "in" and at once threw a hand grenade at him: "Beloved Chairman Mao, you are the red sun *in* our hearts." Encouraged, my father moved his finger back to the second word in the sentence. This time I looked at the word more closely but couldn't recognize it. "It's an 'is,'" he said. "You know 'are' but not 'is'! The third word in this sentence is an 'a'. It means 'one.'" It is the first letter in the alphabet and you don't know that either! What a teacher! A well-trained one too!" He then cleared his throat and read the whole sentence aloud: "It is a truth universally acknowledged, that a man in possession of a good fortune, must be in want of a wife."

44   The sounds he uttered reminded me of Chang's opening speech, but they flowed out of my father's mouth smoothly. Without bothering about the meaning of the sentence, I asked my father to repeat it several times because I liked the rhythm. Pleased with my curiosity, my father began to explain the grammatical structure of the sentence. His task turned out to be much harder than he expected, for he had to explain terms such as "subject," "object," "nouns," "verbs" and "adjectives." To help me understand the structure of the English sentence, he had to teach me Chinese grammar first. He realized that the Great Proletarian Culture Revolution had made his youngest son literally illiterate, in Chinese as well as English.

45   That night, our English lessons started. He taught me the letters A through F. By the end of the week, I had learned my alphabet. Afterward he taught the basics of grammar, sometimes using my hand grenades to illustrate the rules. He also taught me the international phonetic symbols and the way to use a dictionary. For reading materials, he excerpted simple passages from whatever books were available. Some were short paragraphs while others just sentences. We started our lessons at a manageable pace, but after a couple of months, for reasons he didn't tell me till the very last, he speeded up the pace considerably. The new words that I had to memorize increased from twenty words per day to fifty. To meet the challenge, I wrote the new words on small, thin slips of paper and hid them in the little red book of Chairman Mao, so that I could memorize them during the political study hours at school. In hole-digging afternoons I recited the sentences and sometimes even little paragraphs—aloud when I was sure that Chang was not around.

46   Before the sounds and shapes of English words became less elusive, before I could confidently study by myself, my father told me that I would have to continue on my own. He was going to join the "Mao

Zedong Thought Study Group" at his university. In those years, "Mao Zedong Thought Study Group" was a broad term that could refer to many
things. Used in reference to my father and people like him, it had only one
meaning: a euphemism for imprisonment. He had been imprisoned once
when my mother and siblings were still in Bejing. Now it had come again.
I asked, "Are you detained or arrested?" "I don't know," he said. "It's just
a Study Group." "Oh," I said, feeling the weight of the words. Legally, detention couldn't be any longer than fifteen days; arrest had to be followed
by a conviction and a sentence, which also had a definite term. "Just a
Study Group" could be a week or a lifetime. I was left on my own in a city
of eight million people, my English lessons indefinitely postponed. What
was worse, some people never returned alive from "Study Groups."

"When are you joining them?"   47

"Tomorrow."   48

I pretended to be "man" enough not to cry, but my father's eyes   49
were wet when he made me promise to finish *Pride and Prejudice* by the
time he came back.

After he left for the "Study Group," bedding roll on his shoulder, I   50
took my first careful look at the book he had thrust into my hands. It was
a small book with dark green cloth covers and gilt designs and letters on
its spine. I lifted the front cover; the frontispiece had a flowery design and
a woman figure on the upper right corner. Floating in the middle of the
flowery design and as a mother, holding a baby, she held an armful of
herbs, two apples or peaches, and a scroll. Her head tilted slightly toward
her right, to an opened scroll intertwined with the flowers on the other side
of the page. On the unrolled scroll, there were some words. I was thrilled
to find that I could understand all the words in the top two lines with no
difficulty except the last word: EVERYMAN, / I WILL GO WITH THEE. . . .

Two months after father entered the "Study Group," I stopped going   51
to his university for my monthly allowance. The Party secretary of the
bursar's office wore me out by telling me that my father and I didn't deserve to be fed by "working people." "Your father has never done any
positive work," meaning the twenty years my father taught at the university undermined rather than contributed to socialist ideology. To avoid
starvation, I picked up horse droppings in the streets and sold them to the
farming communes in the suburb. Between the little cash savings my
father left me and what I earned by selling dung, I managed an independent life. Meanwhile, I didn't forget my promise to my father. When I
saw him again nineteen months later, I boasted of having thumbed his
dictionary to shreds and struggled through Austen's novel from cover to
cover. I hadn't understood the story, but I had learned many words.

My father was not surprised to find that I took pleasure in drudgery.   52
He knew that looking up English words in a dictionary and wrestling with
an almost incomprehensible text could be an exciting challenge. It provided an intellectual relief for a teenager living at a time when the entire

country read nothing but Chairman Mao's works. "Don't worry whether you are red or black," my father said. "Just be yourself. Just be an ordinary everyman. Keep up with your good work, and when you learn English well enough, you'll be sure of a guide 'in your most need.'"

Content

1. An essay of dividing its subject often draws rigid boundaries between its categories so that they are mutually exclusive. Is that true in Ning Yu's essay? Are the "reds" in total opposition to the "blacks"? If there is any overlap or inter-mingling among these groups, where does it occur (see, for instance, ¶ 15)? Explain your answer.

2. What sorts of comparisons can Ning Yu count on his American readers to make between his childhood, schooling, living conditions, and their own? What sorts of information does he need to supply each time he introduces an unfamiliar concept? Has he done this successfully?

3. For what reasons—political, cultural, ethical—can Ning Yu expect Western readers to be sympathetic to the plight of himself and his father? Illustrate your answer with specific examples.

Strategies/Structures/Language

4. Much of the humor in this essay depends on the students' failure to understand the English slogans their equally uncomprehending teachers oblige them to memo-rize. Find some examples. What would these strike English-speaking readers as funny, but not the pupils?

For Writing

5. Have you ever been given a "label"—based on your race, social class, gender, political or religious affiliation, place of residence (street or area, city or town, state)? If so, what was (or is) that label? How accurate are its connotations? Are they favorable, unfavorable, or a mixture? Does the label stereotype or limit the ways people are expected to react to it? Did (or do) you feel comfortable with that label? If not, what can you do to change it? Write a paper exploring these issues for an audience which includes at least some people whom that label doesn't fit.

6. Have you or anyone you know well ever experienced persecution or harass-ment—intellectual, political, economic, racial, religious, or for other reasons? If so, write a paper explaining the causes, effects, and resolution (if any) of the problem. If it's extremely complex, select one or two aspects to concentrate on in your paper. Can you count on your audience to be sympathetic to your point of view? If not, what will you need to do to win them to your side?

 For comprehension, writing, and research activities and resources, please visit the companion website at <college.hmco.com/english>.

Additional Topics for Writing Process Analysis

(For strategies for writing process analysis, see 130)

MULTIPLE STRATEGIES FOR WRITING
PROCESS ANALYSIS

In writing on any of the process analysis topics below, you can choose among a variety of strategies to help explain a process and interpret its consequences:

- *definitions, explanations* of terms, equipment involved in the process
- a *narrative* of how the process proceeds, from start to finish
- *illustrations* and *examples:* to show what happens, and in what sequence
- *diagrams, drawings, flow charts, graphs* to clarify and explain
- *cause* and *effect*: to show why the process is justified or recommended, with what anticipated consequences
- *comparison* and *contrast,* between your recommendation and alternative ways of achieving the same or a similar result
- consideration of *short term* and *long term consequences* of a particular process

1. Write an essay in which you provide directions on how to perform a process—how to do or make something at which you are particularly skilled. In addition to the essential steps, you may wish to explain your own special technique or strategy that makes your method unique or better. Some possible subjects (which may be narrowed or adapted as you and your instructor wish) are these:

    a. How to get a good job, permanent or summer
    b. How to live meaningfully in a post 9/11 world (See the chapters "Terrorism" and "World Peace.")
    c. How to scuba dive, hang-glide, rappel, jog, lift weights, train for a marathon or triathlon
    d. How to make a good first impression (on a prospective employer, on a date, on your date's parents)
    e. How to do good for others, short term or long term
    f. How to be happy
    g. How to build a library of books, music, DVDs (see Gorry's "Steal This MP3 File," 512–15)
    h. How to lose (or gain) weight, or stabilize a gain or loss
    i. How to shop at a garage sale or secondhand store
    j. How to repair your own car, bicycle, computer, or other machine
    k. How to live cheaply (but enjoyably)
    l. How to study for a test—in general or in a specific subject
    m. How to administer first aid for choking, drowning, burns, or some other medical emergency
    n. How to get rich
    o. Anything else you know that others might want to learn

2. Write an informative essay in which you explain how one of the following occurs or works. Although you should pick a subject you know something about, you may need to supplement your information by consulting outside sources.

    a. How I made a major decision (to be—or not to be—a member of a particular profession, to practice a particular religion or lifestyle . . .)

    b. How a computer (or amplifier, piano, microwave oven, or other machine) works

    c. How to save energy through using a "green" product, such as a bicycle (specify kind), hybrid car, solar heating, and show how the device works

    d. How a professional develops skill in his or her chosen field—that is, how one becomes a skilled electrical engineer, geologist, chef, tennis coach, surgeon . . . ; pick a field in which you're interested

    e. How birds fly (or learn to fly), or some other process in the natural world

    f. How a system of the body (circulatory, digestive, respiratory, skeletal, neurological) works

    g. How the earth (or the solar system) was formed

    h. How the scientific method (or a particular variation of it) functions in a particular field

    i. How a well-run business (pick one of your choice—manufacturing, restaurant, clothing or hardware store, television repair service . . .) functions

    j. How a specific area of our federal government (or your particular local or state government legislative, executive, judicial) came into existence, or has changed over time

    k. How a system or process has gone wrong (may be satiric or humorous)

    l. How a particular drug or other medicine was developed and/or how it works, including its benefits and hazards

    m. How a great idea (on the nature of love, justice, truth, beauty . . .) found acceptance in a particular religion, culture, or smaller group

    n. How a particular culture (ethnic, regional, tribal, religious) or subculture (preppies, yuppies, pacifists, punk rockers, motorcycle gangs . . .) developed, rose, and/or declined in a larger or smaller group

3. Write a humorous paper explaining a process of the kind identified below. You will need to provide a serious analysis of the method you propose, even though the subject itself is intended to be amusing. (See Verge's "The Habs," 119–23.)

    a. How to make or do anything badly or inelegantly, without expertise or ability

    b. How to be popular

    c. How to survive in college

    d. How to survive a broken love affair

    e. How to be a model babysitter/son/daughter/student/employee/lover/spouse/parent

    f. How to become a celebrity

    g. Any of the topics in Writing Suggestions 1 or 2 above

    h. How a process can go dreadfully wrong

Cause and Effect

Writers often explore the relationships between cause and effect. Sometimes they simply list the causes or the consequences, and then either assume the consequences are obvious or let the readers draw their own conclusions. This is a common strategy of short poetry. Mary Oliver's "August" (190), for example, cites many natural causes that in combination create this perfect day of acceptance of nature and acceptance of self, epitomized in "this happy tongue."

Or they can probe more intensively, asking, "*Why* did something happen?" or "*What* are its consequences?" or both. Both questions can be used to interpret the 1995 photograph of a Bosnian wedding celebration (above), held, judging from the rifle raised aloft by one of the celebrants, in a state of siege. Why did the United States develop as a democracy rather than as some other form of government? What have the effects of this form of government been on its population? Or you, as a writer, may choose to examine a chain reaction in which, like a Rube Goldberg cartoon device, Cause *A* produces Effect *B*, which in turn causes *C*, which produces Effect *D*: Peer pressure (Cause *A*) causes young men to drink to excess (Effect *B*), which causes them to drive unsafely (Cause *C*, a corollary of Effect *B*) and results in high accident rates in unmarried males under age twenty-five (Effect *D*).

Process analysis can also deal with events or phenomena in sequence, focusing on the *how* rather than the *why*. To analyze the process of drinking and driving would be to explain, as an accident report might, how Al C. O'Hall became intoxicated (he drank seventeen beers and a bourbon chaser in two hours at the Dun Inn) and how he then roared off at 120 miles an hour, lost control of his lightweight sports car on a curve, and plowed into an oncoming sedan.

Two conditions have to be met to prove a given cause:

B cannot occur without *A*.
Whenever *A* occurs, *B* must also occur.

Thus a biologist who observed, repeatedly, that photosynthesis *(B)* occurred in green plants whenever a light source *(A)* was present and that it only occurred under this condition could infer that light causes photosynthesis. This would be the immediate cause. The more *remote* or *ultimate cause* might be the source of the light if it were natural (the sun). Artificial light (electricity) would have a yet more remote cause, such as water or nuclear power.

But don't be misled by a coincidental time sequence. Just because *A* preceded *B* in time doesn't necessarily mean that *A* caused *B*. Although it may appear to rain every time you wash your car, the car wash doesn't cause the rain. To blame the car wash would be an example of the *post hoc, ergo propter hoc* fallacy (Latin for "after this, therefore because of this").

Indeed, in cause and effect papers ultimate causes may be of greater significance than immediate ones, especially when you're considering social, political, or psychological causes rather than exclusively physical phenomena. Looking for possible causes from multiple perspectives is a good way to develop ideas to write about. It's also a sure way to avoid oversimplification, attributing a single cause to an effect that results from several. Thus if you wanted to probe the causes of Al C. O'Hall's excessive drinking, looking at the phenomenon from the following perspectives would give you considerable breadth for discussion.

Perspective	*Reason (Attributed cause)*
Al, a twenty-one-year-old unmarried male:	"Because I like the taste."
Al's best friend:	"Because he thinks drinking is cool."
Al's mother:	"Because Al wants to defy me."
Al's father:	"Because Al wants to be my pal."
Physician:	"Because Al is addicted to alcohol. There's a strong probability that this is hereditary."
Sociologist:	"Because 79.2 percent of American males twenty-one and under drink at least once a week. It's a social trend encouraged by peer pressure."

| Criminologist: | "Because Al derives antisocial pleasure from breaking the law." |
| Brewer or distiller: | "Because of my heavy advertising campaign." |

All of these explanations may be partly right; none—not even the genetic explanation—is in itself sufficient. (Even if Al were genetically predisposed to alcoholism as the child of an alcoholic parent, he'd have to drink to become an alcoholic.) Taken together they, and perhaps still other explanations, can be considered the complex cause of Al's behavior. To write a paper on the subject, using Al as a case in point, you might decide to discuss all the causes. Or you might concentrate on the most important causes and weed out those that seem irrelevant or less significant. Or to handle a large, complex subject in a short paper you could limit your discussion to a particular cause or type of causes—say, the social or the psychological. You have the same options for selectivity in discussing multiple effects.

The essays that follow treat cause and effect in a variety of ways. Because causes and effects are invariably intertwined, writers usually acknowledge the causes even when they're emphasizing the effects, and vice versa.

Two of the essays in this section—as well as others (see, for instance, Sanders, "The Inheritance of Tools" [148–54] and Yu, "Red and Black, or One English Major's Beginning" [173–82])—deal with the causes and effects of education, formal and informal, on the students involved, and with the consequences of that education—or lack of it—not only to the individual, but to society. Excerpts from Zitkala-Sa's *The School Days of an Indian Girl* (196–202) illustrate a host of constraints that are placed on Native American children uprooted from their homes and sent far away to boarding schools run by whites. These are reflected in the photograph of young girls from Omaha at a boarding school in Carlisle, Pennsylvania, in the 1880s (199). Whether the efforts to acclimate these children to white middle-class culture (symbolized by cutting off their braids, making them wear Anglo clothing, and obliging them to speak English rather than their tribal languages) were made from benign or more sinister motives, the effects were the same: alienation from and marginalization in both cultures. In re-creating the child's point of view, intended to represent all children in such schools, the author does not offer solutions, though she implies them.

Jonathan Kozol's "The Human Cost of an Illiterate Society" (204–11) focuses on the enormous social costs—effects—of illiteracy on the 16 million Americans who cannot read or do math well enough to read or interpret prescriptions, insurance policies, medical warnings, bank regulations, telephone books, cookbooks, and a host of other printed materials that provide directions and information for everyday living. Illiteracy causes people to involuntarily relinquish their freedom of choice, their independence, their self-respect, their citizenship. The costs, in human, ethical, social, economic, and political terms, are enormous.

Two other pieces in this chapter, Amanda N. Cagle's stunning creative nonfiction interpretation of her family's heritage and life, "On the Banks of the Bogue Chitto" (191–95), and Megan McGuire's "Wake Up Call" (225–31), also incorporate the themes of their informal education under the influence of their respective fathers (and McGuire's mother), for better and for worse. Cagle's heritage as a Jena Choctaw growing up in a Louisiana bayou is a thousand miles and a century away from Zitkala-Sa, yet pressures from the white cultures constrain both, threatening to destroy not only their way of life, but the Indians themselves. Why did Jason, Cagle's brother, commit suicide? What caused the grief and breakdowns of Cagle's father? What made him go AWOL as a truck driver but stay on his dull, demeaning job as a mail carrier? What did Cagle, as a child and growing adolescent, learn from the example of this man who had also taught her to shoot panthers with a bow and arrow? How could Megan McGuire, as explained in "Wake Up Call," grow up to be levelheaded, self-reliant, and directed toward positive goals (a college education, a military career) when reared by parents so different—from both these goals and from each other? Her father was loving but on a disability pension, and her mother was underpaid, overworked, and—at best—inattentive. These authors show readers a number of causes and their effects and then let us figure out the interconnections ourselves.

Other essays deal more explicitly with the causes and consequences of social problems. Both Stephanie Coontz, in "Blaming the Family for Economic Decline" (213–16), and Atul Gawande, in "The Cancer-Cluster Myth" (218–23), argue that Americans consistently confuse the effects with the causes. For instance, Coontz contends that people wrongly blame families' economic distress on "divorce and unwed motherhood." She offers considerable evidence to demonstrate that "in the majority of cases, it is poverty and social deprivation that cause unwed motherhood, not the other way around." There is no incentive for poor women to marry poor men. Marriage would not raise the poverty-level wages of undereducated men and women from low-income communities, and even if both parents were present, "two-thirds of the children who are poor today would *still* be poor." The scanty clothing and substandard housing in Walker Evans's striking portrait of a rural American family during the Depression (214) puts a human face on poverty. Two-thirds of all families need more than one income to survive. The majority of single-parent heads of households are women, who are "paid far less than men." A woman's income plummets after divorce, whereas a man's rises. The solution, Coontz says, "does not lie in getting parents back together again but in raising real wages, equalizing the pay of men and women, and making child support . . . more fair."

"The Cancer-Cluster Myth" (218–23) by physician Atul Gawande examines a different sort of confusion between cause and effect. "A community that is afflicted with an unusual number of cancers quite naturally looks for a cause in the environment—in the ground, the water, the air." Because public health officials earnestly investigate outbreaks of other sorts of diseases—"Legionnaires' disease; mercury poisoning from contaminated fish; and HIV infection"—people also expect epidemiologists to come up with causes of local cancer "outbreaks." Citizens have a high stake in finding an environmental cause and thus look for meaning in the random variations that appear by chance in small samples. They misperceive patterns where none exist and become frustrated by the lack of conclusive evidence. The fault doesn't lie in the research but in the way cancer cells behave: "To produce a cancer cluster, a carcinogen has to hit a great many cells in a great many people. A brief, low-level exposure to a carcinogen is unlikely to do the job."

A paper of cause and effect analysis requires you, as a thoughtful and careful writer, to know your subject well enough to avoid oversimplification and to shore up your analysis with specific, convincing details. You won't be expected to explain all the causes or effects of a particular phenomenon; that might be impossible for most humans, even the experts. But you can do a sufficiently thorough job with your chosen segment of the subject to satisfy yourself and help your readers to see it your way. Maybe they'll even come to agree with your interpretation. Why? Because. . . .

STRATEGIES FOR WRITING—
CAUSE AND EFFECT

1. What is the purpose of my cause-and-effect paper? Will I be focusing on the cause(s) of something, or its effect(s), short- or long-term? Will I be using cause and effect to explain a process? Analyze a situation? Present a prediction or an argument?
2. How much does my audience know about my subject? Will I have to explain some portions of the cause-and-effect relationship in more detail than others to compensate for their lack of knowledge? Or do they have sufficient background so I can focus primarily on new information or interpretations?
3. Is the cause-and-effect relationship I'm writing about valid? Or might there be other possible causes (or effects) that I'm overlooking? If I'm emphasizing causes, how far back do I want to go? If I'm focusing on effects, how many do I wish to discuss, and with how many examples?
4. Will I be using narration, description, definition, process analysis, argument, or other strategies in my explanation or analysis of cause(s) and effect(s)?
5. How technical or nontechnical will my language be? Will I need to qualify any of my claims or conclusions with "probably," or "in most cases," or other admissions that what I'm saying is not absolutely certain? What will my tone be—explanatory, persuasive, argumentative, humorous?

MARY OLIVER

Born in Cleveland, Ohio (1935), Mary Oliver attended both Ohio State University and Vassar College. In her first book of poems, *No Voyage, and Other Poems* (1963), the influence of moderns such as Edna St. Vincent Millay, William Carlos Williams, and James Wright was clearly evident, but her distinctive style and vision emerged in *Twelve Moons* (1979); *American Primitive* (1983), which won the Pulitzer Prize; *Dream Work* (1986); *House of Light* (1990); and *New and Selected Poems* (1992), which won a National Book Award. Oliver's main poetic interest is the natural world—its landscapes and especially its wealth of living things. Yet, as she explained to *The Bloomsbury Review,* she employs nature "in an emblematic way" to explore "the human condition." Oliver has taught writing at Bucknell University and Sweet Briar College (in Virginia), and shares her advice to aspiring poets in *Rules for the Dance: A Handbook for Writing and Reading Metrical Verse* (1998). Recent volumes of poetry and essays include *The Leaf and the Cloud* (2000), *Owls and other Fantasies* (2003), and *New and Selected Poems, Volume Two* (2004).

In "August," from *American Primitive,* late-summer ripeness draws the poet into the brambles, compelling the reader to follow. There is a sense of rapture and realization ("there is this happy tongue"), yet the reader is left with unresolved mysteries. If, amidst the blackberries, her body "accepts what it is," what is her body, then, and what relation does it bear to the undertone of dark and black images that haunts this poem?

August

When the blackberries hang
swollen in the woods, in the brambles
nobody owns, I spend

all day among the high
branches, reaching
my ripped arms, thinking

of nothing, cramming
the black honey of summer
into my mouth; all day my body

accepts what it is. In the dark
creeks that run by there is
this thick paw of my life darting among

the black bells, the leaves; there is
this happy tongue.

AMANDA N. CAGLE

> Amanda N. Cagle was born in Louisiana in 1979. She earned a BA in French (2000) and an MA in English (2001) at Mississippi State University. She is currently completing a PhD in English at the University of Connecticut, where she is writing a dissertation on American Indian women's poetry. Cagle's essays and poetry have appeared in *Ontario Review*, *Louisiana Review*, and *Revista Atenea*.
>
> "On the Banks of the Bogue Chitto" won the Aetna Creative Nonfiction Award at the University of Connecticut and appeared in the Spring 2005 issue of the *Ontario Review*. The Bogue Chitto, which means "Big Creek" in Choctaw, winds through southern Louisiana and Mississippi.

❄ *On the Banks of the Bogue Chitto*

I was born on the banks of the Bogue Chitto. It was no accident. My mother wasn't caught miles from a hospital when she found herself in labor. She and my father purposefully walked from our plank-walled shotgun house into those woods and down to that bank. His arms supported her, and hers fitted over her taut belly like an insect's wings. It was early morning, and the light seemed false, my father used to say, like lamplight. Hung together in the gray were crows that fell lightly on the pines like a covering of ash. Even in January, the green kudzu vines curled tightly around the black bones of the cypress and the willow oak. My mother had already given birth to two children on the banks of the Bogue Chitto, and my father's mother, and her mothers, and many mothers before them had come to the same place.

This river is all the truth I've ever needed. It's where most of my family was born, where we were named, where we've found our food, where two of us have since chosen to die. It's where I've gone when the world's seemed too much. In this river, my grandmother proved herself to be the greatest catfish grabber in history by pulling an eighty-three-pound flathead to the banks. It's where my father was taught by his father to be a warrior. Where he taught me. I remember him standing on the bank beside me while I peered through the thickets and the dark roots of the forest floor to the slightest shift of shade and light. I stepped a few paces forward sure the very silence of the earth would follow me. I gently notched my arrow, pulled the bow taut, released the narrow shaft, and watched the panther's paw break into red blossoms.

When I think of my father, I like to remember times like these. I like to imagine that he is still the greatest of all the Jena Choctaw warriors. For many years, my brother Jason and I were convinced he was. When the

Arrow Trucking Company would not let my father off work for Jason's seventh birthday, he came ripping through our pasture at 5:00 in the morning with the big rig and its goods in tow. My father, Jason and I spent the morning picking Satsumas and the afternoon sitting on the banks of the Bogue Chitto chewing sugar cane which was heavy with the scent of hay and syrup.

4   That night, Jason and I slept in the cab of the 18-wheeler. We were not afraid that someone would steal up on us in the night to enter this mighty truck parked in our field. We knew our father would find a way to make things okay. Maybe the owner would come with a gun, and our father would tell a joke so funny that the man would laugh, pat him on the back and forget all about his truck. Maybe our father would hear the man coming and speed off into the night before he even arrived.

5   Of course, my father was fired from this job, as he would be from many others. He was not a very good employee. He wasn't good at making money or keeping it. He couldn't stand to be indoors, and as much as he tried to conform to an employer's schedule, the rhythm of his own life always got in the way. No job could hold him. When the needle-tooth gar made ripples in the river, my father forgot about work and headed out on the pirogue. When the cornfields stretched skyward and the watermelons grew too heavy for the vines, he could be found not at work but in the fields.

6   Somehow, I always expected him to be out there. When I was a child, I used to love to search for him through the dim and unreal morning shadows. He would be listening to the murmur of earthworms beneath his feet, tasting the first tomatoes, watching the swirls and ripples on the Bogue Chitto. These were his greatest moments. These were the times when he allowed himself to be free of the world. The water of the Bogue Chitto opened itself up to him, and he spent every day trapping and fishing along her banks.

7   I never thought nor hoped that there would come a time when the world owned him, when the water of the Bogue Chitto no longer flowed through him like a vein. But that time came when the state threatened to seize our land after my father had failed to come up with the money for the property taxes. He had lived on those thirty-three acres all of his life. The land had belonged to his father, his grandfather, and many fathers before them. He had tried to borrow money and to sell rebuilt car engines, but he couldn't get enough.

8   After the state assessed my father's land, they sent a social worker to assess his children. Jason, two cousins, and I ran into the woods when the social worker arrived. We watched the house from the tree line, unsure of what we were watching for. All I could picture was the man running after us with a giant net, scooping us up, and throwing us into his car.

9   Before long, we decided to head for the safety of our clubhouse, hidden deep in the tangled woods. Here we kept the bones we hunted and found like treasure. Most of them were from a neighbor's herd. The big

This mangrove swamp, with Spanish moss dripping from the branches, presents striking images of trees ethereal and eerie. Where is this located? Where is the shore? What's under the water? What time of day is it? What's the temperature? The humidity level? If people were in this picture, who would they be, and what would they be doing? Tell a story that interprets either the seen or the unseen (or both) in this photograph, and then see how closely your story corresponds to Amanda N. Cagle's "On the Banks of the Bogue Chitto" (191–95).

bones came from sick cows that wandered off and starved or lay down between close trees and died. We had femurs, long and polished by the heat to a metallic whiteness. There were crescent ribs thin and pale as the edges of the moon, a smooth hip bone with deep indentions as carefully hollowed out as the bowl of a pipe, and a skull nearly whole and full of black teeth with splintered roots. In these bones, we traced the lines of everything that had happened to us and everything that would.

One September Jason and I found a dog half eaten. His stomach was   10 ballooning out like a full sail, and we ran straight to the house. A panther, our father told us. In those woods, waiting for our father to send the social worker away, the wild moan of that panther stretched taut through the dim air like a scar.

We entered the house that night reluctantly. Our father was sitting on   11 the couch flipping through the phone book and writing down names and numbers. Early the next morning he went to town and did not return until nightfall. He continued to do this until he landed a job at the post office.

12   At first, he was just a temp, but he was scared and so he worked hard to convince the post office to hire him full time. After a few years, he was given his own route. He arrived at dawn and returned home too late in the evening to work the fields or check the lines on the Bogue Chitto. But, for the first time in his life, he had a steady job, which meant the state would leave his land and his children alone.

13   My mother constantly praised his efforts. She was happy with the steady check and the health insurance. She had grown weary of his jumps between jobs and the anxious wait and hope for food upon his return from the woods. At first, he complained about the hours and the menial task of putting letters in a box, but my mother would simply rub his shoulders and tell him to suck it up. He did just that.

14   Over the next twelve years, he stopped telling stories about how to track deer, about when to plunge the arm deep into the mounded earth to feel for potatoes, and about how to interpret the cold and thin moan of the panther. Instead, he told us about who lived in what neighborhood and about the kind of mail they received. He especially liked to talk about the residents of the Indian Hills subdivision. There were no hills, he would say, and no Indians unless you counted Mr. Gupta.

15   If he had grown restless with the job, he didn't let us know it. He had settled into the expected routine. It was not the routine of a warrior, but I, more than my brother, understood what he had to lose. Nevertheless, I, like Jason, secretly hoped that he would turn in his uniforms. We longed for the days when we relied only on the Bogue Chitto to meet all of our needs. We missed the afternoons of sitting on her banks with our father and spitting muscadine seeds into the water. Sweet potato season passed us by; we harvested a few mustard greens but not enough to sell or freeze; there was squash, but no one stopped to watch it grow heavy with hips. The fall wind blew through the bald cypress, red maple, willow oak, and loblolly pine—the fragrance of death surrounded us, but none of us detected it.

16   In fact, it was a complete surprise. It still is and probably always will be. My father was the first to find out. Two officers arrived at the post office in an unmarked car, walked in and told him Jason was found on the bank of the Bogue Chitto. They were sure because there was a wallet beside the boy's body. There was a shotgun wound, self-inflicted. These things were a matter of fact. My father was so sure the officers were mistaken that he turned down a ride with them and drove himself to the morgue to confirm that the body was not that of his son. He later had to drive back to work to tell his supervisor that he would need a little time off from work; he was not sure how much.

17   He then told mother, the rest of the children, the grandparents and the cousins, and before long the entire Jena Choctaw tribe seemed to have descended on our house. I wondered for a moment if we would perform an old ceremony. The bone pickers of my grandfather's generation knew

that in every bone there was an answer, but this was a different time. My father could do little more than pick out the nicest coffin he could afford. He purchased a plot of land that none of us had ever seen before. The man who sold it to him had a big round face and tight red fingers. He drew his boot heel across the plot and shook my father's hand.

My father spent the days following the funeral in the pastures cutting   18 down what remained of the butterbeans, purple hulls and Satsuma. He paced along the banks of the Bogue Chitto and stared into its water. The large animals living in the swamp water moved now like great shadows of a larger mystery. The river mud flaked in big cracks. My father sat on the bank like a smooth stone made by the waters of many a rain-lit night.

He returned to work too soon, and whatever he did there caused   19 two more men in suits and an unmarked car to approach him. This time they came to our house, and they were not police but some type of high-ranking post office employees. They told him that he was in the midst of a nervous breakdown and that if he wanted to keep his job, he needed to check himself into the Woodland Hills Hospital for psychiatric treatment. When the men left, my cousins and I chased after them and threw small gravel rocks at their car. I didn't think for a moment that my father would go. I somehow expected him to follow behind us and to throw the furthest rock himself, but he did not. He sat inside on the couch while my mother pulled a suitcase from beneath their bed.

When I visited him at the hospital, his room was sterile and white.   20 All of the blinds were down and the only sound was that of the hum of fluorescent lights. Sitting in the corner chair, under the falseness of the lamplight, he didn't look like anyone I had ever seen.

The family was invited to sit in on a few of the therapy sessions.   21 Once the psychiatrist asked me to leave because she thought that I was interfering with my father's progress and disrupting the session. I had lashed out at him for taking the pills the psychiatrist had prescribed. I knew that neither the pills nor the stay at the white and sterile hospital would help him regain his balance. I wanted more than anything to be able to see him again as a warrior. I wanted him to leave the confines of the institution and return home to the ripening of the muscadines and the bedding of the catfish.

He did not stay long in that hospital. He returned to his job and to   22 the routines of his life. The water of the Bogue Chitto must still run through him as it does through me, but he can no longer make the walls and ceilings that surround him vanish into fields of corn and horses, grain and cows, wandering ants and squirrels. There, where we used to sit, the marsh grass dances in the wind. Missing are the marks of our feet in the soft mud on the bank of the Bogue Chitto. Missing are the small prints that should hold the form of our bodies among the ancient creases and folds.

ZITKALA-SA

Zitkala-Sa (1878–1938) was the first Native American woman to write her autobiography by herself, without the help of an intermediary, such as an ethnographer, translator, editor, or oral historian. This unmediated authenticity gives her work unusual authority. She was a Yankton, born on the Pine Ridge Reservation in South Dakota, daughter of a full-blooded Sioux mother and a white father.

Zitkala-Sa wrote a number of autobiographical essays to call attention to the cultural dislocation and hardships caused when the whites in power sent Native American children to boarding schools hundreds of miles away from home and imposed western culture on them. In her own case, as she explains in "The Land of Red Apples," at the age of eight she left the reservation to attend a boarding school in Wabash, Indiana, run by Quaker missionaries. On her return, "neither a wild Indian nor a tame one," her distress and cultural displacement were acute, as "Four Strange Summers" makes clear. These were originally published in *Atlantic Monthly* (1900), as portions of *Impressions of an Indian Childhood* and *The School Days of an Indian Girl*.

Zitkala-Sa remained unhappily on the reservation for four years, then returned to the Quaker school, and at nineteen enrolled in the Quaker-run Earlham College in Indiana. Her marriage to Raymond Bonnin, a Sioux, enhanced her activism for Indian rights. She served as secretary of the Society of American Indians, and also edited *American Indian Magazine.* As a lobbyist and spokesperson for the National Council of American Indians, which she founded in 1926, she helped to secure passage of the Indian Citizenship Bill and other reforms. Yet she was an integrationist, not a separatist, and attempted to forge meaningful connections between cultures.

from The School Days of an Indian Girl

I   The Land of Red Apples

1   There were eight in our party of bronzed children who were going East with the missionaries. Among us were three young braves, two tall girls, and we three little ones, Judéwin, Thowin, and I.

2   We had been very impatient to start on our journey to the Red Apple Country, which, we were told, lay a little beyond the great circular horizon of the Western prairie. Under a sky of rosy apples we dreamt of roaming as freely and happily as we had chased the cloud shadows on the Dakota plains. We had anticipated much pleasure from a ride on the iron horse, but the throngs of staring palefaces disturbed and troubled us.

On the train, fair women, with tottering babies on each arm, stopped
their haste and scrutinized the children of absent mothers. Large men,
with heavy bundles in their hands, halted near by, and riveted their glassy
blue eyes upon us.

I sank deep into the corner of my seat, for I resented being watched.
Directly in front of me, children who were no larger than I hung themselves upon the backs of their seats, with their bold white faces toward
me. Sometimes they took their forefingers out of their mouths and pointed
at my moccasined feet. Their mothers, instead of reproving such rude
curiosity, looked closely at me, and attracted their children's further notice to my blanket. This embarrassed me, and kept me constantly on the
verge of tears.

I sat perfectly still, with my eyes downcast, daring only now and then
to shoot long glances around me. Chancing to turn to the window at my
side, I was quite breathless upon seeing one familiar object. It was the tele-
graph pole which strode by at short paces. Very near my mother's dwelling,
along the edge of a road thickly bordered with wild sunflowers, some poles
like these had been planted by white men. Often I had stopped, on my way
down the road, to hold my ear against the pole, and, hearing its low moaning, I used to wonder what the paleface had done to hurt it. Now I sat
watching for each pole that glided by to be the last one.

In this way I had forgotten my uncomfortable surroundings, when I
heard one of my comrades call out my name. I saw the missionary standing very near, tossing candies and gums into our midst. This amused us
all, and we tried to see who could catch the most of the sweet-meats. The
missionary's generous distribution of candies was impressed upon my
memory by a disastrous result which followed. I had caught more than
my share of candies and gums, and soon after our arrival at the school I
had a chance to disgrace myself, which, I am ashamed to say, I did.

Though we rode several days inside of the iron horse, I do not recall
a single thing about our luncheons.

It was night when we reached the school grounds. The lights from
the windows of the large buildings fell upon some of the icicled trees that
stood beneath them. We were led toward an open door, where the bright-
ness of the lights within flooded out over the heads of the excited palefaces
who blocked the way. My body trembled more from fear than from the
snow I trod upon.

Entering the house, I stood close against the wall. The strong glaring
light in the large whitewashed room dazzled my eyes. The noisy hurry-
ing of hard shoes upon a bare wooden floor increased the whirring in my
ears. My only safety seemed to be in keeping next to the wall. As I was
wondering in which direction to escape from all this confusion, two warm
hands grasped me firmly, and in the same moment I was tossed high in
midair. A rosy-checked paleface woman caught me in her arms. I was both
frightened and insulted by such trifling. I stared into her eyes, wishing

her to let me stand on my own feet, but she jumped me up and down with increasing enthusiasm. My mother had never made a plaything of her wee daughter. Remembering this I began to cry aloud.

10   They misunderstood the cause of my tears, and placed me at a white table loaded with food. There our party were united again. As I did not hush my crying, one of the older ones whispered to me, "Wait until you are alone in the night."

11   It was very little I could swallow besides my sobs, that evening.

12   "Oh, I want my mother and my brother Dawée! I want to go to my aunt!" I pleaded; but the ears of the palefaces could not hear me.

13   From the table we were taken along an upward incline of wooden boxes, which I learned afterward to call a stairway. At the top was a quiet hall, dimly lighted. Many narrow beds were in one straight line down the entire length of the wall. In them lay sleeping brown faces, which peeped just out of the coverings. I was tucked into bed with one of the tall girls, because she talked to me in my mother tongue and seemed to soothe me.

14   I had arrived in the wonderful land of rosy skies, but I was not happy, as I had thought I should be. My long travel and the bewildering sights had exhausted me. I fell asleep, heaving deep, tired sobs. My tears were left to dry themselves in streaks, because neither my aunt nor my mother was near to wipe them away.

II   The Cutting of My Long Hair

15   The first day in the land of the apples was a bitter-cold one; for the snow still covered the ground, and the trees were bare. A large bell rang for breakfast, its loud metallic voice crashing through the belfry overhead and into our sensitive ears. The annoying clatter of shoes on bare floors gave us no peace. The constant clash of harsh noises, with an undercurrent of many voices murmuring an unknown tongue, made a bedlam within which I was securely tied. And though my spirit tore itself in struggling for its lost freedom, all was useless.

16   A paleface woman, with white hair, came up after us. We were placed in a line of girls who were marching into the dining room. These were Indian girls, in stiff shoes and closely clinging dresses. The small girls wore sleeved aprons and shingled hair. As I walked noiselessly in my soft moccasins, I felt like sinking to the floor, for my blanket had been stripped from my shoulders. I looked hard at the Indian girls, who seemed not to care that they were even more immodestly dressed than I, in their tightly fitting clothes. While we marched in, the boys entered at an opposite door. I watched for the three young braves who came in our party. I spied them in the rear ranks, looking as uncomfortable as I felt.

17   A small bell was tapped, and each of the pupils drew a chair from under the table. Supposing this act meant they were to be seated, I pulled

How do you know these girls are Native Americans? What attributes of white middle-class culture are manifest in this photograph? How might the girls be expected to react to these attributes? How might their families be expected to regard the Anglicization of their daughters? How would the school personnel—then and now—interpret the girls' clothing, postures, and hair styles?

out mine and at once slipped into it from one side. But when I turned my head, I saw that I was the only one seated, and all the rest at our table remained standing. Just as I began to rise, looking shyly around to see how chairs were to be used, a second bell was sounded. All were seated at last, and I had to crawl back into my chair again. I heard a man's voice at one end of the hall, and I looked around to see him. But all the others hung their heads over their plates. As I glanced at the long chain of tables, I caught the eyes of a paleface woman upon me. Immediately I dropped my eyes, wondering why I was so keenly watched by the strange woman. The man ceased his mutterings, and then a third bell was tapped. Every one picked up his knife and fork and began eating. I began crying instead, for by this time I was afraid to venture anything more.

But this eating by formula was not the hardest trial in that first day. 18 Late in the morning, my friend Judéwin gave me a terrible warning. Judéwin knew a few words of English; and she had overheard the paleface woman talk about cutting our long, heavy hair. Our mothers had taught us that only unskilled warriors who were captured had their hair shingled by the enemy. Among our people, short hair was worn by mourners, and shingled hair by cowards!

19   We discussed our fate some moments, and when Judéwin said, "We have to submit, because they are strong," I rebelled.

20   "No, I will not submit! I will struggle first!" I answered.

21   I watched my chance, and when no one noticed I disappeared. I crept up the stairs quietly as I could in my squeaking shoes,—my moccasins had been exchanged for shoes. Along the hall I passed, without knowing whither I was going. Turning aside to an open door, I found a large room with three white beds in it. The windows were covered with dark green curtains, which made the room very dim. Thankful that no one was there, I directed my steps toward the corner farthest from the door. On my hands and knees I crawled under the bed, and cuddled myself in the dark corner.

22   From my hiding place I peered out, shuddering with fear whenever I heard footsteps near by. Though in the hall loud voices were calling my name, and I knew that even Judéwin was searching for me, I did not open my mouth to answer. Then the steps were quickened and the voices became excited. The sounds came nearer and nearer. Woman and girls entered the room. I held my breath, and watched them open closet doors and peep behind large trunks. Some one threw up the curtains, and the room was filled with sudden light. What caused them to stoop and look under the bed I do not know. I remember being dragged out, though I resisted by kicking and scratching wildly. In spite of myself, I was carried downstairs and tied fast in a chair.

23   I cried aloud, shaking my head all the while until I felt the cold blades of the scissors against my neck, and heard them gnaw off one of my thick braids. Then I lost my spirit. Since the day I was taken from my mother I had suffered extreme indignities. People had stared at me. I had been tossed about in the air like a wooden puppet. And now my long hair was shingled like a coward's! In my anguish I moaned for my mother, but no one came to comfort me. Not a soul reasoned quietly with me, as my own mother used to do: for now I was only one of many little animals driven by a herder. . . .

VI   Four Strange Summers[1]

24   After my first three years of school, I roamed again in the Western country through four strange summers.

25   During this time I seemed to hang in the heart of chaos, beyond the touch or voice of human aid. My brother, being almost ten years my senior, did not quite understand my feelings. My mother had never gone inside of a schoolhouse, and so she was not capable of comforting her daughter who could read and write. Even nature seemed to have no place for me. I

---

[1] Sections III, IV, and V are omitted.

was neither a wee girl nor a tall one; neither a wild Indian nor a tame one. This deplorable situation was the effect of my brief course in the East, and the unsatisfactory "teenth" in a girl's years.

It was under these trying conditions that, one bright afternoon, as I sat restless and unhappy in my mother's cabin, I caught the sound of the spirited step of my brother's pony on the road which passed by our dwelling. Soon I heard the wheels of a light buckboard, and Dawée's familiar "Ho!" to his pony. He alighted upon the bare ground in front of our house. Tying his pony to one of the projecting corner logs of the low-roofed cottage, he stepped upon the wooden doorstep. 26

I met him there with a hurried greeting, and, as I passed by, he looked a quiet "What?" into my eyes. 27

When he began talking with my mother, I slipped the rope from the pony's bridle. Seizing the reins and bracing my feet against the dashboard, I wheeled around in an instant. The pony was ever ready to try his speed. Looking backward, I saw Dawée waving his hand to me. I turned with the curve in the road and disappeared. I followed the winding road which crawled upward between the bases of little hillocks. Deep water-worn ditches ran parallel on either side. A strong wind blew against my cheeks and fluttered my sleeves. The pony reached the top of the highest hill, and began an even race on level lands. There was nothing moving within that great circular horizon of the Dakota prairies save the tall grasses, over which the wind blew and rolled off in long, shadowy waves. 28

Within this vast wigwam of blue and green I rode reckless and insignificant. It satisfied my small consciousness to see the white foam fly from the pony's mouth. 29

Suddenly, out of the earth a coyote came forth at a swinging trot that was taking the cunning thief toward the hills and the village beyond. Upon the moment's impulse, I gave him a long chase and a wholesome fright. As I turned away to go back to the village, the wolf sank down upon his haunches for a rest, for it was a hot summer day; and as I drove slowly homeward, I saw his sharp nose still pointed at me, until I vanished below the margin of the hilltops. 30

In a little while I came in sight of my mother's house. Dawée stood in the yard, laughing at an old warrior who was pointing his forefinger, and again waving his whole hand, toward the hills. With his blanket drawn over one shoulder, he talked and motioned excitedly. Dawée turned the old man by the shoulder and pointed me out to him. 31

"Oh han!" (Oh yes) the warrior muttered, and went his way. He had climbed the top of his favorite barren hill to survey the surrounding prairies, when he spied my chase after the coyote. His keen eyes recognized the pony and driver. At once uneasy for my safety, he had come running to my mother's cabin to give her warning. I did not appreciate his kindly interest, for there was an unrest gnawing at my heart. 32

As soon as he went away, I asked Dawée about something else. 33

34   "No, my baby sister. I cannot take you with me to the party to-night," he replied. Though I was not far from fifteen, and I felt that before long I should enjoy all the privileges of my tall cousin, Dawée persisted in calling me his baby sister.

35   That moonlight night, I cried in my mother's presence when I heard the jolly young people pass by our cottage. There were no more young braves in blankets and eagle plumes, nor Indian maids with prettily painted cheeks. They had gone three years to school in the East, and had become civilized. The young men wore the white man's coat and trousers, with bright neckties. The girls wore tight muslin dresses, with ribbons at neck and waist. At these gatherings they talked English. I could speak English almost as well as my brother, but I was not properly dressed to be taken along. I had no hat, no ribbons, and no close-fitting gown. Since my return from school I had thrown away my shoes, and wore again the soft moccasins.

36   While Dawée was busily preparing to go I controlled my tears. But when I heard him bounding away on his pony, I buried my face in my arms and cried hot tears.

37   My mother was troubled by my unhappiness. Coming to my side, she offered me the only printed matter we had in our home. It was an Indian Bible, given her some years ago by a missionary. She tried to console me. "Here, my child, are the white man's papers. Read a little from them," she said most piously.

38   I took it from her hand, for her sake; but my enraged spirit felt more like burning the book, which afforded me no help, and was a perfect delusion to my mother. I did not read it, but laid it unopened on the floor, where I sat on my feet. The dim yellow light of the braided muslin burning in a small vessel of oil flickered and sizzled in the awful silent storm which followed my rejection of the Bible.

39   Now my wrath against the fates consumed my tears before they reached my eyes. I sat stony, with a bowed head. My mother threw a shawl over her head and shoulders, and stepped out into the night.

40   After an uncertain solitude, I was suddenly aroused by a loud cry piercing the night. It was my mother's voice wailing among the barren hills which held the bones of buried warriors. She called aloud for her brothers' spirits to support her in her helpless misery. My fingers grew icy cold, as I realized that my unrestrained tears had betrayed my suffering to her, and she was grieving for me.

41   Before she returned, though I knew she was on her way, for she had ceased her weeping, I extinguished the light, and leaned my head on the window sill.

42   Many schemes of running away from my surroundings hovered about in my mind. A few more moons of such a turmoil drove me away to the Eastern school. I rode on the white man's iron steed, thinking it would bring me back to my mother in a few winters, when I should be grown tall, and there would be congenial friends awaiting me. . . .

Content

1. To an extent, leaving the security of home and its familiar culture to go to school, with its inevitably somewhat different culture, presents problems for any child. To what extent are Zitkala-Sa's memories of being uprooted and sent away to school similar to those of any child in a similar circumstance, and to what extent are they exacerbated by the alien culture to which she is expected to adapt?

2. What was the rationale of those in power for sending Native American children away to boarding school? Why did parents allow their children to be sent away (see "The Land of Red Apples")? In what ways did this contribute to the adulteration and breakup of Native American culture (see all sections)?

3. Historically, the Quakers have a reputation for being respectful of civil rights and very sympathetic to the preservation of minority cultures. Quaker households, for instance, were often places of shelter for slaves escaping along the Underground Railway. Was the Quaker school to which Zitkala-Sa went an exception? What factors influenced her perception of the school when she was in residence and later when she wrote about it?

Strategies/Structures/Language

4. Zitkala-Sa is writing in standard English for an educated Anglo-American audience in 1900, many of whom might never have met a Native American, and who would have known very little about their schooling. What information does she need to supply to make the context of her narrative clear? Has she done this?

5. Zitkala-Sa's readers might be expected to share the viewpoint of the school personnel, in opposition to her own point of view, both as a character in her own story and as its narrator. By what means does she try to win readers to her point of view? Is she successful?

6. What are the effects of occasional passages in the language the Anglos attribute to Native Americans? See, for example, "palefaces" (¶ 2 and *passim*); "A few *more moons*. . . . I rode on the white man's *iron steed,* thinking it would bring me back to my mother in a *few winters*" (¶ 42).

For Writing

7. Today many Native American children living on reservations can go to school there, sometimes from kindergarten through college. Write an essay for parents (of a particular ethnicity or culture—your own, perhaps) trying to decide what's best for their children in which you weigh the advantages of cultural integrity versus ghettoization that are inherent in this, or any system, of a closed-culture education—public or private (including parochial schooling). You may need to do some research on a particular school system to provide information for your argument.

8. As Zitkala-Sa does, tell the story of an experience of cultural displacement that you or someone you know well has experienced. Identify its causes and interpret its consequences, short- and long-term.

For comprehension, writing, and research activities and resources, please visit the companion website at <college.hmco.com/english>.

JONATHAN KOZOL

Kozol's first critique of American education, *Death at an Early Age: The Destruction of the Hearts and Minds of Negro Children in the Boston Public Schools* in 1967, won the National Book Award. Written during the civil rights and school desegregation movements in the 1960s, this book documents the repressive teaching methods in Boston's unintegrated public schools designed, Kozol claimed, to reinforce a system that would keep the children separate but unequal. Kozol, himself a Harvard graduate (1958), Rhodes Scholar, and recipient of numerous prestigious fellowships transcends his privileged background to address what he considers to be the failure of American education to reach minorities and the poor. His recent books, *Savage Inequalities: Children in America's Schools* (1991), *Amazing Grace: The Lives of Children and the Conscience of a Nation* (1995), and *The Shame of the Nation: The Restoration of Apartheid Schooling in America* (2005) extend and reinforce these concerns.

  Illiterate America (1985) analyzes the nature, causes, and effects of illiteracy, the ultimate and pervasive failure that, says Kozol, denies sixty million people "significant participation" in the government that "is neither of, nor for, nor by, the people." Kozol concludes with a call to action, a nationwide army of neighborhood volunteers who would teach people to read. Part of his strategy in arousing his own readers to action is to make them understand what it's like to be illiterate, on which this chapter (reprinted in full) focuses. Characteristically, Kozol interprets both the causes of illiteracy and the effects—discussed here—in human, moral terms. Kozol says, "I write as a witness. . . . This is what we have done. This is what we have permitted."

The Human Cost of an Illiterate Society

1   *PRECAUTIONS. READ BEFORE USING.*
     Poison: Contains sodium hydroxide (caustic soda-lye).
     Corrosive: Causes severe eye and skin damage, may cause blindness.
     Harmful or fatal if swallowed.
     If swallowed, give large quantities of milk or water.
     Do not induce vomiting.
     Important: Keep water out of can at all times to prevent contents from violently erupting . . .

                                        WARNING ON A CAN OF DRĀNO

2   We are speaking here no longer of the dangers faced by passengers on Eastern Airlines or the dollar costs incurred by U.S. corporations and taxpayers. We are speaking now of human suffering and of the ethical dilemmas that are faced by a society that looks upon such suffering with qualified concern

but does not take those actions which its wealth and ingenuity would seemingly demand.

Questions of literacy, in Socrates' belief, must at length be judged as 3 matters of morality. Socrates could not have had in mind the moral compromise peculiar to a nation like our own. Some of our Founding Fathers did, however, have this question in their minds. One of the wisest of those Founding Fathers (one who may not have been most compassionate but surely was more prescient than some of his peers) recognized the special dangers that illiteracy would pose to basic equity in the political construction that he helped to shape.

"A people who mean to be their own governors," James Madison 4 wrote, "must arm themselves with the power knowledge gives. A popular government without popular information or the means of acquiring it, is but a prologue to a farce or a tragedy, or perhaps both."

Tragedy looms larger than farce in the United States today. Illiterate 5 citizens seldom vote. Those who do are forced to cast a vote of questionable worth. They cannot make informed decisions based on serious print information. Sometimes they can be alerted to their interests by aggressive voter education. More frequently, they vote for a face, a smile, or a style, not for a mind or character or body of beliefs.

The number of illiterate adults exceeds by 16 million the entire vote 6 cast for the winner in the 1980 presidential contest. If even one third of all illiterates could vote, and read enough and do sufficient math to vote in their self-interest, Ronald Reagan would not likely have been chosen president. There is, of course, no way to know for sure. We do know this: Democracy is a mendacious term when used by those who are prepared to countenance the forced exclusion of one third of our electorate. So long as 60 million people are denied significant participation, the government is neither of, nor for, nor by, the people. It is a government, at best, of those two thirds whose wealth, skin color, or parental privilege allows them opportunity to profit from the provocation and instruction of the written word.

The undermining of democracy in the United States is one "expense" 7 that sensitive Americans can easily deplore because it represents a contradiction that endangers citizens of all political positions. The human price is not so obvious at first.

Since I first immersed myself within this work I have often had the 8 following dream: I find that I am in a railroad station or a large department store within a city that is utterly unknown to me and where I cannot understand the printed words. None of the signs or symbols is familiar. Everything looks strange: like mirror writing of some kind. Gradually I understand that I am in the Soviet Union. All the letters on the walls around me are Cyrillic. I look for my pocket dictionary but I find that it has been mislaid. Where have I left it? Then I recall that I forgot to bring it with me when I packed my bags in Boston. I struggle to remember the name of my hotel. I try to ask somebody for directions. One person stops and looks at me in a peculiar way. I lose the nerve to ask. At last I reach into my wallet for an ID card. The card is missing. Have I lost it? Then I remember that my card was confiscated for some reason, many years before. Around this point, I wake up in a panic.

9   This panic is not so different from the misery that millions of adult illiterates experience each day within the course of their routine existence in the U.S.A.

10   Illiterates cannot read the menu in a restaurant.

11   They cannot read the cost of items on the menu in the *window* of the restaurant before they enter.

12   Illiterates cannot read the letters that their children bring home from their teachers. They cannot study school department circulars that tell them of the courses that their children must be taking if they hope to pass the SAT exams. They cannot help with homework. They cannot write a letter to the teacher. They are afraid to visit in the classroom. They do not want to humiliate their child or themselves.

13   Illiterates cannot read instructions on a bottle of prescription medicine. They cannot find out when a medicine is past the year of safe consumption; nor can they read of allergenic risks, warnings to diabetics, or the potential sedative effect of certain kinds of nonprescription pills. They cannot observe preventive health care admonitions. They cannot read about "the seven warning signs of cancer" or the indications of blood-sugar fluctuations or the risks of eating certain foods that aggravate the likelihood of cardiac arrest.

14   Illiterates live, in more than literal ways, an uninsured existence. They cannot understand the written details on a health insurance form. They cannot read the waivers that they sign preceding surgical procedures. Several women I have known in Boston have entered a slum hospital with the intention of obtaining a tubal ligation and have emerged a few days later after having been subjected to a hysterectomy. Unaware of their rights, incognizant of jargon, intimidated by the unfamiliar air of fear and atmosphere of ether that so many of us find oppressive in the confines even of the most attractive and expensive medical facilities, they have signed their names to documents they could not read and which nobody, in the hectic situation that prevails so often in those overcrowded hospitals that serve the urban poor, had even bothered to explain.

15   Childbirth might seem to be the last inalienable right of any female citizen within a civilized society. Illiterate mothers, as we shall see, already have been cheated of the power to protect their progeny against the likelihood of demolition in deficient public schools and, as a result, against the verbal servitude within which they themselves exist. Surgical denial of the right to bear that child in the first place represents an ultimate denial, an unspeakable metaphor, a final darkness that denies even the twilight gleamings of our own humanity. What greater violation of our biological,

our biblical, our spiritual humanity could possibly exist than that which takes place nightly, perhaps hourly these days, within such overburdened and benighted institutions as the Boston City Hospital? Illiteracy has many costs; few are so irreversible as this.

Even the roof above one's head, the gas or other fuel for heating that 16 protects the residents of northern city slums against the threat of illness in the winter months become uncertain guarantees. Illiterates cannot read the lease that they must sign to live in an apartment which, too often, they cannot afford. They cannot manage check accounts and therefore seldom pay for anything by mail. Hours and entire days of difficult travel (and the cost of bus or other public transit) must be added to the real cost of whatever they consume. Loss of interest on the check accounts they do not have, and could not manage if they did, must be regarded as another of the excess costs paid by the citizen who is excluded from the common instruments of commerce in a numerate society.

"I couldn't understand the bills," a woman in Washington, D.C., re- 17 ports, "and then I couldn't write the checks to pay them. We signed things we didn't know what they were."

Illiterates cannot read the notices that they receive from welfare offices 18 or from the IRS. They must depend on word-of-mouth instruction from the welfare worker—or from other persons whom they have good reason to mistrust. They do not know what rights they have, what deadlines and requirements they face, what options they might choose to exercise. They are half-citizens. Their rights exist in print but not in fact.

Illiterates cannot look up numbers in a telephone directory. Even if 19 they can find the names of friends, few possess the sorting skills to make use of the yellow pages; categories are bewildering and trade names are beyond decoding capabilities for millions of nonreaders. Even the emergency numbers listed on the first page of the phone book—"Ambulance," "Police," and "Fire"—are too frequently beyond the recognition of nonreaders.

Many illiterates cannot read the admonition on a pack of cigarettes. 20 Neither the Surgeon General's warning nor its reproduction on the package can alert them to the risks. Although most people learn by word of mouth that smoking is related to a number of grave physical disorders, they do not get the chance to read the detailed stories which can document this danger with the vividness that turns concern into determination to resist. They can see the handsome cowboy or the slim Virginia lady lighting up a filter cigarette; they cannot heed the words that tell them that this product is (not "may be") dangerous to their health. Sixty million men and women are condemned to be the unalerted, high-risk candidates for cancer.

Illiterates do not buy "no-name" products in the supermarkets. They 21 must depend on photographs or the familiar logos that are printed on the packages of brand-name groceries. The poorest people, therefore, are denied the benefits of the least costly products.

22   Illiterates depend almost entirely upon label recognition. Many labels, however, are not easy to distinguish. Dozens of different kinds of Campbell's soup appear identical to the nonreader. The purchaser who cannot read and does not dare to ask for help, out of the fear of being stigmatized (a fear which is unfortunately realistic), frequently comes home with something which she never wanted and her family never tasted.

23   Illiterates cannot read instructions on a pack of frozen food. Packages sometimes provide an illustration to explain the cooking preparations; but illustrations are of little help to someone who must "boil water, drop the food—*within* its plastic wrapper—in the boiling water, wait for it to simmer, instantly remove."

24   Even when labels are seemingly clear, they may be easily mistaken. A woman in Detroit brought home a gallon of Crisco for her children's dinner. She thought that she had bought the chicken that was pictured on the label. She had enough Crisco now to last a year—but no more money to go back and buy the food for dinner.

25   Recipes provided on the packages of certain staples sometimes tempt a semiliterate person to prepare a meal her children have not tasted. The longing to vary the uniform and often starchy content of low-budget meals provided to the family that relies on food stamps commonly leads to ruinous results. Scarce funds have been wasted and the food must be thrown out. The same applies to distribution of food-surplus produce in emergency conditions. Government inducements to poor people to "explore the ways" by which to make a tasty meal from tasteless noodles, surplus cheese, and powdered milk are useless to nonreaders. Intended as benevolent advice, such recommendations mock reality and foster deeper feelings of resentment and of inability to cope. (Those, on the other hand, who cautiously refrain from "innovative" recipes in preparation of their children's meals must suffer the opprobrium of "laziness," "lack of imagination" . . .)

26   Illiterates cannot travel freely. When they attempt to do so, they encounter risks that few of us can dream of. They cannot read traffic signs and, while they often learn to recognize and to decipher symbols, they cannot manage street names which they haven't seen before. The same is true for bus and subway stops. While ingenuity can sometimes help a man or woman to discern directions from familiar landmarks, buildings, cemeteries, churches, and the like, most illiterates are virtually immobilized. They seldom wander past the streets and neighborhoods they know. Geographical paralysis becomes a bitter metaphor for their entire existence. They are immobilized in almost every sense we can imagine. They can't move up. They can't move out. They cannot see beyond. Illiterates may take an oral test for drivers' permits in most sections of America. It is a questionable concession. Where will they go? How will they get there? How will they get home? Could it be that some of us might like it better if they stayed where they belong?

Travel is only one of many instances of circumscribed existence.   27
Choice, in almost all of its facets, is diminished in the life of an illiterate
adult. Even the printed TV schedule, which provides most people with
the luxury of preselection, does not belong within the arsenal of options
in illiterate existence. One consequence is that the viewer watches only
what appears at moments when he happens to have time to turn the
switch. Another consequence, a lot more common, is that the TV set remains in operation night and day. Whatever the program offered at the
hour when he walks into the room will be the nutriment that he accepts
and swallows. Thus, to passivity, is added frequency—indeed, almost uninterrupted continuity. Freedom to select is no more possible here than in
the choice of home or surgery or food.

"You don't choose," said one illiterate woman. "You take your wishes   28
from somebody else." Whether in perusal of a menu, selection of highways,
purchase of groceries, or determination of affordable enjoyment, illiterate
Americans must trust somebody else: a friend, a relative, a stranger on the
street, a grocery clerk, a TV copywriter.

"All of our mail we get, it's hard for her to read. Settin' down and   29
writing a letter, she can't do it. Like if we get a bill . . . we take it over to my
sister-in-law . . . My sister-in-law reads it."

Billing agencies harass poor people for the payment of the bills for   30
purchases that might have taken place six months before. Utility companies offer an agreement for a staggered payment schedule on a bill past
due. "You have to trust them," one man said. Precisely for this reason, you
end up by trusting no one and suspecting everyone of possible deceit. A
submerged sense of distrust becomes the corollary to a constant need to
trust. "They are cheating me . . . I have been tricked . . . I do not know . . ."

Not knowing: This is a familiar theme. Not knowing the right word   31
for the right thing at the right time is one form of subjugation. Not knowing the world that lies concealed behind those words is a more terrifying
feeling. The longitude and latitude of one's existence are beyond all easy
apprehension. Even the hard, cold stars within the firmament above one's
head begin to mock the possibilities for self-location. Where am I? Where
did I come from? Where will I go?

"I've lost a lot of jobs," one man explains. "Today, even if you're a   32
janitor, there's still reading and writing . . . They leave a note saying, 'Go
to room so-and-so . . .' You can't do it. You can't read it. You don't know."

"The hardest thing about it is that I've been places where I didn't   33
know where I was. You don't know where you are . . . You're lost."

"Like I said: I have two kids. What do I do if one of my kids starts   34
choking? I go running to the phone . . . I can't look up the hospital phone
number. That's if we're at home. Out on the street, I can't read the sign. I
get to a pay phone. 'Okay, tell us where you are. We'll send an ambulance.'
I look at the street sign. Right there, I can't tell you what it says. I'd have to

spell it out, letter for letter. By that time, one of my kids would be dead . . . These are the kinds of fears you go with, every single day . . ."

35   "Reading directions, I suffer with. I work with chemicals . . . That's scary to begin with . . ."

36   "You sit down. They throw the menu in front of you. Where do you go from there? Nine times out of ten you say, 'Go ahead. Pick out something for the both of us.' I've eaten some weird things, let me tell you!"

37   Menus. Chemicals. A child choking while his mother searches for a word she does not know to find assistance that will come too late. Another mother speaks about the inability to help her kids to read: "I can't read to them. Of course that's leaving them out of something they should have. Oh, it matters. You *believe* it matters! I ordered all these books. The kids belong to a book club. Donny wanted me to read a book to him. I told Donny: 'I can't read.' He said: 'Mommy, you sit down. I'll read it to you.' I tried it one day, reading from the pictures. Donny looked at me. He said, 'Mommy, that's not right.' He's only five. He knew I couldn't read . . ."

38   A landlord tells a woman that her lease allows him to evict her if her baby cries and causes inconvenience to her neighbors. The consequence of challenging his words conveys a danger which appears, unlikely as it seems, even more alarming than the danger of eviction. Once she admits that she can't read, in the desire to maneuver for the time in which to call a friend, she will have defined herself in terms of an explicit impotence that she cannot endure. Capitulation in this case is preferable to self-humiliation. Resisting the definition of oneself in terms of what one cannot do, what others take for granted, represents a need so great that other imperatives (even one so urgent as the need to keep one's home in winter's cold) evaporate and fall away in face of fear. Even the loss of home and shelter, in this case, is not so terrifying as the loss of self.

39   "I come out of school. I was sixteen. They had their meetings. The directors meet. They said that I was wasting their school paper. I was wasting pencils . . ."

40   Another illiterate, looking back, believes she was not worthy of her teacher's time. She believes that it was wrong of her to take up space within her school. She believes that it was right to leave in order that somebody more deserving could receive her place.

41   Children choke. Their mother chokes another way: on more than chicken bones.

42   People eat what others order, know what others tell them, struggle not to see themselves as they believe the world perceives them. A man in California speaks about his own loss of identity, of self-location, definition:

43   "I stood at the bottom of the ramp. My car had broke down on the freeway. There was a phone. I asked for the police. They was nice. They said to tell them where I was. I looked up at the signs. There was one that I had seen before. I read it to them: ONE WAY STREET. They thought it was a joke. I told them I couldn't read. There was other signs above the ramp.

They told me to try. I looked around for somebody to help. All the cars was going by real fast. I couldn't make them understand that I was lost. The cop was nice. He told me: 'Try once more.' I did my best. I couldn't read. I only knew the sign above my head. The cop was trying to be nice. He knew that I was trapped. 'I can't send out a car to you if you can't tell me where you are.' I felt afraid. I nearly cried. I'm forty-eight years old. I only said: 'I'm on a one-way street . . .'"

Perhaps we might slow down a moment here and look at the realities described above. This is the nation that we live in. This is a society that most of us did not create but which our President and other leaders have been willing to sustain by virtue of malign neglect. Do we possess the character and courage to address a problem which so many nations, poorer than our own, have found it natural to correct? 44

The answers to these questions represent a reasonable test of our belief in the democracy to which we have been asked in public school to swear allegiance. 45

Content

1. In earlier eras, explanations for illiteracy often implied considerable blame for the victims—they were seen as stupid, lazy, shiftless, imprudent, living only for the day but with no concern for the future. To what extent do these explanations confuse the effects of illiteracy with the causes? In what ways does Kozol's essay refute these stereotypes? In his opinion, who's to blame?

2. How does Kozol's chapter illustrate his assertion that 60 million illiterates in America are "denied significant participation" in the government "of those two thirds whose wealth, skin color, or parental privilege allows them the opportunity to profit from the provocation and instruction of the written word" (¶ 6)? What's provocative about literacy?

Strategies/Structures/Language

3. Why does Kozol begin his chapter on the costs of illiteracy with the warning on a can of Drāno (a caustic chemical to unclog drains)? Why doesn't he say anything more about it—or about a great many of his other examples? To what extent can these (or any) examples be counted on to speak for themselves?

4. Kozol constructs his argument by using a myriad of examples of the effects of illiteracy. What determines the order of the examples? Which are the most memorable? Where in this chapter do they appear?

5. Why does Kozol use so many direct quotations from the illiterate people whose experiences he cites as examples?

For Writing

6. "Questions of literacy, in Socrates' belief, must at length be judged as matters of morality" (¶ 3). Write an essay in which you explain the connection between literacy

and a moral society (and the converse, illiteracy and an immoral society), either for an audience you expect to agree with you or for readers who will disagree.

7. In the concluding vignette of the man unable to read the road signs to guide the police to his disabled car on the freeway (¶s 42–43), Kozol implicitly equates literacy with a sense of self-identity, self-location, self-definition. Write an essay exploring the question, How does being literate enable one to realize one's full human potential? When you're thinking about this, imagine what your life would be like if you couldn't read, write, or do math.

 For comprehension, writing, and research activities and resources, please visit the companion website at <college.hmco.com/english>.

STEPHANIE COONTZ

Coontz (born 1944) was educated at the University of California, Berkeley (BA, 1966), and the University of Washington (MA, 1970). A faculty member since 1975 at Evergreen State College in Olympia, Washington, her research in history and women's studies coalesces in work intended to correct misconceptions about American families. Her influential research includes *The Way We Never Were: American Families and the Nostalgia Trap* (1992) and *The Way We Really Are: Coming to Terms with America's Changing Families* (1997), and *Marriage: A History* (2005). Coontz is critical of the nostalgia that she sees as "very tempting to political and economic elitists who would like to avoid grappling with new demographic challenges. My favorite example," she told an interviewer, "is when people get nostalgic about the way elders were cared for in the past. Well, good Lord! Elders were the poorest, most abused sector of the population until the advent of Social Security."

The mythical American family, autonomous and independent, lives in legends from the early Puritans to the midwestern homesteaders to the rugged ranchers who "tamed" the Wild West. But people confuse the effect with the cause; the mythological characteristics of hard work and self-reliance are at odds with the facts—that the American family actually succeeded only with considerable outside help, particularly through federal policies. "Blaming the Family for Economic Decline" is an excerpt from Chapter 7, "Looking for Someone to Blame: Families and Economic Change," in *The Way We Really Are*. Here Coontz examines the popular and media confusion of the relationship between "poverty and single parenthood."

Blaming the Family for Economic Decline

T he fallback position for those in denial about the socioeconomic   1
transformation we are experiencing is to admit that many families
are in economic stress but to blame their plight on divorce and unwed
motherhood. Lawrence Mead of New York University argues that economic inequalities stemming from differences in wages and employment
patterns "are now trivial in comparison to those stemming from family
structure." David Blankenhorn claims that the "primary fault line" dividing privileged and nonprivileged Americans is no longer "race, religion,
class, education, or gender" but family structure. Every major newspaper
in the country has published editorials and opinion pieces along these
lines. This "new consensus" produces a delightfully simple, inexpensive
solution to the economic ills of America's families. From Republican Dan
Quayle to the Democratic Party's Progressive Policy Institute, we hear the
same words: "Marriage is the best anti-poverty program for children."

Now I am as horrified as anyone by irresponsible parents who yield   2
to the temptations of our winner-take-all society and abandon their family obligations. But we are kidding ourselves if we think the solution to
the economic difficulties of America's children lies in getting their parents
back together. Single-parent families, it is true, are five to six times more
likely to be poor than two-parent ones. But correlations are not the same
as causes. The association between poverty and single parenthood has
several different sources, suggesting that the battle to end child poverty
needs to be fought on a number of different fronts.

One reason that single-parent families are more liable to be poor than   3
two-parent families is because falling real wages have made it increasingly
difficult for one earner to support a family. More than one-third of all *two-
parent* families with children would be poor if both parents didn't work. In
this case, the higher poverty rates of one-parent families are not caused by
divorce or unwed motherhood per se but by the growing need for more
than one income per household. Thus a good part of the gap between two-
parent and one-parent families, which is much higher today than it was in
the past, is the consequence rather than the cause of economic decline.

Another reason that one-parent families are likely to be poor is be-   4
cause the vast majority of single-parent heads of household are women,
who continue to be paid far less than men. One study conducted during the
highest period of divorce rates found that if women were paid the same as
similarly qualified men, the number of poor families would be cut in half.

Many single-parent families fall into poverty, at least temporarily,   5
because of unfair property divisions or inadequate enforcement of child
support after a divorce. Although the figures were exaggerated in past

How many evidences of poverty can you find in this family portrait? What might be its causes? What would photographer Walker Evans's aims be in taking and publishing such a picture? Compare and contrast this with a favorite photograph of your own family.

studies, the fact remains that women, especially women with children, usually lose income after a divorce. The most recent data show a 27 percent drop in women's standard of living in the first year after divorce and a 10 percent increase in that of men. In 1995, only 56 percent of custodial mothers were awarded child support, and only half of these received the full amount they were due.

6   In these examples, the solution to poverty in single-parent families does not lie in getting parents back together again but in raising real wages, equalizing the pay of men and women, and making child support and maintenance provisions more fair. In many cases, though, parents who don't earn enough to support two households *could* adequately support one. In such circumstances, it may be technically correct to say that marriage is the solution to child poverty. But even here, things are not always so simple.

7   Sometimes, for example, the causal arrow points in the opposite direction. Poor parents are twice as likely to divorce as more affluent ones, and job loss also increases divorce even among nonpoor families. Sociologist Scott South calculates that every time the unemployment rate rises by 1 percent, approximately 10,000 extra divorces occur. Jobless individuals are two to three times less likely to marry in the first place. And regardless

of their individual values or personal characteristics, teens who live in areas of high unemployment and inferior schools are five to seven times more likely to become unwed parents than more fortunately situated teens.

In the majority of cases, it is poverty and social deprivation that   8 cause unwed motherhood, not the other way around. The fall in real wages and employment prospects for youth after 1970 *preceded* the rise in teen childbearing, which started after 1975 and accelerated in the 1980s. Indeed, reports researcher Mike Males, "the correlation between child-hood poverty and later teenage childbearing is so strong that during the 1969–1993 period, the teen birth rate could be calculated with 90 percent accuracy from the previous decade's child poverty rate." According to a two-year study conducted by the Alan Guttmacher Institute, 38 percent of America's 15- to 19-year-old youths were poor in 1994. But of the one in forty teens who became an unwed parent, 85 percent were poor.

Of course causal relationships seldom flow entirely in one direction.   9 Single parenthood can worsen poverty, educational failure, and low earn-ings capacity, creating a downward spiral. And I certainly wouldn't deny that values regarding marriage have changed, so that more men and women refuse to get married than in the past. But it's also true, as one poverty researcher has put it, that "almost no one volunteers for roles and duties they cannot fulfill." The fact is that fewer and fewer young men from low-income communities can *afford* to get married, or can be regarded by women as suitable marriage partners.

Today the real wages of a young male high school graduate are lower   10 than those earned by a comparable worker back in 1963. Between 1972 and 1994 the percentage of men aged 25 to 34 with incomes *below* the poverty level for a family of four increased from 14 percent to 32 percent. When you realize that almost a third of all young men do not earn more than $15,141 a year, which is the figure defined as poverty level for a family of four in 1994, it's easier to understand why many young men are not rush-ing to get married, and why many young women don't bother to pursue them. By 1993, nearly half the African-American and Latino men aged 25 to 34 did not earn enough to support a family of four.

For African-American families in particular, the notion that family   11 structure has replaced class and race as the main cause of poverty is absurd. The head of the U.S. Census Department Bureau of Marriage and Family Statistics estimates that at least one-half to three-fourths—perhaps more—of the black–white differential in childhood poverty would remain even if *all* children in African-American families had two parents present in the home. Nor do other family and cultural variations explain the high rates of African-American poverty: Youth poverty rates for African Americans have grown steadily over a period during which black teenage birth rates have dropped and high school graduation rates and test scores have risen.

The most recent and thorough review of the research on the links   12 between poverty and family structure was issued by the Tufts University

Center on Hunger, Poverty and Nutrition in 1995. After reviewing seventy-three separate scholarly studies of the subject, the researchers concluded that "single-parent families are not a primary cause of the overall growth of poverty." Rather, poverty is increasing because of declines in employment, wages, and job training opportunities—"far-reaching changes in the economy . . . which hurt both poor and non-poor Americans." Most poverty, in other words, comes from our changing earnings structure, not our changing family structure.

13   Obviously, single parenthood and family instability intensify pre-existing financial insecurity, throwing some people into economic distress and increasing the magnitude of poverty for those already impoverished. And equally obviously, those exceptional individuals who can construct a stable two-parent family in the absence of a stable community or a stable job will usually benefit from doing so. But marriage will not resolve this crisis of child well-being in our country. According to Donald Hernandez, chief of the U.S. Census Department Bureau of Marriage and Family Statistics, even if we could reunite every child in America with both biological parents—and any look at abuse statistics tells you that's certainly not in the best interest of every child—two-thirds of the children who are poor today would *still* be poor.

Content

1. "Most poverty," says Coontz, "comes from our changing earnings structure, not our changing family structure" (¶ 12), as people commonly believe. What kinds of evidence does Coontz provide to support her argument that the causes of family poverty are misunderstood and confused with the effects? Is her evidence convincing?

2. On what basis does Coontz dispute the claim that marriage is "'the best anti-poverty program for children'" (¶ 1)? She argues, "The association between poverty and single parenthood has several different sources, suggesting that the battle to end child poverty needs to be fought on a number of different fronts" (¶ 2). What are these fronts (see ¶ 6)?

3. What does Coontz suggest as appropriate remedies for the problems she identifies?

4. Which groups are responsible for the continued misunderstanding of the causes of poverty in families? Which groups are attempting to redress this misunderstanding—and what are they doing to make changes? In what ways has this essay affected your thinking about the relationship between cause and effect?

Strategies/Structures/Language

5. At what point(s) does Coontz insert herself into her discussion? In what roles does she appear (expert authority, public citizen, private person of humanitarian views, other)? Explain how and why her presence either contributes to, or detracts from, the effectiveness of her argument.

6. Identify some of the places where Coontz uses figures and statistics, and show how these reinforce her point. Why don't these (or any) numbers speak for themselves? What sorts of analyses does the author need in order to give the numbers an eloquent voice?

7. That "correlations are not the same as causes" (¶ 2) is an axiom of logic and of social science. What does this concept mean, and why is it so important? (For clues, see ¶s 3 and 8.)

For Writing

8. The causes of poverty in families may change over time and nationality, but it is a problem that continues to plague many societies. Consider the causes and solutions Jonathan Swift outlines in his "A Modest Proposal" (497–503) and write an essay that discusses the similarities and differences between the causes of the poverty Swift identifies and the causes of the poverty with which Coontz is concerned. If you have firsthand knowledge of a particular family or community in which these problems are present, draw on this to illustrate your analysis.

9. As Coontz's essays illustrate, much of the confusion surrounding complex social problems results from a lack of the type of solid evidence she provides in her essay. Identify a commonly misunderstood social problem (such as hate crimes, the causes of illiteracy, or welfare reform) and, with classmates, research additional facets of that problem. Finally, present your findings to your classmates in either an oral or a written report that explains both the misconceptions surrounding the problem and the real causes you have identified through your research.

 For comprehension, writing, and research activities and resources, please visit the companion website at <college.hmco.com/english>.

ATUL GAWANDE

Gawande (born 1965) earned an MA in politics, philosophy, and economics from Oxford in 1989. From Harvard Medical School he earned an MD in 1995 and a Master's in Public Health in 1999. He holds a joint appointment at both schools, in surgery and in health policy, and is a surgeon at Brigham and Women's Hospital in Boston and a staff writer for *The New Yorker*. His collection of essays, *Complications: A Surgeon's Notes on an Imperfect Science* (2002), performs "exploratory surgery on medicine itself, laying bare a science not in its idealized form but as it actually is—complicated, perplexing, profoundly human." Gawande takes readers into dramatic territory, the operating room, "where science is ambiguous, information is limited, the stakes are high, yet decisions must be made."

In "The Cancer-Cluster Myth," which originally appeared in *The New Yorker* (1999), Gawande considers the social implications of cancer-clusters—"communities in which there seems to be an unusual number of cancers"—whose residents suspect environmental factors in the water, soil, or air. However, identifying such environmental causes can be difficult because of the multitude of possible variables, including the length of the victim's exposure to the carcinogen. The costs are high, and the rate of success is nearly zero. Because people, as Gawande says, "have a deep-seated tendency to see meaning in the ordinary [random] variations that are bound to appear in small samples," the communities afflicted become frustrated and suspicious when correlations between, for example, cancer deaths and environmental conditions don't lead to the discovery of the causes.

The Cancer-Cluster Myth

1   Is it something in the water? During the past two decades, reports of cancer clusters—communities in which there seems to be an unusual number of cancers—have soared. The place-names and the suspects vary, but the basic story is nearly always the same. The Central Valley farming town of McFarland, California, came to national attention in the eighties after a woman whose child was found to have cancer learned of four other children with cancer in just a few blocks around her home. Soon doctors identified six more cases in the town, which had a population of 6,400. The childhood-cancer rate proved to be four times as high as expected. Suspicion fell on groundwater wells that had been contaminated by pesticides, and lawsuits were filed against six chemical companies.

2   In 1990, in Los Alamos, New Mexico, a local artist learned of seven cases of brain cancer among residents of a small section of the town's Western Area. How could seven cases of brain cancer in one neighborhood be merely a coincidence? "I think there is something seriously wrong with the Western Area," the artist, Tyler Mercier, told the *Times*. "The neighborhood may be contaminated." In fact, the Los Alamos National Laboratory, which was the birthplace of the atomic bomb, had once dumped millions of gallons of radioactive and toxic waste in the surrounding desert, without providing any solid documentation about precisely what was dumped or where. In San Ramon, California, a cluster of brain cancers was discovered at a high-school class reunion. On Long Island, federal, state, and local officials are currently spending $21 million to try to find out why towns like West Islip and Levittown have elevated rates of breast cancer.

3   I myself live in a cancer cluster. A resident in my town—Newton, Massachusetts—became suspicious of a decades-old dump next to an elementary school after her son developed cancer. She went from door to door and turned up forty-two cases of cancer within a few blocks of her home. The cluster is being investigated by the state health department.

4   No doubt, one reason for the veritable cluster of cancer clusters in recent years is the widespread attention that cases like those in McFarland and Los Alamos received, and the ensuing increase in public awareness and concern. Another reason, though, is the way in which states have

responded to that concern: they've made available to the public data on potential toxic sites, along with information from "cancer registries" about local cancer rates. The result has been to make it easier for people to find worrisome patterns, and, more and more, they've done so. In the late eighties, public-health departments were receiving between 1,300 and 1,600 reports of feared cancer clusters, or "cluster alarms," each year. Last year, in Massachusetts alone, the state health department responded to between 3,000 and 4,000 cluster alarms. Under public pressure, state and federal agencies throughout the country are engaging in "cancer mapping" to find clusters that nobody has yet reported.

A community that is afflicted with an unusual number of cancers quite   5 naturally looks for a cause in the environment—in the ground, the water, the air. And correlations are sometimes found: the cluster may arise after, say, contamination of the water supply by a possible carcinogen. The problem is that when scientists have tried to confirm such causes, they haven't been able to. Raymond Richard Neutra, California's chief environmental health investigator and an expert on cancer clusters, points out that among hundreds of exhaustive, published investigations of residential clusters in the United States, not one has convincingly identified an underlying environmental cause. Abroad, in only a handful of cases has a neighborhood cancer cluster been shown to arise from an environmental cause. And only one of these cases ended with the discovery of an unrecognized carcinogen. It was in a Turkish village called Karain, where twenty-five cases of mesothelioma, a rare form of lung cancer, cropped up among fewer than eight hundred villagers. (Scientists traced the cancer to a mineral called erionite, which is abundant in the soil there.) Given the exceedingly poor success rate of such investigations, epidemiologists tend to be skeptical about their worth.

When public-health investigators fail to turn up any explanation for the   6 appearance of a cancer cluster, communities can find it frustrating, even suspicious. After all, these investigators are highly efficient in tracking down the causes of other kinds of disease clusters. "Outbreak" stories usually start the same way: someone has an intuition that there are just too many people coming down with some illness and asks the health department to investigate. With outbreaks, though, such intuitions are vindicated in case after case. Consider the cluster of American Legionnaires who came down with an unusual lung disease in Philadelphia in 1976; the startling number of limb deformities among children born to Japanese women in the sixties; and the appearance of rare *Pneumocystis carinii* pneumonia in five young homosexual men in Los Angeles in 1981. All these clusters prompted what are called "hot-pursuit investigations" by public-health authorities, and all resulted in the definitive identification of a cause: namely, *Legionella* pneumonitis, or Legionnaires' disease; mercury poisoning from contaminated fish; and HIV infection. In fact, successful hot-pursuit investigations of disease clusters take place almost every day. A typical recent issue of the Centers for Disease Control's *Morbidity and Mortality Weekly Report* described a cluster of six patients who developed muscle pain after eating fried fish. Investigation by health authorities identified the condition as Haff disease, which is caused by a toxin sometimes present in buffalo fish. Four of the cases were traced to a single Louisiana wholesaler, whose suppliers fished the same tributaries of the Mississippi River.

7   What's more, for centuries scientists have succeeded in tracking down the causes of clusters of cancers that aren't residential. In 1775 the surgeon Percivall Pott discovered a cluster of scrotal-cancer cases among London chimney sweeps. It was common practice then for young boys to do their job naked, the better to slither down chimneys, and so high concentrations of carcinogenic coal dust would accumulate in the ridges of their scrota. Pott's chimney sweeps proved to be a classic example of an "occupational" cluster. Scientists have also been successful in investigating so-called medical clusters. In the late 1960s, for example, the pathologist Arthur Herbst was surprised to come across eight women between the ages of fifteen and twenty-two who had clear-cell adenocarcinoma, a type of cervical cancer that had never been seen in women so young. In 1971 he published a study linking the cases to an anti-miscarriage drug called diethylstilbestrol, or DES, which the mothers of these women had taken during pregnancy. Subsequent studies confirmed the link with DES, which was taken by some 5 million pregnant women between 1938 and 1971. The investigation of medical and occupational cancer clusters has led to the discovery of dozens of carcinogens, including asbestos, vinyl chloride, and certain artificial dyes.

8   So why don't hot-pursuit investigations of neighborhood cancer clusters yield such successes? For one thing, many clusters fall apart simply because they violate basic rules of cancer behavior. Cancer develops when a cell starts multiplying out of control, and the process by which this happens isn't straightforward. A carcinogen doesn't just flip some cancer switch to "on." Cells have a variety of genes that keep them functioning normally, and it takes an almost chance combination of successive mutations in these genes—multiple "hits," as cancer biologists put it—to make a cell cancerous rather than simply killing it. A carcinogen provides one hit. Other hits may come from a genetic defect, a further environmental exposure, a spontaneous mutation. Even when people have been subjected to a heavy dose of a carcinogen and many cells have been damaged, they will not all get cancer. (For example, DES causes clear-cell adenocarcinoma in only one out of a thousand women exposed to it in utero.) As a rule, it takes a long time before a cell receives enough hits to produce the cancer, and so, unlike infections or acute toxic reactions, the effect of a carcinogen in a community won't be seen for years. Besides, in a mobile society like ours, cancer victims who seem to be clustered may not all have lived in an area long enough for their cancers to have a common cause.

9   To produce a cancer cluster, a carcinogen has to hit a great many cells in a great many people. A brief, low-level exposure to a carcinogen is

unlikely to do the job. Raymond Richard Neutra has calculated that for a carcinogen to produce a sevenfold increase in the occurrence of a cancer (a rate of increase not considered particularly high by epidemiologists) a population would have to be exposed to 70 percent of the maximum tolerated dose in the course of a full year, or the equivalent. "This kind of exposure is credible as part of chemotherapy or in some work settings," he wrote in a 1990 paper, "but it must be very rare for most neighborhood and school settings." For that reason, investigations of occupational cancer clusters have been vastly more successful than investigations of residential cancer clusters.

Matters are further complicated by the fact that cancer isn't one dis-   10 ease. What turns a breast cell into breast cancer isn't what turns a white blood cell into leukemia: the precise combination of hits varies. Yet some clusters lump together people with tumors that have entirely different biologies and are unlikely to have the same cause. The cluster in McFarland, for example, involved eleven children with nine kinds of cancer. Some of the brain-cancer cases in the Los Alamos cluster were really cancers of other organs that had metastasized to the brain.

If true neighborhood clusters—that is, local clusters arising from a com-   11 mon environmental cause—are so rare, why do we see so many? In a sense, we're programmed to: nearly all of them are the result of almost irresistible errors in perception. In a pioneering article published in 1971, the cognitive psychologists Daniel Kahneman and Amos Tversky identified a systematic error in human judgment, which they called the Belief in the Law of Small Numbers. People assume that the pattern of a large population will be replicated in all its subsets. But clusters will occur simply through chance. After seeing a long sequence of red on the roulette wheel, people find it hard to resist the idea that black is "due"—or else they start to wonder whether the wheel is rigged. We assume that a sequence of R-R-R-R-R-R is somehow less random than, say, R-R-B-R-B-B. But the two sequences are equally likely. (Casinos make a lot of money from the Belief in the Law of Small Numbers.) Truly random patterns often don't appear random to us. The statistician William Feller studied one classic example. During the Germans' intensive bombing of South London in the Second World War, a few areas were hit several times and others were not hit at all. The places that were not hit seemed to have been deliberately spared, and, Kahneman says, people became convinced that those places were where the Germans had their spies. When Feller analyzed the statistics of the bomb hits, however, he found that the distribution matched a random pattern.

Daniel Kahneman himself was involved in a similar case. "During   12 the Yom Kippur War, in 1973, I was approached by people in the Israeli Air Force," he told me. "They had two squads that had left base, and when the squads came back one had lost four planes and the other had lost none. They wanted to investigate for all kinds of differences between the squadrons, like whether pilots in one squadron had seen their wives more than in the other. I told them to stop wasting their time." A difference of four lost planes could easily have occurred by chance. Yet Kahneman knew that if Air Force officials investigated they would inevitably find some measurable differences between the squadrons and feel compelled to act on them.

13   Human beings evidently have a deep-seated tendency to see meaning in the ordinary variations that are bound to appear in small samples. For example, most basketball players and fans believe that players have hot and cold streaks in shooting. In a paper entitled "The Hot Hand in Basketball," Tversky and two colleagues painstakingly analyzed the shooting of individual players in more than eighty games played by the Philadelphia 76ers, the New Jersey Nets, and the New York Knicks during the 1980–1981 season. It turned out that basketball players—even notorious "streak shooters"—have no more runs of hits or misses than would be expected by chance. Because of the human tendency to perceive clusters in random sequences, however, Tversky and his colleagues found that "no amount of exposure to such sequences will convince the player, the coach, or the fan that the sequences are in fact random. The more basketball one watches and plays, the more opportunities one has to observe what appears to be streak shooting."

14   In epidemiology, the tendency to isolate clusters from their context is known as the Texas sharpshooter fallacy. Like a Texas sharpshooter who shoots at the side of a barn and then draws a bull's-eye around the bullet holes, we tend to notice cases first—four cancer patients on one street—and then define the population base around them. With rare conditions, such as Haff disease or mercury poisoning, even a small clutch of cases really would represent a dramatic excess, no matter how much Texas sharpshooting we did. But most cancers are common enough that noticeable residential clusters are bound to occur. Raymond Richard Neutra points out that given a typical registry of eighty different cancers, you could expect 2,750 of California's 5,000 census tracts to have statistically significant but perfectly random elevations of cancer. So if you check to see whether your neighborhood has an elevated rate of a specific cancer, chances are better than even that it does—and it almost certainly won't mean a thing. Even when you've established a correlation between a specific cancer and a potential carcinogen, scientists have hardly any way to distinguish the "true" cancer cluster that's worth investigating from the crowd of cluster impostors.

15   One helpful tip-off is an extraordinarily high cancer rate. In Karain, Turkey, the incidence of mesothelioma was more than *seven thousand times* as high as expected. In even the most serious cluster alarms that public-health departments have received, however, the cancer rate has been nowhere near that high. (The lawyer Jan Schlichtmann, of *Civil Action* fame, is now representing victims of a cancer cluster in Dover Township, New Jersey, where the childhood-cancer rate is 30 percent higher than expected.)

16   This isn't to say that carcinogens in the local environment can't raise cancer rates; it's just that such increases disappear in all the background

variation that occurs in small populations. In larger populations, it's a different story. The 1986 Chernobyl disaster exposed hundreds of thousands of people to radiation; scientists were able to establish that it caused a more than one-hundredfold increase in thyroid cancer among children years later. By contrast, investigating an isolated neighborhood cancer cluster is almost always a futile exercise. Investigators knock on doors, track down former residents, and check medical records. They sample air, soil, and water. Thousands, sometimes millions, of dollars are spent. And with all those tests, correlations inevitably turn up. Yet, years later, in case after case, nothing definite is confirmed.

"The reality is that they're an absolute, total, and complete waste of tax-   17
payer dollars," says Alan Bender, an epidemiologist with the Minnesota Department of Health, which investigated more than 1,000 cancer clusters in the state between 1984 and 1995. The problem of perception and politics, however, remains. If you're a public-health official, try explaining why a dozen children with cancer in one neighborhood doesn't warrant investigation. According to a national study, health departments have been able to reassure people by education in more than 70 percent of cluster alarms. Somewhere between 1 and 3 percent of alarms, however, result in expensive on-site investigations. And the cases that are investigated aren't even the best-grounded ones: they are the cases pushed by the media, enraged citizens, or politicians. "Look, you can't just kiss people off," Bender says. In fact, Minnesota has built such an effective public-response apparatus that it has not needed to conduct a formal cluster investigation in three years.

Public-health departments aren't lavishly funded, and scientists are   18
reluctant to see money spent on something that has proved to be as unproductive as neighborhood cluster alarms or cancer mapping. Still, public confidence is poorly served by officials who respond to inquiries with a scientific brushoff and a layer of bureaucracy. To be part of a cancer cluster is a frightening thing, and it magnifies our ordinary response when cancer strikes: we want to hold something or someone responsible, even allocate blame. Health officials who understand the fear and anger can have impressive success, as the ones in Minnesota have shown. But there are times when you cannot maintain public trust without acting on public concerns. Science alone won't put to rest questions like the one a McFarland mother posed to the *Los Angeles Times*: "How many more of our children must die before something is done?"

Content

1. What should point investigators toward the "true" cancer clusters worth investigating and enable them to distinguish these "from the crowd of cluster impostors" (¶s 14–15)?

2. Why do the investigators of local cancer clusters so often confuse causes with effects? (Is that the same as confusing correlation with causation?) What does Gawande mean when he says, "Truly random patterns often don't appear random to us" (¶ 11)?

Strategies/Structures/Language

3. Examine Gawande's evidence. From where does he draw the variety of examples he uses to illustrate his points? Has Gawande persuaded you that "investigating an isolated neighborhood cancer cluster is almost always a futile exercise" (¶ 16)? Would you agree with him if you lived "in a cancer cluster," as Gawande himself does (¶ 3)? On what basis would you decide whether the investigation was worth the time and money?

4. What is the "Texas sharpshooter fallacy" (¶ 14)? Explain why it is or is not an effective analogy for the problem Gawande describes.

5. What is a myth? Why has Gawande entitled his piece "The Cancer-Cluster Myth"? Consider the kind of social myths Coontz investigates in "Blaming the Family for Economic Decline" (213–16). In what ways are they similar to the myths Gawande addresses in his work? In what ways are they different?

For Writing

6. Investigate the occurrence of some unusual phenomenon (cancer clusters in your area—this can be a neighborhood, a town, a county, a state) and the ways in which local or state officials (such as the police, social workers, school officials, public health departments) have handled such occurrences. What does your investigation reveal about its possible causes? Have these been addressed adequately by the investigators? Have they taken all of the major effects into account? Is their emphasis in the investigation appropriate? If not, what have they missed that you've discovered?

7. Gawande claims that "public confidence is poorly served by officials who respond to inquiries with a scientific brushoff and a layer of bureaucracy" (¶ 18). How can nonscientists—for instance, the residents of an affected area—deal with local matters of potential life-and-death that depend on both their trust of scientific investigations and the accuracy of these? Write an essay that considers the importance of maintaining public confidence and addressing public concerns when instances of a major social problem or danger appear (see "Institutionalizing Imagination: The Case of Aircraft as Weapons" [559–65], or consider Hurricane Katrina's effects), and offer suggestions for how to accomplish this. Write a letter either to your representative in the state legislature or Congress, in which you analyze the appropriateness of the investigators' response in light of budget constraints, public concern, and other possibilities the investigation might have considered. Send a copy to the editor of your local newspaper.

 For comprehension, writing, and research activities and resources, please visit the companion website at <college.hmco.com/english>.

MEGAN McGUIRE

McGuire was born in 1983, grew up in Connecticut, and earned a BA in English and political science from the University of Connecticut in 2005. A member of the Army National Guard in college, she was commissioned as a Second Lieutenant soon after graduation. But this just scratches the surface.

Of her essay, she writes, "I generally do not reflect that often on my life growing up or how I got to where I am. I'm satisfied with what I've accomplished, who I am, and where I'm headed. I count myself lucky to have lived in two very different kinds of environments while growing up, one of which that was filled with love and support and fulfilled all the stereotypical ideas of childhood. I played outside until the street-lights came on and spent my summers at my grandparents' lake house. The other portion of my late childhood and adolescence was somewhat of a culture shock. Its forced independence created self-sufficiency and responsibility that, although acquired in a less than favorable way, have just as adequately contributed to my general successes in life as the more cushioned existence I experienced earlier. I never intended to record any portions of my life, but as a class assignment I began to do so and was surprised at the flooding of memories that I had almost forgotten. I was also surprised at how liberating it was to put parts of my life on paper. I felt as if I had inadvertently explained myself and who I am, answering some questions I didn't even know I had and revealing even more—a fulfilling experience that I plan to pursue further."

❄ *Wake Up Call*

*I*t was morning. My father just left my room. He had come in, as he came in   1
every morning Monday through Friday, to inform me that it was no longer time
for dreaming, the time had come to wake up and prepare for another monotonous
day at school. Even at the age of ten the ability to wake up early eluded me. I gradually forced my eyes open, first briefly, then for a period of thirty seconds. Each
time I opened my eyes I would stay awake a little longer. I did this every morning,
partially denying that I had to leave the comfort of my warm bed, waiting for my
second warning yell from down the hall that I was going to be late if I didn't wake
up soon. I stared up at the canopy that covered my bed. I had begged for a canopy
bed for years and one summer my father found one at a tag sale for a price we could
afford. I loved that bed. It had a white frame and a royal blue canopy, with a
miniature floral print. There were many times that I greatly desired something,
and although I may have had to wait, I almost always got what I asked for if I
wanted it long enough. Everyone has fleeting wants, but if the need was persistent,
my father always came through.

2   *Along with the bed, I had always wanted a typewriter. As far back as I can remember I loved books. I don't remember learning to read, but I remember sitting on my father's lap while he read one of his big books, following along to the sound of his voice. We made constant trips to the local library; just being around books was exciting. I don't remember struggling to read but I remember the first book I ever read, an early learning book, a "Spot, the Dog" book, and I read it cover to cover. I became an insatiable reader and decided very young that I wanted to be a writer. For my birthday one year I was given an old typewriter, an antique. The keys were the traditional punch keys and I spent a good week figuring out how to insert the paper and not have my words type diagonally across the page. I soon learned that being a writer was not an easy task. First I actually needed to have something to write about and second, it was very time consuming. I decided, therefore, to enjoy my love of books and revisit the profession of writing at a later date, when I had something of significance to say.*

3   *School allowed an outlet for my desire to write by providing me topics to write about so I didn't have to think them up on my own. I enjoyed school but could never figure out why it required being up so early in the morning. It was a struggle, to be sure. This particular morning was no different. I eventually rolled out of bed. My clothes were still in a laundry basket by the door to my room. Dad was great, but he never seemed to get the hang of putting clothes away. I sifted through until I found something to wear. I chose a pair of jeans with a patch across the knee that my grandmother had sewn on for me and a black t-shirt decorated by yours truly using crafty puff paint, a trend at the time and very cool. I managed to find a pair of somewhat matching socks and donned them as well. I learned to do my own hair very early on. Dad never seemed to master anything beyond a lopsided ponytail and my older sister was far too busy being thirteen to help me, so I quickly braided my long blond hair and stepped off toward the kitchen, wishing I knew how to French-braid so I could have a nice hair-do like my girly classmates. Instead I looked as if I couldn't decide whether or not I wanted to be Barbie or Ken.*

4   *Breakfast consisted of a bowl of cereal which I inhaled quickly. My brother was still in bed. It might have been difficult waking me up for school, but it was impossible to wake up my brother. There was actually a time when he was dragged physically to school by my father and upon arriving he jumped out of the car, ran away, was chased down, caught and physically dragged into the building, kicking and screaming, by not only my father but the principal as well. It was disconcerting at the time and is now merely comical. I kissed Dad goodbye and hurried out of our apartment to the bus stop. My Dad was home when I left for school and I knew he would be home waiting for me at 3:20 when I stepped through the door. We were on state, I wasn't sure at the time what that meant, but I knew it meant Dad didn't have to work and at the grocery store we paid for food with colorful stamps that looked like my play money but apparently had more value. It also meant that during the holidays we went to the town hall and were given presents that were labeled "Girl 8–10" and "Boy 11–12" and we got to meet Santa. I knew we didn't have a lot of money, certainly not like my friend Lauren who lived in a big old colonial house, had a playroom in addition to her own room,*

but I had a canopy bed, a typewriter, and I knew my Dad was always home if I needed him. There was never a day when I wasn't hugged or kissed or told I was loved. I was happy.

It is morning. My alarm clock is blaring in my ear from across the   5
room for the second time. Snooze is a wonderful thing. I'm lucky this
morning, my alarm clock actually works. It is possibly the oldest alarm
clock, most certainly older then I am even at ten. The digital numbers
sometimes fade on and off, but if I am lucky, it will burst to life at the
appointed time in the morning and emit the most horrendous static
sound, eventually forcing me awake. Rolling out of bed is easy, my bed
consists of a mattress on the floor, the box spring adds some elevation to
the mattress and acts as a substitute for a real frame. I sort through a
large brown plastic garbage bag filled with clothes and find something
suitable to wear. I put on a pair of stretchy elastic pants that were purchased at Ames as part of my back to school shopping and an oversized
t-shirt that belonged to my mother. I can't seem to find a pair of socks.
I vaguely remember leaving my laundry in the washing machine overnight. I walk into my older sister's room quietly and softly open her top
drawer and steal a clean pair of socks. I stealthily exit the room and return
to my own.

I share my room with my younger sister. I don't think our room was   6
designed as a bedroom. The stairs lead directly to our room from the bottom
floor and the two actual bedrooms and bathroom branch off our room that
is something akin to a loft. My brother has one of the bedrooms and my
older sister has the other. I hop into the bathroom, hairspray my hair into
some wavelike fashion statement that epitomizes coolness and head downstairs. I spend a good twenty minutes leashing our four dogs up outside
and as a result leave myself no time for breakfast. I head into the kitchen
to see if there is anything quick I can grab and take with me. I try to be
quiet, only a curtain separates my mother's room from the kitchen and I
don't want to wake her up. She must have made it home late last night,
I don't remember hearing her come in. I open the fridge, no milk. I grab a
couple of pieces of bread and head out to the bus.

On the way down the dirt driveway I drag one of the large garbage   7
barrels from the back of the house, Monday, trash day. It tips over when
I snag it on a rock and all the contents spill out into the drive. Fabulous. I
pick up what I can, trying not to get dirty. I stain my shirt. I don't have
time to change and I don't think I have anything else clean to wear. My
brother follows me outside, along with my younger sister. We wait outside the house for the bus. Our house is an old colonial that was moved
from one side of town to its current location at some point in its history. It
was placed on an unstable rocky foundation and as a result has settled
nicely so that all the floors are bowed in one way or another. The paint is
a yellowish color and is excessively chipped, giving the surface a textured

appearance. The house is blocked from sight on one side by large bushes and from the front by a large tree. I am ashamed of our house. It looks dilapidated and old, nothing like the nicely vinyl sided homes on the rest of our street. I am happy there are bushes and trees hiding it from sight.

8   I sit in the back corner of the class. In my other school it was cool to sit in the back, but apparently here the cool kids sit in front. Bad move. Everyone here wears jeans. If I had bought jeans I would have only been allowed to pick one outfit at Ames, so I bought stretch pants so I could have two outfits when school started. I still haven't determined how I am going to alternate what I wear. If I interchange tops with bottoms I still only have four outfits. There are five days in a school week, so I will have to repeat at least once. The other kids will remember what I wear. I want a pair of dark blue jeans like the pretty girl in the front row. She has dark hair in a French-braid, blue jeans and a pretty clean white shirt with ruffles on the collar. Her name is Kate. I know the answers to all the questions the teacher asks but I don't raise my hand. Smart kids are not cool. In my other school they called me Webster. I was like a dictionary. I get put in a remedial math level due to my less than enthusiastic effort but wish I had tried harder, all the cool kids were in advanced math. Tricky, tricky.

9   It is morning. I am freezing. I could swear the cold breeze outside comes right through the drafty closed window of my room. What time is it? My alarm clock didn't go off. I look across the room and the digital numbers are not there. No one is up. If I don't get up, no one gets up. My brother doesn't bother if I don't force him and my little sister relies on the same clock that we share in our room. My older sister doesn't need to get up. Her boyfriend and she sleep until he has to go to work at noon. She feels better now; the morning sickness isn't so bad anymore. I climb out of bed; the floor feels like a sheet of ice against my bare feet. I grab the oversized robe on the floor and put it over my already layered clothing. I flick the light switch and nothing happens. Was there a storm? How come there isn't any power?

10   The bathroom has a little more light; the window is on the one side of the house not smothered by vegetation. I glance in the mirror and notice that there is a black substance crusted under my nose and on my eyelashes. My little sister has it on her nose too. I wash my face off and head downstairs. The kerosene heater is covered in the black substance too; it must be some kind of soot. The TV won't turn on. I still have no idea what time it is. The thermostat is turned all the way down. We must be out of oil again. The living room houses the kerosene heater and is the warmest room in the house. Mom isn't home; she must have left for work already. On the dining room table is my permission slip that is due today. She forgot to sign it. I grab a pen and sign her name as authoritatively as I can, and I realize it doesn't matter since I missed the bus anyway. I go to the bathroom downstairs, the ceramic on the toilet is ice cold so I try to hover over it in the same manner as I would a public bathroom. I try to flush,

the water goes down but nothing replenishes the bowl, this seems somewhat odd. I crank the handle on the sink and the faucet responds with a funny noise and no water comes out.

I pick up the phone and dial Mom at work. At least something works. I'm on hold for about five minutes and she finally picks up. I get yelled at for not being in school. How could I have missed the bus? Does she have to be home to do everything? I'm ten years old, I should be able to wake up and get to school without her holding my hand. Where is Amber? Mom, we have no electricity and no water for some reason and the kerosene heater is broken and we need to go to the store when you get home, there isn't anything to eat. There's plenty to eat, make something, I'll be home around seven.

The fridge has milk and eggs and various condiments. It feels warm and the light doesn't turn on when I open the door. I go into the mudroom to look for something to make. The shelves are lined with jars filled with tomatoes, green beans and mixed vegetables. I remember the Saturday during the summer when Mom showed me how to jar the vegetables from the garden to preserve them. It was fun. I had never jarred vegetables before. Now they were the only things that looked back at me, the jars of vegetables and a box of brownie mix. At ten years old vegetables are still the less appetizing of the two, so I grab the box of brownie mix and head to the kitchen. I forget we have an electric stove. I take a couple of pieces of bread and head to the living room, still no TV.

I put on some clothes and take four dollars of change out of the change jar in my Mom's room. I walk the two miles to Cumberland Farms and buy some cookies and a couple of Airheads, my favorite kind of candy. I pass the library on the way back, situated in the old center of town, next to the police station and the old town hall. No TV, might as well get a book. I take out *The Witch of Blackbird Pond*. I love this book because it mentions the meadows near my house, the great expanse of fields that stretch from Rocky Hill to Wethersfield and through Glastonbury. I love going there when I want to feel alone and put my life into perspective. In the summer I lie in the field and watch the clouds float by.

When I get home everyone is up. I hear Amber yelling. She needs to get out of this place, this is bullshit, she can't wait to move out. She doesn't go to school right now, she'd be a freshman this year. I can't wait until high school. I spend my afternoon reading my book. Mom gets home at about 8:30. She's carrying a Styrofoam to-go container. She stopped at Angellino's for dinner on the way home with a girlfriend from work. The house is dark. I was able to find a candle and it was flickering on the dining room table. She smiles and takes three oil lamps out of a paper bag and sets them on the table. Late one month and they just shut you off. I have a feeling we were late more than just one month but I don't say it. I learn that if you fill the toilet bowl with enough snow it will flush automatically. The pipes must have froze, when the hell is he going to come and fix that damn furnace, I pay way too much for this place. She says this, but I know I haven't seen the oil truck here in weeks. I use a towel and a bowl of water from a bottle to wash up by the light of the oil lamp. Amber and Mom are fighting. How can you go out for dinner? We have no food here, no electricity, no water. The argument continues until Mom slaps her. Amber leaves. I go downstairs and Mom shows me the jeans she bought. I think about the pair I've been industriously saving for every week by cleaning an old lady's house: four floors for $13.50. I wonder how much hers cost.

15   After a certain length of time if a family is without heat or running water the town lets you stay in a hotel for free. The four of us share a room at the Suisse Chalet. I don't know where Amber is. I call it the Sleazy Chalet and everybody laughs. It's nice to watch TV. I haven't seen the Simpsons in four weeks. We stay at the Chalet for a week. Sometimes Mom would work really early and we wouldn't have a ride to school. It is a nice vacation. When we get home on Friday there is a pink notice on our back door. On Monday we are at the Howard Johnson's and our household goods are in storage. It is a much better motel. Bickford's is right at the bottom of the hill so I can walk and get pancakes if I'm hungry. Mike works there and now Amber does too, so I don't have to pay. I start at my new school next week. It's cool because it's the same town my Dad grew up in. He said some of his old teachers are still there. I'll be happy to get back to school. I've missed a lot.

16   It is afternoon. I just walked home from school. There's a pink note on our door. Looks like I'm not graduating here, good thing I didn't order a class ring. I've seen four pink notes since eighth grade, this is nothing new. I'm an expert packer. It's just like Tetris, everything will fit if you do it right. I make sure I leave out everything that I'll need, clothes and schoolbooks. I also throw anything with sentimental value into a bag. So much gets lost.

17   Three weeks I have been living in New Britain. I can't stand it here. I don't like this guy, Mom's friend or not. I'm sleeping on the floor living out of my duffel bag. Amber should be here any minute. She moved back to Connecticut from North Carolina just this week. What a relief. Should I leave a note for Mom? I wonder how long it will take her to notice I'm gone? I'm a coward. I have every reason to leave but I can't force myself to tell her I'm going. I need to get back to school or I won't graduate. What if she cries? What if she tries to make me feel guilty, like I'm abandoning her? She always "tries" so hard for us but it's not enough. I know I can do better on my own. No matter how hard I have to work, I will give myself stability.

18   I missed three weeks of school. Fortunately my new school doesn't know this so I'm still on track to graduate. Mom hasn't called yet. I got a job. Maybe I'll have enough money to buy a car soon. Getting to work is difficult having no transportation other than my own two feet. Location severely limits my job options. My apartment is nice. My job has time and a half on Sunday so if I work every Sunday and at least five nights I'm

hoping I'll be able to save a little. I wake up, go to school, go to work and study into the waning hours of the night. I'm always exhausted, only one more year until college. My grandmother always said that if I wanted to go to college I would have to work hard. Your mother won't help you and your father can't help you so you better study hard and get a scholarship. I study hard. I'm graduating in the top ten of my class but I haven't gotten any scholarships.

It's late. I just got home from work. My feet hurt. I'm 21 years old. I   19 am a full-time student. I have two jobs and I am in the Army National Guard. I've lived on my own since I was 17. I'm always tired and always busy. My apartment is always warm, even if it means working more hours and there is food in my house. Sometimes I sit in my apartment and wonder what my life would be like if Dad hadn't gotten sick and I never moved in with my mother. We didn't have money, but I had a lot. I moved away and learned what it meant to work, what it meant to be hungry and cold, and what the world is really like. I saw what selfishness and bad habits could do. I learned about everything I didn't want to be. Maybe it was the combination of the two worlds. The beginning of my life was filled with love and support and I truly believed I could be anything I wanted to be as long as I worked hard. The latter portion of my adolescence taught me how to work hard. If I was never truly in want of anything would I be as motivated to be so much more than what I came from? I don't resent any part of my life. Everything that was has made me what I am. I'm lucky.

Content

1. McGuire presents examples of good and poor parenting. What are the components of each? Can you infer from her essay the factors that contribute to each parent's "style" of parenting? From the details McGuire presents, is it possible for readers to construct a more sympathetic interpretation of her mother than might initially meet the eye?

2. What kind of personality and character does McGuire have? Is this consistent throughout her childhood? How would you account for her strength of character and purpose?

3. Megan and her older sister appear to be turning out very differently during adolescence. To what extent can this be attributed to the parenting they have experienced? By the end of the narrative, McGuire is clearly headed for professional success and personal happiness. Has she overridden her upbringing, benefited from it, or both?

Strategies/Structures/Language

4. What is the tone of this piece? Is it consistent throughout? Self-pity and self-congratulation generally turn off readers; do you detect any shred of either in this piece? If so, where? If not, why not?

5. Throughout the essay, material objects assume symbolic value: how are readers expected to interpret the canopy bed (¶ 1), the "colorful stamps" (¶ 4), "presents labeled 'Girl 8–10'" (¶ 4), the various items of Megan's clothing (¶s 3, 4, 5, 8) and her mother's new jeans (¶ 8), the "dilapidated" old colonial house (¶ 7), the "pink notice" (¶s 15, 16)?

For Writing

6. This essay implies an ideal of parenting. With a partner, construct the definition of an ideal parent (or father or mother) whose good parenting would produce an ideal child. Identify and explain several characteristics of the ideal, both parent and child.

7. How can people emerge from disastrous upbringing as strong, capable, and powerful adults? Explain, analyzing the example of your own life or that of someone you know, or the life of a public figure, such as Frederick Douglass (109–13), Richard Wright, Sherman Alexie (93–95) and others. You may wish to consult some of the writings on resilience, or positive psychology, by authors such as Martin Seligman and Mihaly Csikszentmihalyi (see, for example, *The American Psychologist,* January 2000 and March 2001 issues).

 For comprehension, writing, and research activities and resources, please visit the companion website at <college.hmco.com/english>.

Additional Topics for Writing
Cause and Effect

(For strategies for writing cause and effect, see 189.)

MULTIPLE STRATEGIES FOR WRITING
CAUSE AND EFFECT

In writing on any of the cause-and-effect topics below, you can employ assorted strategies to help explain either the causes or the effects, and to interpret their consequences:

- *definitions, explanations* of terms, equipment involved in the process
- *illustrations* and *examples:* to show what happens, and in what sequence
- *diagrams, drawings, flow charts, graphs* to clarify and explain
- *logical sequence of interrelated steps or ideas*
- consideration of *short-term* and *long-term consequences* of a particular effect—literal, material, psychological, emotional, economic, ethical, ecological, political or other
- examination of whether there is a *confusion* or *lack of clarity* between cause and effect; sometimes effects are mistaken for causes, and vice versa, or the wrong people or phenomena are credited with or blamed for a particular cause or effect

1. Write an essay, adapted to an audience of your choice, explaining either the causes or the effects of one of the following:

    a. Substance abuse by teenagers, young adults, or another group (see Sanders, "Under the Influence . . . ," 249–59)

    b. America's 50 percent divorce rate (see Hall, "Killing Chickens," 242–45; McGuire, "Wake Up Call," 225–31)

    c. Genetic engineering (see McKibben, "Designer Genes," 413–23)

    d. Teenage pregnancy

    e. The popularity of a given television show, movie or rock star, film, book, or type of book (such as romance, Gothic, Western)

    f. Current taste in clothing, food, cars, architecture, interior decoration

    g. The Civil War, the Great Depression, World War II, the Vietnam War, the attack on the World Trade Center (see the chapter "Terrorism"), or other historical event

    h. The popularity of a particular spectator or active sport

    i. Your personality or temperament

    j. Success in college or in business

    k. Being "born again" or losing one's religious faith

    l. Racial, sexual, or religious discrimination

    m. An increasingly higher proportion of working women (or mothers of young children)

    n. Illiteracy (see Kozol, "The Human Cost . . . ," 204–11)

    o. The American Dream that "if you work hard you're bound to succeed" (see Coontz, "Blaming the Family . . . ," 213–16)

p. The actual or potential consequences of nuclear leaks, meltdowns, global warming, or natural disaster

q. Vanishing animal or plant species; or the depletion of natural resources

r. The effects of outsourcing

s. Decrease in the number of people in training for skilled labor—electricians, plumbers, carpenters, tool and die makers, and others

t. A sudden change in personal status (from being a high school student to being a college freshman; from living at home to living away from home; from being dependent to being self-supporting; from being single to being married; from being childless to being a parent; from being married to being divorced . . .)

2. Write a seemingly objective account of a social phenomenon or some other aspect of human behavior of which you actually disapprove, either because the form and context seem at variance, or because the phenomenon itself seems to you wrong, or to cause unanticipated problems, such as Anne Fadiman illustrates in "Under Water" (104–7), Deborah Tannen identifies in "Fast Forward: Technologically Enhanced Aggression" (297–304), and Bill McKibben analyzes in "Designer Genes" (413–23). You can justify your opinion (and convince your readers) through your choice of details and selection of a revealing incident or several vignettes. Ethical issues are suitable for a serious essay that examines the consequences of a process or set of beliefs, such as those Peter Singer addresses in "The Singer Solution to World Poverty" (505–10) and Anthony Gorry raises in"Steal This MP3 File" (512–15). Social and cultural phenomena are particularly suitable subjects for a comic essay—the causes or consequences of nerd or geek or yuppie or twenty-something behaviors—ways of spending money and leisure time and foolish, trivial, or wasteful things to spend it on.

CLARIFYING IDEAS

Description

"By George, you're right! I <u>thought</u> there was something familiar about it."

When you describe a person, place, thing, experience, or phenomenon, you want your readers to understand it as you do and to experience its sounds, tastes, smells, or textures, both physical and emotional. You want to put your reader there—where you are, where your subject is—and enable them to see it through your eyes, interpret it through your understanding. Because you can't include everything, the details you select, the information you impart, will determine your emphasis, so pick the information that matters most to your point of view. You may decide to focus on only the big picture, the outline, the bare essentials, as seen from a distance as in the cartoon map of the United States that opens this chapter (235). Or you may choose a close-up, concentrating on the small, revealing details.

Your description can *exist for its own sake,* though in fact, few do. Most descriptions, however, function in more than one way, for more than one purpose. A description, perhaps accompanied by a photograph or diagram, can exist *to show*—no surprise—*what something looks like or how it works.* Thus Linda Villarosa's "How Much of the Body Is Replaceable?" (246–47) simply presents the evidence to demonstrate that "from the top of the head to the tips of the toes, nearly every part of the body can be replaced. . . ." The accompanying diagram identifies the nature of the many replacement options—hair, brain, eyes, skin, heart, blood vessels, joints—with captions that explain the nature of the replacement and some of the research in progress. Issues of medical ethics, longevity, cost and allocation of medical time and resources, rationing, theology, and psychology—all of which would involve interpretation and might affect whether the replacements would actually be used—are off the table in this presentation.

Or *a description can serve as an argument,* with or without words. For instance, compare Villarosa's diagram with another diagram of the human body, Istvan Banyai's "Inflation" (264). With only dates—1929–2050—and prices from 3¢ to 1,000,000¢, Banyai's line drawings of the expanding body make his case.

A description can entertain. Another commentary on people's bodies, Suzanne Britt's "That Lean and Hungry Look" (261–63) concentrates on the temperaments, pastimes, and lifestyles of fat and thin people, rather than on the specifics of their bodies. Her generalizations—"Thin people believe in logic. Fat people see all sides. The sides fat people see are rounded blobs"—are intended to provide a humorous defense of the "convivial" fat, in comparison with the "oppressive" thin, whom readers will identify as general characters and personality types, rather than as specific individuals.

Other descriptions tell stories, of people or places, re-creating the *emotional sense* of a person, place, or experience. Sometimes the author writes to understand the subject for herself, as does Meredith Hall in "Killing Chickens" (242–45), focusing on the events that lead to the breakup of her marriage. Scott Russell Sanders's "Under the Influence: Paying the Price of My Father's Booze" (249–59) analyzes his alcoholic father's influence on the family, partly to understand it for himself but partly to convey this understanding to an audience of alcoholics and their families. In both of these highly detailed, specific stories, the precise information the authors provide enables readers to understand the emotional and psychological events in terms of their own experiences and the people they know. Even if we haven't met Hall's adulterous soon-to-be-ex-husband or Sanders's father and would not recognize them in person, we know what they're like. We can recognize the fathers' powerful personalities even when they're not at home, sense their wives' distress, the children's uneasiness and fear. Although Hall's personal story might not prevent others' divorces, Sanders's account is intended as a cautionary tale as well, and thus becomes an argument not only against drinking, but a form of advocacy for the families of alcoholics who must contend with substance abuse.

Other descriptions are inviting, welcoming. Mark Twain serves up nostalgia as he invites readers to visit "Uncle John's Farm" (265–71), in a section of his *Autobiography* with its appeal to the senses, for an abundance of sensory details are often the mainstay of description. Thus Twain evokes *sound* ("I know the crackling sound [a ripe watermelon] makes when the carving knife enters its end"); *smell* ("I can call back . . . [from] the deep woods, the earthy smells"); *touch* ("I can feel the thumping rain, upon my head, of hickory nuts and walnuts"); *taste* ("I know the taste of the watermelon which has been honestly come by, and I know the taste of the watermelon which has been acquired by art"); and *sight* ("I can see the white and black children grouped on the hearth, with the firelight playing on their faces and the shadows flickering upon the walls"). Twain calls on all our senses to take us to his beloved farm—and to love it as he does.

Indeed, most descriptions of places, like descriptions of people, phenomena, processes, and other subjects, are strongly influenced by the observer's aims, experiences, and values. Thus in much nontechnical writing the descriptions you provide are bound to be subjective, intended both to guide and influence your readers to see the topic your way rather than theirs. As a writer you can't afford to leave critical spaces blank; you must provide direction to influence your readers' interpretations, as you would need to do when looking at the cartoon on page 235. Although we have heard, to the point of cliché, that one picture is worth a thousand words, very often pictures need some words to expand and focus the interpretation to which the picture invites us. This is true not only of the cartoon on page 235, for which we could come up with a variety of captions, and the photo of binge drinking on page 255, but also of Linda Villarosa's schematic diagram of replaceable parts of the body (246–47). Although the diagram shows us what parts are replaceable, we need written explanations to flesh out the figure.

Linda Hogan's "Dwellings" (273–76) reflects on a variety of places to live from a range of perspectives—close up to long distance, immediate to remote in time, personal to anecdotal and legendary. This combination of points of view is common in description, just as it is in photography, where the interpreter employs a variety of angles and focuses to convey her personal vision. (In fact, the style of a distinctive photographer—Ansel Adams, Dorothea Lange, Cindy Sherman—is as individual and as immediately recognizable as a writer's characteristic literary style.) In her writing Hogan is always concerned with "the deepest questions, those of spirit, of shelter, of growth and movement toward peace and liberation, inner and outer," and it is these qualities she seeks in the environment, natural and manmade. As she explores the possibilities of ideal dwellings, Hogan looks first from long distance at "a broken wall of earth that contains old roots and pebbles woven together and exposed." Close up, however, this "rise of raw earth" becomes a bees' cliff dwelling, Anasazi-like, a sheltering hill of "tunneling rooms" that becomes a catacomb as the bees die. Inspired by this "intelligent architecture of memory," Hogan describes her own "dreams of peace," escaping to a wilderness sanctuary, a "nest inside stone or woods," "where a human hand has not been in everything." As she meditates on the goodness of fit between various shelters and their occupants—caves, fanciful bird houses, barn swallows' cluster nesting— Hogan discovers a great horned owl's nest adorned with a blue thread from one of Hogan's skirts and a "gnarl" of her daughter's hair. These specific details, primarily visual, lead her to contemplate the shelter that all living things find in the integrated universe, throbbing with life and possibility. Although Hogan's description throughout concentrates on precise physical details, the literal serves as a metaphor for the world beyond this world, and its effect is intensely spiritual: "The whole world was a nest . . . in the maze of the universe, holding us."

Poignant events can occur anywhere, in places as familiar as one's own backyard or in exotic spots halfway around the world. As intense as the message of Hogan's "Dwellings," but with complicated political undercurrents is Asiya S. Tschannerl's "One Remembers Most What One Loves" (278–81). Here she recalls incidents from her early childhood in Beijing to depict her life as a foreign schoolchild, "a little black [American] kid" who soon learned to speak "perfect Mandarin." She juxtaposes these with images of Tiananmen Square, initially a place of happy socialization, later tainted with the bloody massacre of the Chinese people by Chinese soldiers. Having become acculturated to life in China, she undergoes culture shock on return to her native country, with its noise, racism, and lack of respect for elders.

Rarely do any literary techniques occur in isolation. Although the chapters in *The Essay Connection* are intended to highlight many of the major techniques of nonfiction writing, it is rare to find relatively pure types. Hogan's "Dwellings," for instance, may be interpreted as an implied argument in favor of preserving a vulnerable, perhaps vanishing, ecosystem.

Essays that blend different techniques are far more common, as you may already have experienced if you've tried to write a narrative or, for example, an explanation, of cause and effect.

Scott Russell Sanders's description of his father in "Under the Influence: Paying the Price of My Father's Booze" (249–59) presents an argument—and an *explanation*—and uses *comparison and contrast* to *illustrate cause-and-effect.* Sanders uses the single example of his father's alcoholism and its numerous, devastating effects on his family to serve as a description of alcoholism in general: the secret drinking, the reckless driving, the weaving walk, his mother's accusations and his father's rage, the children cowering in fear—at the fights, the sneakiness, the unseemly behavior. Sanders's reaction to his father's drinking, as both a child and as an adult, may also be generalized to describe the impact of parental drinking on the children of alcoholics: "I lie there [in bed] hating him, loving him, fearing him, knowing I have failed him. I tell myself he drinks to ease the ache . . . I must have caused by disappointing him somehow, a murderous ache I should be able to relieve by doing all my chores, earning A's in school. . . . He would not . . . drink himself to death, if only I were perfect." The accompanying photograph of a bartender in Cancun (255) pouring tequila down the willing throat of an American college student engaging in a spring break ritual, implies an argument that corroborates Sanders's view of alcohol abuse, even if the participants in the ritual would disagree with this interpretation. Sanders's account of alcoholism is personal and biographical, not medical. As these authors and illustrators show us, there is a world of difference in descriptions, a compelling, complex world to explore. Whether we want the pictures wide-angled or narrow, distant or close up, sharply focused or fuzzy, is up to us—and our readers.

STRATEGIES FOR WRITING— DESCRIPTION

1. What is my main purpose in writing this descriptive essay? To present and interpret factual information about the subject? To recreate its essence as I have experienced it, or the person, as I have known him or her? To form the basis for a story, a cause-and-effect sequence, or an argument—overt or implied? What mixture of objective information and subjective impressions will best fit my purpose?

2. If my audience is completely unfamiliar with the subject, how much and what kinds of basic information will I have to provide so they can understand what I'm talking about? (Can I assume that they've seen lakes, but not necessarily Lake Tahoe, the subject of my paper? Or that they know other grandmothers, but not mine, about whom I'm writing?) If my readers are familiar with the subject, in what ways can I describe it so they'll discover new aspects of it?

3. What particular characteristics of my subject do I wish to emphasize? Will I use in this description details revealed by the senses—sight, sound, taste, smell, touch? Any other sort of information, such as a person's characteristic behavior, gestures, ways of speaking or moving or dressing, values, companions, possessions, occupation, residence, style of spending money, beliefs, hopes, vulnerabilities? Nonsensory details will be particularly necessary in describing an abstraction, such as somebody's temperament or state of mind.

4. How will I organize my description? From the most dominant to the least dominant details? From the most to the least familiar aspects (or vice versa)? According to what an observer is likely to notice first, second . . . last? Or according to some other pattern?

5. Will I use much general language, or will my description be highly specific throughout? Do I want to evoke a clear, distinct image of the subject? Or a mood—nostalgic, thoughtful, happy, sad, or otherwise?

MEREDITH HALL

Hall was born in 1949 and grew up in New Hampshire. She quit college at eighteen and returned only after "forced to" by divorce as the only full-time nontraditional student at Bowdoin College. This experience ("my great intellectual hungers were fed"), enhanced by a full scholarship, changed her life and launched her career as a teacher and writer. Graduating at age forty-four, she earned an MA in writing from the University of New Hampshire (1995) and has taught there ever since. Her prize-winning essays have been published in *Creative Nonfiction* and the *New York Times*. In 2005, she received the Gift of Freedom Award, a two-year writing grant from A Room of Her Own Foundation. She lives on the coast of Maine.

About writing "Killing Chickens"—her first published work—and another intensely personal essay, "Shunned," she says, "I suspect that each of us has obsessive images about difficulties in our lives. They get hazy in our memory of happiness [but] are jarring to us because we're not yet at peace with them. Writing is a way, in part, to come to terms with them. These are stories I have not told friends; these are not stories I talk about, and so there's an instinct to finally share these with strangers." She adds, "I tell my students that you don't have to write anything. . . . But when you do, you must be frighteningly honest with your reader. If you're not willing to expose yourself completely and risk everything in that honesty, then . . . go write about something else. I don't care about writing that doesn't commit a writer fully." Of "Killing Chickens" itself, Hall says, "The image of the soft, dusty light in the chicken coop and my little hens laid out one by one has come to embody for me the difficulties of our family breakup. Love and violence tangle in this essay. My children were unaware of what I was doing outside, of my first desperate efforts to take charge of my new life. Inside the house, they had already started their own young reckoning. That it was such a beautiful spring day, so full of promise, and my birthday, plays in my memory against the finality and trauma of the deaths and the impending divorce."

As you read this piece of creative nonfiction—a true story and so-labeled—compare this with the fictional short stories you have read—or Tallent's "No One's a Mystery" (388–90). What, if any, aspects of "Killing Chickens" itself—events, characters, dialogue, setting, details of everyday life—tell you this is a true story rather than a work of fiction? Or does your understanding that this is a true story arise from the fact that the author identifies it as truth rather than fiction? Suppose Hall had called it "fiction." Would you have read it any differently?

Killing Chickens

1   I tucked her wings tight against her heaving body, crouched over her, and covered her flailing head with my gloved hand. Holding her neck hard against the floor of the coop, I took a breath, set something deep and hard inside my heart, and twisted her head. I heard her neck break with a crackle. Still she fought me, struggling to be free of my weight, my gloved hands, my need to kill her. Her shiny black beak opened and closed, opened and closely silently, as she gasped for air. I didn't know this would happen. I was undone by the flapping, the dust rising and choking me, the disbelieving little eye turned up to mine. I held her beak closed, covering that eye. Still she pushed, her reptile legs bracing against mine, her warmth, her heart beating fast with mine. I turned her head on her floppy neck again, and again, corkscrewing her breathing tube, struggling to end the gasping. The eye, turned around and around, blinked and studied me. The early spring sun flowed onto us through a silver stream of dust, like a stage light, while we fought each other. I lifted my head and saw that the other birds were eating still, pecking their way around us for stray bits of corn. This one, this twisted and broken lump of gleaming black feathers, clawed hard at the floor, like a big stretch, and then deflated like a pierced ball. I waited, holding her tiny beak and broken neck with all my might.

2   I was killing chickens. It was my 38th birthday. My best friend, Ashley, had chosen that morning to tell me that my husband had slept with her a year before. I had absorbed the rumors and suspicions about other women for 10 years, but this one, I knew, was going to break us. When I roared upstairs and confronted John, he told me to go fuck myself, ran downstairs and jumped into the truck. Our sons, Sam and Ben, were making a surprise for me at the table; they stood behind me silently in the kitchen door while John gunned the truck out of the yard. "It's okay, guys," I said. "Mum and Dad just had a fight. You better go finish my surprise before I come peeking."

3   I carried Bertie's warm, limp body outside and laid her on the grass. Back inside the coop, I stalked my hens and came up with Tippy-Toes. I gathered her frantic wings and crouched over her. John was supposed to kill off our beautiful but tired old hens, no longer laying, last month to make way for the new chicks that were arriving tomorrow. But he was never around, and the job had not been done. I didn't know how to do this. But I was going to do it myself. This was just a little thing in all the things I was going to have to learn to do alone.

4   I had five more to go. Tippy-Toes tried to shriek behind my glove. I clamped my hand over her beak and gave her head a hard twist. I felt her body break deep inside my own chest.

5   Two down. I felt powerful, capable. I could handle whatever came to me.

But I needed a rest. I was tired, exhausted, with a heavy, muffled 6 weight settling inside. "I'm coming in," I called in a false, singsong voice from the kitchen door. "Better hide my surprise." Ten and 7, the boys knew something was up, something bigger than the moody, dark days John brought home, bigger than the hushed, hissing fights we had behind our bedroom door, bigger than the days-long silent treatment John imposed on me if I asked too many questions about where he had been and why. Sam and Ben were working quietly in the kitchen, not giggling and jostling the way they usually did. Their downy blond heads touched as they leaned over their projects. I felt a crush of sadness, of defeat. We were exploding into smithereens on this pretty March day, and we all knew it.

"I have to make a cake!" I sang from the doorway. "When are you 7 guys going to be done in there?"

"Wait! Wait!" they squealed. It was an empty protest, their cheer as 8 hollow as mine.

Our old house smelled good, of wood and the pancakes the three of 9 us had eaten this morning, in that other world of hope and tight determination before Ashley's phone call. We lived on a ridge high over the mouth of the Damariscotta River on the coast of Maine. From our beds, we could all see out over Pemaquid Point, over Monhegan Island, over the ocean to the edge of the Old World. The rising sun burst into our sleep each morning. At night, before bed, we lay on my bed together—three of us—naming Orion and Leo and the Pleiades in whispers. Monhegan's distant light swept the walls of our rooms all night at 36-second intervals. Our little house creaked in the wind during February storms. Now spring had come, and the world had shifted.

"Help me make my cake," I said to the boys. They dragged their 10 chairs to the counter.

"Mum, will Dad be home for your birthday tonight?" Sam asked. 11 Both boys were so contained, so taut, so helpless. They leaned against me, quiet.

Guilt and fear tugged me like an undertow. I started to cry. 12

"I don't know, my loves. I think this is a really big one." 13

Bertie and Tippy-Toes lay side by side on the brown grass, their eyes 14 open, necks bent. I closed the coop door behind me and lunged for the next hen.

"It's all right," I said softly. "It's all right. Everything's going to be all 15 right. Shhh, Silly, shh." I crouched over her. Silly was the boys' favorite because she let them carry her around the yard. I hoped they would forget her when the box of peeping balls of fluff arrived tomorrow.

"It's okay, Silly," I said quietly, wrapping my gloved fingers around 16 her hard little head. She was panting, her eyes wild, frantic, betrayed. I covered them with my fingers and twisted her neck hard. Her black wings, iridescent in the dusty sunlight, beat against my legs. I held her close to me while she scrabbled against my strong hands. I started to cry again.

17   When I went back up to the house, Bertie and Tippy-Toes and Silly and Mother Mabel lay on the grass outside the coop.

18   Benjamin came into the kitchen and leaned against my legs. "What are we going to do?" he asked.

19   "About what, Sweetheart?" I hoped he was not asking me about tomorrow. Or the next day.

20   "Nothing," he said, drifting off to play with Sam upstairs.

21   We frosted the cake blue, Ben's favorite color, and put it on the table next to their presents for me, wrapped in wallpaper. I wanted to call someone, to call my mother or my sister. Yesterday I would have called Ashley, my best friend, who had listened to me cry and rail about John again and again. Instead, I brought in three loads of wood and put them in the box John had left empty.

22   "Sam, will you lay up a fire for tonight? And Ben, go down to the cellar and get a bunch of kindling wood."

23   Like serious little men, my children did what I asked.

24   "What are we going to make for my birthday supper?"

25   "I thought we were going to Uncle Stephen's and Aunt Ashley's," Sam said.

26   "Know what?" I said. "Know what I want to do? Let's just stay here and have our own private little party. Just us."

27   I felt marooned with my children. I sat at the table, watching while they did their chores, then headed back out to finish mine.

28   Minnie Hen was next. She let me catch her and kill her without much fight. I laid her next to the others in the cold grass.

29   Itty-Bit was last. She was my favorite. The others had chewed off her toes, one by one, when she was a chick. I had made a separate box for her, a separate feeder, separate roost, and smeared antibiotic ointment four times a day on the weeping stubs. She survived, and ate from my hand after that. She had grown to be fierce with the other hens, never letting them too close to her, able to slip in, grab the best morsels and flee before they could peck her. I had come to admire her very much, my tough little biddie.

30   She cowered in the corner, alone. I sat next to her, and she let me pull her up into my lap. I stroked her feathers smooth, stroke after stroke. Her comb was pale and shriveled, a sign of her age. I knew she hadn't laid an egg for months. She was shaking. I held her warmth against me, cooing to her, "It's all right, Itty-Bit. Everything's going to be all right. Don't be scared." My anger at John centered like a tornado on having to kill this hen. "You stupid, selfish son of a bitch," I said. I got up, crying again,

holding Itty-Bit tight to me. I laid her gently on the floor and crouched over her. The sun filled the coop with thick light.

That night, after eating spaghetti and making a wish and blowing 31
out 38 candles and opening presents made by Sam and Benjamin—a mail holder made from wood slats, a sculpture of 2-by-4s and shells; after baths and reading stories in bed and our sweet, in-the-dark, whispered good nights; after saying "I don't know what is going to happen" to my scared children; after banking the fire and turning off the lights, I sat on the porch in the cold, trying to imagine what had to happen next. I could see the outline of the coop against the dark, milky sky. I touched my fingers, my hands, so familiar to me. Tonight they felt like someone else's. I wrapped my arms around myself—thin, tired—and wished it were yesterday.

Tomorrow morning, I thought, I have to turn over the garden and go 32
to the dump. Tomorrow morning, I have to call a lawyer. I have to figure out what to say to Sam and Benjamin. I have to put Ben's sculpture on the mantel and put some mail in Sam's holder on the desk. I have to clean out the coop and spread fresh shavings.

LINDA VILLAROSA

Linda Villarosa (born 1959) is a graduate of the University of Colorado and a former executive editor of *Essence Magazine.* She currently works as a freelance journalist based in New York City and has edited or coedited several books on parenting, adolescence, and health.

How Much of the Body Is Replaceable?

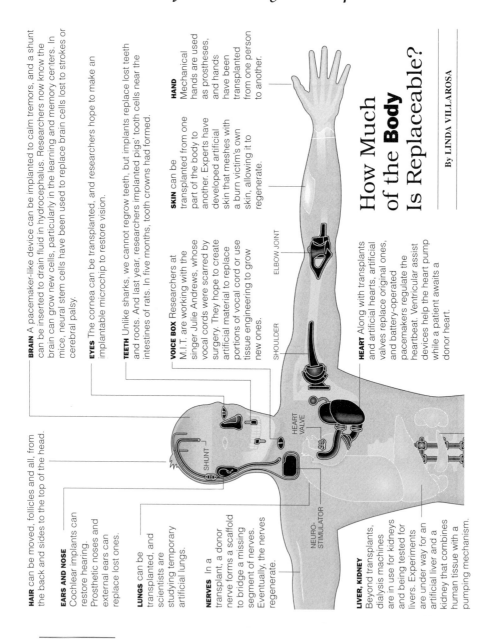

How Much of the Body Is Replaceable?

BY LINDA VILLAROSA

BRAIN A pacemaker-like device can be implanted to calm tremors, and a shunt can be inserted to drain fluid in hydrocephalus. Researchers now know the brain can grow new cells, particularly in the learning and memory centers. In mice, neural stem cells have been used to replace brain cells lost to strokes or cerebral palsy.

EYES The cornea can be transplanted, and researchers hope to make an implantable microchip to restore vision.

TEETH Unlike sharks, we cannot regrow teeth, but implants replace lost teeth and roots. And last year, researchers implanted pigs' tooth cells near the intestines of rats. In five months, tooth crowns had formed.

VOICE BOX Researchers at M.I.T. are working with the singer Julie Andrews, whose vocal cords were scarred by surgery. They hope to create artificial material to replace portions of vocal cord or use tissue engineering to grow new ones.

SKIN can be transplanted from one part of the body to another. Experts have developed artificial skin that meshes with a burn victim's own skin, allowing it to regenerate.

HAND Mechanical hands are used as prostheses, and hands have been transplanted from one person to another.

HAIR can be moved, follicles and all, from the back and sides to the top of the head.

EARS AND NOSE Cochlear implants can restore hearing. Prosthetic noses and external ears can replace lost ones.

LUNGS can be transplanted, and scientists are studying temporary artificial lungs.

NERVES In a transplant, a donor nerve forms a scaffold to bridge a missing segment of nerves. Eventually, the nerves regenerate.

LIVER, KIDNEY Beyond transplants, dialysis machines are in use for kidneys and being tested for livers. Experiments are under way for an artificial liver and a kidney that combines human tissue with a pumping mechanism.

HEART Along with transplants and artificial hearts, artificial valves replace original ones, and battery-operated pacemakers regulate the heartbeat. Ventricular assist devices help the heart pump while a patient awaits a donor heart.

SHUNT
HEART VALVE
SHOULDER
ELBOW JOINT
NEURO-STIMULATOR

Copyright © 2003 by The *New York Times Company*. Reprinted with permission. *Sources:* Dr. Robert Langer, M.I.T.; Dr. Denise Faustman, Harvard Medical School; Dr. Alan J. Russell, University of Pittsburgh School of Engineering; Dr. James Herndon, Harvard Medical School; Dr. Todd Kuiken, Rehabilitation Institute of Chicago.

Legend has it that in the fifth century A.D., a beautiful woman kissed the hand of Pope Leo I during Mass. The pope, mortified at feeling desire for the woman, ordered a servant to cut off the offending hand. The Virgin Mary later restored the limb by performing the Miracle of the Severed Hand, an act immortalized in stained glass at the Church of Orsanmichele in Florence.

Many centuries later, replacing a body part is no longer miraculous, but simply commonplace. From the top of the head to the tips of the toes, nearly every part of the body can be replaced by transplanting organs and tissues from one person to the next or substituting artificial parts for weakened or damaged tissue. And research in several areas — from building better medical devices to creating artificial organs to growing new ones with the help of stem cells — is progressing at a pace only Steve Austin, the Six Million Dollar Man, could match.

"How much of the body is replaceable? I have not come across a part of the body that someone somewhere isn't working on," said Dr. Robert Langer, professor of chemical and biomedical engineering at M.I.T. and a pioneer of tissue engineering. "Someday every part will be replaceable, even if that day is centuries away."

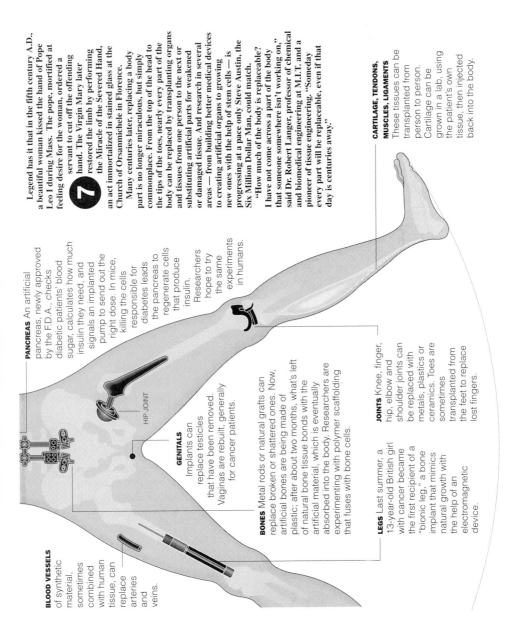

BLOOD VESSELS of synthetic material, sometimes combined with human tissue, can replace arteries and veins.

PANCREAS An artificial pancreas, newly approved by the F.D.A., checks diabetic patients' blood sugar, calculates how much insulin they need, and signals an implanted pump to send out the right dose. In mice, killing the cells responsible for diabetes leads the pancreas to regenerate cells that produce insulin. Researchers hope to try the same experiments in humans.

HIP JOINT

GENITALS Implants can replace testicles that have been removed. Vaginas are rebuilt, generally for cancer patients.

BONES Metal rods or natural grafts can replace broken or shattered ones. Now, artificial bones are being made of plastic; after about two months, what's left of natural bone tissue bonds with the artificial material, which is eventually absorbed into the body. Researchers are experimenting with polymer scaffolding that fuses with bone cells.

LEGS Last summer, a 13-year-old British girl with cancer became the first recipient of a "bionic leg," a bone implant that mimics natural growth with the help of an electromagnetic device.

JOINTS Knee, finger, hip, elbow and shoulder joints can be replaced with metals, plastics or ceramics. Toes are sometimes transplanted from the feet to replace lost fingers.

CARTILAGE, TENDONS, MUSCLES, LIGAMENTS These tissues can be transplanted from person to person. Cartilage can be grown in a lab, using the patient's own tissue, then injected back into the body.

Questions for discussion and writing

1. Villarosa refers to "the Six Million Dollar Man," from a television show about an action hero, who, after having been severely injured, was "put back together"— better than new—using artificial parts. *The Bionic Woman* took up a similar theme. What other shows or movies use this idea, and why is it a popular subject? If you have read Mary Shelley's *Frankenstein*, discuss to what extent it belongs to this tradition.

2. Many people currently alter their body voluntarily through plastic surgery. Do you suppose that at some time in the future people will elect to replace healthy body parts with stronger, more durable artificial ones? Explore the ethical implications of this possibility. For example, if professional athletes could buy themselves better knees, arms, or legs, what would the implications of this trend be for professional sports? What about students who might want to implant computing devices into their brain to enhance math ability? (See Bill McKibben, "Designer Genes," 413–23 for an extension of this discussion.)

 For comprehension, writing, and research activities and resources, please visit the companion website at <college.hmco.com/english>.

SCOTT RUSSELL SANDERS

"Under the Influence," from *Secrets of the Universe* (1991), is full of examples that describe the effects of alcoholism—on the alcoholic father, on his wife, alternately distressed and defiant, and on his children, cowering with guilt and fear. Sanders uses especially the example of himself, the eldest son, who felt responsible for his father's drinking, guilty because he couldn't get him to stop, and obligated to atone for his father's sins through his own perfection and accomplishment. Although at the age of forty-four Sanders knows that his father was "consumed by disease rather than by disappointment," he writes to understand "the corrosive mixture of helplessness, responsibility, and shame that I learned to feel as the son of an alcoholic." Through the specific example of his family's behavior, Sanders illustrates the general problem of alcoholism that afflicts some "ten or fifteen million people." He expects his readers to generalize and to learn from his understanding.

Under the Influence: Paying the Price of My Father's Booze

My father drank. He drank as a gut-punched boxer gasps for breath, as a starving dog gobbles food—compulsively, secretly, in pain and trembling. I use the past tense not because he ever quit drinking but because he quit living. That is how the story ends for my father, age sixty-four, heart bursting, body cooling, slumped and forsaken on the linoleum of my brother's trailer. The story continues for my brother, my sister, my mother, and me, and will continue as long as memory holds. 1

In the perennial present of memory, I slip into the garage or barn to see my father tipping back the flat green bottles of wine, the brown cylinders of whiskey, the cans of beer disguised in paper bags. His Adam's apple bobs, the liquid gurgles, he wipes the sandy-haired back of a hand over his lips, and then, his bloodshot gaze bumping into me, he stashes the bottle or can inside his jacket, under the workbench, between two bales of hay, and we both pretend the moment has not occurred. 2

"What's up, buddy?" he says, thick-tongued and edgy. 3

"Sky's up," I answer, playing along. 4

"And don't forget prices," he grumbles. "Prices are always up. And taxes." 5

In memory, his white 1951 Pontiac with the stripes down the hood and the Indian head on the snout lurches to a stop in the driveway; or it is the 1956 Ford station wagon, or the 1963 Rambler shaped like a toad, or the sleek 1969 Bonneville that will do 120 miles per hour on straightaways; or it is the robin's-egg-blue pickup, new in 1980, battered in 1981, the year of his death. He climbs out, grinning dangerously, unsteady on his legs, and we children interrupt our game of catch, our building of snow forts, our picking of plums, to watch in silence as he weaves past us into the house, where he drops into his overstuffed chair and falls asleep. Shaking her head, our mother stubs out a cigarette he has left smoldering in the ashtray. All evening, until our bedtimes, we tiptoe past him, as past a snoring dragon. Then we curl fearfully in our sheets, listening. Eventually he wakes with a grunt, Mother slings accusations at him, he snarls back, she yells, he growls, their voices clashing. Before long, she retreats to their bedroom, sobbing—not from the blows of fists, for he never strikes her, but from the force of his words. 6

Left alone, our father prowls the house, thumping into furniture, rummaging in the kitchen, slamming doors, turning the pages of the newspaper with a savage crackle, muttering back at the late-night drivel from television. The roof might fly off, the walls might buckle from the pressure of his rage. Whatever my brother and sister and mother may be thinking on their own rumpled pillows, I lie there hating him, loving 7 him, fearing him, knowing I have failed him. I tell myself he drinks to ease the ache that gnaws at his belly, an ache I must have caused by disappointing him somehow, a murderous ache I should be able to relieve by doing all my chores, earning A's in school, winning baseball games, fixing the broken washer and the burst pipes, bringing in the money to fill his empty wallet. He would not hide the green bottles in his toolbox, would not sneak off to the barn with a lump under his coat, would not fall asleep in the daylight, would not roar and fume, would not drink himself to death, if only I were perfect.

8   I am forty-four, and I know full well now that my father was an alcoholic, a man consumed by disease rather than by disappointment. What had seemed to me a private grief is in fact, of course, a public scourge. In the United States alone, some ten or fifteen million people share his ailment, and behind the doors they slam in fury or disgrace, countless other children tremble. I comfort myself with such knowledge, holding it against the throb of memory like an ice pack against a bruise. Other people have keener sources of grief: poverty, racism, rape, war. I do not wish to compete to determine who has suffered most. I am only trying to understand the corrosive mixture of helplessness, responsibility, and shame that I learned to feel as the son of an alcoholic. I realize now that I did not cause my father's illness, nor could I have cured it. Yet for all this grownup knowledge, I am still ten years old, my own son's age, and as that boy I struggle in guilt and confusion to save my father from pain.

9   Consider a few of our synonyms for *drunk*: tipsy, tight, pickled, soused, and plowed; stoned and stewed, lubricated and inebriated, juiced and sluiced; three sheets to the wind, in your cups, out of your mind, under the table; lit up, tanked up, wiped out; besotted, blotto, bombed, and buzzed; plastered, polluted, putrefied; loaded or looped, boozy, woozy, fuddled, or smashed; crocked and shit-faced, corked and pissed, snockered and sloshed.

10   It is a mostly humorous lexicon, as the lore that deals with drunks— in jokes and cartoons, in plays, films and television skits—is largely comic. Aunt Matilda nips elderberry wine from the sideboard and burps politely during supper. Uncle Fred slouches to the table glassy-eyed, wearing a lampshade for a hat and murmuring, "Candy is dandy, but liquor is quicker." Inspired by cocktails, Mrs. Somebody recounts the events of her day in a fuzzy dialect, while Mr. Somebody nibbles her ear and croons a bawdy song. On the sofa with Boyfriend, Daughter Somebody giggles, licking gin from her lips, and loosens the bows in her hair. Junior knocks back some brews with his chums at the Leopard Lounge and stumbles home to the wrong house, wonders foggily why he cannot locate his pajamas, and crawls naked into bed with the ugliest girl in school. The family dog slurps from a neglected martini and wobbles to the nursery, where he vomits in Baby's shoe.

It is all great fun. But if in the audience you notice a few laughing 11
faces turn grim when the drunk lurches onstage, don't be surprised, for
these are the children of alcoholics. Over the grinning mask of Dionysus,
the leering face of Bacchus, these children cannot help seeing the bloated
features of their own parents. Instead of laughing, they wince, they mourn.
Instead of celebrating the drunk as one freed from constraints, they pity
him as one enslaved. They refuse to believe *in vino veritas*, having seen
their befuddled parents skid away from truth toward folly and oblivion.
And so these children bite their lips until the lush staggers into the wings.

My father, when drunk, was neither funny nor honest; he was pa- 12
thetic, frightening, deceitful. There seemed to be a leak in him somewhere,
and he poured in booze to keep from draining dry. Like a torture victim who
refuses to squeal, he would never admit that he had touched a drop, not
even in his last year, when he seemed to be dissolving in alcohol before our
very eyes. I never knew him to lie about anything, ever, except about this
one ruinous fact. Drowsy, clumsy, unable to fix a bicycle tire, balance a grocery sack, or walk across a room, he was stripped of his true self by drink.
In a matter of minutes, the contents of a bottle could transform a brave man
into a coward, a buddy into a bully, a gifted athlete and skilled carpenter
and shrewd businessman into a bumbler. No dictionary of synonyms for
drunk would soften the anguish of watching our prince turn into a frog.

Father's drinking became the family secret. While growing up, we 13
children never breathed a word of it beyond the four walls of our house.
To this day, my brother and sister rarely mention it, and then only when I
press them. I did not confess the ugly, bewildering fact to my wife until
his wavering and slurred speech forced me to. Recently, on the seventh
anniversary of my father's death, I asked my mother if she ever spoke of
his drinking to friends. "No, no, never," she replied hastily. "I couldn't
bear for anyone to know."

The secret bores under the skin, gets in the blood, into the bone, and 14
stays there. Long after you have supposedly been cured of malaria, the
fever can flare up, the tremors can shake you. So it is with the fevers of
shame. You swallow the bitter quinine of knowledge, and you learn to feel
pity and compassion toward the drinker. Yet the shame lingers and, because of it, anger.

For a long stretch of my childhood we lived on a military reservation in 15
Ohio, an arsenal where bombs were stored underground in bunkers and
vintage airplanes burst into flames and unstable artillery shells boomed
nightly at the dump. We had the feeling, as children, that we played within
a minefield, where a heedless footfall could trigger an explosion. When
Father was drinking, the house, too, became a minefield. The least bump
could set off either parent.

The more he drank, the more obsessed Mother became with stopping 16
him. She hunted for bottles, counted the cash in his wallet, sniffed at his

breath. Without meaning to snoop, we children blundered left and right into damning evidence. On afternoons when he came home from work sober, we flung ourselves at him for hugs and felt against our ribs the tell-tale lump in his coat. In the barn we tumbled on the hay and heard beneath our sneakers the crunch of broken glass. We tugged open a drawer in his workbench, looking for screwdrivers or crescent wrenches, and spied a gleaming six-pack among the tools. Playing tag, we darted around the house just in time to see him sway on the rear stoop and heave a finished bottle into the woods. In his good-night kiss we smelled the cloying sweet-ness of Clorets, the mints he chewed to camouflage his dragon's breath.

17   I can summon up that kiss right now by recalling Theodore Roethke's lines about his own father:

> The whiskey on your breath
> Could make a small boy dizzy;
> But I hung on like death:
> Such waltzing was not easy.

Such waltzing was hard, terribly hard, for with a boy's scrawny arms I was trying to hold my tipsy father upright.

18   For years, the chief source of those incriminating bottles and cans was a grimy store a mile from us, a cinderblock place called Sly's, with two gas pumps outside and a mangy dog asleep in the window. Inside, on rusty metal shelves or in wheezing coolers, you could find pop and Pop-sicles, cigarettes, potato chips, canned soup, raunchy postcards, fishing gear, Twinkies, wine, and beer. When Father drove anywhere on errands, Mother would send us along as guards, warning us not to let him out of our sight. And so with one or more of us on board, Father would cruise up to Sly's, pump a dollar's worth of gas or plump the tires with air, and then, telling us to wait in the car, he would head for the doorway.

19   Dutiful and panicky, we cried, "Let us go with you!"

20   "No," he answered. "I'll be back in two shakes."

21   "Please!"

22   "No!" he roared. "Don't you budge or I'll jerk a knot in your tails!"

23   So we stayed put, kicking the seats, while he ducked inside. Often, when he had parked the car at a careless angle, we gazed in through the window and saw Mr. Sly fetching down from the shelf behind the cash register two green pints of Gallo wine. Father swigged one of them right there at the counter, stuffed the other in his pocket, and then out he came, a bulge in his coat, a flustered look on his reddened face.

24   Because the mom and pop who ran the dump were neighbors of ours, living just down the tar-blistered road, I hated them all the more for poi-soning my father. I wanted to sneak in their store and smash the bottles and set fire to the place. I also hated the Gallo brothers, Ernest and Julio, whose jovial faces beamed from the labels of their wine, labels I would find, torn and curled, when I burned the trash. I noted the Gallo brothers' address in California and studied the road atlas to see how far that was from Ohio,

because I meant to go out there and tell Ernest and Julio what they were doing to my father, and then, if they showed no mercy, I would kill them.

While growing up on the back roads and in the country schools and 25 cramped Methodist churches of Ohio and Tennessee, I never heard the word *alcoholic*, never happened across it in books or magazines. In the nearby towns, there were no addiction-treatment programs, no community mental-health centers, no Alcoholics Anonymous chapters, no therapists. Left alone with our grievous secret, we had no way of understanding Father's drinking except as an act of will, a deliberate folly or cruelty, a moral weakness, a sin. He drank because he chose to, pure and simple. Why our father, so playful and competent and kind when sober, would choose to ruin himself and punish his family we could not fathom.

Our neighborhood was high on the Bible, and the Bible was hard on 26 drunkards. "Woe to those who are heroes at drinking wine and valiant men in mixing strong drink," wrote Isaiah. "The priest and the prophet reel with strong drink, they are confused with wine, they err in vision, they stumble in giving judgment. For all tables are full of vomit, no place is without filthiness." We children had seen those fouled tables at the local truck stop where the notorious boozers hung out, our father occasionally among them. "Wine and new wine take away the understanding," declared the prophet Hosea. We had also seen evidence of that in our father, who could multiply seven-digit numbers in his head when sober but when drunk could not help us with fourth-grade math. Proverbs warned: "Do not look at wine when it is red, when it sparkles in the cup and goes down smoothly. At the last it bites like a serpent and stings like an adder. Your eyes will see strange things, and your mind utter perverse things." Woe, woe.

Dismayingly often, these biblical drunkards stirred up trouble for 27 their own kids. Noah made fresh wine after the flood, drank too much of it, fell asleep without any clothes on, and was glimpsed in the buff by his son Ham, whom Noah promptly cursed. In one passage—it was so shocking we had to read it under our blankets with flashlights—the patriarch Lot fell down drunk and slept with his daughters. The sins of the fathers set their children's teeth on edge.

Our ministers were fond of quoting St. Paul's pronouncement that 28 drunkards would not inherit the kingdom of God. These grave preachers assured us that the wine referred to in the Last Supper was in fact grape juice. Bible and sermons and hymns combined to give us the impression that Moses should have brought down from the mountain another stone tablet, bearing the Eleventh Commandment: Thou shalt not drink.

The scariest and most illuminating Bible story apropos of drunkards 29 was the one about the lunatic and the swine. We knew it by heart: When Jesus climbed out of his boat one day, this lunatic came charging up from the graveyard, stark naked and filthy, frothing at the mouth, so violent that he broke the strongest chains. Nobody would go near him. Night and day for years, this madman had been wailing among the tombs and bruising himself with stones. Jesus took one look at him and said, "Come out of the man, you unclean spirits!" for he could see that the lunatic was possessed by demons. Meanwhile, some hogs were conveniently rooting nearby. "If we have to come out," begged the demons, "at least let us go into those swine." Jesus agreed, the unclean spirits entered the hogs, and the hogs raced straight off a cliff and plunged into a lake. Hearing the story in Sunday school, my friends thought mainly of the pigs. (How big a splash did they make? Who paid for the lost pork?) But I thought of the redeemed lunatic, who bathed himself and put on clothes and calmly sat at the feet of Jesus, restored—so the Bible said—to "his right mind."

30   When drunk, our father was clearly in his wrong mind. He became a stranger, as fearful to us as any graveyard lunatic, not quite frothing at the mouth but fierce enough, quick-tempered, explosive; or else he grew maudlin and weepy, which frightened us nearly as much. In my boyhood despair, I reasoned that maybe he wasn't to blame for turning into an ogre: Maybe, like the lunatic, he was possessed by demons.

31   If my father was indeed possessed, who would exorcise him? If he was a sinner, who would save him? If he was ill, who would cure him? If he suffered, who would ease his pain? Not ministers or doctors, for we could not bring ourselves to confide in them; not the neighbors, for we pretended they had never seen him drunk; not Mother, who fussed and pleaded but could not budge him; not my brother and sister, who were only kids. That left me. It did not matter that I, too, was only a child, and a bewildered one at that. I could not excuse myself.

32   On first reading a description of delirium tremens—in a book on alcoholism I smuggled from a university library—I thought immediately of the frothing lunatic and the frenzied swine. When I read stories or watched films about grisly metamorphoses—Dr. Jekyll and Mr. Hyde, the mild husband changing into a werewolf, the kindly neighbor inhabited by a brutal alien—I could not help but see my own father's mutation from sober to drunk. Even today, knowing better, I am attracted by the demonic theory of drink, for when I recall my father's transformation, the emergence of his ugly second self, I find it easy to believe in being possessed by unclean spirits. We never knew which version of Father would come home from work, the true or the tainted, nor could we guess how far down the slope toward cruelty he would slide.

33   How far a man *could* slide we gauged by observing our backroad neighbors—the out-of-work miners who had dragged their families to our corner of Ohio from the desolate hollows of Appalachia, the tightfisted farmers, the surly mechanics, the balked and broken men. There was, for example, whiskey-soaked Mr. Jenkins, who beat his wife and kids so hard we could hear their screams from the road. There was Mr. Lavo the wino, who fell asleep smoking time and again, until one night his disgusted wife bundled up the children and went outside and left him in his easy chair to burn; he awoke on his own, staggered out coughing into the yard,

Describe and interpret this picture, with relevance to Sanders's essay "Under the Influence" and to your own experience. In what ways can this picture be read—and by whom—as an invitation to party? In what ways—and by whom—can this picture be read as a cautionary tale?

and pounded her flat while the children looked on and the shack turned to ash. There was the truck driver, Mr. Sampson, who tripped over his son's tricycle one night while drunk and got mad, jumped into his semi, and drove away, shifting through the dozen gears, and never came back. We saw the bruised children of these fathers clump onto our school bus, we saw the abandoned children huddle in the pews at church, we saw the stunned and battered mothers begging for help at our doors.

Our own father never beat us, and I don't think he beat Mother, but   34
he threatened often. The Old Testament Yahweh was not more terrible in His rage. Eyes blazing, voice booming, Father would pull out his belt and swear to give us a whipping, but he never followed through, never needed to, because we could imagine it so vividly. He shoved us, pawed us with the back of his hand, not to injure, just to clear a space. I can see him grabbing Mother by the hair as she cowers on a chair during a nightly quarrel. He twists her neck back until she gapes up at him, and then he lifts over her skull a glass quart bottle of milk, and milk spilling down his forearm, and he yells at her, "Say just one more word, one goddamn word, and I'll shut you up!" I fear she will prick him with her sharp tongue, but she is terrified into silence, and so am I, and the leaking bottle quivers in the air, and milk seeps through the red hair of my father's uplifted arm, and the entire scene is there to this moment, the head jerked back, the club raised.

35   When the drink made him weepy, Father would pack, kiss each of us children on the head, and announce from the front door that he was moving out. "Where to?" we demanded, fearful each time that he would leave for good, as Mr. Sampson had roared away for good in his diesel truck. "Someplace where I won't get hounded every minute," Father would answer, his jaw quivering. He stabbed a look at Mother, who might say, "Don't run into the ditch before you get there," or "Good riddance," and then he would slink away. Mother watched him go with arms crossed over her chest, her face closed like the lid on a box of snakes. We children bawled. Where could he go? To the truck stop, that den of iniquity? To one of those dark, ratty flophouses in town? Would he wind up sleeping under a railroad bridge or on a park bench or in a cardboard box, mummied in rags like the bums we had seen on our trips to Cleveland and Chicago? We bawled and bawled, wondering if he would ever come back.

36   He always did come back, a day or a week later, but each time there was a sliver less of him.

37   In Kafka's *Metamorphosis*, which opens famously with Gregor Samsa waking up from uneasy dreams to find himself transformed into an insect, Gregor's family keep reassuring themselves that things will be just fine again "when he comes back to us." Each time alcohol transformed our father we held out the same hope, that he would really and truly come back to us, our authentic father, the tender and playful and competent man, and then all things would be fine. We had grounds for such hope. After his tearful departures and chapfallen returns, he would sometimes go weeks, even months, without drinking. Those were glad times. Every day without the furtive glint of bottles, every meal without a fight, every bedtime without sobs encouraged us to believe that such bliss might go on forever.

38   Mother was fooled by such a hope all during the forty-odd years she knew Greeley Ray Sanders. Soon after she met him in a Chicago delicatessen on the eve of World War II and fell for his butter-melting Mississippi drawl and his wavy red hair, she learned that he drank heavily. But then so did a lot of men. She would soon coax or scold him into breaking the nasty habit. She would point out to him how ugly and foolish it was, this bleary drinking, and then he would quit. He refused to quit during their engagement, however, still refused during the first years of marriage, refused until my older sister came along. The shock of fatherhood sobered him, and he remained sober through my birth at the end of the war and right on through until we moved in 1951 to the Ohio arsenal. The arsenal had more than its share of alcoholics, drug addicts, and other varieties of escape artists. There I turned six and started school and woke into a child's flickering awareness, just in time to see my father begin sneaking swigs in the garage.

39   He sobered up again for most of a year at the height of the Korean War, to celebrate the birth of my brother. But aside from that dry spell, his only breaks from drinking before I graduated from high school were just long enough to raise and then dash our hopes. Then during the fall of my

senior year—the time of the Cuban Missile Crisis, when it seemed that the nightly explosions at the munitions dump and the nightly rages in our household might spread to engulf the globe—Father collapsed. His liver, kidneys, and heart all conked out. The doctors saved him, but only by a hair. He stayed in the hospital for weeks, going through a withdrawal so terrible that Mother would not let us visit him. If he wanted to kill himself, the doctors solemnly warned him, all he had to do was hit the bottle again. One binge would finish him.

Father must have believed them, for he stayed dry the next fifteen   40 years. It was an answer to prayer, Mother said, it was a miracle. I believe it was a reflex of fear, which he sustained over the years through courage and pride. He knew a man could die from drink, for his brother Roscoe had. We children never laid eyes on doomed Uncle Roscoe, but in the stories Mother told us he became a fairy-tale figure, like a boy who took the wrong turn in the woods and was gobbled up by the wolf.

The fifteen-year dry spell came to an end with Father's retirement in   41 the spring of 1978. Like many men, he gave up his identity along with his job. One day he was a boss at the factory, with a brass plate on his door and a reputation to uphold; the next day he was a nobody at home. He and Mother were leaving Ontario, the last of the many places to which his job had carried them, and they were moving to a new house in Mississippi, his childhood stomping ground. As a boy in Mississippi, Father sold Coca-Cola during dances while the moonshiners peddled their brew in the parking lot; as a young blade, he fought in bars and in the ring, winning a state Golden Gloves championship; he gambled at poker, hunted pheasant, raced motorcycles and cars, played semiprofessional baseball, and, along with all his buddies—in the Black Cat Saloon, behind the cotton gin, in the woods—he drank hard. It was a perilous youth to dream of recovering.

After his final day of work, Mother drove on ahead with a car full of   42 begonias and violets, while Father stayed behind to oversee the packing. When the van was loaded, the sweaty movers broke open a six-pack and offered him a beer.

"Let's drink to retirement!" they crowed. "Let's drink to freedom! to   43 fishing! hunting! loafing! Let's drink to a guy who's going home!"

At least I imagine some such words, for that is all I can do, imagine,   44 and I see Father's hand trembling in midair as he thinks about the fifteen sober years and about the doctors' warning, and he tells himself, *Goddammit, I am a free man,* and *Why can't a free man drink one beer after a lifetime of hard work?* and I see his arm reaching, his fingers closing, the can tilting to his lips. I even supply a label for the beer, a swaggering brand that promises on television to deliver the essence of life. I watch the amber liquid pour down his throat, the alcohol steal into his blood, the key turn in his brain.

Soon after my parents moved back to Father's treacherous stomping   45 ground, my wife and I visited them in Mississippi with our four-year-old daughter. Mother had been too distraught to warn me about the return of the demons. So when I climbed out of the car that bright July morning and saw my father napping in the hammock, I felt uneasy, and when he lurched upright and blinked his bloodshot eyes and greeted us in a syrupy voice, I was hurled back into childhood.

46   "What's the matter with Papaw?" our daughter asked.

47   "Nothing," I said. "Nothing!"

48   Like a child again, I pretended not to see him in his stupor, and behind my phony smile I grieved. On that visit and on the few that remained before his death, once again I found bottles in the workbench, bottles in the woods. Again his hands shook too much for him to run a saw, to make his precious miniature furniture, to drive straight down back roads. Again he wound up in the ditch, in the hospital, in jail, in the treatment center. Again he shouted and wept. Again he lied. "I never touched a drop," he swore. "Your mother's making it up."

49   I no longer fancied I could reason with the men whose names I found on the bottles—Jim Beam, Jack Daniel's—but I was able now to recall the cold statistics about alcoholism: ten million victims, fifteen million, twenty. And yet, in spite of my age, I reacted in the same blind way as I had in childhood, by vainly seeking to erase through my efforts whatever drove him to drink. I worked on their place twelve and sixteen hours a day, in the swelter of Mississippi summers, digging ditches, running electrical wires, planting trees, mowing grass, building sheds, as though what nagged at him was some list of chores, as though by taking his worries upon my shoulders I could redeem him. I was flung back into boyhood, acting as though my father would not drink himself to death if only I were perfect.

50   I failed of perfection; he succeeded in dying. To the end, he considered himself not sick but sinful. "Do you want to kill yourself?" I asked him. "Why not?" he answered. "Why the hell not? What's there to save?" To the end, he would not speak about his feelings, would not or could not give a name to the beast that was devouring him.

51   In silence, he went rushing off to the cliff. Unlike the biblical swine, however, he left behind a few of the demons to haunt his children. Life with him and the loss of him twisted us into shapes that will be familiar to other sons and daughters of alcoholics. My brother became a rebel, my sister retreated into shyness, I played the stalwart and dutiful son who would hold the family together. If my father was unstable, I would be a rock. If he squandered money on drink, I would pinch every penny. If he wept when drunk—and only when drunk—I would not let myself weep at all. If he roared at the Little League umpire for calling my pitches balls, I would throw nothing but strikes. Watching him flounder and rage, I came to dread the loss of control. I would go through life without making anyone mad. I vowed never to put in my mouth or veins any chemical that would banish my everyday self. I would never make a scene, never lash out at the ones I loved, never hurt a soul. Through hard work, relentless work, I would achieve something dazzling—in the classroom, on the basketball court, in the science lab, in the pages of books—and my achievement

would distract the world's eyes from his humiliation. I would become a worthy sacrifice, and the smoke of my burning would please God.

It is far easier to recognize these twists in my character than to undo 52 them. Work has become an addiction for me, as drink was an addiction for my father. Knowing this, my daughter gave me a placard for the wall: WORKAHOLIC. The labor is endless and futile, for I can no more redeem myself through work than I could redeem my father. I still panic in the face of other people's anger, because his drunken temper was so terrible. I shrink from causing sadness or disappointment even to strangers, as though I were still concealing the family shame. I still notice every twitch of emotion in those faces around me, having learned as a child to read the weather in faces, and I blame myself for their least pang of unhappiness or anger. In certain moods I blame myself for everything. Guilt burns like acid in my veins.

I am moved to write these pages now because my own son, at the age of 53 ten, is taking on himself the griefs of the world, and in particular the griefs of his father. He tells me that when I am gripped by sadness, he feels responsible; he feels there must be something he can do to spring me from depression, to fix my life and that crushing sense of responsibility is exactly what I felt at the age of ten in the face of my father's drinking. My son wonders if I, too, am possessed. I write, therefore, to drag into the light what eats at me—the fear, the guilt, the shame—so that my own children may be spared.

I still shy away from nightclubs, from bars, from parties where the 54 solvent is alcohol. My friends puzzle over this, but it is no more peculiar than for a man to shy away from the lions' den after seeing his father torn apart. I took my own first drink at the age of twenty-one, half a glass of burgundy. I knew the odds of my becoming an alcoholic were four times higher than for the children of nonalcoholic fathers. So I sipped warily.

I still do—once a week, perhaps, a glass of wine, a can of beer, noth- 55 ing stronger, nothing more. I listen for the turning of a key in my brain.

Content

1. This essay abounds in examples of alcoholism. Which examples are the most memorable? Are these also the most painful? The most powerful? Explain why.

2. Sanders says that in spite of all his "grown-up knowledge" of alcoholism, "I am still ten years old, my own son's age" (¶ 8) as he writes this essay. What does he mean by this? What kind of a character is Sanders in this essay? What kind of a character is his father? Is there any resemblance between father and son?

Strategies/Structures/Language

3. Is Sanders writing for alcoholic readers? Their families? People unfamiliar with the symptoms of alcoholism? Or is he writing mostly for himself, to try to come to terms with the effects of his father's alcoholism on him then and now?

4. Each section of this essay (¶s 1–8, 9–14, 15–24, 25–31, 32–36, 37–44, 45–52, 53–55) focuses on a different sort of example. What are they, and why are they arranged in this particular order?

5. Why does Sanders wait until late in the essay (¶ 39) to discuss his father's sobriety, and then devote only three paragraphs to a state that lasted fifteen years?

6. What is the tone of this essay? How does Sanders, one of the victims of alcoholism as both a child and an adult, avoid being full of self-pity? Is he angry at his father? How can you tell?

For Writing

7. "Father's drinking became the family secret," says Sanders (¶ 13). Every family has significant secrets. Explain one of your family secrets, illustrating its effects on various family members, particularly on yourself. If you wish to keep the secret, don't show your essay to anyone; the point of writing this is to help yourself understand or come to terms with the matter.

8. Define an economic, political, ecological, social, or personal problem (unemployment, waste disposal, AIDS, hunger, housing, racism, or another subject of your choice) so your readers can understand it from an unusual perspective—your own or that of your sources. Illustrate its causes, effects, or implications with several significant examples—perhaps those of a perpetrator or victim.

 For comprehension, writing, and research activities and resources, please visit the companion website at <college.hmco.com/english>.

SUZANNE BRITT

Britt was born in 1946 in Winston-Salem, North Carolina, and educated at Salem College and Washington University. A newspaper columnist and essayist, Britt, who describes herself as "stately, plump," says, "I talk, eat, drink, walk around the block, read, have a stream of company, and sit on the grass outside. I try not to preach, do handicrafts, camp, bowl, argue, visit relatives, or serve on committees." "That Lean and Hungry Look," first published in *Newsweek,* is a contemporary example of a classical mode of literature—the "character"—a common form of description in which the stereotypical features of a character type ("the angry man") or role ("the schoolboy," "the housewife") are identified and often satirized.

Britt's humorous defense of fat people was first published in 1978, before obesity became a national epidemic. At that time, it would have been read as a lighthearted reinforcement of people's right to indulge in hot fudge sundaes and "two doughnuts and a big orange drink anytime they wanted it," augmented by double fudge brownies. But three decades later, obesity is considered a national epidemic. Sixty-five percent of American adults—127 million—are estimated to be overweight, and 31 percent of those are categorized as "obese" (having more than 30 percent body fat). These figures do not include the 15 percent of overweight school-age children. Complications from obesity, including strokes, heart disease, high blood pressure, diabetes, some cancers, and kidney and gallbladder disorders, contribute to 300,000 deaths a year, lowering life expectancy and dramatically increasing health care costs—currently by over $100 billion a year. How do these sobering statistics affect the reading of "That Lean and Hungry Look" today?

That Lean and Hungry Look

Caesar was right. Thin people need watching. I've been watching them for most of my adult life, and I don't like what I see. When these narrow fellows spring at me, I quiver to my toes. Thin people come in all personalities, most of them menacing. You've got your "together" thin person, your mechanical thin person, your condescending thin person, your tsk-tsk thin person, your efficiency expert thin person. All of them are dangerous.

In the first place, thin people aren't fun. They don't know how to goof off, at least in the best, fat sense of the word. They've always got to be a doing. Give them a coffee break, and they'll jog around the block. Supply them with a quiet evening at home, and they'll fix the screen door and lick S&H green stamps. They say things like "there aren't enough hours in the day." Fat people never say that. Fat people think the day is too damn long already.

Thin people make me tired. They've got speedy little metabolisms that cause them to bustle briskly. They're forever rubbing their bony hands together and eying new problems to "tackle." I like to surround myself with sluggish, inert, easygoing fat people, the kind who believe that if you clean it up today, it'll just get dirty again tomorrow.

Some people say the business about the jolly fat person is a myth, that all of us chubbies are neurotic, sick, sad people. I disagree. Fat people may not be chortling all day long, but they're a hell of a lot *nicer* than the wizened and shriveled. Thin people turn surly, mean and hard at a young age because they never learn the value of a hot-fudge sundae for easing tension. Thin people don't like gooey soft things because they themselves are neither gooey nor soft. They are crunchy and dull, like carrots. They go straight to the heart of the matter while fat people let things stay all blurry and hazy and vague, the way things actually are. Thin people want to face the truth. Fat people know there is no truth. One of my thin friends is always staring at complex, unsolvable problems and saying, "The key thing is . . ." Fat people never say that. They know there isn't any such thing as the key thing about anything.

5   Thin people believe in logic. Fat people see all sides. The sides fat people see are rounded blobs, usually gray, always nebulous and truly not worth worrying about. But the thin persons persists. "If you consume more calories than you burn," says one of my thin friends, "you will gain weight. It's that simple." Fat people always grin when they hear statements like that. They know better.

6   Fat people realize that life is illogical and unfair. They know very well that God is not in his heaven and all is not right with the world. If God was up there, fat people could have two doughnuts and a big orange drink anytime they wanted it.

7   Thin people have a long list of logical things they are always spouting off to me. They hold up one finger at a time as they reel off these things, so I won't lose track. They speak slowly as if to a young child. The list is long and full of holes. It contains tidbits like "get a grip on yourself," "cigarettes kill," "cholesterol clogs," "fit as a fiddle," "ducks in a row," "organize" and "sound fiscal management." Phrases like that.

8   They think these 2,000-point plans lead to happiness. Fat people know happiness is elusive at best and even if they could get the kind thin people talk about, they wouldn't want it. Wisely, fat people see that such programs are too dull, too hard, too off the mark. They are never better than a whole cheesecake.

9   Fat people know all about the mystery of life. They are the ones acquainted with the night, with luck, with fate, with playing it by ear. One thin person I know once suggested that we arrange all the parts of a jigsaw puzzle into groups according to size, shape and color. He figured this would cut the time needed to complete the puzzle by at least 50 per cent. I said I wouldn't do it. One, I like to muddle through. Two, what good would it do to finish early? Three, the jigsaw puzzle isn't the important thing. The important thing is the fun of four people (one thin person included) sitting around a card table, working a jigsaw puzzle. My thin friend had no use for my list. Instead of joining us, he went outside and mulched the boxwoods. The three remaining fat people finished the puzzle and made chocolate, double-fudge brownies to celebrate.

10   The main problem with thin people is they oppress. Their good intentions, bony torsos, tight ships, neat corners, cerebral machinations and pat solutions loom like dark clouds over the loose, comfortable, spread-out, soft world of the fat. Long after fat people have removed their coats and shoes and put their feet up on the coffee table, thin people are still sitting on the edge of the sofa, looking neat as a pin, discussing rutabagas. Fat people are heavily into fits of laughter, slapping their thighs and whooping it up, while thin people are still politely waiting for the punch line.

11   Thin people are downers. They like math and morality and reasoned evaluating of the limitations of human beings. They have their skinny little acts together. They expound, prognose, probe and prick.

Fat people are convivial. They will like you even if you're irregular 12
and have acne. They will come up with a good reason why you never wrote
the great American novel. They will cry in your beer with you. They will
put your name in the pot. They will let you off the hook. Fat people will
gab, giggle, guffaw, gallumph, gyrate and gossip. They are generous, giving and gallant. They are gluttonous and goodly and great. What you want
when you're down is soft and jiggly, not muscled and stable. Fat people
know this. Fat people have plenty of room. Fat people will take you in.

Content

1. Britt is describing two categories of people, thin and fat. Does she stereotype
them? If so, what does she gain from stereotyping? If not, how does she individ-
ualize each category? Is her depiction accurate? Why or why not?

2. Why has she chosen to overlook characteristics typical of either group—for instance, the effects on one's health of being either too fat or too thin? Does she treat
thin people fairly? Does she intend to do so?

3. For the purpose of contrast, Britt has concentrated on the differences between
fat and thin people. What similarities, if any, do they have? Are these related to
their weight?

Strategies/Structures/Language

4. Throughout, Britt makes blanket generalizations about both thin and fat people.
Does she support these? Is her evidence appropriate? Is it sufficiently comprehensive to make her case?

5. At what point in the essay do you realize that Britt is being humorous? Does
her humor reinforce or undermine her point? Explain your answer. Is the humor
appropriate for today's readers?

6. Britt's language is conversational, sometimes slangy: "Thin people are downers.
. . . They have their skinny little acts together" (¶ 11). In what ways does the language reinforce what Britt says about fat people?

For Writing

7. Write a humorous essay in which you divide a larger category (such as students, parents, Southerners, Easterners, Californians) into subcategories as Britt
does in the first paragraph, and then characterize each subcategory through comparing and contrasting its parts (working students, athletes, nerds, partiers). Writing collaboratively, each partner could describe one category or subcategory.
Photographs, drawings, or cartoons can enhance the descriptions.

8. By yourself or with a partner, select one major cause of obesity in America
today, research its causes, and provide a workable solution to the problem.

 For comprehension, writing, and research activities and resources, please visit
the companion website at <college.hmco.com/english>.

ISTVAN BANYAI

Inflation

What's the story here? What changes—in the figure and in the cost of the postage stamp—occur in the successive panels? Do they need any captions? What's the point of using "Inflation" as a title? Can you think of any alternate titles that would work as well?

MARK TWAIN

Mark Twain (a riverman's term for "two fathoms deep," the pen name of Samuel Clemens) celebrated in his writing a lifelong love affair with the Mississippi River and with the rural life along its banks. In *The Adventures of Tom Sawyer* (1876) and *The Adventures of Huckleberry Finn* (1885), he immortalized the riverfront town of Hannibal, Missouri, where he was born (1835) and whose folkways he absorbed. A prolific writer, Twain's works grew increasingly pessimistic as he experienced grief (the death of his beloved daughter) and economic reversals later in life. Nevertheless, in his *Autobiography* (published in 1924, fourteen years after his death), Twain depicted an idyllic but comically realistic picture of a country childhood, specific in time (pre–Civil War) and place (in the country, four miles from Florida, Missouri), yet timeless and ubiquitous. The autobiography shows us two central characters, the boy Sam Clemens, who enjoyed every aspect of his Uncle John Quarles's farm, and Mark Twain, the older, wiser, and sometimes more cynical author, who writes these reminiscences after alerting readers to bear in mind that he can "remember anything, whether it had happened or not." What he remembers is the spirit of the farm, the people who lived there, white and black, and how they lived in abiding harmony.

Twain reinforces that spirit with an abundance of sensory details— often the mainstay of description, as they are here. Thus he evokes a rich sensory intermingling in descriptions such as the following: "I can call back the solemn twilight [*sight*] and mystery of the deep woods, the earthy smells, the faint odors of the wild flowers [*smell*], the sheen of rain-washed foliage [*sight*], the rattling clatter of drops when the wind shook the trees, the far-off hammering of woodpeckers [*sound*]. . . . I can see the blue clusters of wild grapes . . . and I remember the taste of them and the smell" [*sight, taste, smell*] (¶ 13).

Uncle John's Farm[1]

For many years I believed that I remembered helping my grandfather   1
drink his whiskey toddy when I was six weeks old, but I do not tell about that any more, now; I am grown old, and my memory is not as active as it used to be. When I was younger I could remember anything, whether it had happened or not; but my faculties are decaying, now, and soon I shall be so I cannot remember any but the things that [never] happened. It is sad to go to pieces like this, but we all have to do it.

My uncle, John A. Quarles, was a farmer, and his place was in the   2
country four miles from Florida. He had eight children, and fifteen or twenty negroes, and was also fortunate in other ways. Particularly in his character.

---

[1]Title supplied.

I have not come across a better man than he was. I was his guest for two or three months every year, from the fourth year after we removed to Hanni-bal till I was eleven or twelve years old. I have never consciously used him or his wife in a book, but his farm has come very handy to me in literature, once or twice. In *Huck Finn* and in *Tom Sawyer Detective* I moved it down to Arkansas. It was all of six hundred miles, but it was no trouble, it was not a very large farm; five hundred acres, perhaps, but I could have done it if it had been twice as large. And as for the morality of it, I cared nothing for that; I would move a State if the exigencies of literature required it.

3   It was a heavenly place for a boy, that farm of my uncle John's. The house was a double log one, with a spacious floor (roofed in) connecting it with the kitchen. In the summer the table was set in the middle of that shady and breezy floor, and the sumptuous meals—well, it makes me cry to think of them. Fried chicken, roast pig, wild and tame turkeys, ducks and geese; venison just killed; squirrels, rabbits, pheasants, partridges, prairie-chickens; biscuits, hot batter cakes, hot buckwheat cakes, hot "wheat bread," hot rolls, hot corn pone; fresh corn boiled on the ear, suc-cotash, butterbeans, string-beans, tomatoes, pease, Irish potatoes, sweet-potatoes; buttermilk, sweet milk, "clabber"; watermelons, muskmelons, cantaloupe—all fresh from the garden—apple pie, peach pie, pumpkin pie, apple dumplings, peach cobbler—I can't remember the rest. The way that the things were cooked was perhaps the main splendor—particularly a certain few of the dishes. For instance, the corn bread, the hot biscuits and wheat bread, and the fried chicken. These things have never been properly cooked in the North—in fact, no one there is able to learn the art, so far as my experience goes. The North thinks it knows how to make corn bread, but this is gross superstition. Perhaps no bread in the world is quite as good as Southern corn bread, and perhaps no bread in the world is quite so bad as the Northern imitation of it. The North seldom tries to fry chicken, and this is well; the art cannot be learned north of the line of Mason and Dixon, nor anywhere in Europe. . . .

4   It seems a pity that the world should throw away so many good things merely because they are unwholesome. I doubt if God has given us any refreshment which, taken in moderation, is unwholesome, except microbes. Yet there are people who strictly deprive themselves of each and every eatable, drinkable and smokable which has in any way acquired a shady reputation. They pay this price for health. And health is all they get for it. How strange it is; it is like paying out your whole fortune for a cow that has gone dry. . . .

5   The farmhouse stood in the middle of a very large yard, and the yard was fenced on three sides with rails and on the rear side with high palings; against these stood the smokehouse; beyond the palings was the orchard; beyond the orchard were the negro quarter and the tobacco-fields. The front yard was entered over a stile, made of sawed-off logs of graduated heights; I do not remember any gate. In a corner of the front

yard were a dozen lofty hickory-trees and a dozen black-walnuts, and in the nutting season riches were to be gathered there.

Down a piece, abreast the house, stood a little log cabin against the rail 6 fence; and there the woody hill fell sharply away, past the barns, the corn-crib, the stables and the tobacco-curing house, to a limpid brook which sang along over its gravelly bed and curved and frisked in and out and here and there and yonder in the deep shade of overhanging foliage and vines—a divine place for wading, and it had swimming-pools, too, which were forbidden to us and therefore much frequented by us. For we were little Christian children, and had early been taught the value of forbidden fruit. . . .

I can see the farm yet, with perfect clearness. I can see all its belong- 7 ings, all its details; the family room of the house, with a "trundle" bed in one corner and a spinning-wheel in another, a wheel whose rising and falling wail, heard from a distance, was the mournfulest of all sounds to me, and made me homesick and low-spirited, and filled my atmosphere with the wandering spirits of the dead; the vast fireplace, piled high, on winter nights, with flaming hickory logs from whose ends a sugary sap bubbled out but did not go to waste, for we scraped it off and ate it; the lazy cat spread out on the rough hearthstones, the drowsy dogs braced against the jambs and blinking; my aunt in one chimney-corner knitting, my uncle in the other smoking his corn-cob pipe; the slick and carpetless oak floor faintly mirror-ing the dancing flame-tongues and freckled with black indentations where fire-coals had popped out and died a leisurely death; half a dozen children romping in the background twilight; "split"-bottomed chairs here and there, some with rockers; a cradle—out of service, but waiting, with confidence; in the early cold mornings a snuggle of children, in shirts and chemises, occupying the hearthstone and procrastinating—they could not bear to leave that comfortable place and go out on the wind-swept floor-space be-tween the house and kitchen where the general tin basin stood, and wash.

Along outside of the front fence ran the country road; dusty in the 8 summertime, and a good place for snakes—they liked to lie in it and sun themselves; when they were rattlesnakes or puff adders, we killed them; when they were black snakes, or racers, or belonged to the fabled "hoop" breed, we fled, without shame; when they were "house snakes" or "garters" we carried them home and put them in Aunt Patsy's work-basket for a surprise; for she was prejudiced against snakes, and always when she took the basket in her lap and they began to climb out of it it disordered her mind. She never could seem to get used to them; her opportunities went for nothing. And she was always cold toward bats, too, and could not bear them; and yet I think a bat is as friendly a bird as there is. My mother was Aunt Patsy's sister, and had the same wild superstitions. A bat is beautifully soft and silky; I do not know any creature that is pleasanter to the touch, or is more grateful for caressings, if offered in the right spirit. I know all about these coleoptera, because our great cave, three miles below

Hannibal, was multitudinously stocked with them, and often I brought them home to amuse my mother with. It was easy to manage if it was a school day, because then I had ostensibly been to school and hadn't any bats. She was not a suspicious person, but full of trust and confidence; and when I said "There's something in my coat pocket for you," she would put her hand in. But she always took it out again, herself; I didn't have to tell her. It was remarkable, the way she couldn't learn to like private bats. . . .

9   Beyond the road where the snakes sunned themselves was a dense young thicket, and through it a dim-lighted path led a quarter of a mile; then out of the dimness one emerged abruptly upon a level great prairie which was covered with wild strawberry-plants, vividly starred with prairie pinks, and walled in on all sides by forests. The strawberries were fragrant and fine, and in the season we were generally there in the crisp freshness of the early morning, while the dew-beads still sparkled upon the grass and the woods were ringing with the first songs of the birds.

10   Down the forest slopes to the left were the swings. They were made of bark stripped from hickory saplings. When they became dry they were dangerous. They usually broke when a child was forty feet in the air, and this was why so many bones had to be mended every year. I had no ill-luck myself, but none of my cousins escaped. There were eight of them, and at one time and another they broke fourteen arms among them. But it cost next to nothing, for the doctor worked by the year—$25 for the whole family. I remember two of the Florida doctors, Chowning and Meredith. They not only tended an entire family for $25 a year, but furnished the medicines themselves. Good measures, too. Only the largest persons could hold a whole dose. Castor-oil was the principal beverage. The dose was half a dipperful, with half a dipperful of New Orleans molasses added to help it down and make it taste good, which it never did. The next standby was calomel; the next, rhubarb; and the next, jalap. Then they bled the patient, and put mustard-plasters on him. It was a dreadful system, and yet the death-rate was not heavy. The calomel was nearly sure to salivate the patient and cost him some of his teeth. There were no dentists. When teeth became touched with decay or were otherwise ailing, the doctor knew of but one thing to do: he fetched his tongs and dragged them out. If the jaw remained, it was not his fault. Doctors were not called, in cases of ordinary illness; the family's grandmother attended to those. . . .

11   The country schoolhouse was three miles from my uncle's farm. It stood in a clearing in the woods, and would hold about twenty-five boys and girls. We attended the school with more or less regularity once or twice a week, in summer, walking to it in the cool of the morning by the forest paths, and back in the gloaming at the end of the day. All the pupils brought their dinners in baskets—corn-dodger, buttermilk and other good things—and sat in the shade of the trees at noon and ate them. It is the part of my education which I look back upon with the most satisfaction. My first visit to the school was when I was seven. A strapping girl of fifteen, in the customary sunbonnet and calico dress, asked me if I "used

tobacco"—meaning did I chew it. I said, no. It roused her scorn. She reported me to all the crowd, and said—

"Here is a boy seven years old who can't chaw tobacco."   12

By the looks and comments which this produced, I realized that I was   13
a degraded object; I was cruelly ashamed of myself. I determined to reform.
But I only made myself sick; I was not able to learn to chew tobacco. I
learned to smoke fairly well, but that did not conciliate anybody, and I remained a poor thing, and characterless. I longed to be respected, but I never
was able to rise. Children have but little charity for each other's defects.

As I have said, I spent some part of every year at the farm until I was   14
twelve or thirteen years old. The life which I led there with my cousins
was full of charm, and so is the memory of it yet. I can call back the solemn
twilight and mystery of the deep woods, the earthy smells, the faint odors
of the wild flowers, the sheen of rain-washed foliage, the rattling clatter
of drops when the wind shook the trees, the far-off hammering of woodpeckers and the muffled drumming of wood-pheasants in the remoteness
of the forest, the snap-shot glimpses of disturbed wild creatures skurrying
through the grass,—I can call it all back and make it as real as it ever was,
and as blessed. I can call back the prairie, and its loneliness and peace, and
a vast hawk hanging motionless in the sky, with his wings spread wide and
the blue of the vault showing through the fringe of their end-feathers. I can
see the woods in their autumn dress, the oaks purple, the hickories washed
with gold, the maples and the sumacs luminous with crimson fires, and I
can hear the rustle made by the fallen leaves as we ploughed through them.
I can see the blue clusters of wild grapes hanging amongst the foliage of the
saplings, and I remember the taste of them and the smell. I know how the
wild blackberries looked, and how they tasted; and the same with the pawpaws, the hazelnuts and the persimmons; and I can feel the thumping rain,
upon my head, of hickory-nuts and walnuts when we were out in the frosty
dawn to scramble for them with the pigs, and the gusts of wind loosed them
and sent them down. I know the stain of blackberries, and how pretty it
is; and I know the stain of walnut hulls, and how little it minds soap and
water; also what grudged experience it had of either of them. I know the
taste of maple sap, and when to gather it, and how to arrange the troughs
and the delivery tubes, and how to boil down the juice, and how to hook the
sugar after it is made; also how much better hooked sugar tastes than any
that is honestly come by, let bigots say what they will. I know how a prize
watermelon looks when it is sunning its fat rotundity among pumpkin-
vines and "simblins"; I know how to tell when it is ripe without "plugging"
it; I know how inviting it looks when it is cooling itself in a tub of water
under the bed, waiting; I know how it looks when it lies on the table in the
sheltered great floor-space between house and kitchen, and the children
gathered for the sacrifice and their mouths watering; I know the crackling
sound it makes when the carving-knife enters its end, and I can see the split
fly along in front of the blade as the knife cleaves its way to the other end;
I can see its halves fall apart and display the rich red meat and the black

seeds, and the heart standing up, a luxury fit for the elect; I know how a boy looks, behind a yard-long slice of that melon, and I know how he feels; for I have been there. I know the taste of the watermelon which has been honestly come by, and I know the taste of the watermelon which has been acquired by art. Both taste good, but the experienced know which tastes best. I know the look of green apples and peaches and pears on the trees, and I know how entertaining they are when they are inside of a person. I know how ripe ones look when they are piled in pyramids under the trees, and how pretty they are and how vivid their colors. I know how a frozen apple looks, in a barrel down cellar in the winter-time, and how hard it is to bite, and how the frost makes the teeth ache, and yet how good it is, notwithstanding. I know the disposition of elderly people to select the specked apples for the children, and I once knew ways to beat the game. I know the look of an apple that is roasting and sizzling on a hearth on a winter's evening, and I know the comfort that comes of eating it hot, along with some sugar and a drench of cream. I know the delicate art and mystery of so cracking hickory-nuts and walnuts on a flatiron with a hammer that the kernels will be delivered whole, and I know how the nuts, taken in conjunction with winter apples, cider and doughnuts, make old people's tales and old jokes sound fresh and crisp and enchanting, and juggle an evening away before you know what went with the time. I know the look of Uncle Dan'l's kitchen as it was on privileged nights when I was a child, and I can see the white and black children grouped on the hearth, with the firelight playing on their faces and the shadows flickering upon the walls, clear back toward the cavernous gloom of the rear, and I can hear Uncle Dan'l telling the immortal tales which Uncle Remus Harris was to gather into his books and charm the world with, by and by; and I can feel again the creepy joy which quivered through me when the time for the ghost-story of the "Golden Arm" was reached—and the sense of regret, too, which came over me, for it was always the last story of the evening, and there was nothing between it and the unwelcome bed.

15   I can remember the bare wooden stairway in my uncle's house, and the turn to the left above the landing, and the rafters and the slanting roof over my bed, and the squares of moonlight on the floor, and the white cold world of snow outside, seen through the curtainless window. I can remember the howling of the wind and the quaking of the house on stormy nights, and how snug and cozy one felt, under the blankets, listening, and how the powdery snow used to sift in, around the sashes, and lie in little ridges on the floor, and make the place look chilly in the morning, and curb the wild desire to get up—in case there was any. I can remember how very dark that room was, in the dark of the moon, and how packed it was with ghostly stillness when one woke up by accident away in the night, and forgotten sins came flocking out of the secret chambers of the memory and wanted a hearing; and how ill chosen the time seemed for this kind of business; and how dismal was the hoo-hooing of the owl and the wailing of the wolf, sent mourning by on the night wind.

I remember the raging of the rain on that roof, summer nights, and 16 how pleasant it was to lie and listen to it, and enjoy the white splendor of the lightning and the majestic booming and crashing of the thunder. It was a very satisfactory room; and there was a lightning-rod which was reachable from the window, an adorable and skittish thing to climb up and down, summer nights, when there were duties on hand of a sort to make privacy desirable.

I remember the 'coon and 'possum hunts, night, and the negroes, and 17 the long marches through the black gloom of the woods, and the excitement which fired everybody when the distant bay of an experienced dog announced that the game was treed; then the wild scramblings and stumblings through briars and bushes and over roots to get to the spot; then the lighting of a fire and the felling of the tree, the joyful frenzy of the dogs and the negroes, and the weird picture it all made in the red glare—I remember it all well, and the delight that every one got out of it, except the 'coon.

I remember the pigeon seasons, when the birds would come in mil- 18 lions, and cover the trees, and by their weight break down the branches. They were clubbed to death with sticks; guns were not necessary, and were not used. I remember the squirrel hunts, and the prairie-chicken hunts, and the wild-turkey hunts, and all that; and how we turned out, mornings, while it was still dark, to go on these expeditions, and how chilly and dismal it was, and how often I regretted that I was well enough to go. A toot on a tin horn brought twice as many dogs as were needed, and in their happiness they raced and scampered about, and knocked small people down, and made no end of unnecessary noise. At the word, they vanished away toward the woods, and we drifted silently after them in the melancholy gloom. But presently the gray dawn stole over the world, the birds piped up, then the sun rose and poured light and comfort all around, everything was fresh and dewy and fragrant, and life was a boon again. After three hours of tramping we arrived back wholesomely tired, overladen with game, very hungry, and just in time for breakfast.

Content

1. Even though Twain's opening two paragraphs warn that he is quite capable of remembering anything, "whether it had happened or not," what he says throughout this essay appears true and convincing. Why? Does anything seem too good to be true? What made the farm a "heavenly place for a boy"? Do his memories of children's broken bones (¶ 10) and his childhood shame at being unable to chew tobacco (¶s 11–13) diminish his pleasant recollections?

Strategies/Structures/Language

2. In places Twain's description involves long lists or catalogues—of foods (¶ 3), of the sights and sounds and activities of farm life (¶s 3–14), and of the seasons and seasonal activities (¶s 15–18). How does he vary the lists to keep them appealing?

3. Why does Twain pack so many details into such a long paragraph (¶ 14)? If he had broken it up, where could he have done so? With what effects?

4. In this largely descriptive account, Twain provides characterizations of the local doctors (¶ 10), many interpretations ("The life was . . . full of charm," [¶ 14]), and narration of incidents—for instance, of Aunt Patsy and the snakes (¶ 8). Explain how these techniques contribute to the overall picture of life on the farm.

5. Twain uses the language of an adult to recall events from his childhood. Find a typical passage in which he enables us to see the experience as a child would but to imply or offer an adult's interpretation.

For Writing

6. Identify a place that had considerable significance—pleasant, indifferent, unpleasant, or a mixture—for you as a child, and describe it for an unfamiliar reader to emphasize your attitude toward it. Use sensory details, where appropriate, to help your readers to recreate your experiences. The essays by Amanda N. Cagle (191–95), Linda Hogan (273–76), Asiya S. Tschannerl (278–81), Megan McGuire (225–31), and Matt Nocton (527–31) provide good examples of how to do this.

7. Pick an aspect of your childhood relationship with a parent or other adult, or a critical experience in your precollege schooling, and describe it so the reader shares your experience. Compare, if you wish, with essays by E. B. White (97–103), Anne Fadiman (104–7), Frederick Douglass (109–13), Scott Russell Sanders (249–59), Ning Yu (173–82), or Megan McGuire (225–31).

 For comprehension, writing, and research activities and resources, please visit the companion website at <college.hmco.com/english>.

LINDA HOGAN

Hogan's Chickasaw Indian heritage informs her work both as a creative writer and as a professor of American Indian studies, currently at the University of Colorado. She was born in Denver in 1947 and earned a BA at the University of Colorado at Colorado Springs and an MA in English and creative writing at the University of Colorado, Boulder, in 1978. *Seeing Through the Sun* (1985) received an American Book Award for poetry. Her novels include *Mean Spirit* (1990), *Solar Storms* (1995), and *Power* (1998). Her recent work includes *The Woman Who Watches Over the World: A Native Memoir* (2001) and *Face to Face* (2004). "Dwellings" is the title essay of her collection *Dwellings: A Spiritual History of the Living World* (1995).

"As an Indian woman," the introduction to her book begins, "I question our responsibilities to the caretaking of the future and to the other species who share our journeys. These writings have grown out of these questions, out of wondering what makes us human, out of lifelong love for the living world and all its inhabitants. They have grown, too, out of my native understanding that there is a terrestrial intelligence that lies beyond our human knowing and grasping." She continues, "It has been my lifelong work to seek an understanding of the two views of the world, one as seen by native people and the other as seen by those who are new and young on this continent. It is clear that we have strayed from the treaties we once had with the land and with the animals. It is also clear, and heartening, that in our time there are many—Indian and non-Indian alike—who want to restore and honor these broken agreements."

Dwellings

N ot far from where I live is a hill that was cut into by the moving   1
water of a creek. Eroded this way, all that's left of it is a broken wall of earth that contains old roots and pebbles woven together and exposed. Seen from a distance, it is only a rise of raw earth. But up close it is some-thing wonderful, a small cliff dwelling that looks almost as intricate and well made as those the Anasazi left behind when they vanished myste-riously centuries ago. This hill is a place that could be the starry skies of night turned inward into the thousand round holes where solitary bees have lived and died. It is a hill of tunneling rooms. At the mouths of some of the excavations, half-circles of clay beetle out like awnings shading a doorway. It is earth that was turned to clay in the mouths of the bees and spit out as they mined deeper into their dwelling places.

This place where the bees reside is at an angle safe from rain. It faces   2
the southern sun. It is a warm and intelligent architecture of memory, learned by whatever memory lives in the blood. Many of the holes still contain the gold husks of dead bees, their faces dry and gone, their flat eyes gazing out from death's land toward the other uninhabited half of the hill that is across the creek from these catacombs.

The first time I found the residence of the bees, it was dusty summer.   3
The sun was hot, and land was the dry color of rust. Now and then a car rumbled along the dirt road and dust rose up behind it before settling back down on older dust. In the silence, the bees made a soft droning hum. They were alive then, and working the hill, going out and returning with pollen, in and out through the holes, back and forth between day-light and the cooler, darker regions of inner earth. They were flying an in-visible map through air, a map charted by landmarks, the slant of light, and a circling story they told one another about the direction of food held inside the center of yellow flowers.

Sitting in the hot sun, watching the small bees fly in and out around the   4
hill, hearing the summer birds, the light breeze, I felt right in the world. I belonged there. I thought of my own dwelling places, those real and those imagined. Once I lived in a town called Manitou, which means "Great Spirit," and where hot mineral springwater gurgled beneath the streets

and rose up into open wells. I felt safe there. With the underground movement of water and heat a constant reminder of other life, of what lives beneath us, it seemed to be the center of the world.

5   A few years after that, I wanted silence. My daydreams were full of places I longed to be, shelters and solitudes. I wanted a room apart from others, a hidden cabin to rest in. I wanted to be in a redwood forest with trees so tall the owls called out in the daytime. I daydreamed of living in a vapor cave a few hours away from here. Underground, warm, and moist, I thought it would be the perfect world for staying out of cold winter, for escaping the noise of living.

6   And how often I've wanted to escape to a wilderness where a human hand has not been in everything. But those were only dreams of peace, of comfort, of a nest inside stone or woods, a sanctuary where a dream or life wouldn't be invaded.

7   Years ago, in the next canyon west of here, there was a man who followed one of those dreams and moved into a cave that could only be reached by climbing down a rope. For years he lived there in comfort, like a troglodyte. The inner weather was stable, never too hot, too cold, too wet, or too dry. But then he felt lonely. His utopia needed a woman. He went to town until he found a wife. For a while after the marriage, his wife climbed down the rope along with him, but before long she didn't want the mice scurrying about in the cave, or the untidy bats that wanted to hang from stones of the ceiling. So they built a door. Because of the closed entryway, the temperature changed. They had to put in heat. Then the inner moisture of earth warped the door, so they had to have air-conditioning, and after that the earth wanted to go about life in its own way and it didn't give in to the people.

8   In other days and places, people paid more attention to the strong-headed will of earth. Once homes were built of wood that had been felled from a single region in a forest. That way, it was thought, the house would hold together more harmoniously, and the family of walls would not fall or lend themselves to the unhappiness or arguments of the inhabitants.

9   An Italian immigrant to Chicago, Aldo Piacenzi, built birdhouses that were dwellings of harmony and peace. They were the incredible spired shapes of cathedrals in Italy. They housed not only the birds, but also his memories, his own past. He painted them the watery blue of his Mediterranean, the wild rose of flowers in a summer field. Inside them was straw and the droppings of lives that layed eggs, fledglings who grew there. What places to inhabit, the bright and sunny birdhouses in dreary alleyways of the city.

10   One beautiful afternoon, cool and moist, with the kind of yellow light that falls on earth in these arid regions, I waited for barn swallows to return from their daily work of food gathering. Inside the tunnel where they live,

hundreds of swallows had mixed their saliva with mud and clay, much like the solitary bees, and formed nests that were perfect as a potter's bowl. At five in the evening, they returned all at once, a dark, flying shadow. Despite their enormous numbers and the crowding together of nests, they didn't pause for even a moment before entering the nests, nor did they crowd one another. Instantly they vanished into the nests. The tunnel went silent. It held no outward signs of life.

But I knew they were there, filled with the fire of living. And what a 11 marriage of elements was in those nests. Not only mud's earth and water, the fire of sun and dry air, but even the elements contained one another. The bodies of prophets and crazy men were broken down in that soil.

I've noticed often how when a house is abandoned, it begins to sag. With- 12 out a tenant, it has no need to go on. If it were a person, we'd say it is depressed or lonely. The roof settles in, the paint cracks, the walls and floorboards warp and slope downward in their own natural ways, telling us that life must stay in everything as the world whirls and tilts and moves through boundless space.

One summer day, cleaning up after long-eared owls where I work at a re- 13 habilitation facility for birds of prey, I was raking the gravel floor of a flight cage. Down on the ground, something looked like it was moving. I bent over to look into the pile of bones and pellets I'd just raked together. There, close to the ground, were two fetal mice. They were new to the planet, pink and hairless. They were so tenderly young. Their faces had swollen blue-veined eyes. They were nestled in a mound of feathers, soft as velvet, each one curled up smaller than an infant's ear, listening to the first sounds of earth. But the ants were biting them. They turned in agony, unable to pull away, not yet having the arms or legs to move, but feeling, twisting away from, the pain of the bites. I was horrified to see them bitten out of life that way. I dipped them in water, as if to take away the sting, and let the ants fall in the bucket. Then I held the tiny mice in the palm of my hand. Some of the ants were drowning in the water. I was trading one life for another, exchanging the lives of ants for those of mice, but I hated their suffering, and hated even more that they had not yet grown to a life, and already they inhabited the miserable world of pain. Death and life feed each other. I know that.

Inside these rooms where birds are healed, there are other lives be- 14 sides those of mice. There are fine gray globes the wasps have woven together, the white cocoons of spiders in a corner, the downward tunneling anthills. All these dwellings are inside one small walled space, but I think most about the mice. Sometimes the downy nests fall out of the walls where their mothers have placed them out of the way of their enemies. When one of the nests falls, they are so well made and soft, woven mostly from the chest feathers of birds. Sometimes the leg of a small quail holds the nest together like a slender cornerstone with dry, bent claws. The mice have adapted to life in the presence of their enemies, adapted to living in the thin wall between beak and beak, claw and claw. They move their nests often, as if a new rafter or wall will protect them from the inevitable fate of all our returns home to the deeper, wider nest of earth that houses us all.

15   One August at Zia Pueblo during the corn dance I noticed tourists picking up shards of all the old pottery that had been made and broken there. The residents of Zia know not to take the bowls and pots left behind by the older ones. They know that the fragments of those earlier lives need to be smoothed back to earth, but younger nations, travelers from continents across the world who have come to inhabit this land, have little of their own to grow on. The pieces of earth that were formed into bowls, even on their way home to dust, provide the new people a lifeline to an unknown land, help them remember that they live in the old nest of earth.

16   It was in early February, during the mating season of the great horned owls. It was dusk, and I hiked up the back of a mountain to where I'd heard the owls a year before. I wanted to hear them again, the voices so tender, so deep, like a memory of comfort. I was halfway up the trail when I found a soft, round nest. It had fallen from one of the bare-branched trees. It was a delicate nest, woven together of feathers, sage, and strands of wild grass. Holding it in my hand in the rosy twilight, I noticed that a blue thread was entwined with the other gatherings there. I pulled at the thread a little, and then I recognized it. It was a thread from one of my skirts. It was blue cotton. It was the unmistakable color and shape of a pattern I knew. I liked it, that a thread of my life was in an abandoned nest, one that had held eggs and new life. I took the nest home. At home, I held it to the light and looked more closely. There, to my surprise, nestled into the gray-green sage, was a gnarl of black hair. It was also unmistakable. It was my daughter's hair, cleaned from a brush and picked up out in the sun beneath the maple tree, or the pit cherry where birds eat from the overladen, fertile branches until only the seeds remain on the trees.

17   I didn't know what kind of nest it was, or who had lived there. It didn't matter. I thought of the remnants of our lives carried up the hill that way and turned into shelter. That night, resting inside the walls of our home, the world outside weighed so heavily against the thin wood of the house. The sloped roof was the only thing between us and the universe. Everything outside of our wooden boundaries seemed so large. Filled with night's citizens, it all came alive. The world opened in the thickets of the dark. The wild grapes would soon ripen on the vines. The burrowing ones were emerging. Horned owls sat in treetops. Mice scurried here and there. Skunks, fox, the slow and holy porcupine, all were passing by this way. The young of the solitary bees were feeding on pollen in the dark. The whole world was a nest on its humble tilt, in the maze of the universe, holding us.

Content

1. Linda Hogan describes a variety of different types of dwellings. Choose two and explain what the relationship of these dwellings is to each other and to the natural setting in which they appear. In what ways does Hogan's selection and organization of information, particularly sensory details, convey her implicit judgments of those dwellings?

2. Why does Hogan describe such a variety of dwellings—human and animal? What elements of nature connect them with one another and with the lives of their occupants? In what ways are the descriptions of animals' dwellings as vivid as those of humans?

Strategies/Structures/Language

3. What determines the essay's overall order? To determine this, identify the topic of each paragraph in sequence. Which dwellings come first, in the middle, last? Which paragraphs don't discuss particular dwellings or types of dwellings—and where do they come? When Hogan is describing a particular dwelling, what sort of details does she begin with? Conclude with? With what effects?

4. Hogan uses many details as she describes both her own and others' dwellings. Is there a difference in the kind of details she uses to describe human dwellings and the kind of details she uses to describe nonhuman dwellings? If so, explain what the differences are. If not, identify the similarities.

5. Toward the conclusion of her essay Hogan accidentally stumbles upon a thread from one of her own skirts and "a gnarl of black hair" from her daughter's brush contained in a bird's nest (¶ 16). Why doesn't it matter to her that she "didn't know what kind of nest it was, or who had lived there" (¶ 17)? What does she mean by ending her essay with "The whole world was a nest on its humble tilt, in the maze of the universe, holding us" (¶ 17)? In what ways throughout the essay has Hogan prepared her readers for this conclusion? Compare and contrast Hogan's version of Indian history with Alexie's "What Sacagawea Means to Me" (94–95).

For Writing

6. Write an essay that describes your own dwelling (house, apartment, dorm room), or the house of another—human or animal. What details will you choose to include, and with what emphasis? What kinds of details will you leave out? Why? Do you want your readers to be attracted to your dwelling, or not? For what reasons?

Once you've written your essay, ask another student to read it and draw a sketch of the dwelling you've written about as she understands it. Does the sketch contain all the essential features? In the right proportions? Does it capture your attitude toward the dwelling? If not, what do you need to add to your essay, including diagrams, photographs, or floor plans, to convey its meaning?

7. Draw up a detailed outline for a descriptive essay of, say, a person or place you know well, and then revise that outline to reflect a different organizational pattern (see pages 285–89 for a discussion of types of organizational patterns). In a brief essay, consider the differences between the two organizational outlines.

What sorts of information do they highlight? For what types of audience might each be appropriate?

 For comprehension, writing, and research activities and resources, please visit the companion website at <college.hmco.com/english>.

ASIYA S. TSCHANNERL

Asiya Tschannerl was adopted soon after her birth in Philadelphia in 1977 by parents of Indian and Austrian nationalities (her Austrian last name, *Tschannerl,* rhymes with *chunnel,* as in the name of the tunnel under the English Channel). Having lived in China, India, and parts of Africa and Europe, she feels that her ethnicity extends well beyond her African-American roots. In 1998 she earned a BSc in medical biochemistry from Royal Holloway, University of London, to which she has returned for graduate study in pursuit of an MD. She is currently a certified emergency medical technician, as well as an artist, composer, singer, cellist, and writer.

Asiya believes that her best writing stems from subjects she knows well. In composing short autobiographical pieces, she "retraces thoughts, smells, and touches from the past, since doing so usually brings a wealth of other memories along with the initial association." Through the "domino effect of remembrance," she claims even to remember her adoption at three months, the moment when her adoptive mother first held her. Her memories are evocative of the senses ("I remember leaning back against that wind and not being able to fall"), of pride, terror, disillusionment, and love. Through writing sketches such as "One Remembers Most What One Loves," Asiya hopes to "inspire readers with a willingness to embrace and love other cultures as their own."

❄ One Remembers Most What One Loves

1   I have often been commended for my memory. I can even remember being held when I was adopted at three months of age. Perhaps one only recalls events which profoundly change one's life.

2   I remember my youth very clearly. How the seasons would change! September would bring its chilly air and a nervous start of a new school year. November would be full of excitement, with its strong gusts of wind and swirling sandstorms. It was amazing to look at a grain of sand and

know that it had come from over two thousand miles away, from the Gobi desert. I remember leaning back against that wind and not being able to fall. I can still see that stream of bicycles going to the city, every head clad with a thin scarf to protect against the sand.

How well I know that bitter coldness of the winter, bringing snow- 3 balls and ice-skating on the lake at the Summer Palace. February fireworks, noodles and mooncakes for the New Year, our home always filled with friendly visits. I remember the monsoon rains of April and how the rice fields behind our apartment would sway as if they had a life of their own. And how could I forget the long, hot summers of badminton, evening walks, and mosquito nets?

Perhaps my memory is fostered by the countless nights I spent mem- 4 orizing Chinese characters, stroke after stroke. In any case, I cannot forget. I love my childhood. I love Beijing.

Bei sha tan nong ji xue yuan. This is the name of the Chinese com- 5 pound we lived in, an agricultural mechanization institute on the out-skirts of Beijing. During the day, my father worked there while I would accompany my mother into the city. My mother taught sociology at the Beijing Foreign Languages Institute and I attended its adjoining Chinese elementary school. At age nine, I was in a country I had not lived in since I was a toddler and my Chinese was very poor. Hence, I entered first grade having already had four years of American grade school.

I remember my apprehension when my teacher introduced me on 6 the first day of school. A hush fell over the classroom as forty pairs of wide eyes beheld for the first time a person of African descent. After what seemed a long time, class went on as usual, and finding myself amidst a maze of unintelligible dialogue, I took out my coloring pencils and began to draw. The children around me smiled shyly at me, curious to see what I was drawing. Such was the beginning of enduring friendships.

As the months rolled by, the sea of gibberish slowly became a wealth 7 of vocabulary. I never knew that a language could describe things so pre-cisely—but this is not to be wondered at when one considers the 15,000 characters that comprise the Chinese language, of which one must know at least 3,000 to be literate.

There was a routine common to each day. Upon arriving at school in 8 the morning, everyone assembled in the playground and did the morning exercises. This involved dance-like movements and several laps around the school, rain or shine. Once inside the building we would do a series of mental math computations as quickly as possible. Then everyone would assume the "correct posture" of arms folded behind the back—a posture I found exceedingly uncomfortable at first. This position had to be main-tained throughout class except when raising a hand, which was done by putting the right elbow on the desk.

Chinese class would involve reading passages from our textbooks 9 and learning new characters. Breaks between every class would be used to clean the classroom—sprinkling water on the concrete floor to dampen the famous Beijing dust before sweeping, washing the blackboards with wet cloths and neatening up the teacher's desk. One of these breaks was used for everyone to massage their heads while relaxing music wafted down from the announcement speaker attached to the ceiling. In the middle of the day, everybody went home to eat lunch and nap for a few hours, after which classes would continue till four in the afternoon.

10   After school I would always get a snack while I waited for my mother to pick me up. In the fall there were glazed apple-like fruit which were put on sticks, kebab style. In the winter there were dried, seasoned fish slices, and dried plums. Summer always meant popsicles, peaches and watermelon. I would eat my snack on the way home, watching the city change into the corn and rice fields of our institute.

11   At first I found the idea of Saturday classes repelling but I soon forgot that I ever had a two-day weekend. Sundays I looked forward to the hour of Disney cartoons in Chinese. Every other weekend I visited a nearby cow farm and helped feed the cows and calves. I remember talking at length with a milkmaid who had never before heard of the African slave trade, and her subsequent wishful disbelief.

12   I remember the proud feeling of putting on my red scarf for the first time. By then, I had read a lot about Chairman Mao and talked to people about the history of China. I felt a nationalist pride wearing this scarf, as the Little Red Guards had forty years ago in helping to defeat the Japanese militarists. The red scarf meant that one was committed to helping all those in difficulty and I proceeded to do this with great zeal—picking up watermelons for a man whose wheelbarrow wheels had split, helping old people across busy roads, etc.

13   Third grade brought the advent of the English class. I was inwardly amused by the children's accents but when I corrected them, I was astonished to find that my words differed very little from theirs. In fact, as a grain of desert sand that has traveled many miles is indistinguishable from surrounding indigenous earth, I felt no different from any other Chinese child.

14   I can still see the faces of shopkeepers who had had their backs turned when I had asked for an item and when they turned around, were astounded to see a little black kid speaking perfect Mandarin. I think I even delighted in shocking people, purposefully going on a raid of the local shops. But I found that people were genuinely touched that I had taken the time to study their difficult language. I was warmly embraced as one of their children.

15   Fourth grade brought the Tiananmen massacre. Before the shootings, my mother and I had gone every day to visit her students and friends at the square. My heart felt like it was bursting with love, so strong was the feeling of community. There were so many people there that every part of your body was in contact with someone else. Once I

looked triumphantly at my mother and exclaimed, "See? When you're with the people, you can't fall!" I remember drawing an analogy between the people and the November winds I could lean back against. Of course it was also a political statement.

The night of the massacre, I could hear the firing of guns from our home. My mother, who had been in the square at the time, managed to get back safely. The silence the next day pervaded the whole city and the sadness was unbearable. I remember feeling betrayed. How could this happen to my people? For the first time in forty years, the army had gone against its people. The young said that this was what socialism had come to, but the elders, recognizing that this was a form of fascism, muttered softly that this would never have happened under Chairman Mao.

The vision of black marks on the roads made from burning vehicles is engraved in my mind. The pools of blood were quickly washed away, bullet holes patched and death tolls revised. Near our institute there was the distinct scent of decomposing bodies brought from the city. These may have been buried or set fire to—no one knew, no one asked or verified. No one dared to speak, but in everyone was a mixture of anger, anguish and horror.

My parents' following separation accentuated the sadness. I spent months trying to heal our broken family, almost believing that that achievement would heal the outside world as well. Fourth grade ended early and I longed to get away from the sadness. It was at this point that my mother decided to return to the U.S. I dreaded leaving but I anticipated the change of atmosphere. I was in for a surprise.

For more than a year, I experienced culture shock. Everything was familiar but new—the clothes, hairstyles, houses, toilets. People had so many things they never used or took for granted, and yet they considered themselves not to be well-off. I was incensed how little respect my peers had for their parents and elders. How anyone could hear what the teachers were saying when classes were so noisy was beyond me. Everyone seemed arrogant and ignorant of other cultures. Kids wouldn't believe I was American because they thought I "spoke weird." They asked me, "Why can't you talk normal?" I grew tired of explaining. Even African Americans thought I was from elsewhere. The pride I had felt when I represented Black America in China suffered a pang. I was disgusted by the racism against the Orient which I discovered to be rampant. I found myself pining for the comfortable existence I had come from.

Seven years later, I still like to surprise Chinese people with my knowledge of the language when I happen to meet them. I think it is important to show that cultural gaps can be crossed, and without much difficulty as long as there is an open mind. I go back to China when money is available—I visit Beijing and the cow farm, reliving old memories and making new ones. Perhaps one remembers most what one loves.

Content

1. If you were to form your understanding of China only from Tschannerl's description, what would your impression of the country be?

2. What kind of a character is Tschannerl herself? What details, what incidents does she specifically present (as, for example, "a little black kid speaking perfect Mandarin," ¶ 14)? What else do you infer about her from reading between the lines?

3. Why did returning to the United States present such a culture shock (¶ 19) for Tschannerl?

Strategies/Structures/Language

4. Throughout the essay (except for the last paragraph) Tschannerl appropriately sticks to her child's perspective. What would she have gained—or lost—if she had incorporated her more adult understanding of the country and the subject?

5. The prevailing tone of Tschannerl's recollection of China is one of love. How does she manage to convey this while at the same time acknowledging the harshness of the political climate?

6. Tschannerl uses only a single Chinese expression, the name of the compound where her family lived (¶ 5), yet her immersion in China depends on fishing "a wealth of vocabulary" out of "a sea of gibberish" (¶ 7). This technique, of using a small fragment to indicate a much larger picture, delicate as a calligraphed scroll, conveys a wealth of meaning. Find other instances where she has used this technique effectively.

For Writing

7. Many of the essays in *The Essay Connection,* such as this one (see also Fadiman, 104–7; White, 97–103; Sanders, 249–59; and Spinner 333–34) rely on the memories of young children for their details, incidents, even interpretations—though the meanings are often enhanced by the adult author's understanding. With a partner, discuss a significant memory of your own. Does s/he find it credible? Coherent? Is any crucial information missing? Based on your discussion, examine Tschannerl's essay and two others of your choice in terms of their credibility, and propose a set of criteria for evaluating the validity of child memories. You may wish to consult celebrated court cases concerning child abuse or Binjamin Wilkomirski's disputed account of his alleged holocaust experiences before the age of five (since indisputable evidence shows that he was living in Switzerland at the time).

8. Drawing primarily on your childhood memories, describe a place that is important to you, providing sufficient detail to convey its significance to readers who are unfamiliar with it. Can you rely entirely on your own memory, or do you need to consult other sources? If so, for what kinds of information? You could use E. B. White's "Once More to the Lake" (97–103) as a model of split perception—past and present superimposed on one another.

 For comprehension, writing, and research activities and resources, please visit the companion website at <college.hmco.com/english>.

Additional Topics for Writing
Description

(For strategies for writing description, see 239–40.)

MULTIPLE STRATEGIES FOR WRITING
DESCRIPTION

In writing on any of the description topics below, you can employ a number of options to enable your readers to interpret the subject according to the dimensions you present—those accessible by sight, sound, touch, taste, and smell or in psychological or emotional terms:

- *illustrations* and *examples*, to show the whole, its components, and to interpret them
- *photographs, drawings, diagrams*, to clarify and explain
- *symbolic* use of literal details
- a *narrative*, or *logical sequence*, to provide coherence of interrelated parts
- *definitions, explanations, analyses* of the evidence
- *an implied argument* derived from the evidence and dependent on any of the above techniques

1. Places, for readers who haven't been there:

   a. Your dream house (or room)
   b. Your favorite spot on earth—or the place from hell
   c. A ghost town, or a dying or decaying neighborhood
   d. A foreign city or country you have visited
   e. A shopping mall or a particular store or restaurant
   f. A factory, farm, store, or other place where you've worked
   g. The waiting room of an airport, hospital, physician's or dentist's office, or welfare office
   h. A mountain, beach, lake, forest, desert, field, or other natural setting you know well
   i. Or compare and contrast two places you know well—two churches, houses, restaurants, vacation spots, schools, or any of the places identified in parts a–h, above; or a place before or after a renovation, a natural disaster, a long gap in time

   See essays and poetry by E. B. White, 97–103; Lee, 156–64; Shange, 166–71; Yu, 173–82; Oliver, 190; Cagle, 191–95; Zitkala-Sa, 196–202; Twain, 265–71; Hogan, 273–76; Tschannerl, 278–81; Asayesh and Khan, 318–24; Barry, 354–63; Innerarity and Verghese, 365–72; Nocton, 527–31; O'Brien, 543–50; and Tayebi, 554–58.

2. People you know for readers who don't know them:

   a. A close relative or friend
   b. A friend or relative with whom you were once very close but from whom you are presently separated, physically or psychologically
   c. An antagonist

  d. Someone with an occupation or skill you want to know more about—
     you may want to interview the person to learn what skills, training, and
     personal qualities the job or activity requires
  e. Someone who has participated, voluntarily or involuntarily, in a signifi-
     cant historical event
  f. A bizarre or eccentric person, a "character"
  g. A high achiever, mentor or role model, in business, education, sports, the
     arts or sciences, politics, religion
  h. A person whose reputation, public or private, has changed dramatically,
     for better or worse

See essays and poetry by Lamott, 39–40; Kingston, 60–61; Ruffin, 76–82; Pelizzon, 91–92; Alexie, 93–95; White, 97–103; Sanders, 249–59; Lee, 156–64; Cagle,
191–95; McGuire, 225–31; Britt, 261–63; and Spinner, 333–34.

3. Situations or events, for readers who weren't there:

  a. A holiday, birthday, or community celebration; a high school or college
     party
  b. a crucial job interview
  c. A farmer's market, flea market, garage sale, swap meet, or auction
  d. An argument, brawl, or fight
  e. A performance of a play, concert, or athletic event
  f. A ceremony—a graduation, wedding, christening, bar or bat mitzvah, an
     initiation, the swearing-in of a public official
  g. A family or school reunion
  h. A confrontation—between team members and referees or the coach,
     strikers and scabs, protesters and police

See essays, poetry, fiction, and creative nonfiction by Fadiman, 104–7; Nelson,
132–32; Hall, 242–45; Sedaris, 306–8; Rodriguez, 310–16; Tallent, 388–90; Loomis,
425–29; King, Jr., 444–57; O'Brien, 543–50; Fendrich, 551–53; and Tayebi, 554–58.

4. Experiences or feelings, for readers with analogous experiences:

  a. Love—romantic, familial, patriotic, or religious (see Sanders, 249–59;
     Rodriguez, 310–16; Spinner, 333–34; Lee, 156–64)
  b. Isolation or rejection (see Zitkala-Sa, 196–202; Kozol, 204–11; Loomis,
     425–59)
  c. Fear (see Fadiman, 104–7)
  d. Aspiration (see Douglass, 109–13)
  e. Success (see McGuire, 225–31)
  f. Anger (see Douglass, 109–13)
  g. Peace, contentment, or happiness (see White, 97–103)
  h. An encounter with birth or death (see Lee, 156–64)
  i. Coping with a handicap or disability—yours or that of someone close to
     you (see Lamott, 39–40; Sanders, 249–59)
  j. Knowledge and understanding—but after the fact (Fadiman, 104–7;
     Sanders, 249–59)
  k. Being a stranger in a strange land, as a traveler, immigrant, minority, or
     displaced person (Cagle, 191–95; Asayesh, 318–20; Khan, 321–24)

Division and Classification

To divide something is to separate it into its component parts, as the above cartoon "Deconstructing Lunch" indicates. As a writer you can divide a large, complex subject into smaller segments, easier for you and your readers to deal with individually than to consider in a large, complicated whole: whole wheat bread, bologna and mayo, lettuce, American cheese. An even further refined analysis would interpret each component, as the small print in the cartoon does. "A sandwich" thus indicates, in this analysis, that the eater is "a *normal* child from a *normal* family." As the section on process analysis indicates (see 126–30), writers usually employ division to explain the individual stages of a process—how the earth was formed, how a professional jockey (or potter or surgeon) performs his or her job, how a heat pump works. Process analysis also underlies explanations of how to make or do something, how to train your dog, or make a cake, or cut gems.

You could also divide your subject in other ways—according to types of dogs, cakes, or gems. And there would be still different ways to divide a discussion of dogs—by their size (miniature, small, medium, large); by the length of their hair (short or long); or according to their suitability as working dogs, pets, or show dogs.

As you start to divide your subject, you almost naturally begin to *classify* it as well, to sort it into categories of groups or families. You'll probably determine the subcategories according to some logical principle or according to characteristics common to members of particular subgroups. Don't stretch to create esoteric groupings (dogs by hair color, for example) if your common sense suggests a more natural way. Some categories simply make more sense than others. A discussion of dogs by breeds could be logically arranged in alphabetical order—Afghan, borzoi, bulldog, collie, Weimaraner. But a discussion that grouped dogs by type first and then breed would be easier to understand and more economical to write. For instance, you could consider all the common features of spaniels first, before dividing them into breeds of spaniels—cocker, springer, water— and discussing the differences.

How minutely you refine the subcategories of your classification system depends on the length of your writing, your focus, and your emphasis. You could use a *binary* (two-part) *classification*. This is a favorite technique of classifiers who wish to sort things into two categories, those with a particular characteristic and those without it (drinkers and nondrinkers, swimmers and nonswimmers). Thus, in an essay discussing the components of a large structure or organization—a farm, a corporation, a university—a binary classification might lead you to focus on management and labor or the university's academic and nonacademic functions. Alexander Pope's satiric couplet "I am his Highness' dog at Kew/Pray tell me, sir, whose dog are you?" (290) assumes that men, like dogs, are bought and sold to owners who treat them like the dogs they are. This binary division sorts the world into men and dogs, the owners and the servile, though neither category is particularly honorable. In "Make That a Double," satirist David Sedaris makes the assumption that gender in French grammar is a straightforward binary classification scheme. In fact, as Sedaris correctly understands, a noun is indeed either masculine or feminine—and its gender "affects both its articles and its adjectives." The comic complication is one of logic—that if something is feminine or masculine in real life, its grammatical gender, or "sexual assignment," will logically correspond to that reality. Not so, as Sedaris discovers, "*Vagina* is masculine . . . while the word *masculinity* is feminine." His solution to the problem hinges on another classification system, singular and plural, for "the plural article does not reflect gender" and is consequently "the same for both the masculine and the feminine." That this requires him to buy two of everything, creating still other problems, seems a small price to pay for solving the grammatical dilemma.

Sometimes the divisions get more complicated because they are less clear-cut. The two essays on wearing the *hijab*, Gelareh Asayesh's "Shrouded in Contradiction" (318–20) and Sumbul Khan's "'Mirror, Mirror on the Wall'" (321–24) examine the combination of restrictions and freedom, comfort and discomfort, that wearing the veil allows women in (and out of) Islamic societies. This is an issue freighted with intense religious, social, and political implications, and so full of controversy that the personal stories here can only begin to touch on it. All of these complications are reinforced by a photograph taken in Pakistan in 2002 (319), in which veiled women, one carrying a child, pass in front of a phalanx of armed men in uniform.

In "Family Values" (310–16) Richard Rodriguez analyzes the subject from his perspective as a gay man about to come out to his parents. Each label of classification that he might use—*gay, queer, homosexual, joto, maricon*—has different connotations, as does each definition of *family* and, consequently, of *family values*. He then speculates on what it means for society to be arbitrarily divided into straight and gay, pointing out that each group performs overlapping roles and has varied sorts of investment in the family as they define it. Other definitions of family and family values are provided by still other categories of people: grandparents, parents, children (young and adult), politicians, immigrant groups from Asia and Mexico, Catholics and Protestants. Do so many labels, so many divisions and classifications, render them all insignificant? he implies. Are we not all one people? "My father opens the door to welcome me in."

In "Why Men Don't Last: Self-Destruction as a Way of Life" (291–94), Natalie Angier makes distinctions, based on biological and psychological research and statistical reports, between the self-destructive behavior of men and women—"women are about three times more likely than men to express suicidal thoughts or to attempt to kill themselves . . . but in the United States, four times more men than women die from the act each year." However, there are, she indicates, different ways to interpret these facts to show either that men are the greater risk takers ("given to showy displays of bravado, aggression and daring all for the sake of attracting a harem of mates") or that women are (because those who talk about suicide are more open to experience, including taking risks and seeking novelties). She makes other distinctions between men's and women's risk-taking behavior concerning homicide, alcohol and drug use, and gambling. For instance, although both men and women gamble, their "methods and preferences for throwing away big sums of money" are very different. Men try to "overcome the odds and beat the system" at table games "where they can feel powerful and omnipotent while everybody watches them," whereas women prefer "the solitary forms of gambling, the slot machines or video poker, where there isn't as much social scrutiny." Angier concludes by citing research that classifies boys by the extent to which they uphold traditional versus egalitarian views of masculinity; presumably the traditionalists would grow up to be more self-destructive than those who favored equal rights and responsibilities for women.

Deborah Tannen's works for general readers are characterized by numerous short divisions of the general topic, as both "Fast Forward: Technologically Enhanced Aggression" (297–304) and "Communication Styles" (391–95) indicate (both essays are graphically represented in the photograph of the tense angry man on page 300). Each division makes her work easy to read and to understand. In particular, each division serves to classify the points in the arguments she makes, and each division is headed by a title that reinforces the point of that section. Although Tannen begins "Fast Forward" with positive examples of e-mail communication among coworkers and family members at short and long distance, the division titles reveal the way these divisions become an argument, that e-mail is really a form of "Technologically Enhanced Aggression" conducted through rapid and anonymous electronic communication. Thus the division titles claim, as they argue: "E-Mail Aggravates Aggression," "One-Way Communication Breeds Contempt," "Not So Fast!," "Stop That Law!" (what appears to legislators to be a "groundswell of popular protest is often the technologically enhanced protest of a few"—by fax, phone, letter, or e-mail), "Through the Magnifying Glass" (technology makes it much easier for critics of public figures to "ferret out inconsistencies" and make them look "unreliable" or "dishonest"), "'Who Is This? Why Are You Calling Here?'" (new technology makes it easier to act on the anger toward intrusive phone calls), and "Training Our Children to Kill" (by allowing them to play war video games).

Obviously, you can create as many categories and subcategories as are useful in enabling you and your readers to understand and interpret the subject. If you wanted to concentrate on the academic aspects of your own university, you might categorize them according to academic divisions—arts and sciences, business, education, music, public health. A smaller classification would examine the academic disciplines within a division—biology, English, history, mathematics. Or smaller yet, depending on your purpose—English literature, American literature, creative writing, linguistics—*ad infinitum*, as the anonymous jingle observes:

> Big fleas have little fleas, and these
> Have littler fleas to bite 'em,
> And these have fleas, and these have fleas,
> And so on ad infinitum.

In all six of the essays in this chapter, the classification system provides the basis for the overall organization; but here as in most essays, the authors use many other techniques of writing in addition—narration, definition, description, analysis, illustration, and comparison and contrast.

In writing essays based on division, you might ask the following questions to help organize your materials: What are the parts of the total unit? How can these be subdivided to make the subject more understandable to my readers? In essays of classification, where you're sorting or grouping two or more things, you can ask: Into what categories can I sort these items? According to what principles—of logic, common characteristics, "fitness"? Do I want my classification to emphasize the similarities among groups or their differences? Once I've determined the groupings, am I organizing my discussion of each category in the same way, considering the same features in the same order? In many instances divisions and classifications are in the mind of the beholder. Is the glass half full or half empty? Your job as a writer is to help your readers recognize and accept the order of your universe.

STRATEGIES FOR WRITING— DIVISION AND CLASSIFICATION

1. Am I going to explain an existing system of classification, or am I going to invent a new one? Do I want to define a system by categorizing its components? Explain a process by dividing it into stages? Argue in favor of one category or another? Entertain through an amusing classification?
2. Do my readers know my subject but not my classification system? Know both subject and system? Or are they unacquainted with either? How will their knowledge (or lack of knowledge) of the subject or system influence how much I say about either? Will this influence the simplicity or complexity of my classification system?
3. According to what principle am I classifying or dividing my subject? Is it sensible? Significant? Does it emphasize the similarities or the differences among groups? Have I applied the principle consistently with respect to each category? How have I integrated my paper (to keep it from being just a long list), through providing interconnections among the parts and transitions between the divisions?
4. Have I organized my discussion of each category in the same way, considering the same features in the same order? Have I illustrated each category? Are the discussions of each category the same length? Should they be? Why or why not?
5. Have I used language similar in vocabulary level (equally technical, or equally informal) in each category? Have I defined any needed terms?

ALEXANDER POPE

Alexander Pope (1688–1744) was the first Englishman to earn a substantial living from writing prose and poetry. His translations of Homer's *Iliad* and *Odyssey*—at a time when good translations were valued as much as original works—were published in installments beginning in 1713, earning him fame and fortune. Today he is usually remembered as one of the most brilliant verse satirists in the Western tradition. His mock epic, *The Rape of the Lock* (1712), treated the theft of a lock of a young girl's hair as if it were the subject of a Homeric epic. His *Dunciad* (1728) deflated the pretensions and nonsense he perceived to be rampant in English society—especially among the intellectual class. Pope had good cause to resent social folly; as a Catholic he was forbidden by law to attend a university, vote, or hold public office. Yet his satire is relatively devoid of bitterness and has been read with enjoyment for close to 300 years.

"On the Collar of a Dog" is an epigram that Pope actually engraved on the collar of a dog he gave to Frederick Louis, Prince of Wales (the son of King George II and Queen Wilhelmina-Caroline). Pope's satirical depth is condensed to diamondlike sharpness. The lines work as an animal fable— we picture a dog's life on the streets of London, where animals sniff out each other's affiliations, but humans are prone to ask each other this question, too. The poem implies that everyone belongs to someone. Are we deceiving ourselves when we say, "I am my own person"?

On the Collar of a Dog

1   I am his Highness'[1] dog at Kew;
       Pray tell me, sir, whose dog are you?

NATALIE ANGIER

Angier (born 1958), grew up in New York City and graduated from Barnard College in 1978. After working as a magazine staff writer at *Discover* and *Time* and as an editor at *Savvy*, she became a science reporter for the *New York Times* in 1990 and won a Pulitzer Prize in the following year. Her columns were published in 1995 as *The Beauty of the Beastly: New Views on the Nature of Life*. Topics include evolutionary biology ("Mating for Life?") DNA, scorpions, and central issues of life, death (by suicide

---

[1]Frederick, Prince of Wales

or AIDS), and creativity. *Woman: An Intimate Geography* (1999) offers a spirited and controversial celebration of "the female body—its anatomy, its chemistry, its evolution, and its laughter," including both traditional (the womb, the egg) and nontraditional elements ("movement, strength, aggression, and fury"). Angier, who lists her hobby as "weightlifting," recently became a mother; her work reflects the strengths of both.

Angier's writing is characteristically clear, precise, and witty. She explains the unfamiliar in terms of the familiar, giving research a memorably human perspective. Thus, in "Why Men Don't Last," first published in the *New York Times* (Feb. 17, 1999), Angier examines significant differences between the biology of men and women, translating statistical and psychological research (on risk taking, compulsive gambling, suicidal behavior, masculinity) into language and concepts general readers can readily understand—without oversimplifying the subject or demeaning the audience.

Why Men Don't Last: Self-Destruction as a Way of Life

M y father had great habits. Long before ficus trees met weight machines, he was a dogged exerciser. He did push-ups and isometrics. He climbed rocks. He went for long, vigorous walks. He ate sparingly and avoided sweets and grease. He took such good care of his teeth that they looked fake.

My father had terrible habits. He was chronically angry. He threw 2 things around the house and broke them. He didn't drink often, but when he did, he turned more violent than usual. He didn't go to doctors, even when we begged him to. He let a big, ugly mole on his back grow bigger and bigger, and so he died of malignant melanoma, a curable cancer, at 51.

My father was a real man—so good and so bad. He was also Everyman. 3

Men by some measures take better care of themselves than women 4 do and are in better health. They are less likely to be fat, for example; they exercise more, and suffer from fewer chronic diseases like diabetes, osteoporosis and arthritis.

By standard measures, men have less than half the rate of depression 5 seen in women. When men do feel depressed, they tend to seek distraction in an activity, which, many psychologists say, can be a more effective technique for dispelling the mood than is a depressed woman's tendency to turn inward and ruminate. In the United States and many other industrialized nations, women are about three times more likely than men to express suicidal thoughts or to attempt to kill themselves.

And yet . . . men don't last. They die off in greater numbers than 6 women do at every stage of life, and thus their average life span is seven years shorter. Women may attempt suicide relatively more often, but in the United States, four times more men than women die from the act each year.

7   Men are also far more likely than women to die behind the wheel or to kill others as a result of their driving. From 1977 to 1995, three and a half times more male drivers than female drivers were involved in fatal car crashes. Death by homicide also favors men; among those under 30, the male-to-female ratio is 8 to 1.

8   Yes, men can be impressive in their tendency to self-destruct, explosively or gradually. They are at least twice as likely as women to be alcoholics and three times more likely to be drug addicts. They have an eightfold greater chance than women do of ending up in prison. Boys are much more likely than girls to be thrown out of school for a conduct or antisocial personality disorder, or to drop out on their own surly initiative. Men gamble themselves into a devastating economic and emotional pit two to three times more often than women do.

9   "Between boys' suicide rates, dropout rates and homicide rates, and men's self-destructive behaviors generally, we have a real crisis in America," said William S. Pollack, a psychologist at Harvard Medical School and co-director of the Center for Men at McLean Hospital in Belmont, Mass. "Until recently, the crisis has gone unheralded."

10   It is one thing to herald a presumed crisis, though, and to cite a ream of gloomy statistics. It is quite another to understand the crisis, or to figure out where it comes from or what to do about it. As those who study the various forms of men's self-destructive behaviors realize, there is not a single, glib, overarching explanation for the sex-specific patterns they see.

11   A crude evolutionary hypothesis would have it that men are natural risk-takers, given to showy displays of bravado, aggression and daring all for the sake of attracting a harem of mates. By this premise, most of men's self-destructive, violent tendencies are a manifestation of their need to take big chances for the sake of passing their genes into the river of tomorrow.

12   Some of the data on men's bad habits fit the risk-taker model. For example, those who study compulsive gambling have observed that men and women tend to display very different methods and preferences for throwing away big sums of money.

13   "Men get enamored of the action in gambling," said Linda Chamberlain, a psychologist at Regis University in Denver who specializes in treating gambling disorders. "They describe an overwhelming rush of feelings and excitement associated with the process of gambling. They like the feeling of being a player, and taking on a struggle with the house to show that they can overcome the odds and beat the system. They tend to prefer the table games, where they can feel powerful and omnipotent while everybody watches them."

14   Dr. Chamberlain noted that many male gamblers engage in other risk-taking behaviors, like auto racing or hang gliding. By contrast, she said, "Women tend to use gambling more as a sedative, to numb themselves and

escape from daily responsibilities, or feelings of depression or alienation. Women tend to prefer the solitary forms of gambling, the slot machines or video poker, where there isn't as much social scrutiny."

Yet the risk-taking theory does not account for why men outnumber   15
women in the consumption of licit and illicit anodynes. Alcohol, heroin and marijuana can be at least as numbing and sedating as repetitively pulling the arm of a slot machine. And some studies have found that men use drugs and alcohol for the same reasons that women often overeat: as an attempt to self-medicate when they are feeling anxious or in despair.

"We can speculate all we want, but we really don't know why men   16
drink more than women," said Enoch Gordis, the head of the National Institute on Alcohol Abuse and Alcoholism. Nor does men's comparatively higher rate of suicide appear linked to the risk-taking profile. To the contrary, Paul Duberstein, an assistant professor of psychiatry and oncology at the University of Rochester School of Medicine, has found that people who complete a suicidal act are often low in a personality trait referred to as "openness to experience," tending to be rigid and inflexible in their behaviors. By comparison, those who express suicidal thoughts tend to score relatively high on the openness-to-experience scale.

Given that men commit suicide more often than women, and women   17
talk about it more, his research suggests that, in a sense, women are the greater risk-takers and novelty seekers, while the men are likelier to feel trapped and helpless in the face of changing circumstances.

Silvia Cara Canetto, an associate professor of psychology at Colo-   18
rado State University in Fort Collins, has extensively studied the role of gender in suicidal behaviors. Dr. Canetto has found that cultural narratives may determine why women attempt suicide more often while men kill themselves more often. She proposes that in Western countries, to talk about suicide or to survive a suicidal act is often considered "feminine," hysterical, irrational and weak. To actually die by one's own hand may be viewed as "masculine," decisive, strong. Even the language conveys the polarized, weak-strong imagery: a "failed" suicide attempt as opposed to a "successful" one.

"There is indirect evidence that there is negative stigma toward men   19
who survive suicide," Dr. Canetto said. "Men don't want to 'fail,' even though failing in this case means surviving." If the "suicidal script" that identifies completing the acts as "rational, courageous and masculine" can be "undermined and torn to pieces," she said, we might have a new approach to prevention.

Dr. Pollack of the Center for Men also blames many of men's self-   20
destructive ways on the persistent image of the dispassionate, resilient, action-oriented male—the Marlboro Man who never even gasps for breath. For all the talk of the sensitive "new man," he argues, men have yet to catch up with women in expanding their range of acceptable emotions and

behaviors. Men in our culture, Dr. Pollack says, are pretty much limited to a menu of three strong feelings: rage, triumph, lust. "Anything else and you risk being seen as a sissy," he said.

21   In a number of books, most recently "Real Boys: Rescuing Our Sons From the Myths of Boyhood," he proposes that boys "lose their voice, a whole half of their emotional selves," beginning at age 4 or 5. "Their vulnerable, sad feelings and sense of need are suppressed or shamed out of them," he said—by their peers, parents, the great wide televised fist in their face.

22   He added: "If you keep hammering it into a kid that he has to look tough and stop being a crybaby and a mama's boy, the boy will start creating a mask of bravado."

23   That boys and young men continue to feel confused over the proper harmonics of modern masculinity was revealed in a study that Dr. Pollack conducted of 200 eighth-grade boys. Through questionnaires, he determined their scores on two scales, one measuring their "egalitarianism"— the degree to which they think men and women are equal, that men should change a baby's diapers, that mothers should work and the like—and the other gauging their "traditionalism" as determined by their responses to conventional notions, like the premise that men must "stand on their own two feet" and must "always be willing to have sex if someone asks."

24   On average, the boys scored high on both scales. "They are split on what it means to be a man," said Dr. Pollack.

25   The cult of masculinity can beckon like a siren song in baritone. Dr. Franklin L. Nelson, a clinical psychologist at the Fairbanks Community Mental Health Center in Alaska, sees many men who get into trouble by adhering to sentimental notions of manhood. "A lot of men come up here hoping to get away from a wimpy world and live like pioneers by old-fashioned masculine principles of individualism, strength and ruggedness," he said. They learn that nothing is simple; even Alaska is part of a wider, interdependent world and they really do need friends, warmth and electricity.

26   "Right now, it's 35 degrees below zero outside," he said during a January interview. "If you're not prepared, it doesn't take long at that temperature to freeze to death."

Content

1. Angier uses several categories of division in this piece: the "so good and so bad" habits of "Everyman" (¶ 3); the self-destructive habits and rates of men versus women (throughout); the division between the rugged individual versus the egalitarian helpmeet roles today's men are expected to play (¶s 23–25). Why do such divisions enable readers to clearly recognize similarities as well as differences?

2. Angier's explanations for these divisions are equally divided. What evidence does she offer to support the "crude evolutionary hypothesis" that "men are natural risk-takers, given to showy display of bravado, aggression and daring all for the sake of attracting a harem of mates" (¶ 11)? What evidence does she offer to contradict this hypothesis?

3. What do you make of the fact that women talk about committing suicide more than men do, but that men actually have a higher rate of suicide than women do (¶s 16–19)?

Strategies/Structures/Language

4. What are the dangers and difficulties of categorizing behavior by gender? Why aren't the divisions and classifications Angier uses more clear-cut? Is this a phenomenon of the research she cites, of her writing, of the way things are in real life, or of some combination of the three?

5. Angier is writing as a reporter of other people's research. Do we know where she stands on the subject—which hypothesis for men's risk-taking behavior she believes? Is her essay slanted in favor of one opinion or another, either in terms of her examples or her language?

6. Should a reporter be neutral? Isn't the selection of evidence in itself a form of tipping the scale in favor of one side or another?

For Writing

7. Have you ever done anything risky or dangerous to avoid looking like a wimp or to avoid falling into one or another stereotypical role for either men or women? Write a paper for an audience different from yourself; for instance, if you're a risk-taking man, write for a more prudent audience of women or men (if it makes a difference to your argument, specify which gender), and have such a reader critique your paper before you revise it.

8. Angier, like other science writers, has the difficult job of translating scientific research into language that newspaper readers can understand. From the following list of authors she cites on the role of gender in suicidal behaviors, choose one source and identify, with illustrations, the principles by which Angier works. Consider aspects such as document format, uses of evidence, presentation of data (via graphs, charts, statistics), technicality of language, definitions of scientific terms, citation of supporting research. Use illustrations, graphic as well as written, to clarify.

> Canetto, Silvia Sara, and David Lester. "Gender, Culture, and Suicidal Behavior." *Transcultural Psychiatry* 35.2 (1998): 163–90.
>
> Canetto, Silvia Sara, and Issac Sakinofsky. "The Gender Paradox in Suicide." *Suicide and Life-Threatening Behavior* 28.1 (Spring 1998): 1–23.
>
> Chamberlain, Linda, Michael R. Ruetz, and William G. McCown. *Strange Attractors: Chaos, Complexity, and the Art of Family Therapy.* New York: Wiley, 1997.
>
> Duberstein, Paul R., Yeates Conwell, and Christopher Cox. "Suicide in Widowed Persons." *American Journal of Geriatric Psychiatry* 6.4 (Fall 1998): 328–34.

Gordis, Enoch. "Alcohol Problems in Public Health Policy." *Journal of the American Medical Association* (Dec. 1997): 1781–87.

Pollack, William S. *Real Boys: Rescuing Our Sons from the Myths of Boyhood.* New York: Random, 1998.

Pollack, William S., and Ronald F. Levant, eds. *New Psychotherapy for Men.* New York: Wiley, 1998.

For comprehension, writing, and research activities and resources, please visit the companion website at <college.hmco.com/english>.

DEBORAH TANNEN

Tannen, born in Brooklyn in 1945, was partially deafened by a childhood illness. Her consequent interest in nonverbal communication and other aspects of conversation led ultimately to a doctorate in linguistics (University of California, Berkeley, 1979) and professorship at Georgetown University. Tannen's numerous studies of gender-related speech patterns draw on the combined perspectives of anthropology, sociology, psychology, and women's studies, as well as linguistics. Tannen brings a sensitive ear and keen analysis to communication related to gender, power, and status in the best-selling *That's Not What I Meant!: How Conversational Style Makes or Breaks Your Relations with Others* (1986), *You Just Don't Understand: Women and Men in Conversation* (1990), *Talking from 9 to 5* (1994), *I Only Say This Because I Love You* (2001), and *Conversational Style: Analyzing Talk Among Friends* (2005).

"Fast Forward: Technologically Enhanced Aggression" comes from *The Argument Culture: Moving from Debate to Dialogue*, (1998) a book devoted to analyzing the "pervasive warlike atmosphere that makes us approach public dialogue, and just about anything we need to accomplish, as if it were a fight." Our spirits, she says, are "corroded by living in an atmosphere of unrelenting contention—an argument culture" that "urges us to approach the world—and the people in it—in an adversarial frame of mind." Although argument can be useful, it often creates "more problems than it solves," as Tannen's analysis of various types of e-mail communication indicates. Each division of her analysis can be further categorized according to those who behave in the aggressive ways the section addresses and those who don't.

Fast Forward: Technologically Enhanced Aggression

I was the second person in my department to get a computer. The first
  was my colleague Ralph. The year was 1980. Ralph got a Radio Shack
TRS 80; I got a used Apple 2-Plus. He helped me get started and before
long helped me get on e-mail, the precursor of the Internet. Though his
office was next to mine, we rarely had extended conversations except
about department business. Shy and soft-spoken, Ralph mumbled so, I
could barely tell he was speaking. But when we both were using e-mail,
we started communicating daily in this (then) leisurely medium. We could
send each other messages without fear of imposing, since the receiver determines when to log on and read and respond. Soon I was getting long,
self-revealing messages from Ralph. We moved effortlessly among discussions of department business, our work, and our lives. Through e-mail
Ralph and I became friends.

Ralph recently forwarded to me a message he had received from his
niece, a college freshman. "How nice," I commented, "that you have such
a close relationship with your niece. Do you think you'd be in touch with
her if it weren't for e-mail?" "No," he replied. "I can't imagine we'd write
each other letters regularly or call on the phone. No way." E-mail makes
possible connections with relatives, acquaintances, or strangers that would
not otherwise exist. And it enables more and different communication with
people you are already close to. One woman discovered that e-mail brought
her closer to her father. He would never talk much on the phone (as her
mother would), but they have become close since they both got online.

Everywhere e-mail is enhancing or even transforming relationships.
Parents keep in regular touch with children in college who would not be
caught dead telephoning home every day. When I spent a year and a half
in Greece in the late 1960s, I was out of touch with my family except for the
mail—letters that took hours to compose and weeks to arrive. When my
sister spent a year in Israel in the mid-1990s, we kept in touch nearly every
day—and not only she and I. Prodded by her absence, within a month of
her departure our third sister and my sisters' daughters all started using
e-mail. Though she was so far away, my sister was in some ways in closer
touch with the family than she would have been had she stayed home.

And another surprise: My other sister, who generally is not eager to
talk about her feelings, opened up on e-mail. One time I called her and we
spoke on the phone; after we hung up, I checked my e-mail and found she
had revealed information there that she hadn't mentioned when we spoke.
I asked her about it (on e-mail), and she explained, "The telephone is so
impersonal." At first this seemed absurd: How could the actual voice of a
person right there be impersonal and the on-screen little letters detached

from the writer be more personal? When I asked her about this, she explained: "The big advantage to e-mail is that you can do it at your time and pace; there is never the feeling that the phone is ringing and interrupting whatever it is you are doing." Writing e-mail is like writing in a journal; you're alone with your thoughts and your words, safe from the intrusive presence of another person.

E-Mail Aggravates Aggression

5   E-mail, and now the Internet and the World Wide Web, are creating networks of human connection unthinkable even a few years ago. But at the same time that technologically enhanced communication enables previously impossible loving contact, it also enhances hostile and distressing communication. Along with the voices of family members and friends, telephone lines bring into our homes the annoying voices of solicitors who want to sell something—generally at dinnertime. (My father-in-law startles a telephone solicitor by saying, "We're eating dinner, but I'll call you back. What's your home phone number?" To the nonplussed caller, he explains, "Well, you're calling me at home; I thought I'd call you at home, too.") Even more unnerving, in the middle of the night may come frightening obscene calls and stalkers. From time to time the public is horrified to learn that even the most respected citizens can succumb to the temptation of anonymity that the telephone seems to offer—like the New York State Supreme Court chief justice who was harassing a former lover by mail and phone and the president of American University in Washington, D.C., who was found to be the source of obscene telephone calls to a woman he didn't even know.

6   But telephone lines can be traced (as President Richard Berendzen learned) and voices can be recognized (as Judge Sol Wachtler discovered). The Internet ratchets up anonymity by homogenizing all messages into identical-appearing print and making it almost impossible to trace messages back to the computer that sent them. As the ease of using the Internet has resulted in more and more people logging on and sending messages to more and more others with whom they have a connection, it has also led to increased communication with strangers—and this has resulted in "flaming": vituperative messages that verbally attack. Flaming results from the anonymity not only of the sender but also of the receiver. It is easier to feel and express hostility against someone far removed whom you do not know personally, like the rage that some drivers feel toward an anonymous car that cuts them off. If the anonymous driver to whom you've flipped the finger turns out to be someone you know, the rush of shame you experience is evidence that anonymity was essential for your expression—and experience—of rage.

7   One of the most effective ways to defuse antagonism between two groups is to provide a forum for individuals from those groups to get to

know each other personally. This is the logic behind programs that bring together, for example, African-American and Jewish youths or Israeli and Palestinian women. It was the means by which a troubled Vietnam veteran finally achieved healing: through a friendship with a man who had been the enemy he was trying to kill—a retired Vietnamese officer whose diary the American had found during the war and managed to return to its owner nearly twenty-five years later. When you get to know members of an "enemy" group personally, it is hard to demonize them, to see them as less than human.

What is happening in our lives is just the opposite: More and more   8
of our communication is not face to face, and not with people we know. The proliferation and increasing portability of technology isolate people in a bubble. When I was a child, my family got the first television on our block, and the neighborhood children gathered in our dining room to watch Howdy Doody. Before long, every family had its own TV—but each had just one, so, in order to watch it, families came together. Now it is common for families to have more than one television, so the adults can watch what they like in one room and the children can watch their choice in another—or maybe each child has a private TV to watch alone. The spread of radio has followed the same pattern. Early radios were like a piece of furniture around which a family had to gather in order to listen. Now radio listeners may have a radio in every room, one in the car, and yet another, equipped with headphones, for walking or jogging. Radio and television began as sources of information that drew people together physically, even if their attention was not on each other. Now these technologies are exerting a centrifugal force, pulling people apart—and, as a result, increasing the likelihood that their encounters will be agonistic.

One-Way Communication Breeds Contempt

The head of a small business had a reputation among his employees as   9
being a Jekyll-and-Hyde personality. In person he was always mild-mannered and polite. But when his employees saw a memo from him in their mail, their backs stiffened. The boss was famous for composing angry, even vicious memos that he often had to temper and apologize for later. It seemed that the presence of a living, breathing person in front of him was a brake on his hostility. But seated before a faceless typewriter or computer screen, his anger built and overflowed. A woman who had worked as a dean at a small liberal arts college commented that all the major problems she encountered with faculty or other administrators resulted from written memos, not face-to-face communication.

Answering machines are also a form of one-way communication. A   10
piano teacher named Craig was president of a piano teachers' association that sponsored a yearly competition. Craig had nothing to do with the competition—someone else had organized and overseen it. So he felt

"Read" the picture as an illustration of either Angier's "Why Men Don't Last" or Tannen's "Fast Forward: Technologically Enhanced Aggression," or both. How can you tell he's angry? Would you interpret the picture the same way if the figure were a woman rather than a man? Or if the figure looked more like a college student than a career person?

helpless and caught off guard when he came home to a message that laid out in detail the caller's grievances about how the competition had been handled, and ended, "That's no way to run an organization!" Slam! When he heard the message, Craig thought, "Here I am, being the president as a service to keep things together, and I'm being attacked for something I had no control over. It made me wonder," he commented, "why I was doing it at all." Craig refused a second term in large part because of attacks like this—even though they were infrequent, while he frequently received lavish praise. Being attacked is perhaps unavoidable for those in authority, but in this case the technology played a role as well. It is highly unlikely the caller would have worked herself up into quite this frenzy, or concluded the conversation by hanging up on Craig, if she had gotten Craig himself and not his answering machine, let alone if she had talked to him in person.

11   In the heat of anger, it is easy to pick up a phone and make a call. But when talking directly to someone, most people feel an impulse to tone down what they say. Even if they do not, the person they are attacking will respond after the first initial blast—by explaining, apologizing, or counterattacking. Whatever the response, it will redirect the attacker's speech, perhaps aggravating the anger but also perhaps deflating it. If you write

an angry letter, you might decide later not to send it or to tone it down. But if you make a call and reach voice mail or an answering machine, it's the worst of both worlds: You spout off in the heat of anger, there is no way to take back what you said or correct misinterpretations, and there is no response to act as a brake. In my research on workplace communication, I found that a large percentage of serious conflicts had been sparked by one-way communication such as memos, voice mail, and e-mail.

An experienced reporter at a newspaper heard that one of his colleagues, a feature writer, was working on a story about a topic he knew well. He had done extensive research on a related topic in the course of his own reporting. So he thought he'd be helpful: He sent her a long e-mail message warning her of potential pitfalls and pointing out aspects she should bear in mind. Rather than thanks, he received a testy reply informing him that she was quite capable of watching out for these pitfalls without his expert guidance, and that she too was a seasoned reporter, even though she had been at the paper a shorter time than he. Reading her angry reply, he gulped and sent an apology. 12

An advantage of e-mail is its efficiency: The reporter was able to send his ideas without taking the time to walk to another floor and talk face to face with his colleague. But had he done so, he would probably have presented his ideas differently, and she would have seen the spirit in which the advice was given. If not, it is unlikely he would have gotten so far in his advice giving before picking up that he was not coming across the way he intended, that she was taking offense. He then could have backtracked and changed the tone of his communication rather than laying it on thicker and thicker, continuing and expanding in a vein that was making her angrier by the second. What's more, if people meet regularly face to face, friendships begin to build that lay the foundation for future communication. It's harder for e-mail and memos to do that. 13

Not So Fast!

The potential for misunderstandings and mishaps with electronic communication expands in proportion to the potential for positive exchanges. For example, two workers exchanged e-mail about a report that had to be submitted. One of them wrote that a portion could better be handled by a third person—but added an unflattering remark about her. The recipient received the message at a busy time, noticed that it called for Person 3 to do something—and quickly and efficiently forwarded it to her, disparaging remark and all. E-mail makes it too easy to forward messages, too easy to reply before your temper cools, too easy to broadcast messages to large numbers of people without thinking about how every sentence will strike every recipient. And there's plenty of opportunity for error: sending a message to the wrong person or having a message mysteriously appear on the screen of an unintended recipient. 14

15   Every improvement in technology makes possible new and scarier kinds of errors. In one company, a manager set up an e-mail user-group list, so his messages would go to everyone in the department at once and their replies would also get distributed to everyone on the list. But several people sent him replies that they thought were private, not realizing everyone in the office would see them. Like a private conversation overheard, these "overread" messages to the manager came across to colleagues as kissing up, since people tend to use a more deferential tone in addressing a boss than a peer. It was embarrassing, but not as bad as the job applicant who mistakenly sent a message including his uncensored judgment about the person who interviewed him to that person. . . .

Who's to Judge?

16 One of the great contributions of the Internet is that it enables ordinary people to put out information that previously would have been limited by such gatekeepers as newspaper editors and book publishers, or that would have required enormous amounts of time and money to publish and disseminate independently. In a few moments, anyone with the equipment and expertise can post information on the World Wide Web, and anyone else with the equipment and expertise can read it. This can be invaluable—for example, when individuals who have unusual medical conditions and their families exchange information and personal experience through specialized user groups. But there is a danger here as well. Editors, publishers, and other gatekeepers impose their judgment—for better or worse—on the accuracy of the material they publish. Those who download information from the Internet may be unable to judge the veracity and reliability of information.

17   A professor at a public university was assigned a student assistant who had excellent computer skills. The assistant offered to help her make reading materials available to her class by placing them on a class Web site. He began by putting on the site readings and secondary sources that the professor had assigned or recommended. But he did not stop there. He went on to scour the Internet for anything related to the course topic and import it into the class Web site, too. When the professor discovered what he had done, she told him to remove these materials, since she did not have time to read everything he had imported to determine whether it was appropriate for the students to read. Some of it might have been irrelevant to the class and would distract them from the material she felt they should read. And some of it might be factually wrong. The idea that the professor thought she should read the material she was making available to her students in order to judge its accuracy and suitability was foreign to the student assistant—and offensive. He argued that she was trying to infringe on the students' First Amendment right to have access to any kind of information at all.

This is a danger inherent in the Internet: At the same time that the ease of posting makes available enormous amounts of useful information, it also makes possible the dissemination of useless, false, or dangerous information—and makes it more difficult to distinguish between the two. To be sure, publishers and editors often make mistakes in publishing material they should not and rejecting material they should accept (as any author whose work has been rejected can tell you—and as evidenced by the many successful books that were rejected by dozens of editors before finally finding a home). Yet readers of reputable newspapers and magazines or books published by established presses know that what they are reading has been deemed reliable by professional editors. The Internet makes it more difficult for consumers to distinguish the veracity and reliability of information they come across.

The Internet can function as a giant and unstoppable rumor mill or as a conduit for such dangerous information as how to build a bomb. It can also facilitate aggressive behavior, as author Elaine Showalter discovered when she published a book, *Hystories,* in which she included chronic fatigue syndrome among a list of phenomena, such as alien abduction and satanic ritual abuse, that she identified as hysterical epidemics. Sufferers from chronic fatigue syndrome who were angered by the label "hysterical" used the Internet to share information about the author's public appearances, so they could turn out in force to harass and even threaten her. Law enforcement authorities have been unable to identify members of the Animal Liberation Front, who use violence and terrorism in their efforts to halt what they see as cruelty to animals, because their communication with one another takes place for the most part on the Internet rather than at face-to-face meetings. . . .

Like Peas Out of a Pod

Flaming is only one aspect of electronic communication. E-mail makes possible extended interaction among people who are physically distant from each other. But it also makes possible anonymity and in some cases—as with young people (mostly boys) who become computer "nerds"—begins to substitute for human interaction. Following a tragic incident in which a fifteen-year-old boy sexually assaulted and then murdered an eleven-year-old boy who happened to ring his doorbell selling candy and wrapping paper to raise money for his school, many people felt that the Internet shared a portion of the blame, because the murderer had himself been sexually abused by a pedophile he had met through the Internet. An aspect of this harrowing and bizarre event which received less comment was that as the older boy had become obsessed with the Internet, he had gradually withdrawn from social interaction with his peers.

Advances in technology are part of a larger complex of forces moving people away from face-to-face interaction and away from actual experience—from hearing music performed, to hearing recordings of performances, to hearing digital re-creations of performances that some believe bear little resemblance to music as performed. From live dramatic performances in theaters, to silent movies shown in theaters with the accompaniment of live orchestras, to sound movies, to videos watched in the isolation of one's home. From local stores privately owned and owner-operated to chains owned by huge corporations based far away and staffed by minimum-wage employees who know little about the merchandise and have much less stake in whether customers leave the store happy or offended.

22   All of these trends have complex implications—many positive, but many troubling. Each new advance makes possible not only new levels of connection but also new levels of hostility and enhanced means of expressing it. People who would not dream of cutting in front of others waiting in a line think nothing of speeding along an empty traffic lane to cut ahead of others waiting in a line of cars. It is easy to forget that inside the car, or facing a computer screen, is a living, feeling person.

23   The rising level of public aggression in our society seems directly related to the increasing isolation in our lives, which is helped along by advances in technology. This isolation—and the technology that enhances it—is an ingredient in the argument culture. We seem to be better at developing technological means of communication than at finding ways to temper the hostility that sometimes accompanies them. We have to work harder at finding those ways. That is the challenge we now face.

Content

1. What connections does Tannen make between "advances in technology," "the increasing isolation in our lives," and "the rising level of public aggression in our society" (¶ 23)? Which types of evidence that she uses to make her case do you find the most convincing: personal anecdotes, contemporary news events, issues of public policy, or analyses of the way Americans in general live and behave? Why?

2. What are some of the advantages of technology as outlined by Tannen? Some of its disadvantages? Do the gains outweigh the losses in Tannen's analysis? In yours?

3. Tannen opens her essay with a discussion of the advantages of e-mail in building and maintaining close relationships (¶s 1–4). In paragraph 13, she claims that "if people meet regularly face to face, friendships begin to build that lay the foundation for future communication. It's harder for e-mail and memos to do that." These positions are seemingly at odds with each other. Does she address or account for this apparent contradiction at any point in her essay?

4. What relationship does Tannen see between expressions of hostility such as "flaming" and "road rage" and the "anonymity not only of the sender but also of the receiver" (¶ 6)? Does your own experience corroborate her claim that "It is easier to feel and express hostility against someone far removed whom you do not know personally" (¶ 6) than it is to treat people with whom one has a personal

connection in a hostile manner? Does Tannen offer any solutions to this problem? Can you or your fellow students resolve this issue, in discussion or in writing (see question 9).

Strategies/Structures/Language

5. Each division of Tannen's analysis can be further divided according to people who behave in the aggressive ways the section addresses and people who don't. Is anonymity, coupled with the ease and speed of sending insults by e-mail, the most compelling reason for such hostile behavior? What evidence does she offer that personal acquaintance with "members of an 'enemy' group" will humanize them (¶ 7) and thus have the potential for transforming a hostile relationship into a friendly one? Under what circumstances could personal acquaintance make relations worse rather than better?

6. Tannen's writing here and in "Communication Styles" (391–95) is characterized by numerous subdivisions of her topic, identified by witty slogans ("One-Way Communication Breeds Contempt") and breezy captions ("Not So Fast!"). What is the effect on the total piece of these subdivisions and of the language in which they're written?

For Writing

7. Do you use different language in e-mails than you do in conversation? In hardcopy letters? What consistencies do you find in the language and other conventions of all three forms of communication? What differences? (For evidence you could look at some messages you've written and perhaps tape a conversation for analysis.) Tabulate your results in lists or a chart.

8. Use the data you and your classmates have collected in answering question 7 to write an essay that analyzes the use of technology by college students. You might, for example, set up a system of division and classification based on the categories suggested in question 7. Do you need to add other categories? You may wish to interview classmates to expand on their answers.

9. Tannen notes, "We seem to be better at developing technological means of communication than at finding ways to temper the hostility that sometimes accompanies them. We have to work harder at finding those ways. That is the challenge we now face" (¶ 23). If you use e-mail a lot (say, twenty or more messages a day), in collaboration with other e-mail users, draft a policy statement of appropriate e-mail etiquette for dealing with messages from people you don't know personally, such as those in your school or workplace to whom you are accountable. Would you recommend treating people you know personally any different from strangers? Incorporate some of the evidence you've gleaned in your answer to question 7.

 For comprehension, writing, and research activities and resources, please visit the companion website at <college.hmco.com/english>.

DAVID SEDARIS

Sedaris was born in 1957 and reared in North Carolina. He graduated from the School of the Art Institute of Chicago in 1987. His national reputation as a humorist began in 1993 when he read excerpts from "The SantaLand Diaries" on National Public Radio, in a "nicely nerdy, quavering voice." These monologues, praised for their wit and deadpan delivery, anatomized various odd jobs he held after moving to New York—an elf in SantaLand at Macy's department store, an office worker, and an apartment cleaner. He explained to the *New York Times,* "I can only write when it's dark, so basically, my whole day is spent waiting for it to get dark. Cleaning apartments gives me something to do when I get up. Otherwise, I'd feel like a bum." His NPR appearances led to job offers—for both cleaning and writing—as well as contracts for *Barrel Fever* (1994) and *Naked* (1997).

In *Naked* and later books—*Me Talk Pretty One Day* (2000) and *Dress Your Family in Corduroy and Denim* (2004)—Sedaris has drawn his most memorable material from bittersweet renderings of his family: his father, "an eccentric IBM engineer who ruins miniature golf with dissertations on wind trajectory"; his mother, a secret alcoholic ("Drinking didn't count if you followed a glass of wine with a cup of coffee") who pushed her children outside on a snow day so she could drink in secret; and his siblings, alternately attractive and pathetic. Sedaris's presentations of his relationship with his partner, Hugh, are more mellow, as in "Make That a Double," which emphasizes the illogical and irrational (to English speakers) attributions of gender in French grammar: "Because it is a female and lays eggs, a chicken is masculine . . . while the word *masculinity* is feminine."

Make That a Double

1   There are, I have noticed, two basic types of French spoken by Americans vacationing in Paris: the Hard Kind and the Easy Kind. The Hard Kind involves the conjugation of wily verbs and the science of placing them alongside various other words in order to form such sentences as "I go him say good afternoon" and "No, not to him I no go it him say now."

2   The second, less complicated form of French amounts to screaming English at the top of your lungs, much the same way you'd shout at a deaf person or the dog you thought you could train to stay off the sofa. Doubt and hesitation are completely unnecessary, as Easy French is rooted in the premise that, if properly packed, the rest of the world could fit within the confines of Reno, Nevada. The speaker carries no pocket dictionary and never suffers the humiliation that inevitably comes with pointing to the menu and ordering the day of the week. With Easy French, eating out involves a simple "BRING ME A STEAK."

Having undertaken the study of Hard French, I'll overhear such 3
requests and glare across the room, thinking, "That's *Mister* Steak to you,
buddy." Of all the stumbling blocks inherent in learning this language, the
greatest for me is the principle that each noun has a corresponding sex
that affects both its articles and its adjectives. Because it is a female and
lays eggs, a chicken is masculine. *Vagina* is masculine as well, while the
word *masculinity* is feminine. Forced by the grammar to take a stand one
way or the other, *hermaphrodite* is male and *indecisiveness* female.

I spent months searching for some secret code before I realized that 4
common sense has nothing to do with it. *Hysteria, psychosis, torture, depression:* I was told that if something is unpleasant, it's probably feminine.
This encouraged me, but the theory was blown by such masculine nouns
as *murder, toothache,* and *Rollerblade.* I have no problem learning the words
themselves, it's the sexes that trip me up and refuse to stick.

What's the trick to remembering that a sandwich is masculine? 5
What qualities does it share with anyone in possession of a penis? I'll tell
myself that a sandwich is masculine because if left alone for a week or
two, it will eventually grow a beard. This works until it's time to order
and I decide that because it sometimes loses its makeup, a sandwich is
undoubtedly feminine.

I just can't manage to keep my stories straight. Hoping I might learn 6
through repetition, I tried using gender in my everyday English. "Hi, guys,"
I'd say, opening a new box of paper clips, or "Hey, Hugh, have you seen my
belt? I can't find her anywhere." I invented personalities for the objects on
my dresser and set them up on blind dates. When things didn't work out
with my wallet, my watch drove a wedge between my hairbrush and my
lighter. The scenarios reminded me of my youth, when my sisters and I
would enact epic dramas with our food. Ketchup-wigged french fries would
march across our plates, engaging in brief affairs or heated disputes over
carrot coins while burly chicken legs guarded the perimeter, ready to jump
in should things get out of hand. Sexes were assigned at our discretion and
were subject to change from one night to the next—unlike here, where the
corncob and the string bean remain locked in their rigid masculine roles.
Say what you like about southern social structure, but at least in North
Carolina a hot dog is free to swing both ways.

Nothing in France is free from sexual assignment. I was leafing 7
through the dictionary, trying to complete a homework assignment, when
I noticed the French had prescribed genders for the various land masses
and natural wonders we Americans had always thought of as sexless,
Niagara Falls is feminine and, against all reason, the Grand Canyon is masculine. Georgia and Florida are female, but Montana and Utah are male.
New England is a she, while the vast area we call the Midwest is just one
big guy. I wonder whose job it was to assign these sexes in the first place.
Did he do his work right there in the sanitarium, or did they rent him a
little office where he could get away from all the noise?

8   There are times when you can swallow the article and others when it must be clearly pronounced, as the word has two different meanings, one masculine and the other feminine. It should be fairly obvious that I cooked an omelette in a frying pan rather than in a wood stove, but it bothers me to make the same mistakes over and over again. I wind up exhausting the listener before I even get to the verb.

9   My confidence hit a new low when my friend Adeline told me that French children often make mistakes, but never with the sex of their nouns. "It's just something we grow up with," she said. "We hear the gender once, and then think of it as part of the word. There's nothing to it."

10   It's a pretty grim world when I can't even feel superior to a toddler. Tired of embarrassing myself in front of two-year-olds, I've started referring to everything in the plural, which can get expensive but has solved a lot of my problems. In saying a *melon,* you need to use the masculine article. In saying *the melons,* you use the plural article, which does not reflect gender and is the same for both the masculine and the feminine. Ask for two or ten or three hundred melons, and the number lets you off the hook by replacing the article altogether. A masculine kilo of feminine tomatoes presents a sexual problem easily solved by asking for two kilos of tomatoes. I've started using the plural while shopping, and Hugh has started using it in our cramped kitchen, where he stands huddled in the corner, shouting, "What do we need with four pounds of tomatoes?"

11   I answer that I'm sure we can use them for something. The only hard part is finding someplace to put them. They won't fit in the refrigerator, as I filled the last remaining shelf with the two chickens I bought from the butcher the night before, forgetting that we were still working our way through a pair of pork roasts the size of Duraflame logs. "We could put them next to the radios," I say, "or grind them for sauce in one of the blenders. Don't get so mad. Having four pounds of tomatoes is better than having no tomatoes at all, isn't it?"

12   Hugh tells me that the market is off-limits until my French improves. He's pretty steamed, but I think he'll get over it when he sees the CD players I got him for his birthday.

Content

1. What is the underlying logic of Sedaris's premises, as a speaker of English, about the gender designations of a language? How does the French use of gender defy this logic? Grammar books don't treat this division humorously; why not? What's the difference between grammatical gender and sexual gender? Why does Sedaris find this contrast humorous?

2. Sedaris allegedly solves the problem by resorting to "referring to everything in the plural" (¶ 10), which, of course, since this is a comic piece, causes other problems. The solution is appropriate to comedy, but is it suitable for application to real-life situations? Explain.

Strategies/Structures/Language

3. Humorists often exaggerate, as Sedaris does in "Make That a Double." Find some instances of this. Why doesn't the obvious exaggeration trouble the humorist's readers or cause them to distrust the narrator?

4. What's the point of inventing "personalities for the objects" on the dresser and setting "them up on blind dates" and other stratagems for learning grammatical gender? Do they work?

5. Having come to the logical conclusion of his humorous point, Sedaris stops. Is there more he could say? If so, what might that be? If not, what does this piece illustrate about why humorous writing is often short?

For Writing

6. As Sedaris does in "Make That a Double" and Britt does in "That Lean and Hungry Look" (261–63), write a brief humorous essay that derives much of its humor from the system of division and classification of its subject. No topic is immune from outrageously irreverent humor; in "Possession" Sedaris, while visiting Anne Frank's secret annex, imagines how he would remodel it: "I'd get rid of the countertop and of course redo all the plumbing . . . and reclaim the fireplace. 'That's your focal point, there.'" Nevertheless, some topics are easier to work with than others; pick one you can handle comfortably, even though it might make your readers uncomfortable. Before turning it in, test it out on a classmate—on whose paper you will comment in turn.

 For comprehension, writing, and research activities and resources, please visit the companion website at <college.hmco.com/english>.

RICHARD RODRIGUEZ

How Richard Rodriguez, born in San Francisco in 1944, the son of Mexican immigrants, should and can deal with his dual heritage is the subject of his autobiographical *Hunger of Memory: The Education of Richard Rodriguez* (1982). He spoke Spanish at home and didn't learn English until he began grammar school in Sacramento. Although for a time he refused to speak Spanish, he studied that language in high school as if it were a foreign language. Nevertheless, classified as Mexican-American, Rodriguez benefited from Affirmative Action programs, and on scholarships he earned a BA from Stanford (1967) and an MA from Columbia (1969). After that he studied Renaissance literature at the University of California, Berkeley. In 1992 he published *Days of Obligation: An Argument with my Mexican Father*, a collection of essays focusing on his complicated relations to the cultures of the Catholic Church, San Francisco's gay Castro District, and Mexico. His book, *Brown: The Last Discovery of America* followed in 2002.

For nearly three decades Rodriguez has been a nationally known commentator—in print and on radio and television—on issues of immigration, race, ethnicity, multiculturalism, and gender, but he did not come out as gay in his writings until around 1990. He opposes bilingual education and has consistently—and controversially—argued against the arbitrary and divisive classification of people into categories by race, religion, or ethnic origin for the purposes of Affirmative Action. In this essay Rodriguez turns his customarily critical gaze onto *family values;* he finds that American beliefs about family closeness and intimacy conflict with the centrifugal realities of American life.

Family Values

1   I am sitting alone in my car, in front of my parents' house—a middle-aged man with a boy's secret to tell. What words will I use to tell them? I hate the word *gay,* find its little affirming sparkle more pathetic than assertive. I am happier with the less polite *queer.* But to my parents I would say *homosexual,* avoid the Mexican slang *joto* (I had always heard it said in our house with hints of condescension), though *joto* is less mocking than the sissy-boy *maricon.*

2   The buzz on everyone's lips now: Family values. The other night on TV, the vice president of the United States, his arm around his wife, smiled into the camera and described homosexuality as "mostly a choice." But how would he know? Homosexuality never felt like a choice to me.

3   A few minutes ago Rush Limbaugh, the radio guy with a voice that reminds me, for some reason, of a butcher's arms, was banging his console and booming a near-reasonable polemic about family values. Limbaugh was not very clear about which values exactly he considers to be family values. A divorced man who lives alone in New York?

4   My parents live on a gray, treeless street in San Francisco not far from the ocean. Probably more than half of the neighborhood is immigrant. India lives next door to Greece, who lives next door to Russia. I wonder what the Chinese lady next door to my parents makes of the politicians' phrase *family values.*

5   What immigrants know, what my parents certainly know, is that when you come to this country, you risk losing your children. The assurance of family—continuity, inevitably—is precisely what America encourages its children to overturn. *Become your own man.* We who are native to this country know this too, of course, though we are likely to deny it. Only a society so guilty about its betrayal of family would tolerate the pieties of politicians regarding family values.

6   On the same summer day that Republicans were swarming in Houston (buzzing about family values), a friend of mine who escaped family values awhile back and who now wears earrings resembling intrauterine

This photograph was taken on October 11, 2003, National Coming Out Day, at a gay rights rally at the University of Texas, Austin. The middle student's T-shirt, the focal point of the picture, invites a reading. How do you "read" it? Does your interpretation of the message influence your interpretation of the student's sunglasses and his smile? Of his companions? Suppose the T-shirt were plain white. How would that affect your interpretation of the people in the photograph? Would you even remember it? By analogy, how could such a photograph, with and without messages on the T-shirt, illustrate Richard Rodriguez's "Family Values"? Now, look at David Sedaris's "Make That a Double," 306–8); is the author, who is openly gay, appearing in the equivalent of an unmarked shirt, or is he sending messages on the subject to his readers?

devices, was complaining to me over coffee about the Chinese. The Chinese will never take over San Francisco, my friend said, because the Chinese do not want to take over San Francisco. The Chinese do not even see San Francisco! All they care about is their damn families. All they care about is double-parking smack in front of the restaurant on Clement Street and pulling granny out of the car—and damn anyone who happens to be in the car behind them or the next or the next.

Politicians would be horrified by such as American opinion, of course. 7
But then what do politicians, Republicans or Democrats, really know of our family life? Or what are they willing to admit? Even in that area where they could reasonably be expected to have something to say—regarding the relationship of family life to our economic system—the politician say nothing. Republicans celebrate American economic freedom, but Republicans don't seem to connect that economic freedom to the social breakdown they find appalling. Democrats, on the other hand, if more tolerant of the drift from familial tradition, are suspicious of the very capitalism that creates social freedom.

8   How you become free in America: Consider the immigrant. He gets a job. Soon he is earning more money than his father ever made (his father's authority is thereby subtly undermined). The immigrant begins living a life his father never knew. The immigrant moves from one job to another, changes houses. His economic choices determine his home address—not the other way around. The immigrant is on his way to becoming his own man.

9   When I was broke a few years ago and trying to finish a book, I lived with my parents. What a thing to do! A major theme of America is leaving home. We trust the child who forsakes family connections to make it on his own. We call that the making of a man.

10   Let's talk about this man stuff for a minute. America's ethos is anti-domestic. We may be intrigued by blood that runs through wealth—the Kennedys or the Rockefellers—but they seem European to us. Which is to say, they are movies. They are Corleones. Our real pledge of allegiance: We say in America that nothing about your family—your class, your race, your pedigree—should be as important as what you yourself achieve. We end up in 1992 introducing ourselves by first names.

11   What authority can Papa have in a country that formed its identity in an act of Oedipal rebellion against a mad British king? Papa is a joke in America, a stock sitcom figure—Archie Bunker or Homer Simpson. But my Mexican father went to work every morning, and he stood in a white smock, making false teeth, oblivious of the shelves of grinning false teeth mocking his devotion.

12   The nuns in grammar school—my wonderful Irish nuns—used to push Mark Twain on me. I distrusted Huck Finn, he seemed like a gringo kid I would steer clear of in the schoolyard. (He was too confident.) I realize now, of course, that Huck is the closest we have to a national hero. We trust the story of a boy who has no home and is restless for the river. (Huck's Pap is drunk.) Americans are more forgiving of Huck's wildness than of the sweetness of the Chinese boy who walks to school with his mama or grandma. (There is no worse thing in America than to be a mama's boy, nothing better than to be a real boy—all boy—like Huck, who eludes Aunt Sally, and is eager for the world of men.)

13   There's a bent old woman coming up the street. She glances nervously as she passes my car. What would you tell us, old lady, of family values in America?

14   America is an immigrant country, we say. Motherhood—parenthood— is less our point than adoption. If I had to assign gender to America, I would note the consensus of the rest of the world. When America is burned in effigy, a male is burned. Americans themselves speak of Uncle Sam.

15   Like the Goddess of Liberty, Uncle Sam has no children of his own. He steals children to make men of them, mocks all reticence, all modesty, all memory. Uncle Sam is a hectoring Yankee, a skinflint uncle, gaunt, uncouth, unloved. He is the American Savonarola—hater of moonshine, destroyer of stills, burner of cocaine. Sam has no patience with mama's boys.

You betray Uncle Sam by favoring private over public life, by seeking 16 to exempt yourself, by cheating on your income taxes, by avoiding jury duty, by trying to keep your boy on the farm.

Mothers are traditionally the guardians of the family against America— 17 though even Mom may side with America against queers and deserters, at least when the Old Man is around. Premature gray hair. Arthritis in her shoulders. Bowlegged with time, red hands. In their fiercely flowered housedresses, mothers are always smarter than fathers in America. But in reality they are betrayed by their children who leave. In a thousand ways. They end up alone.

We kind of like the daughter who was a tomboy. Remember her? It was 18 always easier to be a tomboy in America than a sissy. Americans admired Annie Oakley more than they admired Liberace (who, nevertheless, always remembered his mother). But today we do not admire Annie Oakley when we see Mom becoming Annie Oakley.

The American household now needs two incomes, everyone says. 19 Meaning: Mom is *forced* to leave home out of economic necessity. But lots of us know lots of moms who are sick and tired of being mom, or only mom. It's like the nuns getting fed up, teaching kids for all those years and having those kids grow up telling stories of how awful Catholic school was. Not every woman in America wants her life's work to be forgiveness. Today there are moms who don't want their husbands' names. And the most disturbing possibility: What happens when Mom doesn't want to be Mom at all? Refuses pregnancy?

Mom is only becoming an American like the rest of us. Certainly, 20 people all over the world are going to describe the influence of feminism on women (all over the world) as their "Americanization." And rightly so.

Nothing of this, of course, will the politician's wife tell you. The poli- 21 tician's wife is careful to follow her husband's sentimental reassurances that nothing has changed about America except perhaps for the sinister influence of deviants. Like myself.

I contain within myself an anomaly at least as interesting as the Re- 22 publican Party's version of family values. I am a homosexual Catholic, a communicant in a tradition that rejects even as it upholds me.

I do not count myself among those Christians who proclaim them- 23 selves protectors of family values. They regard me as no less an enemy of the family than the "radical feminists." But the joke about families that all homosexuals know is that we are the ones who stick around and make families possible. Call on us. I can think of 20 or 30 examples. A gay son or daughter is the only one who is "free" (married brothers and sisters are too busy). And, indeed, because we have admitted the inadmissible about ourselves (that we are queer)—we are adepts at imagination—we can even imagine those who refuse to imagine us. We can imagine Mom's loneliness, for example. If Mom needs to be taken to church or to the doctor or ferried between Christmas dinners, depend on the gay son or lesbian daughter.

24   I won't deny that the so-called gay liberation movement, along with feminism, undermined the heterosexual household, if that's what politicians mean when they say family values. Against churchly reminders that sex was for procreation, the gay bar as much as the birth-control pill taught Americans not to fear sexual pleasure. In the past two decades—and, not coincidentally, parallel to the feminist movement—the gay liberation movement moved a generation of Americans toward the idea of a childless adulthood. If the women's movement was ultimately more concerned about getting out of the house and into the workplace, the gay movement was in its way more subversive to puritan America because it stressed the importance of play.

25   Several months ago, the society editor of the morning paper in San Francisco suggested (on a list of "must haves") that every society dame must have at least one gay male friend. A ballet companion. A lunch date. The remark was glib and incorrect enough to beg complaints from homosexual readers, but there was a truth about it as well. Homosexual men have provided women with an alternate model of masculinity. And the truth: The Old Man, God bless him, is a bore. Thus are we seen as preserving marriages? Even Republican marriages?

26   For myself, homosexuality is a deep brotherhood but does not involve domestic life. Which is why, my married sisters will tell you, I can afford the time to be a writer. And why are so many homosexuals such wonderful teachers and priests and favorite aunts, if not because we are freed from the house? On the other hand, I know lots of homosexual couples (male and female) who model their lives on the traditional heterosexual version of domesticity and marriage. Republican politicians mock the notion of a homosexual marriage, but ironically such marriages honor the heterosexual marriage by imitating it.

27   "The only loving couples I know," a friend of mine recently remarked, "are all gay couples."

28   This woman was not saying that she does not love her children or that she is planning a divorce. But she was saying something about the sadness of American domestic life: the fact that there is so little joy in family intimacy. Which is perhaps why gossip (public intrusion into the private) has become a national industry. All day long, in forlorn houses, the television lights up a freakish parade of husbands and mothers-in-law and children upon the stage of Sally or Oprah or Phil. They tell on each other. The audience ooohhhs. Then a psychiatrist-shaman appears at the end to dispense prescriptions—the importance of family members granting one another more "space."

29   The question I desperately need to ask you is whether we Americans have ever truly valued the family. We are famous, or our immigrant ancestors were famous, for the willingness to leave home. And it is ironic that a crusade under the banner of family values has been taken up by those who would otherwise pass themselves off as patriots. For they seem not to understand America, nor do I think they love the freedoms America grants.

Do they understand why, in a country that prizes individuality and is suspicious of authority, children are disinclined to submit to their parents? You cannot celebrate American values in the public realm without expecting them to touch our private lives. As Barbara Bush remarked recently, family values are also neighborhood values. It may be harmless enough for Barbara Bush to recall a sweeter America—Midland, Texas, in the 1950s. But the question left begging is why we chose to leave Midland, Texas. Americans like to say that we can't go home again. The truth is that we don't want to go home again, don't want to be known, recognized. Don't want to respond in the same old ways. (And you know you will if you go back there.)

Little 10-year-old girls know that there are reasons for getting away   30 from the family. They learn to keep their secrets—under lock and key—addressed to Dear Diary. Growing up queer, you learn to keep secrets as well. In no place are those secrets more firmly held than within the family house. You learn to live in closets. I know a Chinese man who arrived in America about 10 years ago. He got a job and made some money. And during that time he came to confront his homosexuality. And then his family arrived. I do not yet know the end of this story.

The genius of America is that it permits children to leave home, it per-   31 mits us to become different from our parents. But the sadness, the loneliness of America, is clear too.

Listen to the way Americans talk about immigrants. If, on the one   32 hand, there is impatience when today's immigrants do not seem to give up their family, there is also a fascination with this reluctance. In Los Angeles, Hispanics are considered people of family. Hispanic women are hired to be at the center of the American family—to babysit and diaper, to cook and to clean and to ease the dying. Hispanic attachment to family is seen by many Americans, I think, as the reason why Hispanics don't get ahead. But if Asians privately annoy us for being so family oriented, they are also stereotypically celebrated as the new "whiz kids" in school. Don't Asians go to college, after all, to honor their parents?

More important still is the technological and economic ascendancy   33 of Asia, particularly Japan, on the American imagination. Americans are starting to wonder whether perhaps the family values of Asia put the United States at a disadvantage. The old platitude had it that ours is a vibrant, robust society for being a society of individuals. Now we look to Asia and see team effort paying off.

In this time of national homesickness, of nostalgia, for how we imag-   34 ine America used to be, there are obvious dangers. We are going to start blaming each other for the loss. Since we are inclined, as Americans, to think of ourselves individually, we are disinclined to think of ourselves as creating one another or influencing one another.

But it is not the politician or any political debate about family values   35 that has brought me here on a gray morning to my parents' house. It is some payment I owe to my youth and to my parents' youth. I imagine us sitting in the living room, amid my mother's sentimental doilies and the family photographs, trying to take the measure of the people we have turned out to be in America.

36   A San Francisco poet, when he was in the hospital and dying, called a priest to his bedside. The old poet wanted to make his peace with Mother Church. He wanted baptism. The priest asked why. "Because the Catholic Church has to accept me," said the poet. "Because I am a sinner."

37   Isn't willy-nilly inclusiveness the point, the only possible point to be derived from the concept of family? Curiously, both President Bush and Vice President Quayle got in trouble with their constituents recently for expressing a real family value. Both men said that they would try to dissuade a daughter or granddaughter from having an abortion. But, finally, they said they would support her decision, continue to love her, never abandon her.

38   There are families that do not accept. There are children who are forced to leave home because of abortions or homosexuality. There are family secrets that Papa never hears. Which is to say there are families that never learn the point of families.

39   But there she is at the window. My mother has seen me and she waves me in. Her face asks: Why am I sitting outside? (Have they, after all, known my secret for years and kept it, out of embarrassment, not knowing what to say?) Families accept, often by silence. My father opens the door to welcome me in.

Content

1. One of Rodriguez's main points in "Family Values" is that American beliefs about families clash with American realities. For example, politicians praise "family values," but "when you come to this country, you risk losing your children" (¶ 5) because they grow up to be different or move away. Identify several other beliefs about American families in this essay, and show how Rodriguez challenges these beliefs.

2. How does Rodriguez's status as a second-generation American affect his perception of American life? Give some examples of things he notices that less recent immigrants might not perceive. Similarly, consider his status as a gay man; does his sexual orientation allow him to perceive what others might miss?

3. This essay asserts that some American values cause results that are the opposite of what they intend to promote. For example, economic freedom and family traditions are both key values, but economic freedom means that "a major theme of America is leaving home" (¶ 9). What American traditions cause unintended results, according to Rodriguez?

Strategies/Structures/Language

4. "Family Values" begins and ends with a framing narrative—the episode in Rodriguez's life when he is just about to come out to his parents about his homosexuality. How effective is his use of a story to launch an argumentative essay?

5. Rodriguez uses generalizations that may provoke thought—or stretch the reader's credibility. For example, his friend states, "The only loving couples I know

are all gay couples." What other generalizations play a role in the argument? To what extent do they help, or detract from, the essay's effectiveness?

6. Humor plays an important role in "Family Values." Consider passages such as "India lives next door to Greece, who lives next door to Russia" (¶ 4); or the moralizing of Rush Limbaugh, "a divorced man who lives alone in New York" (¶ 3); or "a friend of mine who escaped family values awhile back and who now wears earrings resembling intrauterine devices" (¶ 6). What other examples of humor did you notice? How is Rodriguez's use of humor effective in persuading the reader to accept his point of view?

For Writing

7. To what extent do you agree or disagree with Rodriguez's argument about American family values? With a friend, discuss what the most important values are in your respective families. On the basis of this discussion, explain whether Rodriguez does or doesn't succeed in convincing you that some American beliefs actually weaken the American family tradition or that family values are out of step with realities.

8. Research some of the issues that Rodriguez discusses to learn more about the trends that he sees. For example, you could find data or articles about adult children who move away from their place of birth or whose ability to outearn their parents greatly interferes with family cohesion. Or you could focus on the stability or instability of immigrant families (compare with Chang-rae Lee's "Coming Home Again," 156–64). Determine whether or not your findings confirm Rodriguez's conclusions, and discuss why this is so.

9. Use a framing narrative, like Rodriguez's story about coming out to his parents, to discuss your own experiences with, and beliefs about, family. You may focus on your family experience or families in general.

 For comprehension, writing, and research activities and resources, please visit the companion website at <college.hmco.com/english>.

GELAREH ASAYESH

"When a natural disaster hits, people talk for years about . . . the power of the earth tremor that remade the landscape of their lives. But the emotional disasters in our lives go largely unacknowledged, their repercussions unclaimed," says Asayesh, in *Saffron Sky*, of her parents' decision in 1977 to move the family from Tehran, Iran (where she was born in 1961), to Chapel Hill, North Carolina. In Iran they lived in material comfort but in political opposition to the repressive Shah. In Chapel Hill, as graduate students, they became outsiders, "wrenched from all that was loved and familiar" in Iran, "faced with an unspoken choice: to be alienated from the world around us or from our innermost selves." Although Asayesh was educated at the

University of North Carolina-Chapel Hill, and went on to become a journalist, working for *The Boston Globe, The Miami Herald,* and *The Baltimore Sun,* the appeals and tensions of these contradictory cultures have never been fully resolved.

In *Saffron Sky: A Life Between Iran and America* (1999), Asayesh explores the contrasts between these two ways of life, her ambivalent attitude toward her homeland intensified by her marriage to an American and her own parenthood. Returning to Iran in October 1990, just before the Persian Gulf war, Asayesh is newly aware of the world of "rigidity and restriction"— rules against wearing lipstick, or too sheer stockings, or letting the hair show—enforced by the intrusive gender police. Yet, as "Shrouded in Contradiction," published in the *New York Times Magazine* (November 2001), reveals, "To wear *hijab* is to invite contradiction. Sometimes I hate it. Sometimes I value it"—as a covering of both restriction and freedom.

Shrouded in Contradiction

1   I grew up wearing the miniskirt to school, the veil to the mosque. In the Tehran of my childhood, women in bright sundresses shared the sidewalk with women swathed in black. The tension between the two ways of life was palpable. As a schoolgirl, I often cringed when my bare legs got leering or contemptuous glances. Yet, at times, I long for the days when I could walk the streets of my country with the wind in my hair. When clothes were clothes. In today's Iran, whatever I wear sends a message. If it's a chador, it embarrasses my Westernized relatives. If it's a skimpy scarf, I risk being accused of stepping on the blood of the martyrs who died in the war with Iraq. Each time I return to Tehran, I wait until the last possible moment, when my plane lands on the tarmac, to don the scarf and long jacket that many Iranian women wear in lieu of a veil. To wear *hijab*—Islamic covering—is to invite contradiction. Sometimes I hate it. Sometimes I value it.

2   Most of the time, I don't even notice it. It's annoying, but so is wearing pantyhose to work. It ruins my hair, but so does the humidity in Florida, where I live. For many women, the veil is neither a symbol nor a statement. It's simply what they wear, as their mothers did before them. Something to dry your face with after your ablutions before prayer. A place for a toddler to hide when he's feeling shy. Even for a woman like me, who wears it with a hint of rebellion, *hijab* is just not that big a deal.

3   Except when it is.

4   "Sister, what kind of get-up is this?" a woman in black, one of a pair, asks me one summer day on the Caspian shore. I am standing in line to ride a gondola up a mountain, where I'll savor some ice cream along with vistas of sea and forest. Women in chadors stand wilting in the heat, faces gleaming with sweat. Women in makeup and clunky heels wear knee-length jackets with pants, their hair daringly exposed beneath sheer scarves.

In what ways is this photograph a graphic illustration of the elements of division and classification? Explain how it is a commentary on both "Shrouded in Contradiction" and "Mirror, Mirror on the Wall."

None have been more daring than I. I've wound my scarf into a tur- 5 ban, leaving my neck bare to the breeze. The woman in black is a government employee paid to police public morals. "Fix your scarf at once!" she snaps.

"But I'm hot," I say. 6

"You're hot?" she exclaims. "Don't you think we all are?" 7

I start unwinding my makeshift turban. "The men aren't hot," I 8 mutter.

Her companion looks at me in shocked reproach. "Sister, this isn't 9 about men and women," she says, shaking her head. "This is about Islam."

I want to argue. I feel like a child. Defiant, but powerless. Burning 10 with injustice, but also with a hint of shame. I do as I am told, feeling acutely conscious of the bare skin I am covering. In policing my sexuality, these women have made me more aware of it.

The veil masks erotic freedom, but its advocates believe *hijab* tran- 11 scends the erotic—or expands it. In the West, we think of passion as a fever of the body, not the soul. In the East, Sufi poets used earthly passion as a metaphor; the beloved they celebrated was God. Where I come from, people are more likely to find delirious passion in the mosque than in the bedroom.

12   There are times when I feel a hint of this passion. A few years after my encounter on the Caspian, I go to the wake of a family friend. Sitting in a mosque in Mashhad, I grip a slippery black veil with one hand and a prayer book with the other. In the center of the hall, there's a stack of Koranic texts decorated with green-and-black calligraphy, a vase of white gladioluses and a large photograph of the dearly departed. Along the walls, women wait quietly.

13   From the men's side of the mosque, the mullah's voice rises in lament. His voice is deep and plaintive, oddly compelling. I bow my head, sequestered in my veil while at my side a community of women pray and weep with increasing abandon. I remember from girlhood this sense of being exquisitely alone in the company of others. Sometimes I have cried as well, free to weep without having to offer an explanation. Perhaps they are right, those mystics who believe that physical love is an obstacle to spiritual love; those architects of mosques who abstained from images of earthly life, decorating their work with geometric shapes that they believed freed the soul to slip from its worldly moorings. I do not aspire to such lofty sentiments. All I know is that such moments of passionate abandon, within the circle of invisibility created by the veil, offer an emotional catharsis every bit as potent as any sexual release.

14   Outside, the rain pours from a sullen sky. I make my farewells and walk toward the car, where my driver waits. My veil is wicking muddy water from the sidewalk. I gather up the wet and grimy folds with distaste, longing to be home, where I can cast off this curtain of cloth that gives with one hand, takes away with the other.

[Suggestions for reading and writing about this essay are combined with those pertaining to Sumbul Khan's "Mirror, Mirror on the Wall" and appear on pages 324–25.]

SUMBUL KHAN

Sumbul Khan, born in Karachi, Pakistan, in 1978, attended the Indus Valley School of Art and Architecture for three years before transferring to the University of Connecticut and earning a BFA. "Mirror, Mirror on the Wall" was written in a freshman composition class during her first year at an American university. This was, Kahn says, "a tumultuous and yet very enriching time as it entailed adjusting to a completely different culture and finding my place in it as an international student." In writing the essay, she says, "I made a conscious effort to convey lucidly the logic behind the Muslim practice of wearing the veil and addressing the stereotypes that make it difficult sometimes to adhere to the practice, without alienating an audience that might have had varied perceptions of it."

❄ *Mirror, Mirror on the Wall, Who's the Fairest of Them All?*

"One of those international students, can't help looking at them, can you?"

The snigger repeats itself in her mind as her fingers fasten the dark strands of hair in silver barrettes. She looks at the girl on the other side of the mirror and watches her face change as the white folds of cloth crop her countenance closely around its contours. The resemblance is evident and yet it is not her she sees today but the girl they see.

Rambling through her mind, seeking to find words that describe her to them, she sets herself on a plane outside of herself. It is as if she does not reside in her own body anymore but somewhere beyond its physical dimensions, from where she stares down at the effigy she calls, I. Is it the I that keeps coming in the way of adopting their ways? What is the I? What is it made of?

The I, for the moment, is only the piece of cloth that covers her hair, the *hejaab*. The garb of bondage, the symbol of primitive conformity, the virgin white *hejaab* that enshrouds her body that breathes every breath in self-abnegation. She wonders if that is what it really is? She peers into her eyes for an answer but the two pairs of eyes, both her own, stare transfixed at each other, neither knowing what to expect of which.

I was seventeen when it all began. Dunya had come home one day in tears: her husband had put a knife to her throat and threatened to kill her. They had been in the marriage for two years and not a day had gone by that he hadn't called her a whore and not meant it. *Was* Dunya a whore? Dunya was as untouched and pure as they come. Dunya was, however, a better doctor than him and, worse still, she belonged to a family that believed its daughters to be individual entities, not their husbands' doormats. The man was insecure. Having risen from adversity by dint of a little luck and a little help from kind relatives, his views were still as inflexible, as was typical of the men of his strata. Dunya, for him, was too self-sufficient for her culture and so Dunya was a whore. "It can't work, *Ammi*," she wept hysterically in their mother's arms.

That was the first failed marriage in the family and that too on the eve of the second daughter's wedding. Iman's wedding was fraught with uncertainty. It would have been postponed, for no one was up to celebrating, but putting off a wedding was said to bring bad luck. Hence it was decided that the wedding would be held the very day that it had been scheduled. It was the day after Dunya's divorce papers were filed.

The irony of it all did not go unnoticed and much was said in the neighborhood about *Miyan Saheb's* misfortune. Of course the punch line was, "When girls get sent to college they lose sight of their real station in life. How then, can marriages last?" After a year and a half of turning a deaf ear to such shows of sympathy and keeping their chins up with all the integrity parents with girls can have in South Asia, they hadn't the faintest idea what more was about to come their way.

8   It wasn't long before Iman came home too. Her divorce was not stomached as well as Dunya's, after all there was a third's marriage prospects to consider: who would marry her knowing both her elder sisters had failed to keep their husbands happy. They wouldn't see that the decision to opt out had been the girls' in both cases because there was something wrong with the men, but that didn't matter. No matter what the men were like, the girls had failed. The third will probably not make it either. It took six months of Iman being tossed back and forth between her father's and husband's house, before it was decided that it was unfair to make Iman live through hell for the sake of the youngest. If Allah willed the youngest to be happy, she would find her happiness regardless of whether her sisters were divorced or not. So that was that.

9   It was sometime in the middle of this frenzy that I, the youngest, struggled with the travails of adolescent girlhood in a male-dominated culture. Disillusioned by my sisters' experiences, I was probably the most cynical nineteen-year-old of my lot. So while my friends were looking for flippant high school sweethearts, I found myself thinking of independence—financial, social, physical and emotional—a career began to take form in my mind. Perhaps it was the need for stability, external and internal, that made me start reading up on Islam, the religion I was born in. And then I woke up one day and donned the *hejaab*. I was not going to be sized up by men, I would take control of my body and defy the objectification I felt as a woman. I would decide who was worthy enough to share my person with. It was a step towards liberation, as the readings on feminism later suggested, from the masculine gaze.

10   America. The land of opportunity. The land where Feminism was born. The land I thought would embrace me with open arms because I had broken the shackles of male dependence by deciding to live on my own. I celebrated my twenty-second birthday here. Life takes a perverse delight, though, in proving us wrong just when we think we're on top of things.

11   Her finger tips trace the circles around her eyes. Age. Is this what they say they feel at the big thirty? She counts her years up to thirty—eight more to go—no, it must be another feeling, she was too far behind to know quite what thirty felt like. It has been a while since she has thought back to a past so carefully locked away in the deep recesses of her mind. Perhaps this is one of those moments, when one feels so overcome by vulnerability that the strength of the everyday façade refuses to stay up, and all one's insecurities

float before one's face laughing demonically, with vengeance. She looks back at them, the tiny specters that loom so large before her.

"Afghanistan wages war on women" had been the subject of the e-mail her   12
friend had forwarded her. It had jabbed like a dagger in her gut. Even now she could feel the bile rising to her throat as she imagined women, covered like herself, being sentenced to death for being out with a male friend.

It's not their fault. How can they help but think of me as a victim? I can't   13
even blame them for seeing me as an accomplice in the savagery of the Muslim world for wearing my *hejaab* so confidently. How can I explain my position against a backdrop of such ignorant transgression? What is wrong with the Afghan government? This is not what Islam propounds. Islam was the religion to give women the right to vote, the right to conduct trade, the right to marry who they pleased when the West was still grappling with corseted, powdered and puffed to perfection, chaperoned, puppets of the male will. What a mockery we make of our religion now! How in the face of this does one propose to anyone the feminist implications of *hejaab?* The fact that it sets a woman free from having to conform to the male standards of feminine beauty. Even in the most traditional of connotations, where it was a symbol of protection at a time against men who were at liberty to take any woman off the street, the *hejaab* was *for* the woman and now it is the very thing our men strangle us with! No, that isn't Islam, not to me, and not to a lot of Muslim men and women I know. There are those of us who still see the teachings in their true spirit. Yet, to a world that is fed only on the media, there appears to be no difference between those of us who understand their faith and those who warp it to suit their own interests.

Haven't there been transgressors in every religion, though? What of   14
the ethnic cleansing in Bosnia? Christ, who died for the sins of mankind, would not have proposed killing every non-Christian left, right and center, yet the world doesn't generalize Christians as bigoted terrorists. Why is that objectivity extended to Christians—the level-headedness that says not all are alike and what is being done is wrong, wrong even to the spirit of the religion, in the name of which it is being done—and not to Muslims?

Her eyes wander from her face to the rest of her form, to her practically   15
non-existent breasts. All through school if anyone had anything to say to her it was, "Honey, you need to let a man get to you." It was one of the gifts of repressed, single-sex, Convent schooling—girls deriding each other more openly than they would have were there boys around. Under the loose T-shirt however, they completely disappeared. Her thoughts drift to the pair of gray-green eyes that she had lately been seeking out in her drawing class. Eyes that barely ever rested on her longer than a second—how could they on a form so covered that it offered little incentive

to look? Yet this is exactly what the point had been, to not allow a man to feast his eyes on her, but this one she was willing to give the prerogative to. The prerogative, however, only came with marriage and an American man was not about to forsake all the pleasures prettier girls may readily offer, just to have her.

16   It's something about the color of his eyes, I think, because in every other sense he's just an ordinary looking male. All that is keeping me from those eyes is my *hejaab*.

17   Is it worth it? This whole deal that I make of it? Can not having pre-marital sex guarantee that the man I ultimately choose to take would be right for me? He wasn't for Dunya or Iman. Yet would succumbing to this desire now guarantee that I would be able to secure a long-term relation-ship with this man-to-be?

18   No, if it failed, it would hurt all the more for then my husband's touch would never suffice. Perhaps then the *hejaab* in a way protects one from getting hurt, too; if there is nothing to compare against, at least the physical aspect of a conjugal bond would most likely be pleasurable with whomever the husband might be.

19   And yet, there is the present, the sordidly hurtful present that yearns, that longs, and that doesn't quite taste that particular mouth.

20   Her mouth curves into a sad wishful smile as her lower lip curls under the sharp bite of her teeth. For now, reverie has seized reign of her conscious self as a whiff of the fresh, sweet air that would waft across her room at home when the window was opened on to the garden. Her senses give in to its heady, tantalizing allure, unable to keep her from smiling. Far, oh-so-far, is the misery, the torment of being misunderstood, being unread. The anticipation of a new day, of the possibility of seeing him, propels her away from the self-analytical mirror to gather her things for the Tuesday morning studio.

Content

1. For what purpose or purposes is the *hijab* (or *hejaab*) worn? Why does Asayesh write, "In today's Iran, whatever I wear sends a message" (¶ 1)? What is the "mes-sage"? To whom is a message being sent? Is the message the same to every viewer? Is this the same message that Khan sends when she wears the *hejaab* to class in America?

2. Both Asayesh and Khan have ambivalent feelings about wearing the *hijab*, the veil-like covering for women mandated in Islamic countries. What are these?

3. Both authors are bicultural: Asayesh is Iranian-American, and Khan, from Karachi, Pakistan, is studying in Connecticut. Are their conflicts related to the fact that they live in dual cultures? Or would these same conflicts exist if they lived in or held the values of a single culture?

Strategies/Structures/Language

4. Asayesh introduces her subject with a reference to wearing both miniskirts and veils. How does this reference help to convey the forms of division and classification she will pursue in her discussion? How does her conclusion help to tie her essay together?

5. The essays by Asayesh and Khan contain several contradictions. Identify them and explain how they contribute to the project of division and classification each undertakes in her essay.

6. Is Asayesh's definition of *hijab* adequate? Is Khan's? Do some research on *hijab* and explain why the definition each provides is either adequate or inadequate for the purposes of her essay.

7. In Asayesh's essay, who is "paid to police public morals" (¶ 5)? What does the policing of public morals entail? What is "the masculine gaze" to which Khan refers in paragraph 9? Is this also a form of control and "policing"? Compare and contrast, in discussion or in writing, the differences in the scrutiny of individual women's dress (and behavior) in the cultures depicted in these papers.

For Writing

8. Choose a particular article of clothing, describe it in detail (fabric, cost, quality, style), and trace the history of the changed messages it (as worn by a particular individual or group) has sent over time. You might consider the original purpose of the article (for example, a baseball cap, a fur coat, blue jeans, a military uniform) and then examine how and why the connotations of wearing this have changed— over time and when worn by different types of people. What message—cultural, economic, political, aesthetic, and/or other—is sent by each type of wearing?

9. Writing as an individual or with a partner, address the subject of what clothes your fellow students wear. You can use the essays by Asayesh and Khan as points of reference. Analyze the clothing of a typical man and woman. In what respects are they similar? Different? Do any articles of clothing predominate? What "messages" do they send to particular audiences in particular contexts? What dictates this dress? Custom? Individual preference? Group behavior? Other factors?

10. Write an essay that proposes answers to Khan's questions in paragraph 13. How can those not familiar with the history of the *hejaab* "help but think of [Khan, Asayesh, or any woman who wears a *hejaab*] as a victim"? How can these and other women who choose to wear a *hejaab* for the reasons these authors identify avoid being seen as "an accomplice in the savagery of the Muslim world for wearing [their] *hejaab* so confidently" (¶ 13)?

 For comprehension, writing, and research activities and resources, please visit the companion website at <college.hmco.com/english>.

Additional Topics for Writing Division and Classification

(For strategies for writing division and classification, see 289)

MULTIPLE STRATEGIES FOR WRITING
DIVISION AND CLASSIFICATION

In writing on any of the following division and classification topics, you can draw on various strategies to reinforce your organization into two or more parts or categories:

- *illustrations* and *examples,* to show the whole, its components, and to interpret them
- a systematic *analysis* of the component elements
- *photographs, drawings, diagrams,* to clarify and explain similarities and differences
- a *time sequence,* to show the formation or consequences of a particular division or classification
- *definitions, explanations, analyses* of the evidence
- an *argument, explicit* or *implicit,* to make the case for the superiority of one or more members of the classification over others—perhaps satiric or humorous

Note: So many of the readings in *The Essay Connection* lend themselves to division and classification that no specific works are identified here; the Table of Contents or Topical Table of Contents should suffice.

1. Write an essay in which you use division to analyze one of the subjects below. Explain or illustrate each of the component parts, showing how each part functions or relates to the functioning or structure of the whole. Remember to adapt your analysis to your reader's assumed knowledge of the subject. Is it extensive? meager? or somewhere in between? Are you, directly or indirectly, arguing for a particular interpretation?

   a. The organization of the college or university you attend
   b. An organization of which you are a member—team, band or orchestra, fraternity or sorority, social or political action group
   c. A typical (or atypical) weekday or weekend in your life
   d. Your budget, or the federal budget
   e. Your family
   f. A farm, factory, or other business
   g. Geologic periods or a zoological phylum
   h. Body types or temperament types
   i. A provocative poem, short story, novel, play, or television or film drama
   j. A hospital, city hall, bank, restaurant, supermarket, shopping mall
   k. The organizational structure of a particular corporation or government office
   l. Reasons for writing (or not writing)

2. Write an essay, adapted to your reader's assumed knowledge of the subject, in which you classify members of one of the following subjects. Make the basis of your classification apparent, consistent, and logical. You may want to identify each

group or subgroup by a name or relevant term, actual or invented. The division or classification scheme could include a rationale for the superiority of one or more of its members.

    a. Types of cars (or SUVs, minivans, or sports cars), boats, bicycles, or surfboards

    b. People's temperaments or personality types

    c. Vacations or holidays—including terrible trips

    d. Styles of music, or types of a particular kind of music (classical, country and western, pop, folk, rock)

    e. People's styles of spending money

    f. Types of restaurants, or subcategories (such as types of fast-food restaurants)

    g. Individual or family lifestyles

    h. Types of post–high school educational institutions, or types of courses a given school offers

    i. Religions or other systems of beliefs or values

    j. Athletes or media celebrities

    k. Computers—types of hardware or software, or types of computer (or Internet) users

    l. Types of stores or shopping malls

    m. Some phenomenon, activity, types of people or literature or entertainment that you like or dislike a great deal

    n. Social or political groups

Definition

A definition can set limits or expand them. An objective definition may settle an argument; a subjective definition can provoke one. In either case, they answer the definer's fundamental question, What is X? The photograph above of the couple in the kitchen, for instance, might be interpreted as a visual definition of "love," "marriage," "domesticity," "home office," "sex roles," "materialism," "technology," "cleanliness," "wealth," or "the good life," among many possibilities. The easiest way to define something is to identify it as a member of a class and then specify the characteristics that make it distinctive from all the other members of that class. You could define yourself as a "student," but that wouldn't be sufficient to discriminate between you as a college undergraduate and pupils in kindergarten, elementary, junior high, or high school, graduate students, or, for that matter, a person independently studying aardvarks, gourmet cooking, or the nature of the universe.

As you make any kind of writing more specific, you lower the level of abstraction, usually a good idea in definition. So you could identify—and thereby define—yourself by specifying "college student," or more specifically yet, your class status, "first-year college student," or "freshman." That might be sufficient for some contexts, such as filling out an application blank. Or you might need to indicate where you go to school "at Cuyahoga Community College" or "Michigan State University." (Initials won't always work—readers might think MSU means Memphis State, or Mississippi, or Montana.)

But if you're writing an entire essay devoted to defining exactly what kind of student you are, a phrase or sentence will be insufficient, even if expanded to include "a computer science major" or "a business major with an accounting specialty, and a varsity diver." Although the details of that definition would separate and thereby distinguish you from, certainly, most other members of your class, they wouldn't convey the essence of what you as a person are like in your student role.

You could consider that sentence your core definition, and expand each key word into a separate paragraph to create an essay-length definition that could include "college student," "accounting major," and "varsity diver." But that still might not cover it. You could approach the subject through considering *cause-and-effect*. Why did you decide to go to college? Because you love to learn? Because you need to get specialized training for your chosen career? To get away from home? What have been the short-term effects of your decision to attend college? What are the long-term effects likely to be—on yourself, on your chosen field, perhaps on the world?

Or you might define yourself as a college student by *comparing and contrasting* your current life with that of a friend still in high school, or with someone who hasn't gone to college, or with a person you admire who has already graduated. If you work part- or full-time while attending college, you could write an *analysis* of its effect on your studying; or an *argument*, using yourself as an *extended example*, stating why it's desirable (or undesirable) for college students to work. Or, among many other possibilities, you could write a *narrative* of a typical week or semester at college. Each of these modes of writing could be an essay of definition. Each could be only partial, unless you wrote a book, for every definition is, by definition, selective. But each would serve your intended purpose. Each essay in this section represents a different common type of definition, but most use other types as well.

Definition According to Purpose. A definition according to purpose specifies the fundamental qualities an object, principle or policy, role, or literary or artistic work has—or should have—in order to fulfill its potential. Thus, such a definition might explicitly answer such questions as, What is the purpose of X? ("A parable is a simple story designed to teach a moral truth.") What is X for? ("Horror movies exist to scare the spectators.") What does X do? What is the role of X?

Descriptive Definition. A descriptive definition identifies the distinctive characteristics of an individual or group that set it apart from others. Thus a descriptive definition may begin by *naming* something, answering the question, What is X called? A possible answer might be Eudora Welty (unique among all other women); a walnut (as opposed to all other species of nuts); or *The Sound and the Fury* (and no other novel by William Faulkner). A descriptive definition may also *specify the relationship among the parts of a unit or group*, responding to the questions, What is the structure of X? How is X organized? How is X put together or constituted—as in the periodic table or a diagram of the body, an engine, or any other mechanical device? Lynda Barry's "Common Scents" (354–63) also, through a series of cartoon panels, offers many combinations of smells, "mint, tangerines, and library books," "fried smelt, garlic, onions; 9,000 cigarettes; "½ a can of Adorne hair spray"; Jade East aftershave" and more. . . . She uses these to evoke people's reactions both to the smells themselves and to the cultures and people who either denigrate or appreciate them, concluding, "Our house smelled like grease and fish and cigs, like Jade East and pork and dogs, like all the wild food my grandma boiled and fried. And if they could get *that* into a spray can, I'd buy it." The literal, descriptive definition might be, "You are what you smell like," but the connotative definition would depend not only on what the definers thought of the smells, but also on their opinions of the culture associated with that particular combination of odors.

Logical Definitions.   Logical definitions answer two related questions: Into what general category does X fall? and How does it differ from all other members of that category? ("A porpoise is a marine mammal but differs from whales, seals, dolphins, and the others in its. . . .") Logical definitions are often used in scientific and philosophical writing, and indeed form the basis for the functional definition Howard Gardner presents in "Who Owns Intelligence?" (342–52).

There are five key principles for writing logical definitions:

1. For economy's sake, use the most specific category to which the item to be defined belongs, rather than broader categories. Thus Gardner confines his discussion to human beings, not animals nor even all primates.
2. Any division of a class must include all members of that class. *Negative definitions* explain what is excluded from a given classification and what is not.
3. Subdivisions must be smaller than the class divided. Intelligence, says Gardner, can be divided into various functional categories: "linguistic and logical-mathematical, musical, spatial, bodily-kinesthetic, naturalist, interpersonal, and intrapersonal."
4. Categories should be mutually exclusive; they should not overlap.
5. The basis for subdividing categories must be consistent throughout each stage of subdivision. Thus, claiming that Daniel Goleman, in his "otherwise admirable *Emotional Intelligence*," confuses emotional intelligence with "certain preferred patterns of behavior," Gardner prefers

the term "emotional sensitivity" because this includes both "interpersonal and intrapersonal intelligences" and therefore applies to "people who are sensitive to emotions in themselves and in others."

Essential or Existential Definition. An essential definition might be considered a variation of a descriptive definition as it answers the question, "What is the essence, the fundamental nature of X?"—love, beauty, truth, justice, for instance. An existential definition presents the essence of its subject by answering the question, "What does it mean to be X?" or "What does it mean to live as an X" or "in a state of X?"—perhaps Chinese, supremely happy, married (or not), an AIDS victim.

In "Together in the Old Square Print, 1976" Jenny Spinner explores what it means not only to be a twin, but an identical twin, and, in "In Search of Our Past," adopted twins, as well, and thus each other's only known blood relative when they were growing up. As Spinner shows us through the examples in her poem and in her creative nonfiction essay, the definition of *twin* depends a great deal on its context as well as on who's doing the defining. The biological definition is unvarying, but the social definition is shifting and complicated and as unique as each pair of twins or as its individual members—for Jenny and Jackie do not think alike. Indeed, their significance to one another changes and deepens through time, understanding, maturity—and independence from each other, though still intertwined, convinced that "no one, that nothing, can destroy us." They mean one set of things to their adoptive parents, and perhaps to their brother. They mean something else to acquaintances, who respond essentially to their identical appearance or to the label "twin." What *twin* means to their biological parents, the sisters choose never to know, as "together, separately we live."

Process Definitions. These are concerned with how things or phenomena get to be the way they are. How is X produced? What causes X? How does it work? What does it do, or not do? With what effects? How does change affect X itself? Such questions are often the basis for scientific definitions, as Charles Darwin's "Understanding Natural Selection" (335–40) illustrates. Darwin's definition is composed of a series of illustrations of natural phenomena and processes (such as stags' horns, cocks' spurs, lions' manes, male peacocks' plumage) that lead to demonstrable effects, such as the propagation and survival of the species, as depicted in the photograph of the cape gannet pairs on page 337. The two essays on "Code Blue" provide very different definitions of a dramatic medical process. In "Code Blue: The Process" (365–69), Jasmine Innerarity carefully explains, from her experience as a pediatric oncology nurse, the conditions for calling a "Code Blue," "the alert signal for a patient who has stopped breathing or whose heart has stopped." She identifies the medical personnel summoned in the process, the equipment needed, the processes involved ("sedating and intubating the patient"), the speed required, the decisions to be made (to take a patient to the operating room, or off a respirator), and the likely outcomes. Innerarity's language, precise and careful, identifies medical crises and explains the medical team's appropriate reactions—definition in the abstract. "Code Blue: The Story" (370–72), Dr. Abraham Verghese's fast-paced narrative, takes readers into the emergency room for a breathless reenactment of the race to snatch life from death—definition in action.

Ultimately, when you're writing an extended definition, you'll need to make it as clear, real, and understandable as possible. You could define a dog as "a clawed, domesticated, carnivorous mammal, *Canis familiaris.*" But would that abstract, technical definition get at your intended focus on working dogs (for instance, sheepherding border collies or seeing-eye German shepherds), or convey the essence of the family setter, Serendipity, who rescued you from drowning when you were five and has been your security blanket ever since? Your choices of specific details, illustrations, analogies, anecdotes, and the like will enable your readers to accept your definition, the ways you see the subject, the boundaries you set.

STRATEGIES FOR WRITING— DEFINITION

1. What is the purpose of the definition (or definitions) I'm writing about? Do I want to explain the subject's particular characteristics? Identify its nature? Persuade readers of my interpretation of its meaning? Entertain readers with a novel, bizarre, or highly personal meaning? How long will my essay be? (A short essay will require a restricted subject that you can cover in the limited space.)
2. For whom am I providing the definition? Why are they reading it? Do they know enough about the background of the subject to enable me to deal with it in a fairly technical way? Or must I stick to the basics—or at least begin there? If I wish to persuade or entertain my readers, can I count on them to have a pre-existing definition in mind against which I can match my own?
3. Will my entire essay be a definition, or will I incorporate definition(s) as part of a different type of essay? What proportion of my essay will be devoted to definition? Where will I include definitions? As I introduce new terms or concepts? Where else, if at all?
4. What techniques of definition will I use: naming; providing examples, brief or extended; comparing and contrasting; considering cause and effect; analysis; argument; narrative; analogy; or a mixture? Will I employ primarily positive or negative means (i.e., X is, or X is not)?
5. How much denotative (objective) definition will I use in my essay? How much connotative (subjective) definition? Will my tone be serious? Authoritative? Entertaining? Sarcastic? Or otherwise?

JENNY SPINNER

Spinner (born 1970) grew up in Decatur, Illinois, a sprawling factory town on the central Illinois prairie. She earned a BA at Millikin University (1992), an MFA in nonfiction writing at Pennsylvania State University (1995), and an MA (1999) and PhD at the University of Connecticut (2004). She is currently Assistant Professor of English at St. Joseph's University in Philadelphia. Spinner's dissertation focused on women essayists. Her essays, often about her sister and her family in Illinois, have appeared in the *Washington Post* and on National Public Radio. "Together in the Old Square Print, 1976" and "In Search of Our Past" (374–79), both written when Spinner was a doctoral student, address her profound and intimate relationship with Jackie, her identical twin sister—and, until she became a mother, her only known blood relative, since the twins were adopted at birth.

Spinner explains the genesis of the poem: "In a creative writing class several semesters ago, I asked my students . . . to write a poem based on a photograph of themselves as children. I decided to give the assignment a whirl myself. I have scores of photographs of my twin sister Jackie and me from when we were children. Every year, on the first day of school, my mom would pose us in front of the wooden French doors that lead to our kitchen. The photograph upon which this poem is based was taken in 1976, the day we began first grade. I knew as soon as I touched it that this photo contained a poem. I remember vividly that traumatic day, the first day I was separated from my beloved sister and forced to make my way in the world as an individual. The poem attempts to describe what anyone looking at the picture can see—two look-alike little girls dressed in matching outfits, holding hands, posed and poised. It also attempts to fill in what is beyond the physical edges of the photograph, the narrative of our first day of school. Finally, the poem brings in the seer, the adult poet who reflects on what she sees and emerges with some sort of truth. In this case, the truth is that I love(d) being a twin as much as I love(d) my sister. It made me feel unique, but that uniqueness, perhaps ironically, was bound to another. I was the first-born, scrambling out of the womb two minutes before my sister. Yet, I am the one who looked back, who was afraid to make her way in the world without her sister. Writing this poem taught me something I'd never before been able to articulate. It was a powerful, personal discovery."

❄ *Together in the Old Square Print, 1976*

> Summer-brown, armed against
> our inaugural day of first grade,
> we are so alike in our *dernier cri:*
> knee-high gingham dresses—
> hers red, mine blue—
> with coordinating tights
> and brass-buckled Mary Janes.

5

Framed by the sleek pectinate line of our bangs,
our identical faces sprout, determined,
10   from our lace-ringed necks.
On the french doors behind us,
the camera flash forms a bright cross,
each of our heads hanging off an arm.
In just one hour, we will be led
15   into different classrooms,
our first separation since birth.
I will suffer through introductions
alone, hardly knowing
who I am without her,
20   and then I will cry.
And I won't stop until Mrs. Parnell
drags me across the hall
into the other first grade.
When my sister sees me
25   standing in the doorway, eyes aflame,
she looks up bewildered,
only then recognizing my absence.
For the rest of the day, I share
her small seat, drying my tears
30   in the heat of her body.
I don't feel shame, only
love bound back together.

But in the old print, all is yet to come.
At ease in our symmetry,
35   puffed sleeve against puffed sleeve,
we look out into the deceptive morning
that arrives with vague hints
of promises and premonitions:
Without her, I would be ordinary.
40   Afraid—and ordinary.

CHARLES DARWIN

Darwin (1809–1882) descended from a distinguished British scientific family; his father was a physician, and his grandfather was the renowned Erasmus Darwin, amateur naturalist. As a youth Darwin was most alert when studying natural phenomena, particularly beetles, even popping a rare specimen into his mouth to preserve it when his hands were full of other newly collected insects. So, despite his lackadaisical study of medicine at Edinburgh University (1825–1828) and equally indifferent preparation for the clergy at Cambridge (BA, 1831), he shipped aboard the HMS *Beagle* on a scientific expedition around South America, 1831–1836. As the ship's naturalist, he recorded careful observations of plants, animals, and human behavior that were published in *The Voyage of the Beagle* (1839), and eventually led to his theories of natural selection (roughly translated as "the survival of the fittest") and evolution. The publication of the earthshaking *On the Origin of Species by Means of Natural Selection, or the Preservation of Favored Races in the Struggle for Life* (1859) was based on his painstaking observations of animals and plants, on land and sea and in the air.

"Understanding Natural Selection," a small portion of this work, contains the essence of Darwin's best-known and most revolutionary principles, that in natural selection those variations, "infinitesimally small inherited modifications," endure if they aid in survival. The claim that these modifications occur gradually, rather than being produced at a single stroke by a divine creator, is the basis for Darwin's theory of evolution, extended to humans in *The Descent of Man* (1871). Darwin's theories provoked the enormous controversy between theologians and scientists that continues to this day—as Gould's "Evolution as Fact and Theory" (404–11) makes clear.

Darwin's work continues to be read, as much for its clear and elegant literary style as for its content. Using the techniques of popular literature to explain sophisticated scientific concepts and to present mountains of detailed information, Darwin is a highly engaging writer. He uses the first person, metaphors, anecdotes, and numerous illustrations that overlap and reinforce one another—here as ways to define his subject. Because he is explaining a theory and concepts totally new to his audience, he has to ground them in the reality of numerous natural phenomena that can be seen and studied.

Understanding Natural Selection

I t may be said that natural selection is daily and hourly scrutinizing, throughout the world, every variation, even the slightest; rejecting that which is bad, preserving and adding up all that is good; silently and insensibly working, whenever and wherever opportunity offers, at the improvement of each organic being in relation to its organic and inorganic conditions of life. We see nothing of these slow changes in progress, until the hand of time has marked the long lapses of ages, and then so imperfect is our view into long past geological ages, that we only see that the forms of life are now different from what they formerly were.

Although natural selection can act only through and for the good of each being, yet characters and structures, which we are apt to consider as of very trifling importance, may thus be acted on. When we see leaf-eating insects green, and bark-feeders mottled-grey; the alpine ptarmigan white in winter, the red-grouse the color of heather, and the black-grouse that of peaty earth, we must believe that these tints are of service to these birds and insects in preserving them from danger. Grouse, if not destroyed at some period of their lives, would increase in countless numbers; they are known to suffer largely from birds of prey; and hawks are guided by eyesight to their prey—so much so, that on parts of the Continent persons are warned not to keep white pigeons, as being the most liable to destruction. Hence I can see no reason to doubt that natural selection might be most effective in giving the proper color to each kind of grouse, and in keeping that color, when once acquired, true and constant. Nor ought we to think that the occasional destruction of an animal of any particular color would produce little effect: we should remember how essential it is in a flock of white sheep to destroy every lamb with the faintest trace of black. In plants the down on the fruit and the color of the flesh are considered by botanists as characters of the most trifling importance: yet we hear from an excellent horticulturist, Downing, that in the United States smooth-skinned fruits suffer far more from a beetle, a curculio, than those with down; that purple plums suffer far more from a certain disease than yellow plums; whereas another disease attacks yellow-fleshed peaches far more than those with other colored flesh. If, with all the aids of art, these slight differences make a great difference in cultivating the several varieties, assuredly, in a state of nature, where the trees would have to struggle with other trees and with a host of enemies, such differences would effectually settle which variety, whether a smooth or downy, a yellow or purple fleshed fruit, should succeed.

3   In looking at many small points of difference between species, which, as far as our ignorance permits us to judge, seem to be quite unimportant, we must not forget that climate, food, and so on probably produce some slight and direct effect. It is, however, far more necessary to bear in mind that there are many unknown laws of correlation to growth, which, when one part of the organization is modified through variation, and the modifications are accumulated by natural selection for the good of the being, will cause other modifications, often of the most unexpected nature.

4   As we see that those variations which under domestication appear at any particular period of life, tend to reappear in the offspring of the same period; for instance, in the seeds of the many varieties of our culinary and agricultural plants; in the caterpillar and cocoon stages of the varieties of the silkworm; in the eggs of poultry, and in the color of the down of their chickens; in the horns of our sheep and cattle when nearly adult; so in a state of nature, natural selection will be enabled to act on and modify organic beings at any age, by the accumulation of profitable variations at that age, and by their inheritance at a corresponding age. If it profit a plant to have its seeds more and more widely disseminated by the wind, I can see no greater difficulty in this being effected through natural selection, than in the cotton-planter increasing and improving by selection the down in the pods on his cotton-trees. Natural selection may modify and adapt the larva of an insect to a score of contingencies, wholly different from those which concern the mature insect. These modifications will no doubt affect, through the laws of correlation, the structure of the adult; and probably in the case of those insects which live only for a few hours, and which never

What Darwinian observations or principles does this photograph illustrate? Does each species, whose members bear a strong family resemblance, have ways of detecting individuals that members of other species are unaware of? How does this detection—and pairing—contribute to their survival?

feed, a large part of their structure is merely the correlated result of successive changes in the structure of their larvae. So, conversely, modifications in the adult will probably often affect the structure of the larva; but in all cases natural selection will ensure that modifications consequent on other modifications at a different period of life, shall not be in the least degree injurious: for if they became so, they would cause the extinction of the species.

Natural selection will modify the structure of the young in relation   5
to the parent, and of the parent in relation to the young. In social animals it will adapt the structure of each individual for the benefit of the community; if each in consequence profits by the selected change. What natural selection cannot do, is to modify the structure of one species, without giving it any advantage, for the good of another species; and though statements to this effect may be found in works of natural history, I cannot find one case which will bear investigation. A structure used only once in an animal's whole life, if of high importance to it, might be modified to any extent by natural selection; for instance, the great jaws possessed by certain insects, and used exclusively for opening the cocoon—or the hard tip to the beak of nestling birds, used for breaking the egg. It has been asserted, that of the best short-beaked tumbler pigeons more perish in the egg than are able to get out of it; so that fanciers assist in the act of hatching. Now, if nature had to make the beak of a full-grown pigeon very short for the

bird's own advantage, the process of modification would be very slow, and there would be simultaneously the most rigorous selection of the young birds within the egg, which had the most powerful and hardest beaks, for all with weak beaks would inevitably perish: or, more delicate and more easily broken shells might be selected, the thickness of the shell being known to vary like every other structure.

Sexual Selection

6 Inasmuch as peculiarities often appear under domestication in one sex and become hereditarily attached to that sex, the same fact probably occurs under nature, and if so, natural selection will be able to modify one sex in its functional relations to the other sex, or in relation to wholly different habits of life in the two sexes, as is sometimes the case with insects. And this leads me to say a few words on what I call sexual selection. This depends, not on a struggle for existence, but on a struggle between the males for possession of the females; the result is not death to the unsuccessful competitor, but few or no offspring. Sexual selection is, therefore, less rigorous than natural selection. Generally, the most vigorous males, those which are best fitted for their places in nature, will leave most progeny. But in many cases, victory will depend not on general vigor, but on having special weapons, confined to the male sex. A hornless stag or spurless cock would have a poor chance of leaving offspring. Sexual selection by always allowing the victor to breed might surely give indomitable courage, length to the spur, and strength to the wing to strike in the spurred leg, as well as the brutal cock-fighter, who knows well that he can improve his breed by careful selection of the best cocks. How low in the scale of nature this law of battle descends, I know not; male alligators have been described as fighting, bellowing, and whirling round, like Indians in a war dance, for the possession of the females; male salmons have been seen fighting all day long; male stag-beetles often bear wounds from the huge mandibles of other males. The war is, perhaps, severest between the males of polygamous animals, and these seem oftenest provided with special weapons. The males of carnivorous animals are already well armed; though to them and to others, special means of defence may be given through means of sexual selection, as the mane to the lion, the shoulder-pad to the boar, and the hooked jaw to the male salmon, for the shield may be as important for victory, as the sword or spear.

7   Amongst birds, the contest is often of a more peaceful character. All those who have attended to the subject, believe that there is the severest rivalry between the males of many species to attract by singing the females. The rock-thrush of Guiana, birds of Paradise, and some others, congregate; and successive males display their gorgeous plumage and perform strange antics before the females, which standing by as spectators, at last choose the most attractive partner. Those who have closely attended to birds in confinement well know that they often take individual preferences and

dislikes: thus Sir R. Heron has described how one pied peacock was eminently attractive to all his hen birds. It may appear childish to attribute any effect to such apparently weak means: I cannot here enter on the details necessary to support this view; but if man can in a short time give elegant carriage and beauty to his bantams, according to his standard of beauty, I can see no good reason to doubt that female birds, by selecting, during thousands of generations, the most melodious or beautiful males, according to their standard of beauty, might produce a marked effect. I strongly suspect that some well-known laws with respect to the plumage of male and female birds, in comparison with the plumage of the young, can be explained on the view of plumage having been chiefly modified by sexual selection, acting when the birds have come to the breeding age or during the breeding season; the modifications thus produced being inherited at corresponding ages or seasons, either by the males alone, or by the males and females; but I have not space here to enter on this subject.

Thus it is, as I believe, that when the males and females of any animal [8] have the same general habits of life, but differ in structure, color, or ornament, such differences have been mainly caused by sexual selection; that is, individual males have had, in successive generations, some slight advantage over other males, in their weapons, means of defence, or charms; and have transmitted these advantages to their male offspring. Yet, I would not wish to attribute all such sexual differences to this agency: for we see peculiarities arising and becoming attached to the male sex in our domestic animals (as the wattle in male carriers, horn-like protuberances in the cocks of certain fowls, and so on), which we cannot believe to be either useful to the males in battle, or attractive to the females. We see analogous cases under nature, for instance, the tuft of hair on the breast of the turkey-cock, which can hardly be either useful or ornamental to this bird; indeed, had the tuft appeared under domestication, it would have been called a monstrosity.

Illustration of the Action of Natural Selection

. . . Let us take the case of a wolf, which preys on various animals, securing [9] some by craft, some by strength, and some by fleetness; and let us suppose that the fleetest prey, a deer for instance, had from any change in the country increased in numbers, or that other prey had decreased in numbers, during that season of the year when the wolf is hardest pressed for food. I can under such circumstances see no reason to doubt that the swiftest and slimmest wolves would have the best chance of surviving, and so be preserved or selected—provided always that they retain strength to master their prey at this or at some other period of the year, when they might be compelled to prey on other animals. I can see no more reason to doubt this, than that man can improve the fleetness of his greyhounds by careful and methodical selection, or by that unconscious selection which results from each man trying to keep the best dogs without any thought of modifying the breed.

10   Even without any change in the proportional numbers of the animals on which our wolf preyed, a cub might be born with an innate tendency to pursue certain kinds of prey. Nor can this be thought very improbable; for we often observe great differences in the natural tendencies of our domestic animals; one cat, for instance, taking to catch rats, another mice; one cat . . . bringing home winged game, another hares or rabbits, and another hunting on marshy ground and almost nightly catching woodcocks or snipes. The tendency to catch rats rather than mice is known to be inherited. Now, if any slight innate change of habit or of structure benefited an individual wolf, it would have the best chance of surviving and of leaving offspring. Some of its young would probably inherit the same habits or structure, and by the repetition of this process, a new variety might be formed which would either supplant or coexist with the parent-form of wolf. Or, again, the wolves inhabiting a mountainous district, and those frequenting the lowlands, would naturally be forced to hunt different prey; and from the continued preservation of the individuals best fitted for the two sites, two varieties might slowly be formed. These varieties would cross and blend where they met; but to this subject of intercrossing we shall soon have to return. I may add, that . . . there are two varieties of the wolf inhabiting the Catskill Mountains in the United States, one with a light greyhoundlike form, which pursues deer, and the other more bulky, with shorter legs, which more frequently attacks the shepherd's flocks.

Content

1. What does Darwin mean by "natural selection" (¶s 1–5)? How does "natural selection" differ from "sexual selection" (¶s 6–8)?

2. Although Darwin doesn't use the term "evolution," this piece clearly illustrates that concept. Define that term, using some of Darwin's illustrations. Does your definition anticipate creationists' objections? Should it? If you believe in creationism, how does this belief influence the way you define "evolution"?

3. Distinguish between theory, opinion, and fact in Darwin's presentation of the concepts of natural selection (¶s 1–5, 9–10).

Strategies/Structures/Language

4. Darwin offers arguments on behalf of both natural selection and sexual selection. Which argument has the better supporting evidence? Which argument makes its case more compellingly? Why?

5. Darwin builds his case for the existence of natural selection by using numerous illustrations. Identify some. Explain how an argument can also, as in this case, be a definition.

6. What kind of authorial persona does Darwin present? In what ways is this "scientist figure" familiar today? How does this persona differ from the stereotype of the "mad scientist"?

7. Is Darwin writing for an audience of other scientists? For a general readership? Or for both? What aspects of his language (choice of vocabulary, familiar or unfamiliar language and illustrations), tone, and sentence structure reinforce your answer?

For Writing

8. Either by yourself or in collaboration with a partner or team, write a definition of something (a natural phenomenon, human or animal behavior you have observed carefully over time) for an audience of nonscientists. If you are writing about the behavior of college students in a particular type of situation—for example, some aspect(s) of test-taking, dating, dressing, eating—record your observations in as objective and "scientific" a manner as you can. Each team member could conduct the research for a particular characteristic.

9. Every definition is an argument, overt or implied, for the definer's particular way of looking at the subject (for example, see Gould's "Evolution as Fact and Theory" [404–11]). For readers who might disagree with you, write a controversial definition of a subject about which you feel passionate—friendship, love, marriage, violence, war, an ideal—you name it (place to live, job to have, family life, public policy). If you are dealing in abstractions, as you are likely to do in an extended definition, you will need to shore up your generalizations with specific information and illustrations.

 For comprehension, writing, and research activities and resources, please visit the companion website at <college.hmco.com/english>.

HOWARD GARDNER

Gardner (born 1943) studied cognitive and social psychology at Harvard (BA, 1965, PhD, 1971) and became codirector of Project Zero at the Harvard Graduate School of Education, studying the ways children and adults learn. He is currently the Hobbs Professor in Cognition and Education at Harvard and an adjunct research professor of neurology at Boston University School of Medicine. Gardner has written over twenty books and hundreds of articles, most of them focusing on creativity and intelligence. His most recent work is *Changing Minds: The Art and Science of Changing Our Own and Other People's Minds* (2004).

In his best-known book, *Frames of Mind: The Theory of Multiple Intelligences* (1983), he postulates that there are seven distinct cognitive realms in the human brain and that each governs a particular kind of intelligence. Those intelligences most commonly considered—and tested—by the American educational establishment are *linguistic*, the ability to communicate through language, and *logical-mathematical*, the ability to come up with and use abstract concepts. To these Gardner adds five other intelligences: *spatial*, the ability to perceive and reimage the physical world;

bodily-kinesthetic, the ability to use the body in skilled or creative ways; *musical,* the ability to distinguish, remember, and manipulate tone, melody, and rhythm; *interpersonal,* the ability to understand other people; and *intrapersonal,* the ability to understand one's self and have a conscious awareness of one's emotions. A decade later Gardner added an eighth intelligence: *naturalist,* the ability to have an intuitive understanding about plants and animals. Despite criticism from people who say Gardner's multiple intelligences are really talents (something we can get along without, as opposed to traditionally defined intelligence, which is indispensable) and that they can't be easily measured, to many educators he evokes "the reverence teenagers lavish on a rock star." "Who Owns Intelligence?" first published in the *Atlantic Monthly* in February 1999, addresses these issues in attempting, once again, to pin down intelligence and who owns it—a particularly significant issue as the twenty-first century grapples with expanding concepts of intellectual property, ranging from book manuscripts, musical compositions, and mechanical inventions to websites, applications of gene therapy, and esoteric chemical and technical processes.

Who Owns Intelligence?

1   Almost a century ago Alfred Binet, a gifted psychologist, was asked by the French Ministry of Education to help determine who would experience difficulty in school. Given the influx of provincials to the capital, along with immigrants of uncertain stock, Parisian officials believed they needed to know who might not advance smoothly through the system. Proceeding in an empirical manner, Binet posed many questions to youngsters of different ages. He ascertained which questions when answered correctly predicted success in school, and which questions when answered incorrectly foretold school difficulties. The items that discriminated most clearly between the two groups became, in effect, the first test of intelligence.

2   Binet is a hero to many psychologists. He was a keen observer, a careful scholar, an inventive technologist. Perhaps even more important for his followers, he devised the instrument that is often considered psychology's greatest success story. Millions of people who have never heard Binet's name have had aspects of their fate influenced by instrumentation that the French psychologist inspired. And thousands of psychometricians—specialists in the measurement of psychological variables—earn their living courtesy of Binet's invention.

3   Although it has prevailed over the long run, the psychologists' version of intelligence is now facing its biggest threat. Many scholars and observers—and even some iconoclastic psychologists—feel that intelligence is too important to be left to the psychometricians. Experts are extending the breadth of the concept—proposing many intelligences, including emotional intelligence and moral intelligence. They are experimenting with new methods of ascertaining intelligence, including some that avoid tests altogether in favor of direct measures of brain activity. They are forcing citizens

everywhere to confront a number of questions: What is intelligence? How ought it to be assessed? And how do our notions of intelligence fit with what we value about human beings? In short, experts are competing for the "ownership" of intelligence in the next century.

The outline of the psychometricians' success story is well known. Binet's colleagues in England and Germany contributed to the conceptualization and instrumentation of intelligence testing—which soon became known as IQ tests. (An IQ, or intelligence quotient, designates the ratio between mental age and chronological age. Clearly we'd prefer that a child in our care have an IQ of 120, being smarter than average for his or her years, than an IQ of 80, being older than average for his or her intelligence). Like other Parisian fashions of the period, the intelligence test migrated easily to the United States. First used to determine who was "feeble-minded," it was soon used to assess "normal" children, to identify the "gifted," and to determine who was fit to serve in the Army. By the 1920s the intelligence test had become a fixture in educational practice in the United States and much of Western Europe.

Early intelligence tests were not without their critics. Many enduring concerns were first raised by the influential journalist Walter Lippmann, in a series of published debates with Lewis Terman, of Stanford University, the father of IQ testing in America. Lippmann pointed out the superficiality of the questions, their possible cultural biases, and the risks of trying to determine a person's intellectual potential with a brief oral or paper-and-pencil measure.

Perhaps surprisingly, the conceptualization of intelligence did not advance much in the decades following Binet's and Terman's pioneering contributions. Intelligence tests came to be seen, rightly or wrongly, as primarily a tool for selecting people to fill academic or vocational niches. In one of the most famous—if irritating—remarks about intelligence testing, the influential Harvard psychologist E. G. Boring declared, "Intelligence is what the tests test." So long as these tests did what they were supposed to do (that is, give some indication of school success), it did not seem necessary or prudent to probe too deeply into their meaning or to explore alternative views of the human intellect.

Psychologists who study intelligence have argued chiefly about three questions. The first: Is intelligence singular, or does it consist of various more or less independent intellectual faculties? The purists—ranging from the turn of-the-century English psychologist Charles Spearman to his latter-day disciples Richard J. Herrnstein and Charles Murray (of *The Bell Curve* fame)— defend the notion of a single overarching "g," or general intelligence. The pluralists—ranging from L. L. Thurstone, of the University of Chicago, who posited seven vectors of the mind, to J. P. Guilford, of the University of Southern California, who discerned 150 factors of the intellect—construe intelligence as composed of some or even many dissociable components. In his much cited *The Mismeasure of Man* (1981) the paleontologist Stephen Jay

Gould argued that the conflicting conclusions reached on this issue reflect alternative assumptions about statistical procedures rather than the way the mind is. Still, psychologists continue the debate, with a majority sympathetic to the general-intelligence perspective.

8   The public is more interested in the second question: Is intelligence (or are intelligences) largely inherited? This is by and large a Western question. In the Confucian societies of East Asia individual differences in endowment are assumed to be modest, and differences in achievement are thought to be due largely to effort. In the West, however, many students of the subject sympathize with the view—defended within psychology by Lewis Terman, among others—that intelligence is inborn and one can do little to alter one's intellectual birthright.

9   Studies of identical twins reared apart provide surprisingly strong support for the "heritability" of psychometric intelligence. That is, if one wants to predict someone's score on an intelligence test, the scores of the biological parents (even if the child has not had appreciable contact with them) are more likely to prove relevant than the scores of the adoptive parents. By the same token, the IQs of identical twins are more similar than the IQs of fraternal twins. And, contrary to common sense (and political correctness), the IQs of biologically related people grow closer in the later years of life. Still, because of the intricacies of behavioral genetics and the difficulties of conducting valid experiments with human child-rearing, a few defend the proposition that intelligence is largely environmental rather than heritable, and some believe that we cannot answer the question at all.

10   Most scholars agree that even if psychometric intelligence is largely inherited, it is not possible to pinpoint the sources of differences in average IQ between groups, such as the fifteen-point difference typically observed between African-American and white populations. That is because in our society the contemporary—let alone the historical—experiences of these two groups cannot be equated. One could ferret out the differences (if any) between black and white populations only in a society that was truly color-blind.

11   One other question has intrigued laypeople and psychologists: Are intelligence tests biased? Cultural assumptions are evident in early intelligence tests. Some class biases are obvious—who except the wealthy could readily answer a question about polo? Others are more subtle. Suppose the question is what one should do with money found on the street. Although ordinarily one might turn it over to the police, what if one had a hungry child? Or what if the police force were known to be hostile to members of one's ethnic group? Only the canonical response to such a question would be scored as correct.

12   Psychometricians have striven to remove the obviously biased items from such measures. But biases that are built into the test situation itself are far more difficult to deal with. For example, a person's background affects his or her reaction to being placed in an unfamiliar locale, being instructed

by someone dressed in a certain way, and having a printed test booklet thrust into his or her hands. And as the psychologist Claude M. Steele has argued in these pages (see "Race and the Schooling of Black Americans," April, 1992), the biases prove even more acute when people know that their academic potential is being measured and that their racial or ethnic group is widely considered to be less intelligent than the dominant social group. . . .

Paradoxically, one of the clearest signs of the success of intelligence 13 tests is that they are no longer widely administered. In the wake of legal cases about the propriety of making consequential decisions about education on the basis of IQ scores, many public school officials have become test-shy. By and large, the testing of IQ in the schools is restricted to cases involving a recognized problem (such as a learning disability) or a selection procedure (determining eligibility for a program that serves gifted children).

Despite this apparent setback, intelligence testing and the line of 14 thinking that underlies it have actually triumphed. Many widely used scholastic measures, chief among them the SAT (renamed the Scholastic Assessment Test a few years ago), are thinly disguised intelligence tests that correlate highly with scores on standard psychometric instruments. Virtually no one raised in the developed world today has gone untouched by Binet's seemingly simple invention of a century ago.

Multiple Intelligences

The concept of intelligence has in recent years undergone its most robust 15 challenge since the days of Walter Lippmann. Some who are informed by psychology but not bound by the assumptions of the psychometricians have invaded this formerly sacrosanct territory. They have put forth their own ideas of what intelligence is, how (and whether) it should be measured, and which values should be invoked in considerations of the human intellect. For the first time in many years the intelligence establishment is clearly on the defensive—and the new century seems likely to usher in quite different ways of thinking about intelligence.

One evident factor in the rethinking of intelligence is the perspec- 16 tive introduced by scholars who are not psychologists. Anthropologists have commented on the parochialism of the Western view of intelligence. Some cultures do not even have a concept called intelligence, and others define intelligence in terms of traits that we in the West might consider odd—obedience, good listening skills, or moral fiber, for example. Neuroscientists are skeptical that the highly differentiated and modular structure of the brain is consistent with a unitary form of intelligence. Computer scientists have devised programs deemed intelligent; these programs often go about problem-solving in ways quite different from those embraced by human beings or other animals.

Even within the field of psychology the natives have been getting rest- 17 less. Probably the most restless is the Yale psychologist Robert J. Sternberg. A prodigious scholar, Sternberg, who is forty-nine, has written dozens of books and hundreds of articles, the majority of them focusing in one or another way on intelligence. Sternberg began with the strategic goal of understanding the actual mental processes mobilized by standard test items, such as the solving of analogies. But he soon went beyond standard intelligence testing by insisting on two hitherto neglected forms of intelligence: the "practical" ability to adapt to varying contexts (as we all must in these days of divorcing and downsizing), and the capacity to automate familiar activities so that we can deal effectively with novelty and display "creative" intelligence.

18   Sternberg has gone to greater pains than many other critics of standard intelligence testing to measure these forms of intelligence with the paper-and-pencil laboratory methods favored by the profession. And he has found that a person's ability to adapt to diverse contexts or to deal with novel information can be differentiated from success at standard IQ-test problems. . . .

19   The psychologist and journalist Daniel Goleman has achieved worldwide success with his book *Emotional Intelligence* (1995). Contending that this new concept (sometimes nicknamed EQ) may matter as much as or more than IQ, Goleman draws attention to such pivotal human abilities as controlling one's emotional reactions and "reading" the signals of others. In the view of the noted psychiatrist Robert Coles, author of *The Moral Intelligence of Children* (1997), among many other books, we should prize character over intellect. He decries the amorality of our families, hence our children; he shows how we might cultivate human beings with a strong sense of right and wrong, who are willing to act on that sense even when it runs counter to self-interest. Other, frankly popular accounts deal with leadership intelligence (LQ), executive intelligence (EQ or ExQ), and even financial intelligence.

20   Like Coles's and Goleman's efforts, my work on "multiple intelligences" eschews the psychologists' credo of operationalization and test-making. I began by asking two questions: How did the human mind and brain evolve over millions of years? and How can we account for the diversity of skills and capacities that are or have been valued in different communities around the world?

21   Armed with these questions and a set of eight criteria, I have concluded that all human beings possess at least eight intelligences: linguistic and logical-mathematical (the two most prized in school and the ones central to success on standard intelligence tests), musical, spatial, bodily-kinesthetic, naturalist, interpersonal, and intrapersonal.

22   I make two complementary claims about intelligence. The first is universal. We all possess these eight intelligences—and possibly more. Indeed, rather than seeing us as "rational animals," I offer a new definition of what it means to be a human being, cognitively speaking: *Homo sapiens sapiens* is the animal that possesses these eight forms of mental representation.

23   My second claim concerns individual differences. Owing to the accidents of heredity, environment, and their interactions, no two of us exhibit

the same intelligences in precisely the same proportions. Our "profiles of intelligence" differ from one another. This fact poses intriguing challenges and opportunities for our education system. We can ignore these differences and pretend that we are all the same; historically, that is what most education systems have done. Or we can fashion an education system that tries to exploit these differences, individualizing instruction and assessment as much as possible.

Intelligence and Morality

As the century of Binet and his successors draws to a close, we'd be wise to take stock of, and to anticipate, the course of thinking about intelligence. Although my crystal ball is no clearer than anyone else's (the species may lack "future intelligence"), it seems safe to predict that interest in intelligence will not go away.   24

To begin with, the psychometric community has scarcely laid down its arms. New versions of the standard tests continue to be created, and occasionally new tests surface as well. Researchers in the psychometric tradition churn out fresh evidence of the predictive power of their instruments and the correlations between measured intelligence and one's life chances. And some in the psychometric tradition are searching for the biological basis of intelligence: the gene or complex of genes that may affect intelligence, and neural structures that are crucial for intelligence, or telltale brain-wave patterns that distinguish the bright from the less bright.   25

Beyond various psychometric twists, interest in intelligence is likely to grow in other ways. It will be fed by the creation of machines that display intelligence and by the specific intelligence or intelligences. Moreover, observers as diverse as Richard Herrnstein and Robert B. Reich, President Clinton's first Secretary of Labor, have agreed that in coming years a large proportion of society's rewards will go to those people who are skilled symbol analysts—who can sit at a computer screen (or its technological successor), manipulate numbers and other kinds of symbols, and use the results of their operations to contrive plans, tactics, and strategies for enterprises ranging from business to science to war games. These people may well color how intelligence is conceived in decades to come—just as the need to provide good middle-level bureaucrats to run an empire served as a primary molder of intelligence tests in the early years of the century.   26

Surveying the landscape of intelligence, I discern three struggles between opposing forces. The extent to which, and the manner in which, these various struggles are resolved will influence the lives of millions of people. I believe that the three struggles are interrelated; that the first struggle provides the key to the other two; and that the ensemble of struggles can be resolved in an optimal way.   27

The first struggle concerns the breadth of our definition of intelligence. One camp consists of the purists, who believe in a single form of intelligence—one that basically predicts success in school and in school-like   28 activities. Arrayed against the purists are the progressive pluralists, who believe that many forms of intelligence exist. Some of these pluralists would like to broaden the definition of intelligence considerably, to include the abilities to create, to lead, and to stand out in terms of emotional sensitivity or moral excellence.

29   The second struggle concerns the assessment of intelligence. Again, one readily encounters a traditional position. Once chiefly concerned with paper-and-pencil tests, the traditionally oriented practitioner is now likely to use computers to provide the same information more quickly and more accurately. But other positions abound. Purists disdain psychological tasks of any complexity, preferring to look instead at reaction time, brain waves, and other physiological measures of intellect. In contrast, simulators favor measures closely resembling the actual abilities that are prized. And skeptics warn against the continued expansion of testing. They emphasize the damage often done to individual life chances and self-esteem by a regimen of psychological testing, and call for less technocratic, more humane methods—ranging from self-assessment to the examination of portfolios of student work to selection in the service of social equity.

30   The final struggle concerns the relationship between intelligence and the qualities we value in human beings. Although no one would baldly equate intellect and human worth, nuanced positions have emerged on this issue. Some (in the *Bell Curve* mold) see intelligence as closely related to a person's ethics and values; they believe that brighter people are more likely to appreciate moral complexity and to behave judiciously. Some call for a sharp distinction between the realm of intellect on the one hand, and character, morality, or ethics on the other. Society's ambivalence on this issue can be discerned in the figures that become the culture's heroes. For every Albert Einstein or Bobby Fischer who is celebrated for his intellect, there is a Forrest Gump or a Chauncey Gardiner who is celebrated for human—and humane—traits that would never be captured on any kind of intelligence test. . . .

The Borders of Intelligence

31   Writing as a scholar rather than as a layperson, I see two problems with the notion of emotional intelligence. First, unlike language or space, the emotions are not contents to be processed; rather, cognition has evolved so that we can make sense of human beings (self and others) that possess and experience emotions. Emotions are part and parcel of all cognition, though they may well prove more salient at certain times or under certain circumstances: they accompany our interactions with others, our listening to great music, our feelings when we solve—or fail to solve—a difficult mathematical problem. If one calls some intelligences emotional, one suggests that other intelligences are not—and that implication flies in the face of experience and empirical data.

The second problem is the conflation of emotional intelligence and a $_{32}$ certain preferred pattern of behavior. This is the trap that Daniel Goleman sometimes falls into in his otherwise admirable *Emotional Intelligence.* Goleman singles out as emotionally intelligent those people who use their understanding of emotions to make others feel better, to solve conflicts, or to cooperate in home or work situations. No one would dispute that such people are wanted. However, people who understand emotion may not necessarily use their skills for the benefit of society.

For this reason I prefer the term "emotional sensitivity"—a term (en- $_{33}$ compassing my interpersonal and intrapersonal intelligences) that could apply to people who are sensitive to emotions in themselves and in others. Presumably, clinicians and salespeople excel in sensitivity to others, poets and mystics in sensitivity to themselves. And some autistic or psycho-pathological people seem completely insensitive to the emotional realm. I would insist, however, on a strict distinction between emotional sensitivity and being a "good" or "moral" person. A person may be sensitive to the emotions of others but use that sensitivity to manipulate or to deceive them, or to create hatred.

I call, then, for a delineation of intelligence that includes the full range $_{34}$ of contents to which human beings are sensitive, but at the same time desig-nates as off limits such valued but separate human traits as creativity, moral-ity, and emotional appropriateness. I believe that such a delineation makes scientific and epistemological sense. It reinvigorates the elastic band with-out stretching it to the breaking point. It helps to resolve the two remaining struggles: how to assess, and what kinds of human beings to admire.

Once we decide to restrict intelligence to human information- $_{35}$ processing and product-making capacities, we can make use of the estab-lished technology of assessment. That is, we can continue to use paper-and-pencil or computer-adapted testing techniques while looking at a broader range of capacities, such as musical sensitivity and empathy with others. And we can avoid ticklish and possibly unresolvable questions about the assessment of values and morality that may well be restricted to a particular culture and that may well change over time.

Still, even with a limited perspective on intelligence, important ques- $_{36}$ tions remain about which assessment path to follow—that of the purist, the simulator, or the skeptic. Here I have strong views. I question the wisdom of searching for a "pure" intelligence—be it general intelligence, musical intelligence, or interpersonal intelligence. I do not believe that such al-chemical intellectual essences actually exist; they are a product of our pen-chant for creating terminology rather than determinable and measurable entities. Moreover, the correlations that have thus far been found between supposedly pure measures and the skills that we actually value in the world are too modest to be useful.

What does exist is the use of intelligences, individually and in concert, $_{37}$ to carry out tasks that are valued by a society. Accordingly, we should be assessing the extent to which human beings succeed in carrying out tasks of consequence that presumably involve certain intelligences. To be concrete, we should not test musical intelligence by looking at the ability to discriminate between two tones or timbres; rather, we should be teaching people to sing songs or play instruments or transform melodies and seeing how readily they master such feats. At the same time, we should abjure a search for pure emotional sensitivity—for example, a test that matches facial expressions to galvanic skin response. Rather, we should place (or observe) people in situations that call for them to be sensitive to the aspirations and motives of others. For example, we could see how they handle a situation in which they and colleagues have to break up a fight between two teenagers, or persuade a boss to change a policy of which they do not approve.

38   Here powerful new simulations can be invoked. We are now in a position to draw on technologies that can deliver realistic situations or problems and also record the success of subjects in dealing with them. A student can be presented with an unfamiliar tune on a computer and asked to learn that tune, transpose it, orchestrate it, and the like. Such exercises would reveal much about the student's intelligence in musical matters.

39   Turning to the social (or human, if you prefer) realm, subjects can be presented with simulated interactions and asked to judge the shifting motivations of each actor. Or they can be asked to work in an interactive hypermedia production with unfamiliar people who are trying to accomplish some sort of goal, and to respond to their various moves and countermoves. The program can alter responses in light of the moves of the subject. Like a high-stakes poker game, such a measure should reveal much about the interpersonal or emotional sensitivity of a subject.

40   A significant increase in the breadth—the elasticity—of our concept of intelligence, then, should open the possibility for innovative forms of assessment far more realistic than the classic short-answer examinations. Why settle for an IQ or an SAT test, in which the items are at best remote proxies for the ability to design experiments, write essays, critique musical performances, and so forth? Why not instead ask people actually (or virtually) to carry out such tasks? And yet by not opening up the Pandora's box of values and subjectivity, one can continue to make judicious use of the insights and technologies achieved by those who have devoted decades to perfecting mental measurement.

41   To be sure, one can create a psychometric instrument for any conceivable human virtue, including morality, creativity, and emotional intelligence in its several senses. Indeed, since the publication of Daniel Goleman's book dozens of efforts have been made to create tests for emotional intelligence. The resulting instruments are not, however, necessarily useful. Such instruments are far more likely to satisfy the test maker's desire for reliability (a subject gets roughly the same score on two separate administrations of the test) than the need for validity (the test measures the trait that it purports to measure).

Such instruments-on-demand prove dubious for two reasons. First, beyond some platitudes, few can agree on what it means to be moral, ethical, a good person: consider the differing values of Jesse Helms and Jesse Jackson, Margaret Thatcher and Margaret Mead. Second, scores on such tests are much more likely to reveal test-taking savvy (skills in language and logic) than fundamental character.

In speaking about character, I turn to a final concern: the relationship between intelligence and what I will call virtue—those qualities that we admire and wish to hold up as examples for our children. No doubt the desire to expand intelligence to encompass ethics and character represents a direct response to the general feeling that our society is lacking in these dimensions; the expansionist view of intelligence reflects the hope that if we transmit the technology of intelligence to these virtues, we might in the end secure a more virtuous population.

I have already indicated my strong reservations about trying to make the word "intelligence" all things to all people—the psychometric equivalent of the true, the beautiful, and the good. Yet the problem remains: how, in a post-Aristotelian, post-Confucian era in which psychometrics looms large, do we think about the virtuous human being?

My analysis suggests one promising approach. We should recognize that intelligences, creativity, and morality—to mention just three desiderata—are separate. Each may require its own form of measurement or assessment, and some will prove far easier to assess objectively than others. Indeed, with respect to creativity and morality, we are more likely to rely on overall judgments by experts than on any putative test battery. At the same time, nothing prevents us from looking for people who combine several of these attributes—who have musical and interpersonal intelligence, who are psychometrically intelligent and creative in the arts, who combine emotional sensitivity and a high standard of moral conduct.

Let me introduce another analogy at this point. In college admissions much attention is paid to scholastic performance, as measured by College Board examinations and grades. However, other features are also weighed, and sometimes a person with lower test scores is admitted if he or she proves exemplary in terms of citizenship or athletics or motivation. Admissions officers do not confound these virtues (indeed, they may use different scales and issue different grades), but they recognize the attractiveness of candidates who exemplify two or more desirable traits.

We have left the Eden of classical times, in which various intellectual and ethical values necessarily commingled, and we are unlikely ever to re-create it. We should recognize that these virtues can be separate and will often prove to be remote from one another. When we attempt to aggregate them, through phrases like "emotional intelligence," "creative intelligence," and "moral intelligence," we should realize that we are expressing a wish rather than denoting a necessary or even a likely coupling.

We have an aid in converting this wish to reality: the existence of powerful examples—people who succeed in exemplifying two or more cardinal human virtues. To name names is risky—particularly when one generation's heroes can become the subject of the next generation's pathographies. Even so, I can without apology mention Niels Bohr, George C. Marshall, Rachel Carson, Arthur Ashe, Louis Armstrong, Pablo Casals, Ella Fitzgerald.

49   In studying the lives of such people, we discover human possibilities. Young human beings learn primarily from the examples of powerful adults around them—those who are admirable and also those who are simply glamorous. Sustained attention to admirable examples may well increase the future incidence of people who actually do yoke capacities that are scientifically and epistemologically separate.

50   In one of the most evocative phrases of the century the British novelist E. M. Forster counseled us, "Only connect." I believe that some expansionists in the territory of intelligence, though well motivated, have prematurely asserted connections that do not exist. But I also believe that as human beings, we can help to forge connections that may be important for our physical and psychic survival.

51   Just how the precise borders of intelligence are drawn is a question we can leave to scholars. But the imperative to broaden our definition of intelligence in a responsible way goes well beyond the academy. Who "owns" intelligence promises to be an issue even more critical in the next century than it has been in this era of the IQ test.

Content

1. What is intelligence? Compare and contrast some of the types Gardner refers to, which may be divided into two groups, the sort that "predicts success in school and in school-like activities" (¶s 4–10, 28) and all other kinds, including "the abilities to create, to lead, and to stand out in terms of emotional sensitivity or moral excellence" (¶ 28).

2. How can intelligence of a particular sort best be measured?

3. Who owns intelligence? The people who possess it? The society or social subgroup that determines what sorts of intelligence are valuable, necessary, appreciated—and those that aren't? The testers? How does Gardner's essay address this issue?

Strategies/Structures/Language

4. Find examples in Gardner's essay of the following common techniques of definition, and comment on their effectiveness in conveying one or more meanings of intelligence:

   a. Illustration
   b. Comparison and contrast
   c. Negation (saying what something is not)
   d. Analysis
   e. Explanation of a process (how something is measured or works)
   f. Identification of causes or effects

g. Simile, metaphor, or analogy

h. Reference to authority or the writer's own expertise

i. Reference to the writer's or others' personal experience or observation

5. Gardner's essay is full of arguments: for his definition of intelligence, against competing definitions; for various practical ways of measuring intelligence, against particular sorts of testing. Identify some of the assertions and evidence he uses to support his claims. Are they credible?

6. Does Gardner believe it's possible to expand the definition of *intelligence* to include virtue (¶ 43), to make it encompass qualities he'd like it to have?

7. Can people change definitions of words to make them mean what they want them to mean? Or does every term have a border around it (¶ 50)? If so, who creates and enforces the boundaries?

For Writing

8. Write your own definition either of *intelligence* in general or of a specific type of intelligence such as one that Gardner discusses in his essay. You may need to define some of these yourself or consult other sources for the intelligences Gardner only touches on: a. psychometric intelligence (¶s 4–10); b. the "'practical'" ability to adapt to varying contexts (¶ 17); the "ability to deal with novel information" (¶ 18); emotional intelligence (¶s 19, 31–33); moral intelligence (¶s 19, 41–45); or creativity (¶s 41–45). Or define a form of intelligence on Gardner's personal list that includes "linguistic, logical-mathematical, musical, spatial, bodily-kinesthetic, naturalist, interpersonal, and intrapersonal." (See Gardner's book *Frames of Mind* [1983] or any other of Gardner's numerous writings on the subject.) Use one or more techniques of definition identified in Strategies above, and, assuming that you yourself fulfill your own definition of *intelligent*, supplement your more general definition with a specific firsthand example, and abundant illustrations, verbal and graphic.

9. Write a definition of an abstract concept for readers who may not have thought much about it—such as *love, truth, beauty, justice, greed, pride,* or *the good life*—but who have probably used it often in everyday life, something intangible that can be identified in terms of its effects, causes, manifestations, or other nonphysical properties. Use one or more techniques of definition identified above and illustrate your definition with one or two specific examples with which you are familiar. Then use the examples as a basis for making generalizations that apply to other aspects of the concept.

 For comprehension, writing, and research activities and resources, please visit the companion website at <college.hmco.com/english>.

LYNDA BARRY

Lynda Barry (born 1956), daughter of a Filipino mother and an American father, grew up in an interracial neighborhood in Seattle. When she began Evergreen State College Barry "wanted to be a fine artist." "Cartoons to me were really base." Then she realized that her drawings could make her friends laugh, and shortly after she graduated, in 1978, she created "Ernie

Pook's Comeek," a wry, witty, and feminist strip now syndicated in over sixty newspapers in the United States, Canada, Russia, and Hungary. Barry's eighth comic collection is *It's So Magic* (1994); her second novel is *Cruddy* (1998). *One! Hundred! Demons!*, her autobiography in graphic novel format, was published in 2003.

"Common Scents" (from *One! Hundred! Demons!*) illustrates what Barry told an interviewer, "There was always a lot of commotion in the house, mostly in the kitchen. We didn't have a set dinner or lunch or breakfast time; when we wanted to eat there was always food on the stove. . . . At the time it was a little frustrating for me, because I looked to all the world like a regular little white American kid, but at home we were eating real different food and there was sometimes octopus in the refrigerator and stuff that was scary looking to my friends. . . . We ate with our hands, and when you say that, people think that you're also squatting on the floor . . . but it wasn't like that. There's a whole etiquette to the way that you eat with your hands, just like you hold a fork. And it was lively and unusual, an atmosphere where I . . . could pretty much do whatever I wanted to do."

Common Scents

SOME SMELLS WERE MYS-TERIOUSLY WONDERFUL LIKE AT THE PALINKI'S WHERE IT WAS A COMBINATION OF MINT, TAN-GERINES, AND LIBRARY BOOKS. BUT HOW? I NEVER SAW ANY OF THOSE THINGS THERE.

WHAT'S YOUR KIND OF AIR FRESHENER, BECAUSE THAT'S THE KIND I WANT MY MOM TO GET.

I DON'T USE AIR FRESHENER, DEAR.

WELL, THAT'S WEIRD BECAUSE YOUR HOUSE SMELLS PERFECT.

5

BUT THERE WERE BAD MYS-TERIES TOO, LIKE THE MYSTERY OF THE BLEACH PEOPLE WHOSE HOUSE GAVE OFF FUMES YOU COULD SMELL FROM THE STREET. WE KEPT WAITING FOR THAT HOUSE TO EXPLODE. THE BUGS DIDN'T EVEN GO IN THEIR YARD.

HEYA, JANINA. HEYA.

'N I ASK YOU A PERSONAL THING?

POSSIBLY.

HOW COME YOUR HOUSE SMELLS LIKE THAT?

SMELLS LIKE WHAT?

ALSO GIVING OFF BLEACH FUMES

4

THE GIRL WHO SHOCKED ME WITH THE NEWS ABOUT THE SMELL OF MY HOUSE WAS THE ONE WHOSE HOUSE SMELLED LIKE THE FRESH BUS BATHROOM. HER MOTHER WAS THE MOST DISINFECTING, AIR FRESHENER SPRAYING PERSON THAT EVER LIVED.

THE TRUTH WAS WE DID SAVE OUR GREASE IN A HILLS BROTHERS COFFEE CAN AND YES, MY GRANDMA DID COOK THINGS LIKE PIGS BLOOD STEW. BOILING AND FRYING WENT ON IN THE HOUSE EVERY DAY.

THAT'S WHY I'M NOT SPOSTA COME OVER, 'CAUSE THE SMELL GETS ON MY CLOTHES, MAKES MY MOM SICK.

10

SHE HAD THOSE CAR FRESHENER CHRISTMAS TREE THINGS HANGING EVERYWHERE. EVEN THE MARSHMALLOW TREATS SHE MADE HAD A FRESH PINE-SPRAY FLAVOR. SHE WAS FREE WITH HER OBSERVATIONS ABOUT THE SMELL OF OTHERS.

YOUR ORIENTALS HAVE AN ARRAY, WITH YOUR CHINESE SMELLING STRONGER THAN YOUR JAPANESE AND YOUR KOREANS FALLING SOMEWHERES IN THE MIDDLE AND DON'T GET ME STARTED ON YOUR FILIPINOS.

11

SHE DETAILED THE SMELLS OF BLACKS, MEXICANS, ITALIANS, SOME PEOPLE I NEVER HEARD OF CALLED "BO-HUNKS" AND THE DIFFERENCE IT MADE IF THEY WERE WET OR DRY, FAT OR SKINNY. NATURALLY I BROUGHT THIS INFORMATION HOME.

AIE N'AKO! WHITE LADIES SMELL BAD TOO, NAMAN! SHE NEVER WASH HER POOKIE! HER KILI-KILI ALWAYS SWEAT-SWEATING! THE OLD ONES SMELL LIKE E-HEE! THAT LADY IS TUNG-AH!

Panel 16:

I'VE NEVER HEARD A SINGLE PERSON EVER SAY THEY LOVED THE SMELL OF AIR FRESHENER AND YET THERE ARE SO MANY PEOPLE WHO FILL THEIR HOMES WITH IT.

AIR WICKS

CAT PEE INCENSE

LIGHT BULB SCENT RINGS

SCENTED CANDLE NIGHTMARE

POTPOURRI MIXES

POP UPS

STICK ONS

PLUG-INS

DANGLERS

Panel 17:

WHEN COMBINED WITH NATURAL BUT POWER-FILLED SMELLS, THE RESULTS CAN BE TRAUMATIC.

TROPICAL PASSION AROMA THERAPY CAT BOX

PINEY WOODS PIG'S BLOOD STEW BREAK DOWN

STRAWBERRY-DREAMSCAPE PLUG-IN FRIED FLOUNDER

CHERRY POP-UP FRIED LIVER

VANILLA-SPICE DIAPER PAIL

EVEN MY GRANDMA WAS DRAWN IN BY THE PROMISES OF FRESHNESS THE ADS GAVE, ALTHOUGH NOT FOR LONG.

ONE QUICK SRRAY AND YOUR HOUSE IS SPRINGTIME FRESH!

AIE NAKO, LADY. I TRIED IT. IT SMELLS WORSE THAN THE PUEET OF A VAMPIRE!

YOU'LL NEVER WORRY ABOUT FRYING FISH AGAIN!

IF I HAVE FISH, I AM NOT WORRIED! I AM THANKING GOD!

OUR HOUSE SMELLED LIKE GREASE AND FISH AND CIGS, LIKE JADE EAST AND PORK AND DOGS, LIKE ALL THE WILD FOOD MY GRANDMA BOILED AND FRIED. AND IF THEY COULD GET THAT INTO A SPRAY CAN, I'D <u>BUY</u> IT.

N'AKO, LYNDA! THIS DURAN FRUITS SMELLS SO BADLY BUT TASTE SO GOODLY! YOU TRY IT! GOD MADE IT! MY GOLLY! EAT! EAT!

18

19

Content

1. Good works of visual art, like good essays or stories, stand up to careful reread-ing; they can't be entirely taken in or understood at a single glance. Skim "Common Scents" and then go back and review it carefully. What topics and meanings come into sharp focus on the second reading?

2. Explain the meaning of the caption of panel 7: "I probably had the strongest-smelling house in the neighborhood except for the bleach people, but I had no idea what it smelled like to others until I heard a comment about it." Can you identify some of the more exotic smells, such as "pigs blood stew" (panel 8) and duran (panel 19)?

Strategies/Structures/Language

3. None of Barry's characters look very attractive—in fact, by some criteria they'd be considered ugly. In what respects are they sympathetic or unsympathetic—just as characters are in a totally verbal story? In what ways does their appearance re-inforce Barry's point?

4. What latitude does Barry have in using drawings with dialogue that she wouldn't have if the story were told entirely in writing?

For Writing/Drawing

5. If you're artistically inclined, tell a story that presents a social commentary through a series of six to eight pictures (or more, if you get carried away) with cap-tions that reinforce the pictures and perhaps explain them. If your artistic abilities are limited, either work with a partner who can draw or use someone else's cartoons or drawings and substitute your own captions. In either case, write an analysis of what you've done, and why, to show how the illustrations and the text reinforce one another.

6. "Common Scents" obliges readers to think about smells—of people (and ethnic stereotypes of their smells), of food, of environments: "[The air freshener lady] de-tailed the smells of blacks, Mexicans, Italians . . . 'bo-hunks' and the difference it made if they were wet or dry, fat or skinny" (panel 11)—and to examine their preju-dices concerning these smells. In fact, American culture in general may be prejudiced against most odors, given the fact that in the United States many people try to re-move all odors except those of some flowers and some foods. Explain why this is so. In what ways have Barry's drawings raised your critical awareness of this prac-tice? Would a national culture with a greater range and variety of acceptable smells be preferable?

7. If you're not an artist, write a paper in which you analyze and explain Barry's "Common Scents" or another cartoon sequence with a social point, such as Art Spiegelman's "Mein Kampf" (116–17), another sequence by Spiegelman, or one of Garry Trudeau's *Doonesbury* comic strips.

 For comprehension, writing, and research activities and resources, please visit the companion website at <college.hmco.com/english>.

Code Blue: Two Definitions

JASMINE INNERARITY

Innerarity, born (1968) and raised in Jamaica, studied at the University of
Toronto and earned from the University of Connecticut a BS in nursing
(1989) and an MS in nursing/public health (1999). A pediatric oncology
nurse, she has served as president of the Connecticut chapter of the Society
of Pediatric Nurses and has written movingly of her compassionate care of
young patients—those who would survive, and those who would not.

The writing of "Code Blue: The Process" presented problems for
Innerarity. She wanted to present an accurate and precise definition of
what happens during this emergency procedure that would be clear to
an audience of undergraduates, who needed further definitions of terms
such as "intubation," "crash cart," and "ambu bag." During the course
of several revisions, to ensure that her writing was both accurate and
ethical, she checked her work with nursing colleagues (was she revealing
medical secrets? no!). She also provided additional definitions of key terms
and more illustrations because of her realization that what she as a professional nurse could take for granted was not always common knowledge.
To avoid giving the impression of medical infallibility, her last revision
was to include an example of the fact that despite a medical team's best
efforts Code Blue procedures do not always succeed.

❄ *Code Blue: The Process*

An unforgettable moment in caring for the sick in the hospital or any 1
institutional setting is the Code Blue Process. Code Blue is the alert
signal for a patient who has stopped breathing or whose heart has stopped.
This signal is universal throughout hospitals in the U.S. The alert is given
via the physicians' private beepers and the overhead intercom within hospitals. This process is always associated with what seems like chaos to the
outsider but to the health team, it is well organized and well executed.

Code Blue is usually initiated by the nurse. There are many reasons 2
for this. First, the nurse spends more time with the patient than any other
member of the health team. In addition, the nurse is continuously assessing the patient's condition. The nurse usually detects small changes in vital
signs or physical conditions at crucial times when other members of the
health team are absent.

Within the hospital, a patient who has stopped breathing or who is in 3
cardiac arrest is quickly discovered because the circular arrangement of
the floor allows all patients to be seen from the nursing station. In addition,
those patients who are unstable are placed on cardiac monitors with audio

alarms which alert the medical team to changes in their health status if medical personnel is not present in the room.

4   A cart which is equipped with all the necessary equipment to initiate the Code Blue response is also placed in a central region on each hospital floor. This cart called the "Code cart," usually contains intravenous fluids, emergency medications, and equipment used for intubating the patient. In the event of a Code Blue, this cart is immediately brought into the patient's room.

Example of Code Blue Process

5   Timmy was a two-year-old boy. He was in the Intensive Care Unit for a neurological condition which affects his breathing patterns. He has been doing well. I have been caring for him for the past week and have watched his progress with great joy. He was still being monitored before being released from the Intensive Care Unit to the regular Hospital Unit.

6   One morning, I walked in to see Timmy five minutes after his mother had left the room. I had heard them playing together minutes before she left. As I entered the room, I noticed that Timmy was lying still and his lips were turning blue. "Timmy! Timmy!" I shouted, while shaking him. He did not respond. "I have a Code Blue," I called out.

7   My shout of "Code Blue!" was the warning to the rest of the health team to get someone else into the room while the secretary announces the alert to the Code Blue team. In a Code Blue situation, a member from several different medical teams appears. The teams are designed to ensure that in an emergency situation, such as this one, each physician or health care member essential to getting this patient back to health is present. Although the medical personnel who arrive vary by hospitals, there is usually a surgeon, a cardiologist, a respiratory therapist, an anesthesiologist, an intensivist, and the patient's primary or attending physician for the day. The primary physician leads the Code team by getting a quick history of what precipitated the patient's cessation of breathing and tries to determine how to reverse this crisis. His role is to give the orders in the code.

8   The surgeon arrives to insert central lines—a plastic tubing going from the outside of the body to the inside that is used to infuse medication, fluids, and blood products quickly into the body and heart. A cardiologist has the role of prescribing medications to ensure that the most central organ in the body (the heart) is functioning.

9   The anesthesiologist has the role of sedating and intubating the patient who has stopped breathing. Intubation involves placing a plastic tubing through the patient's mouth and into his or her lungs. This process requires considerable skill, because one has to take care to insert the tube into the trachea, and not into the esophagus which leads to the stomach. Once the tube is placed into the lungs, an X-ray is taken of the chest to confirm that this tube is in fact where it belongs, in the lungs. The end of

the tubing which projects from the mouth is connected to a respirator, a computerized machine that breathes for the patient. The respiratory therapist is in charge of monitoring the respirator.

Accessory personnel, such as members of the fire department or EMT team from the hospital, may arrive to assist in a Code Blue situation. In fact, it is not unusual after the initial assessment of the situation to ask some health personnel who are not needed to leave the room. The aim is to prevent clutter and maximize efficiency in responding to the Code. 10

A series of quick actions is executed within a minute of the Code Blue call. A team of health professionals rushes into the room. As I try to instill air into Timmy's lungs, using a mechanical device called an "ambu bag," another nurse feels for pulses, and the physician prepares to intubate Timmy. An ambu bag is a pressure bag made of rubber (it looks like an inflated balloon) that has two ends. One end has a long plastic tubing which connects to an oxygen tank or oxygen outlet in the wall, and the other end has a mouthpiece which fits over the patient's face and mouth. When the middle part of the balloon is squeezed, oxygen is expelled into the patient's mouth and ultimately into the lungs. 11

The physician in charge of Timmy gives the orders: 12

"500 ml of I.V. fluids wide open stat!"
"What's his pressure?"
"Does he have a pulse?"
"Yes."
"Okay, let's have a blood gas."

Each member of the team rushes to fulfill their role.

The series of quick necessary motions, as well as the numerous health professionals in the patient's room, give the impression of disorder. On the contrary, the process is very orderly: Blood is being drawn, phone calls are being made to get lab results quickly, and the physician is speaking loudly so that everyone can hear what to do and when. There is no time for mishaps. It is an assembly line and everyone must be alert. Each team member must mesh into this new team, the team of people trying to save the patient's life. 13

Timmy starts to cry after three minutes of resuscitation. His lips are no longer blue. "Good job, team," says the physician. 14

The team rushes out and back to their original stations. The nurses stay behind to do what they do best, care for Timmy and comfort his family. Timmy's mother has been brought down to the lounge during the code. Timmy will be in an oxygen tent for the night. "What's that?" she asks, pointing to the tent. The oxygen tent is made of plastic and is in the shape of a tent (hence the name). It delivers a continuous supply of oxygen to Timmy, which will help with his breathing overnight. I sit to explain to her what just happened to Timmy and to answer any questions she may have. Timmy's mother takes my hand, "Thanks for saving him." 15

16   The process of Code Blue in this instance is short, lasting for fifteen minutes only. Timmy responded well to the medical interventions. In other cases, however, the outcome can be grave. Mark was a twelve-year-old boy with a brain tumor. His family had agonized about the decision to make him a "Do not resuscitate" (DNR) patient. This status implies that if he should stop breathing, then the Code Blue process would not be initiated. DNR is attributed to patients who are gravely ill and for whom medical interventions have proven ineffective. The decision to make a patient a DNR however, is ultimately that of the family. Mark's parents wanted everything to be done for him despite the recommendation of DNR status by the physicians. Thus, Mark was not a DNR.

17   When Mark stopped breathing one evening, a Code Blue was called. Again the group of medical personnel arrived to save Mark's life. In this case and unlike Timmy, Mark responded poorly to the use of the ambu bag. His heart stopped. He was intubated by the anesthesiologist and was placed on a respirator. The private physician shouted: "We need to take him to the operating room (OR), he's bleeding." The physicians debated whether Mark's heart was strong enough for the OR. Despite several medications, Mark's heart would not return to the normal sinus rhythm.

18   The health team rushed to get blood into his body. The surgeons debated whether they could stop the bleeding, which they found was in his brain. After forty-five minutes of medications and mechanical ventilation, Mark still did not respond. The primary physician and the family talked about the grave outcome for Mark. After a half hour had passed since the Code Blue, the parents decided to let Mark go. He was taken off the respirator and died immediately.

19   The timing for the Code Blue process is as varied as the patients involved in the process. The two examples above showed the difference in response to medical interventions, which determine how long the process is continued. In many instances, the team will continue the process for up to an hour if the patient responds to medication. The patient will then be transferred to an Intensive Care Unit where he will be monitored closely until he is stable.

20   There are many emotions involved in a Code Blue process, depending on whether the outcome is good or poor. Initially, the team members experience a rush of adrenalin. This occurs because a Code Blue does not happen daily, so the nervousness, yet urgency of the situation takes one by surprise. There is also the continuous struggle with the ethical issues involved in Code Blue situations. For example, in each Code Blue situation, the determination must be made whether or not that patient is a DNR status. Usually the primary nurse and physician are aware of this status. At times, however, the determination must be made immediately. Nurses as well as family members struggle with the decision to make someone a DNR or a full code status.

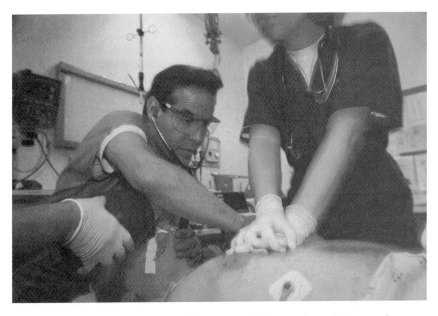

What's going on here? How many people are present? What are the mode, tone, and energy level of the activities depicted here? What is the relation of teamwork to this matter of life and death?

One of the biggest rewards in caring for the sick is the miracle of see-   21
ing a person who has stopped breathing and who looks lifeless return to
life. After ten years of being involved in the nursing process, my natural instinct is to care for those who are sick. I genuinely believe that caring for the
sick makes them better. Of course, the Code Blue process shows that this is
not always true. However, in my experience, the positive outcomes dis-
proportionately overshadow the very small number of morbid outcomes.

[Suggestions for reading and writing about this essay are combined with those pertaining to Abraham Verghese's "Code Blue: The Story" and appear on pages 372–73.]

ABRAHAM VERGHESE

Verghese was born in Addis Ababa, Ethiopia (1955), where his expatriate
Indian parents were teachers, but he returned to India to study medicine (MD, Madras University, 1979). During his residency at East Tennessee
State University (1980–1983), Verghese concentrated on infectious diseases
because, he says, "it offered the promise of a cure. In the early 1980s infectious disease was the one discipline where a cure was common." But in

August 1985, the local hospital in rural Johnson City treated its first AIDS patient, and soon the crisis that had once seemed an urban problem spread to the small town, as well. *My Own Country: A Doctor's Story* (1994) describes how Verghese, as a specialist in infectious diseases, gradually became drawn into the treatment of the "shocking number" of male and female patients who took over not only his professional life but also his compassionate imagination.

Of this experience, Verghese, now chief of infectious diseases at Texas Technological Regional Academic Health Center in El Paso, says, "Today I am a doctor who is unable to cure." He explains, "You're suddenly dealing with people your own age whose plight makes you reflect on your ideas about sex, about social issues and, of course, about your own mortality. Almost every emotion is magnified and brought into sharp relief with AIDS." He began writing nonfiction, now published in the *New Yorker* and many other places, aided by a year's Michener Fellowship to the Writers' Workshop at the University of Iowa (1990–1991), as a way to deal with "some of my frustrations at work. I can't reverse death, I can't get into a patient's mind and think his thoughts. But with writing, the boundaries are virtually limitless," as Verghese's most recent book, *The Tennis Partner: A Doctor's Story of Friendship and Loss* (1998) also illustrates. "Code Blue: The Story" opens *My Own Country,* putting into dramatic action—with characters, dialogue, and frenetic activity—the definition that Innerarity has explained in a more formal manner.

Code Blue: The Story

1   In the early evening of August 11, 1985, he was rolled into the emergency room (ER) of the Johnson City Medical Center—the "Miracle Center," as we referred to it when we were interns. Puffing like an overheated steam engine, he was squeezing in forty-five breaths a minute. Or so Claire Bellamy, the nurse, told me later. It had shocked her to see a thirty-two-year-old man in such severe respiratory distress.

2   He sat bolt upright on the stretcher, his arms propped behind him like struts that braced his heaving chest. His blond hair was wet and stuck to his forehead; his skin, Claire recalled, was gunmetal gray, his lips and nail beds blue.

3   She had slapped an oxygen mask on him and hollered for someone to pull the duty physician away from the wound he was suturing. A genuine emergency was at hand, something she realized, even as it overtook her, she was not fully comprehending. She knew what it was not: it was *not* severe asthma, status asthmaticus; it was *not* a heart attack. She could not stop to take it all in. Everything was happening too quickly.

4   With every breath he sucked in, his nostrils flared. The strap muscles of his neck stood out like cables. He pursed his lips when he exhaled, as if he was loath to let the oxygen go, hanging on to it as long as he could.

Electrodes placed on his chest and hooked to a monitor showed his ₅ heart fluttering at a desperate 160 beats per minute.

On his chest x-ray, the lungs that should have been dark as the night ₆ were instead whited out by a veritable snowstorm.

My friend Ray, a pulmonary physician was immediately summoned. ₇ While Ray listened to his chest, the phlebotomist drew blood for serum electrolytes and red and white blood cell counts. The respiratory therapist punctured the radial artery at the wrist to measure blood oxygen levels. Claire started an intravenous line. And the young man slumped on the stretcher. He stopped breathing.

Claire punched the "Code Blue" button on the cubicle wall and an ₈ operator's voice sounded through the six-story hospital building: "Code Blue, emergency room!"

The code team—an intern, a senior resident, two intensive care unit ₉ nurses, a respiratory therapist, a pharmacist—thundered down the hallway.

Patients in their rooms watching TV sat up in their beds; visitors ₁₀ froze in place in the corridors.

More doctors arrived; some came in street clothes, having heard the ₁₁ call as they headed for the parking lot. Others came in scrub suits. Ray was "running" the code; he called for boluses of bicarbonate and epinephrine, for a second intravenous line to be secured, and for Claire to increase the vigor but slow down the rate of her chest compressions.

The code team took their positions. The beefy intern with Nautilus ₁₂ shoulders took off his jacket and climbed onto a step stool. He moved in just as Claire stepped back, picking up the rhythm of chest compressions without missing a beat, calling the cadence out loud. With locked elbows, one palm over the back of the other, he squished the heart between breastbone and spine, trying to squirt enough blood out of it to supply the brain.

The ER physician unbuttoned the young man's pants and cut away ₁₃ the underwear, now soiled with urine. His fingers reached for the groin, feeling for the femoral artery to assess the adequacy of the chest compressions.

A "crash cart" stocked with ampules of every variety, its defibrillator ₁₄ paddles charged and ready, stood at the foot of the bed as the pharmacist recorded each medication given and the exact time it was administered.

The clock above the stretcher had been automatically zeroed when ₁₅ the Code Blue was called. A code nurse called out the elapsed time at thirty-second intervals. The resident and another nurse from the code team probed with a needle for a vein to establish the second "line."

Ray "bagged" the patient with a tight-fitting mask and hand-held ₁₆ squeeze bag as the respiratory therapist readied an endotracheal tube and laryngoscope.

At a signal from Ray, the players froze in midair while he bent the ₁₇ young man's head back over the edge of the stretcher. Ray slid the laryngoscope in between tongue and palate and heaved up with his left hand, pulling the base of the tongue up and forward until the leaf-shaped epiglottis appeared.

18   Behind it, the light at the tip of the laryngoscope showed glimpses of the voice box and the vocal cords. With his right hand, Ray fed the endotracheal tube alongside the laryngoscope, down the back of the throat, past the epiglottis, and past the vocal cords—this part done almost blindly and with a prayer—and into the trachea. Then he connected the squeeze bag to the end of the endotracheal tube and watched the chest rise as he pumped air into the lungs. He nodded, giving the signal for the action to resume.

19   Now Ray listened with his stethoscope over both sides of the chest as the respiratory therapist bagged the limp young man. He listened for the muffled *whoosh* of air, listened to see if it was equally loud over both lungs.

20   He heard sounds only over the right lung. The tube had gone down the right main bronchus, a straighter shot than the left.

21   He pulled the tube back an inch, listened again, and heard air entering both sides. The tube was sitting above the carina, above the point where the trachea bifurcates. He called for another chest x-ray; a radiopaque marker at the end of the tube would confirm its exact position.

22   With a syringe he inflated the balloon cuff at the end of the endotracheal tube that would keep it snugly in the trachea. Claire wound tape around the tube and plastered it down across the young man's cheeks and behind his neck.

23   The blue in the young man's skin began to wash out and a faint pink appeared in his cheeks. The ECG machine, which had spewed paper into a curly mound on the floor, now showed the original rapid heart rhythm restored.

24   At this point the young man was alive again, but just barely. The Code Blue had been a success.

Content

1. What is *Code Blue* according to Innerarity's definition?
2. Is it possible to infer a definition of *Code Blue* from Verghese's illustration of Code Blue in action? What additional information do you need?
3. After she had written several versions of "Code Blue" that contained only positive examples, Innerarity added a negative example—of Code Blue not working—at her teacher's insistence. Does the negative example undercut the positive?
4. Why, in medical and science writing, are there usually many more positive examples (successful processes and procedures) than negative ones? Do the essays by Innerarity and Verghese bear this out?

Strategies/Structures/Language

5. Why would nonmedical people want to know the details of a procedure that can be performed only by a medical team?

6. Innerarity offers a textbook definition of the process, personnel, and equipment used to carry out a Code Blue. In contrast, Verghese shows Code Blue in action. Explain how his narrative also functions as a definition. Which version of "Code Blue" are you more likely to remember? Why?

7. Innerarity had difficulty translating medical terminology into everyday language and wrote several drafts to simplify and clarify the language. Has she succeeded? Has she used any terms that still need definition?

For Writing

8. Define a specialized technical or scientific term or process so a nonspecialist can understand it. See the Magliozzis (142–46), Innerarity and Verghese (365–72), Gardner (342–52), Turkle (397–402), and McKibben (413–23).

9. Write/draw a segment of your life in the form of a graphic novel, as Spiegelman (116–17) and Barry (354–63) do.

10. Write a narrative (that is, tell a true story), as Innerarity and Verghese do, that through its characters and action implies a definition of a significant term—such as *love* (or *hate*), *beauty* (or *ugliness*), *fidelity* (or *betrayal*), *honesty* (or *dishonesty*)—or of a process (how to form or destroy a friendship, how to travel); or of some other concept that you expect to learn to understand in the process of writing about it. See Britt (261–63), Spinner (374–79), White (97–103), Sanders (249–59), and Rodriguez (310–16).

 For comprehension, writing, and research activities and resources, please visit the companion website at <college.hmco.com/english>.

JENNY SPINNER

> For biographical information, see page 333. The most frequently appearing "character" in Spinner's personal essays—besides herself—is her twin sister Jackie. In fact, Jenny Spinner has written interchapters to Jackie's book, *Tell Them I Didn't Cry: A Young Journalist's Story of Joy, Loss and Survival in Iraq* (2006), where Jackie was *Washington Post* Bureau Chief in Baghdad, 2003–2004. "I use the word *character* on purpose," Spinner explains. "In many of my essays, Jackie is a true wit. Of course she's charming and funny in reality, but she's extraordinarily charming and funny in my essays. She's there to make the reader laugh, to make me look good. . . .
>
> "It is when I write seriously about her, when I try to describe our unique relationship as adopted twins, that I most struggle. I was twenty-eight when I began writing 'In Search of Our Past.' I had been writing since I was eighteen. It took me ten years to find the courage to write the story of our beginning. Our relationship is so powerful, and so powerfully embedded in who I am, that I was almost afraid to touch it, as if doing so would either cheapen it or prove entirely inadequate.

"I had to remind myself, as I remind my students, that 'I am not the page.' My writing is a construction of myself, of my sister, of our relationship. I am not writing a life; I am writing *about* a life (and thereby creating a new life, in print). To that end, I cannot possibly write about our life in a single essay, or even in a book of essays. The initial drafts of 'In Search of Our Past' include too much detail, too many stories, too many angles on our relationship. . . . I'd lost track of my readers—who didn't need them— and of my focus for this essay: to write about our adoption.

"When revising 'In Search of Our Past,' as is the case each time I write about my sister, I had to forgive myself: for not being able to write perfectly about what means most to me. In the process, I also felt relieved. After all, my readers have access only to that which I give them. I, the writer and chief engineer, remain in control of construction. My writing represents many choices, to include some details, leave behind others. I choose to make my sister savvy and myself a bit awkward. These choices are grounded in reality, in what is true, but they remain creations. I create."

❄ *In Search of Our Past*

1   When we were young, my twin sister Jackie and I shared everything. Although our childhood years were not the last we shared, they were the least divided. We had the same Baby Alives dolls that burbled slime which Grandpa Spinner once heroically ate; same Buster Browns, brown, narrow, fitted with arch supports for flat feet; same cotton dresses that barely touched the knees; same Trixie Belden books bought for us to share. And share we did: the dresser, its drawers; bathroom towels; gum sometimes; earrings, make-up, the car during high school; perfectionism, ambition and eating disorders after that. But what really mattered is that we shared the door to our bedroom, the way in, the way out, the lock that could be opened with a toothpick: one door, one way, one lock. There is little dignity in running to a room mid-tantrum, sobbing, slamming a door so hard that the second-floor windows rattle, only to turn around and find someone sitting in the middle of her bed watching you unfold.

2   It seems fitting that we shared so much of our lives together in our strawberry pink room with its strawberry walls, strawberry carpet, strawberry gingham bedspreads and curtains. What came before the pink was colorless, blank, *tabula rasa* in its purest sense, and we shared that blankness, too. Unlike our brother Tim, twenty months younger and biological child of our parents, we had no roots before birth. The first few weeks following that birth hinged on tiny, gathered bits of information. Adopted at twenty-three days old, we came into the world free of any heritage other than the one we chose for ourselves.

3   It was something we always knew: adoption. One of my earliest memories is of the two of us begging my parents to "tell the story." "Don't

you ever get tired of hearing it?" my mother asked, amused. "No." No, even though there was not much to it, or to the answers we sought: A poor young woman and her husband could not afford two infants. They loved them, yes, enough to give them up—because that is what you do, when you love something more than yourself. And so, after repeated tellings, the myth of our birth evolved, out of one "lady," whom we carefully never called mother and one man who soon disappeared from the stories we told ourselves.

For my parents, the story actually began two years before my sister   4
and I were born. In June 1968, three years after they were married, my mother lay in bed trying not to bleed. She was three months pregnant with their first child. Trying hard to save the baby, to go twenty-four hours without spotting, she stayed in bed for several days. On the black-and-white Zenith at the edge of the bed, she watched as Sirhan B. Sirhan shot Bobby Kennedy two thousand miles away in a Los Angeles hotel. Kennedy did not survive; neither did my parents' baby. For a long time, my sister and I celebrated quietly the death of this child. Beneath a blanket tent on one of our beds, we whispered our understanding: Had the baby lived, we would not have—at least not in the lives we knew.

In 1969, after four years of trying to conceive, my parents contacted   5
Lutheran Child and Family Services—a private adoption agency affiliated with the Lutheran Church Missouri Synod. At that time, my mother's oldest sister already had three children; my father's oldest brother, two. My parents so desperately wanted to contribute a baby to the family that when their adoption counselor asked if they were willing to adopt multiple birth babies, they agreed. So rare was this possibility that the question was more formality than reality.

That reality soon reordered itself, however, when my mother re-   6
ceived a telephone call from their counselor on July 28, 1970. Would she and my father be interested in adopting twin girls born on the fifteenth? This phone call is the closest thing my sister and I have to a conception. It is the moment in which the idea of us was first presented to our parents, and it is the moment we call birth. Details about the days before are scattered and incomplete. According to information given to my parents by the adoption agency, I had been living in a foster home in the Chicago area since July 24. Not released until July 31, my sister (four pounds at birth compared to my plumper five) was still in the hospital when my mother received the counselor's phone call.

Thinking about these early days creates questions for which there are   7
few answers. We do know on July 15, 1970, at 2:08 and 2:10 P.M. we were delivered by cesarean in the former Chicago Masonic Medical Center (now Illinois Masonic Medical Center). Cesarean is important because it indicates a trace of permanence, a visible scar. On our birthday each year, we imagined her, "the lady," running her fingers across that scar, feeling the hard skin, wondering. Because of the scar, she can't forget. The hospital is

important, too, because it means a place exists, means in some building we were there, all three of us. One year, during a visit to Chicago relatives, our parents drove us by the Medical Center. Intimidated by the hospital's reality, we didn't ask to go inside. Behind closed eyes, I imagined pale green walls and gray filing cabinets hiding manila folders. In those folders were names—and a past. A few years later I ventured inside, just to see, but I wasn't allowed on the maternity ward. A nurse told me visitors might infect new mothers and babies. I paced the main lobby for an hour trying to find something that "she" saw, too. When my parents, waiting in the car, came in to find me, my mother tried to cheer me by buying me a pink baby shirt that she would have bought herself had I been hers at that hospital. Back in the car, I hid my face from her good intentions and swallowed sobs.

8   When I was twelve, I went searching for names and didn't find them. I did discover several pages of biographical data which the adoption agency had given to my parents and which my parents chose not to share with us—perhaps because we never asked, careful not to hurt their feelings by reminding them that we were not biologically theirs. In the bottom drawer of a filing cabinet, behind tax records, insurance papers and department store bills, I found a folder marked in my dad's neat block-letter hand: "GIRLS ADOPTION." I sat on his office floor for several minutes, unable to open the folder, the weight of my past leaning hard against my chest. When I finally peered inside, a twenty-seven-year-old man and a twenty-three-year-old woman stepped out to greet me, brushing the dust from their clothes—or trying to pull it back around them. She was tiny with dark brown hair and blue-green eyes. He was tall, had blond hair and blue eyes. These physical details were important. Ever since we were old enough to realize what we were doing, my sister and I had been searching crowds for the woman who gave birth to us. At the World's Fair in Tennessee we thought we saw her, but she disappeared before we could be sure.

9   When we were younger, a number of people told us we looked like our adoptive mother, and we did. We shared her straight brown hair, cut boyishly short like hers, parted in the middle, her brown eyes and fair skin. Our father and brother, with their dark blond hair and green eyes, were their own perfect match. When required to fill out heredity worksheets during what became the dreaded genetics unit in grade- and high-school science classes, we came close, pretending our parents' and grandparents' blood was really ours, at least by association. But the widows' peaks never matched; neither did the blood. In the end, those nights we spent in our pink room filling out our biological family trees were unhappy ones, and we wondered why it never occurred to our teachers that not everyone lived by science.

10   I memorized other details in the file, adding them to the pictures in my head and measuring myself. A talented cartoonist and fiction writer, the woman graduated from college and planned to attend graduate school.

The man was a college graduate, manager of a bank, dabbled in photography and art. They both swam and played tennis. The tomboy in me who loved taking pictures and writing beamed—until I read the next lines. Although they were college sweethearts and intended to marry, the man changed his mind after learning about the woman's pregnancy. "He didn't reject her but tried to help," the black ink scrawled onto my heart. "Mother felt best thing to do was give up for adoption." I realized then that my biological parents were not married, that what changed the man's mind was my sister and me. Moreover, the vision of them sharing a life together was a myth, even though my mother always referred to him as the lady's husband. Probably she gave birth, they parted and went on with their lives, trying not to remind themselves of what they had done. Probably. Nothing is sure. It was a lot to swallow at twelve, especially for someone surrounded in school and at home by a conservative religious doctrine that demanded men and women have sex only after marriage, that chastised people who ran from pregnancies. Until I was old enough to establish my own rules, make mistakes, understand, then forgive, I lived with the burden of sin. At the very least, I knew we were a mistake.

Near the bottom of the papers I found a physical description of Jackie   11 and me at birth: petite feminine build, fair complexions, brown hair with blond highlights, dark blue eyes. When I shared my findings with my sister, we wondered if that description was all the woman knew. How soon did they take us away? Did she ask to hold us? Did she cry? We wondered, of course, if she now wondered, too. But most of our questions were not grounded in a dramatic fairy tale of two happy people ready to apologize and explain once discovered by their progeny. We simply wanted to color in a black hole that swallowed the beginning of our lives. "Dear Lady," I wrote to her when I was thirteen, "Some day my sister and I will open our adoption records and find out your name. We won't try to contact you. We just want a name. We're not looking for a mother because we have one. We're looking for some answers to questions we've had for a long time, questions that might remain unanswered forever." Every year I wrote to her a version of that letter, always addressed "Dear Lady." I never put the letter in an envelope, and every year it asked fewer questions and told more about me and my sister. I wasn't bragging as much as insisting: that we turned out okay, that she would be proud.

Although the darkness surrounding our birth bothered us, my sister   12 and I never opened our adoption records, even after we turned twenty-one and were old enough to do so. The desire for name finally lost its pull. Mostly we didn't want to hurt our parents. The hole, after all, had nothing to do with them, and we had no intention of creating a new one—in their hearts. A few years ago, I ran into a childhood friend in a bar in my hometown. She had recently been hired by Lutheran Child and Family Services, and, she told me excitedly, she'd read our file. She knew our original names. Leaning close, smiling, she asked, "Do you want to know anything else?" I set my glass on the table and told her I needed a minute to think. I walked to the back of the bar, found a pay phone and called my sister. At first I thought she couldn't hear me over the juke box. Neither of us said anything for a long time. Finally I understood her silence as "no," told our friend "no" and left. Our past stayed behind in the bar, washed down by glass after glass of ordinary beer.

13   From the time we began attending elementary school and our class-mates learned of our adoption—how, I don't remember—we knew we were different. One morning in third grade, I stood in front of a long mir-ror in the girls' bathroom alongside Karen, both of us examining our faces.

14   "Do you ever wonder if you look like her?" she asked.

15   "Who?" I replied, avoiding her eyes, and my own.

16   "Your mother."

17   "I do look like my mother."

18   "Really? Have you seen a picture?"

19   "No."

20   "Then how do you know?"

21   "Because I see her every day." I knew what she was asking but I was determined not to let her make me feel different than she, the tall, skinny girl with long brown flapping braids who was a miniature version of her mother.

22   "I mean your real mother, not Mrs. Spinner," she said, turning away from the mirror.

23   "She is my real mother."

24   "It's not the same," she said, walking away and tossing her braids.

25   Although I hated Karen then, I knew she was right. But my sister and I were good at pretending.

26   Our brother Tim was not always as skilled. In angry moods, he re-minded us that we did not belong as much as he did. We, too, were good at throwing an occasional "You love him better because he's yours" tantrum. Usually, however, we kept such comparisons inside. In trips to the grocery store or K Mart, Tim pushed ahead of us, pointing out boxes of cold cereal and stuffed bears he wanted. Jackie and I hung back, reluctant to ask for too much, afraid the expense would force my parents to give us back. We were eleven before we understood adoption well enough to know they couldn't return us. "Don't ask for anything," I whispered to my sister beneath a row of blonde Barbies. "Timmy can afford to, but not us."

27   One afternoon, we kneeled in front of the couch in our basement, tallying how much we had cost our parents since they brought us home. "Did you pay anything to get us?" my sister asked, nervously eyeing the lengthening expense column. "A little," my father said, buried in his own stack of bills and unaware of why she asked. In actuality, they paid $1,000 to the adoption agency and about $300 in lawyer's fees. The thought of any money at all, however, even "a little," was a shock to my sister and

me who viewed the transaction as one of love—poor parents handing over their babies to richer ones. Money turned love into business. It made us bought.

"All things considered," I asked my father when I was older, "do 28 you think your investment has paid off?"

"Of course," he laughed. It wasn't always that easy. Yet it was. The 29 adoption story we lived was nothing like the dramas that entertained television audiences in the late 1980s, especially following the Baby M and Baby Jessica cases. For people who know nothing about it, adoption is fascinating, embarrassing or sad; for people who do, it just is. No woman ever demanded us back. We never considered going back. Our parents loved us completely, loved us as much as our brother. We also had a wonderful relationship with both sets of grandparents with whom we spent a great deal of time and considered best friends as we grew older. Only once did I feel the awkwardness of being an adopted child in my family. I had just returned home from the first three weeks of my freshman year at college—they were actually my only three weeks as I withdrew, homesick and disenchanted, a failure. I'd always made good grades and given my family reasons to be proud. Now, in the dark of my grandmother's living room, I tried to explain what went wrong. Reaching out from her chair to touch my hand, she told me, "We don't know certain things about you girls that could explain a lot. There could be ugly things in your past." Her explanation startled me. Later I realized she was right, not about why I left college, but in some sense still right. My sister and I didn't know anything beyond what we created for ourselves.

What we *had* created was each other. Eventually I learned there would be 30 gaps even in what we constructed, times when I would be left alone to make sense of the absence that thrust us into this world. Until that time, the only world I knew contained my sister and what we held together—and I could not imagine any experience outside that bond. What lay outside was nothing we could name, touch, hold onto. Nothing would belong only to me, or to her, until we moved away from one another and began to create our own lives.

Those lives remain a curious mix of fervent attachment and the desire 31 to be individuals. We are both writers, she a journalist, I, an essayist. We both run, physically and emotionally, until exhausted. She injures herself, and hundreds of miles away, I feel her pain. I cry, and she calls to ask what's wrong. We fight tortured fights. We make up like lovers, whispering over and over, "Don't leave me," "I won't," until we are convinced that we will be okay, that no one, that nothing, can destroy us. Together, separately we live, stepping carefully from our shared past, from that dry well falling deep into the dark.

Content

1. What couldn't the adopted Spinner twins take for granted, or even know, that children living with their birth parents know and accept? Why, when Spinner finally has the chance to learn her birth parents' names and other information about them (¶ 12), does she reject the opportunity?

2. Why did Spinner write this essay? What is its thesis? Is it implied or stated explicitly?

3. This essay could be interpreted from the perspective of contrasts: insiders/outsiders; people with an identifiable past/people without; people with twin siblings/people without; adoptive siblings/birth siblings living in the same family. Explain how these divisions govern what Spinner tells us about these relationships, and what she implies.

Strategies/Structures/Language

4. What's the meaning of Spinner's concluding paradox, "Together, separately we [Jenny and her twin sister] live, stepping carefully from our shared past, from that dry well falling deep into the dark" (¶ 31)? Is the essay's ending optimistic, pessimistic, realistic?

For Writing

5. What problems exist for school children who are asked to write family histories when they don't know those histories? Or when the family stories are difficult to understand or full of problems? How can teachers adjust their assignments to be sensitive to issues of individual and family heritages? Construct such an assignment, and explain why you've written it in the way you have. Elicit responses to it from your fellow students before showing it to your instructor.

6. Write an essay that explores the relations between outsiders and a particular insider group such as a family; a group united by race, religion, ethnicity, class, or immigrant status; a gang; a club, a residence-hall group, a sorority or fraternity; or people of a particular geographic area whether urban, suburban, or rural, in a particular state or country. See essays by Tan (13–18), Wiesel (23–27), Yu (173–82), among others. Consider your audience to be outsiders to the group you are discussing.

 For comprehension, writing, and research activities and resources, please visit the companion website at <college.hmco.com/english>.

Additional Topics for Writing
Definition

(For strategies for writing definition, see 332)

MULTIPLE STRATEGIES FOR WRITING
DEFINITION

Definition is an essential component of many kinds of writing; it is often necessary to define terms, components, or concepts as the basis for explaining something or conducting an argument. Conversely, you may employ a variety of other strategies in writing definitions:

- *illustrations* and *examples*, to show the meaning of the entire term or its components, and to interpret them
- *photographs, drawings, diagrams, maps* as alternatives to "a thousand words"
- a *time sequence*, to show the formation or consequences of a particular term
- *explanations* and *analyses* of the term
- *comparison* and *contrast; division* and *classification*, to illustrate the parts of the whole
- a *narrative*, on occasion, to allow the meaning of the term to emerge gradually as the tale unfolds
- *negation*—what a term isn't

1. Write an extended definition of one or more of the following trends, concepts, abstractions, phenomena, or institutions. Be sure to identify your audience, limit your subject, and illustrate your essay with specific examples.

    a. Peace (see the "World Peace" chapter)
    b. Terrorism, national or international (see the "Terrorism" chapter)
    c. Intelligence (see Gardner, 342–52)
    d. Physical fitness
    e. Personality
    f. Character
    g. Optimism
    h Depression (economic or psychological) (see Angier, 291–94)
    i. The nature of friendship
    j. Marriage (either, the ideal marriage, or the ideal versus the reality)
    k. Parenthood (see White, 97–103; Lee, 156–64; Sanders, 249–59; Spinner, 374–79; and Rodriguez, 310–16)
    l. Education—formal or informal (see Kozol, 204–11; Zitkala-Sa, 196–202; Turkle, 397–402; and Sedaris, 306–8)
    m. A good job or profession; work; or a very bad job
    n. A sport, game, hobby, or recreational activity (see Young, 517–25)
    o. A Northerner, Southerner, Midwesterner, Texan, Californian, or person from some other state, region, or country
    p. A scientific or technical phenomenon of your choice (an eclipse, the "big bang" theory of creation, genetic engineering, DNA, the MX missile) (see Darwin, 335–40; Gould 404–11; McKibben, 413–23)

2. Explain a particular value system or belief system, such as the following:

   a. Democracy, communism, socialism, or some other political theory or form of government

   b. Protestantism (or a particular sect), Catholicism, Judaism (or a particular branch—Orthodox, Conservative, Reform), Buddhism (or a particular sort), Islam, or some other religion

   c. A theoretical system and some of its major ramifications (feminism, Marxism, postcolonialism, Freudianism, postmodernism)

3. Prepare a dictionary of fifteen jargon or slang words used in your academic major, in your hobby, or in some other activity you enjoy, such as playing a particular sport or game, listening to a specific type of music, or working on a computer system.

Comparison and
Contrast

Writers compare people, places, things, or qualities to identify their similarities, and contrast them to identify the differences. What you say about one subject usually helps to illuminate or explain the other, as a commentary on the five college graduates pictured above might do. Although all are happy—presumably because they are celebrating graduation—their diverse appearances imply different individualities, heritages, lives. Such explanations have the added advantage of answering questions that hinge on the similarities and differences under consideration. Your commentary can also provide the basis for judging the relative merits and demerits of the subject at hand.

For instance, comparison and contrast can help you determine whether to choose a liberal arts or technical education, and what your future will be like with whichever you select. It can help you explain the resemblances between the works of Faulkner and Hemingway, and the differences—and to justify your preference for one author over the other. Comparison and contrast can help you decide whom to vote for, what movie to see (or avoid), where to spend your next vacation, what car to buy, which person to marry. A thoroughgoing, detailed comparison and contrast of the reasons for the quality of life with and without handguns, conservation of natural resources, or nuclear power can provide a convincing argument for your choice.

But not everything will work. The subjects you select should have some obvious qualities in common to make the comparison and contrast fruitful. If you try to compare very dissimilar things, as the Mad Hatter does in *Alice in Wonderland* ("Why is a raven like a writing desk?"), you'll have to stretch for an answer ("Because they both begin with an *r* sound.") that may be either silly or irrelevant. But other comparisons by their very nature can command appropriate contrasts. Deborah Tannen's "Communication Styles" (391–95) is based on an extended exploration of differences in the way men and women students behave in the classroom. For instance, Tannen has found that men speak in class more often than women do. They're more at ease in the "public" classroom setting and enjoy the "debate-like form that discussion may take," while women students are "more comfortable speaking in private to a small group of people they know well" in nonconfrontational dialogue. Compare this essay with Elizabeth Tallent's short story "No One's a Mystery" (388–90) and Kate Loomis's "Spiderwebs" (425–29), both of which consist of dialogues between older men and younger women. In each narrative the men have very different views of the relationship delineated than the women do. This intriguing contrast permits comparisons between the speakers in each pair, and between the two stories, in addition to possible generalizations about the nature of such relationships. "Whose side are we on in each?" is a question that provokes still more comparisons and contrasts.

In writing an essay of comparison and contrast you'll need to justify your choice of subject, unless the grounds for comparison are obvious. Thus in "Evolution as Fact and Theory" (404–11), the late Stephen Jay Gould explains a contrast that is not necessarily apparent to general readers—that evolution as a theory and evolution as a fact are "different things, not rungs in a hierarchy of increasing certainty." Facts are the data that theories try to explain, as evolutionists have always made clear "from the very beginning, if only because we have always acknowledged how far we are from completely understanding the mechanisms (theory) by which evolution (fact) occurred." He then uses these definitions as the basis for refuting the contrasting view of "scientific creationism," a "self-contradictory, nonsense" set of beliefs. What theory could explain the existence of the 130-million-year-old fossil dinosaur pictured on page 409, covered from head to tail with downy fluff and primitive feathers? Might alternative theories compete for an evolutionary explanation?

You'll also have to limit your comparison, for no single essay—or even an entire book—can fully address the possibilities of most subjects.

For example, from the many angles from which to examine DNA, Bill McKibben chooses in "Designer Genes" to concentrate on social and ethical issues related to "germline genetic engineering" that could be used to create an embryo that would "grow into a genetically engineered child." Once started, where do we stop?, he asks. If we start with "semimedical" genetic intervention "to eliminate nearsightedness or prevent deafness," why stop there? Would not ambitious parents want intelligent offspring? Why not buy the egg of a supersmart coed? Parents who object might find their naturally conceived offspring at a great disadvantage in the "biological arms race," especially if new and improved genetic models come out at intervals. Genetically engineered Sophie might be up-to-date at birth, for example, but the possibility exists that "by the time Sophie is twenty-five and in the job market, she's already more or less obsolete." Moreover, the race for genetic superiority would exacerbate the differences between the rich—the "haves"—and the poor—the "have-nots"—even in America, where one-sixth of the population has no health insurance and can't afford even minimum medical care. Before we let the germline genie out of the bottle, McKibben concludes, making yet other comparisons, we need to think "not as parents but as citizens, not as individuals but as a whole. . . ."

There are several common ways to organize an essay of comparison and contrast. Sherry Turkle's "How Computers Change the Way We Think" (397–402) is based on *before-and-after* considerations of how the omnipresence of computers has changed our ways of seeing and knowing the world and "our place in it." Among the changes are today's dramatically different conceptions of privacy, authentic selves, "powerful ideas" versus Power-Point (which "encourages presentation, not conversation"), and the deleterious effects of rapid word processing on thinking.

Other common patterns become apparent when you examine the ways you might organize your thoughts about buying a new car. Let's say you're making lists that will be the basis of an essay to help you make decisions on type (minivan, pickup, sports car, sedan), make and model, age (new or used), cost, special features (four-wheel drive, built-in CD player), and financing (buy or lease). If you've just begun to think about the subject, you could deal with each issue topic by topic, most usefully in the order listed here: type, make and model, and so on. Or you could deal with each subject as a whole before moving on to the next. If you've already decided on the particular type and price of the car—say, a small used vehicle costing between $8,000 and $10,000— then you might find it more useful to devote one section, say, to the Honda Civic, another to the GEO Prizm, and a third to the Toyota Celica, considering all features of each car in the same order: size, handling, reliability, fuel economy, safety, sportiness, and final cost. Why the same order for each car? Because you'll confuse yourself and your readers if you follow a different organizational pattern for each car; everyone needs to know where to look in each discussion to find comparable information. Another way to organize the information would be to group all the similarities about the cars in one section and all the differences in another, arranged in order from the most important (to you) to the least. Eventually, you'll summarize your conclusion: "While I like the first car better because it's sportier and more fun to drive, and the second is great on hills and curves, I guess I'm stuck with the third because I know I can get a good deal from my great uncle, who kept it in his garage all winter and never drove it over fifty."

The pattern of comparison and contrast that emerges may depend on how long the paper is; the longer the discussion, the less easy it is for readers to remember what they need to. Try out a sample section on members of your class or writing group and see whether they can understand the points of comparison you're trying to make; if they can't, then try another method of arrangement.

Whatever pattern of comparison and contrast you use, a topic outline can help you to organize such papers, and to make sure you've covered equivalent points for each item in the comparison. However you organize the paper, you don't have to give such equal emphasis to the similarities and to the differences; some may simply be more important than others. But you do have to make your chosen points of comparison relevant. Comparison and contrast is particularly useful as a technique in explanations. You can compare something that readers don't know much about (foreign sports cars) with something that's familiar (family sedans).

As we've seen, essays of comparison and contrast may include other types of writing, particularly description, narration, and analysis. Classification and division often determine the points to be covered in such essays: my actual life versus my ideal life, country living versus city living, life on the East (or West) Coast versus life in the Midwest, middle-class life versus upper-class life. . . . And essays of comparison and contrast themselves become, at times, illustrations or arguments, direct or indirect, overt or more subtle. Long live the differences and the zest they provide.

STRATEGIES FOR WRITING— COMPARISON AND CONTRAST

1. Will my essay focus on the similarities between two or more things (comparison) or the differences (contrast), or will I be discussing both similarities and differences? Why do I want to make the comparison or contrast? To find, explore, or deny overt or less apparent resemblances among the items? To decide which one of a pair or group is better or preferable? Or to use the comparison or contrast to argue for my preference?
2. Are my readers familiar with one or more of the objects of my comparison? If they are familiar with them all, then can I concentrate on the unique features of my analysis? (If they are familiar with only one item, start with the known

before discussing the unknown. If they are unacquainted with everything, for purposes of explanation you might wish to begin with a comparison that focuses on the common elements among the items under discussion.)

3. How global or minute will my comparison be (i.e., do I want to make only a few points of comparison or contrast, or many)? Will my essay make more sense to my readers if I present each subject as a complete unit before discussing the next? Or will the comparison or contrast be more meaningful if I proceed point by point?

4. Have I ruled out trivial and irrelevant comparisons? Does each point have a counterpart that I have treated in an equivalent manner, through comparable analysis or illustration, length, and language?

5. Suppose I like or favor one item of the comparison or contrast over the others? Am I obliged to treat every item equally in language and tone, or can my tone vary to reinforce my interpretation?

ELIZABETH TALLENT

Tallent had planned on graduate study in anthropology, but she changed her mind on the way to the University of New Mexico, opting for a career as a fiction writer instead. Born in Washington D.C., in 1954, Tallent grew up in the Midwest and majored in anthropology at Illinois State University (BA, 1975). Her first volume of stories, *In Constant Flight* (1983), centered on characters alienated from each other and detached from their own lives, while her novel *Museum Pieces* (1985) explored a married couple's separation and the reaction of their young daughter. *Time with Children* (1987) and *Honey* (1993) continued this unflinching examination of couples, marriage, children, and houses—the last as objects onto which characters project their ideals and emotions. Tallent's fiction appears regularly in periodicals such as *Granta* and *The New Yorker*, and anthologies such as *Best American Short Stories*. She has also published a critical study, *Married Men and Magic Tricks: John Updike's Erotic Heroes* (1982). Her academic career includes teaching positions at the University of California at Irvine, the Iowa Writers Workshop, and the University of California, Davis. Currently, she is a professor at Stanford University, where she also served as Director of Creative Writing from 1994 to 1996.

"No One's a Mystery," from *Time with Children*, describes a close encounter between an adulterous couple and the husband's wife. With a bit of dialogue and a few images, smells, and sounds, the characters, situation, past, present, and future spring into view. The bittersweet collision between Jack's and the girl's view of the future unfolds in relation to a key object: the five-year diary. Like any good short story, "No One's a Mystery" rewards rereading. A second look helps us better appreciate Tallent's artistry; consider the amount of information we can glean from two pages. It's also a good way to get to know the characters and the situation better. As our experience of the fiction deepens, we may be able to relate this to our own lives or the lives of people we know. What do you notice upon your second or third reading that previously escaped your attention?

No One's a Mystery

1   For my eighteenth birthday Jack gave me a five-year diary with a latch and a little key, light as a dime. I was sitting beside him scratching at the lock, which didn't seem to want to work, when he thought he saw his wife's Cadillac in the distance, coming toward us. He pushed me down onto the dirty floor of the pickup and kept one hand on my head while I inhaled the musk of his cigarettes in the dashboard ashtray and sang along with Rosanne Cash on the tape deck. We'd been drinking tequila and the bottle was between his legs, resting up against his crotch, where the seam of his Levi's was bleached linen-white, though the Levi's were nearly new.

I don't know why his Levi's always bleached like that, along the seams and at the knees. In a curve of cloth his zipper glinted, gold.

"It's her," he said. "She keeps the lights on in the daytime. I can't think of a single habit in a woman that irritates me more than that." When he saw that I was going to stay still he took his hand from my head and ran it through his own dark hair.

"Why does she?" I said.

"She thinks it's safer. Why does she need to be safer? She's driving exactly fifty-five miles an hour. She believes in those signs: 'Speed Monitored by Aircraft.' It doesn't matter that you can look up and see that the sky is empty."

"She'll see your lips move, Jack. She'll know you're talking to someone."

"She'll think I'm singing along with the radio."

He didn't lift his hand, just raised the fingers in salute while the pressure of his palm steadied the wheel, and I heard the Cadillac honk twice, musically; he was driving easily eighty miles an hour. I studied his boots. The elk heads stitched into the leather were bearded with frayed thread, the toes were scuffed, and there was a compact wedge of muddy manure between the heel and the sole—the same boots he'd been wearing for the two years I'd known him. On the tape deck Rosanne Cash sang, "Nobody's into me, no one's a mystery."

"Do you think she's getting famous because of who her daddy is or for herself?" Jack said.

"There are about a hundred pop tops on the floor, did you know that? Some little kid could cut a bare foot on one of these, Jack."

"No little kids get into this truck except for you."

"How come you let it get so dirty?"

"'How come,'" he mocked. "You even sound like a kid. You can get back into the seat now, if you want. She's not going to look over her shoulder and see you."

"How do you know?"

"I just know," he said. "Like I know I'm going to get meat loaf for supper. It's in the air. Like I know what you'll be writing in that diary."

"What will I be writing?" I knelt on my side of the seat and craned around to look at the butterfly of dust printed on my jeans. Outside the window Wyoming was dazzling in the heat. The wheat was fawn and yellow and parted smoothly by the thin dirt road. I could smell the water in the irrigation ditches hidden in the wheat.

"Tonight you'll write, 'I love Jack. This is my birthday present from him. I can't imagine anybody loving anybody more than I love Jack.'"

"I can't."

"In a year you'll write, 'I wonder what I ever really saw in Jack. I wonder why I spent so many days just riding around in his pickup. It's true he taught me something about sex. It's true there wasn't ever much else to do in Cheyenne.'"

19   "I won't write that."

20   "In two years you'll write, 'I wonder what that old guy's name was, the one with the curly hair and the filthy dirty pickup truck and time on his hands.'"

21   "I won't write that."

22   "No?"

23   "Tonight I'll write, 'I love Jack. This is my birthday present from him. I can't imagine anybody loving anybody more than I love Jack.'"

24   "No, you can't," he said. "You can't imagine it."

25   "In a year I'll write, 'Jack should be home any minute now. The table's set—my grandmother's linen and her old silver and the yellow candles left over from the wedding—but I don't know if I can wait until after the trout à la Navarra to make love to him.'"

26   "It must have been a fast divorce."

27   "In two years I'll write, 'Jack should be home by now. Little Jack is hungry for his supper. He said his first word today besides "Mama" and "Papa." He said "kaka."'"

28   Jack laughed. "He was probably trying to finger-paint with kaka on the bathroom wall when you heard him say it."

29   "In three years I'll write, 'My nipples are a little sore from nursing Eliza Rosamund.'"

30   "Rosamund. Every little girl should have a middle name she hates."

31   "'Her breath smells like vanilla and her eyes are just Jack's color of blue.'"

32   "That's nice," Jack said.

33   "So, which one do you like?"

34   "I like yours," he said. "But I believe mine."

35   "It doesn't matter. I believe mine."

36   "Not in your heart of hearts, you don't."

37   "You're wrong."

38   "I'm not wrong," he said. "And her breath would smell like your milk, and it's kind of a bittersweet smell, if you want to know the truth."

For Discussion

1. How many things can you infer from the slice of life Tallent offers you? Use your knowledge of people, relationships, and the information Tallent provides to sum up everything she conveys about the characters and situation *without having to tell you directly.*

2. Is this story mainly about differences or similarities? Certainly the age difference between the two characters is a major issue, yet there may be other contrasts operating as well. Can you draw out any differences in personality, temperament, or values? Is gender a factor? From another point of view, what do Jack and the narrator have in common? Do they share any attitudes toward life?

3. Whose view of the future are you likely to believe? What evidence in the story corroborates your prediction?

 For comprehension, writing, and research activities and resources, please visit the companion website at <college.hmco.com/english>.

DEBORAH TANNEN

For biographical information, see page 296.

Much of Tannen's research, like her writing, is based on comparative analyses of the contrasting behavior of men and women in a variety of situations. "Communication Styles" was originally published as "Teachers' Classroom Strategies Should Recognize that Men and Women Use Language Differently" in the *Chronicle of Higher Education* (June 19, 1991). Here Tannen explores differences in the ways that men and women students interact, and how the size, informality, and composition of the group influences who speaks up and who remains silent.

Communication Styles

When I researched and wrote my book, *You Just Don't Understand: Women and Men in Conversation,* the furthest thing from my mind was reevaluating my teaching strategies. But that has been one of the direct benefits of having written the book.

The primary focus of my linguistic research always has been the language of everyday conversation. One facet of this is conversational style: how different regional, ethnic, and class backgrounds, as well as age and gender, result in different ways of using language to communicate. *You Just Don't Understand* is about the conversational styles of women and men. As I gained more insight into typically male and female ways of using language, I began to suspect some of the causes of the troubling facts that women who go to single-sex schools do better in later life, and that when young women sit next to young men in classrooms, the males talk more. This is not to say that all men talk in class, nor that no women do. It is simply that a greater percentage of discussion time is taken by men's voices.

The research of sociologists and anthropologists such as Janet Lever, Marjorie Harness Goodwin, and Donna Eder has shown that girls and boys learn to use language differently in their sex-separate peer groups. Typically, a girl has a best friend with whom she sits and talks, frequently telling secrets. It's the telling of secrets, the fact and the way that they talk to each other, that makes them best friends. For boys, activities are central: Their best friends are the ones they do things with. Boys also tend to play in larger groups that are hierarchical. High-status boys give orders and push low-status boys around. So boys are expected to use language to seize center stage: by exhibiting their skills, displaying their knowledge, and challenging and resisting challenges.

4   These patterns have stunning implications for classroom interaction. Most faculty members assume that participating in class discussion is a necessary part of successful performance. Yet speaking in a classroom is more congenial to boys' language experience than to girls', since it entails putting oneself forward in front of a large group of people, many of whom are strangers and at least one of whom is sure to judge speakers' knowledge and intelligence by their verbal display.

5   Another aspect of many classrooms that makes them more hospitable to most men than to most women is the use of debate-like formats as a learning tool. Our educational system, as Walter Ong argues persuasively in his book *Fighting for Life* (Cornell University Press, 1981), is fundamentally male in that the pursuit of knowledge is believed to be achieved by ritual opposition: public display followed by argument and challenge. Father Ong demonstrates that ritual opposition—what he calls "adversativeness" or "agonism"—is fundamental to the way most males approach almost any activity. (Consider, for example, the little boy who shows he likes a little girl by pulling her braids and shoving her.) But ritual opposition is antithetical to the way most females learn and like to interact. It is not that females don't fight, but that they don't fight for fun. They don't *ritualize* opposition.

6   Anthropologists working in widely disparate parts of the world have found contrasting verbal rituals for women and men. Women in completely unrelated cultures (for example, Greece and Bali) engage in ritual laments: spontaneously produced rhyming couplets that express their pain, for example, over the loss of loved ones. Men do not take part in laments. They have their own, very different verbal ritual: a contest, a war of words in which they vie with each other to devise clever insults.

7   When discussing these phenomena with a colleague, I commented that I see these two styles in American conversation: Many women bond by talking about troubles, and many men bond by exchanging playful insults and put-downs, and other sorts of verbal sparring. He exclaimed: "I never thought of this, but that's the way I teach: I have students read an article, and then I invite them to tear it apart. After we've torn it to shreds, we talk about how to build a better model."

8   This contrasts sharply with the way I teach: I open the discussion of readings by asking, "What did you find useful in this? What can we use in our own theory building and our own methods?" I note what I see as weaknesses in the author's approach, but I also point out that the writer's

discipline and purposes might be different from ours. Finally, I offer personal anecdotes illustrating the phenomena under discussion and praise students' anecdotes as well as their critical acumen.

These different teaching styles must make our classrooms wildly different places and hospitable to different students. Male students are more likely to be comfortable attacking the readings and might find the inclusion of personal anecdotes irrelevant and "soft." Women are more likely to resist discussion they perceive as hostile, and, indeed, it is women in my classes who are most likely to offer personal anecdotes.

A colleague who read my book commented that he had always taken for granted that the best way to deal with students' comments is to challenge them; this, he felt it was self-evident, sharpens their minds and helps them develop debating skills. But he had noticed that women were relatively silent in his classes, so he decided to try beginning discussion with relatively open-ended questions and letting comments go unchallenged. He found, to his amazement and satisfaction, that more women began to speak up.

Though some women in his class clearly liked this better, perhaps some of the men liked it less. One young man in my class wrote in a questionnaire about a history professor who gave students questions to think about and called on people to answer them: "He would then play devil's advocate . . . *i.e.,* he debated us. . . . That class *really* sharpened me intellectually. . . . We as students do need to know how to defend ourselves." This young man valued the experience of being attacked and challenged publicly. Many, if not most, women would shrink from such "challenge," experiencing it as public humiliation.

A professor at Hamilton College told me of a young man who was upset because he felt his class presentation had been a failure. The professor was puzzled because he had observed that class members had listened attentively and agreed with the student's observations. It turned out that it was this very agreement that the student interpreted as failure: Since no one had engaged his ideas by arguing with him, he felt they had found them unworthy of attention.

So one reason men speak in class more than women is that many of them find the "public" classroom setting more conducive to speaking, whereas most women are more comfortable speaking in private to a small group of people they know well. A second reason is that men are more likely to be comfortable with the debate-like form that discussion may take. Yet another reason is the different attitudes toward speaking in class that typify women and men.

Students who speak frequently in class, many of whom are men, assume that it is their job to think of contributions and try to get the floor to express them. But many women monitor their participation not only to get the floor but to avoid getting it. Women students in my class tell me that if they have spoken up once or twice, they hold back for the rest of the class because they don't want to dominate. If they have spoken a lot one week, they will remain silent the next. These different ethics of participation are, of course, unstated, so those who speak freely assume that those who remain silent have nothing to say, and those who are reining themselves in assume that the big talkers are selfish and hoggish.

15   When I looked around my classes, I could see these differing ethics and habits at work. For example, my graduate class in analyzing conversation had 20 students, 11 women and 9 men. Of the men, four were foreign students: two Japanese, one Chinese, and one Syrian. With the exception of the three Asian men, all the men spoke in class at least occasionally. The biggest talker in the class was a woman, but there were also five women who never spoke at all, only one of whom was Japanese. I decided to try something different.

16   I broke the class into small groups to discuss the issues raised in the readings and to analyze their own conversational transcripts. I devised three ways of dividing the students into groups: one by the degree program they were in, one by gender, and one by conversational style, as closely as I could guess it. This meant that when the class was grouped according to conversational style, I put Asian students together, fast talkers together, and quiet students together. The class split into groups six times during the semester, so they met in each grouping twice. I told students to regard the groups as examples of interactional data and to note the different ways they participated in different groups. Toward the end of the term, I gave them a questionnaire asking about their class and group participation.

17   I could see plainly from my observation of the groups at work that women who never opened their mouths in class were talking away in the small groups. In fact, the Japanese woman commented that she found it particularly hard to contribute to the all-woman group she was in because "I was overwhelmed by how talkative the female students were in the female-only group." This is particularly revealing because it highlights that the same person who can be "oppressed" into silence in one context can become the talkative "oppressor" in another. No one's conversational style is absolute; everyone's style changes in response to the context and others' styles.

18   Some of the students (seven) said that they preferred the same-gender groups; others preferred the same-style groups. In answer to the question "Would you have liked to speak in class more than you did?" six of the seven who said Yes were women; the one man was Japanese. Most startlingly, this response did not come only from quiet women; it came from women who had indicated they had spoken in class never, rarely, sometimes, and often. Of the 11 students who said the amount they had spoken was fine, 7 were men. Of the four women who checked "fine," two added qualifications indicating it wasn't completely fine: One wrote in "maybe more," and one wrote, "I have an urge to participate but often feel I should have something more interesting/relevant/wonderful/intelligent to say!!"

I counted my experiment a success. Everyone in the class found the 19
small groups interesting, and no one indicated he or she would have
preferred that the class not break into groups. Perhaps most instructive,
however, was the fact that the experience of breaking into groups, and of
talking about participation in class, raised everyone's awareness about
classroom participation. After we had talked about it, some of the quietest
women in the class made a few voluntary contributions, though sometimes I had to insure their participation by interrupting the students who
were exuberantly speaking out.

Americans are often proud that they discount the significance of cul- 20
tural differences: "We are all individuals," many people boast. Ignoring
such issues as gender and ethnicity becomes a source of pride: "I treat
everyone the same." But treating people the same is not equal treatment
if they are not the same.

The classroom is a different environment for those who feel comfort- 21
able putting themselves forward in a group than it is for those who find
the prospect of doing so chastening, or even terrifying. When a professor
asks, "Are there any questions?," students who can formulate statements
the fastest have the greatest opportunity to respond. Those who need significant time to do so have not really been given a chance at all, since by
the time they are ready to speak, someone else has the floor.

In a class where some students speak out without raising hands, those who 22
feel they must raise their hands and wait to be recognized do not have
equal opportunity to speak. Telling them to feel free to jump in will not
make them feel free; one's sense of timing, of one's rights and obligations in
a classroom, are automatic, learned over years of interaction. They may be
changed over time, with motivation and effort, but they cannot be changed
on the spot. And everyone assumes his or her own way is best. When I
asked my students how the class could be changed to make it easier for
them to speak more, the most talkative woman said she would prefer it if
no one had to raise hands, and a foreign student said he wished people
would raise their hands and wait to be recognized.

My experience in this class has convinced me that small-group inter- 23
action should be part of any class that is not a small seminar. I also am
convinced that having the students become observers of their own interaction is a crucial part of their education. Talking about ways of talking in
class makes students aware that their ways of talking affect other students,
that the motivations they impute to others may not truly reflect others'
motives, and that the behaviors they assume to be self-evidently right are
not universal norms.

The goal of complete equal opportunity in class may not be attain- 24
able, but realizing that one monolithic classroom-participation structure is
not equal opportunity is itself a powerful motivation to find more-diverse
methods to serve diverse students—and every classroom is diverse.

Content

1. In your experience, are boys (more often than girls) "expected to use language to seize center stage: by exhibiting their skills, displaying their knowledge, and challenging and resisting challenges" (¶ 3)? How does this translate into classroom performance (¶s 4, 7)? In your experience, is Ong's claim true that "ritual opposition . . . is fundamental to the way most males approach almost any activity" (¶ 5)?

2. "Treating people the same is not equal treatment if they are not the same" (¶ 20). Explain how this idea applies in a classroom.

3. Does Tannen argue that the differences between men's and women's communication styles are biologically or culturally determined? Does she equate student talkativeness in class with an inquiring mind? With intelligent preparation? Or does she base her equation exclusively on gender? Explain your answers.

Strategies/Structures/Language

4. Tannen's article follows the format of physical science and social research: statement of the problem, review of the literature, identification of research methodology, explanation of the research procedure, interpretation of the research findings, and generalizations to other situations or recommendations for either further research or practical applications or both. Show where each stage occurs in this article.

5. "No one's conversational style is absolute; everyone's style changes in response to the context and others' styles" (¶ 17). Explain, with reference to your own experience and other students' behavior in your classes—and out.

For Writing

6. By yourself or with a partner, do some primary investigation to replicate Tannen's observation that "when young women sit next to [presumably she means *share the same classroom*, not necessarily *sit in immediate proximity to*] young men in classrooms, the males talk more" (¶ 2). Is this true in any or all of your classes? Typically, do men speak more than women in classes taught by men? Do women speak more or less than men in classes taught by women? Do the ages and life experiences of men and women influence the extent of their class participation? Generalize from your findings and interpret them with regard to Tannen's findings. Do you think the men and women students at your school are typical of students at all American colleges or only at colleges of the type that yours represents (private or public community college, four-year undergraduate school, research university)?

7. Do you agree with Tannen's conclusion that "small-group interaction should be part of any class that is not a small seminar" (¶ 23)? If so, why? If not, why not? What demands does this format place on the students? What does this format imply about the way we learn?

8. Write an essay about any of the Content questions. Base your essay on your own experience, and reinforce it with three interviews—one with a student of a different gender from yours, another with a student of a different racial background, another with a student from a different socio-economic class. (To control for teaching style and content, all the students should be enrolled in the same course at the same time.) To what extent are your conclusions influenced by your informants' class and ethnicity, in comparison with their gender?

9. Examine a class in which you wanted to talk more (or at all), but did not do so. Why were you more silent than you wanted to be? What in the class format—teacher's instructional style, other students' behavior, your own preparation or maturity—would have had to change in order for you to have been willing to talk more? Would you have gained more from the class if you'd been a more talkative (and hence, more active) participant?

 For comprehension, writing, and research activities and resources, please visit the companion website at <college.hmco.com/english>.

SHERRY TURKLE

Turkle is a clinical psychologist and sociology professor at Massachusetts Institute of Technology. She was born in 1948 in New York City, and was educated at Harvard (BA, 1970; PhD, 1976). Her research and writing focus on the cultural and psychological implications of computer technology. She looks at "computers as carriers of culture, as objects that give rise to new metaphors, to new relationships between people and machines, between different people, and most significantly between people and their ways of thinking about themselves." Her books include *The Second Self: Computers and the Human Spirit* (1984) and *Life on the Screen: Identity in the Age of the Internet* (1995) In addition to identities as "Turkle the social scientist," the author, and the professor, she adds others: "the cyberspace explorer, the woman who might log on as a man, or as another woman, or as, simply, ST" (from "Why Am We?"). "How Computers Change the Way We Think" was originally published in *The Chronicle of Higher Education* on January 30, 2004.

How Computers Change the Way We Think

The tools we use to think change the ways in which we think. The invention of written language brought about a radical shift in how we process, organize, store, and transmit representations of the world. Although writing remains our primary information technology, today when we think about the impact of technology on our habits of mind, we think primarily of the computer.

My first encounters with how computers change the way we think came soon after I joined the faculty at the Massachusetts Institute of Technology in the late 1970s, at the end of the era of the slide rule and the beginning of the era of the personal computer. At a lunch for new faculty members, several senior professors in engineering complained that the transition from slide rules to calculators had affected their students' ability to deal with issues of scale. When students used slide rules, they had to insert decimal points themselves. The professors insisted that that required students to maintain a mental sense of scale, whereas those who relied on calculators made frequent errors in orders of magnitude. Additionally, the students with calculators had lost their ability to do "back of the envelope" calculations, and with that, an intuitive feel for the material.

3   That same semester, I taught a course in the history of psychology. There, I experienced the impact of computational objects on students' ideas about their emotional lives. My class had read Freud's essay on slips of the tongue, with its famous first example: The chairman of a parliamentary session opens a meeting by declaring it closed. The students discussed how Freud interpreted such errors as revealing a person's mixed emotions. A computer-science major disagreed with Freud's approach. The mind, she argued, is a computer. And in a computational dictionary—like we have in the human mind—"closed" and "open" are designated by the same symbol, separated by a sign for opposition. "Closed" equals "minus open." To substitute "closed" for "open" does not require the notion of ambivalence or conflict.

4   "When the chairman made that substitution," she declared, "a bit was dropped; a minus sign was lost. There was a power surge. No problem."

5   The young woman turned a Freudian slip into an information-processing error. An explanation in terms of meaning had become an explanation in terms of mechanism.

6   Such encounters turned me to the study of both the instrumental and the subjective sides of the nascent computer culture. As an ethnographer and psychologist, I began to study not only what the computer was doing *for* us, but what it was doing *to* us, including how it was changing the way we see ourselves, our sense of human identity.

7   In the 1980s, I surveyed the psychological effects of computational objects in everyday life—largely the unintended side effects of people's tendency to project thoughts and feelings onto their machines. In the 20 years since, computational objects have become more explicitly designed to have emotional and cognitive effects. And those "effects by design" will become even stronger in the decade to come. Machines are being designed to serve explicitly as companions, pets, and tutors. And they are introduced in school settings for the youngest children.

8   Today, starting in elementary school, students use e-mail, word processing, computer simulations, virtual communities, and PowerPoint software. In the process, they are absorbing more than the content of what appears on their screens. They are learning new ways to think about what it means to know and understand.

9   What follows is a short and certainly not comprehensive list of areas where I see information technology encouraging changes in thinking. There can be no simple way of cataloging whether any particular change is good or bad. That is contested terrain. At every step we have to ask, as educators

and citizens, whether current technology is leading us in directions that serve our human purposes. Such questions are not technical; they are social, moral, and political. For me, addressing that subjective side of computation is one of the more significant challenges for the next decade of information technology in higher education. Technology does not determine change, but it encourages us to take certain directions. If we make those directions clear, we can more easily exert human choice.

Thinking about privacy.   Today's college students are habituated   10
to a world of online blogging, instant messaging, and Web browsing that leaves electronic traces. Yet they have had little experience with the right to privacy. Unlike past generations of Americans, who grew up with the notion that the privacy of their mail was sacrosanct, our children are accustomed to electronic surveillance as part of their daily lives.

I have colleagues who feel that the increased incursions on privacy   11
have put the topic more in the news, and that this is a positive change. But middle-school and high-school students tend to be willing to provide personal information online with no safeguards, and college students seem uninterested in violations of privacy and in increased governmental and commercial surveillance. Professors find that students do not understand that in a democracy, privacy is a right, not merely a privilege. In 10 years, ideas about the relationship of privacy and government will require even more active pedagogy. (One might also hope that increased education about the kinds of silent surveillance that technology makes possible may inspire more active political engagement with the issue.)

Avatars or a self?   Chat rooms, role-playing games, and other tech-   12
nological venues offer us many different contexts for presenting ourselves online. Those possibilities are particularly important for adolescents because they offer what Erik Erikson described as a moratorium, a time out or safe space for the personal experimentation that is so crucial for adolescent development. Our dangerous world—with crime, terrorism, drugs, and AIDS—offers little in the way of safe spaces. Online worlds can provide valuable spaces for identity play.

But some people who gain fluency in expressing multiple aspects for   13
self may find it harder to develop authentic selves. Some children who write narratives for their screen avatars may grow up with too little experience of how to share their real feelings with other people. For those who are lonely yet afraid of intimacy, information technology has made it possible to have the illusion of companionship without the demands of friendship.

From powerful ideas to PowerPoint.   In the 1970s and early 1980s,   14
some educators wanted to make programming part of the regular curriculum for K–12 education. They argued that because information technology carries ideas, it might as well carry the most powerful ideas that computer science has to offer. It is ironic that in most elementary schools today, the ideas being carried by information technology are not ideas from computer science like procedural thinking, but more likely to be those embedded in productivity tools like PowerPoint presentation software.

15   PowerPoint does more than provide a way of transmitting content. It carries its own way of thinking, its own aesthetic—which not surprisingly shows up in the aesthetic of college freshmen. In that aesthetic, presentation becomes its own powerful idea.

16   To be sure, the software cannot be blamed for lower intellectual standards. Misuse of the former is as much a symptom as a cause of the latter. Indeed, the culture in which our children are raised is increasingly a culture of presentation, a corporate culture in which appearance is often more important than reality. In contemporary political discourse, the bar has also been lowered. Use of rhetorical devices at the expense of cogent argument regularly goes without notice. But it is precisely because standards of intellectual rigor outside the educational sphere have fallen that educators must attend to how we use, and when we introduce, software that has been designed to simplify the organization and processing of information.

17   In "The Cognitive Style of PowerPoint" (Graphics Press, 2003), Edward R. Tufte suggests that PowerPoint equates bulleting with clear thinking. It does not teach students to begin a discussion or construct a narrative. It encourages presentation, not conversation. Of course, in the hands of a master teacher, a PowerPoint presentation with few words and powerful images can serve as the jumping-off point for a brilliant lecture. But in the hands of elementary-school students, often introduced to PowerPoint in the third grade, and often infatuated with its swooshing sounds, animated icons, and flashing text, a slide show is more likely to close down debate than open it up.

18   Developed to serve the needs of the corporate boardroom, the software is designed to convey absolute authority. Teachers used to tell students that clear exposition depended on clear outlining, but presentation software has fetishized the outline at the expense of the content.

19   Narrative, the exposition of content, takes time. PowerPoint, like so much in the computer culture, speeds up the pace.

20   **Word processing vs. thinking.**   The catalog for the Vermont Country Store advertises a manual typewriter, which the advertising copy says "moves at a pace that allows time to compose your thoughts." As many of us know, it is possible to manipulate text on a computer screen and see how it looks faster than we can think about what the words mean.

21   Word processing has its own complex psychology. From a pedagogical point of view, it can make dedicated students into better writers because it allows them to revise text, rearrange paragraphs, and experiment with the tone and shape of an essay. Few professional writers would part with their computers; some claim that they simply cannot think without their hands on the keyboard. Yet the ability to quickly fill the page, to see it before you can think it, can make bad writers even worse.

22   A seventh grader once told me that the typewriter she found in her mother's attic is "cool because you have to type each letter by itself. You have to know what you are doing in advance or it comes out a mess." The idea of thinking ahead has become exotic.

Taking things at interface value. We expect software to be easy to use, and we assume that we don't have to know how a computer works. In the early 1980s, most computer users who spoke of transparency meant that, as with any other machine, you could "open the hood" and poke around. But only a few years later, Macintosh users began to use the term when they talked about seeing their documents and programs represented by attractive and easy-to-interpret icons. They were referring to an ability to make things work without needing to go below the screen surface. Paradoxically, it was the screen's opacity that permitted that kind of transparency. Today, when people say that something is transparent, they mean that they can see how to make it work, not that they know how it works. In other words, transparency means epistemic opacity. 23

The people who built or bought the first generation of personal computers understood them down to the bits and bytes. The next generation of operation systems were more complex, but they still invited that old-time reductive understanding. Contemporary information technology encourages different habits of mind. Today's college students are already used to taking things at (inter) face value; their successors in 2014 will be even less accustomed to probing below the surface. 24

Simulation and its discontents. Some thinkers argue that the new opacity is empowering, enabling anyone to use the most sophisticated technological tools and to experiment with simulation in complex and creative ways. But it is also true that our tools carry the message that they are beyond our understanding. It is possible that in daily life, epistemic opacity can lead to passivity. 25

I first became aware of that possibility in the early 1990s, when the first generation of complex simulation games were introduced and immediately became popular for home as well as school use. SimLife teaches the principles of evolution by getting children involved in the development of complex ecosystems; in that sense it is an extraordinary learning tool. During one session in which I played SimLife with Tim, a 13-year-old, the screen before us flashed a message: "Your orgot is being eaten up." "What's an orgot?" I asked. Tim didn't know. "I just ignore that," he said confidently. "You don't need to know that kind of stuff to play." 26

For me, that story serves as a cautionary tale. Computer simulations enable their users to think about complex phenomena as dynamic, evolving systems. But they also accustom us to manipulating systems whose core assumptions we may not understand and that may not be true. 27

We live in a culture of simulation. Our games, our economic and political systems, and the ways architects design buildings, chemists envisage molecules, and surgeons perform operations all use simulation technology. In 10 years the degree to which simulations are embedded in every area of life will have increased exponentially. We need to develop a new form of media literacy: readership skills for the culture of simulation. 28

We come to written text with habits of readership based on centuries of civilization. At the very least, we have learned to begin with the journalist's 29 traditional questions: who, what, when, where, why, and how. Who wrote these words, what is their message, why were they written, and how are they situated in time and place, politically and socially? A central project for higher education during the next 10 years should be creating programs in information-technology literacy, with the goal of teaching students to interrogate simulations in much the same spirit, challenging their built-in assumptions.

30   Despite the ever-increasing complexity of software, most computer environments put users in worlds based on constrained choices. In other words, immersion in programmed worlds puts us in reassuring environments where the rules are clear. For example, when you play a video game, you often go through a series of frightening situations that you escape by mastering the rules—you experience life as a reassuring dichotomy of scary and safe. Children grow up in a culture of video games, action films, fantasy epics, and computer programs that all rely on that familiar scenario of almost losing but then regaining total mastery: There is danger. It is mastered. A still-more-powerful monster appears. It is subdued. Scary. Safe.

31   Yet in the real world, we have never had a greater need to work our way out of binary assumptions. In the decade ahead, we need to rebuild the culture around information technology. In that new socio-technical culture, assumptions about the nature of mastery would be less absolute. The new culture would make it easier, not more difficult, to consider life in shades of gray, to see moral dilemmas in terms other than a battle between Good and Evil. For never has our world been more complex, hybridized, and global. Never have we so needed to have many contradictory thoughts and feelings at the same time. Our tools must help us accomplish that, not fight against us.

32   Information technology is identity technology. Embedding it in a culture that supports democracy, freedom of expression, tolerance, diversity, and complexity of opinion is one of the next decade's greatest challenges. We cannot afford to fail.

33   When I first began studying the computer culture, a small breed of highly trained technologists thought of themselves as "computer people." That is no longer the case. If we take the computer as a carrier of a way of knowing, a way of seeing the world and our place in it, we are all computer people now.

Content

1. What new technologies does Turkle claim are changing the way people think? Have you experienced the changes in thought patterns that she describes, such as reduced discussions caused by PowerPoint presentations or writing faster with a word processor than you can think?

2. Is there any technology or program that Turkle should add to her list, based on your experience? What mind-altering computing experiences have you had that she doesn't mention?

3. At the end of the article, Turkle asserts that current computing habits and software may undermine "democracy, freedom of expression, tolerance, diversity, and complexity of opinion" (¶ 32). Look over the article again to determine the precise reasons she gives to support these conclusions. Which arguments do you find to be the most convincing? Why?

4. Do you ever intentionally try to get away from technology, or have you ever had to be away from the Internet or the computer for an extended period of time? Did you notice any changes in your thinking process or attitudes as a result? Explain what happened and whether the experience was positive or negative.

Strategies/Structures/Language

5. One of the main strategies Turkle uses is the past/present contrast, such as the idea that the typewriter allowed people to put more thought into their writing (¶ 22). What other examples can you find of Turkle comparing current technology to past technology? To what extent are these comparisons effective at persuading the reader to accept her conclusions?

For Writing

6. With a group of classmates, determine how much experience each person has with the technologies that Turkle mentions. For example, how many of your colleagues have experience with PowerPoint? How many participate in chat rooms, role-playing games, simulation games, or use a screen avatar? Discuss with the group whether any of these technologies may be changing or shaping your basic thought processes, and write a collaborative paper reporting on and analyzing your findings.

7. Can you think of some solutions to the issues that Turkle raises in her article? To what extent can we lessen computer technology's negative impact on our thinking? Is the solution technological, or would it help to educate the public about the dangers Turkle outlines? Write a paper explaining how some, or all, of the issues Turkle discusses could be resolved.

8. Can you think of any computing technology that might help humans to *improve* their thought processes? Invent a program or online service that could help enhance mental functioning or perhaps enhance the democratic process, freedom of expression, or tolerance. Write a proposal persuading readers to support your effort to make your invention available to the public, stressing the way it will improve the way we think.

 For comprehension, writing, and research activities and resources, please visit the companion website at <college.hmco.com/english>.

STEPHEN JAY GOULD

Gould (born 1941) graduated from Antioch in 1963, earned a PhD from Columbia in 1967, and then taught paleontology, biology, and history of science at Harvard until his death in 2002. He provided exceptionally clear definitions, explanations, and arguments in his writings for students, colleagues, and general readers of his columns in *Natural History,* which were collected in several volumes; ranging from *Ever Since Darwin* (1977) to *Bully for Brontosaurus* (1991) to *The Lying Stones of Marrakech* (2001). Gould's scientific orientation favors the underdog, as is evident in *The Mismeasure of Man* (1981). There he reinterprets two centuries of IQ testing and other quantitative ways of determining intelligence to show how flawed measurement procedures and wrong interpretations of information invariably favored educated white Anglo-Saxon males and contributed to the oppression of everyone else. He received numerous honors, including a MacArthur Fellowship (a "genius grant").

Gould's analysis of the qualities of great scientific essayists (T. H. Huxley, J. B. S. Haldane, P. B. Medawar) applies equally well to his own writings:

> All write about the simplest things and draw from them a universe of implications. . . . All maintain an unflinching commitment to rationality. . . . [All demystify] science by cutting through jargon; they show by example rather than exhortation that the most complex concepts can be rendered intelligible to everyone.

"Evolution as Fact and Theory," originally published in *Discover* (1981), manifests these qualities. Gould uses the crucial definitions and distinctions between fact and theory as the basis for contrasting the evolutionists' scientific position with the creationists' pseudoscientific position, which he argues against in most of the rest of the essay. He contends—by means of another contrast—that "'scientific creationism' is a self-contradictory, nonsense phrase precisely because it cannot be falsified."

Evolution as Fact and Theory

1   Kirtley Mather, who died last year at age 89, was a pillar of both science and the Christian religion in America and one of my dearest friends. The difference of half a century in our ages evaporated before our common interests. The most curious thing we shared was a battle we each fought at the same age. For Kirtley had gone to Tennessee with Clarence Darrow to testify for evolution at the Scopes trial of 1925. When I think that we are enmeshed again in the same struggle for one of the best documented, most compelling and exciting concepts in all of science, I don't know whether to laugh or cry.

2   According to idealized principles of scientific discourse, the arousal of dormant issues should reflect fresh data that give renewed life to abandoned

notions. Those outside the current debate may therefore be excused for suspecting that creationists have come up with something new, or that evolutionists have generated some serious internal trouble. But nothing has changed; the creationists have not a single new fact or argument. Darrow and Bryan were at least more entertaining than we lesser antagonists today. The rise of creationism is politics, pure and simple; it represents one issue (and by no means the major concern) of the resurgent evangelical right. Arguments that seemed kooky just a decade ago have re-entered the mainstream.

Creationism Is Not Science

The basic attack of the creationists falls apart on two general counts before   3
we even reach the supposed factual details of their complaints against evolution. First, they play upon a vernacular misunderstanding of the word "theory" to convey the false impression that we evolutionists are covering up the rotten core of our edifice. Second, they misuse a popular philosophy of science to argue that they are behaving scientifically in attacking evolution. Yet the same philosophy demonstrates that their own belief is not science, and that "scientific creationism" is therefore meaningless and self-contradictory, a superb example of what Orwell called "newspeak."

In the American vernacular, "theory" often means "imperfect fact"—   4
part of a hierarchy of confidence running downhill from fact to theory to hypothesis to guess. Thus the power of the creationist argument: evolution is "only" a theory, and intense debate now rages about many aspects of the theory. If evolution is less than a fact, and scientists can't even make up their minds about the theory, then what confidence can we have in it? Indeed, President Reagan echoed this argument before an evangelical group in Dallas when he said (in what I devoutly hope was campaign rhetoric): "Well, it is a theory. It is a scientific theory only, and it has in recent years been challenged in the world of science—that is, not believed in the scientific community to be as infallible as it once was."

Well, evolution *is* a theory. It is also a fact. And facts and theories are   5
different things, not rungs in a hierarchy of increasing certainty. Facts are the world's data. Theories are structures of ideas that explain and interpret facts. Facts do not go away when scientists debate rival theories to explain them. Einstein's theory of gravitation replaced Newton's, but apples did not suspend themselves in mid-air pending the outcome. And human beings evolved from apelike ancestors whether they did so by Darwin's proposed mechanism or by some other, yet to be discovered.

Moreover, "fact" does not mean "absolute certainty." The final proofs   6
of logic and mathematics flow deductively from stated premises and achieve certainty only because they are *not* about the empirical world. Evolutionists make no claim for perpetual truth, though creationists often do (and then attack us for a style of argument that they themselves favor). In science,

"fact" can only mean "confirmed to such a degree that it would be perverse to withhold provisional assent." I suppose that apples might start to rise tomorrow, but the possibility does not merit equal time in physics classrooms.

7   Evolutionists have been clear about this distinction between fact and theory from the very beginning, if only because we have always acknowledged how far we are from completely understanding the mechanisms (theory) by which evolution (fact) occurred. Darwin continually emphasized the difference between his two great and separate accomplishments: establishing the fact of evolution, and proposing a theory—natural selection—to explain the mechanism of evolution. He wrote in *The Descent of Man:* "I had two distinct objects in view; firstly, to show that species had not been separately created, and secondly, that natural selection had been the chief agent of change . . . Hence if I have erred in . . . having exaggerated its [natural selection's] power . . . I have at least, as I hope, done good service in aiding to overthrow the dogma of separate creations."

8   Thus Darwin acknowledged the provisional nature of natural selection while affirming the fact of evolution. The fruitful theoretical debate that Darwin initiated has never ceased. From the 1940s through the 1960s, Darwin's own theory of natural selection did achieve a temporary hegemony that it never enjoyed in his lifetime. But renewed debate characterizes our decade, and, while no biologist questions the importance of natural selection, many now doubt its ubiquity. In particular, many evolutionists argue that substantial amounts of genetic change may not be subject to natural selection and may spread through populations at random. Others are challenging Darwin's linking of natural selection with gradual, imperceptible change through all intermediary degrees; they are arguing that most evolutionary events may occur far more rapidly than Darwin envisioned.

9   Scientists regard debates on fundamental issues of theory as a sign of intellectual health and a source of excitement. Science is—and how else can I say it?—most fun when it plays with interesting ideas, examines their implications, and recognizes that old information may be explained in surprisingly new ways. Evolutionary theory is now enjoying this uncommon vigor. Yet amidst all this turmoil no biologist has been led to doubt the fact that evolution occurred; we are debating *how* it happened. We are all trying to explain the same thing: the tree of evolutionary descent linking all organisms by ties of genealogy. Creationists pervert and caricature this debate by conveniently neglecting the common conviction that underlies it, and by falsely suggesting that we now doubt the very phenomenon we are struggling to understand.

10   Using another invalid argument, creationists claim that "the dogma of separate creations," as Darwin characterized it a century ago, is a scientific theory meriting equal time with evolution in high school biology curricula. But a prevailing viewpoint among philosophers of science belies this creationist argument. Philosopher Karl Popper has argued for decades that the primary criterion of science is the falsifiability of its theories. We

can never prove absolutely, but we can falsify. A set of ideas that cannot, in principle, be falsified is not science.

The entire creationist argument involves little more than a rhetorical 11
attempt to falsify evolution by presenting supposed contradictions among its supporters. Their brand of creationism, they claim, is "scientific" because it follows the Popperian model in trying to demolish evolution. Yet Popper's argument must apply in both directions. One does not become a scientist by the simple act of trying to falsify another scientific system; one has to present an alternative system that also meets Popper's criterion—it too must be falsifiable in principle.

"Scientific creationism" is a self-contradictory, nonsense phrase pre- 12
cisely because it cannot be falsified. I can envision observations and experiments that would disprove any evolutionary theory I know, but I cannot imagine what potential data could lead creationists to abandon their beliefs. Unbeatable systems are dogma, not science. Lest I seem harsh or rhetorical, I quote creationism's leading intellectual, Duane Gish, PhD, from his recent (1978) book *Evolution? The Fossils Say No!* "By creation we mean the bringing into being by a supernatural Creator of the basic kinds of plants and animals by the process of sudden, or fiat, creation. We do not know how the Creator created, what processes He used, *for He used processes which are not now operating anywhere in the natural universe* [Gish's italics]. This is why we refer to creation as special creation. We cannot discover by scientific investigations anything about the creative processes used by the Creator." Pray tell, Dr. Gish, in the light of your last sentence, what then is "scientific" creationism?

The Fact of Evolution

Our confidence that evolution occurred centers upon three general argu- 13
ments. First, we have abundant, direct, observational evidence of evolution in action, from both the field and the laboratory. It ranges from countless experiments on change in nearly everything about fruit flies subjected to artificial selection in the laboratory to the famous British moths that turned black when industrial soot darkened the trees upon which they rest. (The moths gain protection from sharp-sighted bird predators by blending into the background.) Creationists do not deny these observations; how could they? Creationists have tightened their act. They now argue that God only created "basic kinds," and allowed for limited evolutionary meandering within them. Thus toy poodles and Great Danes come from the dog kind and moths can change color, but nature cannot convert a dog to a cat or a monkey to a man.

The second and third arguments for evolution—the case for major 14
changes—do not involve direct observation of evolution in action. They rest upon inference, but are no less secure for that reason. Major evolutionary change requires too much time for direct observation on the scale

of recorded human history. All historical sciences rest upon inference, and evolution is no different from geology, cosmology, or human history in this respect. In principle, we cannot observe processes that operated in the past. We must infer them from results that still survive: living and fossil organisms for evolution, documents and artifacts for human history, strata and topography for geology.

15   The second argument—that the imperfection of nature reveals evolution—strikes many people as ironic, for they feel that evolution should be most elegantly displayed in the nearly perfect adaptation expressed by some organisms—the chamber of a gull's wing, or butterflies that cannot be seen in ground litter because they mimic leaves so precisely. But perfection could be imposed by a wise creator or evolved by natural selection. Perfection covers the tracks of past history. And past history—the evidence of descent—is our mark of evolution.

16   Evolution lies exposed in the *imperfections* that record a history of descent. Why should a rat run, a bat fly, a porpoise swim, and I type this essay with structures built of the same bones unless we all inherited them from a common ancestor? An engineer, starting from scratch, could design better limbs in each case. Why should all the large native mammals of Australia be marsupials, unless they descended from a common ancestor isolated on this island continent? Marsupials are not "better," or ideally suited for Australia; many have been wiped out by placental mammals imported by man from other continents. This principle of imperfection extends to all historical sciences. When we recognize the etymology of September, October, November, and December (seventh, eighth, ninth, and tenth, from the Latin), we know that two additional items (January and February) must have been added to an original calendar of ten months.

17   The third argument is more direct: transitions are often found in the fossil record. Preserved transitions are not common—and should not be, according to our understanding of evolution (see next section)—but they are not entirely wanting, as creationists often claim. The lower jaw of reptiles contains several bones, that of mammals only one. The non-mammalian jawbones are reduced, step by step, in mammalian ancestors until they become tiny nubbins located at the back of the jaw. The "hammer" and "anvil" bones of the mammalian ear are descendants of these nubbins. How could such a transition be accomplished? the creationists ask. Surely a bone is either entirely in the jaw or in the ear. Yet paleontologists have discovered two transitional lineages or therapsids (the so-called mammal-like reptiles) with a double jaw joint—one composed of the old quadrate and articular bones (soon to become the hammer and anvil), the other of the squamosal and dentary bones (as in modern mammals). For that matter, what better transitional form could we desire than the oldest human, *Australopithecus afarensis*, with its apelike palate, its human upright stance, and a cranial capacity larger than any ape's of the same body size but a full 1,000 cubic centimeters below ours? If God made each of the half

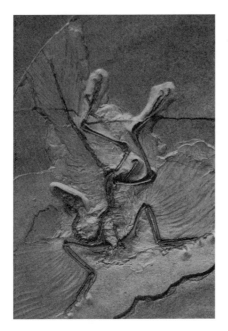

What is the significance of the downy fluff and feathers on this 130 million-year-old dinosaur skeleton? What explanation(s) would Darwin's theory reinforce? What explanation(s) would Gould's analysis address?

dozen human species discovered in ancient rocks, why did he create in an unbroken temporal sequence of progressively more modern features—increasing cranial capacity, reduced face and teeth, larger body size? Did he create to mimic evolution and test our faith thereby?

An Example of Creationist Argument

Faced with these facts of evolution and the philosophical bankruptcy of their own position, creationists rely upon distortion and innuendo to buttress their rhetorical claim. If I should sound sharp or bitter, indeed I am—for I have become a major target of these practices. [18]

I count myself among the evolutionists who argue for a jerky, or episodic, rather than a smoothly gradual, pace of change. In 1972 my colleague Niles Eldredge and I developed the theory of punctuated equilibrium. We argued that two outstanding facts of the fossil record—geologically "sudden" origin of new species and failure to change thereafter (stasis)—reflect the predictions of evolutionary theory, not the imperfections of the fossil record. In most theories, small isolated populations are the source of new species, and the process of speciation takes thousands or tens of thousands of years. This amount of time, so long when measured against our lives, is a geological microsecond. It represents much less than 1 percent of the average life span for a fossil invertebrate species—more than 10 million years. Large, widespread, and well-established species, on the other hand, [19] are not expected to change very much. We believe that the inertia of large populations explains the stasis of most fossil species over millions of years.

20   We proposed the theory of punctuated equilibrium largely to provide a different explanation for pervasive trends in the fossil record. Trends, we argued, cannot be attributed to gradual transformation within lineages, but must arise from the differential success of certain kinds of species. A trend, we argued, is more like climbing a flight of stairs (punctuations and stasis) than rolling up an inclined plane.

21   Since we proposed punctuated equilibria to explain trends, it is infuriating to be quoted again and again by creationists—whether through design or stupidity, I do not know—as admitting that the fossil record includes no transitional forms. Transitional forms are generally lacking at the species level, but are abundant between larger groups. The evolution from reptiles to mammals, as mentioned earlier, is well documented. Yet a pamphlet entitled "Harvard Scientists Agree Evolution Is a Hoax" states: "The facts of punctuated equilibrium which Gould and Eldredge . . . are forcing Darwinists to swallow fit the picture that Bryan insisted on, and which God has revealed to us in the Bible."

22   Continuing the distortion, several creationists have equated the theory of punctuated equilibrium with a caricature of the beliefs of Richard Goldschmidt, a great early geneticist. Goldschmidt argued, in a famous book published in 1940, that new groups can arise all at once through major mutations. He referred to these suddenly transformed creatures as "hopeful monsters." (I am attracted to some aspects of the non-caricatured version, but Goldschmidt's theory still has nothing to do with punctuated equilibrium.) Creationist Luther Sunderland talks of the "punctuated equilibrium hopeful monster theory" and tells his hopeful readers that "it amounts to tacit admission that anti-evolutionists are correct in asserting there is no fossil evidence supporting the theory that all life is connected to a common ancestor." Duane Gish writes, "According to Goldschmidt, and now apparently according to Gould, a reptile laid an egg from which the first bird, feathers and all, was produced." Any evolutionist who believed such nonsense would rightly be laughed off the intellectual stage; yet the only theory that could ever envision such a scenario for the evolution of birds is creationism—God acts in the egg.

Conclusion

23   I am both angry at and amused by the creationists; but mostly I am deeply sad. Sad for many reasons. Sad because so many people who respond to creationist appeals are troubled for the right reason, but venting their anger at the wrong target. It is true that scientists have often been dogmatic and elitist. It is true that we have often allowed the white-coated, advertising image to represent us—"Scientists say that Brand X cures bunions

ten times faster than . . ." We have not fought it adequately because we derive benefits from appearing as a new priesthood. It is also true that faceless bureaucratic state power intrudes more and more into our lives and removes choices that should belong to individuals and communities. I can understand that requiring that evolution be taught in schools might be seen as one more insult on all these grounds. But the culprit is not, and cannot be, evolution or any other fact of the natural world. Identify and fight your legitimate enemies by all means, but we are not among them.

I am sad because the practical result of this brouhaha will not be expanded coverage to include creationism (that would also make me sad), but the reduction or excision of evolution from high school curricula. Evolution is one of the half dozen "great ideas" developed by science. It speaks to the profound issues of genealogy that fascinate all of us—the "roots" phenomenon writ large. Where did we come from? Where did life arise? How did it develop? How are organisms related? It forces us to think, ponder, and wonder. Shall we deprive millions of this knowledge and once again teach biology as a set of dull and unconnected facts, without the thread that weaves diverse material into a supple unity?   24

But most of all I am saddened by a trend I am just beginning to discern among my colleagues. I sense that some now wish to mute the healthy debate about theory that has brought new life to evolutionary biology. It provides grist for creationist mills, they say, even if only by distortion. Perhaps we should lie low and rally round the flag of strict Darwinism, at least for the moment—a kind of old-time religion on our part.   25

But we should borrow another metaphor and recognize that we too have to tread a straight and narrow path, surrounded by roads to perdition. For if we ever begin to suppress our search to understand nature, to quench our own intellectual excitement in a misguided effort to present a united front where it does not and should not exist, then we are truly lost.   26

Content

1. Identify Gould's two different definitions of "theory," one scientific, the other vernacular (common, everyday) (¶s 3–4, and elsewhere). Define what he means by a "fact" (¶s 5–7). Using these definitions, explain what he means by "Well, evolution *is* a theory. It is also a fact." What differentiation does Gould make between evolution as a fact and evolution as a theory (¶s 5–7 and throughout)?

2. What does Gould mean by insisting that any set of scientific ideas must be able to be falsified? Why does he identify creationism as an "unbeatable system" that cannot be falsified?

3. "Scientists regard debates on fundamental issues of theory as a sign of intellectual health and a source of excitement," says Gould (¶ 9). Why is this so? Why is evolutionary theory so much fun, in Gould's view? Why would creationist theories stifle debate and take the "fun" out of doing science (¶s 9–12)?

Strategies/Structures/Language

4. Using Gould's definitions, derive Gould's rules for scientific debate. Does he follow his own rules in this essay?

5. Gould says, "The rise of creationism is politics, pure and simple" (¶ 2). What does he mean by this? How does politics influence the language we use?

6. How does the language we use influence our beliefs about a particular subject? In reference to this essay, you could talk about *science* and *creationism,* but there are many other possibilities for discussion.

7. Gould says, "I am both angry at and amused by the creationists; but mostly I am deeply sad" (¶ 23). Does the language Gould uses in addressing the ideas of his opponents (both creationists and fellow strict Darwinist geologists who dispute his theories and would suppress them for different reasons [¶s 23–26]) reflect any or all of these attitudes? Does he treat his opponents with courtesy? With respect?

For Writing

8. Science, like any other body of knowledge, is ever-changing. Facts can be reassessed, reinterpreted; intellectual constructs can be reconfigured—suppose someone redrew the constellations to represent great works of art instead of mythological stories. New contexts can be provided to enable new ways to understand familiar information. Select a definition of a term central to medicine, psychology, sociology, or an empirically oriented science, that has undergone major changes (*race, homosexual, family,* are among the possible terms). Trace the history of this definition to highlight the changes in the word's meaning, and explore some of the implications of the old and new definitions.

9. With a partner, preferably one with whom you disagree on a salient issue, construct a set of rules for appropriate treatment of one's opponents in an argument. (You could use your answers to Language question 7 as a point of departure.) Under what, if any, circumstances are irony, sarcasm, invective, humor suitable in referring to ideas or people with whom you disagree? You may use Gould's essay as a model.

 For comprehension, writing, and research activities and resources, please visit the companion website at <college.hmco.com/english>.

BILL McKIBBEN

After graduating from Harvard in 1982, McKibben (born 1960) started at the top, becoming a staff writer, and later an editor, for *The NewYorker.* Five years later he turned to writing full time, married, moved to upstate New York, and had a child. His books, such as *The End of Nature* (1989); *Hope, Human and Wild: True Stories of Living Lightly on the Earth* (1995); and *Maybe One: A Case for Smaller Families* (1998), concentrate on "the effects of rampant consumerism on the future of the global ecosystem." All of his books, says commentator Michael Coffey, "pursue the same theme . . . what do we consume, why do we consume it, and what are the consequences?" Answering his own question, McKibben replies, "What I've learned so far is that what is sound and elegant and civilized and respectful of community is also environmentally benign."

   Enough: Staying Human in an Engineered Age (2003) is about the moral ramifications of biological engineering—the topic of "Designer Genes," as well. This essay, first published in *Orion* in 2003, was reprinted in the book *The Best American Spiritual Writing* in 2004. Here McKibben offers a chilling, clearheaded analysis of what could happen if aspiring (and wealthy) parents resort to genetic engineering to create new and ever-newer models of superior children, a "biological arms race." Each new model might seem better than its predecessor in intelligence, say, or appearance or strength, and every one might appear superior to the homegrown babies who receive their DNA naturally. Be careful what you wish for, warns McKibben. "'Suppose parents could add thirty points to their child's IQ? Wouldn't you want to do it?' . . . Deciding not to soup them up . . . well, it could come to seem like child abuse" (¶ 17).

Designer Genes

I grew up in a household where we were very suspicious of dented cans. Dented cans were, according to my mother, a well-established gateway to botulism, and botulism was a bad thing, worse than swimming immediately after lunch. It was one of those bad things measured in extinctions, as in "three tablespoons of botulism toxin could theoretically kill every human on Earth." Or something like that.

   So I refused to believe the early reports, a few years back, that socialites had begun injecting dilute strains of the toxin into their brows in an effort to temporarily remove the vertical furrow that appears between one's eyes as one ages. It sounded like a Monty Python routine, some clinic where they daubed your soles with plague germs to combat athlete's foot. But I was wrong to doubt. As the world now knows, Botox has become, in a few short years, a staple weapon in the cosmetic arsenal—so prevalent that, in the words of one writer, "it is now rare in certain social enclaves to see a woman over the age of thirty-five with the ability to look angry." With their facial muscles essentially paralyzed, actresses are having trouble acting; since the treatment requires periodic booster shots, doctors "warn that you could marry a woman (or a man) with a flawlessly even face and wind up with someone who four months later looks like a Shar-Pei." But never mind—now you can get Botoxed in strip mall storefronts and at cocktail parties.

   People, in other words, will do fairly far out things for less than pressing causes. And more so all the time: public approval of "aesthetic surgery" has grown 50 percent in the United States in the last decade. But why stop there? Once you accept the idea that our bodies are essentially plastic and that it's okay to manipulate that plastic, there's no reason to think that consumers would balk because "genes" were involved instead of, say, "toxins." Especially since genetic engineering would not promote your own vanity, but instead be sold as a boon to your child.

4   The vision of genetic engineers is to do to humans what we have already done to salmon and wheat, pine trees and tomatoes. That is, to make them *better* in some way; to delete, modify, or add genes in developing embryos so that the cells of the resulting person will produce proteins that make them taller and more muscular, or smarter and less aggressive, maybe handsome and possibly straight. Even happy. As early as 1993, a March of Dimes poll found that 43 percent of Americans would engage in genetic engineering "simply to enhance their children's looks or intelligence."

5   Ethical guidelines promulgated by the scientific oversight boards so far prohibit actual attempts at human genetic engineering, but researchers have walked right to the line, maybe even stuck their toes a trifle over. In the spring of 2001, for instance, a fertility clinic in New Jersey impregnated fifteen women with embryos fashioned from their own eggs, their partner's sperm, and a small portion of an egg donated by a second woman. The procedure was designed to work around defects in the would-be mother's egg—but in at least two of the cases, tests showed the resulting babies carried genetic material from all three "parents."

6   And so the genetic modification of humans is not only possible, it's coming fast; a mix of technical progress and shifting mood means it could easily happen in the next few years. Consider what happened with plants. A decade ago, university research farms were growing small plots of genetically modified grain and vegetables. Sometimes activists who didn't like what they were doing would come and rip the plants up, one by one. Then, all of a sudden in the mid-1990s, before anyone had paid any real attention, farmers had planted half the corn and soybean fields in America with transgenic seed.

7   Every time you turn your back this technology creeps a little closer. Gallops, actually, growing and spreading as fast as the internet. One moment you've sort of heard of it; the next moment it's everywhere. But we haven't done it yet. For the moment we remain, if barely, a fully human species. And so we have time yet to consider, to decide, to act. This is arguably the biggest decision humans will ever make.

8   Right up until this decade, the genes that humans carried in their bodies were exclusively the result of chance—of how the genes of the sperm and the egg, the father and the mother, combined. The only way you could intervene in the process was by choosing who you would mate with—and that was as much wishful thinking as anything else, as generation upon generation of surprised parents have discovered.

But that is changing. We now know two different methods to change human genes. The first, and less controversial, is called somatic gene therapy. Somatic gene therapy begins with an existing individual—someone with, say, cystic fibrosis. Researchers try to deliver new, modified genes to some of her cells, usually by putting the genes aboard viruses they inject into the patient, hoping that the viruses will infect the cells and thereby transmit the genes. Somatic gene therapy is, in other words, much like medicine. You take an existing patient with an existing condition, and you in essence try and convince her cells to manufacture the medicine she needs. 9

Germline genetic engineering, on the other hand, is something very novel indeed. "Germ" here refers not to microbes, but to the egg and sperm cells, the germ cells of the human being. Scientists intent on genetic engineering would probably start with a fertilized embryo a week or so old. They would tease apart the cells of that embryo, and then, selecting one, they would add to, delete, or modify some of its genes. They could also insert artificial chromosomes containing predesigned genes. They would then take the cell, place it inside an egg whose nucleus had been removed, and implant the resulting new embryo inside a woman. The embryo would, if all went according to plan, grow into a genetically engineered child. His genes would be pushing out proteins to meet the particular choices made by his parents and by the companies and clinicians they were buying the genes from. Instead of coming solely from the combination of his parents, and thus the combination of their parents, and so on back through time, those genes could come from any other person, or any other plant or animal, or out of the thin blue sky. And once implanted, they will pass to his children and on into time. 10

But all this work will require one large change in our current way of doing business. Instead of making babies by making love, we will have to move conception to the laboratory. You need to have the embryo out there where you can work on it—to make the necessary copies, try to add or delete genes, and then implant the one that seems likely to turn out best. Gregory Stock, a researcher at the University of California and an apostle of the new genetic technologies, says that "the union of egg and sperm from two individuals . . . would be too unpredictable with intercourse." And once you've got the embryo out on the lab bench, gravity disappears altogether. "Ultimately, says Michael West, CEO of Advanced Cell Technology, the firm furthest out on the cutting edge of these technologies, "the dream of biologists is to have the sequence of DNA, the programming code of life, and to be able to edit it the way you can a document on a word processor." 11

Does it sound far-fetched? We began doing it with animals (mice) in 1978, and we've managed the trick with most of the obvious mammals, except one. Some of the first germline interventions might be semi-medical. You might, say some advocates, start by improving "visual and auditory acuity," first to eliminate nearsightedness or prevent deafness, then to "improve artistic potential." But why stop there? "If something 12 has evolved elsewhere, then it is possible for us to determine its genetic basis and transfer it into the human genome," says Princeton geneticist Lee Silver—just as we have stuck flounder genes into strawberries to keep them from freezing, and jellyfish genes into rabbits and monkeys to make them glow in the dark.

13   But would we actually do this? Is there any real need to raise these questions as more than curiosities, or will the schemes simply fade away on their own, ignored by the parents who are their necessary consumers?

14   Anyone who has entered a baby supply store in the last few years knows that even the soberest parents can be counted on to spend virtually unlimited sums in pursuit of successful offspring. What if the "Baby Einstein" video series, which immerses "learning-enabled" babies in English, Spanish, Japanese, Hebrew, German, Russian, and French, could be bolstered with a little gene tweaking to improve memory? What if the Wombsongs prenatal music system, piping in Brahms to your waiting fetus, could be supplemented with an auditory upgrade? One sociologist told the *New York Times* we'd crossed the line from parenting to "product development," and even if that remark is truer in Manhattan than elsewhere, it's not hard to imagine what such attitudes will mean across the affluent world.

15   Here's one small example. In the 1980s, two drug companies were awarded patents to market human growth hormone to the few thousand American children suffering from dwarfism. The PDA thought the market would be very small, so HGH was given "orphan drug status," a series of special market advantages designed to reward the manufacturers for taking on such an unattractive business. But within a few years, HGH had become one of the largest selling drugs in the country, with half a billion dollars in sales. This was not because there'd been a sharp increase in the number of dwarves, but because there'd been a sharp increase in the number of parents who wanted to make their slightly short children taller. Before long the drug companies were arguing that the children in the bottom 5 percent of their normal height range were in fact in need of three to five shots a week of HGH. Take eleven-year-old Marco Oriti. At four foot one, he was about four inches shorter than average, and projected to eventually top out at five foot four. This was enough to convince his parents to start on a six-day-a-week HGH regimen, which will cost them $150,000 over the next four years. "You want to give your child the edge no matter what," said his mother.

16   A few of the would-be parents out on the current cutting edge of the reproduction revolution—those who need to obtain sperm or eggs for in vitro fertilization—exhibit similar zeal. Ads started appearing in Ivy League college newspapers a few years ago: couples were willing to pay $50,000 for an egg, provided the donor was at least five feet, ten inches tall, white, and had scored 1400 on her SATs. There is, in other words, a market just waiting for the first clinic with a catalogue of germline modifications, a market that two California artists proved when they opened a small boutique, Gene Genies Worldwide, in a trendy part of Pasadena. Tran Kim-Trang and

Karl Mihail wanted to get people thinking more deeply about these emerging technologies, so they outfitted their store with petri dishes and models of the double helix and printed up brochures highlighting traits with genetic links: creativity, extroversion, thrill-seeking criminality. When they opened the doors, they found people ready to shell out for designer families (one man insisted he wanted the survival ability of a cockroach). The "store" was meant to be ironic, but the irony was lost on a culture so deeply consumeristic that this land of manipulation seems like the obvious next step. "Generally, people refused to believe this store was an art project," says Tran. And why not? The next store in the mall could easily have been a Botox salon.

But say you're not ready. Say you're perfectly happy with the prospect of a child who shares the unmodified genes of you and your partner. Say you think that manipulating the DNA of your child might be dangerous, or presumptuous, or icky? How long will you be able to hold that line if the procedure begins to spread among your neighbors? Maybe not so long as you think. If germline manipulation actually does begin, it seems likely to set off a kind of biological arms race. "Suppose parents could add thirty points to their child's IQ?" asks MIT economist Lester Thurow. "Wouldn't you want to do it? And if you don't, your child will be the stupidest in the neighborhood." That's precisely what it might feel like to be the parent facing the choice. Individual competition more or less defines the society we've built, and in that context love can almost be defined as giving your kids what they need to make their way in the world. Deciding not to soup them up . . . well, it could come to seem like child abuse. 17

Of course, the problem about arms races is that you never really get anywhere. If everyone's adding thirty IQ points, then having an IQ of one hundred fifty won't get you any closer to Stanford than you were at the outset. The very first athlete engineered to use twice as much oxygen as the next guy will be unbeatable in the Tour de France—but in no time he'll merely be the new standard. You'll have to do what he did to be in the race, but your upgrades won't put you ahead, merely back on a level playing field. You might be able to argue that society as a whole was helped, because there was more total brainpower at work, but your kid won't be any closer to the top of the pack. All you'll be able to do is guarantee she won't be left hopelessly far behind. 18

In fact, the arms race problem has an extra ironic twist when it comes to genetic manipulation. The United States and the Soviet Union could, and did, keep adding new weapons to their arsenals over the decades. But with germline manipulation, you get only one shot; the extra chromosome you stick in your kid when he's born is the one he carries throughout his life. So let's say baby Sophie has a state-of-the-art gene job: her parents paid for the proteins discovered by, say, 2005 that on average yield ten extra IQ points. By the time Sophie is five, though, scientists will doubtless have discovered ten more genes linked to intelligence. Now anyone with 19 a platinum card can get twenty IQ points, not to mention a memory boost and a permanent wrinkle-free brow. So by the time Sophie is twenty-five and in the job market, she's already more or less obsolete—the kids coming out of college plainly just have better hardware.

20   "For all his billions, Bill Gates could not have purchased a single genetic enhancement for his son Rory John," writes Gregory Stock at the University of California. "And you can bet that any enhancements a billion dollars can buy Rory's child in 2030 will seem crude alongside those available for modest sums in 2060." It's not, he adds, "so different from upgraded software. You'll want the new release."

21   The vision of one's child as a nearly useless copy of Windows 95 should make parents fight like hell to make sure we never get started down this path. But the vision gets lost easily in the gushing excitement about "improving" the opportunities for our kids.

22 Beginning the hour my daughter came home from the hospital, I spent part of every day with her in the woods out back, showing her trees and ferns and chipmunks and frogs. One of her very first words was "birch," and you couldn't have asked for a prouder papa. She got her middle name from the mountain we see out the window; for her fifth birthday she got her own child-sized canoe; her school wardrobe may not be relentlessly up-to-date, but she's never lacked for hiking boots. As I write these words, she's spending her first summer at sleepaway camp, one we chose because the kids sleep in tents and spend days in the mountains. All of which is to say that I have done everything in my power to try to mold her into a lover of the natural world. That is where my deepest satisfactions lie, and I want the same for her. It seems benign enough, but it has its drawbacks; it means less time and money and energy for trips to the city and music lessons and so forth. As time goes on and she develops stronger opinions of her own, I yield more and more, but I keep trying to stack the deck, to nudge her in the direction that's meant something to me. On a Saturday morning, when the question comes up of what to do, the very first words out of my mouth always involve yet another hike. I can't help myself.

23   In other words, we already "engineer" our offspring in some sense of the word: we do our best, and often our worst, to steer them in particular directions. And our worst can be pretty bad. We all know people whose lives were blighted trying to meet the expectations of their parents. We've all seen the crazed devotion to getting kids into the right schools, the right professions, the right income brackets. Parents try to pass down their prejudices, their politics, their attitude toward the world ("we've got to toughen that kid up—he's going to get walked all over"). There are fathers who start teaching the curveball at the age of four, and sons made to feel worthless if they don't make the Little League traveling team. People move house so that their kids can grow up with the right band of schoolmates. They threaten to disown them for marrying African Americans, or for not

Twins, particularly identical twins, are special, as Jenny Spinner reminds us in "Together in the Old Square Print, 1976" (333–34) and in "In Search of Our Past" (374–79), capable of having a unique relationship, and intimate understanding not shared with others who lack this common genetic heritage. Explain some of the advantages—and possible disadvantages—of such a relationship. If such twins were conceived as the result of in-vitro fertilization or another method of artificial reproduction, does the method of conception affect your answer? What differences— ethical and relational—exist between natural-born twins and human clones? Now, look again at this picture, very closely. What do the twins resemble? If you sense a resemblance to animals, you are "reading" this photo accurately, for it is composed of manipulated animal images. Does this knowledge affect your answers to any of the above questions? What statement does the manipulated photo make about the subject, which is no longer twins, but cloning?

marrying African Americans. No dictator anywhere has ever tried to rule his subjects with as much attention to detail as the average modern parent.

Why not take this just one small step further? Why not engineer children to up the odds that all that nudging will stick? In the words of Lee Silver, a Princeton geneticist, "Why not seize this power? Why not control what has been left to chance in the past? Indeed, we control all other aspects of our children's lives and identities through powerful social and environmental influences. . . . On what basis can we reject positive genetic influences on a person's essence when we accept the rights of parents to benefit their children in every other way?" If you can buy your kid three years at Deerfield, four at Harvard, and three more at Harvard Law, why shouldn't you be able to turbocharge his IQ a bit?

25   But most likely the answer has already occurred to you as well. Because you know plenty of people who managed to rebel successfully against whatever agenda their parents laid out for them, or who took that agenda and bent it to fit their own particular personality. In our society that's often what growing up is all about—the sometimes excruciatingly difficult, frequently liberating break with the expectations of your parents. The decision to join the Peace Corps (or, the decision to leave the commune where you grew up and go to business school). The discovery that you were happiest davening in an Orthodox shul three hours a day, much to the consternation of your good suburban parents who almost always made it to Yom Kippur services; the decision that, much as you respected the Southern Baptist piety of your parents, the Bible won't be your watchword.

26   Without the grounding offered by tradition, the search for the "authentic you" can be hard; our generations contain the first people who routinely shop religions, for instance. But the sometimes poignant difficulty of finding yourself merely underscores how essential it is. Silver says the costs of germline engineering and a college education might be roughly comparable; in both cases, he goes on, the point is to "increase the chances the child will become wiser in some way, and better able to achieve success and happiness." But that's half the story, at best. College is where you go to be exposed to a thousand new influences, ideas that should be able to take you in almost any direction. It's where you go to get out from under your parents' thumb, to find out that you actually don't have to go to law school if you don't want to. As often as not, the harder parents try to wrench their kids in one direction, the harder those kids eventually fight to determine their own destiny. I am as prepared as I can be for the possibility—the probability—that Sophie will decide she wants to live her life in the concrete heart of Manhattan. It's her life (and perhaps her kids will have a secret desire to come wander in the woods with me).

27   We try to shape the lives of our kids—to "improve" their lives, as we would measure improvement—but our gravity is usually weak enough that kids can break out of it if and when they need to. (When it isn't, when parents manage to bend their children to the point of breaking, we think of them as monstrous.) "Many of the most creative and valuable human lives are the result of particularly difficult struggles" against expectation and influence, writes the legal scholar Martha Nussbaum.

28   That's not how a genetic engineer thinks of his product. He works to ensure absolute success. Last spring an Israeli researcher announced that he had managed to produce a featherless chicken. This constituted an improvement, to his mind, because "it will be cheaper to produce since its lack of feathers means there is no need to pluck it before it hits the shelves." Also, poultry farmers would no longer have to ventilate their vast barns to keep their birds from overheating. "Feathers are a waste," the scientist explained. "The chickens are using feed to produce something

that has to be dumped, and the farmers have to waste electricity to overcome that fact." Now, that engineer was not trying to influence his chickens to shed their feathers because they'd be happier and the farmer would be happier and everyone would be happier. He was inserting a gene that created a protein that made good and certain they would not be producing feathers. Just substitute, say, an even temperament for feathers, and you'll know what the human engineers envision.

"With reprogenetics," writes Lee Silver, "parents can gain *complete control* [emphasis mine] over their destiny, with the ability to guide and enhance the characteristics of their children, and their children's children as well." Such parents would not be calling their children on the phone at annoying frequent intervals to suggest that it's time to get a real job; instead, just like the chicken guy, they would be inserting genes that produced proteins that would make their child behave in certain ways throughout his life. You cannot rebel against the production of that protein. Perhaps you can still do everything in your power to defeat the wishes of your parents, but that protein will nonetheless be pumped out relentlessly into your system, defining who you are. You won't grow feathers, no matter how much you want them. And maybe they can engineer your mood enough that your lack of plumage won't even cross your mind.   29

Such children will, in effect, be assigned a goal by their programmers: "intelligence," "even temper," "athleticism." (As with chickens, the market will doubtless lean in the direction of efficiency. It may be hard to find genes for, say, dreaminess.) Now two possibilities arise. Perhaps the programming doesn't work very well, and your lad spells poorly, or turns moody, or can't hit the inside fastball. In the present world, you just tell yourself that that's who he is. But in the coming world, he'll be, in essence, a defective product. Do you still accept *him* unconditionally? Why? If your new Jetta got thirty miles to the gallon instead of the forty it was designed to get, you'd take it back. You'd call it a lemon. If necessary, you'd sue.   30

Or what if the engineering worked pretty well, but you decided, too late, that you'd picked the wrong package, hadn't gotten the best features? Would you feel buyer's remorse if the kid next door had a better ear, a stronger arm?   31

Say the gene work went a little awry and left you with a kid who had some serious problems; what kind of guilt would that leave you with? Remember, this is not a child created by the random interaction of your genes with those of your partner, this is a child created with specific intent. Does *Consumer Reports* start rating the various biotech offerings?   32

What if you had a second child five years after the first, and by that time the upgrades were undeniably improved: how would you feel about the first kid? How would he feel about his new brother, the latest model?   33

The other outcome—that the genetic engineering works just as you had hoped—seems at least as bad. Now your child is a product. You can take precisely as much pride in her achievements as you take in the   34 achievements of your dishwashing detergent. It was designed to produce streak-free glassware, and she was designed to be sweet-tempered, social, and smart. And what can she take pride in? Her good grades? She may have worked hard, but she'll always know that she was spec'ed for good grades. Her kindness to others? Well, yes, it's good to be kind—but perhaps it's not much of an accomplishment once the various genes with some link to sociability have been catalogued and manipulated. I have no doubt that these qualms would be one of the powerful psychological afflictions of the future—at least until someone figures out a fix that keeps the next generations from having such bad thoughts.

35   Britain's chief rabbi, Jonathan Sacks, was asked a few years ago about the announcement that Italian doctors were trying to clone humans. "If there is a mystery at the heart of human condition, it is otherness: the otherness of man and woman, parent and child. It is the space we make for otherness that makes love something other than narcissism." I remember so well the feeling of walking into the maternity ward with Sue, and walking out with Sue and Sophie: where there had been two there were now, somehow, three, each of us our own person, but now commanded to make a family, a place where we all could thrive. She was so mysterious, that Sophie, and in many ways she still is. There are times when, like every parent, I see myself reflected in her, and times when I wonder if she's even related. She's ours to nurture and protect, but she is who *she is*. That's the mystery and the glory of any child.

36   Mystery, however, is not one of the words that thrills engineers. They try to deliver solid bridges, unyielding dams, reliable cars. We wouldn't want it any other way. The only question is if their product line should be expanded to include children.

37 Right now both the genes, and the limits that they set on us, connect us with every human that came before. Human beings can look at rock art carved into African cliffs and French caves thirty thousand years ago and feel an electric, immediate kinship. We've gone from digging sticks to combines, and from drum circles to symphony orchestras (and back again to drum circles), but we still hear in the same range and see in the same spectrum, still produce adrenaline and dopamine in the same ways, still think in many of the same patterns. We are, by and large, the same people, more closely genetically related to one another than we may be to our engineered grandchildren.

38   These new technologies show us that human meaning dangles by a far thinner thread than we had thought. If germline genetic engineering ever starts, it will accelerate endlessly and unstoppably into the future, as individuals make the calculation that they have no choice but to equip their kids for the world that's being made. The first child whose genes come in part from some corporate lab, the first child who has been "enhanced" from

what came before—that's the first child who will glance back over his shoulder and see a gap between himself and human history.

These would be mere consumer decisions—but that also means that they would benefit the rich far more than the poor. They would take the gap in power, wealth, and education that currently divides both our society and the world at large, and write that division into our very biology. A sixth of the American population lacks health insurance of any kind—they can't afford to go to the doctor for a *check-up*. And much of the rest of the world is far worse off. If we can't afford the fifty cents per person it would take to buy bed nets to protect most of Africa from malaria, it is unlikely we will extend to anyone but the top tax bracket these latest forms of genetic technology. The injustice is so obvious that even the strongest proponents of genetic engineering make little attempt to deny it. "Anyone who accepts the right of affluent parents to provide their children with an expensive private school education cannot use 'unfairness' as a reason for rejecting the use of reprogenetic technologies," says Lee Silver.

These new technologies, however, are not yet inevitable. Unlike global warming, this genie is not yet out of the bottle. But if germline genetic engineering is going to be stopped, it will have to happen now, before it's quite begun. It will have to be a political choice, that is—one we make not as parents but as citizens, not as individuals but as a whole, thinking not only about our own offspring but about everyone.

So far the discussion has been confined to a few scientists, a few philosophers, a few ideologues. It needs to spread widely, and quickly, and loudly. The stakes are absurdly high, nothing less than the meaning of being human. And given the seductions that we've seen—the intuitively and culturally delicious prospect of a *better* child—the arguments against must be not only powerful but also deep. They'll need to resonate on the same intuitive and cultural level. We'll need to feel in our gut the reasons why, this time, we should tell Prometheus thanks, but no thanks.

Content

1. This essay is an excellent example of inductive reasoning that makes its major points in the conclusion (¶s 40–41), after presenting an escalating series of examples. What's the thesis? Is it ever explicitly stated? Explain, with examples, how it can be inferred from virtually every paragraph.

2. How close are humans to achieving "germline genetic engineering" that would enable scientists, or physicians, to construct DNA sequences, "the programming code of life," and "to be able to edit [them] the way you can a document on a word processor" (¶ 11)?

3. What does McKibben speculate the consequences might be of a "biological arms race" devoted to continually enhancing infants' IQ, physical strength, beauty, or other desirable features (¶s 17–20)? What evidence does he offer that people are already

receptive to such genetic enhancements (consider, for instance, the current market for egg donors with specific characteristics of height, color, and SAT scores [¶ 16])?

4. Why is genetic engineering inherently unfair, and why would attempts to level the playing field at the high end inevitably have negative social consequences for the poor (¶s 39–41)?

Strategies/Structures/Language

5. Why does McKibben begin his essay with botulism toxin ("three tablespoons [of which] could theoretically kill every human on Earth") and quickly segue to Botox—a dilute strain of the same toxin and a "staple weapon in the cosmetic arsenal" (¶s 1–2)? What language in these first two paragraphs lets readers know where he stands on the issue?

6. Why does McKibben compare the consequences of germline genetic engineering to upgrading computer software: "The vision of one's child as a nearly useless copy of Windows 95 should make parents fight like hell to make sure we never get started down this path" (¶ 21)? Does McKibben's example of a genetically engineered "featherless chicken" (¶ 28) reinforce his argument? Explain.

For Writing

7. With a partner—preferably one who disagrees with you—explore the question, "On what basis can we reject positive genetic influences on a person's essence when we accept the rights of parents to benefit their children in every other way" (¶ 24)?

8. "'Many of the most creative and valuable human lives are the results of particularly difficult struggles' against expectation and influence," says McKibben, quoting Nussbaum. Yet genetic engineers work "to ensure absolute success" (¶s 27–28). "You cannot rebel against the production of that protein . . . [which] will nonetheless be pumped out relentlessly into your system, defining who you are"— no matter what you might want to be (¶ 29). Where do you stand on issues of free will versus determinism in relation either to your own maturation and development of character and intellect or to that of your actual or prospective children?

 For comprehension, writing, and research activities and resources, please visit the companion website at <college.hmco.com/english>.

KATE LOOMIS

Loomis (born 1986) was raised in Colchester, Connecticut, but spent nearly every summer of her childhood along the shoreline of Long Island Sound. She attended Boston University for her first year and then transferred to the University of Connecticut. She expects to graduate in 2007 with a double major in English and journalism. She aims to travel the world in search of culture, adventure, and a congenial climate.

"Spiderwebs" was written about a neighborhood friend from the Sound who recently enlisted in the Navy. Loomis uses the friend's farewell as a springboard from which to voice her opinions on the occupation of Iraq and the cyclical nature of violence in general. The title refers to Andrew's childhood nickname, Spider, though careful readers will find a spiderweb in the essay, strategically and portentously placed.

❄ *Spiderwebs*

"I can't guarantee you anything," he says, throwing his words toward the water, "but I promise I won't break your heart, kid." *It's already broken.*   1

He is tightening his left calf in gauche contractions as he says this. His muscles jut and flex like they are punching through his skin and I think: the molecules between his knees and ankles must be spastic. I imagine them colliding and exploding right there, two feet, 24 inches away from my sneaker, an imperceptible battlefield. He hates his ankles, he said once.   2

"I'm going to make it fine out there."   3

Right now, the sun is flirting with the horizon—a violent incision slicing apart the sea and the sky. It is bleeding purple and red into the ocean, and she mirrors the hues appreciatively like the tinsel freckles in an eye. She wants in on the love affair.   4

Right now, everything is absurdly symbolic.   5

And so I ask him if this will make him happy, even if he isn't sure, even if he can't be sure. I tell him that I only want him to be happy.   6

Andrew is a rock. He is angular, lean, regal. He is shirtless, now, at sunset, and I study the precision of his spine as it runs down the valley of his back, a seamless fault line. He is shifting. He fixes his posterior directly perpendicular to the bench scaffold (we call this impeccable posture)—his body and the base form the perfect T. T for terrorized. T for *terrified.*   7

George Bush is telling me not to be terrified. We are fighting terror.   8

"So for the four years of active duty, can you get out at any time?" and I already know the answer.   9

"No. I'm tied-in." T for tied-in.   10

He stands up now, presses his granite figure against the dusk. He is carved, chiseled, but not in a movie-star sort of way. (He is far too old-fashioned for that.) No, he has been bronzed and eternalized, erected into the skyline like a warrior statue. His chin scrapes against the twilight, pushing toward the ocean and he is motionless, except for the slightest vein vacillating up and down, up and down above his jawbone.   11

Right now, I am that vein.   12

I tell him that he's fearless and he says he's in good company ("you're cool, too," he'll clarify). But I'm not *fearless.* I am afraid of earthworms and   13 fire and Bloody Mary, so afraid that I can't even face my mirrors at night, that I can't even be left alone in a dimly lit bathroom. I can't even write about it.

14   Ten years ago, Andrew—he was called Spider then—and I would have been dodging through the neighborhood backyards at this hour. I was eight, he was eleven and we exhausted every summer night with furious rounds of hide-and-go-seek. His favorite hideout was the Kenney's low-level rooftop. I see him now, hurtling to the ground like a cannonball, detonating, seizing us—terrifying us. He likes that. I want to tell him, "I can't even recall all those August nights we stayed awake trying to escape the fall," but I can't translate such ambivalence for him right now because a) he's concentrating on the outline of Long Island, and b) nothing I say ever makes sense.

15   Tonight, we are map-less explorers.

16   In later years, when I tell him he owes me another round (for "old time's sake," the saying goes) he says that I better watch out: he'll use marine tactics, and he's ruthless.

17   "You do things that I would never do," he continues. "Have you ever been on a roller coaster?"

18   "You've never been on a roller coaster?!"

19   *Fuck, no! I'll never go on one of those things.*

20   And I say, "Someday, you'll go on one with me," but I know that he won't. He doesn't like rides. We go to carnivals, and Andrew watches by the makeshift fence as we ride the swings and the Ferris wheel. He plays the basketball games and wins us teddy bears and I leave mine in the window of our cottage attic. Andrew says he can see it sometimes when he's out with the dog in his neighboring backyard. I say that I put it there for a reason.

21   George Bush has ensured me that we are waging "war to save civilization itself," but *right now,* my empire is crumbling.

22   I lie down along the bench, propel and extend my body against its wooden planks. I think: in 1943, the Western Union boy must have felt like a leper, distributing devastation in 12-inch envelopes. I'd bet his heart physically broke, just wilted, after so many fatal deliveries. And the scribes of those telegrams, carpal-tunneled to their graves, sipped rubbing alcohol from wine glasses and wept—white-knuckled to their typewriters, waiting, waiting for the end of the world.

23   Who could ever love the Grim Reaper?

24   "Well, I like how you are."

25   "Don't you worry. I'll do what I want," and he always has.

26   *But how are you sure that **this** is what you want?* I want to thrust the question down his throat and into his lower intestines with my right hand. Singe his insides with stomach acid and nail polish residue. I want him to gag on the thought of war. Vomit. Reject it.

"If a man with a bomb strapped to his chest was running into a pre-   27
school, would you shoot him to save the kids?" I read one morning, at 3
a.m., in an online journal. No, I probably wouldn't. I couldn't.

And I never could.   28

I am seven-years-old and powerless. I shrink into the gymnasium   29
corner as a classmate's father explodes through the double doors, red-faced
and massive. He barrels, shatters like a bullet; he wants to kill his daughter;
I think. At once, he seizes her by her neck—her delicate vertebrae cracking,
cracking—and he is spewing, steaming, rabid as he drives her against the
padded wall. His left hand rises, recoils like the belt in a slingshot, and fires
across her right cheekbone. Ten feet away and I can feel the heat reverberate off her four-foot frame in atomic aftershock. She whimpers, contracts.

Violence is a cycle that ends with the world ending.   30

Imagine, ten years ago, what it must have felt like to be the offspring   31
of a Hutu-Tutsi marriage in Rwanda. Families were hacked apart like
chicken breasts, ripped, destroyed, butchered. With primitive tools—yes,
bare hands even—neighbors were mutilating neighbors, literally tearing
off each other's arms and faces with their fingernails, teeth, to audiences
in the street. Parents were spearing their babies in a genocidal fury—*spewing, steaming*—have you ever hated something this much? No. I couldn't.
I never could.

"I haven't felt this good about something in a long time," Andrew   32
says, finally.

"Congratulations," because that's all I can reply. "What happens   33
next?"

"It's down to South Carolina for three months of training. . . . And   34
after boot camp, I'm a marine."

"Will I ever get to see you?"   35

"You could visit me in Korea." Not funny.   36

You have a deformed sense of humor, someone told him once and he   37
laughed because that meant he was the Hunchback of Comedians. I tell him
that's a stupid analogy, one night, on the phone, and he laughs even harder.

When he claims that he is "a bull-shitter and a liar," I say that most   38
bullshit requires intelligence.

"No, it's just more fun," he clarifies. He also claims that he wants to   39
be the ultimate under-achiever, but I know that it's only in a Salinger sense
of the term. The truth is, he's an accidental success.

"I signed up to be in the infantry." Pause. "I'll be the first line."   40

"Does that mean you'll definitely fight overseas?"   41

"If they need me, I get sent over. . . . I scored high on the test so I can   42
have almost any job that I want, from like nuclear and biological stuff to
fixing anything . . . but I chose the bottom job because I think that's where
I'll be the happiest."

"Why do you think that?"   43

44   "Cause that's what I want to do," he says plainly. "I don't want to be in an office or just sit around playing with tanks and helicopters."

45   "I couldn't see you in one of those jobs."

46   "Yah. I feel like I am making the right move."

47   He turns back to me now. Reaches for the cable bracing the adjacent telephone pole. He's climbed that pole before, once, after the family picnic. Tonight, he leans on it. He has been italicized, tilted, sloped in space (and the chorus sings: "it's all downhill from here").

48   I picture Andrew's sailboat, angled against the garage wall in a similar slant, and I remember him at fourteen—so independent, even then—ramming the boat out into the Sound with a visible passion. We were allowed to ride with him only once, one late July afternoon when the jellyfish lined the shore like soldiers. Tonight, spiders lace webs, graveyards, in between his sail and the interior of the vessel.

49   *I feel like I am making the right move.*

50   George Bush graduated college with a 2.35 GPA, one DUI, and an expunged cocaine record. He says, "I am a war president," two years too late.

51   *Right now, the leader of the free world could level humanity with his fingertips.*

52   **Move.**

53   This is my cue. Andrew steps into the crosswalk, and I trail, obediently. I almost invite him to the cemetery (because this is our escape), but the fog has perched itself at eye level, and I can hardly see his face, let alone the sidewalk. Besides, he is four, five, six steps ahead of me, and I can't reach him. I could never reach him.

54   There is a streetlight sputtering by the Duquette's front door when we hit my porch. In Andrew's house, the kitchen light burns alone. Everyone is asleep. I collapse on the couch cushions, damp with sea salt and humidity; there are pearls of sweat decorating my upper lip in delicate rows. I could count every bead if I concentrated.

55   "Do you want to sit down?"

56   Right now, I can feel every fiber in my sweatshirt.

57   "Nah. No. I should go home."

58   This is hyper-reality. But this is *happening.*

59   "Um, ok. Well, not to get all sentimental, because I'm sure that you won't but . . ."

60   "What?"

61   "Let me talk."

62   "Ok."

63   "Well, just so you know, I love you, Andrew. And I hope you find some purpose in the next few months or years or whatever. I'll be thinking about you."

64   "Thanks, kid." He cracks his knuckles uncomfortably. "I remember . . . well, it seems like a thousand years ago now. . . . I remember being at the beach . . . and how I used to have a crush on you. It's *funny,* things

change over the years, and now who knows when I will see you again. . . . It all seems so long ago."

"You'll see me again," I tell him.   65

"Semper fi. Do or die. Things change."   66

"Why do you want to leave it like this?"   67

"Like what?"   68

"Like, 'things change. Good luck. Bet we won't talk again.' "   69

"Ok. Here's reality: I probably won't see you again. I don't plan on   70
being in Connecticut much after I get stationed. I'd rather not come back
here."

And I say I'm the sort of girl that needs closure.   71

"Closure on what?"   72

"Closure on our friendship . . . on the past. . . ."   73

"Don't worry about it. Don't get all worked up or whatever."   74

He hedges the doorframe, now. He seems so big, so unbelievably big   75
and distant, rising before me, that damn streetlight burning his Roman
figure into my retinas with a 1000-watt fury.

"I say, work and believe. That's all you need," and at that, he drifts   76
loudly out my back door and quietly into his front one, as always, as on
any other summer night. His kitchen light flickers, blinks for a second,
and dies. That night, I wrestle beneath bed sheets, frantically recoiling
from every mirror reflection like it's Satan Herself, and in the morning,
Andrew is gone.

Content

1. What is the nature of the relationship of the two characters? How has it changed during the decade they've known one another, the decade when they've both grown up? Is there an imbalance of feeling between them? How can you tell?

2. How typical is this relationship of those you have known? If it were to continue, what indications does this essay provide for the directions in which it might go? Who is saying "goodbye" to whom in this narrative? For what reasons? For how long?

3. To what extent is this a love story? A war story? An antiwar story? Explain, with evidence from the narrative and from your own comparable experience. Use Tim O'Brien's directions on "How to Tell a True War Story" (543–50) in your analysis, if these will help.

Strategies/Structures/Language

4. How does the presence of so many short paragraphs (76!) affect your reading? What would the narrative and the dialogue gain—or lose—if some of these were combined into longer paragraphs?

5. Loomis has rendered a highly charged emotional event in a very understated manner. What are the dominant emotions, and how are they expressed? Does she evoke corresponding emotions in her readers?

For Writing

6. Compare and contrast Tallent's "No One's a Mystery" with Loomis's "Spider-webs"—in themes, characterizations, relationships between the characters, use of dialogue, and projections of past and future events.

7. Write your own true version of "breaking up is hard to do," or easy, or problematic. One of the parties involved should be more sympathetic to the audience than the other, although neither has to be a bad person. In your narrative provide some clues as to what life will be like for at least one of the characters after the relationship has ended.

  For comprehension, writing, and research activities and resources, please visit the companion website at <college.hmco.com/english>.

Additional Topics for Writing
Comparison and Contrast

(For strategies for writing comparison and contrast, see 386–87)

MULTIPLE STRATEGIES FOR WRITING COMPARISON AND CONTRAST

In writing on any of the comparison and contrast topics below, you can employ assorted strategies to make the comparisons more meaningful and the contrasts sharp and distinctive, and to interpret their significance.

- *definitions* of essential terms, component parts
- *illustrations* and *examples,* to show the meaning or significance of the comparison and contrast
- *drawings, diagrams, maps,* to reinforce the illustrations
- *explanations* and *analyses* of the similarities and differences
- *division* and *classification,* to illustrate the parts of the whole
- a *narrative,* on occasion, to allow the meaning of the term to emerge gradually as the tale unfolds
- *negation,* to show why one part is unlike the other

1. Write an essay, full of examples, that compares and contrasts any of the following pairs:

   a. Two people with a number of relevant characteristics in common (two of your teachers, roommates, friends, relatives playing the same role—that is, two of your sisters or brothers, two of your grandparents, a father or mother and a stepparent)
   b. Two cities or regions of the country you know well, or two neighborhoods you have lived in
   c. Two comparable historical figures with similar positions, such as two presidents, two senators, two generals, two explorers, two immigrants from the same home country
   d. Two religions or two sects or churches within the same religion
   e. Two utopian communities (real or imaginary)
   f. Two explanations or interpretations of the same scientific, economic, religious, psychological, or political phenomenon (for instance, creationism versus Darwinism; Freudian versus Skinnerian theory of behavior)
   g. The cuisine of two different countries or two or more parts of a country (Greek versus French cooking; Szechuan, Cantonese, and Peking Chinese food)

2. Write a balanced essay involving a comparison and contrast of one of the subjects below that justifies your preference for one over the other. Write for a reader who is likely to debate your choice.

   a. American-made versus foreign-made cars (specify the country, the manufacturer, and the make/model)
   b. The styles of two performers—musicians, actors or actresses, dancers, athletes participating in the same sport, comedians

c. The work of two writers, painters, theater or film directors; or two (or three) works by the same writer or painter

d. Two political parties, campaigns, or machines, past or present

e. Two colleges or universities (or programs or sports teams within them) that you know well

f. Two styles of friendship, courtship, marriage, or family (both may be contemporary, or you may compare and contrast past and present styles)

g. Two academic majors, professions, or careers

h. Life in the mainstream or on the margin (specify of which group, community, or society)

3. Write an essay, for an audience of fellow students, comparing the reality with the ideal of one of the following:

a. Dating or courtship styles

b. Your current job and the most satisfying job you could have

c. Your current accomplishment in a particular area (sports, a performing art, a skill, or a level of knowledge) with what you hope to attain

d. Friendship

e. Parenthood

f. Your present dwelling and your dream house

g. The way you currently spend your leisure time, or money, and the way you'd like to spend it

h. The present state of affairs versus the future prospects of some issue of social significance, such as world population, ecology, the control of nuclear arms, the activities and treatment of hijackers and other international terrorists, an appropriate climate for world peace

Part IV

ARGUING DIRECTLY
AND INDIRECTLY

Appealing to Reason:
Deductive and
Inductive Arguments

11

When you write persuasively you're trying to move your readers to either belief or action or both, as the Declaration of Independence (439–42) reveals. You can do this through appealing to their reasons, their emotions, or their sense of ethics, as you know if you've ever tried to prove a point on an exam or change an attitude in a letter to the editor. Photographer Gordon Parks's "American Gothic" 1942 that opens this chapter is an homage to Grant Wood's famous "American Gothic" 1929 painting, in which two motionless, iconic figures in front of a plain white wooden farmhouse stare impassively at the viewer, the balding farmer, in overalls and a black suit jacket, holding erect a three-pronged pitchfork as if to protect himself and his aproned wife. By posing the African-American cleaning woman, flanked by an erect broom and mop whose volume nearly equals hers, in front of an American flag, Parks combines title and image to comment on the inequalities of opportunity, ownership, and citizenship in the land of the free, and to argue for change. The next section discusses appeals to emotion and ethics; here we'll concentrate on argumentation.

An argument, as we're using the term here, does not mean a knockdown confrontation over an issue: "Philadelphia is the most wonderful place in the world to live!" "No, it's not. Social snobbery has ruined the City of Brotherly Love." Nor is an argument hard-sell brainwashing that admits of no alternatives: "America—love it or leave it!" When you write an argument, however, as a reasonable writer you'll present a reasonable proposition that states what you believe ("In the twenty-first century, the United States will continue to remain the best country in the world for freedom, democracy, and the opportunity to succeed."). You'll need to offer logic, evidence, and perhaps emotional appeals, to try to convince your readers of the merits of what you say. Sometimes, but not always, you'll also argue that they should adopt a particular course of action. ("Consequently, the United States should establish an 'open door' immigration policy to enable the less fortunate to enjoy these benefits, too." Or "Consequently, the United States should severely restrict immigration, to prevent overcrowding and enable every citizen to enjoy these hard-won benefits.")

Unless you're writing an indirect argument that makes its point through satire, irony, an imagined character whose actions or life story illustrate a point (see Jonathan Swift, "A Modest Proposal," [497–503]), or some other oblique means, you'll probably want to identify the issue at hand and justify its significance early in the essay: "Mandatory drug testing is essential for public officials with access to classified information." If it's a touchy subject, you may wish at this point to demonstrate good will toward readers likely to disagree with you by showing the basis for your common concern: "Most people would agree that it's important to protect children and adolescents from harmful influences." You could follow this by acknowledging the merits of their valid points: "And it's also true that drug abuse is currently a national crisis, and deserves immediate remedy."

You'll need to follow this with an explanation of why, nevertheless, your position is better than theirs: "But mandatory drug testing for everyone would be a violation of their civil liberties, incredibly costly, and subject to abuse through misuse of the data."

There are a number of suitable ways to organize the body of your argument. If your audience is inclined to agree with much of what you say, you might want to put your strongest point first and provide the most evidence for that, before proceeding to the lesser points, arranged in order of descending importance:

1. Mandatory drug testing for everyone is unconstitutional.
   (three paragraphs)
2. Mandatory drug testing would be extremely costly, an expense grossly disproportionate to the results.
   (two paragraphs)
3. The results of mandatory drug testing would be easy to abuse—to falsify, to misreport, to misinterpret.
   (one paragraph)
4. Consequently, mandatory drug testing for everyone would cause more problems than it would solve.
   (conclusion—one paragraph)

For an antagonistic audience you could do the reverse, beginning with the points easiest to accept or agree with and concluding with the most difficult. Or you could work from the most familiar to the least familiar parts.

No matter what organizational pattern you choose, you'll need to provide supporting evidence—through specific examples, facts and figures, the opinions of experts, case histories, narratives, analogies, considerations of cause and effect. Any or all of these techniques can be employed in either *inductive* or *deductive* reasoning. Chances are that most of your arguments will proceed by induction. You might use an individual example intended as representative of the whole, as Scott Russell Sanders does in "Under the Influence: Paying the Price of My Father's Booze" (249–59), anatomizing his father's alcoholism to illustrate the alcoholic's characteristic behavior.

Or you might use a larger number of examples and apply inductive reasoning to prove a general proposition. Research scientists and detectives work this way, as do some social commentators and political theorists. Robert Reich identifies the characteristics of "The Global Elite" (459–66) and uses them both to counteract the myths that the United States is a benevolent, egalitarian society and to argue against the separatism—moral and economic secession—that upper-income Americans currently practice to dissociate themselves from responsibilities toward the rest of society.

An essay of deductive reasoning proceeds from a general proposition to a specific conclusion. The model for a deductive argument is the syllogism, a three-part sequence that begins with a major premise, is followed by a minor premise, and leads to a conclusion. Aristotle's classic example of this basic logical pattern is

> Major premise: All men are mortal.
> Minor premise: Socrates is a man.
> Conclusion: Therefore, Socrates is mortal.

Sometimes an essay will identify all parts of the syllogism; sometimes one or more parts will be implied. In "The Declaration of Independence" (439–42), Thomas Jefferson and his coauthors explore the consequences of the explicitly stated propositions that "all men are created equal" and that, as a consequence, their "unalienable Rights" cannot be denied. Likewise, in "Uncle Sam and Aunt Samantha" (471–73), Anna Quindlen's argument offers a classic example of deductive reasoning, reinforced by the photograph (472) of Cathy De La Garza, one of only seven women F-15 Air Force pilots in 1999.

> Major premise: All U.S. citizens between the ages of eighteen and twenty-five should be subject to the draft.
> Minor premise: Women between the ages of eighteen and twenty-five are citizens of the United States.
> Conclusion: Therefore, women between the ages of eighteen and twenty-five should be subject to the draft.

To do otherwise is insulting to women, deeming them "lesser citizens."

In his classic essay, "Letter from Birmingham Jail" (444–57), Martin Luther King, Jr., shown in a 1960 photograph on page 445 on his way to an Atlanta court as a consequence of his civil rights activities, argues for the proposition that "one has a moral responsibility to disobey unjust laws" and uses a vast range of resources to demonstrate his point. He uses biblical and historical examples to explain the situation in Birmingham; illustrations from his own life and from the lives of his own children and other victims of racial segregation; and more generalized incidents of brutal treatment of "unarmed, nonviolent Negroes."

He identifies the process of nonviolent resistance: "collection of the facts to determine whether injustices exist; negotiation; self-purification; and direct action" (¶ 6). In the course of making his main argument, Dr. King addresses a host of lesser arguments: "Why direct action? . . . Isn't negotiation a better path?" (¶ 10); Why not give local politicians time to act? (¶ 12); Wait! What's the rush? (¶s 13, 23–25); "How can you advocate breaking some laws and obeying others?" (¶ 15), with a related consideration, What is the difference between a just and an unjust law? (¶s 16 ff); "I would agree with St. Augustine that 'an unjust law is no law at all'" (¶ 15). Isn't your nonviolent approach "extremist" (¶s 31 ff)? Why not let the white church handle this (¶s 32–35)? All of Dr. King's illustrations and answers lead to one conclusion: "We will reach the goal of freedom in Birmingham and all over the nation, because the goal of America is freedom. Abused and scorned though we may be, our destiny is tied up with America's destiny" (¶ 44).

No matter what your argumentative strategy, you will want to avoid *logical fallacies,* errors of reasoning that can lead you to the wrong conclusion. The most common logical fallacies to be aware of are the following:

- *Arguing from analogy:* Comparing only similarities between things, concepts, or situations while overlooking significant differences that might weaken the argument. "Having a standing army is just like having a loaded gun in the house. If it's around, people will want to use it."
- *Argumentation ad hominem* (from Latin, "argument to the man"): Attacking a person's ideas or opinions by discrediting him or her as a person. "Napoleon was too short to be a distinguished general." "She was seen at the Kit Kat Lounge three nights last week; she can't possibly be a good mother."
- *Argument from doubtful or unidentified authority:* Treating an unqualified, unreliable, or unidentified source as an expert on the subject at hand. "They say you can't get pregnant the first time." "'History is bunk!' said Henry Ford."
- *Begging the question:* Regarding as true from the start what you set out to prove; asserting that what is true is true. "Rapists and murderers awaiting trial shouldn't be let out on bail" assumes that the suspects have already been proven guilty, which is the point of the impending trial.
- *Arguing in a circle:* Demonstrating a premise by a conclusion and a conclusion by a premise. "People should give 10 percent of their income to charity because that is the right thing to do. Giving 10 percent of one's income to charity is the right thing to do because it is expected."
- *Either/or reasoning:* Restricting the complex aspects of a difficult problem or issue to only one of two possible solutions. "You're not getting any younger. Marry me or you'll end up single forever."
- *Hasty generalization:* Erroneously applying information or knowledge of one or a limited number of representative instances to an entire, much larger category. "Poor people on welfare cheat. Why, just yesterday I saw an SUV parked in front of the tenement at 9th and Main."
- *Non sequitur* (from the Latin, "it does not follow"): Asserting as a conclusion something that doesn't follow from the first premise or premises. "The Senator must be in cahoots with that shyster developer, Landphill. After all, they were college fraternity brothers."
- *Oversimplification:* Providing simplistic answers to complex problems. "Ban handguns and stop murderous assaults in public schools."

- *Post hoc ergo propter hoc* (from Latin, "after this, therefore because of this"): Confusing a cause with an effect and vice versa. "Bicyclists are terribly unsafe riders. They're always getting into accidents with cars." Or confusing causality with proximity: just because two events occur in sequence doesn't necessarily mean that the first caused the second. Does war cause famine, or is famine sometimes the cause of war?

After you've written a logical argument, have someone who disagrees with you read it critically to look for loopholes. Your critic's guidelines could be the same questions you might ask yourself while writing the paper, as indicated in the process strategies below. If you can satisfy yourself and a critic, you can take on the world. Or is that a logical fallacy?

STRATEGIES FOR WRITING— APPEALING TO REASON: DEDUCTIVE AND INDUCTIVE ARGUMENTS

1. Do I want to convince my audience of the truth of a particular matter? Do I want essentially to raise their consciousness of an issue? Do I want to promote a belief or refute a theory? Or do I want to move my readers to action? If action, what kind? To change their minds, attitudes, or behavior? To right a wrong, or alter a situation?
2. At the outset, do I expect my audience to agree with my ideas? To be neutral about the issues at hand? Or to be opposed to my views? Can I build into my essay responses to my readers' anticipated reactions, such as rebuttals to their possible objections? Do I know enough about my subject to be able to do this?
3. What is my strongest (and presumably most controversial) point, and where should I put it? At the beginning, if my audience agrees with my views? At the end, after a gradual buildup, for an antagonistic audience? How much development (and consequent emphasis) should each point have? Will a deductive or inductive format best express my thesis?
4. What will be my best sources of evidence? My own experience? The experiences of people I know? Common sense or common knowledge? Opinion from experts in a relevant field? Scientific evidence? Historic records? Economic, anthropological, or statistical data?
5. What tone will best reinforce my evidence? Will my audience also find this tone appealing? Convincing? Would an appropriate tone be sincere? Straightforward? Objective? Reassuring? Confident? Placating? What language can I use to most appropriately convey this tone?

THOMAS JEFFERSON

Politician, philosopher, architect, inventor, and writer, Jefferson (1743–1826) was born near Charlottesville, Virginia, and was educated at the College of William and Mary. He served as a delegate to the Continental Congress in 1775, as governor of the Commonwealth of Virginia, and as third president of the United States. With help from Benjamin Franklin and John Adams, he wrote *The Declaration of Independence* in mid-June 1776, and after further revision by the Continental Congress in Philadelphia, it was signed on July 4. Frequently called "an expression of the American mind," Jefferson's Declaration is based on his acceptance of democracy as the ideal form of government, a belief also evidenced in his refusal to sign the Constitution until the Bill of Rights was added. Jefferson died at Monticello, his home in Charlottesville, on July 4, 1826, the fiftieth anniversary of the signing of the Declaration.

The Declaration is based on a deductive argument, with the fundamental premises stated in the first sentence of the second paragraph, "We hold these truths to be self-evident. . . ." The rest of the argument follows logically—patriots among the Colonists who read this might say inevitably—from the premises of this emphatic, plainspoken document. What evidence is there in the Declaration that the British might react to it as a hot-headed manifesto, perhaps even a declaration of war? Can a cluster of colonies simply secede by fiat?

The Declaration of Independence

W hen in the course of human events, it becomes necessary for one   1
people to dissolve the political bands which have connected them with another, and to assume among the Powers of the earth, the separate and equal station to which the Laws of Nature and of Nature's God entitle them, a decent respect to the opinions of mankind requires that they should declare the causes which impel them to the separation.

We hold these truths to be self-evident, that all men are created equal,   2
that they are endowed by their Creator with certain unalienable Rights, that among these are Life, Liberty and the pursuit of Happiness. That to secure these rights, Governments are instituted among Men deriving their just powers from the consent of the governed. That whenever any Form of Government becomes destructive of these ends, it is the Right of People to alter or to abolish it, and to institute new Government, laying its foundation on such principles and organizing its powers in such form, as to them shall seem most likely to effect their Safety and Happiness. Prudence, indeed, will dictate that Governments long established should not be changed for light and transient causes; and accordingly all experience hath shown, that mankind are more disposed to suffer, while evils are sufferable, than to

right themselves by abolishing the forms to which they are accustomed. But when a long train of abuses and usurpations pursuing invariably the same Object evinces a design to reduce them under absolute Despotism, it is their right, it is their duty, to throw off such government, and to provide new Guards for their future security. Such has been the patient sufferance of these Colonies; and such is now the necessity which constrains them to alter their former Systems of Government. The history of the present King of Great Britain is a history of repeated injuries and usurpations, all having in direct object the establishment of an absolute Tyranny over these States. To prove this, let Facts be submitted to a candid world.

3   He has refused his Assent to Laws, the most wholesome and necessary for the public good.

4   He had forbidden his Governors to pass Laws of immediate and pressing importance, unless suspended in their operation till his Assent should be obtained; and when so suspended, he has utterly neglected to attend them.

5   He has refused to pass other Laws for the accommodation of large districts of people, unless those people would relinquish the right of Representation in the Legislature, a right inestimable to them and formidable to tyrants only.

6   He has called together legislative bodies at places unusual, uncomfortable, and distant from the depository of their Public Records, for the sole purpose of fatiguing them into compliance with his measures.

7   He has dissolved Representative Houses repeatedly, for opposing with manly firmness his invasions on the rights of the people.

8   He has refused for a long time, after such dissolutions, to cause others to be elected; whereby the Legislative Powers, incapable of Annihilation, have returned to the People at large for their exercise; the State remaining in the mean time exposed to all the dangers of invasion from without, and convulsions within.

9   He has endeavoured to prevent the population of these States; for that purpose obstructing the Laws of Naturalization of Foreigners; refusing to pass others to encourage their migration hither, and raising the conditions of new Appropriations of Lands.

10   He has obstructed the Administration of Justice, by refusing his Assent to Laws for establishing Judiciary Powers.

11   He has made Judges dependent on his Will alone, for the tenure of their offices, and the amount and payment of their salaries.

12   He has erected a multitude of New Offices, and sent hither swarms of Officers to harass our People, and eat out their substance.

13   He has kept among us, in time of peace, Standing Armies without the Consent of our Legislature.

14   He has affected to render the Military independent of and superior to the Civil Power.

He has combined with others to subject us to jurisdictions foreign to our constitution, and unacknowledged by our laws; giving his Assent to their acts of pretended Legislation: 15

For quartering large bodies of armed troops among us: 16

For protecting them, by a mock Trial, from Punishment for any Murders which they should commit on the Inhabitants of these States: 17

For cutting off our Trade with all parts of the world: 18

For imposing Taxes on us without our Consent: 19

For depriving us in many cases, of the benefits of Trial by Jury: 20

For transporting us beyond Seas to be tried for pretended offenses: 21

For abolishing the free System of English Laws in a Neighbouring Province, establishing therein an Arbitrary government, and enlarging its boundaries so as to render it at once an example and fit instrument for introducing the same absolute rule into these Colonies: 22

For taking away our Charters, abolishing our most valuable Laws, and altering fundamentally the Forms of our Governments: 23

For suspending our own Legislatures, and declaring themselves invested with Power to legislate for us in all cases whatsoever. 24

He has abdicated Government here, by declaring us out of his Protection and waging War against us. 25

He has plundered our seas, ravaged our Coasts, burnt our towns and destroyed the Lives of our people. 26

He is at this time transporting large Armies of foreign Mercenaries to compleat works of death, desolation and tyranny, already begun with circumstances of Cruelty & perfidy scarcely paralleled in the most barbarous ages, and totally unworthy the Head of a civilized nation. 27

He has constrained our fellow Citizens taken Captive on the high Seas to bear Arms against their Country, to become the executioners of their friends and Brethren, or to fall themselves by their Hands. 28

He has excited domestic insurrections amongst us, and has endeavoured to bring on the inhabitants of our frontiers, the merciless Indian Savages, whose known rule of warfare, is an undistinguished destruction of all ages, sexes and conditions. 29

In every stage of these Oppressions We Have Petitioned for Redress in the most humble terms: Our repeated petitions have been answered only by repeated injury. A Prince, whose character is thus marked by every act which may define a Tyrant, is unfit to be the ruler of a free People. 30

Not have We been wanting in attention to our British brethren. We have warned them from time to time of attempts by their legislature to extend an unwarrantable jurisdiction over us. We have reminded them of the circumstances of our emigration and settlement here. We have appealed to their native justice and magnanimity and we have conjured them by the ties of our common kindred to disavow these usurpations, which would inevitably interrupt our connections and correspondence. They too 31 have been deaf to the voice of justice and of consanguinity. We must, therefore acquiesce in the necessity, which denounces our Separation, and hold them, as we hold the rest of mankind, Enemies in War, in Peace Friends.

32   We, therefore, the Representatives of the United States of America, in General Congress, Assembled, appealing to the Supreme Judge of the world for the rectitude of our intentions, do, in the Name, and by Authority of the good People of these Colonies, solemnly publish and declare, That these United Colonies are, and of Right ought to be Free and Independent States; that they are Absolved from all Allegiance to the British Crown and that all political connection between them and the State of Great Britain, is and ought to be totally dissolved; and that as Free and Independent States, they have full power to levy War, conclude Peace, contract Alliances, establish Commerce, and to do all other Acts and Things which Independent States may of right do. And for the support of this Declaration, with a firm reliance on the protection of Divine Providence, we mutually pledge to each other our lives, our Fortunes and our sacred Honor.

Content

1. What are "the Laws of Nature and of Nature's God" to which Jefferson refers in paragraph 1? Why doesn't he specify what they are? Is a brief allusion to them in the first paragraph sufficient support for the fundamental premise of the second paragraph?
2. What is Jefferson's fundamental premise (¶ 2)? Does he ever prove it? Does he need to?
3. In paragraphs 3–31 the Declaration states a series of the American colonists' grievances against the British King, George III. What are some of these grievances? Can they be grouped into categories related to the "unalienable rights" Jefferson has specified at the outset, the rights to "Life, Liberty and the pursuit of Happiness"?
4. From the nature of the grievances Jefferson identifies, what ideal of government does he have in mind? Can such a government exist among colonial peoples, or only in an independent nation?
5. Could the American colonists have expected the British simply to agree with what they said? Or is *The Declaration of Independence* in effect a declaration of war? Is the conclusion (¶ 32) the inevitable consequence of the reasoning that precedes it? Are there any feasible alternatives?

Strategies/Structures/Language

6. Why has Jefferson listed the grievances in the order in which they appear?
7. Is *The Declaration of Independence* written primarily for an audience of the British King and his advisors? Who else would be likely to be vitally involved?
8. What is the tone of this document? How would Jefferson have expected this tone to have affected King George III and associates? How might the same tone have affected the American patriots of 1776?

For Writing

9. Write an essay in which you discuss the extent to which the federal government of the United States exhibits one or more of the ideals of government that Jefferson promoted in *The Declaration of Independence.*

10. Write your own "declaration of independence," in which you justify setting yourself (or yourself as a member of a particular social, occupational, economic, ethnic, or cultural group) free from an oppressor or oppressive group.

 For comprehension, writing, and research activities and resources, please visit the companion website at <college.hmco.com/english>.

MARTIN LUTHER KING, JR.

"Letter from Birmingham Jail," a literary and humanitarian masterpiece, reveals why Martin Luther King, Jr. was the most influential leader of the American civil rights movement in the 1950s and 1960s, and, why, with Mahatma Gandhi, he was one of this century's most influential advocates for human rights. King was born in Atlanta in 1929, the son of a well-known Baptist clergyman, educated at Morehouse College, and ordained in his father's denomination.

A forceful and charismatic leader, Dr. King became at twenty-six a national spokesperson for the civil rights movement when in 1955 he led a successful boycott of the segregated bus system of Montgomery, Alabama. Dr. King became president of the Southern Christian Leadership Conference and led the sit-ins and demonstrations—including the 1964 march on Washington, D.C., which climaxed with his famous "I Have a Dream" speech—that helped to ensure passage of the 1964 Civil Rights Act and the Voting Rights Act of 1965. He received the Nobel Peace Prize in 1964, its youngest winner. Toward the end of his life, cut short by assassination in 1968, Dr. King was increasingly concerned with improving the rights and the lives of the nation's poor, irrespective of race, and with ending the war in Vietnam. His birthday became a national holiday in 1986.

In 1963 King wrote the letter reprinted below while imprisoned for "parading without a permit." Though ostensibly replying to eight clergymen—Protestant, Catholic, and Jewish—who feared violence in the Birmingham desegregation demonstrations, King actually intended his letter for the worldwide audience his civil rights activities commanded. Warning that America had more to fear from passive moderates ("the appalling silence of good people") than from extremists, King defended his policy of "nonviolent direct action" and explained why he was compelled to disobey "unjust laws"—supporting his argument with references to Protestant, Catholic, and Jewish examples ("Was not Jesus an extremist for love. . . ."), as well as to the painful examples of segregation in his own life.

Letter from Birmingham Jail[1]

April 16, 1963

My Dear Fellow Clergymen:

1   While confined here in the Birmingham city jail, I came across your recent statement calling my present activities "unwise and untimely." Seldom do I pause to answer criticism of my work and ideas. If I sought to answer all the criticisms that cross my desk, my secretaries would have little time for anything other than such correspondence in the course of the day, and I would have no time for constructive work. But since I feel that you are men of genuine good will and that your criticisms are sincerely set forth, I want to try to answer your statement in what I hope will be patient and reasonable terms.

2   I think I should indicate why I am here in Birmingham, since you have been influenced by the view which argues against "outsiders coming in." I have the honor of serving as president of the Southern Christian Leadership Conference, an organization operating in every southern state, with headquarters in Atlanta, Georgia. We have some eighty-five affiliated organizations across the South, and one of them is the Alabama Christian Movement for Human Rights. Frequently we share staff, educational and financial resources with our affiliates. Several months ago the affiliate here in Birmingham asked us to be on call to engage in a nonviolent direct-action program if such were deemed necessary. We readily consented, and when the hour came we lived up to our promise. So I, along with several members of my staff, am here because I was invited here. I am here because I have organizational ties here.

3   But more basically, I am in Birmingham because injustice is here. Just as the prophets of the eighth century B.C. left their villages and carried their "thus saith the Lord" far beyond the boundaries of their home towns, and, just as the Apostle Paul left his village of Tarsus and carried the gospel of Jesus Christ to the far corners of the Greco-Roman world, so am I compelled to carry the gospel of freedom beyond my own home town. Like Paul, I must constantly respond to the Macedonian call for aid.

---

[1] AUTHOR'S NOTE: This response to a published statement by eight fellow clergymen from Alabama (Bishop C. C. J. Carpenter, Bishop Joseph A. Durick, Rabbi Hilton L. Grafman, Bishop Paul Hardin, Bishop Holan B. Harmon, the Reverend George M. Murray, the Reverend Edward V. Ramage and the Reverend Earl Stallings) was composed under somewhat constricting circumstances. Begun on the margins of the newspaper in which the statement appeared while I was in jail, the letter was continued on scraps of writing paper supplied by a friendly Negro trusty, and concluded on a pad my attorneys were eventually permitted to leave me. Although the text remains in substance unaltered, I have indulged in the author's prerogative of polishing it for publication.

Dr. Martin Luther King, Jr. and other notable figures in the '60s Civil Rights movement—Andy Young (left), Joan Baez, and Hosea Williams (next to Baez)—are escorting black children into a newly-integrated school in Grenada, Mississippi, on September 20, 1966. What arguments are embedded in this picture? What is the point of having such a high profile delegation of escorts? Where would this picture have first been published? Reprinted? Who would be expected to view it? With what reaction(s)? What has happened since this picture was taken to make this a telling scene in American history rather than a typical first-day-of-school picture today?

Moreover, I am cognizant of the interrelatedness of all communities 4 and states. I cannot sit idly by in Atlanta and not be concerned about what happens in Birmingham. Injustice anywhere is a threat to justice everywhere. We are caught in an inescapable network of mutuality, tied in a single garment of destiny. Whatever affects one directly, affects all indirectly. Never again can we afford to live with the narrow, provincial "outside agitator" idea. Anyone who lives inside the United States can never be considered an outsider anywhere within its bounds.

You deplore the demonstrations taking place in Birmingham. But 5 your statement, I am sorry to say, fails to express a similar concern for the conditions that brought about the demonstrations. I am sure that none of you would want to rest content with the superficial kind of social analysis that deals merely with effects and does not grapple with underlying causes. It is unfortunate that demonstrations are taking place in Birmingham, but it is even more unfortunate that the city's white power structure left the Negro community with no alternative.

6   In any nonviolent campaign there are four basic steps: collection of the facts to determine whether injustices exist; negotiation; self-purification; and direct action. We have gone through all these steps in Birmingham. There can be no gainsaying the fact that racial injustice engulfs this community. Birmingham is probably the most thoroughly segregated city in the United States. An ugly record of brutality is widely known. Negroes have experienced grossly unjust treatment in the courts. There have been more unsolved bombings of Negro homes and churches in Birmingham than in any other city in the nation. These are the hard brutal facts of the case. On the basis of these conditions, Negro leaders sought to negotiate with the city fathers. But the latter consistently refused to engage in good-faith negotiation.

7   Then, last September, came the opportunity to talk with leaders of Birmingham's economic community. In the course of the negotiations, certain promises were made by the merchants—for example, to remove the stores' humiliating racial signs. On the basis of these promises, the Reverend Fred Shuttlesworth and the leaders of the Alabama Christian Movement for Human Rights agreed to a moratorium on all demonstrations. As the weeks and months went by, we realized that we were the victims of a broken promise. A few signs, briefly removed, returned; the others remained.

8   As in so many past experiences, our hopes had been blasted, and the shadow of deep disappointment settled upon us. We had no alternative except to prepare for direct action, whereby we would present our very bodies as a means of laying our case before the conscience of the local and the national community. Mindful of the difficulties involved, we decided to undertake a process of self-purification. We began a series of workshops on nonviolence, and we repeatedly asked ourselves: "Are you able to accept blows without retaliating?" "Are you able to endure the ordeal of jail?" We decided to schedule our direct-action program for the Easter season, realizing that except for Christmas, this is the main shopping period of the year. Knowing that a strong economic-withdrawal program would be the by-product of direct action, we felt that this would be the best time to bring pressure to bear on the merchants for the needed change.

9   Then it occurred to us that Birmingham's mayoralty election was coming up in March, and we speedily decided to postpone action until after election day. When we discovered that the Commissioner of Public Safety, Eugene "Bull" Connor, had piled up enough votes to be in the run-off, we decided again to postpone action until the day after the run-off so that the demonstrations could not be used to cloud the issues. Like many others, we waited to see Mr. Connor defeated, and to this end we endured postponement after postponement. Having aided in this community need, we felt that our direct-action program could be delayed no longer.

10   You may well ask: "Why direct action? Why sit-ins, marches and so forth? Isn't negotiation a better path?" You are quite right in calling for negotiation. Indeed this is the very purpose of direct action. Nonviolent

direct action seeks to create such a crisis and foster such a tension that a community which has constantly refused to negotiate is forced to confront the issue. It seeks so to dramatize the issue that it can no longer be ignored. My citing the creation of tension as part of the work of the nonviolent-resister may sound rather shocking. But I must confess that I am not afraid of the word "tension." I have earnestly opposed violent tension, but there is a type of nonviolent tension which is necessary for growth. Just as Socrates felt that it was necessary to create a tension in the mind so that individuals could rise from the bondage of myths and half-truths to the unfettered realm of creative analysis and objective appraisal, so must we see the need for nonviolent gadflies to create the kind of tension in society that will help men rise from the dark depths of prejudice and racism to the majestic heights of understanding and brotherhood.

The purpose of our direct-action program is to create a situation so   11
crisis-packed that it will inevitably open the door to negotiation. I therefore concur with you in your call for negotiation. Too long has our beloved Southland been bogged down in a tragic effort to live in monologue rather than dialogue.

One of the basic points in your statement is that the action that I and   12
my associates have taken in Birmingham is untimely. Some have asked: "Why didn't you give the new city administration time to act?" The only answer that I can give to this query is that the new Birmingham administration must be prodded about as much as the outgoing one, before it will act. We are sadly mistaken if we feel that the election of Albert Boutwell as mayor will bring the millennium to Birmingham. While Mr. Boutwell is a much more gentle person than Mr. Connor, they are both segregationists, dedicated to maintenance of the status quo. I have hope that Mr. Boutwell will be reasonable enough to see the futility of massive resistance to de-segregation. But he will not see this without pressure from devotees of civil rights. My friends, I must say to you that we have not made a single gain in civil rights without determined legal and nonviolent pressure. La-mentably, it is an historical fact that privileged groups seldom give up their privileges voluntarily. Individuals may see the moral light and voluntarily give up their unjust posture; but, as Reinhold Niebuhr has reminded us, groups tend to be more immoral than individuals.

We know through painful experience that freedom is never voluntar-   13
ily given by the oppressor; it must be demanded by the oppressed. Frankly, I have yet to engage in a direct-action campaign that was "well-timed" in the view of those who have not suffered unduly from the disease of segre-gation. For years now I have heard the word "Wait!" It rings in the ear of every Negro with piercing familiarity. This "Wait" has almost always meant "Never." We must come to see, with one of our distinguished jurists, that "justice too long delayed is justice denied."

We have waited for more than 340 years for our constitutional and   14
Godgiven rights. The nations of Asia and Africa are moving with jetlike

speed toward gaining political independence, but we still creep at horse-and-buggy pace toward gaining a cup of coffee at a lunch counter. Perhaps it is easy for those who have never felt the stinging darts of segregation to say, "Wait." But when you have seen vicious mobs lynch your mothers and fathers at will and drown your sisters and brothers at whim; when you have seen hate-filled policemen curse, kick and even kill your black brothers and sisters; when you see the vast majority of your twenty million Negro brothers smothering in an airtight cage of poverty in the midst of an affluent society; when you suddenly find your tongue twisted and your speech stammering as you seek to explain to your six-year-old daughter why she can't go to the public amusement park that has just been adver-tised on television, and see tears welling up in her eyes when she is told that Funtown is closed to colored children, and see ominous clouds of in-feriority beginning to form in her little mental sky, and see her beginning to distort her personality by developing an unconscious bitterness toward white people; when you have to concoct an answer for a five-year-old son who is asking: "Daddy, why do white people treat colored people so mean?"; when you take a cross-country drive and find it necessary to sleep night after night in the uncomfortable corners of your automobile because no motel will accept you; when you are humiliated day in and day out by nagging signs reading "white" and "colored"; when your first name be-comes "nigger," your middle name becomes "boy" (however old you are) and your last name becomes "John," and your wife and mother are never given the respected title "Mrs."; when you are harried by day and haunted by night by the fact that you are a Negro, living constantly at tiptoe stance, never quite knowing what to expect next, and are plagued with inner fears and outer resentments; when you are forever fighting a degenerating sense of "nobodiness"—then you will understand why we find it difficult to wait. There comes a time when the cup of endurance runs over, and men are no longer willing to be plunged into the abyss of despair. I hope, sirs, you can understand our legitimate and unavoidable impatience.

15   You express a great deal of anxiety over our willingness to break laws. This is certainly a legitimate concern. Since we so diligently urge people to obey the Supreme Court's decision of 1954 outlawing segregation in the public schools, at first glance it may seem rather paradoxical for us con-sciously to break laws. One may well ask: "How can you advocate break-ing some laws and obeying others?" The answer lies in the fact that there are two types of laws: just and unjust. I would be the first to advocate obey-ing just laws. One has not only a legal but a moral responsibility to obey just laws. Conversely, one has a moral responsibility to disobey unjust laws. I would agree with St. Augustine that "an unjust law is no law at all."

16   Now, what is the difference between the two? How does one deter-mine whether a law is just or unjust? A just law is a man-made code that squares with the moral law or the law of God. An unjust law is a code that is out of harmony with the moral law. To put it in the terms of St. Thomas Aquinas: An unjust law is a human law that is not rooted in eternal law and

natural law. Any law that uplifts human personality is just. Any law that degrades human personality is unjust. All segregation statutes are unjust because segregation distorts the soul and damages the personality. It gives the segregator a false sense of superiority and the segregated a false sense of inferiority. Segregation, to use the terminology of the Jewish philosopher Martin Buber, substitutes an "I-it" relationship for an "I-thou" relationship and ends up relegating persons to the status of things. Hence segregation is not only politically, economically and sociologically unsound, it is morally wrong and sinful. Paul Tillich has said that sin is separation. Is not segregation an existential expression of man's tragic separation, his awful estrangement, his terrible sinfulness? Thus it is that I can urge men to obey the 1954 decision of the Supreme Court, for it is morally right; and I can urge them to disobey segregation ordinances, for they are morally wrong.

Let us consider a more concrete example of just and unjust laws. An unjust law is a code that a numerical or power majority group compels a minority group to obey but does not make binding on itself. This is *difference* made legal. By the same token, a just law is a code that a majority compels a minority to follow and that it is willing to follow itself. This is *sameness* made legal. 17

Let me give another explanation. A law is unjust if it is inflicted on a minority that, as a result of being denied the right to vote, had no part in enacting or devising the law. Who can say that the legislature of Alabama which set up that state's segregation laws was democratically elected? Throughout Alabama all sorts of devious methods are used to prevent Negroes from becoming registered voters, and there are some counties in which even though Negroes constitute a majority of the population, not a single Negro is registered. Can any law enacted under such circumstances be considered democratically structured? 18

Sometimes a law is just on its face and unjust in its application. For instance, I have been arrested on a charge of parading without a permit. Now, there is nothing wrong in having an ordinance which requires a permit for a parade. But such an ordinance becomes unjust when it is used to maintain segregation and to deny citizens the First-Amendment privilege of peaceful assembly and protest. 19

I hope you are able to see the distinction I am trying to point out. In no sense do I advocate evading or defying the law, as would the rabid segregationist. That would lead to anarchy. One who breaks an unjust law must do so openly, lovingly, and with a willingness to accept the penalty. I submit that an individual who breaks a law that conscience tells him is unjust, and who willingly accepts the penalty of imprisonment in order to arouse the conscience of the community over its injustice, is in reality expressing the highest respect for the law. 20

Of course, there is nothing new about this kind of civil disobedience. It was evidenced sublimely in the refusal of Shadrach, Meshach and Abednego to obey the laws of Nebuchadnezzar, on the ground that a higher moral law was at stake. It was practiced superbly by the early 21

Christians, who were willing to face hungry lions and the excruciating pain of chopping blocks rather than submit to certain unjust laws of the Roman Empire. To a degree, academic freedom is a reality today because Socrates practiced civil disobedience. In our own nation, the Boston Tea Party represented a massive act of civil disobedience.

22   We should never forget that everything Adolf Hitler did in Germany was "legal" and everything the Hungarian freedom fighters did in Hungary was "illegal." It was "illegal" to aid and comfort a Jew in Hitler's Germany. Even so, I am sure that, had I lived in Germany at the time, I would have aided and comforted my Jewish brothers. If today I lived in a Communist country where certain principles dear to the Christian faith are suppressed, I would openly advocate disobeying that country's anti-religious laws.

23   I must make two honest confessions to you, my Christian and Jewish brothers. First, I must confess that over the past few years I have been gravely disappointed with the white moderate. I have almost reached the regrettable conclusion that the Negro's great stumbling block in his stride toward freedom is not the White Citizen's Counciler or the Ku Klux Klanner, but the white moderate, who is more devoted to "order" than to justice; who prefers a negative peace which is the absence of tension to a positive peace which is the presence of justice; who constantly says: "I agree with you in the goal you seek, but I cannot agree with your methods of direct action"; who paternalistically believes he can set the timetable for another man's freedom; who lives by a mythical concept of time and who constantly advises the Negro to wait for a "more convenient season." Shallow understanding from people of good will is more frustrating than absolute misunderstanding from people of ill will. Lukewarm acceptance is much more bewildering than outright rejection.

24   I had hoped that the white moderate would understand that law and order exist for the purpose of establishing justice and that when they fail in this purpose they become the dangerously structured dams that block the flow of social progress. I had hoped that the white moderate would understand that the present tension in the South is a necessary phase of the transition from an obnoxious negative peace, in which the Negro passively accepted his unjust plight, to a substantive and positive peace, in which all men will respect the dignity and worth of human personality. Actually, we who engage in non-violent direct action are not the creators of tension. We merely bring to the surface the hidden tension that is already alive. We bring it out in the open, where it can be seen and dealt with. Like a boil that can never be cured so long as it is covered up but must be opened with all its ugliness to the natural medicines of air and light, injustice must be exposed, with all the tension its exposure creates, to the light of human conscience and the air of national opinion before it can be cured.

25   In your statement you assert that our actions, even though peaceful, must be condemned because they precipitate violence. But is this a logical

assertion? Isn't this like condemning a robbed man because his possession of money precipitated the evil act of robbery? Isn't this like condemning Socrates because his unswerving commitment to truth and his philosophical inquiries precipitated the act by the misguided populace in which they made him drink hemlock? Isn't this like condemning Jesus because his unique God-consciousness and never-ceasing devotion to God's will precipitated the evil act of crucifixion? We must come to see that, as the federal courts have consistently affirmed, it is wrong to urge an individual to cease his efforts to gain his basic constitutional rights because the quest may precipitate violence. Society must protect the robbed and punish the robber.

I had also hoped that the white moderate would reject the myth concerning time in relation to the struggle for freedom. I have just received a letter from a white brother in Texas. He writes: "All Christians know that the colored people will receive equal rights eventually, but it is possible that you are in too great a religious hurry. It has taken Christianity almost two thousand years to accomplish what it has. The teachings of Christ take time to come to earth." Such an attitude stems from a tragic misconception of time, from the strangely irrational notion that there is something in the very flow of time that will inevitably cure all ills. Actually, time itself is neutral; it can be used either destructively or constructively. More and more I feel that the people of ill will have used time much more effectively than have the people of good will. We will have to repent in this generation not merely for the hateful words and actions of the bad people but for the appalling silence of the good people. Human progress never rolls in on wheels of inevitability; it comes through the tireless efforts of men willing to be coworkers with God, and without this hard work, time itself becomes an ally of the forces of social stagnation. We must use time creatively, in the knowledge that the time is always ripe to do right. Now is the time to make real the promise of democracy and transform our pending national elegy into a creative psalm of brotherhood. Now is the time to lift our national policy from the quicksand of racial injustice to the solid rock of human dignity.

You speak of our activity in Birmingham as extreme. At first I was rather disappointed that fellow clergymen would see my nonviolent efforts as those of an extremist. I began thinking about the fact that I stand in the middle of two opposing forces in the Negro community. One is a force of complacency, made up in part of Negroes who, as a result of long years of oppression, are so drained of self-respect and a sense of "somebodiness" that they have adjusted to segregation; and in part of a few middle-class Negroes who, because of a degree of academic and economic security and because in some ways they profit by segregation, have become insensitive to the problems of the masses. The other force is one of bitterness and hatred, and it comes perilously close to advocating violence. It is expressed in the various black nationalist groups that are springing up across the nation, the largest and best-known being Elijah Muhammad's Muslim

26

27

movement. Nourished by the Negro's frustration over the continued existence of racial discrimination, this movement is made up of people who have lost faith in America, who have absolutely repudiated Christianity, and who have concluded that the white man is an incorrigible "devil."

28   I have tried to stand between these two forces, saying that we need emulate neither the "do-nothingism" of the complacent nor the hatred and despair of the black nationalist. For there is the more excellent way of love and nonviolent protest. I am grateful to God that, through the influence of the Negro church, the way of nonviolence became an integral part of our struggle.

29   If this philosophy had not emerged, by now many streets of the South would, I am convinced, be flowing with blood. And I am further convinced that if our white brothers dismiss as "rabble-rousers" and "outside agitators" those of us who employ nonviolent direct action, and if they refuse to support our non-violent efforts, millions of Negroes will, out of frustration and despair, seek solace and security in black-nationalist ideologies—a development that would inevitably lead to a frightening racial nightmare.

30   Oppressed people cannot remain oppressed forever. The yearning for freedom eventually manifests itself, and that is what has happened to the American Negro. Something within has reminded him of his birthright of freedom, and something without has reminded him that it can be gained. Consciously or unconsciously, he has been caught up by the *Zeitgeist,* and with his black brothers of Africa and his brown and yellow brothers of Asia, South America and the Caribbean, the United States Negro is moving with a sense of great urgency toward the promised land of racial justice. If one recognizes this vital urge that has engulfed the Negro community, one should readily understand why public demonstrations are taking place. The Negro has many pent-up resentments and latent frustrations, and he must release them. So let him march; let him make prayer pilgrimages to the city hall; let him go on freedom rides—and try to understand why he must do so. If his repressed emotions are not released in nonviolent ways, they will seek expression through violence; this is not a threat but a fact of history. So I have not said to my people: "Get rid of your discontent." Rather, I have tried to say that this normal and healthy discontent can be channeled into the creative outlet of nonviolent direct action. And now this approach is being termed extremist.

31   But though I was initially disappointed at being categorized as an extremist, as I continued to think about the matter I gradually gained a measure of satisfaction from the label. Was not Jesus an extremist for love: "Love your enemies, bless them that curse you, do good to them that hate you, and pray for them which despitefully use you, and persecute you." Was not Amos an extremist for justice: "Let justice roll down like waters and righteousness like an ever-flowing stream." Was not Paul an extremist for the Christian gospel: "I bear in my body the marks of the Lord

Jesus." Was not Martin Luther an extremist: "Here I stand; I cannot do otherwise, so help me God." And John Bunyan: "I will stay in jail to the end of my days before I make a butchery of my conscience." And Abraham Lincoln: "This nation cannot survive half slave and half free." And Thomas Jefferson: "We hold these truths to be self-evident, that all men are created equal. . . ." So the question is not whether we will be extremists, but what kind of extremists we will be. Will we be extremists for hate or for love? Will we be extremists for the preservation of injustice or for the extension of justice? In that dramatic scene on Calvary's hill three men were crucified. We must never forget that all three were crucified for the same crime—the crime of extremism. Two were extremists for immorality, and thus fell below their environment. The other, Jesus Christ, was an extremist for love, truth and goodness, and thereby rose above his environment. Perhaps the South, the nation and the world are in dire need of creative extremists.

I had hoped that the white moderate would see this need. Perhaps I 32 was too optimistic; perhaps I expected too much. I suppose I should have realized that few members of the oppressor race can understand the deep groans and passionate yearnings of the oppressed race, and still fewer have the vision to see that injustice must be rooted out by strong, persistent and determined action. I am thankful, however, that some of our white brothers in the South have grasped the meaning of this social revolution and committed themselves to it. They are still all too few in quantity, but they are big in quality. Some—such as Ralph McGill, Lillian Smith, Harry Golden, James McBride Dabbs, Ann Braden and Sarah Patton Boyle—have written about our struggle in eloquent and prophetic terms. Others have marched with us down nameless streets of the South. They have languished in filthy, roach-infested jails, suffering the abuse and brutality of policemen who view them as "dirty nigger-lovers." Unlike so many of their moderate brothers and sisters, they have recognized the urgency of the moment and sensed the need for powerful "action" antidotes to combat the disease of segregation.

Let me take note of my other major disappointment. I have been so 33 greatly disappointed with the white church and its leadership. Of course, there are some notable exceptions. I am not unmindful of the fact that each of you has taken some significant stands on this issue. I commend you, Reverend Stallings, for your Christian stand on this past Sunday, in welcoming Negroes to your worship service on a nonsegregated basis. I commend the Catholic leaders of this state for integrating Spring Hill College several years ago.

But despite these notable exceptions, I must honestly reiterate that I 34 have been disappointed with the church. I do not say this as one of those negative critics who can always find something wrong with the church. I say this as a minister of the gospel, who loves the church; who was nurtured in its bosom; who has been sustained by its spiritual blessings and who will remain true to it as long as the cord of life shall lengthen.

35   When I was suddenly catapulted into the leadership of the bus protest in Montgomery, Alabama, a few years ago, I felt we would be supported by the white church. I felt that the white ministers, priests and rabbis of the South would be among our strongest allies. Instead, some have been outright opponents, refusing to understand the freedom movement and misrepresenting its leaders; all too many others have been more cautious than courageous and have remained silent behind the anesthetizing security of stained-glass windows.

36   In spite of my shattered dreams, I came to Birmingham with the hope that the white religious leadership of this community would see the justice of our cause and, with deep moral concern, would serve as the channel through which our just grievances could reach the power structure. I had hoped that each of you would understand. But again I have been disappointed.

37   I have heard numerous southern religious leaders admonish their worshipers to comply with a desegregation decision because it is the law, but I have longed to hear white ministers declare: "Follow this decree because integration is morally right and because the Negro is your brother." In the midst of blatant injustices inflicted upon the Negro, I have watched white churchmen stand on the sideline and mouth pious irrelevancies and sanctimonious trivialities. In the midst of a mighty struggle to rid our nation of racial and economic injustice, I have heard many ministers say: "Those are social issues, with which the gospel has no real concern." And I have watched many churches commit themselves to completely otherworldly religion which makes a strange, un-Biblical distinction between body and soul, between the sacred and the secular.

38   I have traveled the length and breadth of Alabama, Mississippi and all the other southern states. On sweltering summer days and crisp autumn mornings I have looked at the South's beautiful churches with their lofty spires pointing heavenward. I have beheld the impressive outlines of her massive religious-education buildings. Over and over I have found myself asking: "What kind of people worship here? Who is their God? Where were their voices when the lips of Governor Barnett dripped with words of interposition and nullification? Where were they when Governor Wallace gave a clarion call for defiance and hatred? Where were their voices of support when bruised and weary Negro men and women decided to rise from the dark dungeons of complacency to the bright hills of creative protest?"

39   Yes, these questions are still in my mind. In deep disappointment I have wept over the laxity of the church. But be assured that my tears have been tears of love. There can be no deep disappointment where there is not deep love. Yes, I love the church. How could I do otherwise? I am in the rather unique position of being the son, the grandson and the great-grandson of preachers. Yes, I see the church as the body of Christ. But, oh! How we have blemished and scarred that body through social neglect and through fear of being nonconformists.

There was a time when the church was very powerful—in the time when the early Christians rejoiced at being deemed worthy to suffer for what they believed. In those days the church was not merely a thermometer that recorded the ideas and principles of popular opinion; it was a thermostat that transformed the mores of society. Whenever the early Christians entered a town, the people in power became disturbed and immediately sought to convict the Christians for being "disturbers of the peace" and "outside agitators." But the Christians pressed on, in the conviction that they were "a colony of heaven," called to obey God rather than man. Small in number, they were big in commitment. They were too God-intoxicated to be "astronomically intimidated." By their effort and example they brought an end to such ancient evils as infanticide and gladiatorial contests.

Things are different now. So often the contemporary church is a weak, ineffectual voice with an uncertain sound. So often it is an archdefender of the status quo. Far from being disturbed by the presence of the church, the power structure of the average community is consoled by the church's silent—and often even vocal—sanction of things as they are.

But the judgment of God is upon the church as never before. If today's church does not recapture the sacrificial spirit of the early church, it will lose its authenticity, forfeit the loyalty of millions, and be dismissed as an irrelevant social club with no meaning for the twentieth century. Every day I meet young people whose disappointment with the church has turned into outright disgust.

Perhaps I have once again been too optimistic. Is organized religion too inextricably bound to the status quo to save our nation and the world? Perhaps I must turn my faith to the inner spiritual church, the church within the church, as the true *ekklesia* and the hope of the world. But again I am thankful to God that some noble souls from the ranks of organized religion have broken loose from the paralyzing chains of conformity and joined us as active partners in the struggle for freedom. They have left their secure congregations and walked the streets of Albany, Georgia, with us. They have gone down the highways of the South on tortuous rides for freedom. Yes, they have gone to jail with us. Some have been dismissed from their churches, have lost the support of their bishops and fellow ministers. But they have acted in the faith that right defeated is stronger than evil triumphant. Their witness has been the spiritual salt that has preserved the true meaning of the gospel in these troubled times. They have carved a tunnel of hope through the dark mountain of disappointment.

I hope the church as a whole will meet the challenge of this decisive hour. But even if the church does not come to the aid of justice, I have no despair about the future. I have no fear about the outcome of our struggle in Birmingham, even if our motives are at present misunderstood. We will reach the goal of freedom in Birmingham and all over the nation, because the goal of America is freedom. Abused and scorned though we may be, our destiny is tied up with America's destiny. Before the pilgrims landed at Plymouth, we were here. Before the pen of Jefferson etched the majestic words of the Declaration of Independence across the pages of history, we were here. For more than two centuries our forebears labored in this country without wages; they made cotton king; they built the homes of their masters while suffering gross injustice and shameful humiliation— and yet out of a bottomless vitality they continued to thrive and develop. If the inexpressible cruelties of slavery could not stop us, the opposition we now face will surely fail. We will win our freedom because the sacred heritage of our nation and the eternal will of God are embodied in our echoing demands.

45   Before closing I feel impelled to mention one other point in your statement that has troubled me profoundly. You warmly commended the Birmingham police force for keeping "order" and "preventing violence." I doubt that you would have so warmly commended the police force if you had seen its dogs sinking their teeth into unarmed, nonviolent Negroes. I doubt that you would so quickly commend the policemen if you were to observe their ugly and inhumane treatment of Negroes here in the city jail; if you were to watch them push and curse old Negro women and young Negro girls; if you were to see them slap and kick old Negro men and young boys; if you were to observe them as they did on two occasions, re-fuse to give us food because we wanted to sing our grace together. I can-not join you in your praise of the Birmingham police department.

46   It is true that the police have exercised a degree of discipline in handling the demonstrators. In this sense they have conducted them-selves rather "nonviolently" in public. But for what purpose? To preserve the evil system of segregation. Over the past few years I have consistently preached that nonviolence demands that the means we use must be as pure as the ends we seek. I have tried to make clear that it is wrong to use immoral means to attain moral ends. But now I must affirm that it is just as wrong, or perhaps even more so, to use moral means to preserve im-moral ends. Perhaps Mr. Connor and his policemen have been rather non-violent in public, as was Chief Pritchett in Albany, Georgia, but they have used the moral means of nonviolence to maintain the immoral end of racial injustice. As T. S. Eliot has said: "The last temptation is the greatest treason: To do the right deed for the wrong reason."

47   I wish you had commended the Negro sit-inners and demonstrators of Birmingham for their sublime courage, their willingness to suffer and their amazing discipline in the midst of great provocation. One day the South will recognize its real heroes. They will be the James Merediths, with the noble sense of purpose that enables them to face jeering and hostile mobs, and with the agonizing loneliness that characterizes the life of the pioneer. They will be old, oppressed, battered Negro women, symbolized in a seventy-two-year-old woman in Montgomery, Alabama, who rose up with a sense of dignity and with her people decided not to ride segregated buses, and who responded with ungrammatical profundity to one who in-quired about her weariness: "My feet is tired, but my soul is at rest." They

will be the young high school and college students, the young ministers of the gospel and a host of their elders, courageously and nonviolently sitting in at lunch counters and willingly going to jail for conscience' sake. One day the South will know that when these disinherited children of God sat down at lunch counters, they were in reality standing up for what is best in the American dream and for the most sacred values in our Judaeo-Christian heritage, thereby bringing our nation back to those great wells of democracy which were dug deep by the founding fathers in their formulation of the Constitution and the Declaration of Independence.

Never before have I written so long a letter. I'm afraid it is much too long to take your precious time. I can assure you that it would have been much shorter if I had been writing from a comfortable desk, but what else can one do when he is alone in a narrow jail cell, other than write long letters, think long thoughts and pray long prayers? 48

If I have said anything in this letter that overstates the truth and indicates an unreasonable impatience, I beg you to forgive me. If I have said anything that understates the truth and indicates my having a patience that allows me to settle for anything less than brotherhood, I beg God to forgive me. 49

I hope this letter finds you strong in faith. I also hope that circumstances will soon make it possible for me to meet each of you, not as an integrationist or a civil-rights leader but as a fellow clergyman and a Christian brother. Let us all hope that the dark clouds of racial prejudice will soon pass away and the deep fog of misunderstanding will be lifted from our fear-drenched communities, and in some not too distant tomorrow the radiant stars of love and brotherhood will shine over our great nation with all their scintillating beauty. 50

Yours for the cause of Peace and Brotherhood,
Martin Luther King, Jr.

Content

1. In paragraph 4 King makes several assertions on which he bases the rest of his argument. What are they? Does he ever prove them, or does he assume that readers will take them for granted?

2. In paragraph 5 King asserts that Birmingham's "white power structure left the Negro community with no alternative" but to commit civil disobedience. Does he ever prove this? Does he need to? Is it a debatable statement?

3. What, according to King, are the "four basic steps" in "any nonviolent campaign" (¶ 6)? What is the goal of "nonviolent direct action" (¶ 10)? What is the constructive, "nonviolent tension" (¶ 10) King favors?

4. Why has King been disappointed by white moderates (¶s 23–32)? By the white church (¶s 33–44)? What does he want white moderates to do? What does he claim that the church should do?

5. How does King deal with the argument that civil rights activists are too impatient, that they should go slow because "it has taken Christianity almost two thousand years to accomplish what it has" (¶ 26)? How does he refute the argument that he is an extremist (¶ 27)?

Strategies/Structures/Language

6. How does King establish, in the salutation and first paragraph, his reasons for writing? The setting in which he writes? His intended audience? In what ways does he demonstrate a sensitive, reasonable tone?

7. King's letter ostensibly replies to that of the eight clergymen. Find passages in which he addresses them, and analyze the voice he uses. In what relation to the clergymen does King see himself? He also has a secondary audience; who are its members? Locate passages that seem especially directed to this second audience. In what relation to this audience does King see himself?

8. Why does King cite the theologians Aquinas (a Catholic), Buber (a Jew), and Tillich (a Protestant) in paragraph 16? What similarities link the three?

9. After defending his actions against the criticisms of the clergymen, King takes the offensive in paragraphs 23–44. How does he signal this change?

10. Which parts of King's letter appeal chiefly to reason? To emotion? How are the two types of appeals interrelated?

11. King uses large numbers of rhetorical questions throughout this essay (see ¶s 18, 25, 31, 38, 39). Why? With what effects?

12. How does King define a "just law" (¶s 16, 17)? An "unjust law" (¶s 16, 17)? Why are these definitions crucial to the argument that follows?

For Writing

13. With a partner, write a position paper identifying the circumstances, if any, under which breaking the law is justifiable. If you use Dr. King's definition of just and unjust law (¶s 15–20) or make any distinction, say, between moral law and civil law, be sure to explain what you mean. You may, if you wish, use examples with which you are personally familiar. Or you may elaborate on some of the examples King uses (¶ 22) or on examples from King's own civil rights activities, such as the boycotts in the early 1950s of the legally segregated Montgomery bus system (¶ 35).

14. If you are a member of a church, or attend a church regularly, address members of the congregation on what, if any, commitment you think your church should make to better the lives of other groups who do not attend that church. Does this commitment extend to civil disobedience?

15. Would you ever be willing to go to jail for a cause? What cause or types of causes? Under what circumstances? If you knew that a prison record might bar you from some privileges in some states (such as practicing law or medicine), would you still be willing to take such a risk?

 For comprehension, writing, and research activities and resources, please visit the companion website at <college.hmco.com/english>.

ROBERT REICH

Reich (born 1946), earned a BA at Dartmouth College (1968) and a JD degree from Yale Law School (1973), was a Rhodes scholar at Oxford, and taught at Harvard's John F. Kennedy School of Government, and at Brandeis University before moving in 2005 to a professorship at the University of California, Berkeley's Goldman School of Public Policy. In 2003 he received the Václav Havel Prize for his "contributions to social thought." Active in politics since his student days, Reich interned for Senator Robert Kennedy; coordinated Eugene McCarthy's 1968 presidential campaign; and was secretary of labor during Clinton's first term as president (1993–1996). *Locked in the Cabinet* (1997) discusses his experiences.

Many of Reich's books on economics are intended for a general audience, including *Tales of a New America: The Anxious Liberal's Guide to the Future* (1988); and *Reason: Why Liberals will Win the Battle for America* (2004). *The Next American Frontier* (1983) provided a rationale for the Democratic party's economic policy, explaining that "government intervention sets the boundaries, decides what's going to be marketed, sets the rules of the game through procurement policies, tax credits, depreciation allowances, loans and loan guarantees." *Tales of a New America* defines four economic myths: "Mob at the Gate" labels foreigners as adversaries to American citizens; "The Triumphant Individual" reinforces the myth of the American Dream; "The Benevolent Community" claims that Americans act out of social responsibility to one another; and "The Rot at the Top" accuses the elite class of corruption and abuse of their power. "The Global Elite," first published in the *New York Times Magazine* (1991) provides factual information to counteract the myths of a benevolent, egalitarian society and implicitly argues for a more equitable—and democratic—distribution of our country's wealth.

The Global Elite

The idea of "community" has always held a special attraction for Americans. In a 1984 speech, President Ronald Reagan celebrated America's "bedrock"—"its communities where neighbors help one another, where families bring up kids together, where American values are born." Governor Mario M. Cuomo of New York, with a very different political leaning, has been almost as lyrical. "Community . . . is the reality on which our national life has been founded," he said in 1987.

There is only one problem with this picture. Most Americans no longer live in traditional communities. They live in suburban subdivisions bordered by highways and sprinkled with shopping malls, or in tony condominiums and residential clusters, or in ramshackle apartment buildings and housing projects. Most of them commute to work and socialize on some basis other than geographic proximity. And most people pick up and move to a different neighborhood every five years or so.

3   But Americans generally have one thing in common with their neighbors: They have similar incomes. And that simple fact lies at the heart of the new community. This means that their educational backgrounds are likely to be similar, that they pay roughly the same in taxes, and that they indulge in the same consumer impulses. "Tell me someone's ZIP code," the founder of a direct-mail company once bragged, "and I can predict what they eat, drink, drive—even think."

4   Americans who own their homes usually share one political cause with their neighbors: a near obsessive concern with maintaining or upgrading property values. And this common interest is responsible for much of what has brought neighbors together in recent years. Complete strangers, although they may live on the same street or in the same condominium complex, suddenly feel intense solidarity when it is rumored that low-income housing will be constructed in their midst or that a poorer school district will be consolidated with their own.

5   The renewed emphasis on "community" in American life has justified and legitimized these economic enclaves. If generosity and solidarity end at the border of similarly valued properties, then the most fortunate can be virtuous citizens at little cost. Since most people in one neighborhood or town are equally well off, there is no cause for a guilty conscience. If inhabitants of another area are poorer, let them look to one another. Why should *we* pay for *their* schools?

6   So the argument goes, without acknowledging that the critical assumption has already been made: "We" and "they" belong to fundamentally different communities. Through such reasoning, it has become possible to maintain a self-image of generosity toward, and solidarity with, one's "community" without bearing any responsibility to "them"— the other "community."

7   America's high earners—the fortunate top fifth—thus feel increasingly justified in paying only what is necessary to insure that everyone in their community is sufficiently well educated and has access to the public services they need to succeed.

8   Last year, the top fifth of working Americans took home more money than the other four-fifths put together—the highest portion in postwar history. These high earners will relinquish somewhat more of their income to the Federal Government this year than in 1990 as a result of last fall's tax changes, although considerably less than in the late 1970s, when the tax code was more progressive. But the continuing debate over whether the wealthy are paying their fair share of taxes obscures a larger issue, with more profound implications for America: The fortunate fifth is quietly seceding from the rest of the nation.

9   This is occurring gradually, without much awareness by members of the top group—or, for that matter, by anyone else. And the Government is speeding this process as Washington shifts responsibility for many public services to state and local governments.

The secession is taking several forms. In many cities and towns, the   10
wealthy have in effect withdrawn their dollars from the support of public
spaces and institutions shared by all and dedicated the savings to their
own private services. As public parks and playgrounds deteriorate, there
is a proliferation of private health clubs, golf clubs, tennis clubs, skating
clubs, and every other type of recreational association in which costs are
shared among members. Condominiums and the omnipresent residential
communities dun their members to undertake work that financially
strapped local governments can no longer afford to do well—maintaining
roads, mending sidewalks, pruning trees, repairing street lights, cleaning
swimming pools, paying for lifeguards, and, notably, hiring security
guards to protect life and property. (The number of private security guards
in the United States now exceeds the number of public police officers.)

Of course, wealthier Americans have been withdrawing into their   11
own neighborhoods and clubs for generations. But the new secession is
more dramatic because the highest earners now inhabit a different economy
from other Americans. The new elite is linked by jet, modem, fax, satellite,
and fiber-optic cable to the great commercial and recreational centers of the
world, but it is not particularly connected to the rest of the nation.

That is because the work this group does is becoming less tied to the   12
activities of other Americans. Most of their jobs consist of analyzing and
manipulating symbols—words, numbers, or visual images. Among the
most prominent of these "symbolic analysts" are management consultants,
lawyers, software and design engineers, research scientists, corporate
executives, financial advisors, strategic planners, advertising executives,
television and movie producers, and other workers whose job titles include terms like "strategy," "planning," "consultant," "policy," "resources,"
or "engineer."

These workers typically spend long hours in meetings or on the tele-   13
phone and even longer hours in planes or hotels—advising, making
presentations, giving briefings, and making deals. Periodically, they issue
reports, plans, designs, drafts, briefs, blueprints, analyses, memorandums,
layouts, renderings, scripts, or projections. In contrast with people whose
jobs tend to be tedious and repetitive, symbolic analysts find their work
varied and intellectually challenging. In fact, the work is often enjoyable.

These symbolic analysts are in ever greater demand in a world mar-   14
ket that places an increasing value on identifying and solving problems.
Requests for their software designs, financial advice, or engineering blueprints come from all parts of the globe. This largely explains why most (but
by no means all) symbolic analysts have become wealthier, even as the
ever-growing worldwide supply of unskilled labor continues to depress
the wages of other Americans.

Successful Americans have not completely disengaged themselves from   15
the lives of their less fortunate compatriots. Some devote substantial resources and energies to helping the rest of society, not through their tax

payments, but through voluntary efforts. "Generosity is a reflection of what one does with his or her resources—and not what he or she advocates the government do with everyone's money," Ronald Reagan said in 1984.

16   The argument is fair enough. Government is not the only device for redistributing wealth. In his speech accepting the Presidential nomination at the Republican National Convention in 1988, George Bush said that the real magnanimity of America was to be found in a "brilliant diversity" of private charities, "spread like stars, like a thousand points of light in a broad and peaceful sky."

17   No nation congratulates itself more enthusiastically on its charitable acts than America; none engages in a greater number of charity balls, bake sales, benefit auctions, and border-to-border hand holdings for good causes. Much of this is sincerely motivated and admirable.

18   But close examination reveals that many of these acts of benevolence do not help the needy. Particularly suspect is the private givings of those in the top income-tax bracket. Studies have revealed that their largess does not flow mainly to social services for the poor—to better schools, health clinics, or recreational centers. Instead, most voluntary contributions of wealthy Americans go to the places and institutions that entertain, inspire, cure, or educate wealthy Americans—art museums, opera houses, theaters, orchestras, ballet companies, private hospitals, and elite universities.

19   And even these charitable contributions are relatively skimpy. Last year, American households with incomes of less than $10,000 gave an average of 5.5 percent of their earnings to charity or to a religious organization; those making more than $100,000 a year gave only 2.9 percent. After the 1986 tax-code overhaul reduced the benefits of charitable giving, the very rich became even stingier. According to Internal Revenue Service data, taxpayers earning $500,000 or more slashed their average donations to $16,062 in 1988 from $47,432 in 1980.

20   Corporate philanthropy is following the same general pattern. In recent years, the largest American corporations have been sounding the alarm about the nation's fast deteriorating primary and secondary schools. Few are more eloquent and impassioned about the need for better schools than American executives. "How well we educate all of our children will determine our competitiveness globally, and our economic health domestically, and our communities' character and vitality," said a report of The Business Roundtable, a New York–based association of top executives.

21   Accordingly, there are numerous "partnerships" between corporations and public schools: scholarships for poor children qualified to attend college, and programs in which businesses adopt individual schools by making conspicuous donations of computers, books, and, on occasion, even money. That such activities are loudly touted by public relations staffs should not detract from the good they do.

22   Despite the hoopla, business donations to education and charitable causes actually tapered off markedly in the 1980s, even as the economy

boomed. In the 1970s, corporate giving to education jumped an average of 15 percent a year. In 1990, however, giving was only 5 percent over that in 1989; and in 1989 it was 3 percent over 1988. Moreover, most of this money goes to colleges and universities—in particular, to the alma maters of symbolic analysts, who expect their children and grandchildren to follow in their footsteps. Only 1.5 percent of corporate giving in the late 1980s was to public primary and secondary schools.

Notably, these contributions have been smaller than the amounts corporations are receiving from states and communities in the form of subsidies or tax breaks. Companies are quietly procuring such deals by threatening to move their operations—and jobs—to places around the world with a more congenial tax climate. The paradoxical result has been even less corporate revenue to spend on schools and other community services than before. The executives of General Motors, for example, who have been among the loudest to proclaim the need for better schools, have also been among the most relentless in pursuing local tax abatements and in challenging their tax assessments. G.M.'s successful efforts to reduce its taxes in North Tarrytown, N.Y., where the company has had a factory since 1914, cut local revenues by $1 million in 1990, part of a larger shortfall that forced the town to lay off scores of teachers. 23

The secession of the fortunate fifth has been apparent in how and where they have chosen to work and live. In effect, most of America's large urban centers have splintered into two separate cities. One is composed of those whose symbolic and analytic services are linked to the world economy. The other consists of local service workers—custodians, security guards, taxi drivers, clerical aides, parking attendants, salespeople, restaurant employees— whose jobs are dependent on the symbolic analysts. Few blue-collar manufacturing workers remain in American cities. Between 1953 and 1984, for example, New York City lost 600,000 factory jobs; in the same interval, it added about 700,000 jobs for symbolic analysts and service workers. 24

The separation of symbolic analysts from local service workers within cities has been reinforced in several ways. Most large cities now possess two school systems—a private one for the children of the top-earning group and a public one for the children of service workers, the remaining blue-collar workers, and the unemployed. Symbolic analysts spend considerable time and energy insuring that their children gain entrance to good private schools, and then small fortunes keeping them there—dollars that under a more progressive tax code might finance better public education. 25

People with high incomes live, shop, and work within areas of cities that, if not beautiful, are at least esthetically tolerable and reasonably safe; precincts not meeting these minimum standards of charm and security have been left to the less fortunate. 26

Here again, symbolic analysts have pooled their resources to the exclusive benefit of themselves. Public funds have been spent in earnest on 27 downtown "revitalization" projects, entailing the construction of clusters of post-modern office buildings (complete with fiber-optic cables, private branch exchanges, satellite dishes, and other communications equipment linking them to the rest of the world), multilevel parking garages, hotels with glass enclosed atriums, upscale shopping plazas and galleries, theaters, convention centers, and luxury condominiums.

28   Ideally, these complexes are entirely self-contained, with air-conditioned walkways linking residences, businesses, and recreational space. The lucky resident is able to shop, work, and attend the theater without risking direct contact with the outside world—that is, the other city.

29   When not living in urban enclaves, symbolic analysts are increasingly congregating in suburbs and exurbs where corporate headquarters have been relocated, research parks have been created, and where bucolic universities have spawned entrepreneurial ventures. Among the most desirable of such locations are Princeton, N.J.; northern Westchester and Putnam Counties in New York; Palo Alto, Calif.; Austin, Tex.; Bethesda, Md.; and Raleigh-Durham, N.C.

30   Engineers and strategists of American auto companies, for example, do not live in Flint or Saginaw, Mich., where the blue-collar workers reside; they cluster in their own towns of Troy, Warren, and Auburn Hills. Likewise, the vast majority of financial specialists, lawyers, and executives working for the insurance companies of Hartford would never consider living there; after all, Hartford is the nation's fourth-poorest city. Instead, they flock to Windsor, Middlebury, West Hartford, and other towns that are among the wealthiest in the country.

31   This trend, too, has been growing for decades. But technology has accelerated it. Today's symbolic analysts linked directly to the rest of the globe can choose to live and work in the most pastoral of settings.

32   The secession has been encouraged by the Federal Government. For the last decade, Washington has in effect shifted responsibility for many public services to local governments. At their peak, Federal grants made up 25 percent of state and local spending in the late 1970s. Today, the Federal share has dwindled to 17 percent. Direct aid to local governments, in the form of programs introduced in the Johnson and Nixon Administrations, has been the hardest hit by budget cuts. In the 1980s, Federal dollars for clean water, job training and transfers, low-income housing, sewage treatment, and garbage disposal shrank by some $50 billion a year, and Washington's share of spending on local transit declined by 50 percent. (The Bush Administration has proposed that states and localities take on even more of the costs of building and maintaining roads, and wants to cut Federal aid for mass transit.) In 1990, New York City received only 9.6 percent of all its revenue from the Federal Government, compared with 16 percent in 1981.

33   States have quickly transferred many of these new expenses to fiscally strapped cities and towns, with a result that by the start of the 1990s, localities were bearing more than half the costs of water and sewage,

roads, parks, welfare, and public schools. In New York State, the local communities' share has risen to about 75 percent of these costs.

Cities and towns with affluent inhabitants can bear these burdens rel- 34 atively easily. Poorer ones, faced with the twin problem of lower incomes and greater demand for social services, have had far more difficulty. And as the gap between the richest and poorest communities has widened, the shift in responsibility for public services to cities and towns has functioned as another means of relieving wealthier Americans of the cost of aiding less fortunate citizens.

The result has been a growing inequality in basic social and com- 35 munity services. While the city tax rate in Philadelphia, for example, is about triple that of communities around it, the suburbs enjoy far better schools, hospitals, recreation, and police protection. Eighty-five percent of the richest families in the greater Philadelphia area live outside the city limits, and 80 percent of the region's poorest live inside. The quality of a city's infrastructure—roads, bridges, sewage, water treatment—is likewise related to the average income of its inhabitants.

The growing inequality in government services has been most ap- 36 parent in the public schools. The Federal Government's share of the costs of primary and secondary education has dwindled to about 6 percent. The bulk of the cost is divided about equally between the states and local school districts. States with a higher concentration of wealthy residents can afford to spend more on their schools than other states. In 1989, the average public-school teacher in Arkansas, for example, received $21,700; in Connecticut, $37,300.

Even among adjoining suburban towns in the same state the differ- 37 ences can be quite large. Consider three Boston-area communities located within minutes of one another. All are predominantly white, and most residents within each town earn about the same as their neighbors. But the disparity of incomes between towns is substantial.

Belmont, northwest of Boston, is inhabited mainly by symbolic ana- 38 lysts and their families. In 1988, the average teacher in its public schools earned $36,100. Only 3 percent of Belmont's eighteen-year-olds dropped out of high school, and more than 80 percent of graduating seniors chose to go on to a four-year college.

Just east of Belmont is Somerville, most of whose residents are low- 39 wage service workers. In 1988, the average Somerville teacher earned $29,400. A third of the town's eighteen-year-olds did not finish high school, and fewer than a third planned to attend college.

Chelsea, across the Mystic River from Somerville, is the poorest of the 40 three towns. Most of its inhabitants are unskilled, and many are unemployed or only employed part time. The average teacher in Chelsea, facing tougher educational challenges than his or her counterparts in Belmont, earned $26,200 in 1988, almost a third less than the average teacher in the more affluent town just a few miles away. More than half of Chelsea's eighteen-year-olds did not graduate from high school, and only 10 percent planned to attend college.

41   Similar disparities can be found all over the nation. Students at High-land Park High School in a wealthy suburb of Dallas, for example, enjoy a campus with a planetarium, indoor swimming pool, closed-circuit television studio and state-of-the-art science laboratory. Highland Park spends about $6,000 a year to educate each student. This is almost twice that spent per pupil by the towns of Wilmer and Hutchins in southern Dallas County. According to Texas education officials, the richest school district in the state spends $19,300 a year per pupil; its poorest, $2,100 a year.

42   The courts have become involved in trying to repair such imbalances, but the issues are not open to easy judicial remedy.

43   The four-fifths of Americans left in the wake of the secession of the fortunate fifth include many poor blacks, but racial exclusion is neither the primary motive for the separation nor a necessary consequence. Lower-income whites are similarly excluded, and high-income black symbolic analysts are often welcomed. The segregation is economic rather than racial, although economically motivated separation often results in *de facto* racial segregation. Where courts have found a pattern of racially motivated segregation, it usually has involved lower-income white communities bordering on lower-income black neighborhoods.

44   In states where courts have ordered equalized state spending in school districts, the vast differences in a town's property values—and thus local tax revenues—continue to result in substantial inequities. Where courts or state governments have tried to impose limits on what affluent communities can pay their teachers, not a few parents in upscale towns have simply removed their children from the public schools and applied the money they might otherwise have willingly paid in higher taxes to private school tuitions instead. And, of course, even if statewide expenditures were better equalized, poorer states would continue to be at a substantial disadvantage.

45   In all these ways, the gap between America's symbolic analysts and everyone else is widening into a chasm. Their secession from the rest of the population raises fundamental questions about the future of American society. In the new global economy—in which money, technologies, and corporations cross borders effortlessly—a citizen's standard of living depends more and more on skills and insights, and on the infrastructure needed to link these abilities to the rest of the world. But the most skilled and insightful Americans, who are already positioned to thrive in the world market, are now able to slip the bonds of national allegiance, and by so doing disengage themselves from their less-favored fellows. The stark political challenge in the decades ahead will be to reaffirm that, even though America is no longer a separate and distinct economy, it is still a society whose members have abiding obligations to one another.

Content

1. Does Reich prove convincingly that "the fortunate fifth [those Americans with the highest income] is quietly seceding from the rest of the nation" (¶ 8)? To what extent does your receptivity to his argument depend on whether or not you consider yourself or your family a member of the "fortunate fifth"?

2. Who are "symbolic analysts" (¶s 12–14, 25–31)? Does Reich demonstrate that these persons comprise a significant portion of the "fortunate fifth"? Why does he identify their job titles (¶ 12), activities (¶ 13), lifestyles (¶s 25–28), and places of work and residence (¶s 28–30) in long lists? In what ways does he expect his readers to interpret these lists?

3. Reich illustrates many of the points of his argument with reference to the public schools in rich and poor districts (¶s 36–44, for example). Why does he focus on schools?

4. If Reich has convinced you of his premise (see question 1 above), has he also convinced you of his conclusion that "the most skilled and insightful Americans . . . are now able to slip the bonds of national allegiance, and by so doing disengage themselves from their less-favored fellows. The stark political challenge . . . will be to reaffirm that . . . [America] is still a society whose members have abiding obligations to one another" (¶ 45)? If he has convinced you, what does he want you to do as a consequence? If he hasn't convinced you, why hasn't he?

Strategies/Structures/Language

5. The specific statistical information and other figures in Reich's 1991 article change annually, if not more often. Is their alteration within the next decade likely to affect either Reich's argument or your receptivity to it? Since numbers are always in flux, why use them in an argument?

6. Reich's sentences are fairly long, but his paragraphs are short, usually from one to three sentences. (The longest paragraph, ¶ 32, has eight sentences.) This is because the article was originally published in a newspaper, the *New York Times Magazine*; newspapers provide paragraph breaks not to indicate where the material logically breaks or changes course but to rest readers' eyes as they roam the page. What is the effect, if any, of such a large number of short paragraphs in a serious article?

7. Which side does Reich favor? At what point in the argument does he expect his readers to realize this?

8. Does Reich's division of workers into "symbolic and analytic services" and "local service workers" cover most people in cities? Where do "blue-collar manufacturing workers" live (see ¶ 24)? Are such labels necessary or helpful in constructing the argument Reich makes?

For Writing

9. Argue, by yourself or with a team, as Reich does but using your own examples (and some of his factual information, among other sources) that, as Reich concludes, "even though America is no longer a separate and distinct economy, it is still a society whose members have abiding obligations to one another" (¶ 45). One way to

address the subject is to consider the implications of a particular public policy issue (such as, school busing, property taxation, equalization of school funding across rich and poor districts, gated residential communities with private security guards, privatization of Social Security). See, for example, Martin Luther King, Jr.'s, "Letter from Birmingham Jail" (444–57), and the essays by Kozol, Coontz, and Nocton identified in the next question.

10. Is it socially desirable for the upper fifth in income to "secede," however quietly, "from the rest of the nation," as Reich asserts in paragraph 8? Shouldn't everyone have the right to live where they want to? Should people be required to live in the same geographical area where they work? If you wish, supplement your argument with reference to the essays by Kozol, 204–11; Coontz, 213–16; and Nocton, 527–31.

 For comprehension, writing, and research activities and resources, please visit the companion website at <college.hmco.com/english>.

EVAN EISENBERG

Eisenberg (born 1955), educated in philosophy, is a journalist specializing in music and technology. He has published two books. According to reviewer David Hamilton, Eisenberg's *The Recording Angel: Explorations in Phonography* (1987) "grasps the multivalent nature of the recording, that a record is what you do with it, never the same thing to different people—or to the same person at different times and places." Drawing on literature, myth, philosophy, science, and music, continues Hamilton, *The Ecology of Eden* (1988) considers "man's relationship with nature [and offers] a model of how it could be changed to prevent environmental disaster." "Dialogue Boxes You Should Have Read More Carefully" provides a strong critique of Microsoft in a concise form, readily accessible to any computer user. As you read, note not only the text in the dialogue boxes, but the icons and the—very limited—options for response.

Dialogue Boxes You Should Have Read More Carefully

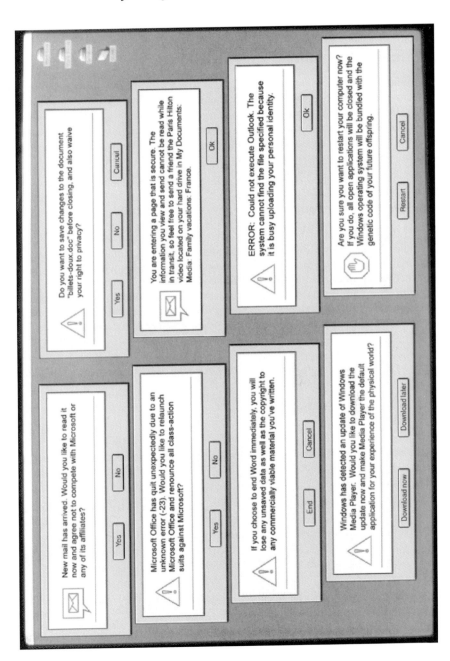

Content

1. Each dialogue box embeds an argument about Microsoft. Identify the argument of each and the specific charge against Microsoft's relation to those who use its operating system.
2. Now consider all the arguments together. What's their point?

Strategies/Structures/Language

3. What's missing from some of the limited choices in the actions the computer user can take? Identify these, and explain what will happen if the user chooses one or another of the permissible alternatives.
4. Eisenberg conducts his argument by letting readers do most of the work and come to all of the conclusions. How can he be sure they'll read the boxes the way he wants them to and arrive at the same conclusions that he does?
5. How closely has Eisenberg imitated Microsoft's language?

For Writing/Drawing

6. Find cartoons that make arguments, and analyze several to show how they do it—either through only visual means or through a combination of words and images. Editorial or political cartoons are a good source. If you work with a partner, you can check your interpretations against each other's.
7. Present an argument of your own in cartoon format, using either a single or multiple panel. If you can't draw, you can provide your own captions for existing cartoons. See, for instance, *The New Yorker's* website., www.cartoonbank.com.

 For comprehension, writing, and research activities and resources, please visit the companion website at <college.hmco.com/english>.

ANNA QUINDLEN

Quindlen, born in Philadelphia in 1953, became a reporter for the *New York Times* within three years of graduating from Barnard (BA, 1974). Her columns "About New York," "Life in the 30s," and "Public & Private"—which won a Pulitzer Prize in 1992—made her "the unintended voice of the baby boom generation." These have been collected in her books *Living Out Loud* (1988) and *Thinking Out Loud* (1993). From a perspective at once incisive and thoroughly alert to the perplexities of being human—a daughter, a happily-married mother of three, a Roman Catholic, a liberal feminist—she focuses on, as *Newsweek* said, "the rocky emotional terrain of marriage, parenthood, secret desires and self-doubts." Leaving the *Times* in 1994 to write fiction and children's stories, she published bestselling novels about complications of family life: *Object Lessons* (1991), on the "dislocations of growing up"; *One True Thing* (1995), on right-to-die issues; *Black and Blue* (1998), on domestic violence, and *Being Perfect* 2005).

In 1999 she became a columnist at *Newsweek,* where "Uncle Sam and Aunt Samantha" appeared on November 5, 2001. Here she argues—as the mother of teenage children—against the sexist U.S. policy of mandatory draft for men only. If men and women truly have equal rights, they should bear equal responsibility to serve their country. A double standard "makes a mockery not only of the standards of this household but of the standards of this nation."

Uncle Sam and Aunt Samantha

One out of every five new recruits in the United States military is   1
female.

The Marines gave the Combat Action Ribbon for service in the Per-   2
sian Gulf to 23 women.

Two female soldiers were killed in the bombing of the USS Cole.   3

The Selective Service registers for the draft all male citizens between   4
the ages of 18 and 25.

What's wrong with this picture?   5

As Americans read and realize that the lives of most women in this   6
country are as different from those of Afghan women as a Cunard cruise is from maximum-security lockdown, there has nonetheless been little attention paid to one persistent gender inequity in U.S. public policy. An astonishing anachronism, really: while women are represented today in virtually all fields, including the armed forces, only men are required to register for the military draft that would be used in the event of a national-security crisis.

Since the nation is as close to such a crisis as it has been in more than   7
60 years, it's a good moment to consider how the draft wound up in this particular time warp. It's not the time warp of the Taliban, certainly, stuck in the worst part of the 13th century, forbidding women to attend school or hold jobs or even reveal their arms, forcing them into sex and marriage. Our own time warp is several decades old. The last time the draft was considered seriously was 20 years ago, when registration with the Selective Service was restored by Jimmy Carter after the Soviet invasion of, yep, Afghanistan. The president, as well as the Army chief of staff, asked at the time for the registration of women as well as men.

Amid a welter of arguments—women interfere with esprit de corps,   8
women don't have the physical strength, women prisoners could be sexually assaulted, women soldiers would distract male soldiers from their mission—Congress shot down the notion of gender-blind registration. So

This young American woman, U.S. Army Spcl. (Specialist) of the 401 MP (Military Police) Company, 720 MP Battalion, is on duty in February 2004 in Samarra, 125 km north of Baghdad, one of two female gunners in this platoon. What appeals to emotion, ethics, prejudices would this photograph elicit, as an illustration of Anna Quindlen's "Uncle Sam and Aunt Samantha"? This essay could have been illustrated with other, more peaceful images, of American women in military uniform, approaching Iraqi women in burnooses with gestures of friendship. Or it could have been illustrated with the now notorious photograph of Private First Class Lynndie England aiding in humiliating naked prisoners in Abu Ghraib prison. In what ways—if any—would either sort of photograph have influenced your answer?

did the Supreme Court, ruling that since women were forbidden to serve in combat positions and the purpose of the draft was to create a combat-ready force, it made sense not to register them.

9   But that was then, and this is now. Women have indeed served in combat positions, in the Balkans and the Middle East. More than 40,000 managed to serve in the Persian Gulf without destroying unit cohesion or failing because of upper-body strength. Some are even now taking out targets in Afghanistan from fighter jets, and apparently without any male soldier's falling prey to some predicted excess of chivalry or lust.

10   Talk about cognitive dissonance. All these military personnel, male and female alike, have come of age at a time when a significant level of parity was taken for granted. Yet they are supposed to accept that only males will be required to defend their country in a time of national emergency. This is insulting to men. And it is insulting to women. Caroline Forell, an expert on women's legal rights and a professor at the University

of Oregon School of Law, puts it bluntly: "Failing to require this of women makes us lesser citizens."

Neither the left nor the right has been particularly inclined to con- 11 sider this issue judiciously. Many feminists came from the antiwar movement and have let their distaste for the military in general and the draft in particular mute their response. In 1980 NOW released a resolution that buried support for the registration of women beneath opposition to the draft, despite the fact that the draft had been redesigned to eliminate the vexing inequities of Vietnam, when the sons of the working class served and the sons of the Ivy League did not. Conservatives, meanwhile, used an equal-opportunity draft as the linchpin of opposition to the Equal Rights Amendment, along with the terrifying specter of unisex bathrooms. (I have seen the urinal, and it is benign.) The legislative director of the right-wing group Concerned Women for America once defended the existing regulations by saying that most women "don't want to be included in the draft." All those young men who went to Canada during Vietnam and those who today register with fear and trembling in the face of the Trade Center devastation might be amazed to discover that lack of desire is an affirmative defense.

Parents face a series of unique new challenges in this more egalitarian 12 world, not the least of which would be sending a daughter off to war. But parents all over this country are doing that right now, with daughters who enlisted; some have even expressed surprise that young women, in this day and age, are not required to register alongside their brothers and friends. While all involved in this debate over the years have invoked the assumed opposition of the people, even 10 years ago more than half of all Americans polled believed women should be made eligible for the draft. Besides, this is not about comfort but about fairness. My son has to register with the Selective Service this year, and if his sister does not when she turns 18, it makes a mockery not only of the standards of this household but of the standards of this nation.

It is possible in Afghanistan for women to be treated like little more 13 than fecund pack animals precisely because gender fear and ignorance and hatred have been codified and permitted to hold sway. In this country, largely because of the concerted efforts of those allied with the women's movement over a century of struggle, much of that bigotry has been beaten back, even buried. Yet in improbable places the creaky old ways surface, the ways suggesting that we women were made of finer stuff. The finer stuff was usually porcelain, decorative and on the shelf, suitable for meals and show. Happily, the finer stuff has been transmuted into the right stuff. But with rights come responsibilities, as teachers like to tell their students. This is a responsibility that should fall equally upon all, male and female alike. If the empirical evidence is considered rationally, if the decision is divested of outmoded stereotypes, that's the only possible conclusion to be reached.

Content

1. Why is it that until now "only men [have been] required to register for the military draft that would be used in the event of a national-security crisis" (¶ 6)? What evidence does Quindlen use to make her point that not requiring women to register for the draft is wrong? What evidence does she cite to make her case that not requiring women to defend their country "in a time of national emergency" is insulting to both men and women (¶ 10)?

2. Why did Quindlen write this essay? To what extent might she believe her readers would agree with her viewpoint at the outset? After reading her essay? Would an audience of college students be expected to respond in the same way?

Strategies/Structures/Language

3. Quindlen begins her essay with a series of factual statements that lead to a question: "What's wrong with this picture?" (¶ 5). What are the advantages of this type of introductory strategy in writing an argumentative essay? Are there disadvantages as well?

4. Quindlen sums up her argument by stating, "If the empirical evidence is considered rationally, if the decision is divested of outmoded stereotypes, that's the only possible conclusion to be reached" (¶ 13). Do most arguments admit of only a single conclusion? Does this one? Explain.

5. What is the point of Quindlen's comparisons between women in America and in Afghanistan (¶s 6, 7, 13)?

6. Quindlen uses straightforward statements, anger, sarcasm, irony, and metaphors in making her argument. Show where these occur and how they work together to reinforce her point.

For Writing

7. Quindlen claims that "even 10 years ago more than half of all Americans polled believed women should be made eligible for the draft" (¶ 12). The results Quindlen cites are derived from a poll of approximately 1,500 respondents in which 52 percent believed women should register for the draft. Conduct your own poll, both on and off campus, to find out whether the figure Quindlen states is still accurate in light of current events.

8. With a peer of the opposite gender, write an essay that discusses your own willingness—whether man or woman—to serve in the military during a period of national emergency.

 For comprehension, writing, and research activities and resources, please visit the companion website at <college.hmco.com/english>.

MATTHEW ALLEN

Allen was born in San Diego in 1980, but he says, "I do not really know where to call home." As a consequence of frequent family moves, he lived in five states (California, Florida, Utah, Georgia, and Virginia) and in ten different cities, and then he spent two years in France, Belgium, and Luxembourg. Allen's summer of 2005 was indeed memorable. He graduated from Brigham Young University (2005), worked in the Department of International Relations in the Mayors' Office at Nice (yes, on the French Riviera), and copresented a paper at an international conference on Forensic Linguistics/Language and Law at Cardiff University in Wales. He is currently preparing for a career in international law at Boston University School of Law.

In several ways, Allen says, "'The Rhetorical Situation of the Scientific Paper' is the culmination of my undergraduate studies. First, I drew on the different disciplines I had studied, including biology, psychology, and English language and linguistics, as I researched and wrote this paper. Second, the countless revisions I went through for this paper showed me how much I had matured as a writer. For years, I dreaded criticism so much that I refused to proofread or redraft my work. After becoming an editor and writing tutor [at BYU's Writing Center], I finally realized the value of feedback and revision." Allen says his paper went through more than six major revisions before it was published in *Young Scholars in Writing: Undergraduate Research in Writing and Rhetoric* (2004). In it, Allen argues that the "experimental report, like all written accounts, is an interpretation, subject to creativity, convention, form, and style" (¶ 26).

❄ *The Rhetorical Situation of the Scientific Paper and the "Appearance" of Objectivity*

Mention the words *rhetoric* and *science* together, and many people see   1
an intrinsic contradiction. After all, two hallmarks of modern science are objectivity and empirical method, whereas rhetoric bears the marks of a long and sometimes sordid history of sophistic oratory and biased argumentation. Gerald Holton describes this distinction: Rhetoric is often perceived as the art of persuasion, while science is generally seen as the art of demonstration (173). This idea implies, to use a figure of speech, that rhetoric and science should not be seen together in public. The distinction between the two, however, is probably more fabricated than genuine. Scholars, especially during the last several decades, have argued that scientific practice and discourse do have rhetorical and persuasive elements.

2   Published scientific papers bridge the gap between a scientist's work and the public's knowledge of that work. Research that goes unpublished, to use an image from Robert Day, is like a tree falling in a forest when no one is around—there is no "sound" without an audience (1). In order for this knowledge to be received and accepted by the intended audience, generally the scientific community, the research or experimental report must follow certain conventions, not the least of which are methodological validity and pertinence to the existing body of scientific knowledge. The authors of scientific papers must demonstrate the validity and objectivity of their findings and make them seem interesting and relevant to already-established conclusions. In effect, this is a rhetorical situation: a speaker (the author) communicates knowledge about a particular subject to an audience via the scientific paper, intending, on some level, to persuade that audience.

3   What is most interesting about the rhetorical situation of the scientific paper is that the writer persuades his or her audience largely through the *appearance of* objectivity. Many people, as Charles Bazerman points out, think that writing based on scientific premises is not really writing at all (14), that it is an unbiased vessel for transmitting truth. But in this essay, I analyze Renske Wassenberg, Jeffrey E. Max, Scott D. Lindgren, and Amy Schatz's article, "Sustained Attention in Children and Adolescents after Traumatic Brain Injury: Relation to Severity of Injury, Adaptive Functioning, ADHD and Social Background" (herein referred to as "Sustained Attention in Children and Adolescents"), recently published in *Brain Injury*, to illustrate that the writer of an experimental report in effect creates an exigence and then addresses it through rhetorical strategies that contribute to the appearance of objectivity.

Scientific Inquiry and Objectivity

4   It would seem that the objective nature of modern science precludes any possibility of rhetoric's entering into scientific writing. The assumption is that writing is interpretive and science is not. This notion results from an apparently sound connection: scientific writing is scientific; science is objective; therefore, scientific writing is objective. Objectivity certainly is one of the key goals and primary assumptions of scientific practice and writing. Nevertheless, it is inaccurate to think that the subjective human element can be completely eliminated through even the most objective scientific method. As Peter Medawar suggests, "There is no such thing as unprejudiced observation. Every act of observation we make is biased. What we see or otherwise sense is a function of what we have seen or sensed in the past" (230).

5   While the historic public face of science may exude objectivity, there is a pervasive, if less openly discussed, subjective side. Even if scientists were able to collect data in a purely objective way, Brent Slife and Richard Williams contend that "we cannot ignore the necessity of *interpreting* the data yielded by scientific method" (5, emphasis in original). Although computer programs may seem to be doing unbiased interpreting in some

cases, human beings must ultimately give meaning to data, however raw they may or may not be. For example, an experiment that measured the brain waves of laboratory rats under certain conditions might yield a group of numbers, a data set. That data set would be virtually meaningless (i.e., it would not tell the researchers what they had found) until it was organized in some coherent way. But what kind of organization would be most coherent? A graph, a table, perhaps a qualitative description? Each organizational approach might produce different findings, but many approaches will be equally valid. The choice of methods and organization of data will ultimately depend on the point of view of the person doing the interpreting and the scientific needs of the project. A computer might flawlessly organize data a particular way, but that computer was programmed by someone. The point is that ideas outside of the actual data set must be projected onto the data set before it means anything. As Slife and Williams explain, "in this sense, data can never be facts until they have been given an interpretation that is dependent on ideas that do not appear in the data themselves" (6).

This type of evidence leads to Bazerman's assertion that the "popular   6
belief of this past century that scientific language is simply a transparent transmitter of natural facts is . . . of course wrong" (14). Medawar goes even further, declaring that the scientific paper gives "a totally misleading narrative of the processes of thought that go into the making of scientific discoveries" (233). One of his points is that there is a creative side to science, a side often sacrificed to an assumed objectivity. Creativity is more subjective than objective, and so alternative interpretations exist.

Experimental Papers and Persuasive Argument

Despite attempts to influence the reader, the type of rhetoric involved in   7
scientific writing does not, as Kristine Hansen emphasizes, involve "bombast, flowery phrases, or appeals to emotion, all aimed at deceiving" (xvi). Rather, contend John Schuster and Richard Yeo, "scientific argumentation is essentially persuasive argument and therefore is rightly termed *rhetorical* in the sense defined by students of 'the new rhetoric,' where 'rhetoric' denotes the entire field of discursive structures and strategies used to render arguments persuasive in given situations" (xii). As scientists write reports of original research, all the while conforming to certain accepted structures and styles, such as logic, clarity, and empiricism, they still give a rhetorical shape to their writing. Gerald Holton describes this process as a "proactive rhetoric of assertion"—when a scientist becomes convinced of something, he or she hopes to persuade others about that same idea or phenomenon when the work is published (176).

There are practical motivations beyond contributing to scientific   8
knowledge for using scientific rhetoric to emphasize the importance of publishable research. Scientists, according to Day, are primarily measured by and known for their publications (ix). In the competitive world of academics and research, scientists need to publish to gain prestige and promotions.

Poorly written, nonstandard, or unconvincing papers are naturally less likely to be chosen for publication.

The Rhetorical Situation and its Exigence

9   According to Lloyd Bitzer, rhetoric is always situational; it is a pragmatic response "to a situation of a certain kind," functioning "ultimately to produce action or change in the world" (3). The rhetorical situation, according to Bitzer, has several key features, but my primary concern is with exigence, which is central to understanding scientific rhetoric. An exigence, as defined by Bitzer, is "an imperfection marked by urgency; it is a defect, an obstacle, something waiting to be done, a thing which is other than it should be" (6). An exigence such as winter or death that cannot be altered through rhetoric or through any other means is not a rhetorical exigence (6). This understanding of exigence is further elucidated by Bitzer's definition of rhetoric:

> In short, rhetoric is a mode of altering reality, not by direct application of energy to objects, but by the creation of discourse which changes reality through the mediation of thought and action. The rhetor alters reality by bringing into existence a discourse of such a character that the audience, in thought and action, is so engaged that it becomes mediator of change. In this sense rhetoric is always persuasive. (3)

10   This concept of rhetoric and exigence is exemplified in many of the speeches and writings of Martin Luther King, Jr. King believed that the racially inequitable social conditions around him could be altered through speech and subsequent action. King helped to change the reality of racial inequality through rhetoric, including his famous "I Have a Dream" speech. His discourse engaged, and continued to engage, his audience, often prompting people to action. King did not himself rewrite legislation or policies, but his rhetoric contributed to the actions of those who did.

11   In a scientific paper, the reality being altered is the accumulating knowledge of the scientific community. The rhetorical exigence is, in Lawrence Prelli's words, the "gap in the collective body of knowledge" (23). Simply put, a scientist performs an experiment to better understand a law, principle, or phenomenon and then creates and publishes a scientific paper to communicate the results to the scientific community. In a sense, the scientist is "fixing" a problem—he or she has come to a better understanding of something than anyone else and is therefore able to fill in that "gap" in knowledge. As Prelli suggests, "[a] scientific orientation inclines one to define rhetorical situations in terms of the presence or absence of objectively verifiable information and the consonance of new evidence with already-accepted knowledge" (23).

12   Prelli seems to imply, justifiably, that scientific rhetoric is secondary to scientific knowledge and practice. If the new knowledge cannot be scientifically verified and reconciled with traditional knowledge, the rhetorical

aspects of the paper alone, the strategies used to make the new knowledge seem like an answer, are useless. The scientist must first have identified a problem in order to propose the answer he or she has found. Experimental reports, Bazerman says, are special in this way because they describe "an event created so that it might be told" (59). Scientists formulated problems, according to their methodologies, in order to solve them—in essence, they create more than discover the rhetorical situation because they construct an exigence.

In "Sustained Attention in Children and Adolescents," the authors   13
express their exigence when they state the study's primary objective: "To examine the relationship of child and family psychological variables and traumatic brain injury (TBI) severity as it relates to sustained attention" (751). The driving question is clear: What, if any, is the relationship between psychosocial variables and TBI? This question certainly is compelling and worthwhile, but was it discovered or created? The authors imply a creative process of arriving at their exigence:

> Attention problems are commonly reported after TBI in children. There is little known about the effects of TBI on specific attentional components: orienting to sensory stimuli, executive functions and maintaining the alert state. The focus of this study is on sustained attention (i.e. the capacity to maintain arousal and alertness over time). According to Dennis et al., sustained attention is a regulator of cognitive activities needed for academic tasks, adaptive function-ing and social interactions. A deficiency in sustained attention may, therefore, have a significant impact on the child's development in the acute and chronic stages of TBI. (752)

As this paragraph from the introduction illustrates, the authors created   14
an exigence by building upon previous research and their own insights and by constructing a logical hypothesis (eventually an entire study) to address that exigence. In essence, they arrived at their research question through inference. The exigence, however valid, was essentially created through a careful, thoughtful, and creative process. The authors' review of the litera-ture did not inevitably lead to their hypothesis. They creatively took two factors (pre-TBI psychological variables and post-TBI sustained attention) and postulated a relationship between them. Yet, the connection is scien-tifically valid: many of their ideas have been discussed or established in previous research, and they can test their new ideas empirically.

Rhetorical Strategies Used to Shape the Persuasive Paper

In effect, the authors of experimental papers address the exigence of the rhe-   15
torical situation through a carefully crafted rhetoric. The writing, as Bazer-man says, "appears to hide itself" (14). This subtle approach is a specific rhetorical strategy: there seems to be no style—hence, no rhetoric—when

in fact there is one. The writing style in most experimental reports intentionally deemphasizes creativity and human voice. The general choice is to use rhetoric that is persuasive through emphasizing logic and objectivity over creativity. Such rhetorical aspects of scientific writing tend to be subsumed or hidden by the larger goal of conveying meaning clearly and impartially.

16   For example, the passive voice, whereby the writer can easily omit the agent (the "doer" in the clause), is more prevalent in scientific writing than in most other genres. The editors of *Merriam Webster's Dictionary of English Usage* point out that while the active voice is generally preferable, "a few [usage] commentators find the passive useful in scientific writing (one even believes it to be necessary) because of the tone of detachment and impersonality that it helps establish" (721).

17   The authors of "Sustained Attention in Children and Adolescents" definitely agree with this remark about the importance of the passive voice. An analysis of the first 118 or so lines of the article (the introduction and part of the method section) attests to the author's careful choice of language: over one-third of the verb constructions are passives (about 26 of 70). For most non-scientific published writing, passive constructions tend to be around 10 to 15 percent, a ratio that the article noticeably surpasses (*Merriam Webster's* 720) The significance of this frequent use of passives is that actions and findings (i.e., non-human elements) are emphasized over human elements. The agent is noticeably missing in the following passive sentences from the article:

- The Paediatric Assessment of Cognitive Efficiency (PACE) was used in this study to test two types of deficits, inattention and impulsiveness. (752)
- Inattention and impulsiveness were not further elucidated because the two error measures, omission and commission errors, were not independently analyzed. (752)
- It was hypothesized that children with severe TBI will produce significantly more errors on the PACE than children with mild/moderate TBI. (753)
- No differences were found between the Mild/Moderate and Severe TBI group in regards to demographic characteristics. (754)

18   For each of these actions, there must have been an agent, someone using the assessment, choosing not to further elucidate certain factors, hypothesizing, and failing to find differences. The authors' use of the passive voice to emphasize the action and deemphasize the agent (the authors omit the agent in nearly every passive construction in the first 118 lines) certainly does create a "tone of detachment and impersonality," even one of objectivity.[1]

19   The standard organization of scientific papers is another way to emphasize the factual and objective over the interpretive and subjective. The

organization helps portray the paper's information logically and persuasively. The modern research paper, as Day explains, has the basic universal form of IMRAD—Introduction, Methods, Results, and Discussion—
because this form is "so eminently logical" (11). Holton dubs this rationale
the "well-tested machinery of logic and analysis, the direct evidence of the
phenomena" (174). Plainly stated, the scientific paper is structured according to a scientific ideal: the method is set forth, and the results are reported,
analyzed, and discussed. The organization by sequential sections is logical;
the analysis is scientific because the discussion (the possibly non-scientific
human element) is kept separate from the results. This type of organization,
Medawar argues, implies an inductive process of unbiased observation
leading to generalization (229). While the accuracy of this method may be
questioned, it is logically convincing because, as Louis Pasteur purportedly
told his students, it makes the results seem inevitable (Holton 174).

   "Sustained Attention in Children and Adolescents" strictly adheres to   20
the IMRAD method of organization. The report contains an introduction;
a methods section, which is further broken down into six subsections; a
results section; and a discussion. The authors could have chosen another
method of organization, but doing so would probably have reduced the
likelihood of their getting the article published, and had it been published
in a novel format, frequent readers of research reports would likely have
been put off to some degree. As it stands, readers of "Sustained Attention
in Children and Adolescents" waste no time getting to the crux of the
study—it's right there in the introduction and discussion—but all the technical evidence is still available. One interesting aspect of this particular
study is that it is essentially part of a "soft" or social science. The variables
in the study are all centered on human beings, studied according to various psychological tests. The patently scientific organization of the paper,
however, seems to leave no question that this study was done according
to "hard" science principles.

   The same type of logical persuasion exemplified in the IMRAD or-   21
ganization is common in the introductions of many papers, a part of the
report designed to emphasize the relevance and necessity of the particular
findings to preexisting scientific evidence. John Swales found that scientists
tend to use a very specific rhetorical strategy, what he termed the Create
a Research Space (CARS) communication move schema (Golebiowski 1).
After analyzing dozens of research paper introductions from various fields
(e.g., physics, biology and medicine, and social sciences), Swales and subsequent researchers found that nearly every one of them contained three
to six rhetorical organization "moves" aimed at making the paper seem
important and relevant.

   Swales' CARS model consists of three principle communicative   22
moves: Move 1—establish centrality within the research; Move 2—establish
a niche within the research; and Move 3—occupy the niche with the present
research (Golebiowski 1–2). These moves help the author clearly state the

exigence (the lack of knowledge) and the proposed solution (the present research). Scientists can use the introduction of the scientific paper to relate their research to others and to show how important the present findings are to the corpus of scientific knowledge. Findings that are relevant and timely should indeed be welcomed and accepted by the larger community, and so carefully introducing one's topic makes all the more sense.

23   These principal CARS communicative moves are central to the introduction of "Sustained Attention in Children and Adolescents." The authors establish centrality within their research area, Move 1, by briefly discussing traumatic brain injury (TBI) in children and adolescents and by stating that "childhood TBI [is] a significant public health problem" because it "is the leading cause of child deaths in the US and one of the most frequent causes of interruption to normal child development" (751). The authors also discuss previous research, eventually building up to their own research, and thereby establish their study's relevance through the implication that they share the same central assumptions and information base.

24   The authors establish a niche within the research, Move 2, primarily by indicating a gap in the research and by claiming that they will build upon the research of a previous study. After reviewing the general topic of TBI, the authors claim, "There is little known about the effects of TBI on specific attentional components: orienting to sensory stimuli, executive functions and maintaining the alert state" (752). They immediately move to occupy this niche, Move 3, by stating. "The focus of this study is on sustained attention (i.e. the capacity to maintain arousal and alertness over time)" (752). After identifying sustained attention as their primary area of interest, the authors continue moving from general to specific and from Move 2 to Move 3. They review the literature dealing with sustained attention and then, in the last paragraph of the introduction, identify one study in particular from which they will proceed: "The present study aims to extend the findings of Taylor et al. in several ways" (753). The authors' intention seems clear: find something new without radically departing from what other researchers have already established.

Conclusion

25   Indubitably, scientific reports further our understanding of the world and the phenomena around us. James Watson and Francis Crick's famous paper that established the double helix structure of DNA, for example, radically altered biological studies (and in many ways, society at large). In "Sustained Attention in Children and Adolescents," the researchers found that people treating children with traumatic brain injury need to "consider pre-injury child and family psychosocial characteristics in addition to severity of injury" (751). While not as revolutionary as Watson and Crick's paper, the authors point out that their study helps fill a dearth of medical knowledge.

Their findings are probably very important to those affected by TBI and those treating them.

    It is important, however, to recognize that just as all scientific data are 26 interpreted, this experimental report, like all written accounts, is an interpretation, subject to creativity, convention, form, and style. For example, the very tests used in the research and the results of those tests may not really show what the authors understood them to show. The authors inferred a connection between the tests and the test results and their eventual interpretations. The tests themselves are fundamentally based on theories, as are all scientific methods, but are essentially treated by the authors as being objective (at least if they are administered under ideal circumstances). A "soft" science experiment, this study is reported in "hard" science fashion.

    Writing experimental reports is an especially provocative practice 27 because through these studies today's hypotheses and theories become tomorrow's scientific facts and laws. In Sundar Sarukkai's words, "The writing of science is not only a representation of the ideas of science; it is also integral to the creation of new meaning and truth claims" (1). In one sense, the "creation of new meaning and truth claims" implies a rhetorical situation, where the writing is meant to persuade. Certainly, scientists and researchers should be aware of embedded rhetorical strategies. But given the profound and pervasive influence of science in Western culture, we should all—scientist or not—be attentive to how our knowledge is shaped.

I would like to thank Beth Hedengren and Kristine Hansen for generously sharing their time and knowledge to help me develop this article.

Notes

    1. By way of comparison, James Watson and Francis Crick's famous article in *Nature* proposing the structure of DNA contains about 24 percent passive constructions, markedly fewer than "Sustained Attention in Children and Adolescents'" approximately 37 percent. Subtract the passive constructions in Watson and Crick's article that include the agent and the number drops to around 17 percent. The comparison between the two articles is useful because it shows that using the passive voice is a choice— a strategy to create a certain ethos, in this case, one of objectivity.

Works Cited

Bazerman, Charles. *Shaping Written Knowledge: The Genre and Activity of the Experimental Article in Science.* Madison: U of Wisconsin P, 1988.

Bitzer, Lloyd F. "The Rhetorical Situation." *Philosophy and Rhetoric* 1 (1968): 1–14.

Day, Robert A. *How to Write and Publish a Scientific Paper.* 4th ed. Phoenix: Oryx, 1994.

Golebiowski, Zosia. "Application of Swales' Model in the Analysis of Research Papers by Polish Authors." *International Review of Applied Linguistics in Language Teaching* 37.3 (1999). Online. *Academic Search Elite.* 14 Mar. 2003.

Hansen, Kristine. *A Rhetoric for the Social Sciences: A Guide to Academic and Professional Communications.* Upper Saddle River, NJ: Prentice Hall, 1998.

Holton, Gerald. "Quanta, Relativity, and Rhetoric." *Persuading Science: The Art of Scientific Rhetoric.* Ed. Marcello Pera and William R. Shea. Canton, MA: Science History, 1991. 173–203.

Medawar, Peter. "Is the Scientific Paper a Fraud?" *BBC Third Programme, Listener.* BBC. London, UK. 1963. Rpt. in *The Threat and the Glory: Reflections on Sciences and Scientists.* Ed. David Pyke. New York: HarperCollins, 1990. 228–33.

Merriam-Webster's Dictionary of English Usage. Springfield: Merriam-Webster, 1994.

Prelli, Lawrence J. *A Rhetoric of Science: Inventing Scientific Discourse.* Columbia: U of South Carolina P, 1989.

Sarukkai, Sundar. *Translating the World: Science and Language.* Lanham: Washington, D.C., 2002.

Schuster, John A., and Richard R. Yeo. Introduction. *The Politics and Rhetoric of Scientific Method: Historical Studies.* Boston: D. Reidel, 1986. ix–xxxvii.

Slife, Brent D., and Richard N. Williams. *What's Behind the Research: Discovering Hidden Assumptions in the Behavioral Sciences.* Thousand Oaks: Sage, 1995.

Wassenberg, Renske, Jeffrey E. Max, Scott D. Lindgren, and Amy Schatz. "Sustained Attention in Children and Adolescents after Traumatic Brain Injury: Relation to Severity of Injury, Adaptive Functioning, ADHD and Social Background." *Brain Injury* 18 (2004): 751–64.

Watson, J. D., and F. H. C. Crick, "Molecular Structure of Nucleic Acids: A Structure for Deoxyribose Nucleic Acid." *Nature* 4356 (1953): 737–38.

Content

1. What evidence does Allen provide to corroborate Peter Medawar's observation that "there is no such thing as unprejudiced observation. Every act of observation we make is biased" (¶ 4)? If this is so, why does scientific writing have the reputation for being objective and unbiased?

2. Is data meaningless without interpretation (¶ 4)? Is objective interpretation—of anything—impossible? What rhetorical strategies do scientists use to present their evidence convincingly?

3. Explain Allen's conclusion that "scientists formulate problems, according to their methodologies, in order to solve them—in essence, they create more than discover the rhetorical situation because they construct an exigence" (¶ 12). What does he mean by "rhetorical situation"? By "exigence"?

4. In what ways has Allen demonstrated his conclusion, that "this experimental report ["Sustained Attention"], like all written accounts, is an interpretation, subject to creativity, convention, form, and style" (¶ 26)?

Strategies/Structures/Language

5. Allen has undertaken the difficult task of trying to summarize a thirteen-page scientific paper and analyze its rhetorical strategies in ten paragraphs (¶s 15–24). Although he has done an exemplary job, this section of the paper is nevertheless difficult to understand. Why?

6. Might some of the difficulties in understanding this paper be due to the specialized vocabularies of (a) rhetorical analysis or (b) the language of "Sustained Attention?" Does Allen define new rhetorical concepts the first time he uses a new word or term?

For Writing

7. Either independently or with a partner, analyze a published scientific or social scientific paper in your field, or one of the scientific or social science essays in *The Essay Connection* (such as those by Kozol (204–11), Coontz (213–16), Gawande 218–23), Darwin (335–40), Gould (404–11), or another) to show why, where, and how they are interpretive (and therefore not objective). *Note:* This does *not* mean these essays are unreliable; indeed, they are all of high quality, though not without controversy.

 For comprehension, writing, and research activities and resources, please visit the companion website at <college.hmco.com/english>.

Additional Topics for Writing Appealing to Reason: Deductive and Inductive Arguments

(For strategies for appealing to reason, see 438.)

MULTIPLE STRATEGIES FOR WRITING ARGUMENTS

Arguments commonly employ assorted strategies to make their points as compelling as possible and to interpret their significance. Among these are the following:

- *definitions* of essential terms, component parts. These may be objective or favorable to the writer's point of view.
- *illustrations* and *examples*, to show the meaning or significance of the key issues
- *explanations* and *analyses* of the salient points
- *comparison* and *contrast* of the pro and con positions
- *division* and *classification* of the relevant subtopics and side issues
- a *narrative*, on occasion, either at the beginning to humanize the abstract or theoretical issue under consideration or at the end to allow the full import of the argument to make a final impact
- *cause* and *effect*, to show the beneficial consequences of the arguer's point of view and the detrimental consequences of the opposition's stance

1. Write a logical, clearly reasoned, well-supported argument appropriate to the subject in organization, language, and tone and appealing to your designated audience. Be sure you have in mind a particular reader or group of readers who you know (or suspect) are likely to be receptive or hostile to your position, or uncommitted people whose opinion you're trying to influence.

    a. A college education is (or is not) worth the effort and expense.

    b. Smoking, drinking, or using "recreational" drugs is (is not) worth the risks.

    c. Economic prosperity is (is not) more important to our country than conservation and preservation of our country's resources.

    d. The Social Security system should (should not) be preserved in its present form for current and future generations.

    e. Everyone should (should not) be entitled to comprehensive medical care (supply one: from the cradle to the grave; in early childhood; while a student; in old age; if they're unable to pay for it).

    f. Drunk drivers should (should not) be jailed, even for a first offense.

    g. Cell phone use should (should not) be prohibited for drivers of motor vehicles when in use.

    h. Companies manufacturing products that may affect consumers' health or safety (such as food, drugs, liquor, automobiles, pesticides) should (should not) have consumer representatives on their boards of directors.

    i. The civil rights, women's liberation, gay liberation, or some comparable movement has (has not) accomplished major and long-lasting benefits for the group it represents.

j. Intercollegiate athletic teams that are big business should (should not) hire their players; intercollegiate athletes should (should not) have professional status.

k. Strong labor unions should (should not) be preserved.

l. The costs of America's space program are worth (far exceed) the benefits.

m. The federal government should (should not) take over the nation's health care system.

n. The Patriot Act should (should not) be repealed.

o. The possibility of identity theft is (is not) a reasonable tradeoff for ease of Internet usage.

2. Write a letter to your campus, city, or area newspaper in which you take a stand on an issue, defending or attacking it. You could write on one of the topics in Additional Topics 1 above or differ with a recent column or editorial. Hot button issues are fine if you have appropriate support for your argument. Send in your letter (keep a copy for yourself), and see if it is published. If so, what kind of response did it attract?

3. Write to your state or federal legislator, urging the passage or defeat of a particular piece of legislation currently being considered. (You will probably find at least one side of the issue being reported in the newspapers or a newsmagazine.) An extra: If you receive a reply, analyze it to see whether it addresses the specific points you raise. In what fashion? Does it sound like an individual response or a form letter?

Appealing to
Emotion and Ethics

The essence of an emotional appeal is passion. You write from passion, and you expect your readers to respond with equal fervor. "I have a dream." "The only thing we have to fear is fear itself." "We have nothing to offer but blood, toil, tears, and sweat." "The West wasn't won with a loaded gun!" "We shall overcome" is illustrated both by the photograph of Dr. Martin Luther King, Jr., Joan Baez, and others escorting African-American school-children to a newly-integrated school in 1966 (445), and here by the well-dressed Chinese schoolgirl standing and waiting amidst rubble in an urban slum neighborhood in Shenghen, beyond which gleam the modern high rise buildings that signal renewal and hope of a way up and out. Both photographs make direct and indirect arguments about children, human rights, and society, appealing to arguments that intertwine appeals to reason, emotion and ethics. You'll be making your case in specific, concrete, memorable ways that you expect to have an unusually powerful impact on your readers. So your writing will probably be more colorful than it might

be in less emotional circumstances, with a high proportion of vivid examples, narratives, anecdotes, character sketches, analogies ("Will Iraq or
North Korea or *X* be another Vietnam?"), and figures of speech, including
metaphors ("a knee-jerk liberal"), and similes ("The Southern Senator had
a face like an old Virginia ham and a personality to match.").

You can't incite your readers, either to agree with you or to take action on behalf of the cause you favor, by simply bleeding all over the page.
The process of writing and rewriting and revising again (see the chapter
"Writing: Re-Vision and Revision") will act to cool your red-hot emotion
and will enable you to modulate in subsequent drafts what you might have
written the first time just to get it out of your system. "Hell, no! We won't
go!" As the essays in this section and elsewhere reveal, writers who appeal
most effectively to their readers' emotions themselves exercise considerable
control over the organization and examples they use to make their points.

They also keep particularly tight rein over their own emotions, as
revealed in the tone and connotations of their language, crucial in an emotional appeal. Tone, the prevailing mood of the essay, like a tone of voice
conveys your attitude toward your subject and toward the evidence you
present in support of your point. It is clear from the tone of all the essays in
this chapter—indeed, all the essays in the entire *Essay Connection*—that the
authors care deeply about their subjects. Matt Nocton's "Harvest of Gold,
Harvest of Shame" (527–31) reports in a relatively objective tone on his
personal experience with an aspect of farming—in this case, the harvesting of tobacco by a business that employs migrant and contract laborers,
racial and ethnic minorities overseen by white bosses. Keeping himself out
of the essay, he does not say in the essay that as a teenager, after two days
on the job he was promoted to "bentkeeper" over the heads of minority
employees with far more experience. Nevertheless, Nocton's concern for
the workers and anger over their exploitation is apparent in the way he recounts the harvesting process, detail by detail, dirty, dusty, hot, and humiliating: each worker "must tie [a burlap sack] around his waist as a source
of protection against the dirt and rocks that he will be dragging himself
through for the next eight hours." Nocton's essay, like the creative nonfiction narratives by Amanda Cagle ("On the Banks of the Bogue Chitto,"
191–95), Meredith Hall ("Killing Chickens," 242–45), and Kandi Tayebi
("Warring Memories," 554–58), illustrate that these days, in nonfiction,
anyway, unless it's satire, readers generally prefer understatement to overkill. To establish a climate that encourages readers to sympathize emotionally, you as a writer can present telling facts and allow the readers to
interpret them, rather than continually nudging the audience with verbal
reminders to see the subject your way.

If you are appealing to your readers' emotions through irony, the
tone of your words, their music, is likely to be at variance with their overt
message—and to intentionally undermine it. Thus the narrator of Swift's
"A Modest Proposal" (497–503) can, with an impassive face, advocate that

year-old children of the poor Irish peasants be sold for "a most delicious, nourishing, and wholesome food, whether stewed, roasted, baked, or broiled"; and, in an additional inhumane observation, "I make no doubt that it will equally serve in a fricassee or a ragout."

The connotations, overtones of the language, are equally significant in emotional appeals, as they subtly (or not so subtly) reinforce the overt, literal meanings of the words. Lincoln, shown (in the photograph on page 495) arriving at Gettysburg in 1863 to deliver the speech that would rank among the most memorable in American history, deliberately uses biblical language ("Fourscore" instead of "eighty"), biblical phrasing, biblical cadences to reinforce the solemnity of the occasion—dedication of the graveyard at Gettysburg. This language also underscores the seriousness of the Civil War, then in progress, and its profound consequences. In contrast to the majesty of Lincoln's language, Swift's narrator depersonalizes human beings, always calling the children *it*, with an impersonal connotation, and never employing the humanizing terms of *he, she,* or *baby.* The *it* emphasizes the animalistic connotations of the narrator's references to a newborn as "a child just dropped from its dam," further dehumanizing both mother and child.

Language, tone, and message often combine to present an *ethical appeal*—a way of impressing your readers that you as the author (and perhaps as a character in your own essay) are a knowledgeable person of good moral character, good will, and good sense. Consequently, you are a person of integrity, and to be believed as a credible, reasonable advocate of the position you take in your essay.

Thus G. Anthony Gorry, in "Steal This MP3 File: What Is Theft?" (512–15) and Peter Singer, in "The Singer Solution to World Poverty" (505–10) employ straightforward language, logic, and clear-cut examples to open their readers' eyes to ethical issues that many people who consider themselves ethical either ignore or disregard. In a matter-of-fact way, Gorry, a business professor, identifies the student perspective: "Students who saw theft" when a student took a high-priced textbook from a bookstore "did not see stealing in the unauthorized copying of music"—though the music industry regards such copying as theft. Singer, an ethicist who is considered controversial because of the logical extent (some would say extremes) his principles lead to, identifies a simple principle for supporting the world's poor: "Whatever money you're spending on luxuries, not necessities, should be given away."

Although ethical appeals usually tap our most profound moral values, they can be made in humorous ways, often by satire, as implied even in the titles of Sherman Alexie's "What Sacagawea Means to Me" (93–95) and Martín Espada's "The Community College Revises its Curriculum in Response to Changing Demographics" (493). Alexie and Espada are using language common in academic writing (one type of "establishment") to criticize the establishment's treatment of minorities (Native Americans for

Alexie, Hispanics for Espada). Social satire—as we can see from these writings as well as from Swift's "Modest Proposal"—always implies the need for reform. Self-satire, however, as Jason Verge presents his Montreal Canadien fanhood in "The Habs" (119–23) and Charles M. Young does in "Losing: An American Tradition" (517–25), may just be poking fun at one's human fallibilities, though Young's ultimate point about our culture that emphasizes winning at all costs makes losers of us all. Young identifies himself early in the essay: "I may not be the worst college football player of all time. . . . I may be only the worst college football player of 1972." Thus he establishes his firsthand understanding of the subject and his orientation to it—profound sympathy for the underdogs, thereby including most of his readers. "Losing" thus becomes an ethical analysis of the phenomenon of losing in sports (and by extrapolation, in the rest of life), the corruption of the language employed in calling people "losers," and other negative consequences of losing. Losers (nearly everyone who plays any sport) suffer from the stigmatizing effects of shame, as depicted in the photograph (520) of two college football players, hunched over on the bench, faces hidden in their hands, suffering the effects of a loss. Winners lose as well, because "The kids who win are being taught that they are good only to the extent that they continue to beat other people." The sense of community is destroyed: "'We're all losers in the race to win.'" Young is not opposed to playing sports per se, but to the emphasis on winning.

Because they usually make their point indirectly, fables, parables, and other stories with subtle moral points are often used to appeal to readers' emotions and ethical sense. The photographs of winsome (never repulsive, never ugly!) waifs often grace fundraising advertisements for famine relief, amplified by biographies of their pitiful lives; only our contributions can save them. One of the dangers in using such poster-child appeals is the possibility that you'll include too many emotional signals or ultraheavy emotional language and thereby write a paper that repels your readers by either excessive sentimentality or overkill. Works by student writers in this book, such as Amanda Cagle's "On the Banks of the Bogue Chitto" (191–95) and Megan McGuire's "Wake Up Call" (225–31), deal directly with the impact of very difficult issues (poverty, instability, divorce, disability, suicide) on their families, particularly as they affected the authors as children growing up—resilient, resourceful, creative. Their language and examples, precise but unsentimental, are more appealing to readers—and ultimately more moving—than any "alas, poor me" approach would be.

Appeals to emotion and ethics are often intertwined. Such appeals are everywhere—for example, in the connotations of descriptions and definitions. Furthermore, if your readers like and trust you, they're more likely to believe what you say and to be moved to agree with your point of view. The evidence in a scientific report, however strong in itself, is buttressed by the credibility of the researcher. The sense of realism, the truth of a narrative, is enhanced by the credibility of the narrator. We believe Lincoln and Nocton, and we trust the spirit of satirist Swift, even if we believe he is exaggerating, if not downright inventing, the substance of his narrative. Hearts compel agreement where minds hesitate. Don't hesitate to make ethical use of this understanding.

STRATEGIES FOR WRITING— APPEALING TO EMOTION AND ETHICS

1. Do I want to appeal primarily to my readers' emotions (and which emotions) or to their ethical sense of how people ought to behave? (Remember that in either case the appeals are intertwined with reason—see the chapter "Appealing to Reason: Deductive and Inductive Arguments.")
2. To what kinds of readers am I making these appeals? What ethical or other personal qualities should I as an author exhibit? How can I lead my readers to believe that I am a person of sound character and good judgment?
3. What evidence can I choose to reinforce my appeals and my authorial image? Examples from my own life? The experiences of others? References to literature or scientific research? What order of arrangement would be most convincing? From the least emotionally moving or involving to the most? Or vice versa?
4. How can I interpret my evidence to move my readers to accept it? Should I explain very elaborately, or should I let the examples speak for themselves? If you decide on the latter, try out your essay on someone unfamiliar with the examples to see if they are in fact self-evident.
5. Do I want my audience to react with sympathy? Pity? Anger? Fear? Horror? To accomplish this, should I use much emotional language? Should my appeal be overt, direct? Or would indirection, understatement, be more effective? Would irony—saying the opposite of what I really mean (as Swift does)—be more appropriate than a direct approach? Could I make my point more effectively with a fable, parable, comic tale, or invented persona than with a straightforward analysis and overt commentary?

MARTÍN ESPADA

Espada was born in Brooklyn, New York, in 1957. Although he has worked at a variety of jobs, ranging from bouncer to tenant lawyer, Espada published his first book of poetry, *The Immigrant Iceboy's Bolero,* when he was twenty-five years old. He is currently an English professor at the University of Massachusetts, Amherst, teaching creative writing, Latino poetry, and the work of Pablo Neruda. His poetry has won numerous awards. *Rebellion Is in the Circle of a Lover's Hands* (1990) received the PEN/Revson Fellowship. *Imagine the Angels of Bread* (1996) won the American Book Award. His most recent book is *Alabanza: New and Selected Poems, 1982–2002* (2003). His work is characterized by its strong sympathy for the "immigrant and working-class experience. Whether it be Puerto Ricans and Chicanos adjusting to life in the United States or Central and South American Latinos struggling against their own repressive governments to achieve social justice, Espada has put their "'otherness,' their powerlessness, poverty, and enmity" into poetry distinguished by powerful imagery and a strong voice. Espada speaks for those who cannot, as in the ironically titled poem that follows.

The Community College Revises Its Curriculum in Response to Changing Demographics

SPA 100 Conversational Spanish
2 credits

The course
is especially concerned
with giving police
the ability
to express themselves
tersely
in matters of interest
to them

ABRAHAM LINCOLN

Lincoln (1809–1865) was a self-made, self-taught son of Kentucky pioneers. He served four terms in the Illinois state legislature before being elected to Congress in 1847. As sixteenth president of the United States (1861–1865), Lincoln's supreme efforts were devoted to trying to secure the passage of the Thirteenth Amendment to outlaw slavery and to preserve the still young United States of America from the forces expressed through and beyond the bloody Civil War that threatened to destroy its young men, its economy, and the very government itself.

The Gettysburg Address

1   Four score and seven years ago our fathers brought forth on this continent, a new nation, conceived in liberty, and dedicated to the proposition that all men are created equal.

2   Now we are engaged in a great civil war, testing whether that nation, or any nation so conceived and so dedicated, can long endure. We are met on a great battlefield of that war. We have come to dedicate a portion of that field, as a final resting place for those who here gave their lives that the nation might live. It is altogether fitting and proper that we should do this.

3   But, in a larger sense, we cannot dedicate—we cannot consecrate—we cannot hallow—this ground. The brave men, living and dead, who struggled here, have consecrated it, far above our poor power to add or detract. The world will little note, nor long remember what we say here, but it can never forget what they did here. It is for us the living, rather, to be dedicated here to the unfinished work which they who fought here have thus far so nobly advanced. It is rather for us to be here dedicated to the great task remaining before us—that from these honored dead we take increased devotion—that we here highly resolve that these dead shall not have died in vain—that this nation, under God, shall have a new birth of freedom—and that government of the people, by the people, for the people, shall not perish from the earth.

Content

1. What principles of the founding of the United States does Lincoln emphasize in the first sentence? Why are these so important to the occasion of his address? To the theme of this address?

2. What does Lincoln imply and assert is the relation of life and death? Birth and rebirth?

This classic photograph of President Abraham Lincoln arriving at Gettysburg, a significant event in American history, requires the viewer to know and understand both the event at hand and its historical context. Drawing on your understanding of the events that goes well beyond this photograph, interpret its emotional as well as its historical impact.

Strategies/Structures/Language

3. Why would Lincoln, knowing that his audience expected longer orations, deliberately have decided to make his speech so short? Lincoln's speech commemorated a solemn occasion: the dedication of a major battlefield of the ongoing Civil War. Wouldn't such a short speech have undermined the significance of the event?

4. Identify the language and metaphors of birth that Lincoln uses throughout this address. For what purpose? With what effect?

5. Why did Lincoln use biblical language and phrasing conspicuously at the beginning and end of the address, such as "four score and seven years ago" instead of the more common "eighty-seven"?

6. Lincoln uses many *antitheses*—oppositions, contrasts. Identify some and show how they reinforce the meaning.

7. Another important rhetorical device is the *tricolon*, "the division of an idea into three harmonious parts, usually of increasing power,"—for example, "government of the people, by the people, for the people. . . ." Find others and show why they are so memorable.

For Writing

8. Write a short, dignified speech for a solemn occasion, real or imaginary. Let the majesty of your language and the conspicuous rhetorical patterns of your

sentences and paragraphs (through such devices as antithesis and parallelism) reinforce your point.

9. Rewrite the "Gettysburg Address" as it might have been spoken by a more recent president or other politician, using language, paragraphing, and sentence structures characteristic of the speaker and the times. One such speech, a parody, is William Safire's "Carter's Gettysburg Address," which begins: "Exactly two hundred and one years, five months and one day ago, our forefathers—and our foremothers, too, as my wife, the First Lady, reminds me—our highly competent Founding Persons brought forth on this land mass a new nation, or entity, dreamed up in liberty and dedicated to the comprehensive program of insuring that all of us are created with the same basic human rights."

 For comprehension, writing, and research activities and resources, please visit the companion website at <college.hmco.com/english>.

JONATHAN SWIFT

Swift, author of *Gulliver's Travels* (1726) and other satiric essays, poems, and tracts, was well acquainted with irony. Born in Dublin in 1667, the son of impoverished English Anglicans, he obtained a degree from Trinity College, Dublin, in 1685 only by "special grace." When James II arrived in Ireland in 1688, he initiated pro-Catholic, anti-Protestant policies that remained in force until the ascendancy of William III. Swift, along with many Anglo-Irish, was forced to flee to England, was eventually ordained as an Anglican priest, and rose prominently in London literary and political circles until 1713. Although he had hoped for a church appointment in England, his desertion of the Whig Party for the Tories was ironically rewarded with an appointment as dean of St. Patrick's (Anglican) Cathedral in Dublin, which he regarded as virtual exile. Nevertheless, despite his religious differences with the Irish people, Swift became a beloved leader in the Irish resistance to English oppression, motivated less by partisan emotions than by his own "savage indignation" against injustice. He died in 1745.

Swift wrote "A Modest Proposal" in the summer of 1729, after three years of drought and crop failure had forced over 35,000 peasants to leave their homes and wander the countryside looking for work, food, and shelter for their starving families, ignored by the insensitive absentee landowners. The "Proposal" carries the English landowners' treatment of the Irish to its logical—but repugnant—extreme: if they are going to devour any hope the Irish have of living decently, why don't they literally eat the Irish children? The persona Swift creates is logical, consistent, seemingly rational—and utterly inhumane, an advocate of infanticide and cannibalism. Yet nowhere in the "Proposal" does the satirist condemn the speaker; he relies on the readers' sense of morality for that. This tactic can be dangerous, for a reader who misses the irony may take the "Proposal" at face value. But Swift's intended readers, English (landlords included) as well as Irish who could act to alleviate the people's suffering, understood very well what he meant. The victims themselves, largely illiterate, would probably have been unaware of this forceful plea on their behalf.

A Modest Proposal

I t is a melancholy object to those who walk through this great town or travel in the country, when they see the streets, the roads, and cabin doors, crowded with beggars of the female sex, followed by three, four, or six children, all in rags and importuning every passenger for an alms. These mothers, instead of being able to work for their honest livelihood, are forced to employ all their time in strolling to beg sustenance for their helpless infants: who as they grow up either turn thieves for want of work, or leave their dear native country to fight for the pretender in Spain, or sell themselves to the Barbadoes.

I think it is agreed by all parties that this prodigious number of children in the arms, or on the backs, or at the heels of their mothers, and frequently of their fathers, is in the present deplorable state of the kingdom a very great additional grievance; and, therefore, whoever could find out a fair, cheap, and easy method of making these children sound, useful members of the commonwealth, would deserve so well of the public as to have his statue set up for a preserver of the nation.

But my intention is very far from being confined to provide only for the children of professed beggars; it is of a much greater extent, and shall take in the whole number of infants at a certain age who are born of parents in effect as little able to support them as those who demand our charity in the streets.

As to my own part, having turned my thoughts for many years upon this important subject, and maturely weighed the several schemes of our projectors, I have always found them grossly mistaken in their computation. It is true, a child just dropped from its dam may be supported by her milk for a solar year, with little other nourishment; at most not above the value of two shillings, which the mother may certainly get, or the value in scraps, by her lawful occupation of begging; and it is exactly at one year old that I propose to provide for them in such a manner as instead of being a charge upon their parents or the parish, or wanting food and raiment for the rest of their lives, they shall on the contrary contribute to the feeding, and partly to the clothing, of many thousands.

There is likewise another great advantage in my scheme, that it will prevent those voluntary abortions, and that horrid practice of women murdering their bastard children, alas! too frequent among us! sacrificing the poor innocent babes I doubt more to avoid the expense than the shame, which would move tears and pity in the most savage and inhuman breast.

6   The number of souls in this kingdom being usually reckoned one million and half, of these I calculate there may be about two hundred thousand couple whose wives are breeders; from which number I subtract thirty thousand couple who are able to maintain their own children (although I apprehend there cannot be so many, under the present distress of the kingdom); but this being granted, there will remain an hundred and seventy thousand breeders. I again subtract fifty thousand for those women who miscarry, or whose children die by accident or disease within the year. There only remain an hundred and twenty thousand children of poor parents annually born. The question therefore is, how this number shall be reared and provided for? which, as I have already said, under the present situation of affairs, is utterly impossible by all the methods hitherto proposed. For we can neither employ them in handicraft or agriculture; we neither build houses (I mean in the country) nor cultivate land; they can very seldom pick up a livelihood by stealing, till they arrive at six years old, except where they are of towardly parts; although I confess they learn the rudiments much earlier; during which time they can, however, be properly looked upon only as probationers; as I have been informed by a principal gentleman in the country of Cavan, who protested to me that he never knew above one or two instances under the age of six, even in a part of the kingdom so renowned for the quickest proficiency in that art.

7   I am assured by our merchants, that a boy or a girl before twelve years old is no saleable commodity; and even when they come to this age they will not yield above three pounds, or three pounds and a half a crown at most on the Exchange; which cannot turn to account either to the parents or kingdom, the charge of nutriment and rags having been at least four times that value.

8   I shall now therefore humbly propose my own thoughts, which I hope will not be liable to the least objection.

9   I have been assured by a very knowing American of my acquaintance in London, that a young healthy child well nursed is at a year old the most delicious, nourishing, and wholesome food, whether stewed, roasted, baked, or broiled; and I make no doubt that it will equally serve in a fricassee or a ragout.

10   I do therefore humbly offer it to public consideration that of the hundred and twenty thousand children already computed, twenty thousand may be reserved for breed, whereof only one fourth part to be males; which is more than we allow to sheep, black cattle, or swine; and my reason is, that these children are seldom the fruits of marriage, a circumstance not much regarded by our savages; therefore, one male will be sufficient to serve four females. That the remaining hundred thousand may, at a year old, be offered in sale to the persons of quality and fortune through the kingdom; always advising the mother to let them suck plentifully in the last month, so as to render them plump and fat for a good table. A child will make two dishes at an entertainment for friends; and when the family dines alone, the fore or hind quarter will make a reasonable dish, and seasoned

with a little pepper or salt will be very good boiled on the fourth day, especially in winter.

I have reckoned upon a medium that a child just born will weigh 11 twelve pounds, and in a solar year, if tolerably nursed, will increase to twenty-eight pounds.

I grant this food will be somewhat dear, and therefore very proper 12 for landlords, who, as they have already devoured most of the parents, seem to have the best title to the children.

Infant's flesh will be in season throughout the year, but more plenti- 13 ful in March, and a little before and after: for we are told by a grave author, an eminent French physician, that fish being a prolific diet, there are more children born in Roman Catholic countries about nine months after Lent than at any other season; therefore, reckoning a year after Lent, the markets will be more glutted than usual, because the number of popish infants is at least three to one in this kingdom: and therefore it will have one other collateral advantage, by lessening the number of papists among us.

I have already computed the charge of nursing a beggar's child (in 14 which list I reckon all cottagers, laborers, and four-fifths of the farmers) to be about two shillings per annum, rags included; and I believe no gentleman would repine to give ten shillings for the carcass of a good fat child, which, as I have said, will make four dishes of excellent nutritive meat, when he has only some particular friend or his own family to dine with him. Thus the squire will learn to be a good landlord, and grow popular among the tenants; the mother will have eight shillings net profit, and be fit for work till she produces another child.

Those who are more thrifty (as I must confess the times require) may 15 flay the carcass; the skin of which artificially dressed will make admirable gloves for ladies, and summer boots for fine gentlemen.

As to our city of Dublin, shambles may be appointed for this purpose 16 in the most convenient parts of it, and butchers we may be assured will not be wanting: although I rather recommend buying the children alive, and dressing them hot from the knife as we do roasting pigs.

A very worthy person, a true lover of his country, and whose virtues 17 I highly esteem, was lately pleased in discoursing on this matter to offer a refinement upon my scheme. He said that many gentlemen of this kingdom, having of late destroyed their deer, he conceived that the want of venison might be well supplied by the bodies of young lads and maidens, not exceeding fourteen years of age nor under twelve; so great a number of both sexes in every country being now ready to starve for want of work and service; and these to be disposed of by their parents, if alive, or otherwise by their nearest relations. But with due deference to so excellent a friend and so deserving a patriot, I cannot be altogether in his sentiments; for as to the males, my American acquaintance assured me from frequent experience that their flesh was generally tough and lean, like that of our schoolboys by continual exercise, and their taste disagreeable; and to fatten them would not answer the charge. Then as to the females, it would,

I think, with humble submission be a loss to the public, because they soon would become breeders themselves: and besides, it is not improbable that some scrupulous people might be apt to censure such a practice (although indeed very unjustly), as a little bordering upon cruelty; which, I confess, has always been with me the strongest objection against any project, how well soever intended.

18   But in order to justify my friend, he confessed that this expedient was put into his head by the famous Psalmanazar, a native of the island Formosa, who came from thence to London about twenty years ago: and in conversation told my friend, that in his country when any young person happened to be put to death, the executioner sold the carcass to persons of quality as a prime dainty; and that in his time the body of a plump girl of fifteen, who was crucified for an attempt to poison the emperor, was sold to his imperial majesty's prime minister of state, and other great mandarins of the court, in joints from the gibbet, at four hundred crowns. Neither indeed can I deny, that if the same use were made of several plump young girls in this town, who without one single groat to their fortunes cannot stir abroad without a chair, and appear at the playhouse and assemblies in foreign fineries which they never will pay for, the kingdom would not be the worse.

19   Some persons of a desponding spirit are in great concern about that vast number of poor people, who are aged, diseased, or maimed, and I have been desired to employ my thoughts what course may be taken to ease the nation of so grievous an encumbrance. But I am not in the least pain upon that matter, because it is very well known that they are every day dying and rotting by cold and famine, and filth and vermin, as fast as can be reasonably expected. And as to the young laborers, they are now in as hopeful a condition: they cannot get work, and consequently pine away for want of nourishment, to a degree that if at any time they are accidentally hired to common labor, they have not strength to perform it; and thus the country and themselves are happily delivered from the evils to come.

20   I have too long digressed, and therefore shall return to my subject. I think the advantages by the proposal which I have made are obvious and many, as well as of the highest importance.

21   For first, as I have already observed, it would greatly lessen the number of papists, with whom we are yearly overrun, being the principal breeders of the nation as well as our most dangerous enemies; and who stay at home on purpose to deliver the kingdom to the Pretender, hoping to take their advantage by the absence of so many good Protestants, who have chosen rather to leave their country than stay at home and pay tithes against their conscience to an Episcopal curate.

22   Secondly, The poor tenants will have something valuable of their own, which by law may be made liable to distress and help to pay their landlord's rent, their corn and cattle being already seized, and money a thing unknown.

Thirdly, Whereas the maintenance of a hundred thousand children 23
from two years old and upward, cannot be computed at less than ten
shillings a piece per annum, the nation's stock will be thereby increased
fifty thousand pounds per annum, beside the profit of a new dish introduced to the tables of all gentlemen of fortune in the kingdom who have
any refinement in taste. And the money will circulate among ourselves,
the goods being entirely of our own growth and manufacture.

Fourthly, The constant breeders beside the gain of eight shillings 24
sterling per annum by the sale of their children, will be rid of the charge
of maintaining them after the first year.

Fifthly, This food would likewise bring great custom to taverns, 25
where the vintners will certainly be so prudent as to procure the best re-
ceipts for dressing it to perfection, and consequently have their houses
frequented by all the fine gentlemen, who justly value themselves upon
their knowledge in good eating; and a skillful cook who understands how
to oblige his guests, will contrive to make it as expensive as they please.

Sixthly, This would be a great inducement to marriage, which all 26
wise nations have either encouraged by rewards or enforced by laws and
penalties. It would increase the care and tenderness of mothers toward
their children, when they were sure of a settlement for life to the poor
babes, provided in some sort by the public, to their annual profit instead
of expense. We should see an honest emulation among the married women,
which of them would bring the fattest child to the market. Men would become as fond of their wives during the time of their pregnancy as they are
now of their mares in foal, their cows in calf, their sows when they are ready
to farrow; nor offer to beat or kick them (as is too frequent a practice) for
fear of a miscarriage.

Many other advantages might be enumerated. For instance, the ad- 27
dition of some thousand carcasses in our exportation of barreled beef, the
propagation of swine's flesh, and improvement in the art of making good
bacon, so much wanted among us by the great destruction of pigs, too frequent at our table; which are no way comparable in taste or magnificence
to a well-grown, fat, yearling child, which roasted whole will make a considerable figure at a lord mayor's feast or any other public entertainment.
But this and many others I omit, being studious of brevity.

Supposing that one thousand families in this city would be constant 28
customers for infants' flesh, besides others who might have it at merry-
meetings, particularly at weddings and christenings, I compute that Dublin
would take off annually about twenty thousand carcasses; and the rest of
the kingdom (where probably they will be sold somewhat cheaper) the remaining eighty thousand.

I can think of no one objection that will possibly be raised against 29
this proposal, unless it should be urged that the number of people will be
thereby much lessened in the kingdom. This I freely own, and it was indeed one principal design in offering it to the world. I desire the reader

will observe, that I calculate my remedy for this one individual kingdom of Ireland and for no other that ever was, is, or I think ever can be upon earth. Therefore let no man talk to me of other expedients; of taxing our absentees at five shillings a pound: of using neither clothes nor household furniture except what is of our own growth and manufacture: of utterly rejecting the materials and instruments that promote foreign luxury: of curing the expensiveness of pride, vanity, idleness, and gaming in our women: of introducing a vein of parsimony, prudence, and temperance: of learning to love our country, in the want of which we differ even from Laplanders and the inhabitants of Topinamboo: of quitting our animosities and factions, nor acting any longer like the Jews, who were murdering one another at the very moment their city was taken: of being a little cautious not to sell our country and conscience for nothing: of teaching landlords to have at least one degree of mercy toward their tenants; lastly, of putting a spirit of honesty, industry, and skill into our shopkeepers; who, if a resolution could now be taken to buy only our native goods, would immediately unite to cheat and exact upon us in the price, the measure, and the goodness, nor could ever yet be brought to make one fair proposal of just dealing, though often and earnestly invited to it.

30　　Therefore I repeat, let no man talk to me of these and the like expedients, till he has at least some glimpse of hope that there will be ever some hearty and sincere attempts to put them in practice.

31　　But as to myself, having been wearied out for many years with offering vain, idle, visionary thoughts, and at length utterly despairing of success, I fortunately fell upon this proposal; which, as it is wholly new, so it has something solid and real, of no expense and little trouble, full in our own power, and whereby we can incur no danger in disobliging England. For this kind of commodity will not bear exportation, the flesh being of too tender a consistence to admit a long continuance in salt, although perhaps I could name a country which would be glad to eat up our whole nation without it.

32　　After all, I am not so violently bent upon my own opinion as to reject any offer proposed by wise men, which shall be found equally innocent, cheap, easy, and effectual. But before something of that kind shall be advanced in contradiction to my scheme, and offering a better, I desire the author or authors will be pleased maturely to consider two points. First, as things now stand, how they will be able to find food and raiment for a hundred thousand useless mouths and backs. And secondly, there being a round million of creatures in human figure throughout this kingdom, whose subsistence put into a common stock would leave them in debt two millions of pounds sterling, adding those who are beggars by profession to the bulk of farmers, cottagers, and laborers, with the wives and children who are beggars in effect; I desire those politicians who dislike my overture, and may perhaps be so bold as to attempt an answer, that they will first ask the parents of these mortals, whether they would not at this day think it a great happiness to have been sold for food at a year old in the manner I prescribe, and thereby have avoided such a perpetual scene of misfortunes as they have since gone through by the oppression of landlords, the impossibility of paying rent without money or trade, the want of common sustenance, with neither house nor clothes to cover them from the inclemencies of the weather, and the most inevitable prospect of entailing the like or greater miseries upon their breed for ever.

I profess, in the sincerity of my heart, that I have not the least per-   33
sonal interest in endeavoring to promote this necessary work, having no other motive than the public good of my country, by advancing our trade, providing for infants, relieving the poor, and giving some pleasure to the rich. I have no children by which I can propose to get a single penny; the youngest being nine years old, and my wife past child-bearing.

Content

1. What is the overt thesis of Swift's essay? What is its implied (and real) thesis? In what ways do these theses differ?
2. What are the primary aims and values of the narrator of the essay? Identify the economic advantages of his proposal that he offers in paragraphs 9–16. How do the narrator's alleged aims and values differ from the aims and values of Swift as the essay's author?
3. What do the advantages that the narrator offers for his proposal (¶s 21–26) reveal about the social and economic conditions of Ireland when Swift was writing?
4. Why is it a "very knowing *American*" who has assured the narrator of the suitability of year-old infants for food (¶ 9)?
5. Swift as the author of the essay expects his readers to respond to the narrator's cold economic arguments on a humane, moral level. What might such an appropriate response be?

Strategies/Structures/Language

6. What persona (a created character) does the speaker of Swift's essay have? How are readers to know that this character is not Swift himself?
7. Why does the narrator use so many mathematical computations throughout? How do they reinforce his economic argument? How do they enhance the image of his cold-bloodedness?
8. Why did Swift choose to present his argument indirectly rather than overtly? What advantages does this indirect, consistently ironic technique provide? What disadvantages does it have (for instance, do you think Swift's readers are likely to believe he really advocated eating babies)?
9. What is the prevailing tone of the essay? How does it undermine what the narrator says? How does the tone reinforce Swift's implied meaning?
10. Why does Swift say "a child just dropped from its dam" (¶ 4) instead of "just born from his mother"? What other language reinforces the animalistic associations (see, for instance, "breeders" in ¶ 17)?

For Writing

11. Either individually or as part of a team, write a modest proposal of your own. Pick some problem that you think needs to be solved, and propose, for a critical audience, a radical solution—perhaps a dramatic way to bring about world peace, preserve endangered species, dispose of chemical or nuclear waste, or use genetic engineering.

12. Write an essay in which a created character, a narrative persona, speaks ironically (as Swift's narrator does) about your subject. The character's values should be at variance with the values you and your audience share. For instance, if you want to propose stiff penalties for drunk driving, your narrator could be a firm advocate of drinking, and of driving without restraint, and could be shown driving unsafely while under the influence of alcohol, indifferent to the dangers.

 For comprehension, writing, and research activities and resources, please visit the companion website at <college.hmco.com/english>.

PETER SINGER

Designated in 2005 by *Time* magazine as one of the "world's most influential people," philosopher Peter Singer is known for challenging conventional notions of ethical correctness. Born in Melbourne, Australia, in 1946 to a family decimated by the Nazi holocaust, Singer was educated at the University of Melbourne (BA, 1967; MA, 1969) and Oxford University (B Phil, 1971). After teaching at Oxford and New York University, he served as Chair of the Philosophy Department at Monash University in Australia and led the Centre for Human Bioethics there (1983–1998). Currently, he is a professor of Bioethics at Princeton University. Singer first gained attention as a protector of animal rights with *Animal Liberation* (1975), in which he criticized "speciesism"—the valuing of human rights above those of other species. He continued to explore the ethics of human–animal relations with *In Defense of Animals* (1985), *Animal Factories* (1990), and *The Great Ape Project* (1994). In *Making Babies* (1985), *Should the Baby Live?* (1985), and *Rethinking Life and Death* (1995), he addressed problems of science, technology, conception, and human life. Singer's views on end-of-life issues are consistent with his utilitarian approach to wealth advocated in "The Singer Solution to World Poverty"—that what is the greatest good for the greatest number should prevail. Their application, to animals, infants, and the elderly has aroused considerable controversy. More recent books include *One World* (2002), about globalization, and *President Of Good & Evil* (2004), about George Bush's ethical stance.

    "The Singer Solution to World Poverty" is a wake-up call for ethical responsibility—a reminder that serious questions of right and wrong behavior lie just beyond the horizon of middle-class awareness. Singer starkly presents the death and degradation that come with child poverty, creates the "Bugatti senario" to test the reader's ethical commitments (to saving an expensive car or a child's life), and even provides an 800 number for immediate action.

The Singer Solution to World Poverty

I n the Brazilian film *Central Station,* Dora is a retired schoolteacher who 1 makes ends meet by sitting at the station writing letters for illiterate people. Suddenly she has an opportunity to pocket a thousand dollars. All she has to do is persuade a homeless nine-year-old-boy to follow her to an address she has been given. (She is told he will be adopted by wealthy foreigners.) She delivers the boy, gets the money, spends some of it on a television set, and settles down to enjoy her new acquisition. Her neighbor spoils the fun, however, by telling her that the boy was too old to be adopted—he will be killed and his organs sold for transplantation. Perhaps Dora knew this all along, but after her neighbor's plain speaking, she spends a troubled night. In the morning Dora resolves to take the boy back.

Suppose Dora had told her neighbor that it is a tough world, other 2 people have nice new TVs too, and if selling the kid is the only way she can get one, well, he was only a street kid. She would then have become, in the eyes of the audience, a monster. She redeems herself only by being prepared to bear considerable risks to save the boy.

At the end of the movie, in cinemas in the affluent nations of the 3 world, people who would have been quick to condemn Dora if she had not rescued the boy go home to places far more comfortable than her apartment. In fact, the average family in the United States spends almost one third of its income on things that are no more necessary to them than Dora's new TV was to her. Going out to nice restaurants, buying new clothes because the old ones are no longer stylish, vacationing at beach resorts—so much of our income is spent on things not essential to the preservation of our lives and health. Donated to one of a number of charitable agencies, that money could mean the difference between life and death for children in need.

All of which raises a question: in the end, what is the ethical distinc- 4 tion between a Brazilian who sells a homeless child to organ peddlers and an American who already has a TV and upgrades to a better one, knowing that the money could be donated to an organization that would use it to save the lives of kids in need?

Of course, there are several differences between the two situations 5 that could support different moral judgments about them. For one thing, to be able to consign a child to death when he is standing right in front of you takes a chilling kind of heartlessness; it is much easier to ignore an appeal for money to help children you will never meet. Yet for a utilitarian philosopher like myself—that is, one who judges whether acts are right or wrong

How typical is this scene in an electronics store? May we assume that this is taking place in America? At any particular time of year? Interpret as many aspects of this scene as you can: the numbers, age range, and income level of the shoppers, what they're buying, how you think they'll pay for their purchases, what lifestyle and/or occupations their purchases represent. Then use your interpretation to comment on "The Singer Solution to World Poverty." Is there any material item you use regularly that you'd be willing to forgo in order to alleviate another's poverty? Is there a category of expensive items—say, diamond jewelry, luxury yachts—that is disposable in the interest of implementing Singer's solution?

by their consequences—if the upshot of the American's failure to donate the money is that one more kid dies on the streets of a Brazilian city, then it is in some sense just as bad as selling the kid to the organ peddlers. But one doesn't need to embrace my utilitarian ethic to see that at the very least, there is a troubling incongruity in being so quick to condemn Dora for taking the child to the organ peddlers while at the same time not regarding the American consumer's behavior as raising a serious moral issue.

6   In his 1996 book, *Living High and Letting Die*, the New York University philosopher Peter Unger presented an ingenious series of imaginary examples designed to probe our intuitions about whether it is wrong to live well without giving substantial amounts of money to help people who are hungry, malnourished, or dying from easily treatable illnesses like diarrhea. Here's my paraphrase of one of these examples:

7   Bob is close to retirement. He has invested most of his savings in a very rare and valuable old car, a Bugatti, which he has not been able to

insure. The Bugatti is his pride and joy. In addition to the pleasure he gets from driving and caring for his car, Bob knows that its rising market value means that he will always be able to sell it and live comfortably after retirement. One day when Bob is out for a drive, he parks the Bugatti near the end of a railway siding and goes for a walk up the track. As he does so, he sees that a runaway train, with no one aboard, is running down the railway track. Looking farther down the track, he sees the small figure of a child very likely to be killed by the runaway train. He can't stop the train and the child is too far away to warn of the danger, but he can throw a switch that will divert the train down the siding where his Bugatti is parked. Then nobody will be killed—but the train will destroy his Bugatti. Thinking of his joy in owning the car and the financial security it represents, Bob decides not to throw the switch. The child is killed. For many years to come, Bob enjoys owning his Bugatti and the financial security it represents.

Bob's conduct, most of us will immediately respond, was gravely   8
wrong. Unger agrees. But then he reminds us that we too have opportunities to save the lives of children. We can give to organizations like UNICEF or Oxfam America. How much would we have to give one of these organizations to have a high probability of saving the life of a child threatened by easily preventable diseases? (I do not believe that children are more worth saving than adults, but since no one can argue that children have brought their poverty on themselves, focusing on them simplifies the issues.) Unger called up some experts and used the information they provided to offer some plausible estimates that include the cost of raising money, administrative expenses, and the cost of delivering aid where it is most needed. By his calculation, $200 in donations would help a sickly two-year-old transform into a healthy six-year-old—offering safe passage through childhood's most dangerous years. To show how practical philosophical argument can be, Unger even tells his readers that they can easily donate funds by using their credit card and calling one of these toll-free numbers: (800) 367-5437 for UNICEF; (800) 693-2687 for Oxfam America.

Now you too have the information you need to save a child's life.   9
How should you judge yourself if you don't do it? Think again about Bob and his Bugatti. Unlike Dora, Bob did not have to look into the eyes of the child he was sacrificing for his own material comfort. The child was a complete stranger to him and too far away to relate to in an intimate, personal way. Unlike Dora too, he did not mislead the child or initiate the chain of events imperiling him. In all these respects, Bob's situation resembles that of people able but unwilling to donate to overseas aid and differs from Dora's situation.

If you still think that it was very wrong of Bob not to throw the switch   10
that would have diverted the train and saved the child's life, then it is hard to see how you could deny that it is also very wrong not to send money to one of the organizations listed above. Unless, that is, there is some morally important difference between the two situations that I have overlooked.

11   Is it the practical uncertainties about whether aid will really reach the people who need it? Nobody who knows the world of overseas aid can doubt that such uncertainties exist. But Unger's figure of $200 to save a child's life was reached after he had made conservative assumptions about the proportion of the money donated that will actually reach its target.

12   One genuine difference between Bob and those who can afford to donate to overseas aid organizations but don't is that only Bob can save the child on the tracks, whereas there are hundreds of millions of people who can give $200 to overseas aid organizations. The problem is that most of them aren't doing it. Does this mean that it is all right for you not to do it?

13   Suppose that there were more owners of priceless vintage cars—Carol, Dave, Emma, Fred, and so on, down to Ziggy—all in exactly the same situation as Bob, with their own siding and their own switch, all sacrificing the child in order to preserve their own cherished car. Would that make it all right for Bob to do the same? To answer this question affirmatively is to endorse follow-the-crowd ethics—the kind of ethics that led many Germans to look away when the Nazi atrocities were being committed. We do not excuse them because others were behaving no better.

14   We seem to lack a sound basis for drawing a clear moral line between Bob's situation and that of any reader of this article with $200 to spare who does not donate it to an overseas aid agency. These readers seem to be acting at least as badly as Bob was acting when he chose to let the runaway train hurtle toward the unsuspecting child. In the light of this conclusion, I trust that many readers will reach for the phone and donate that $200. Perhaps you should do it before reading further.

15 Now that you have distinguished yourself morally from people who put their vintage cars ahead of a child's life, how about treating yourself and your partner to dinner at your favorite restaurant? But wait. The money you will spend at the restaurant could also help save the lives of children overseas! True, you weren't planning to blow $200 tonight, but if you were to give up dining out just for one month, you would easily save that amount. And what is one month's dining out compared to a child's life? There's the rub. Since there are a lot of desperately needy children in the world, there will always be another child whose life you could save for another $200. Are you therefore obliged to keep giving until you have nothing left? At what point can you stop?

16   Hypothetical examples can easily become farcical. Consider Bob. How far past losing the Bugatti should he go? Imagine that Bob had got his foot stuck in the track of the siding, and if he diverted the train, then before it rammed the car it would also amputate his big toe. Should he still throw the switch? What if it would amputate his foot? His entire leg?

17   As absurd as the Bugatti scenario gets when pushed to extremes, the point it raises is a serious one: only when the sacrifices become very significant indeed would most people be prepared to say that Bob does nothing

wrong when he decides not to throw the switch. Of course, most people could be wrong; we can't decide moral issues by taking opinion polls. But consider for yourself the level of sacrifice that you would demand of Bob, and then think about how much money you would have to give away in order to make a sacrifice that is roughly equal to that. It's almost certainly much, much more than $200. For most middle-class Americans, it could easily be more like $200,000.

Isn't it counterproductive to ask people to do so much? Don't we run the risk that many will shrug their shoulders and say that morality, so conceived, is fine for saints but not for them? I accept that we are unlikely to see, in the near or even medium-term future, a world in which it is normal for wealthy Americans to give the bulk of their wealth to strangers. When it comes to praising or blaming people for what they do, we tend to use a standard that is relative to some conception of normal behavior. Comfortably off Americans who give, say, 10 percent of their income to overseas aid organizations are so far ahead of most of their equally comfortable fellow citizens that I wouldn't go out of my way to chastise them for not doing more. Nevertheless, they should be doing much more, and they are in no position to criticize Bob for failing to make the much greater sacrifice of his Bugatti. 18

At this point various objections may crop up. Someone may say, "If every citizen living in the affluent nations contributed his or her share, I wouldn't have to make such a drastic sacrifice, because long before such levels were reached the resources would have been there to save the lives of all those children dying from lack of food or medical care. So why should I give more than my fair share?" Another, related objection is that the government ought to increase its overseas aid allocations, since that would spread the burden more equitably across all taxpayers. 19

Yet the question of how much we ought to give is a matter to be decided in the real world—and that, sadly, is a world in which we know that most people do not, and in the immediate future will not, give substantial amounts to overseas aid agencies. We know too that at least in the next year, the United States government is not going to meet even the very modest United Nations–recommended target of 0.7 percent of gross national product; at the moment it lags far below that, at 0.09 percent, not even half of Japan's 0.22 percent or a tenth of Denmark's 0.97 percent. Thus, we know that the money we can give beyond that theoretical "fair share" is still going to save lives that would otherwise be lost. While the idea that no one need do more than his or her fair share is a powerful one, should it prevail if we know that others are not doing their fair share and that children will die preventable deaths unless we do more than our fair share? That would be taking fairness too far. 20

Thus, this ground for limiting how much we ought to give also fails. In the world as it is now, I can see no escape from the conclusion that each 21 one of us with wealth surplus to his or her essential needs should be giving most of it to help people suffering from poverty so dire as to be life-threatening. That's right: I'm saying that you shouldn't buy that new car, take that cruise, redecorate the house, or get that pricy new suit. After all, a thousand-dollar suit could save five children's lives.

22   So how does my philosophy break down in dollars and cents? An American household with an income of $50,000 spends around $30,000 annually on necessities, according to the Conference Board, a nonprofit economic research organization. Therefore, for a household bringing in $50,000 a year, donations to help the world's poor should be as close as possible to $20,000. The $30,000 required for necessities holds for higher incomes as well. So a household making $100,000 could cut a yearly check for $70,000. Again, the formula is simple: whatever money you're spending on luxuries, not necessities, should be given away.

23   Now, evolutionary psychologists tell us that human nature just isn't sufficiently altruistic to make it plausible that many people will sacrifice so much for strangers. On the facts of human nature, they might be right, but they would be wrong to draw a moral conclusion from those facts. If it is the case that we ought to do things that, predictably, most of us won't do, then let's face that fact head-on. Then, if we value the life of a child more than going to fancy restaurants, the next time we dine out we will know that we could have done something better with our money. If that makes living a morally decent life extremely arduous, well, then that is the way things are. If we don't do it, then we should at least know that we are failing to live a morally decent life—not because it is good to wallow in guilt but because knowing where we should be going is the first step toward heading in that direction.

24   When Bob first grasped the dilemma that faced him as he stood by that railway switch, he must have thought how extraordinarily unlucky he was to be placed in a situation in which he must choose between the life of an innocent child and the sacrifice of most of his savings. But he was not unlucky at all. We are all in that situation.

Content

1. What was your reaction to the "Bugatti scenario," which Singer describes as a "hypothetical example" designed to test the reader's ethics? Do you agree that Bob's conduct was "gravely wrong" (¶ 8)? What about the incremental version of the scenario—how much is the child's life worth? A toe, a foot, a leg? (¶ 16).

2. Singer describes his philosophical stance as utilitarian; he "judges whether acts are right or wrong by their consequences" (¶ 5). How does the utilitarian point of view inform "The Singer Solution"? What actions and what consequences is the article concerned with? Where does Singer stress consequences as a criterion for decision making?

Strategies/Structures/Language

3. Emotion can lead to motion: Authors can move readers to action by arousing intense feelings and then providing an outlet for them. Singer appeals to emotion with the *Central Station* example and the idea of children starving to death. However, he expects the reader to rationally test their ethics in the "Bugatti scenario" and the call for overseas aid donations. Did your emotional reactions to the portrayals of poverty help you make up your mind, or did they get in the way of your ethical deliberations?

4. Consider to what extent Singer uses visual images in his argument. What are some scenes or pictures that remained in your mind after you read the article? Why does Singer rely on imagery? Do you think his use of imagery is effective?

For Writing

5. Do you think that Singer presents a highly effective solution to world poverty? Should his ideas perhaps replace current methods of poverty relief? Write an argument explaining why you agree with Singer's program, or explain how you disapprove of the "Singer Solution" and why.

6. To what extent do you sympathize with the utilitarian philosophy on which Singer bases his argument? (see question 1). Can you give an example of an ethical problem, aside from world poverty, that can be addressed using the utilitarian perspective? Is there any ethical situation to which you feel that a utilitarian point of view does *not* apply?

7. With a classmate, develop an ethical test to help readers confront an issue that you feel is important. Using Singer's methods, construct a hypothetical example that offers the readers choices and helps them come to a decision about a difficult moral problem. Test it out on several classmates, and write a paper reporting and interpreting your findings. What values do these allocations represent? Do you share these? Why or why not?

 For comprehension, writing, and research activities and resources, please visit the companion website at <college.hmco.com/english>.

G. ANTHONY GORRY

G. Anthony Gorry is a leading expert on the impact of information technology on organizations, society, and living systems. A graduate of Yale (BA, 1962), he earned advanced degrees at the University of California at Berkeley (MS, 1963) and MIT (PhD, 1967). Currently a professor of business management at Rice University, Gorry also directs Rice's Center for Technology in Teaching and Learning and the Center for Computational Biology. He has been elected to membership in the Institute of Medicine of the National

Academy of Sciences (1991). Gorry has researched how artificial intelligence can be applied to the practice of medicine and how decision support systems can be developed to assist managers. His publications include articles on computer applications in organizations and in classroom settings.

Gorry explains that he is "interested in the ways in which information technology is changing the ways in which we know about the world and about each other." "Steal This MP3 File," published in *Chronicle of Higher Education* (2003), claims that advances in computer technology have changed people's ethical perception of theft. Specifically, is it wrong to copy and share music files?

Steal This MP3 File: What Is Theft?

1   Sometimes when my students don't see life the way I do, I recall the complaint from *Bye Bye Birdie*, "What's the matter with kids today?" Then I remember that the "kids" in my class are children of the information age. In large part, technology has made them what they are, shaping their world and what they know. For my students, the advance of technology is expected, but for me, it remains both remarkable and somewhat unsettling.

2   In one course I teach, the students and I explore the effects of information technology on society. Our different perspectives on technology lead to engaging and challenging discussions that reveal some of the ways in which technology is shaping the attitudes of young people. An example is our discussion of intellectual property in the information age, of crucial importance to the entertainment business.

3   In recent years, many users of the Internet have launched an assault on the music business. Armed with tools for "ripping" music from compact discs and setting it "free" in cyberspace, they can disseminate online countless copies of a digitally encoded song. Music companies, along with some artists, have tried to stop this perceived pillaging of intellectual property by legal and technical means. The industry has had some success with legal actions against companies that provide the infrastructure for file sharing, but enthusiasm for sharing music is growing, and new file-sharing services continue to appear.

4   The Recording Industry Association of America recently filed lawsuits against four college students, seeking huge damages for "an emporium of music piracy" run on campus networks. However, the industry settled those lawsuits less than a week after a federal judge in California ruled against the association in another case, affirming that two of the Internet's most popular music-swapping services are not responsible for copyright infringements by their users. (In the settlement, the students admitted no wrongdoing but agreed to pay amounts ranging from $12,000 to $17,500 in annual installments over several years and to shut down their file-sharing systems.)

With so many Internet users currently sharing music, legal maneu- 5
vers alone seem unlikely to protect the industry's way of doing business.
Therefore, the music industry has turned to the technology itself, seeking
to create media that cannot be copied or can be copied only in prescribed
circumstances. Finding the right technology for such a defense, however,
is not easy. Defensive technology must not prevent legitimate uses of the
media by customers, yet it must somehow ward off attacks by those seeking to "liberate" the content to the Internet. And each announcement of a
defensive technology spurs development of means to circumvent it.

In apparent frustration, some companies have introduced defective 6
copies of their music into the file-sharing environment of the Internet,
hoping to discourage widespread downloading of music. But so far, the
industry's multifaceted defense has failed. Sales of CDs continue to decline.
And now video ripping and sharing is emerging on the Internet, threatening to upset another industry in the same way.

Music companies might have more success if they focused on the 7
users instead of the courts and technology. When they characterize file
sharing as theft, they overlook the interplay of technology and behavior
that has altered the very idea of theft, at least among young people. I got
a clear demonstration of that change in a class discussion that began with
the matter of a stolen book.

During the '60s, I was a graduate student at a university where stu- 8
dent activism had raised tensions on and around the campus. In the midst
of debates, demonstrations, and protests, a football player was caught leaving the campus store with a book he had not bought. Because he was well
known, his misadventure made the school newspaper. What seemed to be
a simple case of theft, however, took on greater significance. A number of
groups with little connection to athletics rose to his defense, claiming that
he had been entrapped: The university required that he have the book, the
publisher charged an unfairly high price, and the bookstore put the book
right in front of him, tempting him to steal it. So who could blame him?

Well, my students could. They thought it was clear that he had stolen 9
the book. But an MP3 file played from my laptop evoked a different response. Had I stolen the song? Not really, because a student had given me
the file as a gift. Well, was that file stolen property? Was it like the book
stolen from the campus bookstore so many years ago? No again, because
it was a copy, not the original, which presumably was with the student.
But then what should we make of the typical admonition on compact-disc
covers that unauthorized duplication is illegal? Surely the MP3 file was a
duplication of the original. To what extent is copying stealing?

The readings for the class amply demonstrated the complexity of the 10
legal, technical, and economic issues surrounding intellectual property in
the information age and gave the students much to talk about. Some students argued that existing regulations are simply inadequate at a time
when all information "wants to be free" and when liberating technology

is at hand. Others pointed to differences in the economics of the music and book businesses. In the end, the students who saw theft in the removal of the book back in the '60s did not see stealing in the unauthorized copying of music. For me, that was the most memorable aspect of the class because it illustrates how technology affects what we take to be moral behavior.

11   The technology of copying is closely related to the idea of theft. For example, my students would not take books from a store, but they do not consider photocopying a few pages of a book to be theft. They would not copy an entire book, however, perhaps because they vaguely acknowledge intellectual-property rights but probably more because copying would be cumbersome and time-consuming. They would buy the book instead. In that case, the very awkwardness of the copying aligns their actions with moral guidelines and legal standards.

12   But in the case of digital music, where the material is disconnected from the physical moorings of conventional stores and copying is so easy, many of my students see matters differently. They freely copy and share music. And they copy and share software, even though such copying is often illegal. If their books were digital and thus could be copied with comparable ease, they most likely would copy and share them.

13   Of course, the Digital Millennium Copyright Act, along with other laws, prohibits such copying. So we could just say that theft is theft, and complain with song, "Why can't they be like we were, perfect in every way? . . . Oh, what's the matter with kids today?" But had we had the same digital technology when we were young, we probably would have engaged in the same copying and sharing of software, digital music, and video that are so common among students today. We should not confuse lack of tools with righteousness.

14   The music industry would be foolish to put its faith in new protective schemes and devices alone. Protective technology cannot undo the changes that previous technology has caused. Should the industry aggressively pursue legal defenses like the suits against the four college students? Such highly publicized actions may be legally sound and may even slow music sharing in certain settings, but they cannot stop the transformation of the music business. The technology of sharing is too widespread, and my students (and their younger siblings) no longer agree with the music companies about right and wrong. Even some of the companies with big stakes in recorded music seem to have recognized that lawsuits and technical defenses won't work. Sony, for example, sells computers with "ripping and burning" capabilities, MP3 players, and other devices that gain much of their appeal from music sharing. And the AOL part of AOL Time Warner is promoting its new broadband service for faster downloads, which many people will use to share music sold by the Warner part of the company.

15   The lesson from my classroom is that digital technology has unalterably changed the way a growing number of customers think about recorded music. If the music industry is to prosper, it must change, too—perhaps

offering repositories of digital music for downloading (like Apple's newly announced iTunes Music Store), gaining revenue from the scope and quality of its holdings, and from a variety of new products and relationships, as yet largely undefined. Such a transformation will be excruciating for the industry, requiring the abandonment of previously profitable business practices with no certain prospect of success. So it is not surprising that the industry has responded aggressively, with strong legal actions, to the spread of file sharing. But by that response, the industry is risking its relationship with a vital segment of its market. Treating customers like thieves is a certain recipe for failure.

Content

1. What evidence does Gorry provide to support his claim that "technology affects what we take to be moral behavior" (¶ 10)?
2. Copying MP3 files is illegal, yet many people do it. What arguments do people use to justify copying music files, according to Gorry? Have you or people you know used any of these? Are these arguments appropriate? If so, according to what criteria? If not, why not?
3. Gorry details several legal and technological measures that the music industry has adopted to prevent the illegal reproduction of music files. Why haven't these methods been successful?
4. Students have told Gorry that the music file on his laptop should not be considered stolen because it was a copy (¶ 9). This implies a clear ethical distinction between copying and stealing. However, if copying is okay, explain why copying a classmate's exam answer is an infraction of academic rules.
5. Gorry's title, "Steal This MP3 File" is a reference to 1960s radical Abbie Hoffman's book entitled *Steal This Book*. According to Gorry, many of his classmates in the 1960s didn't blame a student who took a book without paying for it (¶ 8). Gorry's students, however, consider it a crime. How do you account for the shift in ethical standards?

Strategies/Structures/Language

6. Gorry uses specific examples, such as the anecdote about the student who stole a book (¶ 8) and students' reactions to the pirated MP3 file on Gorry's laptop (¶ 9). Explain the role these examples play in supporting his argument.
7. To what audience is this article addressed? How can you tell? How might the wording and the ideas be different if it were written for *Rolling Stone* magazine or your campus newspaper?

For Writing

8. Do you copy music files or accept them from friends? Discuss this issue with a classmate, and in collaboration, write an essay explaining why doing so should—or should not—be considered a crime. Specify the principles on which your argument is based, and illustrate the potential consequences.

9. Are musical and visual artists and industry employees victimized when their products are illegally reproduced? Research the impact of copying from musical or visual sources on various individuals or groups, and write an argument persuading the reader that this should be either stopped, or allowed to continue, depending on your findings.

10. Write a paper about Gorry's claim that advancements in technology are changing the ways people view their ethical choices. Discuss a technological change that has impacted ethical decision making. For example, you might focus on whether the availability of contraceptives is changing attitudes about sexual conduct or whether the production of steroid drugs is changing sports. Support your claims with evidence and detailed arguments.

 For comprehension, writing, and research activities and resources, please visit the companion website at <college.hmco.com/english>.

CHARLES M. YOUNG

Young (born 1951), grew up in Waukesha, Wisconsin, and graduated from Macalester College in 1973. For two years, as "the only guy on third string" on the Macalester Scots, a football team with "barely enough players for one string," Young says although he may not have been "the worst college football player of all time," he "may be only the worst player on the Macalester College Scots" in 1972. But, he says, "I do think I made a huge contribution to the atmosphere of despair and futility" that led to the team's NCAA record losing streak of "fifty straight losses."

Cutting his own losses, he headed for Columbia University, where he earned an MS in 1975 and soon got a job as an editor at *Rolling Stone* magazine. At the time he commented, "I try to write from a rock and roll sensibility, which at its best finds humor in the absurdity of life. A friend once accused me of liking punk rock because I never outgrew being fourteen. This is true, and there is nothing more absurd than being an adolescent in America." "Losing," first published in *Men's Journal,* was selected for inclusion in *Best American Sports Writing 2000.* Young says he's "grateful to win an award for losing." In this essay Young analyzes the concepts embedded in the language of "losing"—"to call someone a loser is probably the worst insult in the United States today," the shame associated with losing, and the hypocritical paradox of athletic contests that produce losers in abundance, yet stigmatize the losers, those who call them "losers," and the winners as well. "We're all losers in the race to win."

Losing: An American Tradition

Somebody's got to lose. Don't we all know the feeling? —B.C.

J ust north of the north end zone of Blackshear Stadium at Prairie View   1
A&M University in Texas is an unmarked grave.

"We buried last season," said Greg Johnson, the Prairie View Pan-   2
thers' coach, during a break in football practice. "In March, just before the
start of spring practice, we had them write down everything they didn't
like about the past—being 0–9 last season, the record losing streak. We
used the example of Superman, this guy that nobody could stop unless
you got him near some green kryptonite. We asked them, 'Well, what's
your green kryptonite? What is it that keeps you from doing what you
need to do in the classroom and on the football field? Is it a female? Is it
your friends? Is it a drug? Is it alcohol? Lack of dedication? Not enough
time in the weight room? You got a nagging injury that you didn't rehab?'
Whatever they wanted to bury, they wrote it down on a piece of paper.
And the last thing we did, we looked at the HBO tape. The segment that
Bryant Gumbel did on us for *Real Sports*, where they laughed at us and
ridiculed us as the worst team in the country—'How does it feel to be
0–75 since 1989?' or whatever it was at that point. I said, 'That's the last
we'll ever see of that tape,' and I put it in a big plastic trash bag with the
paper. We took it to a hole I had dug near the gate, and we threw it in. All
the players and all the coaches walked by. Some of them kicked dirt on it,
some of them spit on it. Some of them probably thought I was crazy. I
said, 'This is the last time we're going to talk about last year. This is the
last time we're going to talk about the losing streak. The past is dead, and
anything that's dead ought to be buried. It's history. It's gone.'"

That took place in September 1998, when Prairie View's NCAA-   3
record losing streak stood at 0–77. Now skip ahead to the postgame interviews of the January 9, 1999, AFC playoff game, in which the Denver
Broncos beat the Miami Dolphins 38–3. Shannon Sharpe, the Broncos' tight
end, called Miami's Dan Marino a "loser." Universally, this was viewed as
a mortal insult, far beyond the bounds of acceptable trash talk.

"I cringed when I read that," said Mike Shanahan, the Broncos'   4
coach. "I was really disappointed. Dan Marino's no loser."

So Sharpe, much humbled (and probably at Shanahan's insistence),   5
groveled after the next Denver practice: "In no way, shape, or form is Dan
Marino a loser. Dan, if I offended you or your family, your wife, your kids,
your mother or father, your brothers or sisters, I apologize. I stand before
you and sincerely apologize. I would never disrespect you as a person."

---

6   Which is odd. Football, along with every other major sport, is constructed to create losers. On any given game day, half the teams win, and half the teams lose. By the end of the playoffs, exactly one team can be called a winner, while thirty other teams are, literally, losers. So given that 96.7 percent of the players in the NFL can't help but be losers, why should calling somebody a loser be considered such an egregious violation of propriety that the guy who won must debase himself in public for pointing out that the guy who lost, lost?

7   Consider *Patton*, winner of the 1971 Academy Award for Best Picture and a favorite of coaches, team owners, and politicians ever since. It opens with George C. Scott standing in front of a screen-size American flag in the role of General George S. Patton, giving a pep talk to his troops. Using sports imagery to describe war (mirroring the sportswriters who use war imagery to describe sports), Patton delivers a succinct sociology lesson: "Americans love a winner, and will not tolerate a loser. Americans play to win all the time. I wouldn't give a hoot in hell for a man who lost and laughed. That's why Americans have never lost, and will never lose a war—because the very thought of losing is hateful to Americans."

8   Which is a view of most Americans that's shared by most Americans. Certain women of my acquaintance refer to men who score low on the Multiphasic Boyfriend Potentiality Scale as losers. *Cosmopolitan* has run articles on how to identify and dump losers before they have a chance to inseminate the unwary.

9   In *Jerry Maguire*, Tom Cruise suffers his worst humiliation when he spots his former girlfriend dating a rival agent at a *Monday Night Football* game. She makes an L with her fingers and mouths, "Loser."

10   In *American Beauty*, Kevin Spacey announces during his midlife crisis: "Both my wife and daughter think I'm this gigantic loser."

11   In *Gods and Monsters*, Lolita Davidovich, playing a bartender, dismisses the possibility of sex with her sometime lover, played by Brendan Fraser: "From now on, you're just another loser on the other side of the bar."

12   In *200 Cigarettes*, set in the ostensibly alternative subculture of Manhattan's Lower East Side, Martha Plimpton works herself into a state of despair considering the idea that no one will come to her New Year's Eve party. Then, considering an even worse possibility, she weeps: "All the losers will be here!"

13   At the real-life sentencing last February of Austin Offen for bashing a man over the head with a metal bar outside a Long Island night club, Assistant District Attorney Stephen O'Brien said that Offen was "vicious and brutal. He's a coward and a loser." Offen, displaying no shame over having crippled a man for life, screamed back: "I am not a loser!"

14   In his book *Turbo Capitalism: Winners and Losers in the Global Economy*, Edward Luttwak equates losing with poverty and observes that Americans believe that "failure is the result not of misfortune or injustice, but of divine disfavor."

I could list a hundred more examples, but you get the point.   15

Shannon Sharpe, in using the word *loser*, implied that Dan Marino   16
was: unworthy of sex or love or friendship or progeny, socially clueless,
stupid, parasitical, pathetic, poverty-stricken, cowardly, violent, felonious,
bereft of all forms of status, beneath all consideration, hated by himself,
hated by all good Americans, hated by God. And Dan Marino is one of the
best quarterbacks ever to play football. . . .

The literal truth is, I may not be the worst college football player of all   17
time. I've claimed that occasionally in the course of conversation, but I
may be only the worst college football player of 1972. I was definitely the
worst player on the Macalester College of Scots of St. Paul, Minnesota,
and we lost all of our games that season by an aggregate score of 312–46.
The team went on to win one game in each of the following two seasons
(after I graduated), then set the NCAA record with fifty straight losses. So,
strictly speaking, the losing streak wasn't my fault. I do think I made a
huge contribution to the atmosphere of despair and futility that led to the
losing streak. I think that as Prairie View was to the '90s, Macalester was
to the '70s. But in the final analysis, I think that over two decades at both
schools, some athlete may have failed more than I did.

I may therefore merely be one of the worst, a weaker distinction that   18
makes me even more pathetic than whoever it is who can make the case for
sole possession of the superlative—if someone wants to make that case. . . .

A couple weeks after I left PVU, the Panthers won a football game, 14–12,   19
against Langston University, ending the losing streak at eighty. The campus erupted in a victory celebration that was typical of the orgiastic outpourings that people all over the world feel entitled to after an important
win. I was happy for them. I felt bad for Langston, having to carry the
stigma of losing to the losers of all time.

There being virtually no literature of losing, I became obsessed with   20
reading books about winning, some by coaches and some by self-help
gurus. All of them advised me to forget about losing. If you want to join
the winners, they said, don't dwell on your past humiliations. Then I
thought of George Santayana's dictum: "Those who forget the past are
condemned to repeat it." So if I remembered losing, I'd be a loser. And if
I forgot losing, I'd be a loser. Finally, I remembered a dictum of my own:
"Anybody who quotes George Santayana about repeating the past will
soon be repeating even worse clichés."

That Christmas, my local Barnes & Noble installed a new section   21
called "Lessons from the Winners." Publishers put out staggering numbers of books with "win" in the title (as they do with *Zen and Any Stupid
Thing*), and they make money because there's a bottomless market of
losers who want to be winners. Almost all of these books are incoherent
lists of aphorisms and advice on how to behave like a CEO ("Memorize

How do you know that this photograph depicts losers? Could it represent anything else? Although it depicts two Florida State players in 1997, do the date, location, even the sport itself, actually matter in this portrait of losing?

the keypad on your cell phone so you dial and drive without taking your eyes off the road"). Most of these books are written by men who have made vast fortunes polluting the groundwater and screwing people who work for a living, and these men want to air out their opinions, chiefly that they aren't admired enough for polluting the groundwater and screwing people who work for a living. I thought of the ultimate winner, Howard Hughes, who was once the richest man in the world, who had several presidents catering to his every whim, who stored his feces in jars. I got more and more depressed.

22   Maybe I was just hypnotized by my own history of failure, character defects, and left-wing politics. Maybe what I needed was a pep talk. Maybe what I needed was Ray Pelletier, a motivational speaker who has made a lot of money raising morale for large corporations and athletic teams. Pelletier, a member of the National Speakers Association Hall of Fame, wrote a book, *Permission to Win*, that Coach Johnson had recommended to me. Basically an exhortation to feel like a winner no matter how disastrous your circumstances happen to be, the book deals with losing as a problem of individual psychology. I asked Pelletier if he thought that the emphasis American culture places on competition was creating vast numbers of people who, on the basis of having lost, quite logically think of themselves as losers.

23   "I don't think you have to think of yourself as a loser," he said. "I think competition causes you to reach down inside and challenges you to be at your very best. The key is not to beat yourself. If you're better than I am and

you're more prepared to play that day, you deserve to win. I have no problem with that. Every time I give a presentation, I want it to be better than the last one. I want to be sure I'm winning in everything that I do."

Yeah, but wasn't there a difference between excellence and winning? 24

"No, that's why I say that if I get beat by a team that's more talented, 25 I don't have a problem with that."

When one guy won, was he not inflicting defeat on the other guy? 26

"No. I'll give you an example. The first time I worked with a female 27 team before a big game, I was getting them all riled up and playing on their emotions, telling them how they deserved this win and how they worked really hard. A rah-rah, goose-pimple kind of speech. Just before we went on the court, the point guard said, 'Can I ask a question? Haven't the girls in the other locker room worked really hard, too? Don't they deserve to win, too?'"

Pelletier then veered off into a discussion of how the game teaches 28 you about life, of how his talks are really for fifteen years down the line when your wife leaves you, or the IRS calls for an audit, or you can't pay your mortgage. I asked him how he replied to the point guard in the locker room.

"I said, 'Absolutely the other team deserves to win, too. What we 29 have to do is find out if we can play together tonight as a team.' See, that's the biggest challenge facing corporate America today. We talk about teamwork but we don't understand the concept of team. Most of us have never been coached in anything. We've been taught, but not coached. There's a big difference. Great coaches challenge you to play at your best. The key is, you're in the game, trying to better yourself."

But Bill Parcells, the former coach of the Jets, is famous for saying 30 that you are what the standings say you are . . .

"Winning is playing at your best. Do you know the number-one rea- 31 son why an athlete plays his sport? Recognition. Once you understand that, everything else becomes easy. Lou Holtz says that win means 'What's Important Now.'"

That's just standard practice in books about winning, I told him. 32 They redefine the word to include all human behavior with a good connotation. In *The Psychology of Winning*, Dr. Denis Waitley writes that winning is "unconditional love." Winning could hardly be a more conditional form of love. You are loved if you win, and scorned if you lose.

"I don't believe that." 33

If athletes play for recognition, don't they want to be recognized as 34 winners? And if you've lost, won't you be recognized as a loser?

"I don't think they're labeled that way." 35

By the press? By the fans? 36

"To me, unconditional love is an aspect of winning. The problem 37 is that you and I have not been trained to think positively. In one of my corporate seminars, I ask people to write down all the advantages there are to being negative. I want them to think about it seriously. It's an exercise that can take fifteen or twenty minutes, and then they have the 'Aha!' There is no advantage to negative thinking. None. And yet the biggest problem we face in America is low self-esteem."

38   Low self-esteem has its uses, though. Whenever you see a couple of male animals on a PBS nature special duking it out for the privilege of having sex with some female of the species, one of the males is going to dominate and the other male is either going to die or get low self-esteem and crawl off making obsequious gestures to the winner. The evolutionary value is obvious: Fight to the death and your genes die with you; admit you're a loser and you may recover to fight again or find another strategy for passing on your genes through some less selective female. Species in which one alpha male gets to have sex with most of the females—elephant seals are a good example—need a lot of low self-esteem among the beta males for social stability.

39   With 1 percent of the population possessing more wealth than the bottom 95 percent, the American economy operates a lot like a bunch of elephant seals on a rock in the ocean. And it simply must mass-produce low self-esteem in order to maintain social stability amidst such colossal unfairness.

40   According to the World Health Organization, mood disorders are the number-one cause worldwide of people's normal activities being impaired. In the United States alone, the WHO estimates, depression costs $53 billion a year in worker absenteeism and lost productivity. While that's a hell of a market for Ray Pelletier and the National Speakers Association, which has more than three thousand people giving pep talks to demoralized companies and sports teams, doled-out enthusiasm is a palliative, not a curative. In fact, demoralization is a familiar management tool; the trick is creating just enough. Too much and you have work paralysis, mass depression, and suicide. Too little and you have a revolution. Ever hear a boss brag that he doesn't *have* ulcers, he *gives* them? He's making sure his employees are demoralized enough to stay in their place.

41   Consider the book *Shame and Pride*, by Dr. Donald L. Nathanson, a psychiatrist and the executive director of the Silvan S. Tomkins Institute in Philadelphia. Starting in the mid-1940s, Dr. Tomkins watched babies for thousands of hours and made a convincing case that humans are born preprogrammed with nine "affects"—potential states of emotion that can be triggered by a stimulus or memory. These affects are: interest-excitement, enjoyment-joy, surprise-startle, fear-terror, distress-anguish, anger-rage, dissmell (*dissmell* is similar to *distaste,* but related to the sense of smell), disgust, and shame-humiliation. These affects "amplify" an outside stimulus or memory to give you an increase in brain activity that eventually becomes full-blown emotion.

Until recent years, shame was the "ignored emotion" in psychol-   42
ogy. But a few people, Nathanson most prominently, built on Tomkins
and discovered the key to . . . well, not quite everything, but an awful lot.
According to Tomkins and Nathanson, shame erupts whenever "desire
outruns fulfillment." An impediment arises to the two positive affects
(interest-excitement and enjoyment-joy), and suddenly your eyes drop,
your head and body slump, your face turns red, and your brain is confused to the point of paralysis. . . .

I called up Nathanson and asked if he had any thoughts about [ath-   43
letes and shame]. . . .

Sports events are often described as a morality play, I said, but there's   44
nothing moral about it. Sports decide who will participate in power and
who will be humiliated.

"That's understandable when you recognize that our sense of place   45
in society is maintained by shame. Keeping people in their place is maintaining them at certain levels of shaming interaction at which they can be
controlled. This issue of winning and losing, it throws us. It defines our
identity, doesn't it?"

Calling someone a loser is probably the worst insult in the United   46
States today.

"If you're calling someone that, the person must live in a perpetual   47
state of shame. The only way he can live with himself is to have massive
denial, disavowal of his real identity. He has to make his way in the
world somehow, and he can't walk around constantly thinking of himself as a loser. Yet if someone in our eyes is a loser and he refuses to admit
it, this is narcissism. He has an identity that can't be sustained by con-
sensual validation."

Is there some value in competition, in creating all these losers?   48

"When you're young and you're learning and it's just a bunch of   49
guys playing a game, that's not shame. That's just figuring out that Billy
is faster than Johnny. When parents and schools and bureaucracies start
getting involved and demanding wins, then it gets pathological."

Playing for the Chicago Bears, the Philadelphia Eagles, and the Dallas   50
Cowboys from 1961 to 1972, Mike Ditka was All-Pro five times as a tight
end, won an NFL championship with the Bears in 1963, won Super Bowl
VI with the Cowboys, and was elected to the Hall of Fame. As the coach
of the Bears from 1982 to 1992, he won Super Bowl XX with an 18–1 team
generally acknowledged as one of the greatest ever and was named Coach
of the Year twice. As the coach of the New Orleans Saints for the past three
seasons, he had a 15–33 record and is now most vividly remembered for
flipping off the fans and grabbing his crotch during and after an especially inept defeat. (He was fined $20,000.) I asked him if he thinks that
football fans are inherently interested in the game, or in the hallucination
of power they get when their team wins?

51   "They relate to the winning. Well, you can't say they aren't interested in the game. They watch the game. But the excitement comes from winning."

52   When football players snap at journalists in the locker room after a loss . . .

53   "That's only human nature. They probably snap at their wives when they get home, too. Are you saying, Does losing bother people? Sure it does. It's no different from a guy at IBM who loses a sale to a competitor. You just don't like to lose. Most people want to be associated with winning. When you work your butt off and don't get the results you want, you might be a little short-tempered as a coach. That's only life. But that's no different than any other segment of life. Football parallels society, period."

54   I've noticed that the worst thing you can call somebody in the United States is a loser.

55   "No. The word *quitter* is the worst thing you can call somebody. Lemme ask you something: If two teams play all year, and they reach the Super Bowl, the one that loses is a loser? Come on.

56   "I don't like the term. . . . It's not fair. I think as long as you compete and you do your best, if the other team is better, I don't think you really lose. I think you lose when you quit trying."

57   The problem with declaring a quitter to be a lower form of dirt than a loser is that you're still stigmatizing almost everybody. Studies indicate that up to 90 percent of children drop out of organized competitive sports by the age of fifteen. Extrapolating from my own experience, I would guess that they don't enjoy feeling like losers so that the jocks can feel like winners. Since they associate intense physical activity with feeling rotten, they grow up having problems with obesity and depression, both of which have become epidemic in the United States.

58   As Mike Ditka would say, it's not fair. But I think there's a way out. And I think that Alfie Kohn has seen it. Kohn, an educational philosopher, has helped inspire the opposition to standardized tests, an especially pernicious form of competition. His first book, *No Contest: The Case Against Competition*, cites study after study demonstrating that competition hinders work, play, learning, and creativity in people of all ages. (In fact, there is almost no evidence to the contrary in the social sciences.) The book is wonderfully validating for anyone who ever had doubts about the ostensible fun of gym class and spelling bees. I told Kohn that in my experience, people get unhinged when you question the value of making other people fail.

59   "Absolutely. It calls into question America's state religion, which is practiced not only on the playing field but in the classroom and the workplace, and even in the family. The considerable body of evidence demonstrating that this is self-defeating makes very little impression on people who are psychologically invested in a desperate way in the idea of winning. The real alternative to being number one is not being number two, but

being able to dispense with these pathological ratings altogether. If people accepted the research on the destructiveness of competition, you wouldn't see all these books teaching how to compete more effectively. I hear from a lot of teachers and parents whose kids fall apart after losing in spelling bees and awards assemblies, and they feel dreadful about it. The adults start to think, *Hmm, maybe competition isn't such a good thing, at least for those kids.* It took me years to see that the same harms were being visited upon the winners. The kids who win are being taught that they are good only to the extent that they continue to beat other people. They're being taught that other people are obstacles to their own success, which destroys a sense of community as effectively as when we teach losers that lesson. And finally, the winners are being taught that the point of what they are doing is to win, which leads to diminished achievement and interest in what they are doing. What's true for kids is also true for adults. It's not a problem peculiar to those who lose. We're all losers in the race to win."

I'm very blessed that way. I didn't have the perspective to spell it out like Alfie Kohn, but I've known I was a total loser since my first college football practice. I've admitted it here publicly, and I am free. You, you're probably holding on to some putrefying little shred of self-esteem, denying that you're a loser in a country inhabited by Bill Gates and 260 million losers. You're still hoping to beat your friend at racquetball and make him feel as bad as you do when you lose, still looking to flatten some rival with just the right factoid in an argument, still craving the sports car in the commercial that accurately announces, "There's no such thing as a gracious winner." Give up, I say. Join me. Losers of the world, unite! You have nothing to lose but your shame. 60

Content

1. Young asserts, "Calling someone a loser is probably the worst insult in the United States today" (¶ 46) and "Football, along with every other major sport, is constructed to create losers" (¶ 6). Explain why you either agree or disagree with Young's assertions. If most athletes are in fact losers, why is it such an insult to call them losers (¶ 6)?

2. How, as Young points out, can "books about winning" get away with redefining "the word to include all human behavior with a good connotation," such as "winning is 'unconditional love.' Winning could hardly be a more conditional form of love. You are loved if you win, and scorned if you lose" (¶ 32)? Which definition of winning is more accurate—Young's or those books'? Cite the best evidence you can to prove your point.

3. Young asserts, "Sports events are often described as a morality play . . . but there's nothing moral about it. Sports decide who will participate in power and who will be humiliated" (¶ 44). Do you agree or disagree? On what evidence? How can a country such as the United States, which promises "freedom and justice to all," perpetuate a sports culture devoted to the exercise of power and humiliation as Young describes?

Strategies/Structure/Language

4. In his final paragraph Young proudly declares himself a "total loser," thereby departing from our traditional conception of equating shame with losing (¶ 60). He then makes a direct appeal to his audience with "Give up, I say. Join me. Losers of the world, unite! You have nothing to lose but your shame." Discuss the effectiveness of such a concluding strategy in an essay that appeals to emotions and ethics.

5. Young's definition of the word *loser* (¶ 16) includes "unworthy of sex or love or friendship or progeny, socially clueless, stupid, parasitical, pathetic, poverty-stricken, cowardly. . . ." Compare his definition to a dictionary definition. Do they contain common elements? What are the significant differences? Are there qualities that should either be added to or deleted from Young's definition? What are these?

6. In many respects this entire essay is about language, slippery definitions of losing and winning, low self-esteem, shame, and quitting. Given that "Losing" was originally published in *Men's Journal,* does this mean that Young thinks men in general hold definitions of these terms in some commonly accepted sense? How does Young redefine these terms? Does he expect women as well as men to agree with him?

7. Young's tone varies throughout the essay, from comic to dead serious and in between. What is the tone of his opening examples of the Prairie View Panthers' burial of their losing streak (¶ 2) and the discussion of "losers" that begins and ends with Dan Marino (¶s 3–16)? At what points is he the most serious? In what ways does his variable tone reinforce his argument?

For Writing

8. Alfie Kohn, an educational philosopher, argues that "kids who win are being taught that they are good only to the extent that they continue to beat other people. They're being taught that other people are obstacles to their own success, which destroys a sense of community as effectively as when we teach losers that lesson" and that "we're all losers in the race to win" (¶ 59). Drawing on your own experiences in elementary or high school, would you say that American elementary or secondary education has changed recently in ways designed to ensure cooperation, rather than competition, among its pupils? Write an essay that uses a wide variety of examples, ranging from the personal to examples from the media to those provided by experts, in arguing for or against Kohn's position.

9. With a partner, write an essay in which you discuss two or three key experiences you have each had with winning and losing in light of Young's argument. (You will need to identify the significant features of these experiences. One person's experiences may corroborate the other's, or they may differ significantly.) In what ways has Young reinforced what you already believed to be true in relation to these experiences with winning and losing? In what ways has Young helped you to see these experiences in a new light? What advice for others can you draw from your analysis?

 For comprehension, writing, and research activities and resources, please visit the companion website at <college.hmco.com/english>.

MATT NOCTON

For biographical information, see page 29.

Nocton himself worked harvesting tobacco in Connecticut; the tobacco fields are adjacent to the state's largest airport, Bradley International Airport. "Harvest of Gold, Harvest of Shame" is the seventh revision Nocton submitted, every draft reinforcing the gulf between the bosses and the workers in the tobacco fields and sheds, every draft increasing his own awareness of the workers' exploited and powerless condition.

❄ *Harvest of Gold, Harvest of Shame*

S imsbury is a small affluent town located in the heart of the Connecticut River Valley. It is not a particularly exciting place and its high school students refer to it as "Simsboring." But in fact there is something unique about this quiet town. Simsbury is home to Culbro Tobacco Company's Farm No. 2. The Culbro Tobacco Company prides itself on growing the finest shade tobacco in the world. Its leaves are used to wrap expensive cigars.

Culbro employs three kinds of people: migrant workers, most of whom are from Jamaica and live on the farm headquarters, inner-city people, most of whom are Hispanic and are bussed from Hartford to Simsbury at 6:15 in the morning; and finally, a few local white residents. The latter are typically the men who oversee all of the other employees. Each supervisor is referred to as the "boss man" by the less fortunate workers. When a boss man speaks to one of his subordinates, the usual response comes either in the form of Spanglish, which most of the Hispanics speak, or Patoi, which is what the Jamaicans speak.

Working in tobacco fields is demanding and repetitious and the pay is minimum wage. In a typical day, a field worker is bussed to the field where he will be working with his group of roughly fifty to two hundred workers. When he gets off the bus he will find a pick-up truck parked nearby full of burlap and twine. He must tie this burlap around his waist as a source of protection against the dirt and rocks that he will be dragging himself through for the next eight hours. He will then find another pick-up truck containing wooden stakes with numbers on them. There he will find the stake with his number and stick it into the ground before the row of tobacco plants where he is about to work. A recorder or "bentkeeper" (so called because the distance between two tobacco posts is called a bent) stands under the blazing sun and monitors all the workers. He does this by looking at the numbers of each stake in each row. He flips through the pages on his clipboard until he finds the corresponding employee number.

Then he checks the number of poles in the row and adds the number of "bents" in the row to a particular worker's sum total. He does this for fifty to two hundred laborers. At times when the rows are very short it is difficult to add all of the numbers fast enough to keep up with the pace of the pickers. The pickers who complete the most bents earn the most money. The bentkeeper is the only one authorized to carry the clipboard and add the bent numbers. Every so often the unshaven field boss man with the coarse black mustache and cowboy hat calls the bentkeeper. "Hey, who was working in this row? Twelve six-four-five is still staked in here. Who was working next to twelve six-four-five?" The bentkeeper nervously hands over his clipboard and the boss man takes off his sunglasses and draws on his cigarette while he examines it.

4   "What the hell is this!?! This is an eight bent row! You've been adding nine! It changed from nine to eight way the hell back there! Look at the goddamn post! Goddamn are you blind or can't you read!?! Go fix it!" He shoves the clipboard into the bentkeeper's stomach and jumps in his truck. The truck kicks up dirt and a cloud of dust as it speeds down the rocky dirt road. It comes to an abrupt halt about one hundred yards down. As the bentkeeper tries to figure out where the bents changed from nine to eight and from which numbers he must deduct points, he hears the boss man in the distance. "Hey eleven two-nine-two! Were you working next to twelve six-four-five?! You're bruising the leaves! Look at this? See this? This is from your row! We can't use these! You're going too fast. Stop bruising the goddamn leaves or I'm going to dock ten bents from your total!"

5   The humiliated bentkeeper tries not to listen as he attempts to correct his blunder while keeping pace with the pickers at the same time. A tough looking Hispanic kid breaks his concentration. "Hey bentkeeper! How many I got?" He holds up his stake so the bentkeeper can see the number.

6   The bentkeeper flips through the pages, "Uhhmm . . . sixty-eight."

7   "What!? I got more than that!"

8   "No, you've got sixty-eight."

9   "Ahh man this is bullshit. How'd you get that job anyway?" The complaining worker walks over to the water truck to get a drink.

10   In the middle of two towering tobacco plants under the white netting eleven two-nine-two mumbles slowly in a deep raspy voice with smoke in his breath "Duh boss mon is crazy mon." He finishes his row and approaches the bentkeeper. "Hey mon, eleven two-nine-two, how many I got now?"

11   The bentkeeper replies "Yeah I know your number Stanley, you have one-hundred and fifteen."

12   Stanley's smile reveals a gold front tooth with a black clover on it, "Ohkay mon, yuh shades uh looking fat mon. All shades uh fat in my book mon."

13   After field "asparagus 1032," is finished, the nets are dropped and the boss man selects two unlucky souls to spray the field. They reluctantly

don cumbersome yellow suits that resemble something NASA designed for the planned mission to Mars. The only obvious difference is that the sprayers wear back packs of insecticides rather than oxygen.

Beneath the foggy mask of his suit, David's pockmarked hairy face contorts into a nasty expression as he argues with his partner. Everyone hated David. He talked in the belligerent tongue of a junkyard dog. He was likened to a Neanderthal, though an allusion to something more ancient would probably suit him better. In the middle of the argument David blurts out, "I was in prison you know. . . .you know why I was there? . . . I killed a cop. . . . strangled him. . . . I'm on parole now." The significance of his comment seemed to bear no relation to the argument and his partner ignored it. He wasn't afraid of David.

All of the leaves from "asparagus 1032" are transported to the shed on a trailer pulled by a big blue Ford tractor. The shed operations are run by a short stocky Hispanic man who wears a blue Hawaiian tee shirt with buttons and flowers. Working in the shed is better than working in the field. Many women work in the shed. There, by means of a giant sewing machine, they monotonously sew tobacco leaves to a stick called a "lath." Every time a worker finishes fifty laths she gets credit for one bundle. That is recorded by the bundlekeeper who patrols the shed monitoring daily progress. When a sewer calls out "bundle!" the bundlekeeper acknowledges "bundle!" and he hurries over to the end of the shed and hoists the heavy bundle from the bundle stockpile onto his shoulder. He then carries it to the idle sewer and he drops the bundle of fifty laths on top of her sewing machine. He then withdraws his hole puncher and he punches a hole in her card. Every time he punches a sewer's card he punches the master card which he wears around his neck. The master card shows how many bundles the shed completes on a daily basis. The bundlekeeper is the only one authorized to carry the hole puncher and the master card. Every so often a "boss man" will summon the bundlekeeper over and yank the master card from the bundlekeeper's neck to examine it. Then the boss man marches up and down the shed to exercise his authority. Then he stops in a thick cloud of dust to bark his favorite motivational speech "you not gonna get paid if you don't speed up!" The sewers ignore him and try to keep up with their mindless sewing machines. Those who complete the most bundles make the most money.

Every time a lath is completed it is racked. Then a man who has precariously positioned himself on the bottom level of rafters in the shed reaches down to the rack and picks it up. He then passes it to his partner above him on the next level who passes it up to the man above him and so on until the lath reaches the highest level that is available for another row of lath. Each lath is suspended between two rafters in the barn. They are carefully packed about a foot and a half apart across the width of the shed on every level of rafters and along the length of the barn. It normally takes about three days or a million and a half tobacco leaves to fill a shed.

17   On the dry dusty floor of the shed, the sweaty bundlekeeper looks up and admires the beautiful ceiling as it is painted with enormous green leaves with a splotch of a red shirt on one level and a yellow shirt above it and black arms with extended hands reaching to one another. For a moment he is gazing at the ceiling of the Sistine Chapel in Rome. He can imagine he is actually witnessing Michelangelo paint his masterpiece. For a moment the two men with extended hands remind the bundlekeeper of God in the heavens reaching to Adam. His imagination is suddenly snapped by a falling lath misplaced by an imperfect human being hanging from the rafters. The bundlekeeper ducks and after a loud 'thump!' he thanks God for his green hard hat.

18   As the clock rolls onto ten o'clock the boss man calls out "Coffee! Last lath!" The sewers finish sewing their last fifty leaves and the squeaky machines fall silent. The silence is invaded by the chatter of relieved sewers who have temporarily escaped the heat and dust in the shed to drink their coffee outside under the shade of a nearby tree or the side of the barn. The men in the rafters descend to retrieve their coolers to snack on bread and beer for a leisurely ten minutes.

19   Work resumes promptly at ten after ten with the boss man's "back to work!" The dissipating dust is replenished by a fresh cloud churned from the feet of a tired troop heading back to the barn. Next to the crack in the shed where a ray of sunlight illuminates floating dust particles, an old machine resumes its monotonous humming and clicking as a carefree Jamaican man whistles while feeding it leaves.

20   The boss man steps outside his dark shed for a breath of fresh air and a chance to blow his nose and spit the gritty sand from his mouth. Then he sees the next load of green leaves preceding a light brown dust cloud in field "Ketchen 918" with the new hybrid seed. Those leaves cannot be mixed. He grows red in the face because the next shed has not yet been prepared for those leaves. He stomps over to his dust colored pickup truck to call base. After talking to the base coordinator he realizes that he will have to divide his crew into two sections with one half in one shed and another in the other shed. Now the bundlekeeper will have to run back and forth between the two sheds because of the field boss man's mistake. The stressed-out shed boss man invents another motivational speech "Hey, dees is not a carnival! dees is not the beach!" By lunch time the boss man has resumed his composure. He sneaks a peek at his watch and yells "last lath! break time! last lath!"

21   The shed workers rush to the water truck outside to wash their hands before lunch. They sit in the weeds against the shady side of the shed and eat their lunches. The bundlekeeper and the shed boss eat in the pickup truck and listen to the Spanish radio. Out in the field the boss man calls "lunch time! Finish your rows!" The dirty and smelly pickers crawl out from underneath the nets and remove the tape from their fingers and try to wash the sticky tape, tobacco juices, and dirt from their fingertips.

Then they head to the bus to find their coolers of beer and candy bars. They eat and drink for half an hour. Stanley puffs his harsh "Craven A" cigarette between mouthfuls of ham and cheese and tries not to think about tobacco.

The bentkeeper and the field boss eat in the dusty pickup and the ₂₂ field boss lights his Marlboro and explains: "You know, when I yell at you it's nothing personal. I have to yell at you because it's my job. Man I know how it is, I was in your shoes once." The bentkeeper nods in agreement. His mind is on his lunch. It appears inedible. After growing tired of drinks and sandwiches that became warm and soggy in the hot sun for the past month, he has devised an unreliable system to solve that problem. Instead of just packing his lunch in ice, he actually freezes his entire lunch overnight. Unfortunately, when he opened his cooler on this hot day he discovered his peanut butter and jelly to be hard as a brick. Likewise his Boku juice boxes were still frozen solid.

As he sits there listening to his boss's rambling, he places his sand- ₂₃ wich on the dash and he peels away the walls of his juice box and gnaws on it as if it were some kind of primitive popsicle. No matter how he prepares his lunch he can never seem to achieve a proper balance between hot and cold. When the sun is high and it's time to eat, he discovers either a frozen block of bread and jam or a soggy something suffering heat stroke.

At half past the hour Stanley strikes his stake into the dirt with a ₂₄ swift robotic motion. He sucks deeply on his cigarette and marches down to the end of the row. Large veins puff out of his forearm like the veins on the bottom green leaf that he snaps from the lower stalk of a thriving tobacco plant. Three more hours to go.

At the shed yet another blue tractor arrives with its precious load of ₂₅ fresh leaves. The shed boss man orders two rafter men down to disperse the containers of tobacco among the sewers. The bundlekeeper manages to help with the heavy containers between bundle runs. He is thoroughly exhausted and his eyes are bloodshot from the irritating smoke and dust in the shed. Although three hours remain every shed laborer is anticipating the boss man's "last lath! Get on the bus!"

At three-thirty in the hot afternoon three buses and two Chevy pick- ₂₆ up trucks carry exhausted tobacco workers back to farm headquarters where the workers can rest before returning to work early tomorrow in the cool morning hours.

Content

1. Nocton identifies a variety of tasks the tobacco farm workers perform. What similarities are there among the jobs? What differences? Are readers to assume that all jobs are "demanding and repetitive and the pay is minimum wage" (¶ 3)? What's the difference between the tobacco harvesting process and the harvesting activities that Shange describes (166–71)?

2. Which workers are Hispanics and Jamaicans? Are any white Americans? Who performs which tasks?

3. Nocton evidently doesn't expect his readers to know much about the work of harvesting tobacco. What does he expect them to learn from reading his essay? What does he expect them to do as a consequence?

4. Is Nocton himself a worker in the scene he describes? If so, can you ascertain what his job is? What are your clues? In what ways, if any, does the effectiveness of his argument depend on the authority of his personal experience?

Strategies/Structures/Language

5. Nocton's language is slow and repetitive. How does the style fit the subject?
6. Where does Nocton use dialogue? With what effects?

For Writing

7. Have you ever thought about how any crop that provides common raw materials—wheat, sugar, potatoes, rice, coffee, cotton—is grown and harvested? Have you or your relatives ever worked in such harvests? Find out about the production of one of these crops and compare it with the tobacco harvest that Nocton describes. On the basis of your investigation, formulate some principles of how agricultural workers should be treated and what their compensation and protection should be.

8. Have you or any family members or close friends ever held a minimum-wage job, or do you currently hold such a job? With a partner who has had comparable job experience, analyze your respective jobs and determine their common elements. Do they have aspects in common with the jobs Nocton describes? Are there any significant differences? Either together or individually, write a satiric paper about a typical day on the job, intended to serve as a critique and to imply a plan for better working conditions or employee benefits.

 For comprehension, writing, and research activities and resources, please visit the companion website at <college.hmco.com/english>.

Additional Topics for Writing
Appealing to Emotion and Ethics

(For strategies for appealing to emotion and ethics, see 492.)

MULTIPLE STRATEGIES FOR WRITING
THAT APPEALS TO EMOTION AND ETHICS

Implied arguments, appeals to emotion and ethics, commonly employ assorted strategies to make their points as compelling as possible, and to interpret their significance. Among these are the following:

- *definitions* of essential terms, component parts. These are likely to be subjective and favorable to the writer's point of view.
- a *narrative*, which may comprise the entire argument or an interrelated series of narrative examples. The *narrator* is likely to be the author, using characters or events to make the point, *dialogue, a time sequence,* evocative *setting(s),* and *symbolism* to reinforce the implied point.
- *definitions, illustrations,* and *examples,* to show the meaning or significance of the key issues
- *process analysis,* to show either how the subject at hand arose and why it needs to be addressed or to show the process by which a remedy or solution can be effected
- *comparison* and *contrast* of the pro and con positions
- *division* and *classification* of the relevant subtopics and side issues
- *cause* and *effect,* to show the beneficial consequences of the arguer's point of view and the detrimental consequences of the opposition's stance

1. Write an essay that attempts to persuade one of the following audiences through a combination of appeals to reason, emotion, and ethics.

   a. To someone you'd like for a friend, fiancé(e), or spouse, or an enemy with whom you'd like a reconciliation: Love me.
   b. To an athlete, or to an athletic coach: Play according to the rules, even when the referee (umpire, or other judge) isn't looking.
   c. To a prospective employer: I'm the best person for the job. Hire me.
   d. To a police officer: I shouldn't receive this traffic ticket. Or, to a judge or jury: I am innocent of the crime of which I'm accused.
   e. To the voters: Vote for me (or for a candidate of my choice).
   f. To admissions officers of a particular college, university, or of a program within that institution (such as medical or law school, graduate program, or a division with a special undergraduate degree): Let me in.
   g. To the prospective buyer of something you want to sell or service you can perform: Buy this. Trust me.
   h. To an audience prejudiced against a particular group or simply to a majority audience: It is wrong to discriminate against X. (X may be a minority, female, a member of a particular national or religious group, gay, disabled, elderly . . .)

   i. To an antagonist on any issue: As Joan Didion says, *"Listen to me, see it my way, change your mind."*

   j. To people engaging in behavior that threatens their lives or their health: Stop doing X (or stop doing X to excess)—smoking, drinking, overeating, undereating, or using drugs. Or: Start doing X—exercising regularly, using bike helmets or seatbelts, planning for the future by getting an education, a stable job, free of debt, an investment plan, a retirement plan . . .

2. Pick a work of fiction or nonfiction whose content intrigues you and whose style you admire, and write a brief parody (probably involving considerable exaggeration) of it to show your understanding of the content and your appreciation of the style.

3. Write a satire to argue implicity for a point, as Swift does in "A Modest Proposal" (497–503). Use whatever techniques seem appropriate, such as creating a character who does the talking for you; setting a scene (such as of pathos or misery) that helps make your point; using a tone involving understatement, irony, or exaggeration. Be sure to supply enough clues to enable your readers to understand what you really mean.

4. Write a humorous paper primarily for enjoyment—your own and your audience's—on a familiar topic that either shows its pleasant aspects to advantage (White, "Once More to the Lake," 97–103; Twain, "Uncle John's Farm," 265–71) or parodies its subject (Verge, "The Habs," 119–23; Britt, "That Lean and Hungry Look," 261–63).

5. Write a worst-case scenario designed to frighten readers into accepting your argument on any of the above topics or those in Chapter 11 (486–87).

Part V

CONTROVERSY IN CONTEXT:

Implications of World Terrorism and World Peace

AN ARGUMENT CASEBOOK

Terrorism

For most Americans, indeed for much of the world, the attacks on the World Trade Center and the Pentagon on September 11, 2001, like the attack on Pearl Harbor on December 7, 1941, make it a day that like few others, will long live in infamy as we realize, in poet Seamus Heaney's words, "Anything can happen, the tallest things / Be overturned. . . ." This is illustrated in the photograph (535) of the remains of the World Trade Center disintegrating amidst the ash and debris of that fateful attack. As with every other earth-shaking event, we looked at our world one way before the cataclysm and another way—or many other ways—afterward. Did the world change? Or did we? And in what ways—significant, casual, even trivial? Given where we have been, where we are going (and where exactly that will be) depends to an extent on the viewer's stance. Will our sojourn involve nation with (or against) nation; culture with (or against) culture; technology, economy, or ideology with (or against) its counterpart? How will terrorist attacks and the infinite possibilities of future terrorism, specific or vague, affect the ways we live our lives, our plans for the future, and how we look at our neighbors, our friends—and our enemies? What can we, as individuals and as a nation, do to balance the free and open nature of our hospitable society against needs for protection and security? How can we avoid dividing the world into "us" against "them"? How can we temper suspicion and paranoia, and nevertheless be on guard—but against what?

The chapter "Terrorism" explores these questions, with specific issues embedded in the details not only of the terrorist attacks of September 11, but in earlier manifestations of violence and terrorism throughout the world. Ten pieces comprise this chapter: poems by Seamus Heaney and Eliza Griswold bookend the prose, which includes a chapter from Tim O'Brien's war (really peace) stories, *The Things They Carried;* Kandi Tayebi's creative nonfiction," Warring Memories"; four essays (by Laurie Fendrich, Bernard Lewis, Wendell Berry, and Mary Graham); and excerpts from two books, the *9/11 Commission Report* and Mark Juergensmeyer's *Terror in the Mind of God.* They are representative of the more reasoned, balanced, analytic views of events of this incendiary nature, among hundreds of thousands of outpourings. Yet, with the possible exception of Heaney's poem, all of these pieces could be interpreted as incendiary, provocative of argument and conflict by readers who disagree, or who interpret flash-point words such as *terrorism, war,* even *peace,* from different perspectives. Indeed, the thrust of the more creative writings here, like many other creative works on war and peace, is that war is hell, but as Tim O'Brien says, "To generalize about war is like generalizing about peace" (see the excerpts from the Nobel Peace Prize speeches, 592–632). "Almost everything is true. Almost nothing is true. At its core, perhaps, war is just another name for death, and yet any soldier will tell you, if he tells the truth, that proximity to death brings with it a corresponding proximity to life" (¶ 45, 547). And Eliza Griswold reminds us that "any peace / that must be kept by force / contains another name. It's war." In general, distinguished, evocative writings about war, whether Nobelist Heaney's "Horace and Thunder" (541), O'Brien's distinguished "How to Tell a True War Story" (543–50), or

Tayebi's "Warring Memories" (554–58), are as much about peace—with its implied norms of wholeness and healing—as they are about war. Tayebi expresses the authors' common hope that their work "can help the healing process for a world torn by violence and remind each of us of our humanity." Thus much of the material with which this casebook opens—the work by Heaney, O'Brien, Fendrich, Griswold, and Tayebi—could as readily—and as resonantly—belong in the Peace chapter as in its present location.

This first inclination of many, along with a surge of sympathy for the victims, is to try to understand what happened. "Where were you when . . . ?" "What did you do?" "Do you know anybody who . . . ?" We talk about it, we listen to the incessant media reports, we write to try to make sense of things that don't make sense, which Heaney's brief reflection on "Horace and Thunder" attempts to do. The world, says Heaney, is suddenly "overturned." "Capstones shift, nothing resettles right." And in a time of terror, when "telluric ash and fire-spores darken day," it is tempting, as many writers and media commentators do, to divide the world into "us"—the innocent, beleaguered victims of a horrific attack—and "them"—the vile denizens of an evil empire who hate us all and will stop at nothing to destroy our free society (as, for example, Don DeLillo does in "In the Ruins of the Future," *Harper's,* 2002). This is not a good way to conduct any argument, although this kind of thinking is often the basis for initiating and conducting a war, emanating from the halls of Congress, the Oval Office, branches of the military, with reverberations throughout the press and television, domestic and international.

Because the "us" versus "them" view is so popular, it cannot be overlooked. Nevertheless, as the immediate impact of the events is somewhat mitigated by time, we realize that this is not the only perspective and war is not the only alternative. Even if we can't change the past or prevent the World Trade Center's destruction, we can interpret the present in ways that we hope will prepare us for the future. In "History Overcomes Stories" (551–53), an eyewitness commentary on her experience of living ten blocks from "what used to be the World Trade Center towers" (an experience shared by the men fleeing the collapse of the first tower in the photograph on page 552), Laurie Fendrich, a painter and fine arts professor, writes a counternarrative to combat media overkill, to interpret stories that "are polluted and demeaned by having been reduced to fodder for television, movie, and slick magazine entertainment." She looks, as people do in times of trauma, for guidance "to see if we can now act the way we ought to have been acting all along," and finds focus and stability in a reaffirmation of the core values of Western culture, which trendy postmodern theory has undervalued: "individual liberty, coupled with obligations to virtue, democracy coupled with responsibility, the requirement of courage, an acknowledgement—always tempered by reason—of duty, and an assertion of basic, not jingoistic, patriotism."

In 2003 playwright David Mamet published in *Threepenny Review* a brief essay, "Secret Language," which corroborates Fendrich's perspective. Here he critiques the vocabulary of superpatriotic attempts to control the

hearts and minds of the American people. *Weapons of mass destruction*, he claims, is "overlong, clunky, and obviously confected," awkward, nagging, not used often in common conversation and thus doomed to oblivion. Ditto with *homeland security*, for "The Homeland" simply isn't an American construction, it's very European as in "Die Heimat, or The Motherland, or Das Vaterland." Like "homeland security," Mamet argues, "it rings false" and thus will—or should—cause us to "question the motives of those who created it for our benefit."

One of the reasons Tim O'Brien wrote "How to Tell a True War Story," and a host of other highly praised works about the Vietnam War, is to transmit the totality of the experience, sensory, psychological, philosophical, ethical. War, he writes:

> has the feel—the spiritual texture—of a great ghostly fog, thick and permanent. There is no clarity. Everything swirls. The old rules are no longer binding, the old truths no longer true. Right spills over into wrong. Order blends into chaos, love into hate, ugliness into beauty, law into anarchy, civility into savagery. The vapors suck you in. You can't tell where you are, or why you're there, and the only certainty is overwhelming ambiguity.
>
> In war you lose your sense of the definite, hence your sense of truth itself, and therefore it's safe to say that in a true war story nothing is ever absolutely true. (548)

Kandi Tayebi's perspective on war, in "Warring Memories" is compatible with O'Brien's, though she's talking about two different wars in a different part of the world. In fact, she is viewing the U.S. attack on Iraq in 2003 through the lens of her husband's participation in the Iran-Iraq war a decade earlier, as a soldier in the Iranian army. "'They should take off their rings,'" he says, matter-of-factly. "'When they die, their bodies will bloat in the heat. For gold, their fingers will be cut off.'" Tayebi examines her husband's experiences in light of her own. Though she grew up in a military family, her experiences of war are typical of those of many Americans: "I see war as a snapshot—moments flashed across a screen or plastered on the page." Yet there is war of a different sort at home, where a student's "two-year-old sister was killed in a drive-by shooting," and there is peace in her young children's understanding only of "beauty" in the explosions of fireworks. When will they ever learn?

The 9/11 Commission's mammoth—and clear, well-documented—analysis of the "facts and circumstances relating to the terrorist attacks of September 11, 2001" is designed, in part, to help Americans—the people and the government of, by, and for the people—to understand the failure of American intelligence and to promote measures intended to forestall surprise attacks in the future. The section included here, "Institutionalizing Imagination: The Case of Aircraft as Weapons" (559–65), is concerned with the failure of security analysts to analyze how, "from the enemy's

perspective," an aircraft, specifically a large jet, "hijacked or explosives-laden, might be used as a weapon," or how to detect, monitor, or defend against such an attack. The report, published in 2004, is still too recent for its recommendations to have taken effect.

Those who examine the causes of international terrorism, as does Bernard Lewis in "What Went Wrong?" (565–70), are aware that there is no single interpretation and that all explanations are controversial. Even for those who concede the truth of Lewis's first premise, that by the twentieth century "Compared with Christendom, its rival for more than a millennium, the world of Islam had become poor, weak, and ignorant," the reasons for this decline are in dispute. Because "it is usually easier and always more satisfying to blame others for one's misfortunes," the Middle East could blame the thirteenth-century Mongol invasions "for the destruction of both Muslim power and Islamic civilization"; the Arabs, Turks, and Persians could blame each other for "the loss of their ancient glories" and blame the British and French for nineteenth-century depredations. Current scapegoats include America, and "the Jews." Self-blame includes attacks on Islam in general, or on fanatics, or "the relegation of women to an inferior position in Muslim society," thereby depriving "the Islamic world of the talents and energies of half its people." Because "Who did this to us?" leads only to "neurotic fantasies and conspiracy theories," concludes Lewis, the question "What did we do wrong?" leads naturally to the search for a solution. This is difficult because the condition of freedom in the Middle East is fragile and full of complications.

Lewis's answer, that the peoples of the Middle East should establish a free society where people have the freedom "to question and inquire and speak; freedom of the economy from corrupt and pervasive mismanagement; freedom of women from male oppression; freedom of citizens from tyranny," provides the perspective that underlies the interpretation of the subject by many pro-Westerners. Nevertheless, critics such as the late Palestinian scholar Edward Said (not included here) strongly object to such solutions, which they interpret as the efforts of Westerners attempting to dominate an Eastern culture.

Terror in the Mind of God (571–82), Mark Juergensmeyer's analysis of the "exaggerated violence" of terrorist attacks such as the 1993 World Trade Center bombing, eerily prescient of its 2001 successor, explains them as "constructed events: they are mind-numbing, mesmerizing theater. At center stage are the acts themselves—stunning, abnormal, and outrageous murders carried out in a way that graphically displays the awful power of violence—set within grand scenarios of conflict and proclamation." Horrifically violent acts that "surpass the wounds inflicted during warfare" because of their demonstrative "secondary impact . . . elicit feelings of revulsion and anger in those who witness them." Indeed, claims Juergensmeyer, "terrorism is always part of a political strategy," performed not only to "fulfill political ends" but to "have a direct impact on public policy."

Wendell Berry's "Thoughts in the Presence of Fear" (583–87) itemizes twenty-seven reflections on the aftermath of "the horrors of September 11." Each paragraph could be the basis for a policy statement, an argument, an essay, a book, so concentrated is Berry's discussion of topics ranging from the end of "technological and economic optimism" (I), to the view that "The 'developed' nations had given to the 'free market' the status of a god, and were sacrificing to it their farmers, farmlands, and communities" (IV). He questions the view that "the aim and result of war necessarily is not peace but victory, and any victory won by violence necessarily justifies the violence that won it and leads to further violence. If we are serious about innovation," he says, "must we not conclude that we need something new to replace our perpetual 'war to end war'?" (XX). Although Berry's tone is moderate, his rural, agrarian (Berry is a farmer as well as a poet and essayist), pacifistic, Christian views are bound to anger some whose values conflict with these perspectives, however appreciative they might be of peaceful views such as the sunset on Mt. McKinley depicted in the photograph on page 584.

Are there no solutions to matters of terrorism on which all right-minded, principled people can agree? Many of the possible solutions, ranging from all-out war to racial profiling to severe restraints on the freedoms of speech, the press, assembly, worship, and travel—among others—are problematic, as Berry has indicated. How are we, as individuals and a nation, to balance individual needs against the requirements of national security in a world that is never static, but always in motion? In "The Information Wars" (588–90), Mary Graham identifies a number of ways in which the federal government has, swiftly and silently, restricted public access to information, such as removing from its website "maps of the nation's 2.2 million miles of pipelines" that would enable people to "identify places where ruptures in pipes that carry oil, natural gas, or hazardous chemicals could endanger lives, property, or drinking water," on the grounds that these and many other types of reports—"thousands of pages of information about health and safety risks to Americans"—might "somehow aid terrorists." She concludes that in the nominal interest of "national security," "temporary emergency actions have evolved into fundamental changes in the public's right to know, and the restrictions have been driven as much by familiar politics and bureaucratic instincts as by national security"—a threat not only to civil liberties, but to the health and welfare of all of America's residents.

There are no suggestions for reading or writing following the pieces in this chapter; the topic is too fluid to permit closure at this time. More general suggestions for writing about terrorism and/or peace appear at the end of the "World Peace" chapter (633–34). Each raises issues capable of multiple interpretations and debate. Wendell Berry's "Thoughts in the Presence of Fear" permits infinite discussion of a wide range of issues; he raises subjects that the other essayists here deal with at greater length, and he supplies key words and concepts necessary to pursue a train of thought in a subject that continues to change even as we write about it.

SEAMUS HEANEY

Seamus Heaney, Ireland's best-known contemporary poet, was born in 1939 on a farm in County Derry, Northern Ireland. He considers the fact that his heritage includes "both the Ireland of the cattle-herding Gaelic past and the Ulster of the Industrial Revolution" to be significant in his work. For the past thirty years he has lived alternately in Dublin and the United States. Since 1981 he has taught at Harvard for portions of every academic year, currently as Ralph Waldo Emerson Poet in Residence. Like his predecessor and countryman, W. B. Yeats, Heaney's poetry deals in passionate yet clear language with love and loss, peace and war as interpreted through Irish history and lore. And, like Yeats, Heaney received the Nobel Prize in Literature (1985) for his poetry, the year he published *Station Island*. Other books include *The Haw Lantern* (1987), *Seeing Things* (1991), *The Spirit Level* (1996), and translations of Beowulf (1999) and *Antigone* (2004). Heaney's work has won a rare combination of critical esteem— as signaled by numerous awards and prestigious academic appointments (including five years as professor of poetry at Oxford)—and great popular acclaim, as attested by the large sales of his books and the hundreds of fans ("Heaneyboppers" included) who attend his readings.

Horace and the Thunder

After Horace, Odes, 1, 34.

> Anything can happen. You know how Jupiter 1
> Will mostly wait for clouds to gather head
> Before he hurls the lightning? Well, just now,
> He galloped his thunder-cart and his horses
>
> Across a clear blue sky. It shook the earth 2
> And the clogged underearth, the River Styx,
> The winding streams, the Atlantic shore itself.
> Anything can happen, the tallest things
>
> Be overturned, those in high places daunted, 3
> Those overlooked regarded. Stropped-beak Fortune
> Swoops, making the air gasp, tearing off the crest of one,
> Setting it down bleeding on the next.
>
> Ground gives. The heaven's weight 4
> Lifts up off Atlas like a kettle lid,
> Capstones shift, nothing resettles right.
> Smoke-furl and boiling ashes darken day.

===

TIM O'BRIEN

Tim O'Brien's "striking sequence of stories," *The Things They Carried* (1990), is told by a character named—surprise!—Tim O'Brien. Says this narrator, "In June of 1968, a month after graduating from Macalester College [in Minnesota, where the author grew up], I was drafted to fight a war I hated. I was twenty-one years old." In spite of the fact that these are also the facts of the author's life, O'Brien subtitled his book *A Work of Fiction* and says that the fictional O'Brien is not himself. O'Brien the author first came to public notice with the anecdotal *If I Die in a Combat Zone, Box Me Up and Ship Me Home* (1973), followed by a number of other Vietnam War novels. *Going after Cacciato* (1978) won the National Book Award. His most recent novel, *July, July* (2002), is a tale of disillusioned baby boomers— with the Vietnam War hovering in the background "like some unfinished business from the past." In response to an interviewer's query, "What can you teach people, just for having been in a war?," O'Brien said, "By 'teach,' I mean provide insight, philosophy. The mere fact of having wit- nessed violence and death doesn't make a person a teacher. Insight and wisdom are required, and that means reading and hard thought. I didn't intend *If I Die* to stand as a profound statement, and it's not. Teaching is one thing and telling stories is another. I wanted to use stories to alert readers to the complexity and ambiguity of a set of moral issues—but without preaching a moral lesson."

Like all meaningful war fiction, *The Things They Carried* puts a human face on the faceless abstraction of war. Indeed, a reviewer praised *The Things They Carried* as "so searing and immediate you can almost hear the choppers in the background." It is the single book that many say gets closest to the truth of the Vietnam War. Indeed, although "How to Tell a True War Story" is the seventh chapter of a work that is nominally fiction, what O'Brien says about writing the truth is dead accurate, and it applies to all sorts of creative nonfiction and personal essays, as well as to fiction.

- A true war story is never moral. It does not instruct, nor encourage virtue, nor suggest models of proper human behavior, nor restrain men from doing the things men have always done. If a story seems moral, do not believe it. (¶ 8)
- You can tell a true war story if it embarrasses you. If you don't care for obscenity, you don't care for the truth. . . . (¶ 9)
- "In any [true] war story . . . it's difficult to separate what happened from what seemed to happen. What seems to happen becomes its own happening and has to be told that way. The angles of vision are skewed." (¶ 18)
- "You can tell a true war story by the questions you ask. Somebody tells a story, let's say, and afterward you ask, 'Is it true?' and if the answer matters, you've got your answer" (¶ 51)
- "[Yet] absolute occurrence is irrelevant. A thing may happen and be a total lie; another thing may not happen and be truer than the truth." (¶ 55)

- "In war you lose your sense of the definite, hence your sense of the truth itself, and therefore it's safe to say that in a true war story nothing is ever absolutely true." (¶ 47)
- "To generalize about war is like generalizing about peace. Almost everything is true. Almost nothing is true." (¶ 45)
- "True war stories do not generalize. They do not indulge in abstraction or analysis." (¶ 22)
- "It comes down to gut instinct. A true war story, if truly told, makes the stomach believe." (¶ 24)
- "Often in a true war story there is not even a point, or else that point doesn't hit you until twenty years later, in your sleep. . . ." (¶ 48)
- "In the end, of course, a true war story is never about war. It's about sunlight. . . . It's about love and memory. It's about sorrow. It's about sisters who never write back and people who never listen." (¶ 64)

How to Tell a True War Story

T his is true.   1
  I had a buddy in Vietnam. His name was Bob Kiley, but everybody   2
called him Rat.

A friend of his gets killed, so about a week later Rat sits down and   3
writes a letter to the guy's sister. Rat tells her what a great brother she had,
how together the guy was, a number one pal and comrade. A real soldier's
soldier, Rat says. Then he tells a few stories to make the point, how her
brother would always volunteer for stuff nobody else would volunteer for
in a million years, dangerous stuff, like doing recon or going out on these
really badass night patrols. Stainless steel balls, Rat tells her. The guy was
a little crazy, for sure, but crazy in a good way, a real daredevil, because he
liked the challenge of it, he liked testing himself, just man against gook. A
great, great guy, Rat says.

Anyway, it's a terrific letter, very personal and touching. Rat almost   4
bawls writing it. He gets all teary telling about the good times they had
together, how her brother made the war seem almost fun, always raising
hell and lighting up villes and bringing smoke to bear every which way. A
great sense of humor, too. Like the time at this river when he went fishing
with a whole damn crate of hand grenades. Probably the funniest thing in
world history, Rat says, all that gore, about twenty zillion dead gook fish.
Her brother, he had the right attitude. He knew how to have a good time.
On Halloween, this real hot spooky night, the dude paints up his body all
different colors and puts on this weird mask and hikes over to a ville and
goes trick-or-treating almost stark naked, just boots and balls and an M-16.
A tremendous human being, Rat says. Pretty nutso sometimes, but you
could trust him with your life.

5   And then the letter gets very sad and serious. Rat pours his heart out. He says he loved the guy. He says the guy was his best friend in the world. They were like soul mates, he says, like twins or something, they had a whole lot in common. He tells the guy's sister he'll look her up when the war's over.

6   So what happens?

7   Rat mails the letter. He waits two months. The dumb cooze never writes back.

8   A true war story is never moral. It does not instruct, nor encourage virtue, nor suggest models of proper human behavior, nor restrain men from doing the things men have always done. If a story seems moral, do not believe it. If at the end of a war story you feel uplifted, or if you feel that some small bit of rectitude has been salvaged from the larger waste, then you have been made the victim of a very old and terrible lie. There is no rectitude whatsoever. There is no virtue. As a first rule of thumb, therefore, you can tell a true war story by its absolute and uncompromising allegiance to obscenity and evil. Listen to Rat Kiley. Cooze, he says. He does not say bitch. He certainly does not say woman, or girl. He says cooze. Then he spits and stares. He's nineteen years old—it's too much for him—so he looks at you with those big sad gentle killer eyes and says *cooze*, because his friend is dead, and because it's so incredibly sad and true: she never wrote back.

9   You can tell a true war story if it embarrasses you. If you don't care for obscenity, you don't care for the truth; if you don't care for the truth, watch how you vote. Send guys to war, they come home talking dirty.

10   Listen to Rat: "Jesus Christ, man, I write this beautiful fuckin' letter, I slave over it, and what happens? The dumb cooze never writes back."

11   The dead guy's name was Curt Lemon. What happened was, we crossed a muddy river and marched west into the mountains, and on the third day we took a break along a trail junction in deep jungle. Right away, Lemon and Rat Kiley started goofing. They didn't understand about the spookiness. They were kids; they just didn't know. A nature hike, they thought, not even a war, so they went off into the shade of some giant trees—quadruple canopy, no sunlight at all—and they were giggling and calling each other yellow mother and playing a silly game they'd invented. The game involved smoke grenades, which were harmless unless you did stupid things, and what they did was pull out the pin and stand a few feet apart and play catch under the shade of those huge trees. Whoever chickened out was a yellow mother. And if nobody chickened out, the grenade would make a light popping sound and they'd be covered with smoke and they'd laugh and dance around and then do it again.

12   It's all exactly true.

13   It happened, to *me*, nearly twenty years ago, and I still remember that trail junction and those giant trees and a soft dripping sound somewhere

beyond the trees. I remember the smell of moss. Up in the canopy there were tiny white blossoms, but no sunlight at all, and I remember the shadows spreading out under the trees where Curt Lemon and Rat Kiley were playing catch with smoke grenades. Mitchell Sanders sat flipping his yo-yo. Norman Bowker and Kiowa and Dave Jensen were dozing, or half dozing, and all around us were those ragged green mountains.

Except for the laughter things were quiet.   14

At one point, I remember, Mitchell Sanders turned and looked at me,   15
not quite nodding, as if to warn me about something, as if he already *knew,* then after a while he rolled up his yo-yo and moved away.

It's hard to tell you what happened next.   16

They were just goofing. There was a noise, I suppose, which must've   17
been the detonator, so I glanced behind me and watched Lemon step from the shade into bright sunlight. His face was suddenly brown and shining. A handsome kid, really. Sharp gray eyes, lean and narrow-waisted, and when he died it was almost beautiful, the way the sunlight came around him and lifted him up and sucked him high into a tree full of moss and vines and white blossoms.

In any war story, but especially a true one, it's difficult to separate what   18
happened from what seemed to happen. What seems to happen becomes its own happening and has to be told that way. The angles of vision are skewed. When a booby trap explodes, you close your eyes and duck and float outside yourself. When a guy dies, like Curt Lemon, you look away and then look back for a moment and then look away again. The pictures get jumbled; you tend to miss a lot. And then afterward, when you go to tell about it, there is always that surreal seemingness, which makes the story seem untrue, but which in fact represents the hard and exact truth as it *seemed.*

In many cases a true war story cannot be believed. If you believe it, be   19
skeptical. It's a question of credibility. Often the crazy stuff is true and the normal stuff isn't, because the normal stuff is necessary to make you believe the truly incredible craziness.

In other cases you can't even tell a true war story. Sometimes it's just   20
beyond telling. . . .

In a true war story, if there's a moral at all, it's like the thread that makes   21
the cloth. You can't tease it out. You can't extract the meaning without unraveling the deeper meaning. And in the end, really, there's nothing much to say about a true war story, except maybe "Oh."

True war stories do not generalize. They do not indulge in abstraction   22
or analysis.

For example: War is hell. As a moral declaration the old truism seems   23
perfectly true, and yet because it abstracts, because it generalizes, I can't believe it with my stomach. Nothing turns inside.

24   It comes down to gut instinct. A true war story, if truly told, makes the stomach believe.

25   This one does it for me. I've told it before—many times, many versions—but here's what actually happened.

26   We crossed that river and marched west into the mountains. On the third day, Curt Lemon stepped on a booby-trapped 105 round. He was playing catch with Rat Kiley, laughing, and then he was dead. The trees were thick; it took nearly an hour to cut an LZ for the dustoff.

27   Later, higher in the mountains, we came across a baby VC water buffalo. What it was doing there I don't know—no farms or paddies—but we chased it down and got a rope around it and led it along to a deserted village where we set up for the night. After supper Rat Kiley went over and stroked its nose.

28   He opened up a can of C rations, pork and beans, but the baby buffalo wasn't interested.

29   Rat shrugged.

30   He stepped back and shot it through the right front knee. The animal did not make a sound. It went down hard, then got up again, and Rat took careful aim and shot off an ear. He shot it in the hindquarters and in the little hump at its back. He shot it twice in the flanks. It wasn't to kill; it was to hurt. He put the rifle muzzle up against the mouth and shot the mouth away. Nobody said much. The whole platoon stood there watching, feeling all kinds of things, but there wasn't a great deal of pity for the baby water buffalo. Curt Lemon was dead. Rat Kiley had lost his best friend in the world. Later in the week he would write a long personal letter to the guy's sister, who would not write back, but for now it was a question of pain. He shot off the tail. He shot away chunks of meat below the ribs. All around us there was the smell of smoke and filth and deep greenery, and the evening was humid and very hot. Rat went to automatic. He shot randomly, almost casually, quick little spurts in the belly and butt. Then he reloaded, squatted down, and shot it in the left front knee. Again the animal fell hard and tried to get up, but this time it couldn't quite make it. It wobbled and went down sideways. Rat shot it in the nose. He bent forward and whispered something, as if talking to a pet, then he shot it in the throat. All the while the baby buffalo was silent, or almost silent, just a light bubbling sound where the nose had been. It lay very still. Nothing moved except the eyes, which were enormous, the pupils shiny black and dumb.

31   Rat Kiley was crying. He tried to say something, but then cradled his rifle and went off by himself.

32   The rest of us stood in a ragged circle around the baby buffalo. For a time no one spoke. We had witnessed something essential, something brand-new and profound, a piece of the world so startling there was not yet a name for it.

Somebody kicked the baby buffalo.   33

It was still alive, though just barely, just in the eyes.   34

"Amazing," Dave Jensen said. "My whole life, I never seen anything   35
like it."

"Never?"   36

"Not hardly. Not once."   37

Kiowa and Mitchell Sanders picked up the baby buffalo. They hauled   38
it across the open square, hoisted it up, and dumped it in the village well.

Afterward, we sat waiting for Rat to get himself together.   39

"Amazing," Dave Jensen kept saying. "A new wrinkle. I never seen   40
it before."

Mitchell Sanders took out his yo-yo. "Well, that's Nam," he said.   41
"Garden of Evil. Over here, man, every sin's real fresh and original."

How do you generalize?   42

War is hell, but that's not the half of it, because war is also mystery   43
and terror and adventure and courage and discovery and holiness and pity
and despair and longing and love. War is nasty; war is fun. War is thrilling;
war is drudgery. War makes you a man; war makes you dead.

The truths are contradictory. It can be argued, for instance, that war   44
is grotesque. But in truth war is also beauty. For all its horror, you can't
help but gape at the awful majesty of combat. You stare out at tracer
rounds unwinding through the dark like brilliant red ribbons. You crouch
in ambush as a cool, impassive moon rises over the nighttime paddies.
You admire the fluid symmetries of troops on the move, the harmonies of
sound and shape and proportion, the great sheets of metal-fire streaming
down from a gunship, the illumination rounds, the white phosphorus, the
purply orange glow of napalm, the rocket's red glare. It's not pretty, exactly. It's astonishing. It fills the eye. It commands you. You hate it, yes, but
your eyes do not. Like a killer forest fire, like cancer under a microscope,
any battle or bombing raid or artillery barrage has the aesthetic purity of
absolute moral indifference—a powerful, implacable beauty—and a true
war story will tell the truth about this, though the truth is ugly.

To generalize about war is like generalizing about peace. Almost   45
everything is true. Almost nothing is true. At its core, perhaps, war is just
another name for death, and yet any soldier will tell you, if he tells the truth,
that proximity to death brings with it a corresponding proximity to life.
After a firefight, there is always the immense pleasure of aliveness. The trees
are alive. The grass, the soil—everything. All around you things are purely
living, and you among them, and the aliveness makes you tremble. You feel
an intense, out-of-the-skin awareness of your living self—your truest self,
the human being you want to be and then become by the force of wanting
it. In the midst of evil you want to be a good man. You want decency. You
want justice and courtesy and human concord, things you never knew
you wanted. There is a kind of largeness to it, a kind of godliness. Though

it's odd, you're never more alive than when you're almost dead. You recognize what's valuable. Freshly, as if for the first time, you love what's best in yourself and in the world, all that might be lost. At the hour of dusk you sit at your foxhole and look out on a wide river turning pinkish red, and at the mountains beyond, and although in the morning you must cross the river and go into the mountains and do terrible things and maybe die, even so, you find yourself studying the fine colors on the river, you feel wonder and awe at the setting of the sun, and you are filled with a hard, aching love for how the world could be and always should be, but now is not.

46   Mitchell Sanders was right. For the common soldier, at least, war has the feel—the spiritual texture—of a great ghostly fog, thick and permanent. There is no clarity. Everything swirls. The old rules are no longer binding, the old truths no longer true. Right spills over into wrong. Order blends into chaos, love into hate, ugliness into beauty, law into anarchy, civility into savagery. The vapors suck you in. You can't tell where you are, or why you're there, and the only certainty is overwhelming ambiguity.

47   In war you lose your sense of the definite, hence your sense of truth itself, and therefore it's safe to say that in a true war story nothing is ever absolutely true.

48   Often in a true war story there is not even a point, or else the point doesn't hit you until twenty years later, in your sleep, and you wake up and shake your wife and start telling the story to her, except when you get to the end you've forgotten the point again. And then for a long time you lie there watching the story happen in your head. You listen to your wife's breathing. The war's over. You close your eyes. You smile and think, Christ, what's the *point?*

49   This one wakes me up.

50   In the mountains that day, I watched Lemon turn sideways. He laughed and said something to Rat Kiley. Then he took a peculiar half step, moving from shade into bright sunlight, and the booby-trapped 105 round blew him into a tree. The parts were just hanging there, so Dave Jensen and I were ordered to shinny up and peel him off. I remember the white bone of an arm. I remember pieces of skin and something wet and yellow that must've been the intestines. The gore was horrible, and stays with me. But what wakes me up twenty years later is Dave Jensen singing "Lemon Tree" as we threw down the parts.

51   You can tell a true war story by the questions you ask. Somebody tells a story, let's say, and afterward you ask, "Is it true?" and if the answer matters, you've got your answer.

52   For example, we've all heard this one. Four guys go down a trail. A grenade sails out. One guy jumps on it and takes the blast and saves his three buddies.

Is it true? 53

The answer matters. 54

You'd feel cheated if it never happened. Without the grounding 55
reality, it's just a trite bit of puffery, pure Hollywood, untrue in the way all
such stores are untrue. Yet even if it did happen—and maybe it did, anything's possible—even then you know it can't be true, because a true war
story does not depend upon that kind of truth. Absolute occurrence is
irrelevant. A thing may happen and be a total lie; another thing may not
happen and be truer than the truth. For example: Four guys go down a
trail. A grenade sails out. One guy jumps on it and takes the blast, but it's
a killer grenade and everybody dies anyway. Before they die, though, one
of the dead guy says, "The fuck you do *that* for?" and the jumper says,
"Story of my life, man," and the other guy starts to smile but he's dead.

That's a true story that never happened. 56

Twenty years later, I can still see the sunlight on Lemon's face. I can see 57
him turning, looking back at Rat Kiley, then he laughed and took that
curious half step from shade into sunlight, his face suddenly brown and
shining, and when his foot touched down, in that instant, he must've
thought it was the sunlight that was killing him. It was not the sunlight.
It was a rigged 105 round. But if I could ever get the story right, how the
sun seemed to gather around him and pick him up and lift him high into
a tree, if I could somehow recreate the fatal whiteness of that light, the
quick glare, the obvious cause and effect, then you would believe the last
thing Curt Lemon believed, which for him must've been the final truth.

Now and then, when I tell this story, someone will come up to me afterward 58
and say she liked it. It's always a woman. Usually it's an older woman of
kindly temperament and humane politics. She'll explain that as a rule she
hates war stories; she can't understand why people want to wallow in all
the blood and gore. But this one she liked. The poor baby buffalo, it made
her sad. Sometimes, even, there are little tears. What I should do, she'll
say, is put it all behind me. Find new stories to tell.

I won't say it but I'll think it. 59

I'll picture Rat Kiley's face, his grief, and I'll think, *You dumb cooze.* 60

Because she wasn't listening. 61

It *wasn't* a war story. It was a *love* story. 62

But you can't say that. All you can do is tell it one more time, patiently, 63
adding and subtracting, making up a few things to get at the real truth. No
Mitchell Sanders, you tell her. No Lemon, no Rat Kiley. No trail junction.
No baby buffalo. No vines or moss or white blossoms. Beginning to end,
you tell her, it's all made up. Every goddamn detail—the mountains and
the river and especially that poor dumb baby buffalo. None of it happened.
None of it. And even if it did happen, it didn't happen in the mountains,
it happened in this little village on the Batangan Peninsula, and it was

raining like crazy, and one night a guy named Stink Harris woke up screaming with a leech on his tongue. You can tell a true war story if you just keep on telling it.

64   And in the end, of course, a true war story is never about war. It's about sunlight. It's about the special way that dawn spreads out on a river when you know you must cross the river and march into the mountains and do things you are afraid to do. It's about love and memory. It's about sorrow. It's about sisters who never write back and people who never listen.

===

LAURIE FENDRICH

Laurie Fendrich, a professor of fine arts at Hofstra University, was born in Paterson, New Jersey, in 1948. She earned a BA in political science at Mount Holyoke College in 1970 and an MFA in painting at the School of the Art Institute of Chicago in 1978. She is also an abstract painter who lives and works in New York, where she was on September 11, 2001, an eyewitness to the events in "History Overcomes Stories," commissioned by *The Chronicle of Higher Education*. *Why Painting Still Matters* was published in 2000.

She explains, "I began painting while I was in college, in the late 1960s. Since then, painting has steadily declined in cultural importance. Artists have turned to newer art forms, such as photography, sound and video installations, and computer art. The prevailing outlook of artists has also changed—from modern to postmodern. Modern art had been about the free exploration of forms within ever-widening ideas about beauty. Postmodern art turned its back on beauty almost entirely, focusing instead on popular culture, identity politics, social issues, technology and science. It reflects diverse, often previously ignored voices in society, each of which lays claim to a partial or fragmentary truth about a world continuously in flux. My writing focuses on painting's predicament in the postmodern environment.

"The essay 'History Overcomes Stories' was not about painting, however. I had been asked to write something about the images of the imploding World Trade Center towers. Although I had seen the images over and over again, I didn't have any opinion about them other than that they were horrible. After several hours of struggling to write a personal narrative about what I had seen and felt during the attack and its immediate aftermath, I was getting nowhere. The essay seemed puny in the face of what had happened because it did no more than reiterate that we all felt a sense of shock, grief and fear. Suddenly it hit me that my whole approach was wrong. Artists and writers like to make images and stories, but these are limited, especially when used to excess, in helping us to be good citizens. We need something else in order to participate in politics and history."

History Overcomes Stories

I live about 10 blocks north of what used to be the World Trade Center   1
towers, in an area of New York City called Tribeca. Three mornings
ago was September 11, 2001.

My neighborhood is populated with artists like myself and my hus-   2
band. Artists first started living in lofts in this former manufacturing district
sometime in the late 1960s. Later, they started families, and the neighborhood filled up with children and stores and flowers in the windows.
When my own daughter was ready for kindergarten, we walked her to
P.S. 234, then a brand-new school built a few blocks north of the World
Trade Center. To us, it was practically Mr. Rogers's neighborhood.

Ours was a good life. My husband and I have never even had to own   3
a car. Within the past few years, rich newcomers began developing large
luxury lofts in buildings all over the neighborhood. Recently, they've been
adding spectacular penthouses. We artists grumbled, but most of us con-
ceded that cities must change even along these lines in order to stay vibrant.

An account of my life in lower Manhattan, what I've been through in   4
this calamity, and the sights I've seen don't really count for much. There are
thousands of other stories, many very terrible and dramatic, that are unfortunately more representative of the horror that New York, and the country, has suffered. And there is the question of when necessary, informative
storytelling disintegrates into a kind of entertainment. No amount of my
artist's experience in thinking about images adds relevance. In short, my
story contributes nothing to history.

Experiences and stories were once, however, the heart of history. That   5
was how Thucydides told history. Now stories are polluted and demeaned
by having been reduced to fodder for television, movie, and slick magazine
entertainment. At this point, hardly anybody's story can guide us in how to
act. All we know, dimly, is that we have passed the end of an era, and face
a probably very grim new one. The past 25 years, which so many saw as an
eternal history-less present, turn out to have been a fleeting grace, a blip of
peace in an inexorable continuum of war. The only redemption for the sin
of having thought this eternally present tense could be true is to see if we
can now act the way we ought to have been acting all along.

Until Tuesday, I was part of a ridiculously lucky generation. For me,   6
war was what I knew about from movies, reading, and the distant (before
my birth) loss to my mother of her brother in World War II. Now, like all
Americans, I know something directly about war. I know it as a civilian,
having been attacked here, in my own country, my own city, my own
neighborhood. All my strivings as an artist and a teacher seem to have
been deprived of meaning. I've experienced a very small slice of Theodor
Adorno's conclusion that "to write poetry after Auschwitz is barbaric." I,
like many others, must try to figure out all over again what truly matters.

In what ways does this photograph of people running after the collapse of the first tower of the World Trade Center on September 11, 2001, augment and reinforce Fendrich's observations?

After Tuesday, I can no longer speak as a woman, or an artist, or a New Yorker. Speaking in those ways—"speaking personally"—will no longer do. I have to learn how to speak as a citizen.

7   We have been seduced by television and computers into believing it is images and stories, not ideas, that count. We have bought the party line that ours is the age of the computer and simulacra, not nature and physical reality; we've traded slow, sure ideas for "instant communication." We have deluded ourselves that the older, more complicated concepts of good, evil, beauty, and, above all, nature, are old-fashioned. Thinking we could, as Horace put it, drive nature out with a pitchfork, we moved into such quagmires as genetic manipulation. Not that microbiology in the service of medicine is automatically wrong. But Horace was right about the power of things that are the givens in life. In this case, Nature in its simple, oldest form—some people hating others—has come running back in.

8   In the din of postmodernism, we dismissed all voices celebrating Western culture as reactionary and logocentric. Many of those voices revealed a profound bigotry, hatred, and fear of other cultures and ways of life. But the self-castigation that has been going on since the Vietnam War has gotten to the point where we have been throwing out almost everything that is Western except its material goods. What now ought to be clear as a bell is that it is precisely in our freedom to criticize ourselves that we

locate the values of Western culture. Self-criticism is our freedom, but it, too, must be modified by restraint.

The universal values of freedom and democracy, originating with the   9
ancient Greeks, modified by Christianity and Judaism, and maturing with the ideas of humanism and liberalism, are now nourished by the streaming energy and beauty coming from non-Western cultures. That complex structure is the 21st-century foundation for any viable, modern civilization. At its bottom layer still sits our need for the Western values of individual liberty, coupled with obligations to virtue, democracy coupled with responsibility, the requirement of courage, an acknowledgment—always tempered by reason—of duty, and an assertion of basic, not jingoistic, patriotism.

Art and images need to be postponed. (I certainly can't think of   10
painting right now.) We need, I think, to achieve intellectual control of our feelings, and direct our actions according to what is right and just, instead of to what pleases us as "personal expression" or intrigues us as convoluted theory. Our unfamiliarity with how to use history correctly, and our forgetfulness when it comes to our own values, have resulted in this unspeakable historical moment being at risk of degenerating into hundreds of personal "survival" or "coping" stories, the sort that turn into television movies on the Lifetime network. Worse, the images of our current disaster will be aestheticized into "unforgettable" or "iconic" images. As I write, television news is already adding music to montages of horror.

A perhaps impenetrable boundary exists—or should exist—between   11
the thousands of real lives that were brutally destroyed on Tuesday, and art. And that slovenly province of art known as entertainment should not dare to touch what has happened. Mine is not a postmodernist response, of course, and it is, admittedly, written under the stress of being an immediate neighbor to calamity. But I do not see myself ever shrinking from the renewed convictions put forth in this essay—one for which, I wish with all my heart, there had never been an occasion to write.

KANDI TAYEBI

Tayebi was born in San Francisco in 1962 to a career military family that moved all over the United States and Germany before settling in Strasburg, Colorado—population 1,500. The youngest of five children, she quickly learned creative ways to be heard, which led ultimately to BA and MA degrees from the University of Northern Colorado and a PhD in English literature (1999) from the University of Denver. She is currently Associate Dean of Humanities and Social Sciences at Sam Houston State University. Her military father imbued in her both a strong sense of patriotism and a respect for other cultures. The army had allowed her father to travel to countries all over the world: Korea, Germany, France, the Netherlands, and others. In each place, he had learned some of the language, befriended locals, and eaten new foods. Perhaps the wonder and admiration for other people so different from those her family had known back in Indiana made it seem natural for Kandi to marry, in 1988, a man from another country. Her Iranian husband, Javad, was also a military man, having served on the front line during his country's devastating war with Iraq. He knew the destruction of war, and although he escaped with his body intact, he carried the scars internally, as "Warring Memories" intimates. Tayebi says, "We met while both of us were going to school and working in a restaurant to pay for school. He asked me to play basketball, and then promptly beat me 21–16. Since I don't like to lose, I kept going back trying again to win." Soon they started dating, married, and now have two young sons, Bezhan and Shayon, whom they are raising "with love and respect for both countries and their people." The couple plan to live in the United States but to visit Iran every year, where most of Javad's family lives, though if the political relationship continues to worsen, visits will be difficult.

"Warring Memories" was conceived as Tayebi watched her husband cradling their infant son during Fourth of July fireworks, cringing each time the explosions sounded. It was then she realized how devastating violence has been all around the world and how difficult it is for most Americans to understand. She hopes that "Warring Memories" can "help the healing process for a world torn by violence and remind each of us of our humanity."

Warring Memories

1   "They should take off their rings," my husband stated matter-of-factly as we watched CNN broadcasting more trouble in the Middle East. For two years he had fought in the Iran-Iraq war, but he rarely shared his experiences with me, perhaps feeling that his American-born wife might have difficulty relating to the realities of warfare in one's homeland. On the television screen, eighteen-year-old soldiers displayed their bravery, shaking rifles and shooting into the air. Faces crushed too close to the camera triumphantly spoke of victory. Without the tanks lined behind the young men, or the rifles and camouflage, one could easily think the segment centered on a basketball tournament. One young man, sweat streaked across his T-shirt, held his rifle high in the air, tilted his head back, and whooped. His golden wedding ring covered skin not yet whitened by years of being hidden. I turned slowly to my husband after my eyes focused on the wedding ring encircling the finger of a dark, soft-eyed man, the gold scraping against the side of his MG3 and reflecting the sun into the camera lens.

2   My husband, mingling his words with those of the CNN announcer, said quietly, "When they die, their bodies will bloat in the heat. For gold,

their fingers will be cut off." His words were almost drowned out by the victory calls of the young men on the screen.

For me, video-game graphics displaying a target and its destruction constitute war. Generals, in neatly pressed fatigues, stand in front of blackboards like coaches before the big game, explaining the strategic plans behind each assault against the enemy. Occasionally, a screaming mother, sister, or wife lies across someone's body, but the television screen separates her pain from my world, framing her in cinematic neutrality. I try to match my husband's stories with the only other version of war I know, those from the movie screen—*Saving Private Ryan, The Green Berets, Apocalypse Now.*

An olive-skinned boy with just the beginnings of a beard across his chin pushes his way to the front of the crowd and smiles. Two gold teeth define the border of his mouth, and I laugh cautiously, "Should he remove his teeth, too?" My husband tells about men shoving the butts of their rifles against a jaw, splintering bone across the sand, to remove gold teeth for souvenirs. The boy on the television looks fragile.

I want to nullify the horror of my husband's tales by believing these acts occur only in distant lands at the hands of people unlike me, but the boy's eyes look so much like my son's. The camera turns down to show his black and white Nikes. Suddenly, the lens pans through the crowd to a building in the back. Out of the window dangles what appears at first to be a bloody white cloth or, as the camera moves in, an effigy. Standing above the lifeless form, a boy not older than sixteen or seventeen waves his bloodied hands at the camera. Blood smears his white T-shirt, making abstract patterns over the face of an unidentifiable basketball player dunking a ball. The camera zooms in on the battered, pulpy mass of the dead man, now clearly distinguishable as he falls to the ground. The crowd grabs the body—kicking, pulling, tearing. My eyes remain focused on the screen; not even this violence makes me turn away.

I realize I see war as a snapshot—moments flashed across a screen or plastered on the page. Slowly over time, bits of the war have leaked out into the conversations between my husband and me. He informs me that the worst part of war is the waiting, something the snapshots don't show. During the moments when the fighting is most intense, one doesn't have time to think or to worry. Adrenaline pushes the body to action, and the surroundings seem surreal. Yet most of the day is spent listening and waiting. Stray shots go off in the distance, planes fly over, and soldiers practice by shooting rats. After awhile, the older soldiers learn to avoid thinking by filling the air with idle talk. It is the new men, the ones who haven't yet realized where they are, the ones who still dream about normal life, who begin the taboo discussions of home and family.

Almost a year after the CNN broadcast, my husband recounts one memory from the war as we sit watching our children play in the yard under the summer sun. One young soldier, away from home for the first time, sat on the hillside next to my husband during a late-night watch. As point men, they were to listen carefully for the enemy, then stand up and shoot when the enemy crested the hill. For hours they sat, telling stories of their families—an oldest sister's trip to college, a youngest brother's business, a mother's dream for her son to become a doctor. Silence stretched the night, forcing the two men into the thickness of loneliness. Just before dawn, a shot shattered the stillness, and my husband, the wizened experienced soldier at twenty-three, stood and began firing back.

8   "Stand up and shoot," he hollered at his partner, who shook with fear. Grabbing the boy by a shoulder soaked with sweat, my husband tried to force him onto his feet. Finally, in resignation, he dropped the boy back down onto the soft earth.

9   After the battle ended and the silence returned, my husband looked down at the boy lying across his boots. That first shot had drilled a hole through his forehead—his shaking was the last sign of life, the wetness on his shoulder the blood draining from his wound. Pushing the boy off his feet, my husband turned his eyes away.

10 A few weeks after my husband confides this war story to me, while I am cleaning out closets before the rush of the school year begins, I run across a box of old photos he brought with him from Iran. I thumb through pictures of my husband during the war, looking at all of the wan faces for signs of the man I've come to know. I've watched him walk for hours across our bedroom floor, our son cradled against his chest. As the fevered cries of our son filled the room, my husband would patiently sing Persian lullabies and stroke the baby's back. He has deftly bandaged skinned knees, extracted splinters, and chased away scary dreams. When we were refused housing after a woman saw my husband was from the Middle East, I angrily protested while he quietly walked away. When colleagues at work have called him "camel rider," asked him about all the abusive men in his country, and even discussed how they would bomb all those "Arabs," my husband has responded with humor and reminded me that people need time to change. In contrast, I have at times come close to hitting colleagues who have asked, "How could a bright woman like you marry a man from the Middle East?"

11   Yet in these war pictures, the muscular body and soft eyes of my husband are camouflaged by the gaunt, grizzled look of the young man staring out. His eyes sunk deep in his head glare back in desperation. One hand grips an MG 3; the other rests gently on the front of a tank. Men no more than twenty-five years old, aged by the sights of battle, surround him. In another more haunting photo, a soldier smiles childishly; an oddity among his serious compatriots. At his feet lies a body, the head bent awkwardly to the right as a boot steps down on the face. In the soldier's hand are the dog tags of the dead man. Another soldier distractedly tosses dirt clods onto the dead man's chest, already piled with rocks and trash thrown by others. In the background, my husband shares a sandwich with another young man.

This photo wakens my husband's sharpest memory from the war. Out 12 of all the frightening scenes of the fighting, my husband's strongest recollection is of a tomato sandwich. As his unit entered a village devastated by recent bombings, they began to search for food and shelter. Entire walls and roofs were missing from most of the houses that remained. The streets were lined with rubble, stray chickens and goats, and body parts of women, men, and children. Chunks of blackened flesh checkered the cobblestones. Two fingers, still attached to the outside of an arm blown open and swollen by the sun, lay against one wall. Occasionally, around a corner or behind some bodies, a small piece of greenery pushed its way up through the broken stones and trash.

The soldiers were lucky enough to find a few tomatoes left behind 13 by one house's occupants and somehow untouched by the blast that had leveled all of the walls and blown off the roof. In the kitchen, a loaf of fresh-baked bread sat neatly on the counter above the body of an old woman still dressed in a white and red apron. Her arms were twisted awkwardly behind her back. The left side of her face smeared with ashes, her eyes staring at the cupboard, she seemed prepared to greet visitors—except for the large black hole ripped out of the right side of her head.

For weeks, the soldiers had had little but dried army rations to eat. 14 Sitting on the rat-infested floor, the men devoured sandwiches, relishing the red juice streaking the white bread. The smell of yeast mixed with the stench of burnt flesh. The tomato sandwich amid the destruction was a delicacy.

Fall arrives again, bringing the frenzied activity of a new school year. I sip 15 my last drop of tea, kiss my boys goodbye, and head off to teach at the university, where children the age of those in the photographs I looked at this past summer will struggle with their own sets of problems. One young man comes into my office to explain why he won't be able to complete my course. With vacant eyes, he explains that his two-year-old sister was killed in a drive-by shooting, and his mama needs him to help with his four- and five-year-old brothers. He apologizes for letting me down, shakes my hand, and walks out of the office wiping the nose of one of those brothers. I walk outside into the sunshine.

Fall in the South brings cool relief from the torching humidity of sum- 16 mer, and students sit beneath the old oak trees that line the paths winding throughout campus, taking advantage of the pleasant sun, breeze, and fragrant flowers. Walking across the landscaped lawns, I pause to enjoy the newly blossomed hibiscus, the squirrels chasing each other up one tree and around another, and the students clad in jeans and T-shirts sporting fashion designers' names. My mind drifts to scenes of my young son delighted by the pointy-nosed armadillos that dig up slugs in our yard. He and the neighborhood cats chase the armadillos, which dodge their advances while appearing nonchalantly to ignore their existence. Coming from Colorado, we marvel at these unusual spotted creatures, watching them for hours from our porch and finally resorting to the video camera to record their images for those left behind in the Rockies. Texas has exposed us to a whole new array of animals—slimy, slinking, furry, flying, wrinkled, skittering— that are unfamiliar and enticing.

17   Only the playful squirrels seem a familiar sight. Today, they race through the crabgrass and roll down the hills, enjoying the newly crisp air. Almost like a shooting star, seen briefly in one's peripheral vision and then gone, a squirrel falls from the tallest tree in the middle of the court-yard. Unsure what it really was, I join the increasing number of students gathered closely around the damaged body. The squirrel sits on his hind legs, at first appearing to be a movie on pause. Then, with great effort, it thrusts its front legs as if to scurry up the tree. The back legs drag for only an inch, the top half of its body collapses on the ground, and its breaths come in forced bursts. Back broken, the squirrel continues to struggle as I look away. Even after calling someone to come help the animal, I have flashbacks of the squirrel staring at me, reaching towards me with its front paws only to be pulled back against its useless rear legs.

18   When I return home from the university, I find my husband pre-paring sandwiches for a picnic in the park. Our two boys chase each other up and down the stairs, giggling and screaming. I tell my husband about the slow death of the squirrel, and after a moment of silence, he responds, "Imagine if that were a human being." For an instant I can vaguely com-prehend the war he lived.

19   At the park, I find our neighborhood celebrating Safety Night, an event that helps citizens and local police officers come together to protect our children. While the kids play cowboys and Indians, climb on the monkey bars, and collect police officer trading cards, the adults eat and talk. At sundown the fireworks begin, filling the sky with color. My husband cringes at the first few flashes of light and the accompanying loud booms before he can settle in. My youngest son sits on his lap, leans against his chest, and sees only beauty in the explosions.

9/11 COMMISSION

On November 27, 2002, the U.S. Congress and President George W. Bush established the National Commission on Terrorist Attacks Upon the United States, also known as the 9/11 Commission. This independent, bipartisan panel was directed by law (Public Law 107-306) to investigate "facts and circumstances relating to the terrorist attacks of September 11, 2001," includ-ing those relating to intelligence agencies, law enforcement agencies, diplo-macy, immigration issues and border control, the flow of assets to terrorist organizations, commercial aviation, the role of congressional oversight and resource allocation, and more. The panel was chaired by Thomas H. Kean, former New Jersey governor; Lee H. Hamilton, Indiana Ninth District Representative for thirty-four years; Richard Ben-Veniste, former chief of the Watergate Task Force; Bob Kerrey, Nebraska senator from 1988 to 2000; Fred F. Fielding, counsel to several Republican presidents; John H. Lehman, chairman of J. F. Lehman and other businesses; Jamie S. Gorelick, chair of Fannie Mae from 1997 to 2003; Timothy J. Roemer, president of the Center for National Policy; Slade Gorton, senator from Washington State from 1982 to 2000; and James R. Thompson, Illinois's longest-serving governor (1977–1991).

This panel spent approximately two years reviewing more than 2.5 million pages of documents, interviewing over 1,200 individuals, holding 19 days of public hearings, and writing a 567-page report (published inexpensively by W. W. Norton) that is remarkable for its clear concepts and forthright language. It is impossible to excerpt a segment of this report that accurately represents the whole. The thirteen chapters include "We Have Some Planes," "The Foundation of the New Terrorism," "Counterterrorism Evolves," "Al Qaeda Aims at the American Homeland," "The System Was Blinking Red," "Heroism and Horror," "Wartime," "What to Do? A Global Strategy," and "How to Do It? A Different Way of Organizing the Government." "Institutionalizing Imagination: The Case of Aircraft as Weapons" is a relatively self-contained section of the chapter on "Foresight—and Hindsight." It opens with the critical understatement "Imagination is not a gift usually associated with bureaucracies"—and, comparing 9/11 to Japan's surprise attack on Pearl Harbor in 1941—shows how a more imaginative way of thinking about possible means of attack might have led to better defense sixty years later.

Institutionalizing Imagination: The Case of Aircraft as Weapons

Imagination is not a gift usually associated with bureaucracies. For example, before Pearl Harbor the U.S. government had excellent intelligence that a Japanese attack was coming, especially after peace talks stalemated at the end of November 1941. These were days, one historian notes, of "excruciating uncertainty." The most likely targets were judged to be in Southeast Asia. An attack was coming, "but officials were at a loss to know where the blow would fall or what more might be done to prevent it."[1] In retrospect, available intercepts pointed to Japanese examination of Hawaii as a possible target. But, another historian observes, "in the face of a clear warning, alert measures bowed to routine."[2]

It is therefore crucial to find a way of routinizing, even bureaucratizing, the exercise of imagination. Doing so requires more than finding an expert who can imagine that aircraft could be used as weapons. Indeed, since al Qaeda and other groups had already used suicide vehicles, namely truck bombs, the leap to the use of other vehicles such as boats (the *Cole* attack) or planes is not far-fetched.

3   Yet these scenarios were slow to work their way into the thinking of aviation security experts. In 1996, as a result of the TWA Flight 800 crash, President Clinton created a commission under Vice President Al Gore to report on shortcomings in aviation security in the United States. The Gore Commission's report, having thoroughly canvassed available expertise in and outside of government, did not mention suicide hijackings or the use of aircraft as weapons. It focused mainly on the danger of placing bombs onto aircraft—the approach of the Manila air plot. The Gore Commission did call attention, however, to lax screening of passengers and what they carried onto planes.

4   In late 1998, reports came in of a possible al Qaeda plan to hijack a plane. One, a December 4 Presidential Daily Briefing for President Clinton . . . , brought the focus back to more traditional hostage taking; it reported Bin Ladin's involvement in planning a hijack operation to free prisoners such as the "Blind Sheikh," Omar Abdel Rahman. Had the contents of this PDB been brought to the attention of a wider group, including key members of Congress, it might have brought much more attention to the need for permanent changes in domestic airport and airline security procedures.[3]

5   Threat reports also mentioned the possibility of using an aircraft filled with explosives. The most prominent of these mentioned a possible plot to fly an explosives-laden aircraft into a U.S. city. This report, circulated in September 1998, originated from a source who had walked into an American consulate in East Asia. In August of the same year, the intelligence community had received information that a group of Libyans hoped to crash a plane into the World Trade Center. In neither case could the information be corroborated. In addition, an Algerian group hijacked an airliner in 1994, most likely intending to blow it up over Paris, but possibly to crash it into the Eiffel Tower.[4]

6   In 1994, a private airplane had crashed onto the south lawn of the White House. In early 1995, Abdul Hakim Murad—Ramzi Yousef's accomplice in the Manila airlines bombing plot—told Philippine authorities that he and Yousef had discussed flying a plane into CIA headquarters.

7   [Richard] Clarke had been concerned about the danger posed by aircraft since at least the 1996 Atlanta Olympics. There he had tried to create an air defense plan using assets from the Treasury Department, after the Defense Department declined to contribute resources. The Secret Service continued to work on the problem of airborne threats to the Washington region. In 1998, Clarke chaired an exercise designed to highlight the inadequacy of the solution. This paper exercise involved a scenario in which a group of terrorists commandeered a Learjet on the ground in Atlanta, loaded it with explosives, and flew it toward a target in Washington, D.C.

Clarke asked officials from the Pentagon, Federal Aviation Administration (FAA), and Secret Service what they could do about the situation. Officials from the Pentagon said they could scramble aircraft from Langley Air Force Base, but they would need to go to the President for rules of engagement, and there was no mechanism to do so. There was no clear resolution of the problem at the exercise.[5]

In late 1999, a great deal of discussion took place in the media about the crash off the coast of Massachusetts of EgyptAir Flight 990, a Boeing 767. The most plausible explanation that emerged was that one of the pilots had gone berserk, seized the controls, and flown the aircraft into the sea. After the 1999–2000 millennium alerts, when the nation had relaxed, Clarke held a meeting of his Counterterrorism Security Group devoted largely to the possibility of a possible airplane hijacking by al Qaeda.[6]

In his testimony, Clarke commented that he thought that warning about the possibility of a suicide hijacking would have been just one more speculative theory among many, hard to spot since the volume of warnings of "al Qaeda threats and other terrorist threats, was in the tens of thousands—probably hundreds of thousands."[7] Yet the possibility was imaginable, and imagined. In early August 1999, the FAA's Civil Aviation Security intelligence office summarized the Bin Ladin hijacking threat. After a social recitation of all the information available on this topic, the paper identified a few principal scenarios, one of which was a "suicide hijacking operation." The FAA analysts judged such an operation unlikely, because "it does not offer an opportunity for dialogue to achieve the key goal of obtaining Rahman and other key captive extremists. . . . A suicide hijacking is assessed to be an option of last resort."[8]

Analysts could have shed some light on what kind of "opportunity for dialogue" al Qaeda desired.[9] The CIA did not write any analytical assessments of possible hijacking scenarios.

One prescient pre-9/11 analysis of an aircraft plot was written by a Justice Department trial attorney. The attorney had taken an interest, apparently on his own initiative, in the legal issues that would be involved in shooting down a U.S. aircraft in such a situation.[10]

The North American Aerospace Defense Command imagined the possible use of aircraft as weapons, too, and developed exercises to counter such a threat—from planes coming to the Untied States from overseas, perhaps carrying a weapon of mass destruction. None of this speculation was based on actual intelligence of such a threat. One idea, intended to test command and control plans and NORAD's readiness, postulated a hijacked airliner coming from overseas and crashing into the Pentagon. The idea was put aside in the early planning of the exercise as too much of a distraction from the main focus (war in Korea), and as too unrealistic. As we pointed out in chapter 1, the military planners assumed that since such aircraft would be coming from overseas; they would have time to identify the target and scramble interceptors.[11]

13   We can therefore establish that at least some government agencies were concerned about the hijacking danger and had speculated about various scenarios. The challenge was to flesh out and test those scenarios, then figure out a way to turn a scenario into constructive action.

14   Since the Pearl Harbor attack of 1941, the intelligence community has devoted generations of effort to understanding the problem of forestalling a surprise attack. Rigorous analytic methods were developed, focused in particular on the Soviet Union, and several leading practitioners within the intelligence community discussed them with us. These methods have been articulated in many ways, but almost all seem to have at least four elements in common: (1) think about how surprise attacks might be launched; (2) identify telltale indicators connected to the most dangerous possibilities; (3) where feasible, collect intelligence on these indicators; and (4) adopt defenses to deflect the most dangerous possibilities or at least trigger an earlier warning.

15   After the end of the Gulf War, concerns about lack of warning led to a major study conducted for DCI Robert Gates in 1992 that proposed several recommendations, among them strengthening the national intelligence officer for warning. We were told that these measures languished under Gates's successors. Responsibility for warning related to a terrorist attack passed from the national intelligence officer for warning to the CTC. An Intelligence Community Counterterrorism Board had the responsibility to issue threat advisories.[12]

16   With the important exception of analysis of al Qaeda efforts in chemical, biological, radiological, and nuclear weapons, we did not find evidence that the methods to avoid surprise attack that had been so laboriously developed over the years were regularly applied.

17   Considering what was not done suggests possible ways to institutionalize imagination. To return to the four elements of anlaysis just mentioned:

18   1. The CTC did not analyze how an aircraft, hijacked or explosives-laden, might be used as a weapon. It did not perform this kind of analysis from the enemy's perspective ("red team" analysis), even though suicide terrorism had become a principal tactic of Middle Eastern terrorists. If it had done so, we believe such an analysis would soon have spotlighted a critical constraint for the terrorists—finding a suicide operative able to fly large jet aircraft. They had never done so before 9/11.

19   2. The CTC did not develop a set of telltale indicators for this method of attack. For example, one such indicator might be the discovery of possible terrorists pursuing flight training to fly large jet aircraft, or seeking to buy advanced flight simulators.

20   3. The CTC did not propose, and the intelligence community collection management process did not set, requirements to monitor such telltale indicators. Therefore the warning system was not looking for

information such as the July 2001 FBI report of potential terrorist interest in various kinds of aircraft training in Arizona, or the August 2001 arrest of Zacarias Moussaoui because of his suspicious behavior in a Minnesota flight school. In late August, the Moussaoui arrest was briefed to the DCI and other top CIA officials under the heading "Islamic Extremist Learns to Fly."[13] Because the system was not tuned to comprehend the potential significance of this information, the news had no effect on warning.

4. Neither the intelligence community nor aviation security experts [21] analyzed systemic defenses within an aircraft or against terrorist-controlled aircraft, suicidal or otherwise. The many threat reports mentioning aircraft were passed to the FAA. While that agency continued to react to specific, credible threats, it did not try to perform the broader warning functions we describe here. No one in the government was taking on that role for domestic vulnerabilities.

Richard Clarke told us that he was concerned about the danger [22] posed by aircraft in the context of protecting the Atlanta Olympics of 1996, the White House complex, and the 2001 G-8 summit in Genoa. But he attributed his awareness more to Tom Clancy novels than to warnings from the intelligence community. He did not, or could not, press the government to work on the systemic issues of how to strengthen the layered security defenses to protect aircraft against hijackings or put the adequacy of air defenses against suicide hijackers on the national policy agenda.

The methods for detecting and then warning of surprise attack that [23] the U.S. government had so painstakingly developed in the decades after Pearl Harbor did not fail; instead, they were not really tried. They were not employed to analyze the enemy that, as the twentieth century closed, was most likely to launch a surprise attack directly against the United States.

[Notes]

1. Waldo Heinrichs, *Threshold of War: Franklin D. Roosevelt and American Entry into World War II* (Oxford Univ. Press, 1988), p. 215.

2. For the response being routine, see Gordon Prange, *At Dawn We Slept: The Untold Story of Pearl Harbor* (McGraw-Hill, 1981), pp. 732–733. For a brief summary of these routines and the reasons why the intercepts were not properly digested, see Graham Allison and Philip Zelikow, *Essence of Decision*, 2nd ed. (Longman, 1999), p. 194, n. 72.

3. PDBs were not routinely briefed to congressional leaders, though this item could have been in some other intelligence briefing. It was not circulated in the NID or SEIB. For the September 1998 report, see Intelligence report, "Terrorism: Possible Attack on a U.S. City," Sept. 8, 1998.

4. For the August report, see Intelligence report, "Terrorism: Alleged Threat by Arab Terrorists to Attack the World Trade Center in New York," Aug. 12, 1998. An FAA civil aviation security official believed the plan was improbable because Libyan planes were required to operate within airspace limitations and the Libyans did not possess aircraft with the necessary range to make good on the threat. Jack S. interview (June 13, 2004). On September 30, 1999, the FAA closed the file on the August report after investigation could not corroborate the report, and the source's credibility was deemed suspect. FAA report, Transportation Security Intelligence ICF Report 980162, updated; but see FAA/TSA rebuttal to the Joint Inquiry's Sept. 18, 2002, staff statement, undated, p. 1 (stating that the FAA did not formally analyze this threat). The Algerian hijackers had placed explosives in key areas of the cabin. However, there was some speculation in the media based on reports from a passenger aboard the plane that the hijackers had discussed crashing it into the Eiffel Tower. FAA report, FAA Intelligence Case File 94-305, undated.

5. For Clarke's involvement in the 1996 Olympics, see Richard Clarke interview (Dec. 18, 2003). For the 1998 exercise, see Chuck Green interview (Apr. 21, 2004); NSC briefing paper, Nov. 10, 1998.

6. For the report of the National Transportation Safety Board, see NTSB report, "Aircraft Accident Brief," Mar. 13, 2002 (online at www.ntsb .gov/Publictn/2002/aab0201.htm). For the early 2000 CSG discussion, see NSC note, CSG SVTS agenda, Jan. 31, 2000.

7. Richard Clarke testimony, Mar. 24, 2004.

8. FAA memo, Office of Civil Aviation Security Intelligence, "Usama Bin Ladin/World Islamic Front Hijacking Threat," Intelligence Note 99-06, Aug. 4, 1999, pp. 5–6.

9. Ibid.

10. As part of his 34-page analysis, the attorney explained why he thought that a fueled Boeing 747, used as a weapon, "must be considered capable of destroying virtually any building located anywhere in the world." DOJ memo, Robert D. to Cathleen C., "Ariel Intercepts and Shootdowns: Ambiguities of Law and Practical Considerations," Mar. 30, 2000, p. 10. Also, in February 1974, a man named Samuel Byck attempted to commander a plane at Baltimore Washington International Airport with the intention of forcing the pilots to fly into Washington and crash into the White House to kill the president. The man was shot by police and then killed himself on the aircraft while it was still on the ground at the airport.

11. For NORAD's hypothesis of aircraft as weapons, see, e.g., Ralph Eberhardt interview (Mar. 1, 2004). For the 2001 Positive Force 01 exercise, see DOD briefing (Apr. 29, 2004); Tom Cecil and Mark Postgate interview (June 7, 2004).

12. For the Gates report's recommendations, see DCI task force report, "Improving Intelligence Warning," May 29, 1992. For strengthening of the warning official, see DCI memo, "Warning," July 17, 1992. For the

recommendations languishing, see Charles Allen interview (Sept. 22, 2003). For CTC having responsibility for warning, see Robert Vickers interview (Sept. 17, 2003). For the Board's warnings, see, e.g., Community Counter-terrorism Board report, "Intelligence Community Terrorist Threat Advisory: Bin Ladin Orchestrating Possible Anti-US Attacks," June 30, 2000.

    13. CIA briefing materials, "DCI Update," Aug. 23, 2001.

BERNARD LEWIS

Bernard Lewis (born in London, 1916) was educated at the University of London School of Oriental and African Studies, specializing in the history of Islam. He began his lifelong teaching career at his alma mater in 1938, where—with five years' absence during World War II to serve as a special-ist in Middle Eastern matters for the British Foreign Office—he taught until 1974. Thereafter, he taught at Princeton until retirement in 1986, where he remains an emeritus professor of Near Eastern studies. His numerous books on the Middle East span fifty-five years, from *The Arabs in History* (1950) to *The Political Language of Islam* (1988) to *From Babel to Dragomans* (2005). *What Went Wrong?* (2002) deals with issues addressed in the chapter included here. Indeed, this chapter touches briefly on the range of topics Lewis examines in his other works: Islam's thousand-year domination of the West in culture, science, and military prowess and the retreat of Islam from the West after the failed Turkish siege of Vienna in 1683, "dominated and bettered by the West" according to "every possible measure. Because the Islamic world has an acute sense of history and America does not, this reversal has fed centuries of acrimony." America is the current object of Islamic rage because it is seen as "imperialistic," supportive of oppressive Middle Eastern governments for its own ends and fostering "a culture of temptation and seduction."

What Went Wrong?

I n the course of the twentieth century it became abundantly clear that 1 things had gone badly wrong in the Middle East—and, indeed, in all the lands of Islam. Compared with Christendom, its rival for more than a millennium, the world of Islam had become poor, weak, and ignorant. The primacy and therefore the dominance of the West was clear for all to see, invading every aspect of the Muslim's public and even—more painfully— his private life.

    Muslim modernizers—by reform or revolution—concentrated their 2 efforts in three main areas: military, economic, and political. The results achieved were, to say the least, disappointing. The quest for victory by updated armies brought a series of humiliating defeats. The quest for prosperity through development brought in some countries impoverished and corrupt economies in recurring need of external aid, in others an unhealthy dependence on a single resource—oil. And even this was discovered, extracted, and put to use by Western ingenuity and industry, and is doomed, sooner or later, to be exhausted, or, more probably, superseded, as the international community grows weary of a fuel that pollutes the land, the sea, and the air wherever it is used or transported, and that puts the world economy at the mercy of a clique of capricious autocrats. Worst of all are the political results: the long quest for freedom has left a string of shabby tyrannies, ranging from traditional autocracies to dictatorships that are modern only in their apparatus of repression and indoctrination.

3   Many remedies were tried—weapons and factories, schools and parliaments—but none achieved the desired result. Here and there they brought some alleviation and, to limited elements of the population, some benefit. But they failed to remedy or even to halt the increasing imbalance between Islam and the Western world.

4   There was worse to come. It was bad enough for Muslims to feel poor and weak after centuries of being rich and strong, to lose the position of leadership that they had come to regard as their right, and to be reduced to the role of followers of the West. But the twentieth century, particularly the second half, brought further humiliation—the awareness that they were no longer even the first among followers but were falling back in a lengthening line of eager and more successful Westernizers, notably in East Asia. The rise of Japan had been an encouragement but also a reproach. The later rise of other Asian economic powers brought only reproach. The proud heirs of ancient civilizations had gotten used to hiring Western firms to carry out tasks of which their own contractors and technicians were apparently incapable. Now Middle Eastern rulers and businessmen found themselves inviting contractors and technicians from Korea—only recently emerged from Japanese colonial rule—to perform these tasks. Following is bad enough; limping in the rear is far worse. By all the standards that matter in the modern world—economic development and job creation, literacy, educational and scientific achievement, political freedom and respect for human rights—what was once a mighty civilization has indeed fallen low.

5   "Who did this to us?" is of course a common human response when things are going badly, and many in the Middle East, past and present, have asked this question. They have found several different answers. It is usually easier and always more satisfying to blame others for one's misfortunes. For a long time the Mongols were the favorite villains. The Mongol invasions of the thirteen century were blamed for the destruction of both Muslim power and Islamic civilization, and for what was seen as the ensuing weakness and stagnation. But after a while historians, Muslims and others, pointed to two flaws in this argument. The first was that some of the greatest cultural achievements of Islam, notably in Iran, came after, not

before, the Mongol invasions. The second, more difficult to accept but nevertheless undeniable, was that the Mongols overthrew an empire that was already fatally weakened; indeed, it is hard to see how the once mighty empire of the caliphs would otherwise have succumbed to a horde of nomadic horsemen riding across the steppes from East Asia.

The rise of nationalism—itself an import from Europe—produced   6
new perceptions. Arabs could lay the blame for their troubles on the Turks, who had ruled them for many centuries. Turks could lay the blame for the stagnation of their civilization on the dead weight of the Arab past, in which the creative energies of the Turkish people were caught and immobilized. Persians could lay the blame for the loss of their ancient glories on Arabs, Turks, and Mongols impartially.

In the nineteenth and twentieth centuries British and French para-   7
mountcy [*sic*] in much of the Arab world produced a new and more plausible scapegoat—Western imperialism. In the Middle East there have been good reasons for such blame. Western political domination, economic penetration, and—longest, deepest, and most insidious of all—cultural influence changed the face of the region and transformed the lives of its people, turning them in new directions, arousing new hopes and fears, creating new dangers and new expectations without precedent in their cultural past.

But the Anglo-French interlude was comparatively brief, and ended   8
half a century ago; Islam's change for the worse began long before and continued unabated afterward. Inevitably, the role of the British and the French as villains was taken over by the United States, along with other aspects of Western leadership. The attempt to transfer the guilt to America has won considerable support but, for similar reasons, remains unconvincing. Anglo-French rule and American influence, like the Mongol invasions, were a consequence, not a cause, of the inner weakness of Middle Eastern states and societies. Some observers, both inside and outside the region, have pointed to differences in the post-colonial development of former British possessions—for example, between Aden, in the Middle East, and Singapore or Hong Kong; or between the various lands that once made up the British Empire in India.

Another European contribution to this debate is anti-Semitism, and   9
blaming "the Jews" for all that goes wrong. Jews in traditional Islamic societies experienced the normal constraints and occasional hazards of minority status. Until the rise and spread of Western tolerance in the seventeenth and eighteenth centuries, they were better off under Muslim than under Christian rule in most significant respects. With rare exceptions, where hostile stereotypes of the Jew existed in the Islamic tradition, Islamic societies tended to be contemptuous and dismissive rather than suspicious and obsessive. This made the events of 1948—the failure to prevent the establishment of the state of Israel—all the more of a shock. As some writers observed at the time, it was humiliating enough to be defeated by the great

imperial powers of the West; to suffer the same fate at the hands of a contemptible gang of Jews was intolerable. Anti-Semitism and its image of the Jew as a scheming, evil monster provided a soothing antidote.

10   The earliest specifically anti-Semitic statements in the Middle East occurred among Christian minorities, and can usually be traced back to European originals. They had limited impact, during the Dreyfus trial in France, for example, when a Jewish officer was unjustly accused and condemned by a hostile court, Muslim comments usually favored the persecuted Jew against his Christian persecutors. But the poison continued to spread, and starting in 1933, Nazi Germany and its various agencies made a concerted and on the whole remarkably successful effort to promote European-style anti-Semitism in the Arab world. The struggle for Palestine greatly facilitated the acceptance of the anti-Semitic interpretation of history, and led some to attribute all evil in the Middle East—and, indeed, in the world—to secret Jewish plots. This interpretation has pervaded much of the public discourse in the region, including that seen in education, the media, and even entertainment.

11   An argument sometimes adduced is that the cause of the changed relationship between East and West is not a Middle Eastern decline but a Western upsurge—the discoveries and the scientific, technological, industrial, and political revolutions that transformed the West and vastly increased its wealth and power. But this is merely to restate the question: Why did the discoverers of America sail from Spain rather than from a Muslim Atlantic port, out of which such voyages were indeed attempted in earlier times? Why did the great scientific breakthrough occur in Europe and not, as one might reasonably have expected, in the richer, more advanced, and in most respects more enlightened realm of Islam?

12   A more sophisticated form of the blame game finds its targets inside, rather than outside, Islamic society. One such target is religion—for some, specifically Islam. But to blame Islam as such is usually hazardous and not often attempted. Nor is it very plausible. For most of the Middle Ages it was neither the older cultures of the Orient nor the newer cultures of the West that were the major centers of civilization and progress but the world of Islam. There old sciences were recovered and developed and new sciences were created; there new industries were born and manufactures and commerce were expanded to a level without precedent. There, too, governments and societies achieved a freedom of thought and expression that led persecuted Jews and even dissident Christians to flee Christendom for refuge in Islam. In comparison with modern ideals, and even with modern practice in the more advanced democracies, the medieval Islamic world offered only limited freedom, but that was vastly more than was offered by any of its predecessors, its contemporaries, or most of its successors.

13   The point has often been made: If Islam is an obstacle to freedom, to science, to economic development, how is it that Muslim society in the past

was a pioneer in all three—and this when Muslims were much closer in time to the sources and inspiration of their faith than they are now? Some have posed the question in a different form—not "What has Islam done to the Muslims?" but "What have the Muslims done to Islam?"—and have answered by laying the blame on specific teachers and doctrines and groups.

For those known nowadays as Islamists or fundamentalists, the failures and shortcomings of modern Islamic lands afflict those lands because they adopted alien notions and practices. They fell away from authentic Islam and thus lost their former greatness. Those known as modernists or reformers take the opposite view, seeing the cause of this loss not in the abandonment but in the retention of old ways, and especially in the inflexibility and ubiquity of the Islamic clergy, who, they say, are responsible for the persistence of beliefs and practices that might have been creative and progressive a thousand years ago but are neither today. The modernists' usual tactic is not to denounce religion as such, still less Islam in particular, but to level their criticism against fanaticism. It is to fanaticism—and more particularly to fanatical religious authorities—that they attribute the stifling of the once great Islamic scientific movement and, more generally, of the freedom of thought and expression.

A more common approach to this theme has been to discuss a specific problem: the place of religion and of its professional exponents in the political order. In this view a principal cause of Western progress is the separation of Church and State and the creation of a civil society governed by secular laws. Another approach has been to view the main culprit as the relegation of women to an inferior position in Muslim society, which deprives the Islamic world of the talents and energies of half its people and entrusts the other half's crucial early years of upbringing to illiterate and downtrodden mothers. The products of such an education, it has been said, are likely to grow up either arrogant or submissive, and unfit for a free, open society. However one evaluates the views of secularists and feminists, their success or failure will be a major factor in shaping the Middle Eastern future.

Some solutions that once commanded passionate support have been discarded. The two dominant movements in the twentieth century were socialism and nationalism. Both have been discredited—the first by its failure, the second by its success and consequent exposure as ineffective. Freedom, interpreted to mean national independence, was seen as the great talisman that would bring all other benefits. The overwhelming majority of Muslims now live in independent states, but this has brought no solutions to their problems. National socialism, the bastard offspring of both ideologies, persists in a few states that have preserved the Nazi-Fascist style of dictatorial government and indoctrination through a vast security apparatus and a single all-powerful party. These regimes have failed every test except survival, and have brought none of the promised benefits. If anything, their infrastructures are even more antiquated than those of other Muslim states, their armed forces designed primarily for terror and repression.

17   At present two answers to the question of what went wrong command widespread support in the Middle East, each with its own diagnosis and corresponding prescription. One attributes all evil to the abandonment of the divine heritage of Islam and advocates return to a real or imagined past. That is the way of the Iranian revolution and of the so-called fundamentalist movements and regimes in various Muslim countries. The other condemns the past and advocates secular democracy, best embodied in the Turkish Republic, proclaimed in 1923 by Kemal Atatürk.

18   For the oppressive but ineffectual governments that rule much of the Middle East, finding targets to blame serves a useful, indeed an essential, purpose—to explain the poverty that they have failed to alleviate and to justify the tyranny that they have introduced. They seek to deflect the mounting anger of their unhappy subjects toward other, outside targets.

19   But growing numbers of Middle Easterners are adopting a more self-critical approach. The question "Who did this to us?" has led only to neurotic fantasies and conspiracy theories. And the question "What did we do wrong?" has led naturally to a second question: "How do we put it right?" In that question, and in the various answers that are being found, lie the best hopes for the future.

20   During the past few weeks the worldwide exposure given to the views and actions of Osama bin Laden and his hosts the Taliban has provided a new and vivid insight into the eclipse of what was once the greatest, most advanced, and most open civilization in human history.

21   To a Western observer, schooled in the theory and practice of Western freedom, it is precisely the lack of freedom—freedom of the mind from constraint and indoctrination, to question and inquire and speak; freedom of the economy from corrupt and pervasive mismanagement; freedom of women from male oppression; freedom of citizens from tyranny—that underlies so many of the troubles of the Muslim world. But the road to democracy, as the Western experience amply demonstrates, is long and hard, full of pitfalls and obstacles.

22   If the peoples of the Middle East continue on their present path, the suicide bomber may become a metaphor for the whole region, and there will be no escape from a downward spiral of hate and spite, rage and self-pity, poverty and oppression, culminating sooner or later in yet another alien domination—perhaps from a new Europe reverting to old ways, perhaps from a resurgent Russia, perhaps from some expanding superpower in the East. But if they can abandon grievance and victimhood, settle their differences, and join their talents, energies, and resources in a common creative endeavor, they can once again make the Middle East, in modern times as it was in antiquity and in the Middle Ages, a major center of civilization. For the time being, the choice is theirs.

MARK JUERGENSMEYER

Mark Juergensmeyer (born in 1940 in southern Illinois) earned a Master's in divinity from Union Theological Seminary (1965) and a PhD in political science from Berkeley (1974). He is currently Director of Global and International Studies and professor of sociology and religious studies at the University of California, Santa Barbara. An expert on religious violence, conflict resolution, and South Asian religion and politics, he has published more than two hundred articles and fifteen books, three in 2005: *Gandhi's Way, Religion in Global Civil Society,* and *Handbook of Global Religions. The New Cold War? Religious Nationalism Confronts the Secular State* (1993) covers the rise of religious activism and its confrontation with secular modernity. His widely read *Terror in the Mind of God: The Global Rise of Religious Violence* (2000), from which these excerpts are taken, is based on interviews with violent religious activists around the world—including people convicted of the 1993 World Trade Center bombing, leaders of Hamas, and abortion clinic bombers in the United States.

from Terror in the Mind of God

... Instances of exaggerated violence are constructed events: they are mind-numbing, mesmerizing theater. At center stage are the acts themselves—stunning, abnormal, and outrageous murders carried out in a way that graphically displays the awful power of violence—set within grand scenarios of conflict and proclamation. Killing or maiming of any sort is violent, of course, but these acts surpass the wounds inflicted during warfare or death delivered through capital punishment, in large part because they have a secondary impact. By their demonstrative nature, they elicit feelings of revulsion and anger in those who witness them.

Performance Violence

How do we make sense of such theatrical forms of violence? One way of answering this is to view dramatic violence as part of a strategic plan. This viewpoint assumes that terrorism is always part of a political strategy—and, in fact, some social scientists have defined terrorism in just this way: "the use of covert violence by a group for political ends." In some cases this definition is indeed appropriate, for an act of violence can fulfill political ends and have a direct impact on public policy.

The Israeli elections in 1996 provided a case in point. Shortly after the assassination of Yitzhak Rabin, his successor, Shimon Peres, held a 20 percent lead in the polls over his rival, Benjamin Netanyahu, but this lead vanished following a series of Hamas suicide attacks on Jerusalem buses.

Netanyahu narrowly edged out Peres in the May elections. Many observers concluded that Netanyahu—no friend of Islamic radicals—had the terrorists of Hamas to thank for his victory.

4   When the Hamas operative who planned the 1996 attacks was later caught and imprisoned, he was asked whether he had intended to affect the outcome of the elections. "No," he responded, explaining that the internal affairs of Israelis did not matter much to him. This operative was a fairly low-level figure, however, and one might conjecture that his superiors had a more specific goal in mind. But when I put the same question to the political leader of Hamas, Dr. Abdul Aziz Rantisi, his answer was almost precisely the same: these attacks were not aimed at Israeli internal politics, since Hamas did not differentiate between Peres and Netanyahu. In the Hamas view, the two Israeli leaders were equally opposed to Islam. "Maybe God wanted it," the Hamas operative said of Netanyahu's election victory. Even if the Hamas leaders were being disingenuous, the fact remains that most of their suicide bombings have served no direct political purpose.

5   Other examples of religious terrorism have also shown little strategic value. The release of nerve gas in the Tokyo subways and the bombing of the World Trade Center did not provide any immediate political benefits to those who caused them. Although Mahmud Abouhalima, convicted for his part in the World Trade Center bombing, told me that assaults on public buildings did have a long-range strategic value in that they helped to "identify the government as enemy," in general the "political ends" for which these acts were committed seemed distant indeed.

6   A political scientist, Martha Crenshaw, has shown that the notion of "strategic" thinking can be construed in a broad sense to cover not just immediate political achievements but also the internal logic that propels a group into perpetrating terrorist acts. As Abouhalima said, many of those who committed them felt they were justified by the broad, long-range benefits to be gained. My investigations indicate that Crenshaw is right— acts of terrorism are usually the products of an internal logic and not of random or crazy thinking—but I hesitate to use the term *strategy* for all rationales for terrorist actions. *Strategy* implies a degree of calculation and an expectation of accomplishing a clear objective that does not jibe with such dramatic displays of power as the World Trade Center bombing. These creations of terror are done not to achieve a strategic goal but to make a symbolic statement.

7   By calling acts of religious terrorism "symbolic," I mean that they are intended to illustrate or refer to something beyond their immediate target: a grander conquest, for instance, or a struggle more awesome than meets the eye. As Abouhalima said, the bombing of a public building may dramatically indicate to the populace that the government or the economic forces behind the building were seen as enemies, to show the world that they were targeted as satanic foes. The point of the attack, then, was to produce a graphic and easily understandable object lesson. Such explosive

scenarios are not *tactics* directed toward an immediate, earthly, or strategic goal, but *dramatic events* intended to impress for their symbolic significance. As such, they can be analyzed as one would any other symbol, ritual, or sacred drama.

I can imagine a line with "strategic" on the one side and "symbolic"   8
on the other, with various acts of terrorism located in between. The hostage taking in the Japanese embassy by the Tupac Amaru in Peru in 1997—clearly an attempt to leverage power in order to win the release of members of the movement held prisoner by the Peruvian government—might be placed closer to the political, strategic side. The Aum Shinrikyo nerve gas attack in 1995 might be closer to the symbolic, religious side. Each was the product of logical thought, and each had an internal rationale. In cases such as the Tokyo nerve gas attack that were more symbolic than strategic, however, the logic was focused not on an immediate political acquisition, but at a larger, less tangible goal.

The very adjectives used to describe acts of religious terrorism—   9
symbolic, dramatic, theatrical—suggest that we look at them not as tactics but as *performance violence.* In speaking of terrorism as "performance," I am not suggesting that such acts are undertaken lightly or capriciously. Rather, like religious ritual or street theater, they are dramas designed to have an impact on the several audiences that they affect. Those who witness the violence—even at a distance, via the news media—are therefore a part of what occurs. Moreover, like other forms of public ritual, the symbolic significance of such events is multifaceted; they mean different things to different observers. . . .

In addition to referring to drama, the term *performance* also implies the   10
notion of "performative"—as in the concept of "performative acts." This is an idea developed by language philosophers regarding certain kinds of speech that are able to perform social functions: their very utterance has a transformative impact. Like vows recited during marriage rites, certain words not only represent reality but also shape it: they contain a certain power of their own. The same is true of some nonverbal symbolic actions, such as the gunshot that begins a race, the raising of a white flag to show defeat, or acts of terrorism.

Terrorist acts, then, can be both *performance events,* in that they make   11
a symbolic statement, and *performative acts,* insofar as they try to change things. When Yigal Amir aimed his pistol at Israel's prime minister, Yitzhak Rabin, and when Sikh activists targeted Punjab's chief minister with a car bomb in front of the state's office buildings, the activists were aware that they were creating enormous spectacles. They probably also hoped that their actions would make a difference—if not in a direct, strategic sense, then in an indirect way as a dramatic show so powerful as to change people's perceptions of the world.

But the fact that the assassins of Prime Minister Rabin and Chief Min-   12
ister Beant Singh hoped that their acts would make such a statement does

not mean that they in fact did. As I noted, public symbols mean different things to different people, and a symbolic performance may not have the intended effect. The way the act is perceived—by both the perpetrators and those who are affected by it—makes all the difference. In fact, the same is true of performance speech. One of the leading language philosophers, J. L. Austin, has qualified the notion that some speech acts are performative by observing that the power of the act is related to the perception of it. Children, for example, playing at marriage are not wedded by merely reciting the vows and going through the motions, nor is a ship christened by just anyone who gives it a name.[1]

13   The French sociologist Pierre Bourdieu, carrying further the idea that statements are given credibility by their social context, has insisted that the power of performative speech—vows and christenings—is rooted in social reality and is given currency by the laws and social customs that stand behind it.[2] Similarly, an act of terrorism usually implies an underlying power and legitimizing ideology. But whether the power and legitimacy implicit in acts of terrorism are like play-acted marriage vows or are the real thing depends in part on how the acts are perceived. It depends, in part, on whether their significance is believed.

14   This brings us back to the realm of faith. Public ritual has traditionally been the province of religion, and this is one of the reasons that performance violence comes so naturally to activists from a religious background. In a collection of essays on the connection between religion and terrorism published some years ago, one of the editors, David C. Rapoport, observed—accurately, I think—that the two topics fit together not only because there is a violent streak in the history of religion, but also because terrorist acts have a symbolic side and in that sense mimic religious rites. The victims of terrorism are targeted not because they are threatening to the perpetrators, he said, but because they are "symbols, tools, animals or corrupt beings" that tie into "a special picture of the world, a specific consciousness" that the activist possesses.[3]

15   The street theater of performance violence forces those who witness it directly or indirectly into that "consciousness"—that alternative view of the world. This gives the perpetrators of terrorism a kind of celebrity status and their actions an illusion of importance. The novelist Don DeLillo goes so far as to say that "only the lethal believer, the person who kills and dies for faith," is taken seriously in modern society.[4] When we

---

[1] See J. L. Austin, *How to Do Things with Words* (Oxford: Clarendon Press, 1962), 4.

[2] Pierre Bourdieu, *Language and Symbolic Power* (Cambridge, MA: Harvard University Press, 1991) (translated from the 1982 French original by Gino Raymond and Matthew Adamson, edited by John B. Thompson), 117.

[3] David C. Rapoport, "Introduction," in David C. Rapoport and Yonah Alexander, eds., *The Morality of Terrorism: Religious and Secular Justifications* (New York: Pergamon Press, 1982), xiii.

[4] Don DeLillo, *Mao II* (New York: Penguin, 1991), 157.

who observe these acts take them seriously—are disgusted and repelled by them, and begin to distrust the peacefulness of the world around us— the purposes of this theater are achieved.

Setting the Stage

In looking at religious terrorism as theater, the appropriate place to begin is   16 the stage—the location where the acts are committed, or rather, performed. When followers of an expatriate Muslim sheik living in New Jersey chose to make a statement about their unhappiness with American and Jewish support for Middle East leaders whom they perceived to be enemies of Islam, they found the most dramatic stage in sight: the World Trade Center. It turned out to be an apt location for a variety of symbolic reasons.

Designed to be the tallest buildings in New York City, and at one   17 time the highest in the world, the 110-story twin towers of the World Trade Center house the headquarters of international businesses and financial corporations. Among its many offices are quarters for the federal Secret Service and the governor of the state of New York. More than fifty thousand employees daily enter the huge edifice, which also includes a hotel, shops, and several restaurants. From the windows of the penthouse restaurant, Windows on the World, the executives who come to lunch can scarcely identify Jersey City and the other industrial areas stretched out across the Hudson River in a distant haze.

From across the river in Jersey City, the twin towers of the build-   18 ing are so tall that when no other part of the skyline in New York City is visible, the tower tops are seen ethereally suspended above the eastern horizon. When Muhammad A. Salameh came to the Ryder Truck Rental lot on Jersey City's busy Kennedy Boulevard on Wednesday, February 24, 1993, to rent a ten-foot Ford Econoline van, therefore, he could catch glimpses of the World Trade Center in the distance.

Two days later, at noon, shortly after the van was driven to level B2   19 of the parking basement of the World Trade Center, an enormous blast shuddered through the basement levels, collapsing several floors, killing several workers instantly, and ripping a 180-foot hole in the wall of the underground Port Authority Trans-Hudson train station. On the 110th floor, in the Windows on the World restaurant, young executives who were attending a career-launching lunch felt a thump and heard what seemed to be a mild earthquake or a clap of thunder. When the electricity went off and they were told to evacuate the building, they headed downstairs jauntily singing "One Hundred Bottles of Beer on the Wall." Their joviality turned to nervous apprehension when they were greeted with clouds of soot and smoke as they groped their way down 110 flights of stairs into a scene of confusion and suffering on the ground floor.

Throughout the world the news media projected images of American   20 power and civic order undermined. Based on the belief by government officials that the World Trade Center was targeted primarily as a public symbol, security was rushed to federal monuments and memorials in Washington, DC, later that afternoon. Although six people were killed in the blast, it was the assault on the building itself that received the most prominent reportage. Within an hour of the World Trade Center bombing, a coffeehouse in Cairo was attacked—allegedly by the same group implicated in the World Trade Center incident. This bombing killed more people but garnered very little attention outside of Cairo. Regardless of the number killed, a coffeehouse is not the World Trade Center. The towers are in their own way as American as the Statue of Liberty or the Washington Monument, and by assaulting them activists put their mark on a visibly American symbol.

21   The same can be said about the bombing of the Alfred P. Murrah Federal Building in Oklahoma City on April 19, 1995, by Timothy McVeigh and Terry Nichols. In this case the number killed was much greater than at the World Trade Center, and an enormous outpouring of public sympathy for the victims overshadowed any concern about damage done to the building. Yet there were several similarities between the two events: McVeigh and Nichols used a mixture of ammonium nitrate fertilizer and diesel fuel not unlike that used in the World Trade Center blast, and they mimicked the World Trade Center bombers by employing a Ryder rental truck. Like Mahmud Abouhalima and his colleagues, these self-designated soldiers were fighting a quasi-religious war against the American government, and they chose a building that symbolized what they regarded as an oppressive government force. . . .

22   If one had to choose a single building that symbolized the presence of centralized federal governmental power in this region of mid-America, the Murrah building in Oklahoma City would be it. When the dust settled after the devastating roar of the enormous explosion on Wednesday morning, April 19, 1995, the entire front of the building had been sheared off, killing 168 and injuring more than five hundred. Among the dead and injured were scores of children in the building's day care center, but only four ATF officials were injured, and none were killed. Clearly, the target of the attack was not so much the government agents, or even an agency such as the ATF, as it was the building itself and its everyday staff of government workers.

23   What was targeted was a symbol of normal government operations. In this scenario of terrorism, the lives of the workers were, like the building, a part of the scenery: they and the edifice constituted the stage on which the dramatic act was to be performed. If the building were attacked at night without the workers present, the explosion would not have been a serious blow to government operations, nor would the pain of the event be felt as acutely by society at large. If the building's employees had been machine-gunned as they left their offices, with the building itself left unscathed, the symbolism of an attack on normal government operations would have been incomplete. Such targets as the World Trade Center and

the Oklahoma City federal building have provided striking images of a stable, seemingly invulnerable economic and political power. Yet all buildings are ultimately vulnerable, a fact that performers of terror such as Abouhalima and McVeigh have been eager to demonstrate. . . .

Because air traffic itself is indicative of a society's economic vitality, often airplanes rather than airports have provided terrorism's stage. The most dramatic example is Ramzi Yousef's Bojinka plot, aimed at eleven U.S. trans-Pacific passenger airplanes and alleged to have been funded by Saudi millionaire Osama bin Laden, which would have created a catastrophic event on one fateful day in 1995. The term *Bojinka* was one that Yousef himself had chosen and was the label for the file in the hard disk of his white Toshiba laptop computer that listed the details of the plot— where flights would depart, what routes they would take, and where the participants in the plot should deplane in order to escape the explosions caused by the bombs that they were to leave behind. In the trail that convicted him of conspiring to commit these acts of terrorism, Yousef, acting as his own lawyer, offered as his main defense the notion that anyone with computer expertise could have planted such information on his hard disk. Yet he was not able to refute the testimony of witnesses who heard him talk about the plot and the Philippines airline stewardess who saw him sitting in the very seat under which a bomb exploded on a later leg of the flight, after Yousef had departed. In December 1994, Yousef is said to have boarded the plane and, once it was aloft, entered one of the bathrooms and mixed a highly inflammable cocktail involving a liquid form of nitroglycerin. He sealed it in a container and attached a blasting cap and a timer. Returning to his seat, he strapped the device underneath the cushion and departed the plane at its next stop, leaving the bomb beneath the seat to explode in midair as the plane journeyed on to its next destination. . . . [24]

According to a chronology of terrorist acts maintained by Bruce Hoffman at the RAND Corporation and St. Andrews University, twenty-two airliners were bombed worldwide from 1969 to 1996, and many others were hijacked. A nation can feel dishonored by the bombing of one of its airlines even when the plane, such as the downed Pan Am 103, is far from home. In that case the bomb—plastic explosives hidden in a portable radio–tape player, allegedly placed by Libyan intelligence agencies operating out of Malta—blew up the aircraft as it flew above Scotland in 1988, the shredded pieces of the plane landing near the small town of Lockerbie. . . . [25]

The symbolism of other locations has been more general: the locations represented the power and stability of the society itself. As we have seen, buildings such as the World Trade Center and the Oklahoma City federal building, along with transportation systems, are examples of such general symbols. . . . Computer networks and Internet channels are also symbols of a society's centrality—its central communication system. As the Melissa virus in 1999 demonstrated, acts of sabotage can cripple large corporations and government agencies. In response to NATO's bombing [26] in Serbia and Kosovo in May 1999, hackers electronically entered the computer systems of several United States government agencies, leaving antiwar messages in their wake.

27   By revealing the vulnerability of a nation's most stable and powerful entities, movements that undertake these acts of sabotage have touched virtually everyone in the nation's society. Any person in the United States could have been riding the elevator in the World Trade Center, visiting the Oklahoma City federal building, traveling on Pan Am 103, or using a computer when a virus invaded it, and everyone in the United States will look differently at the stability of public buildings, transportation networks, and communication systems as a result of these violent incidents.

28   Why is the location of terrorist events—of performance violence—so important? . . . Such central places—even if they exist only in cyberspace—are symbols of power, and acts of terrorism claim them in a symbolic way. That is, they express for a moment the power of terrorist groups to control central locations—by damaging, terrorizing, and assaulting them—even when in fact most of the time they do not control them at all. Even before the smoke had cleared at the World Trade Center, life inside was returning to normal. Although the Murrah Federal Building was destroyed, the governmental functions that had been conducted there continued unabated. Yet during that brief dramatic moment when a terrorist act levels a building or damages some entity that a society regards as central to its existence, the perpetrators of the act assert that they—and not the secular government—have ultimate control over that entity and its centrality.

29   The very act, however, is sometimes more than symbolic: by demonstrating the vulnerability of governmental power, to some degree it weakens that power. Because power is largely a matter of perception, symbolic statements can lead to real results. On the whole, however, the small degree to which a government's authority is discredited by a terrorist act does not warrant the massive destructiveness of the act itself. More significant is the impression—in most cases it is simply an illusion—that the movements perpetrating the acts have enormous power and that the ideologies behind them have cosmic importance. In the war between religious and secular authority, the loss of a secular government's ability to control and secure public spaces, even for a terrible moment, is ground gained for religion's side. . . .

America as Enemy

30   More than any other government, America has been assigned the role of primary or secondary foe. The wrath has been directed largely toward political leaders and governmental symbols, but the wider circle has included American businessmen, American culture, and the American "system"—a generic term that has included all responsible persons and every entity that has kept the country functioning as a political, economic, and social unit.

According to the RAND Chronicle of International Terrorism, since 1968 the United States each year has headed the list of countries whose citizens and property were most frequently attacked. The U.S. State Department's counterterrorism unit reported that during the 1990s, 40 percent of all acts of terrorism worldwide have been against American citizens and facilities.[5]

Mahmud Abouhalima has said that he regards America as a world-wide enemy. The reason, he says, is not only because the United States supports the secular Egyptian government that he and his colleagues find directly oppressive, but also because of its history of terrorist acts. The bombing of Hiroshima, for instance, Abouhalima compared with the bombing of the Oklahoma City federal building.[6] Abouhalima's spiritual leader, Sheik Omar Abdul Rahman, during a lengthy courtroom speech at the end of the trial convicting him of conspiring to bomb the World Trade Center, predicted that a "revengeful" God would "scratch" America from the face of the earth.[7]

Osama bin Laden, implicated in the bombing of the American embassies in Kenya and Tanzania in 1998, explained in an interview a year before the bombing that America deserved to be targeted because it was "the biggest terrorist in the world."[8] It may be only coincidence that after the embassy bombings U.S. National Security Advisor Samuel Berger called Osama "the most dangerous nonstate terrorist in the world."[9] The reason bin Laden gave for targeting America was its list of "crimes," which included "occupying the lands of Islam in the holist of places, the Arabian Peninsula, plundering its riches, dictating to its rulers, humiliating its people, terrorizing its neighbors and turning its bases in the peninsula into a spearhead through which to fight the neighboring Muslim peoples."[10] In response to what bin Laden regarded as a declaration of war on Muslims by America, he issued a fatwa calling on "every Muslim" as "an individual duty" to join him in a righteous war "to kill the Americans and their allies." Their obligation was not only "to kill the Americans" but also to "plunder their money wherever and whenever they find it." He sealed his fatwa with the reassurance that "this is in accordance with the words of Almighty God" and that "every Muslim who believes in God and wishes to be rewarded" should "comply with God's order."[11]

Why is America the enemy? This question is hard for observers of international politics to answer, and harder still for ordinary Americans to

31

32

33

---

[5] Robin Wright, "Prophetic 'Terror 2000' Mapped Evolving Threat," *Los Angeles Times,* August 9, 1998, A16.

[6] Interview with Abouhalima, September 30, 1997.

[7] John J. Goldman, "Defendants Given 25 years to Life in New York Terror Plot," *Los Angeles Times,* January 18, 1996, A1.

[8] Osama bin Laden, interviewed on an ABC News report rebroadcast on August 9, 1998.

[9] Samel Berger, quoted in *"Jihad* Is an Individual Duty," *Los Angeles Times,* August 13, 1998, B9.

[10] *"Jihad* Is an Individual Duty," B9.

[11] *"Jihad* Is an Individual Duty," B9.

fathom. Many have watched with horror as their compatriots and sym-bols of their country have been destroyed by people whom they do not know, from cultures they can scarcely identify on a global atlas, and for reasons that do not seem readily apparent. From the frames of reference of those who regard America as enemy, however, several motives appear.

34   One reason we have already mentioned: America is often a secondary enemy. In its role as trading partner and political ally, America has a vested interest in shoring up the stability of regimes around the world. This has often put the United States in the unhappy position of being a defender and promoter of secular governments regarded by their religious opponents as primary foes. Long before the bombing of the World Trade Center, Sheik Omar Abdul Rahman expressed his disdain for the United States because of its role in propping up the Mubarak regime in Egypt. "America is behind all these un-Islamic governments," the Sheik explained, arguing that the purpose of American political and economic support was "to keep them strong" and to try to "defeat the Islamic movements."[12] In the case of Iran prior to the Islamic revolution, Ayatollah Khomeini saw the shah and the American government linked as evil twins: America was tarred by its association with the shah, and the shah, in turn, was corrupted by being a "companion of satanic forces"—that is, of America.[13] When Khomeini prayed to his "noble God for protection from the evil of every wicked traitor" and asked Him to "destroy the enemies," the primary traitor he had in mind was the shah and the chief enemy America.[14]

35   A second reason America is regarded as enemy is that both directly and indirectly it has supported modern culture. In a world where vil-lagers in remote corners of the world increasingly have access to MTV, Hollywood movies, and the Internet, the images and values that have been projected globally have been American. It was this cultural threat that brought an orthodox rabbi, Manachem Fruman, who lived in a Jew-ish settlement on the West Bank of Israel near Hebron, to regular meetings with Hamas-related mullahs in nearby villages. What they had in com-mon, Rabbi Fruman told me, was their common dislike of the "American-style" traits of individualism, the abuse of alcohol, and sexy movies that were widespread in modern cities such as Tel Aviv. Rabbi Fruman told me that "when the mullahs asked, who brought all this corruption here, they answered, 'the Jews.' But," Fruman continued, "rabbis like me don't like this corruption either." Hence the rabbi and the mullahs agreed about the degradation of modern urban values, and they concurred over which country was ultimately responsible. When the mullahs asserted that the

---

[12] Sheik Omar Abdul Rahman, quoted in Kim Murphy, "Have the Islamic Militants Turned to a New Battlefront in the US?" *Los Angeles Times*, March 3, 1993, A20.

[13] Ayatollah Khomeini, *Collection of Speeches, Position Statements* (Arlington, VA: Joint Publications Research Service, 1979), 24.

[14] Khomeini, *Collection*, 30.

United States was the "capital of the devil," Rabbi Fruman told me, he could agree.[15] In a similar vein, Mahmud Abouhalima told me he was bitter that Islam did not have influence over the global media the way that secular America did. America, he believed, was using its power of information to promote the immoral values of secular society.[16]

The third reason for the disdain of America is economic. Although most corporations that trade internationally are multinational, with personnel and legal ties to more than one country, many are based in the United States or have American associations. Even those that were identifiably European or Japanese are thought to be American-like and implicitly American in attitude and style. When Ayatollah Khomeini identified the "satanic" forces that were out to destroy Islam, he included not only Jews but also the even "more satanic" Westerners—especially corporate leaders with "no religious belief" who saw Islam as "the major obstacle in the path of their materialistic ambitions and the chief threat to their political power."[17] The ayatollah went on to claim that "all the problems of Iran" were due to the treachery of "foreign colonialists."[18] On another occasion, the ayatollah blended political, personal, and spiritual issues in generalizing about the cosmic foe—Western colonialism—and about "the black and dreadful future" that "the agents of colonialism, may God Almighty abandon them all," have in mind for Islam and the Muslim people."[19]

What the ayatollah was thinking of when he prophesied a "black and dreadful future" for Islam was the global domination of American economy and culture. This fear of globalization is the fourth reason America is often targeted as an enemy. The apprehensions of Ayatollah Khomeini were shared by many not only in the Muslim world but elsewhere, including the United States. There right-wing militias were convinced that the "new world order" proclaimed by President George [H. W.] Bush was more than a mood of global cooperation: it was a conspiratorial plot to control the world. Accepting this paranoid vision of American leaders' global designs, the Aum Shinrikyo master Shoko Asahara linked the U.S. army with the Japanese government, Freemasons, and Jews in the image of a global conspiratorial band.

Like all stereotypes, each of these characterizations holds a certain amount of truth. America's culture and economy have dominated societies around the world in ways that have caused concern to protectors of local

---

[15] Interview with Rabbi Manachem Fruman, Tuqua settlement, West Bank, Israel, August 14, 1995.

[16] Interview with Abouhalima, September 30, 1997.

[17] Imam [Ayatollah] Khomeini, *Islam and Revolution: Writings and Declarations*, Hamid Algar, trans., annot. (London: Routledge and Kegan Paul, 1985) (orig. published by Mizan Press, Berkeley, in 1981), 27–28.

[18] Khomeini, *Collection*, 3.

[19] Khomeini, *Collection*, 25.

societies. The vast financial and media networks of American-backed corporations and information systems have affected the whole of the globe.
There has indeed been a great conflict between secular and religious life
throughout the world, and America does ordinarily support the secular
side of the fight. Financial aid provided to leaders such as Israel's Benjamin Netanyahu and Egypt's Hosni Mubarak has shored up the political
power of politicians opposed to religious nationalism. Moreover, after the
fall of the Soviet Union, the United States has been virtually the only coherent military power in the world. Hence it has been an easy target for
blame when people have felt that their lives were going askew or were
being controlled by forces they could not readily see. Yet to dislike America
is one thing; to regard it as a cosmic enemy is quite another.

39   When the United States has been branded as an enemy in a cosmic
war, it has been endowed with superhuman—or perhaps subhuman—
qualities, ones that have had little to do with the people who actually live
in America. It is the image of the country that has been despised—a reified
notion of Americanism, not its people. Individual Americans have often
been warmly accepted by those who hate the collective image that they
hold as cosmic enemy. This was brought home to me in Gaza when I talked
with Dr. Abdul Aziz Rantisi about the Hamas movement's attitude toward
America and its pro-Israeli stance. As Dr. Rantisi offered me coffee in the
comfortable living room of his home, he acknowledged that the United
States was a secondary enemy because of its complicity in Israel's existence and its oppression of Palestinian Arabs. From his point of view, it deserved to be treated as an enemy. What about individual Americans, I
cautiously asked him, raising the example of American professors. Would
such people be targeted?

40   "You?" Rantisi responded, somewhat surprised. "You don't count.
You're our guest."[20]

WENDELL BERRY

> Called by the *New York Times* the "prophet of rural America," Berry was
> born in 1934 on a farm in Henry County, Kentucky where he has lived for
> most of his life, except for a year at Stanford (1958–1959) on a creative writ-
> ing fellowship and a short stint teaching at New York University. He earned
> a BA (1956) and MA in English (1957) from the University of Kentucky,
> where he taught from 1964 to 1977. He then returned to his 125-acre farm

---

[20] Interview with Rantisi, March 2, 1989.

to devote full time to laboring—literally and figuratively—in the fields as a farmer, conservationist, philosopher, and visionary, and to writing novels (*Remembering*, 1988; *A World Lost*, 1996), poetry (*The Country of Marriage*, 1973), and essays (*The Unsettling of America: Culture and Agriculture*, 1977; *Tobacco Harvest: An Elegy*, 2005). His commitment to the land and community he loves, as expressed in his writings and social philosophy, is intended to inspire others to act for the common good. His many awards include Guggenheim and Rockefeller fellowships and the Thomas Merton Award, given to people who "advance the transformation of the world." Berry's philosophy of education is to "make the standard the health of the community" rather than "the career of the student." Once you do this, he says, "you can't rule out any kind of knowledge. You need to know everything you possibly can know. . . . All the departmental walls fall down, because you can no longer feel that it's safe not to know something. And then you begin to see that . . . these specializations aren't separate at all, but are connected."

"Thoughts in the Presence of Fear," which appeared in the fall of 2001 on the OrionOnline.org website as "Thoughts on America," was published in the *South Atlantic Quarterly* (Spring 2002). This comprehensive response to "the horrors of September 11" represents a distillation of Berry's philosophical principles. Here he reflects on the implications of the end of "the unquestioning technological and economic optimism that ended on that day." He explores the largely undesirable consequences of the belief that "we should go on and on from one technological innovation to the next, which would cause the economy to 'grow' and make everything better and better. This of course implied at every point a hatred of the past, of all things inherited and free" (VI). He patiently explains why these values are wrong, and makes the case for a peaceable, self-sufficient economy, based on "thrift and care, on saving and conserving, not on excess and waste" (XXVII).

Thoughts in the Presence of Fear

I. The time will soon come when we will not be able to remember the horrors   1
of September 11 without remembering also the unquestioning technological and economic optimism that ended on that day.

II. This optimism rested on the proposition that we were living in a "new   2
world order" and a "new economy" that would "grow" on and on, bringing a prosperity of which every new increment would be "unprecedented."

III. The dominant politicians, corporate officers, and investors who   3
believed this proposition did not acknowledge that the prosperity was limited to a tiny percent of the world's people, and to an ever smaller number of people even in the United States; that it was founded upon the oppressive labor of poor people all over the world; and that its ecological

Compare and contrast this photograph of a magnificent natural phenomenon (sunset on Mt. McKinley) with the former and transient magnificence of the man-made World Trade Center. In what ways do Berry's views amplify, reinforce, or contradict your own?

costs increasingly threatened all life, including the lives of the supposedly prosperous.

4   IV. The "developed" nations had given to the "free market" the status of a god, and were sacrificing to it their farmers, farmlands, and communities, their forests, wetlands, and prairies, their ecosystems and watersheds. They had accepted universal pollution and global warming as normal costs of doing business.

5   V. There was, as a consequence, a growing worldwide effort on behalf of economic decentralization, economic justice, and ecological responsibility. We must recognize that the events of September 11 make this effort more necessary than ever. We citizens of the industrial countries must continue the labor of self-criticism and self-correction. We must recognize our mistakes.

6   VI. The paramount doctrine of the economic and technological euphoria of recent decades has been that everything depends on innovation. It was understood as desirable, and even necessary, that we should go on and on from one technological innovation to the next, which would cause the economy to "grow" and make everything better and better. This of course implied at every point a hatred of the past, of all things inherited

and free. All things superceded in our progress of innovations, whatever their value might have been, were discounted as of no value at all.

VII. We did not anticipate anything like what has now happened. We did not foresee that all our sequence of innovations might be at once overridden by a greater one: the invention of a new kind of war that would turn our previous innovations against us, discovering and exploiting the debits and the dangers that we had ignored. We never considered the possibility that we might be trapped in the webwork of communication and transport that was supposed to make us free.

VIII. Nor did we foresee that the weaponry and the war science that we marketed and taught to the world would become available, not just to recognized national governments, which possess so uncannily the power to legitimate large-scale violence, but also to "rogue nations," dissident or fanatical groups and individuals—whose violence, though never worse than that of nations, is judged by the nations to be illegitimate.

IX. We had accepted uncritically the belief that technology is only good; that it cannot serve evil as well as good; that it cannot serve our enemies as well as ourselves; that it cannot be used to destroy what is good, including our homelands and our lives.

X. We had accepted too the corollary belief that an economy (either as a money economy or as a life-support system) that is global in extent, technologically complex, and centralized is invulnerable to terrorism, sabotage, or war, and that is protectable by "national defense."

XI. We now have a clear, inescapable choice that we must make. We can continue to promote a global economic system of unlimited "free trade" among corporations, held together by long and highly vulnerable lines of communication and supply, but now recognizing that such a system will have to be protected by a hugely expensive police force that will be worldwide, whether maintained by one nation or several or all, and that such a police force will be effective precisely to the extent that it oversways the freedom and privacy of the citizens of every nation.

XII. Or we can promote a decentralized world economy which would have the aim of assuring to every nation and region a local self-sufficiency in life-supporting goods. This would not eliminate international trade, but it would tend toward a trade in surpluses after local needs had been met.

XIII. One of the gravest dangers to us now, second only to further terrorist attacks against our people, is that we will attempt to go on as before with the corporate program of global "free trade," whatever the cost in freedom and civil rights, without self-questioning or self-criticism or public debate.

XIV. This is why the substitution of rhetoric for thought, always a temptation in a national crisis, must be resisted by officials and citizens alike. It is hard for ordinary citizens to know what is actually happening in Washington in a time of such great trouble; for all we know, serious and difficult thought may be taking place there. But the talk that we are hearing from politicians, bureaucrats, and commentators has so far tended to reduce the complex problems now facing us to issues of unity, security, normality, and retaliation.

15   XV. National self-righteousness, like personal self-righteousness, is a mistake. It is misleading. It is a sign of weakness. Any war that we may make now against terrorism will come as a new installment in a history of war in which we have fully participated. We are not innocent of making war against civilian populations. The modern doctrine of such warfare was set forth and enacted by General William Tecumseh Sherman, who held that a civilian population could be declared guilty and rightly subjected to military punishment. We have never repudiated that doctrine.

16   XVI. It is a mistake also—as events since September 11 have shown—to suppose that a government can promote and participate in a global economy and at the same time act exclusively in its own interest by abrogating its international treaties and standing apart from international cooperation on moral issues.

17   XVII. And surely, in our country, under our Constitution, it is a fundamental error to suppose that any crisis or emergency can justify any form of political oppression. Since September 11, far too many public voices have presumed to "speak for us" in saying that Americans will gladly accept a reduction of freedom in exchange for greater "security." Some would, maybe. But some others would accept a reduction in security (and in global trade) far more willingly than they would accept any abridgement of our Constitutional rights.

18   XVIII. In a time such as this, when we have been seriously and most cruelly hurt by those who hate us, and when we must consider ourselves to be gravely threatened by those same people, it is hard to speak of the ways of peace and to remember that Christ enjoined us to love our enemies, but this is no less necessary for being difficult.

19   XIX. Even now we dare not forget that since the attack of Pearl Harbor—to which the present attack has been often and not usefully compared—we humans have suffered an almost uninterrupted sequence of wars, none of which has brought peace or made us more peaceable.

20   XX. The aim and result of war necessarily is not peace but victory, and any victory won by violence necessarily justifies the violence that won it and leads to further violence. If we are serious about innovation, must we not conclude that we need something new to replace our perpetual "war to end war"?

21   XXI. What leads to peace is not violence but peaceableness, which is not passivity, but an alert, informed, practiced, and active state of being. We should recognize that while we have extravagantly subsidized the means of war, we have almost totally neglected the ways of peaceableness. We have, for example, several national military academies, but not

one peace academy. We have ignored the teachings and the examples of Christ, Gandhi, Martin Luther King, and other peaceable leaders. And here we have an inescapable duty to notice also that war is profitable, whereas the means of peaceableness, being cheap or free, make no money.

XXII. The key to peaceableness is continuous practice. It is wrong to suppose that we can exploit and impoverish the poorer countries, while arming them and instructing them in the newest means of war, and then reasonably expect them to be peaceable.

XXIII. We must not again allow public emotion or the public media to caricature our enemies. If our enemies are now to be some nations of Islam, then we should undertake to know those enemies. Our schools should begin to teach the histories, cultures, arts, and language of the Islamic nations. And our leaders should have the humility and the wisdom to ask the reasons some of those people have for hating us.

XXIV. Starting with the economies of food and farming, we should promote at home, and encourage abroad, the ideal of local self-sufficiency. We should recognize that this is the surest, the safest, and the cheapest way for the world to live. We should not countenance the loss or destruction of any local capacity to produce necessary goods.

XXV. We should reconsider and renew and extend our efforts to protect the natural foundations of the human economy: soil, water, and air. We should protect every intact ecosystem and watershed that we have left, and begin restoration of those that have been damaged.

XXVI. The complexity of our present trouble suggests as never before that we need to change our present concept of education. Education is not properly an industry, and its proper use is not to serve industries, either by job-training or by industry-subsidized research. [Its] proper use is to enable citizens to live lives that are economically, politically, socially, and culturally responsible. This cannot be done by gathering or "accessing" what we now call "information"—which is to say facts without context and therefore without priority. A proper education enables young people to put their lives in order, which means knowing what things are more important than other things; it means putting first things first.

XXVII. The first thing we must begin to teach our children (and learn ourselves) is that we cannot spend and consume endlessly. We have got to learn to save and conserve. We do need a "new economy," but one that is founded on thrift and care, on saving and conserving, not on excess and waste. An economy based on waste is inherently and hopelessly violent, and war is its inevitable by-product. We need a peaceable economy.

MARY GRAHAM

Mary Graham is co-director of the Transparency Policy Project at Harvard's John F. Kennedy School of Government. Trained as a lawyer (JD George-town University Law Center, 1970) she is also a Visiting Fellow in Gover-nance Studies at the Brookings Institution, specializing in environmental policy, public access to information, regulatory policy, and U.S. politics more generally. Born in 1945, she earned a BA at Harvard/Radcliffe in 1966. Previously, she worked for the federal government as a budget examiner in the U.S. Office of Management and Budget and as a program analyst in the U.S. Department of Transportation. Through the Brookings Institution she has published *The Morning After Earth Day: New Pragmatism in Environ-mental Politics* (1999) and *Democracy by Disclosure: The Rise of Technopopulism* (2002). She has published widely in periodicals such as the *Atlantic Monthly, Issues in Science and Technology,* and *Environment.*

"The Information Wars," first published in the *Atlantic Monthly* (September 2002) cites telling instances of the restrictions, swift and seem-ingly permanent, that the federal government under the Bush adminis-tration has imposed on public access to information since September 11, 2001—vastly extending and expanding practices begun earlier. For instance, "the Justice Department initiated work on a new policy to support agency actions to keep secret *any* government information, as long as agency heads had a 'sound legal basis' for withholding it." Thus the previous policy, of honoring the public's right to know "unless the government could show 'foreseeable harm'" was reversed in a single stroke. Graham's understated conclusion, "the idea that openness can be more effective than secrecy in reducing risks," should, she claims, get far more attention than it currently receives.

The Information Wars

1   Within twenty-four hours of the terrorist attacks on the World Trade Center the federal Department of Transportation had re-moved maps of the nation's 2.2 million miles of pipe lines from its Web site. The government had created the maps only recently, to identify places where ruptures in pipes that carry oil, natural gas, or hazardous chemicals could endanger lives, property, or drinking water. In the 1990s an average of four accidents a week caused property damage of more than $5,000, in-jury, or death.

2   The removal of the maps was hardly an isolated incident. Since Sep-tember federal and state officials have stricken from Web sites and public reports thousands of pages of information about health and safety risks to Americans—information, officials say, that might somehow aid terrorists.

The Environmental Protection Agency withdrew from its Web site information about accidents, risks, and emergency plans at factories that handle dangerous chemicals. Energy regulators removed reports on power plants, transmission lines, and the transportation of radioactive materials. The Federal Aviation Administration stopped posting enforcement information about security breaches at airports and incidents that threatened airline safety. The U.S. Geological Survey removed reports on water resources and asked libraries to destroy all copies of a CD-ROM that described the characteristics of reservoirs.

Some state governments went further. Florida not only restricted access to security plans for hospitals and state facilities but also gave the president of the state senate authority to close formerly public meetings. In a directive that was itself intended to be secret, New York State's directors of public security and state operations ordered agency heads to curb public access to all "sensitive information." What, exactly, was "sensitive"? "Information related to systems, structures, individuals and services essential to the security, government or economy of the State, including telecommunications . . . electrical power, gas and oil storage and transportation, banking and finance, transportation, water supply, emergency services . . . and the continuity of government operations." Just about everything, that is.

These were extraordinary measures for extraordinary times. Administration officials moved quickly and appropriately to remove from the Web maps of nuclear-power plants and defense installations, for example. The Web, they argued, transformed previously scattered information into mosaics of opportunity for extremists. But a year after the terrorist attacks temporary emergency actions have evolved into fundamental changes in the public's right to know, and the restrictions have been driven as much by familiar politics and bureaucratic instincts as by national security. The problem comes because a new and uncertain threat has provided cover for legitimate and opportunistic measures alike.

Even before September 11 the Bush Administration had taken unprecedented steps to expand official secrecy. Early last year Vice President Dick Cheney refused to provide to Congress the names of energy-industry executives who had advised the energy-policy task force he headed. That action provoked the first lawsuit ever by the General Accounting Office against the executive branch. Also before September 11 the Justice Department initiated work on a new policy to support agency actions to keep secret *any* government information, as long as agency heads had a "sound legal basis" for withholding it. This reversed a presumption in favor of disclosure unless the government could show "foreseeable harm."

By October, President Bush was calling for new policies to shield information voluntarily provided by private companies about weaknesses in "critical infrastructure"—a malleable term that the Administration said should include telecommunications, energy, financial services, transportation, and health care. In March, Andrew Card, the White House chief of staff, ordered all agencies to adopt guidelines to prevent inappropriate disclosure of "sensitive but unclassified" information—without actually defining the term.

7   Typically, these new rules have been put into effect by memorandum, without public explanation. Missing has been any forum for weighing the risks of shutting off public access. Recent congressional debate about restricting access to critical infrastructure information under the Freedom of Information Act provided one limited step in the right direction, producing constructive ideas about how to narrow the definition of what is critical while still satisfying the concerns of national-security agencies.

8   Zealous secrecy in response to a foreign threat is not new, of course. In a Harvard commencement address this past June, Senator Daniel Patrick Moynihan reminded students that the Cold War had produced a culture of secrecy that outlived the conflict and at times actually impaired security. That culture had largely disappeared by the end of the 1990s, as a better-informed public and the growth of the Internet drove advances toward openness. The Clinton Administration declassified millions of pages of historical records, and Congress approved the Electronic Freedom of Information Act, which encouraged agencies to put information online even before it was requested.

9   The wholesale censorship of information on Web sites and in government reports carries insidious costs. Current government proposals to bar foreign nationals from working on scientific projects and to restrict publication of government-funded research could actually decrease national security. Relying on partial truths and official conclusions can create needless scares, increase risks, and ultimately change the political process.

10   Compromises that deem some members of the public more worthy than others violate basic fairness. The Environmental Protection Agency, for example, long known for its openness, now requires researchers to register before it gives them direct access to its enormous Envirofacts database. It also requires them to obtain sponsorship from a senior official and have their requests approved in advance. "The danger is that right to know is replaced by need to know," says Gary D. Bass, the director of OMB Watch and the organizer of a new coalition of environmental, health, labor, journalist, and library groups tracking secrecy changes.

11   An administration that prides itself on conducting business like a well-run corporation naturally thinks that sensitive information can and should remain proprietary. But national security is everyone's concern, and the idea that openness can be more effective than secrecy in reducing risks has received too little attention.

ELIZA GRISWOLD

Eliza Griswold, born in 1973, grew up in Philadelphia, and was educated at Princeton (BA, 1995) and Johns Hopkins (MA, in English 1997). She is a journalist who has written for the *New Yorker,* the *New York Review of Books, Harpers* and the *New York Times Magazine,* among others. Her first book of poems will be published in 2007 by Farrar, Straus and Giroux.

Buying Rations in Kabul

The Uzbek boys on Chicken Street
have never had enough to eat.
They stock from shelf to shining shelf
these G.I. meals, which boil themselves
in added water (bottled, please).   5
In twenty minutes, processed cheese
on jambalaya, followed by
a peanut-butter jamboree.
           The boys, polite,
advise on which we might prefer—   10
beef teriyaki, turkey blight—
and thank us twice for bringing peace
as, meals in hand, we leave the store.
Of course they know that any peace
that must be kept by force   15
contains another name. It's war.

World Peace: Nobel Peace Prize Awards and Speeches

14

In this final chapter it is fitting to balance terrorism against tranquillity, war against peace. To focus only on the negative would be to ignore the best that is represented by the recipients of the Nobel Prize, whose acceptance speeches comprise this chapter. Goodness, selflessness, adherence to high moral principles, as the lives and works of the Nobel Prize winners reveal, can emerge even in times of trauma—often in responses to the challenges of trauma itself. Their talks, like their works, are beacons of faith, hope, and good will. If, as Franklin Roosevelt said, "the only thing we have to fear is fear itself," we need to reinforce a value system that will enable us to lead lives governed by principles and values that bring out the best rather than the worst of our common humanity. This is the message, implied and stated overtly, by every one of these Nobel Prize winners, and one of many possible ways to interpret Walt Whitman's "A Noiseless Patient Spider" that begins this chapter (594).

These Nobel winners form an international spectrum of the brave, the bold, the morally beautiful. Some of these Nobelists are people of high visibility and power—United Nations Secretary General Kofi Annan (Egypt; photograph page 592) and national leaders Jimmy Carter (U.S.A.), Yitzak Rabin (Israel), and Frederik Willem de Klerk (South Africa). Others are religious and political leaders who have suffered extensive privations for living their beliefs: the 14th Dalai Lama (Tibet), sentenced by the Chinese to lifetime exile as the embodiment of the Tibetan Buddhists; Nelson Mandela (South Africa; see photograph with de Klerk on page 614), anti-apartheid head of the African National Congress, who was under harsh imprisonment for over a quarter century; and Aung San Suu Kyi (Myanmar; photograph page 619), Burmese pro-democracy leader confined by the military junta to house arrest for nearly ten years. Still others are people of humble origins whose advocacy of human rights and reconciliation catapulted them into international prominence—housewife turned peace activist Betty Williams (Northern Ireland) and Guatemalan champion of Mayan rights and culture, Rigoberta Menchú Tum. Activist humanitarian organizations are represented by Doctors Without Borders (Médecins Sans Frontières), whose members risk their own lives to travel to embattled parts of the world, providing medical aid to victims of genocide, massacre, rape, and other war crimes. "Ours is an ethic of refusal," explains James Orbinski. "It will not allow any moral political failure or injustice to be sanitized or cleansed of its meaning."

All of these Nobel recipients, and others (like Martin Luther King, Jr.), are "witnesses to the truth of injustice," as Orbinski says, willing to lay their lives on the line—and to lose them, as Rabin and Dr. King have done—for a moral cause. Like their lives, their words in these inspiring speeches can guide us to some answers. How we as individuals, family members, friends, and citizens can do our best not only to lead the good life but to make that life better for humankind is one of the aims of a liberal education and of this book.

Following the readings in this chapter you will find suggestions for discussion and writing. As with the readings on terrorism, the individual speeches presented here may be read in connection with or opposition to one another or the essays in the "Terrorism" chapter, and in relation to other works throughout the book, such as "The Declaration of Independence" (439–42), "The Gettysburg Address" (494), and Martin Luther King, Jr.'s "Letter From Birmingham Jail" (444–57).

WALT WHITMAN

Walt Whitman (1819–1892) was born in Long Island, New York, and worked—lazily, it was claimed—in the printing and publishing industries; held down teaching, journalism, and carpentry jobs; and served as a wound dresser during the Civil War and later as a civil servant. But his true calling was poetry, to which he devoted love, determination, and a vision that encompassed cosmic space as well as the joys of nature. Spurning stifling theories and traditions, Whitman championed the natural energy and freedom he saw in the lives of ordinary Americans—whether in city crowds or rural settings. Although his verse challenged convention, and his unashamed portrayal of physical love between men made him the target of censorship, Whitman eventually won the admiration of readers on both sides of the Atlantic. Along with Emily Dickinson, Ralph Waldo Emerson, Nathaniel Hawthorne, and Herman Melville, he helped to raise the literature of a young country to world prominence.

Whitman's poems often juxtapose details of the natural or urban landscape with landscapes of the self, bringing the exterior world into relation with the interior one. In "A Noiseless Patient Spider," written in 1868, published in 1881, the soul attempts to connect to the vast cosmos surrounding it. Perhaps the scope of this poem's vision, and the motion of reaching out beyond oneself, can serve as a model for bridging the gap between people and nations.

A Noiseless Patient Spider

A noiseless patient spider,
I mark'd where on a little promontory it stood isolated,
Mark'd how to explore the vacant vast surrounding,
It launch'd forth filament, filament, filament, out of itself,
5 Ever unreeling them, ever tirelessly speeding them.

And you O my soul where you stand,
Surrounded, detached, in measureless oceans of space,
Ceaselessly musing, venturing, throwing, seeking the spheres to connect them.
Till the bridge you will need be form'd, till the ductile anchor hold,
10 Till the gossamer thread you fling catch somewhere, O my soul.

JIMMY CARTER

Jimmy Carter, the thirty-ninth president of the United States, was born (1924) and raised in Plains, Georgia, where peanut farming, politics, and devotion to the Baptist faith were the pillars of his upbringing and have remained paramount throughout his life. He graduated in 1946 from the U.S. Naval Academy, married Rosalynn Smith, who became his partner in all activities, and served seven years as a naval officer. The Carters then returned to Plains, where they ran the family peanut farm and entered politics. In 1970 Carter was elected governor of Georgia; his administration emphasized ecology, efficiency in government, and civil rights—an orientation that led to his nomination as the Democratic candidate for president and his election in 1976. He served a single term during a period of high inflation and unemployment; although jobs increased by eight million during his presidency, efforts to reduce inflation resulted in a brief recession (coupled with the Iranian holding of the American embassy staff as hostages for fourteen months) that contributed to Ronald Reagan's landslide victory in 1980.

In the years since then, Carter has "stretched the gravitas and star power of the Oval Office to promote democratic values across the world," says the *New York Times* (Oct. 12, 2002, A8). Carter himself agrees that he has been "a better former president than president." In 1982 he founded the Carter Center, a research group at Emory University (noted in the Nobel citation), and in 1984 the Carters became leaders of Habitat for Humanity, an organization that since that time has sponsored house renovation and home ownership for more than 110,000 dwellings worldwide. Carter has been instrumental in conflict resolution throughout the world, including brokering the Camp David accords between Israel and Egypt in 1978 (see Rabin and Arafat, 606–12); seeking to settle the civil war between the Ethiopian central government and Eritrean rebels (1989); attempting to resolve the controversy over the North Korean suspected nuclear weapons program (1994); negotiating a four-month cease-fire in the civil war in Bosnia (1994); and becoming the first sitting or former president to visit Cuba since Fidel Castro took power (2002). Over the years, he has monitored elections in Liberia, Panama, Mexico, Peru, Paraguay, Nicaragua, Venezuela, East Timor, and Jamaica. Although he has written several books, including *Keeping Faith: Memoirs of a President* (1982), *Living Faith* (1996), and *An Hour Before Daylight: Memories of a Rural Boyhood* (2001), Carter has never exploited his world-wide recognition for personal gain.

Citizen of a Troubled World (2002)

... The world has changed greatly since I left the White House. Now there 1
is only one superpower, with unprecedented military and economic strength. The coming budget for American armaments will be greater than those of the next fifteen nations combined, and there are troops from the United States in many countries throughout the world. Our gross national

economy exceeds that of the three countries that follow us, and our nation's voice most often prevails as decisions are made concerning trade, humanitarian assistance, and the allocation of global wealth. This dominant status is unlikely to change in our lifetimes.

2   Great American power and responsibility are not unprecedented, and have been used with restraint and great benefit in the past. We have not assumed that super strength guarantees super wisdom, and we have consistently reached out to the international community to ensure that our own power and influence are tempered by the best common judgment.

3   Within our country, ultimate decisions are made through democratic means, which tend to moderate radical or ill-advised proposals. Constrained and inspired by historic constitutional principles, our nation has endeavored for more than two hundred years to follow the now almost universal ideals of freedom, human rights, and justice for all. . . .

4   Ladies and gentlemen: Twelve years ago, President Mikhail Gorbachev received your recognition for his preeminent role in ending the Cold War that had lasted fifty years.

5   But instead of entering a millennium of peace, the world is now, in many ways, a more dangerous place. The greater ease of travel and communication has not been matched by equal understanding and mutual respect. There is a plethora of civil wars, unrestrained by rules of the Geneva Convention, within which an overwhelming portion of the casualties are unarmed civilians who have no ability to defend themselves. And recent appalling acts of terrorism have reminded us that no nations, even superpowers, are invulnerable.

6   It is clear that global challenges must be met with an emphasis on peace, in harmony with others, with strong alliances and international consensus. Imperfect as it may be, there is no doubt that this can best be done through the United Nations, which Ralph Bunche described here in this same forum as exhibiting a "fortunate flexibility"—not merely to preserve peace but also to make change, even radical change, without violence.

7   He went on to say: "To suggest that war can prevent war is a base play on words and a despicable form of warmongering. The objective of any who sincerely believe in peace clearly must be to exhaust every honorable recourse in the effort to save the peace. The world has had ample evidence that war begets only conditions that beget further war."

8   We must remember that today there are at least eight nuclear powers on earth, and three of them are threatening to their neighbors in areas of great international tension. For powerful countries to adopt a principle of preventive war may well set an example that can have catastrophic consequences.

9   If we accept the premise that the United Nations is the best avenue for the maintenance of peace, then the carefully considered decisions of the United Nations Security Council must be enforced. All too often, the

alternative has proven to be uncontrollable violence and expanding spheres of hostility. . . .

I am not here as a public official, but as a citizen of a troubled world   10
who finds hope in a growing consensus that the generally accepted goals of society are peace, freedom, human rights, environmental quality, the alleviation of suffering, and the rule of law.

During the past decades, the international community, usually under   11
the auspices of the United Nations, has struggled to negotiate global standards that can help us achieve these essential goals. They include: the abolition of land mines and chemical weapons; an end to the testing, proliferation, and further deployment of nuclear warheads; constraints on global warming; prohibition of the death penalty, at least for children; and an international criminal court to deter and to punish war crimes and genocide. Those agreements already adopted must be fully implemented, and others should be pursued aggressively.

We must also strive to correct the injustice of economic sanctions   12
that seek to penalize abusive leaders but all too often inflict punishment on those who are already suffering from the abuse. . . .

Despite theological differences, all great religions share common com-   13
mitments that define our ideal secular relationships. I am convinced that Christians, Muslims, Buddhists, Hindus, Jews, and others can embrace each other in a common effort to alleviate human suffering and to espouse peace.

But the present era is a challenging and disturbing time for those   14
whose lives are shaped by religious faith based on kindness toward each other. We have been reminded that cruel and inhuman acts can be derived from distorted theological beliefs, as suicide bombers take the lives of innocent human beings, draped falsely in the cloak of God's will. With horrible brutality, neighbors have massacred neighbors in Europe, Asia, and Africa.

In order for us human beings to commit ourselves personally to the   15
inhumanity of war, we find it necessary first to dehumanize our opponents, which is in itself a violation of the beliefs of all religions. Once we characterize our adversaries as beyond the scope of God's mercy and grace, their lives lose all value. We deny personal responsibility when we plant landmines and, days or years later, a stranger to us—often a child—is crippled or killed. From a great distance, we launch bombs or missiles with almost total impunity, and never want to know the number or identity of the victims.

. . . The most serious and universal problem [today] is the growing   16
chasm between the richest and poorest people on earth. Citizens of the ten wealthiest countries are now seventy-five times richer than those who live in the ten poorest ones, and the separation is increasing every year, not only between nations but also within them. The results of this disparity are root causes of most of the world's unresolved problems, including

starvation, illiteracy, environmental degradation, violent conflict, and unnecessary illnesses that range from Guinea worm to HIV/AIDS.

17   Most work of The Carter Center is in remote villages in the poorest nations of Africa, and there I have witnessed the capacity of destitute people to persevere under heartbreaking conditions. I have come to admire their judgment and wisdom, their courage and faith, and their awesome accomplishments when given a chance to use their innate abilities.

18   But tragically, in the industrialized world there is a terrible absence of understanding or concern about those who are enduring lives of despair and hopelessness. We have not yet made the commitment to share with others an appreciable part of our excessive wealth. This is a potentially rewarding burden that we should all be willing to assume.

19   Ladies and gentlemen:

20   War may sometimes be a necessary evil. But no matter how necessary, it is always an evil, never a good. We will not learn how to live together in peace by killing each other's children.

21   The bond of our common humanity is stronger than the divisiveness of our fears and prejudices. God gives us the capacity for choice. We can choose to alleviate suffering. We can choose to work together for peace. We can make these changes—and we must.

22   Thank you.

KOFI ANNAN

Since 1997 Kofi Annan of Ghana has been the secretary-general of the United Nations, where he has spent his entire career. Born in 1938 in Kumasi, Ghana, Kofi Annan completed an undergraduate degree in economics at Macalester College in St. Paul, Minnesota, in 1961 and studied economics in Geneva from 1961 to 1962 before beginning work at the UN as a budget officer with the World Health Organization in Geneva. As a Sloan Fellow (1971–1972) he earned an MS in management from M.I.T. He later served with the UN Economic Commission for Africa in Addis Ababa; the UN Emergency Force in Ismailia; and the Office of the UN High Commissioner for Refugees in Geneva. At the UN in New York he held a variety of posts, among them assistant secretary-general for human resources management, controller, assistant secretary-general for peacekeeping, and under secretary-general during a period of unprecedented growth in UN peacekeeping operations around the world. He was chosen as the seventh secretary-general of the UN in January of 1997. The 2001 Nobel Peace Prize was awarded to both the United Nations and to Kofi Annan for "their work for a better organized and more peaceful world. For one hundred years," says the citation, "the Norwegian Nobel Committee has sought to strengthen organized cooperation between states. The end of the cold war has at last made it possible for the UN to perform more fully the part it was originally intended to play. Today the organization is at the forefront of efforts to achieve peace and security in the world," and of international efforts to meet the world's economic, social, and environmental challenges. These include significant action on human rights and providing humanitarian aid to countries experiencing famine, drought, and medical epidemics such as HIV/AIDS. Since 1998 Annan's particular emphasis has been on "The Causes of Conflict and the Promotion of Durable Peace and Sustainable Development in Africa," "the most disadvantaged of the world's regions." During his tenure as under secretary-general, Annan supervised the expansion of UN peacekeeping operations around the world (including Kuwait, Iraq, Bosnia and Herzegovina) to, in 1995, 70,000 military and civilian personnel from seventy-seven countries.

The United Nations in the 21st Century (2001)

We have entered the third millennium through a gate of fire. If today, after the horror of 11 September, we see better, and we see further— we will realize that humanity is indivisible. New threats make no distinction between races, nations or regions. A new insecurity has entered every mind, regardless of wealth or status. A deeper awareness of the bonds that bind us all—in pain as in prosperity—has gripped young and old.

In the early beginnings of the 21st century—a century already violently disabused of any hopes that progress towards global peace and prosperity is inevitable—this new reality can no longer be ignored. It must be confronted.

The 20th century was perhaps the deadliest in human history, devastated by innumerable conflicts, untold suffering, and unimaginable crimes. Time after time, a group or a nation inflicted extreme violence on another, often driven by irrational hatred and suspicion, or unbounded arrogance and thirst for power and resources. In response to these cataclysms, the leaders of the world came together at mid-century to unite the nations as never before.

A forum was created—the United Nations—where all nations could join forces to affirm the dignity and worth of every person, and to secure peace and development for all peoples. Here States could unite to strengthen the rule of law, recognize and address the needs of the poor, restrain man's brutality and greed, conserve the resources and beauty of nature, sustain the equal rights of men *and* women, and provide for the safety of future generations.

We thus inherit from the 20th century the political, as well as the scientific and technological power, which—if only we have the will to use them—give us the chance to vanquish poverty, ignorance and disease.

6   In the 21st Century I believe the mission of the United Nations will be defined by a new, more profound, awareness of the sanctity and dignity of every human life, regardless of race or religion. This will require us to look beyond the framework of States, and beneath the surface of nations or communities. We must focus, as never before, on improving the conditions of the individual men and women who give the state or nation its richness and character. We must begin with the young Afghan girl [born in poverty], recognizing that saving that one life is to save humanity itself.

7   Over the past five years, I have often recalled that the United Nations' Charter begins with the words: "We the peoples." What is not always recognized is that "we the peoples" are made up of individuals whose claims to the most fundamental rights have too often been sacrificed in the supposed interests of the state or the nation.

8   A genocide begins with the killing of one man—not for what he has done, but because of who he is. A campaign of "ethnic cleansing" begins with one neighbour turning on another. Poverty begins when even one child is denied his or her fundamental right to education. What begins with the failure to uphold the dignity of one life, all too often ends with a calamity for entire nations.

9   In this new century, we must start from the understanding that peace belongs not only to states or peoples, but to each and every member of those communities. The sovereignty of States must no longer be used as a shield for gross violations of human rights. Peace must be made real and tangible in the daily existence of every individual in need. Peace must be sought, above all, because it is the condition for every member of the human family to live a life of dignity and security.

10   The rights of the individual are of no less importance to immigrants and minorities in Europe and the Americas than to women in Afghanistan or children in Africa. They are as fundamental to the poor as to the rich; they are as necessary to the security of the developed world as to that of the developing world.

11   From this vision of the role of the United Nations in the next century flow three key priorities for the future: eradicating poverty, preventing conflict, and promoting democracy. Only in a world that is rid of poverty can all men and women make the most of their abilities. Only where individual rights are respected can differences be channelled politically and resolved peacefully. Only in a democratic environment, based on respect for diversity and dialogue, can individual self-expression and self-government be secured, and freedom of association be upheld. . . .

12   The idea that there is one people in possession of the truth, one answer to the world's ills, or one solution to humanity's needs, has done untold harm throughout history—especially in the last century. Today, however, even amidst continuing ethnic conflict around the world, there is a growing understanding that human diversity is both the reality that makes dialogue necessary, and the very basis for that dialogue.

We understand, as never before, that each of us is fully worthy of the   13
respect and dignity essential to our common humanity. We recognize that
we are the products of many cultures, traditions and memories; that mutual respect allows us to study and learn from other cultures; and that we
gain strength by combining the foreign with the familiar.

In every great faith and tradition one can find the values of tolerance   14
and mutual understanding. The Qur'an, for example, tells us that "We
created you from a single pair of male and female and made you into
nations and tribes, that you may know each other." Confucius urged his
followers: "when the good way prevails in the state, speak boldly and act
boldly. When the state has lost the way, act boldly and speak softly." In the
Jewish tradition, the injunction to "love thy neighbour as thyself," is considered to be the very essence of the Torah.

This thought is reflected in the Christian Gospel, which also teaches us   15
to love our enemies and pray for those who wish to persecute us. Hindus
are taught that "truth is one, the sages give it various names." And in the
Buddhist tradition, individuals are urged to act with compassion in every
facet of life.

Each of us has the right to take pride in our particular faith or heri-   16
tage. But the notion that what is ours is necessarily in conflict with what
is theirs is both false and dangerous. It has resulted in endless enmity and
conflict, leading men to commit the greatest of crimes in the name of a
higher power.

It need not be so. People of different religions and cultures live side by   17
side in almost every part of the world, and most of us have overlapping
identities which unite us with very different groups. We *can* love what we
are, without hating what—and who—we are *not*. We can thrive in our own
tradition, even as we learn from others, and come to respect their teachings.

This will not be possible, however, without freedom of religion, of   18
expression, of assembly, and basic equality under the law. Indeed, the lesson of the past century has been that where the dignity of the individual
has been trampled or threatened—where citizens have not enjoyed the
basic right to choose their government, or the right to change it regularly—
conflict has too often followed, with innocent civilians paying the price, in
lives cut short and communities destroyed.

The obstacles to democracy have little to do with culture or religion,   19
and much more to do with the desire of those in power to maintain their
position at any cost. This is neither a new phenomenon nor one confined to
any particular part of the world. People of all cultures value their freedom
of choice, and feel the need to have a say in decisions affecting their lives.

The United Nations, whose membership comprises almost all the   20
States in the world, is founded on the principle of the equal worth of every
human being. It is the nearest thing we have to a representative institution
that can address the interests of all states, and all peoples. Through this
universal, indispensable instrument of human progress, States can serve

the interests of their citizens by recognizing common interests and pursuing them in unity. No doubt, that is why the Nobel Committee says that it "wishes, in its centenary year, to proclaim that the only negotiable route to global peace and cooperation goes by way of the United Nations."

21   I believe the Committee also recognized that this era of global challenges leaves no choice but cooperation at the global level. When States undermine the rule of law and violate the rights of their individual citizens, they become a menace not only to their own people, but also to their neighbours, and indeed the world. What we need today is better governance—legitimate, democratic governance that allows each individual to flourish, and each State to thrive.

JAMES ORBINSKI, M.D., AND MÉDECINS SANS FRONTIÈRES (DOCTORS WITHOUT BORDERS)

"Médecins Sans Frontières" ("Doctors Without Borders") received the Nobel Peace Prize in 1999 for "pioneering humanitarian work on several continents." The Nobel citation explains, "Since its foundation in the early 1970s, Médecins Sans Frontières has adhered to the fundamental principle that all disaster victims, whether the disaster is natural or human in origin, have a right to professional assistance, delivered as quickly and efficiently as possible. National boundaries and political circumstances or sympathies must have no influence on who is to receive humanitarian help." MSF has remained independent. It moves into hostile and dangerous situations rapidly, and in the process of treating victims of crisis, pinpoints the causes of such catastrophes and helps to influence public opinion to oppose violations and abuses of power and to effect reconciliation among warring parties. "At the same time, each fearless and self-sacrificing" helper—doctor, nurse, aide—"shows each victim a human face, stands for respect for that person's dignity, and is a source of hope for peace and reconciliation."

James Orbinski, MD, president of Médecins Sans Frontières from 1998 to 2000, accepted the award on behalf of the organization. Born in the United Kingdom in 1960, Orbinski moved to Montreal in 1968, earned a bachelor's degree from Trent College in 1984 and an MD from McMaster Medical School in 1990. After spending his final year of medical school in Rwanda doing pediatric AIDS research, he formed MSF Canada in 1990 and worked with MSF during the Somalian civil war (1992), in Afghanistan during the civil war (1993), in Rwanda during the genocide (1994), in Zaire during the early stages of the civil war (1996), and in Zaire on the National Immunization program. After a year at the University of Toronto (1997–1998) to earn an MA in international relations, as MSF president Orbinski spent time in—among other places—Sudan, Kosovo, Albania, Russia, Cambodia, and South Africa.

Humanitarianism (1999)

T he honor you give us today could so easily go to so many organiza- 1
tions, or worthy individuals, who struggle in their own society. But
clearly, you have made a choice to recognize MSF. We began formally in
1971 as a group of French doctors and journalists who decided to make
themselves available to assist. This meant sometimes a rejection of the
practices of states that directly assault the dignity of people. Silence has
long been confused with neutrality, and has been presented as a necessary
condition for humanitarian action. From its beginning, MSF was created in
opposition to this assumption. We are not sure that words can always save
lives, but we know that silence can certainly kill. Over our 28 years we
have been—and are today—firmly and irrevocably committed to this ethic
of refusal. This is the proud genesis of our identity, and today we struggle
as an imperfect movement, but strong in thousands of volunteers and national staff, and with millions of donors who support both financially and
morally, the project that is MSF. This honor is shared with all who in one
way or another, have struggled and do struggle every day to make live
the fragile reality that is MSF.

Humanitarianism occurs where the political has failed or is in crisis. 2
We act not to assume political responsibility, but firstly to relieve the inhuman suffering of failure. The act must be free of political influence, and the
political must recognize its responsibility to ensure that the humanitarian
can exist. Humanitarian action requires a framework in which to act.

In conflict, this framework is international humanitarian law. It es- 3
tablishes rights for victims and humanitarian organisations and fixes the
responsibility of states to ensure respect of these rights and to sanction their
violation as war crimes. Today this framework is clearly dysfunctional. Access to victims of conflict is often refused. Humanitarian assistance is even
used as a tool of war by belligerents. And more seriously, we are seeing the
militarisation of humanitarian action by the international community.

In this dysfunction, we will speak-out to push the political to assume 4
its inescapable responsibility. Humanitarianism is not a tool to end war or
to create peace. It is a citizen's response to political failure. It is an immediate, short term act that cannot erase the long term necessity of political
responsibility.

And ours is an ethic of refusal. It will not allow any moral political 5
failure or injustice to be sanitized or cleansed of its meaning. The 1992
crimes against humanity in Bosnia-Herzegovina. The 1994 genocide in
Rwanda. The 1997 massacres in Zaire. The 1999 actual attacks on civilians
in Chechnya. These cannot be masked by terms like "Complex Humanitarian Emergency," or "Internal Security Crisis." Or by any other such euphemism—as though they are some random, politically undetermined event.
Language is determinant. It frames the problem and defines response, rights

and therefore responsibilities. It defines whether a medical or humanitarian response is adequate. And it defines whether a political response is inadequate. No one calls a rape a complex gynecologic emergency. A rape is a rape, just as a genocide is a genocide. And both are a crime. For MSF, this is the humanitarian act: to seek to relieve suffering, to seek to restore autonomy, to witness to the truth of injustice, and to insist on political responsibility.

6   The work that MSF chooses does not occur in a vacuum, but in a social order that both includes and excludes, that both affirms and denies, and that both protects and attacks. Our daily work is a struggle, and it is intensely medical, and it is intensely personal. MSF is not a formal institution, and with any luck at all, it never will be. It is a civil society organization, and today civil society has a new global role, a new informal legitimacy that is rooted in its action and in its support from public opinion. It is also rooted in the maturity of its intent, in for example the human rights, the environmental and the humanitarian movements, and of course, the movement for equitable trade. Conflict and violence are not the only subjects of concern. We, as members of civil society, will maintain our role and our power if we remain lucid in our intent and independence.

7   As civil society we exist relative to the state, to its institutions and its power. We also exist relative to other non-state actors such as the private sector. Ours is not to displace the responsibility of the state. Ours is not to allow a humanitarian alibi to mask the state responsibility to ensure justice and security. And ours is not to be co-managers of misery with the state. If civil society identifies a problem, it is not theirs to provide a solution, but it is theirs to expect that states will translate this into concrete and just solutions. Only the state has the legitimacy and power to do this. Today, a growing injustice confronts us. More than 90% of all death and suffering from infectious diseases occurs in the developing world. Some of the reasons that people die from diseases like AIDS, TB, Sleeping Sickness and other tropical diseases is that life saving essential medicines are either too expensive, are not available because they are not seen as financially viable, or because there is virtually no new research and development for priority tropical diseases. This market failure is our next challenge. The challenge however, is not ours alone. It is also for governments, International Government Institutions, the Pharmaceutical Industry and other NGOs to confront this injustice. What we as a civil society movement demand is change, not charity.

8   We affirm the independence of the humanitarian from the political, but this is not to polarize the "good" NGO against "bad" governments, or the "virtue" of civil society against the "vice" of political power. Such a polemic is false and dangerous. As with slavery and welfare rights, history has shown that humanitarian preoccupations born in civil society have gained influence until they reach the political agenda. But these convergences should not mask the distinctions that exist between the political and the humanitarian. Humanitarian action takes place in the short term, for

limited groups and for limited objectives. This is at the same time both its strength and its limitation. The political can only be conceived in the long term, which itself is the movement of societies. Humanitarian action is by definition universal, or it is not. Humanitarian responsibility has no frontiers. Wherever in the world there is manifest distress, the humanitarian by vocation must respond. By contrast, the political knows borders, and where crisis occurs, political response will vary because historical relations, balance of power, and the interests of one or the other must be considered. The time and space of the humanitarian are not those of the political. These vary in opposing ways, and this is another way to locate the founding principles of humanitarian action: the refusal of all forms of problem solving through sacrifice of the weak and vulnerable. No victim can be intentionally discriminated against, OR neglected to the advantage of another. One life today cannot be measured by its value tomorrow: and the relief of suffering "here," cannot legitimize the abandoning of relief "over there." The limitation of means naturally must mean the making of choice, but the context and the constraints of action do not alter the fundamentals of this humanitarian vision. It is a vision that by definition must ignore political choices.

===========

YITZAK RABIN AND YASSER ARAFAT

Yitzak Rabin (Israel, born in Jerusalem in 1922) and Shimon Peres (Israel, born in Poland in 1923) shared the 1994 Nobel Peace Prize with Yasser Arafat (a Palestinian born in Cairo in 1929) for their efforts to create peace in the Middle East. For years they were military commanders on opposing sides, in a protracted and bloody struggle "among the most irreconcilable and menacing in international politics," acknowledges the Nobel citation: "The parties have caused each other great suffering." For more than thirty years Arafat, in pursuit of his dream of an independent Palestinian homeland, waged war against Israel. His revolutionary leadership of the Palestine Liberation Organization (PLO)—driven out of Jordan by its violent guerrilla attacks on Israel and out of Lebanon by the Israeli army—kept him constantly on the move, always in secret. He survived a plane crash, assassination attempts by Israeli intelligence agencies, and a stroke. In 1988 Arafat announced a major change of policy in a speech to the United Nations. The PLO renounced terrorism, he said, and supported "the right of all parties concerned in the Middle East conflict to live in peace and security, including the state of Palestine, Israel and other neighbors." This trio of military commanders brokered the Oslo Accords of 1993, which, acknowledged the Nobel citation, "called for great courage on both sides, and which opened up opportunities for a new development towards fraternity in the Middle East," including the establishment of a Palestinian state. Arafat died in 2004.

Peres was the director-general of the Ministry of Defense from 1952 to 1959, and minister of defense from 1974 to 1977. He later served in the government as prime minister and a variety of other capacities. At the time of the Nobel award he was serving his second term as Israel's minister of foreign affairs. Always a writer, amidst continuous public service Peres wrote hundreds of articles and essays and seven books, including *David's Sling* (1970) and *Battling for Peace* (1995). Rabin's military career began in 1940, when at eighteen he joined the "Palmach," the elite unit of the Haganah. He served for twenty-eight years in Israel's defense, commanding the Israeli Defense Forces during the Six-Day War. After serving as ambassador to the United States (1968–1973), he became simultaneously active in the Israeli government and in peace efforts in the Middle East, negotiating disengagement agreements with Egypt and Syria (1974). In 1985, as minister of defense (1984–1990), he presented the proposal for withdrawing IDF forces from Lebanon and establishing a security zone to guarantee peace to the settlements along Israel's northern frontier. Despite the activity of suicide bombers in July 1994, and April and October 1995, a peace treaty between Jordan and Israel was signed in October 1995. Sadly, Rabin was assassinated shortly thereafter, on November 4, 1995. Even more sadly, the current disintegration of the Oslo Accords reveals the fragility of the hopes and dreams for permanent peace in the Middle East.

Yitzhak Rabin, The One Radical Solution Is Peace (1994)

1   . . . I wanted to be a water engineer. I studied in an agricultural school and I thought that being a water engineer was an important profession in the parched Middle East. I still think so today. However, I was compelled to resort to the gun.

2   I served in the military for decades. Under my command, young men and women who wanted to live, wanted to love, went to their deaths instead. Under my command, they killed the enemy's men who had been sent out to kill us.

3   In my current position, I have ample opportunity to fly over the state of Israel, and lately over other parts of the Middle East, as well. The view from the plane is breathtaking: deep-blue lakes, dark-green fields, dun-coloured deserts, stone-gray mountains, and the entire countryside peppered with white-washed, red-roofed houses.

4   And cemeteries. Graves as far as the eye can see. . . .

5   I was a young man who has now grown fully in years. And of all the memories I have stored up in my seventy-two years, what I shall remember most, to my last day, are the silences:

6   The heavy silence of the moment after, and the terrifying silence of the moment before.

As a military man, as a commander, I issued orders for dozens, probably hundreds of military operations. And together with the joy of victory and grief of bereavement, I shall always remember the moment just after taking the decision to mount an action: the hush as senior officers or cabinet ministers slowly rise from their seats; the sight of their receding backs; the sound of the closing door; and then the silence in which I remain alone. 7

That is the moment you grasp that as a result of the decision just made, people will be going to their deaths. People from my nation, people from other nations. And they still don't know it. 8

At that hour, they are still laughing and weeping; still weaving plans and dreams about love; still musing about planting a garden or building a house—and they have no idea these are their last hours on earth. Which of them is fated to die? Whose picture will appear in a black border in tomorrow's newspaper? Whose mother will soon be in mourning? Whose world will crumble under the weight of the loss? 9

As a former military man, I will also forever remember the silence of the moment before: the hush when the hands of the clock seem to be spinning forward, when time is running out and in another hour, another minute, the inferno will erupt. 10

In that moment of great tension just before the finger pulls the trigger, just before the fuse begins to burn; in the terrible quiet of that moment, there's still time to wonder, alone: Is it really imperative to act? Is there no other choice? No other way? 11

And then the order is given, and the inferno begins. . . . 12

For decades God has not taken pity on the kindergarteners in the Middle East, or the schoolchildren, or their elders. There has been no pity in the Middle East for generations. . . . 13

A child is born into an utterly undemocratic world. He cannot choose his father and mother. He cannot pick his sex or colour, his religion, nationality, or homeland. Whether he is born in a manor or a manger, whether he lives under a despotic or democratic regime, is not his choice. From the moment he comes, close-fisted, into the world, his fate lies in the hands of his nation's leaders. It is they who will decide whether he lives in comfort or despair, in security or in fear. His fate is given to us to resolve—to the Presidents and Prime Ministers of countries, democratic or otherwise. 14

Just as no two fingerprints are identical, so no two people are alike, and every country has its own laws and culture, traditions and leaders. But there is one universal message which can embrace the entire world, one precept which can be common to different regimes, to races which bear no resemblance, to cultures alien to each other. 15

It is a message which the Jewish people has borne for thousands of years, a message found in the Book of Books . . . in the words in Deuteronomy: "Therefore take good heed to yourselves"—or, in contemporary terms, the message of the Sanctity of Life. 16

17   The leaders of nations must provide their peoples with the conditions—the "infrastructure," if you will—which enables them to enjoy life: freedom of speech and of movement; food and shelter; and most important of all: life itself. A man cannot enjoy his rights if he is not among the living. And so every country must protect and preserve the key element in its national ethos: the lives of its citizens.

18   To defend those lives, we call upon our citizens to enlist in the army. And to defend the lives of our citizens serving in the army, we invest huge sums in planes, and tanks, in armored plating and concrete fortifications. Yet despite it all, we fail to protect the lives of our citizens and soldiers. Military cemeteries in every corner of the world are silent testimony to the failure of national leaders to sanctify human life.

19   There is only one radical means of sanctifying human lives. Not armored plating, or tanks, or planes, or concrete fortifications.

20   The one radical solution is peace.

21   The profession of soldiering embraces a certain paradox. We take the best and bravest of our young men into the army. We supply them with equipment which costs a virtual fortune. We rigorously train them for the day when they must do their duty—and we expect them to do it well. Yet we fervently pray that day will never come—that the planes will never take flight, the tanks will never move forward, the soldiers will never mount the attacks for which they have been trained so well.

22   We pray it will never happen because of the Sanctity of Life.

23   History as a whole, and modern history in particular, has known harrowing times when national leaders turned their citizens into cannon fodder in the name of wicked doctrines: vicious Fascism and fiendish Nazism. Pictures of children marching to the slaughter, photos of terrified women at the gates of crematoria must loom before the eyes of every leader in our generation, and the generations to come. They must serve as a warning to all who wield power.

24   Almost all the regimes which did not place man and the Sanctity of Life at the heart of their world view, all those regimes have collapsed and are no more. You can see it for yourselves in our own day.

25   Yet this is not the whole picture. To preserve the Sanctity of Life, we must sometimes risk it. Sometimes there is no other way to defend our citizens than to fight for their lives, for their safety and sovereignty. This is the creed of every democratic state. . . .

26   In the coming days, a special Commission of the Israel Defence Forces will finish drafting a Code of Conduct for our soldiers. The formulation regarding human life will read as follows, and I quote:

> In recognition of its supreme importance, the soldier will preserve human life in every way possible and endanger himself, or others, only to the extent deemed necessary to fulfil this mission.

"Wars themselves shatter every boundary imaginable," says military scholar Alex Vernon, "from national boundaries to bodily ones, often confusing distinctions between social castes as well as between friends and foes, men and women, humans and animals, humans and machines, the living and the dead" (*Arms and the Self* 6). Natural disasters, such as earthquakes and hurricanes, wreak the same mayhem on civilization as do wars and acts of terrorism. As such disasters threaten and take life itself, they inexorably, inevitably disrupt the survivors' daily lives, ordinary human relations, and normal communication. The heart of one's universe, if not the entire world, beat in a steadily predictable way before disaster struck; afterward, all was "changed, changed utterly." The photographs is this section disclose the inextricable relations between war and peace, explicitly or by implication.

In the midst of destruction people—ordinary and extraordinary folk, victims, survivors, and heroes alike—find perspective and consolation in the familiar, what they know and cherish and where they come from, rather than the void created as these comforts disappear. It is reassuring to wrap oneself in the country's flag, figuratively donning the fabric of patriotism no matter what that very image may symbolize to those antagonistic or indifferent to the nation whose flag is displayed. Indeed, the American flag in the iconic photographs 1 and 2 is a powerful symbol of national unity, signaled by the fact that our flag proudly waves in times of crisis—such as that of the terrorist attacks on the World Trade Center (photograph 2) which became iconic at the moment of its destruction. This potent image of the flag also resonates in the patriotically-painted barn roof in photograph 4. But what are viewers to make of the flag on the lap of the "Bicentennial Indian" (photograph 3)? Although the Indian wears half-glasses and holds a large plume that echoes paintings of our Founding Fathers, were not the Indians themselves America's actual founding people? Who took their land and relegated them to reservations? It is essential to know something of the country's history and current events to fully appreciate the meanings of what we're looking at, even if what we see makes us uncomfortable.

Whether or not Americans are visible in the last three photographs of children in Iraq, Afghanistan, and a mother and baby in Vietnam, their historical presence is palpable in these photographs. In photograph 5, four troops in full battle armor, rifles at the ready, stride through a street in Iraq to the stares of seven young unarmed boys; no matter what nationality the troops, they are there as a consequence of America's foreign policy. The war in Afghanistan is somewhat more distant, in time and in American presence, which remains there to this day in the hunt for Osama Bin Laden, yet the children in photograph 6 play with a balloon against the backdrop of buildings destroyed and never rebuilt. Photograph 7, of a smiling Hmong girl in tribal dress carrying a baby in a frilly pink cap on her back through a rice field in Binh Lu, Vietnam, was taken in 2003, twenty-two years after the end of the Vietnam War. The bitter contrast to this peaceful scene lies in the viewers' minds and memories of this most devastating conflict that ravaged the country from 1954 to 1975.

These photographs and Fritz Scholder's lithograph, taken singly or together, provide a visual political commentary on the United States' self-image, seen from various perspectives, historical and contemporary, gaining resonance—straightforward or ironic—from their juxtaposition. Without romanticizing the subject, the last three photographs also disclose, through the innocence of children, that there is hope for peace and reconciliation, and that many of these great expectations reside with the young.

Photograph 1: Marines Raising the Flag on Mount Suribachi, Iwo Jima, February 25, 1945.
Near the end of World War II Iwo Jima, five miles long and 700 miles south of Tokyo, was occupied by 21,000 Japanese troops living in miles of caves, trenches, and connecting tunnels. Mount Suribachi, its highest point, was taken after twenty days of yard-by-yard fighting, in which 6,821 Americans and all but 200 of the Japanese troops were killed. Joe Rosenthal photographed this scene that marked "an incident in the turn of the battle" that had been touch and go up to that point. Writing in Collier's ten years later, Rosenthal observed that within a decade this was "the most widely reproduced photograph of all time," appearing on 3¢ postage stamps, 3,500,000 postcards, 15,000 outdoor panels, and reproduced in "oils, watercolors, pastels, chalk, and matchsticks," as well as in a prizewinning Rose Bowl parade float. "It has been sculptured in ice and in hamburger and, by the Seabees, in sandstone on Iwo Jima."

CONSIDERING THE IMAGE

1. Although the photograph's patriotic appeal as a symbol of victory—impending and finally achieved in World War II—is obvious, why would this picture, rather than many other illustrations of heroism, become so instantaneously beloved? How do you account for its continued popularity throughout the United States during the subsequent sixty years?

2. Analyze the composition of the photograph. Why is the flag the focal point? What leads the viewer's eyes to it? What does the grouping of the Marines convey about the way they work? About the country they represent? During subsequent wars, what does this picture say in response to divided popular opinion? How can politics dictate interpretation?

Photograph 2: Firefighters Raising the American Flag in the Wreckage of the World Trade Center After the Terrorist Attack on September 11, 2001. *Thomas E. Franklin of the Bergen (Bergen County, New Jersey) Record took this digital news photo that became the cover picture of a special* Newsweek *issue on September 24, 2001. Like Rosenthal's picture of the flag raising at Iwo Jima, this too has become a highly symbolic work, widely-reproduced and greatly admired. Journalism professor Mark Danner comments, "Seldom has an image so clearly marked the turning of the world. One of man's mightiest structures collapses into an immense white blossom of churning, roiling dust, metamorphosing in 14 seconds from hundred-story giant of the earth into towering white plume reaching to heaven. The demise of the World Trade Center gave us an image as newborn to the world of sight as the mushroom cloud must have appeared to those who first cast eyes on it"* (New York Times Magazine, September 11, 2005, p. 46).

CONSIDERING THE IMAGE

1. In what ways does Franklin's photograph gain in meaning for those who have also seen "Flag Raising on Iwo Jima, February 25, 1945"? What are your visual clues that the resemblance of the two photographs is more than coincidental? Are the events commemorated as similar as these photographs make them seem? In what ways are they different?

2. What messages does the Franklin photograph send? Given the differences in time, place, and historical context, are these the same or different from the message of Rosenthal's photograph? Why is it important that the flag is in the process of being raised, rather than say, fully furled on the flagpole?

3. James Nachtwey, whose career is devoted to photographing genocide and destruction around the world, observed "When I saw Ground Zero I was in a state of disbelief. I was in Grozny when it was being pulverized by Russian artillery and aircraft. I spent a couple of years in Beirut during various sieges and bombardments. But now it was literally in my own backyard, and I think one thing Americans are learning from this is that now we are a part of the world in a way we never have been before. . . ." (from "Ground Zero," *American Photo* 13.1 Jan./Feb. 2002). Is Nachtwey right? Has the terrorist attack on the World Trade Center caused Americans to become "part of the world" in ways hitherto inconceivable? If so, in what ways? If not, why not?

Photograph 3: "Bicentennial Indian" from "Spirit of Independence," by Fritz Scholder, 1974–1975. *This lithograph in four colors is characteristic of many of Scholder's works, particularly in the 1970s, during the era of the Vietnam War and its bitter aftermath. These works, with graphic and sardonic humor analogous to Sherman Alexie's writings (92–96), illustrate the jarring intersection of Indian and Anglo history in the United States and attempt to undo the "noble savage" depictions of America's first peoples in paintings, photographs, and written works.*

CONSIDERING THE IMAGE

1. In what ways does this 1974–1975 lithograph of "Bicentennial Indian" comment on the United States Bicentennial? On Indians in the United States? On the relation between U.S. "bicentennial" and "Indian"? What are some typical American knee-jerk reactions to 1776 and how has subsequent history modified these, if at all?

2. This lithograph by Scholder (who was part Indian) rejects the clichés of predictable, romanticized art on Native American themes, and instead fuses abstract expressionism, surrealism, and pop art to provide ironic, sardonic commentary on the position of Indians in contemporary society. Whether or not you feel comfortable with these artistic terms, explain what you see in this painting. What does it mean to you? Does it seem sarcastic? Does it remind you of either portraits of America's Founding Fathers or of Betsy Ross with the first American flag on her lap? Explain your answer. Does your ethnic background and family history influence your interpretation?

Photograph 4: Painting a Flag on a Barn Roof. *This photograph of a man painting a flag on a barn roof was taken sometime between 1990 and 2001, somewhere in the United States. Its very anonymity may reveal the potential of such folk painting for broad declarations of patriotism anywhere, everywhere in the country, at any time. However, such affirmations are most often made explicit when artists feel their values are threatened—particularly in times of war. Whether this barn roof is a response to the American invasion of Iraq in the Persian Gulf War in 1991, or a reaction to the terrorist attacks of September 11 is a matter for speculation, though the glimpse of the model of the car to the left of the barn might argue for the earlier date.*

Considering the Image

1. In rural America it's common to paint ads and slogans on barns. Who is likely to see this representation of the flag? What message is the roof painter intending to send? To what extent is this, or any photograph or painting involving the flag, a political message? Does it call out merely for recognition? Or for action of some sort? If so, what action?

2. Is the photographer merely passing along the roof painter's message, or does the photograph itself convey additional meaning? If so, what? Is the process of painting a flag on a barn roof in any ways comparable to raising the flag at either Iwo Jima or the World Trade Center?

Photograph 5: On Patrol in Baghdad. *Members of the Iraqi National Guard, some wearing masks, and the U.S. Army 256th Brigade Combat Team patrol the former insurgent stronghold of Haifa Street in Baghdad, Iraq, on May 24, 2005, after forcing out the insurgents.*

CONSIDERING THE IMAGE

1. Can you tell the nationality of these troops from their uniforms? From their physical appearance? Given their recent military success, why are they so heavily armed? Where are they going? What are they doing? What do you imagine the troops are thinking? Why are their faces obscured? How does your knowledge that this photograph was taken in Iraq in 2005 to be used as an example of the invaders' military power influence your interpretation of it?

2. In contrast, what are the boys doing? How do they regard the troops? Do they have a common reaction? How can you tell? What is the effect of the boys' casual clothing in contrast with the troops' helmets, rifles, body armor, and uniforms? Their openness and vulnerability in contrast with the covered, unidentifiable troops? Are any of these boys likely to grow up to be soldiers? Why are there no women apparent in this photograph (even with considerable magnification it is impossible to tell whether the third troop from the front is a man or woman)?

finding its true place in today's world, in an atmosphere of democracy, pluralism and prosperity.

Just as war is a great adventure, peace is a challenge and wager. If we fail 8
to endow peace with the wherewithal to withstand the tempest and the storm, if we fail to nurture peace so that it may gain in strength, if we fail to give it scope to grow and gain in strength, the wager could be wasted and lost. So, from this rostrum I call upon my partners in peace to speed up the peace process, to bring about an early withdrawal, to allow elections to be held and to move on rapidly to the next stage, so that peace may become entrenched and grow, become an established reality. . . .

. . . Even though the peace process has not reached its full scope, the 9
new environment of trust as well as the modest steps implemented during the first and second years of the peace agreement are very promising and call for the lifting of reservations, for procedures to be simplified. We must fulfil what remains, especially the transfer of power and taking further steps in Israeli withdrawal from the West Bank and the settlements to achieve full withdrawal. This would provide our society with the opportunity to rebuild its infrastructure and to contribute from its location, with its own heritage, knowledge and know-how in forging our new world. . . .

Peace cannot thrive, and the peace process cannot be consolidated in 10
the absence of the necessary material conditions.

I call on my partners in peace to reinforce the peace process with the necessary 11
comprehensive and strategic vision.

Confidence alone does not make peace. But acknowledging rights 12
and confidence do. Failure to recognize these rights creates a sense of injustice, it keeps the embers burning under the ashes. It moves peace towards the quicksands of danger and rekindles a fuse that is ready to explode.

We view peace as an historic strategic option[,] not a tactical one directed 13
by current calculations of gain or loss. The peace process is not only a political process, it is an integrated operation where national awareness, economic, scientific and technological development play a major role, just as cultural, social and creative merging play essential roles that are of the very essence of the peace process and fortify it. I review all this as I recall the difficult peace journey we have travelled; we have only covered a short distance. We have to arm ourselves with courage and utmost temerity to cover the longer distance ahead, towards the homebase of just and comprehensive peace, and to be able to assimilate that creative force of the deeper meanings of peace.

As long as we have decided to coexist in peace we must do so on a 14
firm basis that will withstand time and for generations. . . .

15   Let us protect this new-born infant from the winter winds, let us nurture it with milk and honey, from the land of milk and honey, and on the land of Salem, Abraham, Ismael and Isaac, the Holy Land, the Land of Peace.

NELSON MANDELA AND FREDERIK WILLEM DE KLERK

Nelson Mandela and Frederik Willem de Klerk shared the Nobel Peace Prize in 1993 for "their work for the peaceful termination of the apartheid regime," the citation explains, "and for laying the foundations of a new democratic South Africa." For twenty-eight years Mandela (born in Transeki, South Africa, in 1918) was the imprisoned leader of the African National Congress and—as time went on—an internationally known symbol of determined resistance to apartheid. His autobiography, *Long Walk to Freedom* (1994), explains, in serenely charitable language, the great physical and psychological fortitude he needed to endure the hard labor (which included several oppressive years of breaking rocks), isolation, and other deprivations of this long and harsh time. De Klerk (born in Johannesburg in 1936, son of Senator Jan de Klerk), who had held a series of ministerial positions in the South African government from 1978 to 1989, "was not known to advocate reform" before his election as state president in September 1989. Nevertheless, says the Nobel Prize committee, "In his first speech after assuming the party leadership he called for a nonracist South Africa and for negotiations about the country's future. He lifted the ban on the ANC and released Nelson Mandela. He brought apartheid to an end and opened the way for the drafting of a new constitution for the country based on the principle of one person, one vote." Thus, coming from very different points of departure, Mandela and de Klerk looked "ahead to South African reconciliation instead of back at the deep wounds of the past," showing "great integrity and great political courage."

Nelson Mandela,
The End of Apartheid (1993)

1   Because of their courage and persistence for many years, we can, today, even set the dates when all humanity will join together to celebrate one of the outstanding human victories of our century.

2   When that moment comes, we shall, together, rejoice in a common victory over racism, apartheid and white minority rule.

3   That triumph will finally bring to a close a history of five hundred years of African colonisation that began with the establishment of the Portuguese empire.

Thus, it will mark a great step forward in history and also serve as a 4
common pledge of the peoples of the world to fight racism, wherever it
occurs and whatever guise it assumes.

At the southern tip of the continent of Africa, a rich reward in the 5
making, an invaluable gift is in the preparation for those who suffered in
the name of all humanity when they sacrificed everything—for liberty,
peace, human dignity and human fulfillment.

This reward will not be measured in money. Nor can it be reckoned 6
in the collective price of the rare metals and precious stones that rest in the
bowels of the African soil we tread in the footsteps of our ancestors.

It will and must be measured by the happiness and welfare of the 7
children, at once the most vulnerable citizens in any society and the greatest of our treasures.

The children must, at last, play in the open veld, no longer tortured 8
by the pangs of hunger or ravaged by disease or threatened with the
scourge of ignorance, molestation and abuse, and no longer required to
engage in deeds whose gravity exceeds the demands of their tender years.

In front of this distinguished audience, we commit the new South 9
Africa to the relentless pursuit of the purposes defined in the World Declaration on the Survival, Protection and Development of Children.

The reward of which we have spoken will and must also be meas- 10
ured by the happiness and welfare of the mothers and fathers of these
children, who must walk the earth without fear of being robbed, killed for
political or material profit, or spat upon because they are beggars.

They too must be relieved of the heavy burden of despair which they 11
carry in their hearts, born of hunger, homelessness and unemployment.

The value of that gift to all who have suffered will and must be meas- 12
ured by the happiness and welfare of all the people of our country, who
will have torn down the inhuman walls that divide them.

These great masses will have turned their backs on the grave insult 13
to human dignity which described some as masters and others as servants,
and transformed each into a predator whose survival depended on the destruction of the other.

The value of our shared reward will and must be measured by the 14
joyful peace which will triumph, because the common humanity that
bonds both black and white into one human race, will have said to each
one of us that we shall all live like the children of paradise.

Thus shall we live, because we will have created a society which rec- 15
ognises that all people are born equal, with each entitled in equal measure
to life, liberty, prosperity, human rights and good governance.

Such a society should never allow again that there should be pris- 16
oners of conscience nor that any person's human right should be violated.

Neither should it ever happen that once more the avenues to peace- 17
ful change are blocked by usurpers who seek to take power away from the
people, in pursuit of their own, ignoble purposes.

South African President Nelson Mandela (on left) and South African
Deputy President F. W. de Klerk (on right) holding their Nobel Peace Prize
gold medals and diplomas on December 10, 1993. Interpret and comment on
the significance of this photograph—historical, ethical, political, human.

18   In relation to these matters, we appeal to those who govern Burma that they release our fellow Nobel Peace Prize laureate, Aung San Suu Kyi, and engage her and those she represents in serious dialogue, for the benefit of all the people of Burma.

19   We pray that those who have the power to do so will, without further delay, permit that she uses her talents and energies for the greater good of the people of her country and humanity as a whole.

20   Far from the rough and tumble of the politics of our own country. I would like to take this opportunity to join the Norwegian Nobel Committee and pay tribute to my joint laureate[,] Mr. F. W. de Klerk.

21   He had the courage to admit that a terrible wrong had been done to our country and people through the imposition of the system of apartheid.

22   He had the foresight to understand and accept that all the people of South Africa must through negotiations and as equal participants in the process, together determine what they want to make of their future.

23   But there are still some within our country who wrongly believe they can make a contribution to the cause of justice and peace by clinging to the shibboleths that have been proved to spell nothing but disaster.

24   It remains our hope that these, too, will be blessed with sufficient reason to realise that history will not be denied and that the new society

cannot be created by reproducing the repugnant past, however refined or enticingly repackaged.

We would also like to take advantage of this occasion to pay tribute to the many formations of the democratic movement of our country, including the members of our Patriotic Front, who have themselves played a central role in bringing our country as close to the democratic transformation as it is today. 25

We are happy that many representatives of these formations, including people who have served or are serving in the "homeland" structures, came with us to Oslo. They too must share the accolade which the Nobel Peace Prize confers. 26

We live with the hope that as she battles to remake herself, South Africa will be like a microcosm of the new world that is striving to be born. 27

This must be a world of democracy and respect for human rights, a world freed from the horrors of poverty, hunger, deprivation and ignorance, relieved of the threat and the scourge of civil wars and external aggression and unburdened of the great tragedy of millions forced to become refugees. 28

The processes in which South Africa and Southern Africa as a whole are engaged, beckon and urge us all that we take this tide at the flood and make of this region as a living example of what all people of conscience would like the world to be. 29

We do not believe that this Nobel Peace Prize is intended as a commendation for matters that have happened and passed. 30

We hear the voices which say that it is an appeal from all those, throughout the universe, who sought an end to the system of apartheid. 31

We understand their call, that we devote what remains of our lives to the use of our country's unique and painful experience to demonstrate, in practice, that the normal condition for human existence is democracy, justice, peace, non-racism, non-sexism, prosperity for everybody, a healthy environment and equality and solidarity among the peoples. 32

Moved by that appeal and inspired by the eminence you have thrust upon us, we undertake that we too will do what we can to contribute to the renewal of our world so that none should, in future, be described as the "wretched of the earth." 33

Let it never be said by future generations that indifference, cynicism or selfishness made us fail to live up to the ideals of humanism which the Nobel Peace Prize encapsulates. 34

Let the strivings of us all prove Martin Luther King Jr. to have been correct, when he said that humanity can no longer be tragically bound to the starless midnight of racism and war. 35

Let the efforts of us all prove that he was not a mere dreamer when he spoke of the beauty of genuine brotherhood and peace being more precious than diamonds or silver or gold. 36

Let a new age dawn! 37

Frederik Willem de Klerk, Reformation and Reconciliation in South Africa (1993)

1   F ive years ago people would have seriously questioned the sanity of anyone who would have predicted that Mr Mandela and I would be joint recipients of the 1993 Nobel Peace Prize.

2   And yet both of us are here before you today.

3   We are political opponents.

4   We disagree strongly on key issues and we will soon fight a strenuous election campaign against one another. But we will do so, I believe, in the frame of mind and within the framework of peace which has already been established.

5   We will do it—and many other leaders will do it with us—because there is no other road to peace and prosperity for the people of our country. In the conflicts of the past, there was no gain for anyone in our country. Through reconciliation all of us are now becoming winners.

6   The compromises we have reached demand sacrifices on all sides. It was not easy for the supporters of Mr Mandela or mine to relinquish the ideals they had cherished for many decades.

7   But we did it. And because we did it, there is hope.

8   The coming election will not be about the past. It will be about the future. It will not be about Blacks or Whites, or Afrikaners and Xhosas. It will be about the best solutions for the future in the interests of all our people. It will not be about apartheid or armed struggle. It will be about future peace and stability, about progress and prosperity, about nation-building.

9   In my first speech about becoming Leader of the National Party, I said on February the 8th, 1989:

10   Our goal is a new South Africa:
A totally changed South Africa;
a South Africa which has rid itself of the
antagonism of the past;
a South Africa free of domination or oppression
in whatever form;
a South Africa within which the democratic
forces—all reasonable people—align themselves
behind mutually acceptable goals and against
radicalism, irrespective of where it comes from.

11   Since then we have made impressive progress, thanks to the cooperation of political, spiritual, business and community leaders over a wide spectrum. To Mr Mandela I sincerely say: Congratulations. And in accepting

this Peace Prize today I wish to pay tribute to all who are working for peace in our land. On behalf of all South Africans who supported me, directly or indirectly, I accept it in humility, deeply aware of my own shortcomings.

I thank those who decided to make the award for the recognition   12
they have granted in doing so—recognition of a mighty deed of reformation and reconciliation that is taking place in South Africa. The road ahead is still full of obstacles and, therefore, dangerous. There is, however, no question of turning back.

AUNG SAN SUU KYI

Aung San Suu Kyi, the daughter of Burma's liberation leader Aung San, was born in Rangoon, then Burma, now Myanmar, in 1945. In 1991 she was awarded the Nobel Peace Prize, which her sons accepted on her behalf because she was under house arrest. Her father, General Aung San, then commander of the Burma Independence Army, was assassinated when Suu Kyi was two years old. Her mother, Daw Khin Kyi, continued to champion the cause, attaining prominence in social planning and social policy, and it was partly through her efforts that the Independent Union of Burma was established in 1948. In 1960 Daw Khin Kyi was appointed Burma's ambassador to India. Suu Kyi, who accompanied her mother, attended preparatory school in New Delhi, followed by a BA in philosophy, politics, and economics at Oxford. Her background, marriage to Michael Aris, a scholar of Tibetan civilization, and friendships with high-ranking officials in England, the United States, Bhutan, Japan, and India, led to work at the UN, study at Oxford, and international visibility as she assumed leadership of the opposition party, the National League for Democracy, in Burma as her mother was dying in 1988.

Harassment of Suu Kyi and her nonviolent party began immediately, with brutal arrests and killings. After facing down troops with rifles aimed at her in April 1989, she was placed under house arrest in July 1989. Her heroic actions had already made her an important symbol in the struggle against oppression. In May 1990, despite Suu Kyi's continued detention, her party won 82 percent of the seats in parliament, but the military state voided the results. It was in this climate that the Nobel Prize committee awarded her the Peace Prize, "to honor her nonviolent struggle for democracy and human rights" and to show "support for the many people throughout the world who are striving to attain democracy, human rights, and ethnic conciliation by peaceful means." As of 2002, Aung San Suu Kyi had spent a total of ten years under house arrest, refusing offers of freedom and reunion with her husband (who died in 1999 without being allowed to visit her) and sons if she would leave the country and withdraw from politics. Like Nelson Mandela, she chose separation from her family as one of the personal sacrifices she had to make in order to work for a larger, more humanitarian cause—in this case, a free Burma. Released in June 2002, her volatile political status offers no assurance of continued freedom.

The Revolution of Spirit (1991)

1 ... I stand before you here today to accept on behalf of my mother, Aung San Suu Kyi, this greatest of prizes, the Nobel Prize for Peace. Because circumstances do not permit my mother to be here in person, I will do my best to convey the sentiments I believe she would express.

2 Firstly, I know that she would begin by saying that she accepts the Nobel Prize for Peace not in her own name but in the name of all the people of Burma. She would say that this prize belongs not to her but to all those men, women and children who, even as I speak, continue to sacrifice their well being, their freedom and their lives in pursuit of a democratic Burma. Theirs is the prize and theirs will be the eventual victory in Burma's long struggle for peace, freedom and democracy.

3 Speaking as her son, however, I would add that I personally believe that by her own dedication and personal sacrifice she has come to be a worthy symbol through whom the plight of all the people of Burma may be recognized.

4 And no one must underestimate that plight. The plight of those in the countryside and towns, living in poverty and destitution, those in prison, battered and tortured; the plight of the young people, the hope of Burma, dying of malaria in the jungles to which they have fled; that of the Buddhist monks, beaten and dishonoured. Nor should we forget the many senior and highly respected leaders besides my mother who are all incarcerated.

5 It is on their behalf that I thank you, from my heart, for this supreme honour. The Burmese people can today hold their heads a little higher in the knowledge that in this far distant land their suffering has been heard and heeded.

6 We must also remember that the lonely struggle taking place in a heavily guarded compound in Rangoon is part of the much larger struggle, worldwide, for the emancipation of the human spirit from political tyranny and psychological subjection. The Prize, I feel sure, is also intended to honour all those engaged in this struggle wherever they may be. It is not without reason that today's events in Oslo fall on the International Human Rights Day, celebrated throughout the world.

7 Mr Chairman, the whole international community has applauded the choice of your Committee. Just a few days ago, the United Nations passed a unanimous and historic resolution welcoming Secretary-General Javier Pérez de Cuéllar's statement on the significance of this award and

"Read" the speech that Aung San Suu Kyi is making. Who is her audience? What does she want to happen as a consequence of her speaking? How do her physical attractiveness, gender, and dress reinforce—or contradict—your interpretation?

endorsing his repeated appeals for my mother's early release from detention. Universal concern at the grave human rights situation in Burma was clearly expressed. Alone and isolated among the entire nations of the world a single dissenting voice was heard, from the military junta in Rangoon, too late and too weak.

This regime has through almost thirty years of misrule reduced the once prosperous "Golden Land" of Burma to one of the world's most economically destitute nations. In their heart of hearts even those in power now in Rangoon must know that their eventual fate will be that of all totalitarian regimes who seek to impose their authority through fear, repression, and hatred. When the present Burmese struggle for democracy erupted onto the streets in 1988 it was the first of what became an international tidal wave of such movements throughout Eastern Europe, Asia and Africa. Today, in 1991, Burma stands conspicuous in its continued suffering at the hands of a repressive, intransigent junta, the State Law and Order Restoration Council. However, the example of those nations which have successfully achieved democracy holds out an important message to the Burmese people: that, in the last resort, through the sheer economic unworkability of totalitarianism this present regime will be swept away. And today in the face of rising inflation, a mismanaged economy and near worthless Kyat, the Burmese Government is undoubtedly reaping as it has sown.

9   However, it is my deepest hope that it will not be in the face of complete economic collapse that the regime will fall, but that the ruling junta may yet heed such appeals to basic humanity as that which the Nobel Committee has expressed in its award of this year's Prize. I know that within the military government there *are* those to whom the present policies of fear and repression are abhorrent, violating as they do the most sacred principles of Burma's Buddhist heritage. This is no empty wishful thinking but a conviction my mother reached in the course of her dealings with those in positions of authority, illustrated by the election victories of her party in constituencies comprised almost exclusively of military personnel and their families. It is my profoundest wish that these elements for moderation and reconciliation among those now in authority may make their sentiments felt in Burma's hour of deepest need.

10   I know that if she were free today my mother would in thanking you also ask you to pray that the oppressors and the oppressed should throw down their weapons and join together to build a nation founded on humanity in the spirit of peace.

11   Although my mother is often described as a political dissident who strives by peaceful means for democratic change, we should remember that her quest is basically spiritual. As she has said, "The quintessential revolution is that of the spirit," and she has written of the "essential spiritual aims" of the struggle. The realization of this depends solely on human responsibility. At the root of that responsibility lies, and I quote, "the concept of perfection, the urge to achieve it, the intelligence to find a path towards it, and the will to follow that path if not to the end, at least the distance needed to rise above individual limitation. . . ." "To live the full life," she says, "one must have the courage to bear the responsibility of the needs of others . . . one must *want* to bear this responsibility." And she links this firmly to her faith when she writes, ". . . Buddhism, the foundation of traditional Burmese culture, places the greatest value on man, who alone of all beings can achieve the supreme state of Buddhahood. Each man has in him the potential to realize the truth through his own will and endeavour and to help others to realize it." Finally she says, "The quest for democracy in Burma is the struggle of a people to live whole, meaningful lives as free and equal members of the world community. It is part of the unceasing human endeavour to prove that the spirit of man can transcend the flaws of his nature."

12   It only remains for me to thank you all from the bottom of my heart. Let us hope and pray that from today the wounds start to heal and that in the years to come the 1991 Nobel Prize for Peace will be seen as a historic step towards the achievement of true peace in Burma. The lessons of the past will not be forgotten, but it is our hope for the future that we celebrate today.

RIGOBERTA MENCHÚ TUM

Rigoberta Menchú Tum received the 1992 Nobel Peace Prize "in recognition of her work for social justice and ethno-cultural reconciliation based on respect for the rights of indigenous peoples." In the 1970s and 1980s Guatemala, like many other countries in South and Central America, was filled with tremendous tension between descendants of European immigrants and the native Indian peoples, who were brutally suppressed and persecuted. Menchú Tum, a social and political activist, said the Nobel committee, "stands out as a vivid symbol of peace and reconciliation across ethnic, cultural and social dividing lines," nationwide and worldwide.

Rigoberta Menchú Tum was born in 1959 to a poor Indian peasant family in Guatemala and raised in the Quiche branch of the Mayan culture. In childhood she helped with the family farm work, which included picking coffee on the large plantations. As a teenager she became involved in social reform activities through the Catholic Church, including becoming an advocate for women's rights—efforts that aroused opposition of those in power, especially after a guerilla organization became active in the area. The Menchú family was accused of guerilla activities; her father was imprisoned and tortured for allegedly having participated in the execution of a local plantation owner. After his release he became a member of the Committee of the Peasant Union (CUC), which Rigoberta joined in 1979—the year her brother was tortured and killed by the army. The following year her father was killed by security forces, and her mother died after being arrested, raped, and tortured. In 1980 Rigoberta, who had taught herself Spanish and a variety of Mayan languages, figured prominently in a strike organized by the CUC to improve conditions for farm workers. In 1981 her activities in educating the Indian peasant population to resist military oppression forced her to go into hiding in Guatemala and then flee to Mexico. She helped to found an opposition body, the United Representation of the Guatemalan Opposition (RUOG). In a week of recorded interviews with anthropologist Elisabeth Burgos-Debray, she told her life story. The book, *I, Rigoberta Menchú*, was published in 1983, translated into a dozen languages, and soon acquired incendiary international fame as the embodiment of the atrocities committed by the Guatemalan army in peasant villages during the civil war.

In 1999 David Stoll, though fully supportive of her Nobel Prize, published a critique of the book—*Menchú and the Story of All Poor Guatemalans* (1999)—demonstrating that parts of her own and her family history are in error, even when she speaks as an eyewitness. Stoll, an anthropologist who studied Mayan peasants, claims he trusted Menchú Tum's presentation of the Guatemalan army atrocities, but he feels that "by inaccurately portraying the events in her own village as representative of what happened in all such indigenous villages in Guatemala, she gives a misleading interpretation of the relationship of the Mayan peasants to the revolutionary movement." The Nobel Prize committee defended its decision to award the prize to Menchú Tum, saying that this "was not based exclusively or primarily on the autobiography," and dismissed any suggestion that the

Committee should consider revoking the prize. *The Rigoberta Menchú Controversy* (2002) is a superb collection of "primary documents—newspaper articles, interviews, and official statements" complemented by assessments by distinguished international scholars of the political, historical, and cultural implications of this debate.

Five Hundred Years of Mayan Oppression (1992)

1   Please allow me, ladies and gentlemen, to say some words about my country and the Civilization of the Mayas. The Maya people developed and spread geographically through some 300,000 square km; they occupied parts of the South of Mexico, Belize, Guatemala, as well as Honduras and El Salvador; they developed a very rich civilization in the area of political organization, as well as in social and economic fields; they were great scientists in the fields of mathematics, astronomy, agriculture, architecture and engineering; they were great artists in the fields of sculpture, painting, weaving and carving. . . .

2   Who can predict what other great scientific conquests and developments these people could have achieved, if they had not been conquered in blood and fire, and subjected to an ethnocide that affected nearly 50 million people in the course of 500 years.

3   I would describe the meaning of this Nobel Prize, in the first place as a tribute to the indian people who have been sacrificed and have disappeared because they aimed at a more dignified and just life with fraternity and understanding among the human beings. To those who are no longer alive to keep up the hope for a change in the situation in respect of poverty and marginalization of the indians, of those who have been banished, of the helpless in Guatemala as well as in the entire American Continent.

4   This growing concern is comforting, even though it comes 500 years later, to the suffering, the discrimination, the oppression and the exploitation that our people has been exposed to, but who, thanks to their own cosmovision—and concept of life, have managed to withstand and finally see some promising prospects. How those roots, that were to be eradicated, now begin to grow with strength, hopes and visions for the future!

5   It also represents a sign of the growing international interest for, and understanding of the original Rights of the People, of the future of more than 60 million indians that live in our America, and their uproar because of the 500 years of oppression that they have endured. For the genocides beyond comparison that they have had to suffer all this time, and from which other countries and the elite of the Americas have profited and taken advantage.

Let there be freedom for the indians, wherever they may be in the 6
American Continent or else in the world, because while they are alive, a
glow of hope will be alive as well as the real concept of life.

The expressions of great happiness by the Indian Organizations in 7
the entire Continent and the worldwide congratulations received for the
award of the Nobel Peace Prize, clearly indicate the great importance of
this decision. It is the recognition of the European debt to the American
indigenous people; it is an appeal to the conscience of Humanity so that
those conditions of marginalization that condemned them to colonialism
and exploitation may be eradicated; it is a cry for life, peace, justice, equality and fraternity between human beings.

The peculiarities of the vision of the indian people are expressed 8
according to the way in which they relate. First of all, between human
being[s], through communication. Second, with the earth, as with our
mother, because she gives us our lives and is not a mere merchandise.
Third, with nature, because we are integral parts of it, and not its owners.

To us mother earth is not only a source of economic riches that give 9
us the maize, which is our life, but she also provides so many other things
that the privileged ones of today strive after. The earth is the root and the
source of our culture. She keeps our memories, she receives our ancestors
and she therefore demands that we honour her and return to her, with
tenderness and respect, those goods that she gives us. We have to take
care of her and look after mother earth so that our children and grandchildren may continue to benefit from her. If the world does not learn
now to show respect to nature, what kind of future will the new generations have?

From these basic features derive behaviour, rights and obligations in 10
the American Continent, for indians as well as for non-indians, whether
they be racially mixed, blacks, whites or Asian. The whole society has the
obligation to show mutual respect, to learn from each other and to share
material and scientific achievements, in the most convenient way. The indians have never had, and they do not have, the place that they should
have occupied in the progress and benefits of science and technology, although they have represented an important basis.

If the indian civilizations and the European civilizations could have 11
made exchanges in a peaceful and harmonious manner, without destruction, exploitation, discrimination and poverty, they could, no doubt, have
achieved greater and more valuable conquests for Humanity.

Let us not forget that when the Europeans came to America, there 12
were flourishing and strong civilizations there. One cannot talk about a
discovery of America, because one discovers that which one does not
know about, or that which is hidden. But America and its native civilizations had discovered themselves long before the fall of the Roman Empire
and the Medieval Europe. The significance of its cultures form part of the
heritage of humanity and continue to astonish the learned ones. . . .

13   We the indians are willing to combine tradition with modernism, but not at all costs. We will not tolerate nor permit that our future be planned as possible guardians of ethno-touristic projects at continental level.

14   At a time when the commemoration of the Fifth Centenary of the arrival of Columbus in America has repercussions all over the world, the revival of hopes for the indian people claims that we reassert to the world our existence and the value of our cultural identity. It demands that we endeavour to actively participate in the decisions that concern our destiny, in the building-up of our countries/nations. Should we, in spite of all, not be taken into consideration, there are factors that guarantee our future: struggle and endurance; courage; the decision to maintain our traditions that have been exposed to so many perils and sufferings; solidarity towards our struggle on the part of numerous countries, governments, organizations and citizens of the world.

15   That is why I dream of the day when the relationship between the indigenous people and other people is strengthened; when they can join their potentialities and their capabilities and contribute to make life on this planet less unequal.

THE 14TH DALAI LAMA, TENZIN GYATSO

The 14th Dalai Lama, Tenzin Gyatso, born to a peasant family in Takster, Tibet, in 1935, was recognized at the age of two as the reincarnation of his predecessor, the 13th Dalai Lama. Dalai Lamas (the name means "Oceans of Wisdom") are the manifestations of the Bodhisattva of Compassion, who chose to reincarnate to serve the people. His monastic education began at six and culminated in a Doctorate of Buddhist Philosophy awarded when he was twenty-five. His political education took place concurrently, for in 1950 he assumed full power as Head of State and Government when Tibet's autonomy was threatened by Communist China. His meetings with Mao Tse-Tung and Chou En-Lai were in vain, for in 1959 he was forced into exile in India by the Chinese military occupation of Tibet—events depicted in the popular film *Kundun* (meaning "The Presence").

Since then the Dalai Lama has conducted the Tibetan government-in-exile from Dharamsala, India, and—unlike many of his predecessors—traveled worldwide on diplomatic missions, in part aiming to preserve the integrity of the Tibetan national identity and cultural heritage. He proposed to the Congressional Human Rights Caucus in 1987 a Five-Point Peace Plan designed to ensure the integrity of Tibet: (1) designate Tibet as a zone of peace, (2) end the massive transfer of ethnic Chinese into Tibet, (3) restore to Tibet fundamental human rights and democratic freedoms, (4) abandon China's use of Tibet to produce nuclear weapons and as a dumping ground for nuclear waste, and (5) create a self-governing Tibet, in association with the People's Republic of China. The Tibetan people themselves, insists His Holiness, "must be the ultimate deciding authority."

It was because of these "constructive and forward-looking proposals for the solution of international conflicts, human rights issues, and global environmental problems" that the 14th Dalai Lama was awarded the Nobel Peace Prize for 1989.

Inner Peace and Human Rights (1989)

P eace, in the sense of the absence of war, is of little value to someone   1
who is dying of hunger or cold. It will not remove the pain of torture inflicted on a prisoner of conscience. It does not comfort those who have lost their loved ones in floods caused by senseless deforestation in a neighbouring country. Peace can only last where human rights are respected, where the people are fed, and where individuals and nations are free. True peace with oneself and with the world around us can only be achieved through the development of mental peace. The other phenomena mentioned above are similarly interrelated. Thus, for example, we see that a clean environment, wealth or democracy mean little in the face of war, especially nuclear war, and that material development is not sufficient to ensure human happiness.

Material progress is of course important for human advancement. In   2
Tibet, we paid much too little attention to technological and economic development, and today we realise that this was a mistake. At the same time, material development without spiritual development can also cause serious problems. In some countries too much attention is paid to external things and very little importance is given to inner development. I believe both are important and must be developed side by side so as to achieve a good balance between them. Tibetans are always described by foreign visitors as being a happy, jovial people. This is part of our national character, formed by cultural and religious values that stress the importance of mental peace through the generation of love and kindness to all other living sentient beings, both human and animal. Inner peace is the key: if you have inner peace, the external problems do not affect your deep sense of peace and tranquility. In that state of mind you can deal with situations with calmness and reason, while keeping your inner happiness. That is very important. Without this inner peace, no matter how comfortable your life is materially, you may still be worried, disturbed or unhappy because of circumstances.

Clearly, it is of great importance, therefore, to understand the inter-   3
relationship among these and other phenomena, and to approach and attempt to solve problems in a balanced way that takes these different aspects into consideration. Of course it is not easy. But it is of little benefit to try to solve one problem if doing so creates an equally serious new one.

So really we have no alternative: we must develop a sense of universal responsibility not only in the geographic sense, but also in respect to the different issues that confront our planet.

4   Responsibility does not only lie with the leaders of our countries or with those who have been appointed or elected to do a particular job. It lies with each one of us individually. Peace, for example, starts with each one of us. When we have inner peace, we can be at peace with those around us. When our community is in a state of peace, it can share that peace with neighbouring communities, and so on. When we feel love and kindness towards others, it not only makes others feel loved and cared for, but it helps us also to develop inner happiness and peace. And there are ways in which we can consciously work to develop feelings of love and kindness. For some of us, the most effective way to do so is through religious practice. For others it may be non-religious practices. What is important is that we each make a sincere effort to take our responsibility for each other and for the natural environment we live in seriously.

5   I am very encouraged by the developments which are taking place around us. After the young people of many countries, particularly in northern Europe, have repeatedly called for an end to the dangerous destruction of the environment which was being conducted in the name of economic development, the world's political leaders are now starting to take meaningful steps to address this problem. The report to the United Nations Secretary-General by the World Commission on the Environment and Development (the Brundtland Report) was an important step in educating governments on the urgency of the issue. Serious efforts to bring peace to war-torn zones and to implement the right to self-determination of some people have resulted in the withdrawal of Soviet troops from Afghanistan and the establishment of independent Namibia. Through persistent nonviolent popular efforts dramatic changes, bringing many countries closer to real democracy, have occurred in many places, from Manila in the Philippines to Berlin in East Germany. With the Cold War era apparently drawing to a close, people everywhere live with renewed hope. Sadly, the courageous efforts of the Chinese people to bring similar change to their country was brutally crushed last June. But their efforts too are a source of hope. The military might has not extinguished the desire for freedom and the determination of the Chinese people to achieve it. I particularly admire the fact that these young people who have been taught that "power grows from the barrel of the gun," chose, instead, to use nonviolence as their weapon.

6   What these positive changes indicate, is that reason, courage, determination, and the inextinguishable desire for freedom can ultimately win. In the struggle between forces of war, violence and oppression on the one hand, and peace, reason and freedom on the other, the latter are gaining the upper hand. This realisation fills us Tibetans with hope that some day we too will once again be free.

The awarding of the Nobel Prize to me, a simple monk from faraway 7
Tibet, here in Norway, also fills us Tibetans with hope. It means, despite
the fact that we have not drawn attention to our plight by means of violence, we have not been forgotten. It also means that the values we cherish,
in particular our respect for all forms of life and the belief in the power of
truth, are today recognised and encouraged. It is also a tribute to my mentor, Mahatma Gandhi, whose example is an inspiration to so many of us.
This year's award is an indication that this sense of universal responsibility is developing. I am deeply touched by the sincere concern shown
by so many people in this part of the world for the suffering of the people
of Tibet. That is a source of hope not only for us Tibetans, but for all oppressed people.

As you know, Tibet has, for forty years, been under foreign occupa- 8
tion. Today, more than a quarter of a million Chinese troops are stationed
in Tibet. Some sources estimate the occupation army to be twice this
strength. During this time, Tibetans have been deprived of their most basic
human rights, including the right to life, movement, speech, worship, only
to mention a few. More than one sixth of Tibet's population of six million
died as a direct result of the Chinese invasion and occupation. Even before
the Cultural Revolution started, many of Tibet's monasteries, temples and
historic buildings were destroyed. Almost everything that remained was
destroyed during the Cultural Revolution. I do not wish to dwell on this
point, which is well documented. What is important to realise, however, is
that despite the limited freedom granted after 1979, to rebuild parts of
some monasteries and other such tokens of liberalisation, the fundamental
human rights of the Tibetan people are still today being systematically violated. In recent months this bad situation has become even worse.

If it were not for our community in exile, so generously sheltered and 9
supported by the government and people of India and helped by organisations and individuals from many parts of the world, our nation would
today be little more than a shattered remnant of a people. Our culture, religion and national identity would have been effectively eliminated. As it
is, we have built schools and monasteries in exile and have created democratic institutions to serve our people and preserve the seeds of our civili-
sation. With this experience, we intend to implement full democracy in a
future free Tibet. Thus, as we develop our community in exile on modern
lines, we also cherish and preserve our own identity and culture and bring
hope to millions of our countrymen and -women in Tibet.

The issue of most urgent concern at this time, is the massive influx 10
of Chinese settlers into Tibet. Although in the first decades of occupation
a considerable number of Chinese were transferred into the eastern parts
of Tibet—in the Tibetan provinces of Amdo (Chinghai) and Kham (most of
which has been annexed by neighboring Chinese provinces)—since 1983
an unprecedented number of Chinese have been encouraged by their government to migrate to all parts of Tibet, including central and western Tibet

(which the People's Republic of China refers to as the so-called Tibet Autonomous Region). Tibetans are rapidly being reduced to an insignificant minority in their own country. This development, which threatens the very survival of the Tibetan nation, its culture and spiritual heritage, can still be stopped and reversed. But this must be done now, before it is too late.

====================

BETTY WILLIAMS

"The violent and intractable Irish problem," as the *Random House Encyclopedia* calls it, has dominated Irish politics, military policy, friendships, and home and civic life throughout much of modern Ireland's history, (see introduction to Swift's "Modest Proposal," 496) but particularly since the Easter uprising of April 24, 1916—a small armed insurrection of Catholics against British rule, with long-lasting political consequences. This led to partition of the island in 1922, establishing the largely Catholic Irish Free State in the South (capital, Dublin), while the Protestant loyalists to the British crown were to live largely in Northern Ireland, whose capital is Belfast. Yet the populations are mixed, and remain under continual tension. As in many other countries with a common culture and bitter religious divisions, the borders are porous; the inhabitants are suspicious of one another, if not possessed of downright hatred; they have enduring bitter memories and itchy trigger fingers. In the early 1970s the Catholic Provisional IRA (Irish Republican Army) began a series of guerilla terrorist attacks to prevent British troops stationed in Northern Ireland from concentrating on Catholic enclaves, with the ultimate aim of driving the British out and reunifying Ireland as a Catholic country.

The incident that provided the impetus for the formation of the movement of the Peace People, an ad hoc coalition of Catholic and Protestant women (and some men) in Northern Ireland, occurred in Belfast on August 10, 1976. In pursuit of a stolen car, driven by Danny Lennon, who may or may not have been a member of the Provisional IRA and who may or may not have fired on a patrol of the King's Own Border Regiment, the King's Own troops mortally wounded Lennon, whose runaway car killed two children on the spot, 8-year-old Joanna Maguire and her six-week-old baby brother Andrew. Their two-year-old brother died the next day.

Mairead Corrigan, their aunt, a Catholic secretary at the Guinness brewery, was interviewed on BBC-TV that evening in a widely rebroadcast commentary: "Only one percent of the people of this province want this slaughter," she said before breaking down in tears. Betty Williams, a Catholic housewife married to a Protestant, had witnessed the accident, and was moved to action by Corrigan's speech. Within forty-eight hours she had circulated a petition signed by 6,000 people, demanding that the Provisional IRA stop its military campaign. Williams and Corrigan met Ciaran McKeown, a young Catholic journalist, at the Maguire children's funeral; he provided organizational strategy to maintain the momentum of this interfaith peace movement. They effected sufficient rapprochement so that in December 1976 northern and southern Irish met on a historic bridge over the River Boyne to pledge an end to sectarian hatred at the spot where it had begun 300 years earlier.

The trio received the Nobel Peace Prize in 1976 for their grassroots efforts. Each of the recipients made an acceptance speech; space permits reprinting only part of one here. Unfortunately, the spirit of reconciliation has not prevailed, though after Muslim suicide bombings in the London transit system in July 2005, the IRA promised to cease its own terrorist attacks. In 2001 Paul Connolly, a sociologist at the University of Ulster, commissioned by the Northern Ireland Community Relations Council, interviewed 352 Northern Irish Catholic and Protestant children between three and six years of age about their attitudes toward the political situation there. Here are their typical replies:

Protestant children, when asked "What do you know about Catholics?"

They rob.

They're bad. They batter Almond Drive people. Almond Drive— that's where I live.

Catholics are different from ordinary human beings because they are badder.

The police come after them. They make petrol bombs, get petrol at garages, throw them, and they blow up.

Catholic children, when asked "What do you know about Protestants?"

They want to kill all the Catholics.

They're like Catholics. They do the same things, only they're stronger.

Protestants would take people hostage. The police give them their weapons and make a deal to get the hostages.

Catholics don't like Protestants, and that's why they don't like them. They're bad.

The Movement of the Peace People (1976)

I feel humble in officially receiving the Nobel Peace Prize, because so many people have been involved in the campaign that drew such attention to our leadership that an award like this could justifiably be made. Mairead Corrigan and I may take some satisfaction with us all the days of our lives that we did make that initial call, a call which unlocked the massive desire for peace within the hearts of the Northern Irish people, and as we so soon discovered, in the hearts of people around the world. . . .

2   But unlocking the desire for peace would never have been enough. All the energy, all the determination to express an overwhelming demand for an end to the sickening cycle of useless violence would have reverberated briefly and despairingly among the people, as had happened so many times before . . . if we had not organized ourselves to use that energy and that determination positively, once and for all.

3   So in that first week Mairead Corrigan, Ciaran McKeown and I founded the Movement of the Peace People, in order to give real leadership and direction to the desire which we were certain was there, deep within the hearts of the vast majority of the people, . . . and even deep within the hearts of those who felt, perhaps still do, feel obliged, to oppose us in public.

4   We are for life and creation, and we are against war and destruction, and in our rage in that terrible week, we screamed that the violence had to stop.

5   But we also began to do something about it besides shouting. Ciaran McKeown wrote "The Declaration of the Peace People" which in its simple words pointed along the path of true peace, and with the publication of that Declaration, we announced the founding of the Movement of the Peace People, and we began planning a series of rallies which would last four months, and through which we would mobilize hundreds of thousands of people and challenge them to take the road of the Declaration.

6   The words are simple but the path is not easy, as all the people ever associated with the historic Nobel Peace Prize must know. It is a path on which we must not only reject the use of all the techniques of violence, but along which we must seek out the work of peace . . . and do it. It is the way of dedication, hard work and courage.

7   Hundreds of thousands of people turned out during those four months and we would not be standing here if they had not. So I feel humble that I should be receiving this award, but I am very proud to be here in the name of all the Peace People to accept it. . . .

8   And with that sense of history, we feel a special sense of honour . . . honour for women, perhaps a little specially at this time. War has traditionally been a man's work, although we know that often women were the cause of violence. But the voice of women, the voice of those most closely involved in bringing forth new life, has not always been listened to when it pleaded and implored against the waste of life in war after war. The voice of women has a special role and a special soul-force in the struggle for a non-violent world. We do not wish to replace religious sectarianism, or ideological division with sexism or any kind of militant feminism. But we do believe, as Ciaran McKeown who is with us in spirit, believes, that women have a leading role to play in this great struggle.

9   So we are honoured, in the name of all women, that women have been honoured especially for their part in leading a non-violent movement for a just and peaceful society. Compassion is more important than intellect, in

calling forth the love that the work of peace needs, and intuition can often be a far more powerful searchlight than cold reason. We have to think, and think hard, but if we do not have compassion before we even start thinking, then we are quite likely to start fighting over theories. The whole world is divided ideologically, and theologically, right and left, and men are prepared to fight over their ideological differences. Yet the whole human family can be united by compassion. And, as Ciaran said recently in Israel, "compassion recognizes human rights automatically . . . it does not need a charter."

Because of the role of women over so many centuries in so many dif- 10 ferent cultures, they have been excluded from what have been called public affairs; for that very reason they have concentrated much more on things close to home . . . and they have kept far more in touch with the true realities . . . the realities of giving birth and love. The moment has perhaps come in human history when, for very survival, those realities must be given pride of place over the vainglorious adventures that lead to war.

But we do not wish to see a division over this . . . merely a natural 11 and respectful and loving co-operation. Women and men together can make this a beautiful people's world, and that is why we called ourselves, "THE PEACE PEOPLE."

So, in humility at the efforts of so many people, I am proud to stand here 12 on their behalf, and accept this honour on behalf of all of us.

But I am also angry. I am as angry today, in a calm and a deep sense 13 at the wastage of human life that continues each day, as I was when I saw young life squashed on a Belfast street.

I am angry, the Peace People are angry that war at home dribbles on, 14 and around the world we see the same stupidity gathering momentum for far worse wars than the little one which the little population of Northern Ireland, has had to endure. We are angry at the waste of resources that goes on every day for militarism while human beings live in misery and sometimes even live in the hope of a quick death to release them from their hopelessness. We rage as $500,000 are spent every minute of every day on war and the preparation for war; while in every one of those minutes human beings, more than 8 people, die of neglect. Every day 12,000 people die of neglect and malnutrition and misery; yet every day, $720 *million* are spent on armaments. Just think of those insane priorities. . . .

We know that this insane and immoral imbalance of priorities cannot 15 be changed overnight; we also know that it will not be changed without the greatest struggle, the incessant struggle to get the human race to stop wasting its vast resources on arms, and start investing in the people who must live out their lives on the planet we share, east and west, north and south. And that struggle must be all the greater because it has to be an unarmed, a non-violent struggle, and requires more courage and more persistence than the courage to squeeze triggers or press murderous buttons.

Men must not only end war, they must begin to have the courage not even to prepare for war.

16   Someday we must take seriously the words of Carl Sandburg: "Someday there will be a war, and no one will come." Won't that be beautiful. Someday there will be a "war" but no one will come. And of course, if no one comes there will be no war. And we don't have to go, we don't have to have war, but it seems to take more courage to say NO to war than to say YES, and perhaps we women have for too long encouraged the idea that it is brave and manly to go to war, often to "defend" women and children. Let women everywhere from this day on encourage men to have the courage not to turn up for war, not to work for a militarized world but a world of peace, a non-violent world.

17   To begin to have that kind of real courage, people must begin to breach the barriers which divide them. We are divided on the surface on this planet, by physical barriers, emotional barriers, ideological barriers, barriers of prejudice and hatreds of every kind. . . .

18   We as Peace People go much further: we believe in taking down the barriers, but we also believe in the most energetic reconciliation among peoples by getting them to know each other, talk each other's languages, understand each other's fears and beliefs, getting to know each other physically, philosophically and spiritually. It is much harder to kill your near neighbour than the thousands of unknown and hostile aliens at the other end of a nuclear missile. We have to create a world in which there are no unknown, hostile aliens at the other end of any missiles, and that is going to take a tremendous amount of sheer hard work.

For Discussion and Writing

Each of the following issues is complicated, for matters of war and peace are never simple, never static, particularly when negotiated in an international arena. Most can be seen not just from two points of view, but from many perspectives embedded in the political, economic, religious, ethical, and cultural values of a great variety of individuals, cultures, and countries. In discussing any of these topics, or others stimulated by your reading and thinking, you will find it helpful to talk with your peers and to consult reliable outside sources, perhaps beginning with one or two of those listed. You will be aiming to write papers informed by accurate information, terms clearly defined, that avoid blanket generalizations and simplistic conclusions.

Rather than trying to cover the gigantic issues embedded in the overall subject, pick a segment of the topic that is small enough to handle in a well-developed paper. The complex nature of the issues embedded in these subjects—terrorism, war, peace, national culture, values, justice, security, civil liberties, vengeance, social action, leadership—lends itself to group projects. Each participant could be assigned to research a specific segment of a larger issue and the results could be combined in a coauthored paper. It is advisable, even when discussing issues on which you feel strongly, to avoid either/or thinking, stereotyping, and incendiary language. It is appropriate, however, to build your case on accurate information, principle, and passion—the principles of communication—and of life—that have guided the Nobel Prize winners and established exemplary models for nations as well as individual citizens.

Because the events related to international terrorism as well as to world peace occur in a constantly changing world, you will need to update your information before discussing either the World Trade Center bombings of 1993 or 2001, or any other terroristic activities or their implications or consequences. The print sources identified in the following list are good places to start. Be aware that all of them, like any other source of information on any subject—especially one as incendiary as international terrorism—contain opinions and other interpretations of fact that support the author's point of view, just as your own writing does. As every reading in *The Essay Connection* illustrates, every author expresses biases; reliable authors also honor the obligation to be fair. Most of these sources on international terrorism, like the readings in the "Terrorism" chapter, are pro-Western, written by authors from the United States or Great Britain. The exception is *Orientalism,* the late Palestinian Edward Said's work that claims Western study of the Middle East is a means of reducing and dominating that culture through continuing the colonial oppression of the nineteenth and twentieth centuries. This pro-Western bias is why it is particularly necessary to balance these views with the views on peace from Nobel Prize winners throughout the world.

The 9/11 Commission Report: Final Report of the National Commission on Terrorist Attacks Upon the United States. New York: W. W. Norton, 2004.

Atlantic Monthly continuing coverage.

Feldman, Noah. *War and the Ethics of Nation Building.* Princeton, NJ: Princeton University Press, 2004.

Griffiths, David Ray. *The 9/11 Commission Report: Omissions and Distortions.* Northampton, MA: Olive Branch Press, 2005.

Hazlitt, William. "On the Pleasure of Hating" (c. 1826). [widely reprinted or see **www.bluepete.com/Literature/Essays/Hazlitt/Hating.htm**]

Ignatieff, Michael. *The Lesser Evil: Political Ethics in an Age of Terror.* Princeton: Princeton UP, 2004.

Juergensmeyer, Mark. *Terror in the Mind of God: The Global Rise of Religious Violence.* Updated ed. Berkeley: U of California Press, 2000.

Laqueur, Walter, ed. *Voices of Terror: Manifestos, Writings, and Manuals of Al Quaeda, Hamas, and Other Terrorists from Around the World and Throughout the Ages.* Naperville, IL: Reed Press, 2004.

Lelyveld, Joseph. "All Suicide Bombers Are Not Alike." *New York Times Magazine* (28 Oct. 2001): 49–53, 62, 78–79.

Lewis, Bernard. *The Middle East: A Brief History of the Last 2,000 Years.* New York: Scribner, 1996.

Lewis, Bernard. *What Went Wrong.* New York: Oxford University Press, 2002.

Mertus, Julie A. *Bait and Switch: Human Rights and United States Foreign Policy.* New York: Routledge, 2004.

Purdum, Todd S. *A Time of Our Own Choosing: America's War in Iraq.* New York: New York Times, 2003.

Said, Edward. *Orientalism.* New York: Random House, 1979.

Singer, P. W. *Children at War.* New York: Pantheon, 2005.

South Atlantic Quarterly (Spring 2002). See the entire issue.

Vollman, William T. "The Taliban," *New Yorker* (15 May 2000): 58–66.

Because much of your information will arrive via an Internet search, it's important to conduct a search that is efficient and focused and that yields reliable results. The following principles should help.

Appendix A:
How to Search for
(and Recognize) Good
Sites on the Internet

Note: You can do any and all of these by yourself, with a partner, or with a group.

1. Pick popular, reliable search engines (for example, Google Scholar, Google, Yahoo!, etc.).
2. Use terms appropriate to your search. If you want more hits or more general information, use broad terms ("philosophy," "peace," "terrorism"); if you want fewer hits or more specific information, use more detail ("Western philosophy," "peace initiatives," "international terrorism"). Keep refining your terms: To "international terrorism" add a country, an event, a time span and so on, with more and more restrictions until your results are a manageable number and many of the entries are recent.
3. Be flexible: Try a couple of different search terms if you don't find what you're looking for the first time, or try your search in another search engine. Look through a couple of pages of results; don't just settle for the first dozen hits. Patience here will pay off in finding the best sites available.
4. Look for reliable sources: Anyone can put a page on the Internet, and sometimes bad or misleading information is not readily apparent. Look for organizations, companies, or names you recognize. Read Web addresses (URLs) carefully to ensure the accuracy of your sources (a page might *look* like the Microsoft website, but check the address for **http://www.microsoft.com** to make sure). Look at the kind of information the site provides. The Web address should represent the actual source name, such as **www.nobel.se/peace/laureates** and date of the particular prizewinner. Exercise caution with an address you don't know; you may be able to check an unfamiliar name on another Internet source.
5. Use the best information you can find, and read it carefully and critically. Blatantly biased websites are often identifiable by their inflammatory language and distorted information. Like junk mail, such biased sources are relatively easy to identify. It's more difficult to recognize less blatant forms of bias in the guise of serious scholarship. Look for balance and fairness—in the choice of evidence and in the

language in which it's presented. So in reading Internet sources, it's wise to be as skeptical as you would in reading your mail. Sources with an axe to grind send out verbal cues to the audience—weird or extreme language, unsupported claims, incendiary or insulting generalizations. Reader, beware!

These sites discuss international terrorism.

The International Policy Institute for Counter-Terrorism (Israel)
http://www.ict.org.il/
The Federation of American Scientists site
http://www.fas.org/index.html
http://www.fas.org/irp/threat/commission.html
http://www.fas.org/irp/threat/terror.htm
The Centre for Defence and International Security Studies (U.K.)
http://www.cdiss.org/
U.S. Department of State's Response to Terrorism page
http://usinfo.state.gov/is/international_security/terrorism.html
FEMA's Fact Sheet on terrorism
http://www.fema.gov/hazards/terrorism/terrorf.shtm
The UN page on terrorism
http://www.un.org/terrorism/

These sites discuss peace initiatives.

The UN page on peace and security
http://www.un.org/peace/
The United States Institute of Peace
http://www.usip.org/
Peace Brigades International (U.K.)
http://www.peacebrigades.org/
The Carnegie Endowment for International Peace
http://www.ceip.org/
Stockholm International Peace Research Institute
http://www.sipri.org/
The Peace Corps
http://www.peacecorps.gov/index.cfm
Volunteers for Peace
http://www.vfp.org/

These are philosophy sites.

Western philosophy
http://www.philosophypages.com/
Chinese philosophy
http://uweb.superlink.net/~fsu/philo.html
This site, out of Hong Kong, deals with both Eastern and Western thought
http://www.arts.cuhk.edu.hk/Philo.html

Ways to Think, Discuss, and Write About the Readings

1. Define *terrorism,* or *war,* based on selected readings in the "Terrorism" and "World Peace" chapters and supplemented by your own understanding of the term. Illustrate your definition with examples from these readings, noting where these conflict with and reinforce one another. Is terrorism a constant term or one that changes with changing interpretations of current events and past history? What are the major differences between *terror* and *terrorism?* Between *terrorism* and *war?*

2. Provide an extended definition of *peace,* using examples from the speeches or lives of two or three of the Nobel Peace Prize recipients and supplemented by your own understanding of the term and reading of O'Brien (543–50), Tayebi (554–58), Griswold (591), or particularly peaceful contexts, such as those described by E. B. White in "Once More to the Lake" (97–103) or Mark Twain in "Uncle John's Farm" (265–71). Is *peace* a constant term or one that changes with changing interpretations of current events and past history? Why do war, imprisonment, torture, genocide, segregation, and other forms of evil figure so prominently in the struggle to find and maintain peace?

3. Is world peace possible? Is long-term prosperity possible without peace? Will our quest involve nation with (or against) nation; culture with (or against) culture; technology, economy, or ideology with (or against) its counterpart?

4. What are—or should be—the highest priorities for our private life in the United States? Security? Freedom? Peace and prosperity? How do—or should—these coincide with our national priorities?

5. What changes will terrorist attacks, and the infinite possibilities of future terrorism—specific or vague—make in the ways we live our lives, plan for our futures, look at our neighbors, our friends, and our enemies? See the *9/11 Commission Report* (558–65).

6. What civil liberties are indispensable to life as guaranteed by the Constitution of the United States? (See also Thomas Jefferson "The Declaration of Independence," 439–42.) What can we, as individuals and as a nation, do to balance the free and open nature of our hospitable society against needs for protection and security?

7. Is it possible for our country to act unilaterally in attaining any of its aims? To what extent do we live in a world in which the interests of all countries are intimately intertwined? Is it even possible for our country to consider autonomy, in light of its global business interests and dependence on foreign oil and a host of other products? You might pick a single area—medicine, automobiles, the Internet—and focus your answer on this.

8. How can we avoid dividing the world into "us" against "them," suspicion and paranoia, and nevertheless be on guard—but against what?

9. What qualities does it take to become a nationally or internationally distinguished leader? What can the rest of us learn from the experiences of the Nobel Peace Prize winners?

10. What would you personally be willing to sacrifice your time and freedom to attain? Would you lay down your life for a cause? If so, what is that cause, and why is it worth this degree of commitment?

11. Pick a historical document, either published (such as the Declaration of Independence [439–42] or the Gettysburg Address [494]) or unpublished. An unpublished document might be a photograph or letter your family may own that concerns an event that has passed into history, such as an invention (the atomic bomb, personal computers, a particular car), the Great Depression or other period of unemployment; or a war (the Civil War, World War I, World War II, the Korean War, the Vietnam War); or a major sporting or literary event; or the outcome of an election. Flesh out the meaning of the event through consulting family members involved in the document (either as its producers or subjects) and appropriate reference works and websites, on- or offline. Then, write a paper explaining what you've come to understand about the event, using the document as the focal point of your discussion.

12. Every one of us has been alive during one or more major historical events somewhere in our own state or country, as well as elsewhere in the world. These include discoveries, explorations, inventions, conflicts, and—with good fortune—resolutions of such conflicts. Perhaps you have been an eyewitness to such an event, or a participant in it, or affected by it—whether this is a manifestation of cloning, a discovery in outer space, the attack on the World Trade Center and the Pentagon of September 11, 2001, or a matter of more local concern. Sometimes the event seems highly significant when it happens; at other times its full meaning becomes apparent only with the passage of time. In all cases, the event is subject to a myriad of interpretations, from many perspectives, which continue to change as time moves on. Either on your own, or with a partner or group, select a memorable event or phenomenon that has occurred during your lifetime and write an interpretation of its significance when it first happened, and its changing meaning(s) over time for different people (perhaps, those in your group of coauthors). If you choose a natural disaster, such as Hurricane Katrina (2005), in what ways does the fact that it was natural rather than instigated by humans change the ways you interpret its causes and effects, both short and long term? If you were an eyewitness, how did you interpret the event at the time you experienced it? How has your understanding deepened and/or changed since that time?

APPENDIX B: GLOSSARY

abstract refers to qualities, ideas, or states of being that exist but that our senses cannot perceive. What we perceive are the concrete by-products of abstract ideas. No single object or action can be labeled *love,* but a warm embrace or a passionate kiss is a visible, concrete token of the abstraction we call "love." In "What Sacagawea Means to Me" (93–95), Sherman Alexie treats Sacagawea as an iconic abstraction of Indian. In many instances abstract words such as *beauty, hatred, stupidity,* or *kindness* are more clearly understood if illustrated with **concrete** examples (*see* **concrete** and **general/specific**).

allusion is a writer's reference to a person, place, thing, literary character, or quotation that the reader is expected to recognize. Because the reader supplies the meaning and the original context, such references are economical; writers don't have to explain them. By alluding to a young man as a *Romeo, Don Juan,* or *Casanova,* a writer can present the subject's amorous nature without needing to say more. To make sure that references will be understood, writers have to choose what their readers can reasonably be expected to recognize.

analogy is a comparison made between two things, qualities, or ideas that have certain similarities although the items themselves may be very different. For example, Scott Russell Sanders characterizes his alcoholic father, "Like a torture victim who refuses to squeal, he would never admit that he had touched a drop, not even in his last year when he seemed to be dissolving in alcohol before our very eyes" ("Under the Influence," 249–59). The emphasis is on the similarities between Mr. Sanders, drunk or sober, and the torture victim; dissimilarities would have weakened the analogy. **Metaphors** and **similes** are two figures of speech that are based on analogies, and such comparisons are often used in argumentation (*see* **figures of speech** *and* **argumentation**).

argument, in a specialized literary sense, is a prose summary of the plot, main idea, or subject of a prose or poetic work. For *argumentation,* see introductions to the chapters "Appeal to Reason: Deductive and Inductive Arguments," "Appealing to Emotion and Ethics," and "Terrorism."

audience consists of the readers of a given writing. Writers may write some pieces solely for themselves; others for their peers, teachers, or supervisors; others for people with special knowledge of the subject. Writers adapt the level of their language and the details of their presentation to readers of different ages, backgrounds, interests, and education. (See Chapter 1, 2.) Gertrude Stein once observed, "I write for myself and strangers." Writers often aim to convert strangers into friends.

cliché is a commonplace expression that reveals the writer's lack of imagination to use fresher, more vivid language. If a person finds himself *between a rock and a hard place,* he might decide to use a cliché, *come hell or high water,* but cliché is *as dead as a mackerel.* Its excessive familiarity dulls the reader's responses. Avoid clichés *like the plague.*

coherence indicates an orderly relationship among the parts in a whole essay or other literary work. Writing is coherent when the interconnections among clauses, sentences, and paragraphs are clearly and logically related to the main subject under discussion. The writer may establish and maintain coherence through the use of transitional words or phrases (however; likewise), a consistent point of view, an ordered chronological or spatial presentation of information, appropriate pronoun references for nouns, or strategic repetition of important words or sentence structures.

colloquial expressions (*see* **diction**)

conclusion refers to sentences, paragraphs, or longer sections of an essay that bring the work to a logical or psychologically satisfying end. Although a conclusion may (**a**) summarize or restate the essay's main point, and thereby refresh the reader's memory, it may also end with (**b**) the most important point, or (**c**) a memorable example, anecdote, or quotation, or (**d**) identify the broader implications or ultimate development of the subject, or (**e**) offer a prediction. Stylistically, it's best to end with a bang, not a whimper; Lincoln's "Gettysburg Address" (494) concludes with the impressive "... and that government of the people, by the people, for the people, shall not perish from the earth." A vigorous conclusion grows organically from the material that precedes it and is not simply tacked on to get the essay over with.

concrete terms give readers something specific to see, hear, touch, smell, or feel, while abstract terms are more general and intangible. Writers employ concrete words to show their subject or characters in action, rather than merely to tell about them. Yet a concrete word does not have to be hard, like cement; anything directly perceived by the senses is considered concrete, including an ostrich plume, the sound of a harp, a smile, or a cone of cotton candy (*see* **abstract** *and* **general/specific**).

connotation and denotation refer to two levels of interpreting the meanings of words. Denotation is the literal, explicit "core" meaning—the "dictionary" definition. Connotation refers to additional meanings implied or suggested by the word, or associated with it, depending on the user's or reader's personal experience, attitudes, and cultural conditioning. For example, the word *athlete* denotes a skilled participant in a sport. But to a sports enthusiast, *athlete* is likely to connote, as well, physical and moral qualities, such as robust physical condition, well-coordinated movements, a wholesome character, a love of the outdoors, and a concern with fair play. Those disenchanted with sports might regard an *athlete* as a marketable commodity, an overpaid exploiter of the public, a drug user, or someone who has developed every part of his anatomy but his brain—a "dumb jock."

creative nonfiction is writing that employs the techniques of fiction to tell a true story—and which readers regard as true. These techniques include a narrator or narrative voice, plot, characters, dialogue, setting, symbolism; they may be found in autobiography, descriptions of a place or experience, personal-sounding interpretations of phenomena, and social commentary with a human face, a human voice. *See* Amanda Cagle's "On the Banks of the Bogue Chitto" (191–95) and Meredith Hall's "Killing Chickens" (242–45).

diction is word choice. Hemingway was talking about diction when he explained that the reason he allegedly rewrote the last page of *A Farewell to Arms* thirty-nine times was because of problems in "getting the words right." Getting the words right means choosing, arranging, and using words appropriate to the purpose, audience, and sometimes the form of a particular piece of writing. Puns are fine in limericks and shaggy-dog stories ("I wouldn't send a knight out on a dog like this"), but they're out of place in technical reports and obituaries. Diction ranges on a continuum from highly formal (a *repast*) to informal writing and conversation (a *meal*) to slang (*eats*), as illustrated below.

formal English words and grammatical constructions used by educated native speakers of English in sermons, oratory, and in many serious books, scientific reports, and lectures. *See* Abraham Lincoln, "The Gettysburg Address" (494).

informal (conversational or colloquial) *English* the more relaxed but still standard usage in polite (but not stuffy) conversation or writing, as in much popular newspaper writing and in many of the essays in this book. In informal writing it's all right to use contractions ("I'll go to the wedding, but I won't wear tails") and some abbreviations, but not all. OK is generally acceptable in conversation, but it's not OK in most formal or informal writing.

slang highly informal (often figurative) word choice in speech or writing. It may be used by specialized groups (*pot, grass, uppers*) or more general speakers to add vividness and humor (often derogatory) to their language. Although some slang is old and sometimes even becomes respectable (*cab*), it often erupts quickly into the language and just as quickly disappears (*twenty-three skidoo*); it's better to avoid all slang than to use outmoded slang.

regionalisms expressions used by people of a certain region of the country, often derived from the native languages of earlier settlers, such as *arroyo* for *deep ditch* used in the Southwest.

dialect the spoken (and sometimes written) language of a group of people that reflects their social, educational, economic, and geographic status ("My mamma done tole me . . ."). Dialect may include regionalisms. In parts of the Northeast, *youse* is a dialect form of *you*, while its counterpart in the South is *y'all*. Even some educated Southerners say *ain't*, but they don't usually write it except to be humorous.

technical terms (jargon) words used by those in a particular trade, occupation, business, or specialized activity. For example, medical personnel use *stat* (immediately) and *NPO* (nothing by mouth); surfers' vocabularies include *shooting the curl, hotdogging,* and *hang ten; hardware* has different meanings for carpenters and computer users.

emphasis makes the most important ideas, characters, themes, or other elements stand out. The principal ways of achieving emphasis are through the use of the following:

proportion saying more about the major issues and less about the minor ones.

position placing important material in the key spots, the beginning or ends of paragraphs or larger units. Arrangement in climactic order, with the main point of an argument or the funniest joke last, can be particularly effective.

repetition   of essential words, phrases, and ideas ("Ask not what your country can do for you; ask what you can do for your country.")

focus   pruning of verbal underbrush and unnecessary detail to accentuate the main features.

mechanical devices   such as capitalization, underlining (italics), and exclamation points, conveying enthusiasm, excitement, and emphasis, as advertisers and new journalists well know. Tom Wolfe's title *Las Vegas (What?) Las Vegas (Can't Hear You! Too Noisy) Las Vegas!!!!* illustrates this practice, as well as the fact that nothing exceeds like excess.

essay refers to a composition, usually or primarily nonfiction, on a central theme or subject, usually brief and written in prose. As the contents of this book reveal, essays come in varied modes—among them descriptive, narrative, analytic, argumentative—and moods, ranging from humorous to grim, whimsical to bitterly satiric. Essays are sometimes categorized as *formal* or *informal,* depending on the author's content, style, and organization. Formal essays, written in formal language, tend to focus on a single significant idea supported with evidence carefully chosen and arranged, such as Robert Reich's "The Global Elite" (459–66). Informal essays sometimes have a less obvious structure than formal essays; the subject may seem less significant, even ordinary; the manner of presentation casual, personal, or humorous. Yet these distinctions blur. Although E. B. White's "Once More to the Lake" (97–103) discusses a personal experience in conversation and humorous language, its apparently trivial subject, the vacation of a boy and his father in the Maine woods, takes on universal, existential significance. *See* Chapter 1, 5–7.

evidence is supporting information that explains or proves a point. General comments or personal opinions that are not substantiated with evidence usually aren't convincing. Skeptical readers require proof. Writers establish credibility by backing general statements with examples, facts, and figures that make evident their knowledge of the subject. We believe what Martin Luther King, Jr. says about racism and segregation in "Letter from Birmingham Jail" (444–57) because his specific examples show that he has experienced these events and has understood their context and implications.

exposition is a mode of discourse that, as its name indicates, exposes information, through explaining, defining, or interpreting its subject. Expository prose is to the realm of writing what the Ford automobile was historically to the auto industry—useful, versatile, accessible to the average person, and heavy duty—for it is the mode of the most research reports, critical analyses, examination answers, case histories, reviews, and term papers. In exposition, writers employ a variety of techniques, such as definition, illustration, classification, comparison and contrast, analogy, and cause-and-effect reasoning. Exposition is not an exclusive mode; it is often blended with **argumentation, description,** and **narration** to provide a more complete or convincing discussion of a subject.

figures of speech are used by writers who want to make their subject unique or memorable through vivid language. Literal language often lacks the connotations of figurative language. Instead of merely conveying information ("The car was messy"), a writer might use a figure of speech to attract attention

("The car was a Dumpster on wheels"). Figures of speech enable the writer to play with words and with the reader's imagination. Some of the most frequently used figures of speech include the following:

metaphor an implied comparison that equates two things or qualities. "No dictionary of synonyms for **drunk** would soften the anguish of watching our prince turn into a frog" (Scott Russell Sanders).

simile a direct comparison; usually with the connecting word *like* or *as*. ". . . inside [the sawed board] there was this smell waiting, as of something freshly baked" (Scott Russell Sanders).

personification humanization of inanimate or nonhuman objects or qualities, as in giving a car, a boat, or a plane a person's name, nickname, or label (The Katz Meow, The Enola Gay).

hyperbole an elaborate exaggeration, often intended to be humorous or ironic. "When I was younger I could remember anything, whether it had happened or not; but my faculties are decaying now, and soon I shall be so I cannot remember any but the things that never happened" (Mark Twain).

understatement a deliberate downplaying of the seriousness of something. As with the *hyperbole,* the antithesis of understatement, this is often done for the sake of humor or irony. [My "Modest Proposal"] is "innocent, cheap, easy, effectual" (Jonathan Swift).

paradox a contradiction that upon closer inspection is actually truthful. ("You never know what you've got until you lose it.")

rhetorical question a question that demands no answer, asked for dramatic impact. In "Letter from Birmingham Jail" (444–57) Martin Luther King, Jr. asks, "Will we be extremists for hate or for love? Will we be extremists for the preservation of injustice or for the extension of justice?"

metonomy the representation of an object, public office, or concept by something associated with it. ("Watergate brought down the White House, as Woodward and Bernstein explain in *All the President's Men.*")

dead metaphor a word or phrase, originally a figure of speech, that through constant use is treated literally (the *arm* of a chair, the *leg* of a table, the *head* of a bed).

focus represents the writer's control and limitation of a subject to a specific aspect or set of features, determined in part by the subject under discussion (*what* the writer is writing about), the audience (to *whom* the writer is writing), and the purpose (*why* the writer is writing). Thus, instead of writing about food in general, someone writing for college students on limited budgets might focus on imaginative but economical meals.

general and specific are the ends of a continuum that designates the relative degree of abstractness or concreteness of a word. General terms identify the class (*house*); specific terms restrict the class by naming its members (a *Georgian mansion,* a *Dutch colonial,* a *brick ranch*). To clarify relationships, words may be arranged in a series from general to specific: writers, twentieth-century authors, Southern novelists, William Faulkner (*see* **abstract** *and* **concrete**).

generalization (*see* **induction/deduction** *and* **logical fallacies**)

illustrations can be visual works—photographs (the photo essay that follows page 608) drawings (Linda Villarosa, 246–47), cartoons (Istvan Banyai, 264), graphic narratives (Art Spiegelman, 116–17; Lynda Barry, 354–64; Evan Eisenberg, 469). All make a statement or combination of statements through lines and shapes, colors, light and shadow, presence and absence, that can be "read"—sometimes with the addition of captions, thought balloons, or other language. *See* Chapter 1, 11–12. Verbal illustrations, such as anecdotes, examples, analyses, and statistical evidence can work in similar ways to clarify, describe, explain, or argue.

induction and deduction refer to two different methods of arriving at a conclusion. Inductive reasoning relies on examining specific instances, examples, or facts in an effort to arrive at a general conclusion. Conversely, deductive reasoning involves examining general principles in order to arrive at a specific conclusion, *see* 434–38, "Appeal to Reason: Deductive and Inductive Arguments."

introduction is the beginning of a written work that is likely to present the author's subject, focus (perhaps including the thesis), attitude toward it, and possibly the plan for organizing supporting materials. The length of the introduction is usually proportionate to the length of what follows; short essays may be introduced by a sentence or two; a book may require an entire introductory chapter. In any case, an introduction should be sufficiently forceful and interesting to let readers know what is to be discussed and entice them to continue reading. An effective introduction might do one or more of the following:

1. state the thesis or topic;
2. present a controversial or startling focus on the topic;
3. offer a witty or dramatic quotation, statement, metaphor, or analogy;
4. provide background information to help readers understand the subject, its history, or significance;
5. give a compelling anecdote or illustration from real life;
6. refer to an authority on the subject.

irony is a technique that enables the writer to say one thing while meaning another, often with critical intention. Three types of irony are frequently used by writers: *verbal, dramatic,* and *situational.* Verbal irony is expressed with tongue in cheek, often implying the opposite of what is overtly stated. The verbal ironist maintains tight control over tone, counting on the alert reader (or listener) to recognize the discrepancy between words and meaning, as does Jonathan Swift in "A Modest Proposal" (497–503), where deadpan advocacy of cannibalism is really a monstrous proposal. Dramatic irony, found in plays, novels, and other forms of fiction, allows readers to see the wisdom or folly of characters' actions in light of information they have—the ace up their sleeve—that the characters lack. For example, readers know Desdemona is innocent of cheating on her husband, Othello, but his ignorance of the truth and of the behavior of virtuous women leads him to murder her in a jealous rage. Situational irony, life's joke on life, entails opposition between what would ordinarily occur and what actually happens in a particular instance. In O. Henry's "The Gift of the Magi," the husband sells his watch to buy his wife combs for her hair, only to find out she has sold her hair to buy him a watch chain.

jargon (*see* **diction**)

logical fallacies are errors in reasoning and often occur in arguments. *See* "Appeal to Reason: Deductive and Inductive Arguments," introduction (434–38).

metaphor (*see* **figures of speech**)

metonomy (*see* **figures of speech**)

modes of discourse are traditionally identified as narration, description, argumentation, and exposition. In writing they are often intermingled. The *narration* of Frederick Douglass's "Resurrection" (109–13), for instance, involves *description of characters* and settings, an explanation (*exposition*) of their motives, while the expression of its theme serves as an *argument*, direct and indirect. Through its characters, actions, and situations it argues powerfully against slavery.

nonfiction is writing based on fact but shaped by the writer's interpretations, point of view, style, and other literary techniques. Nonfiction writings in essay or book form include interviews, portraits, biographies and autobiographies, travel writings, direct arguments, implied arguments in the form of narratives or satires, investigative reporting, reviews, literary criticism, sports articles, historical accounts, how-to instructions, and scientific and technical reports, among other types. These vary greatly in purpose (to inform, argue, entertain . . .), form, length (from a paragraph to multiple volumes), intended audience (from general readers to specialists), mood (somber to joyous, straightforward to parody), and techniques, including those of fiction—scene setting, characterization, dialogue, and so forth. *The Essay Connection* gives examples of most of these. *See* also Chapter 1, 7–9.

non sequitur a conclusion that does not follow logically from the premises. In humorous writing, the *non sequitur* conclusion is illogical, unexpected, and perhaps ridiculous: the resulting surprise startles readers into laughter—as when George Bernard Shaw's Eliza Dolittle says, upon devouring a chocolate, "I wouldn't have eaten it, but I'm too ladylike to take it out of my mouth."

objective refers to the writer's presentation of material in a personally detached, unemotional way that emphasizes the topic, rather than the author's attitudes or feelings about it as would be the case in a **subjective** presentation. Some process analyses, such as many computer instruction manuals, are written objectively. Many other process writings combine objective information with the author's personal, and somewhat subjective, views on how to do it (*see* the chapter "Process Analysis"). The more heavily emotional the writing, the more subjective it is.

oxymoron a contradiction in terms, such as "study date" or "airline food."

paradox (*see* **figures of speech**)

paragraph has a number of functions. Newspaper paragraphs, which are usually short and consist of a sentence or two, serve as punctuation—visual units to break up columns for ease of reading. A paragraph in most other prose is usually a single unified group of sentences that explain or illustrate a central idea, whether expressed overtly in a topic sentence, or merely implied. Paragraphs emphasize ideas; each new topic (or sometimes each important subtopic) demands a new paragraph. Short (sometimes even one-sentence) paragraphs can provide transitions from one major area of discussion to another, or indicate a change of speakers in dialogue.

parallelism is the arrangement of two or more equally important ideas in similar grammatical form ("I came, I saw, I conquered"). Not only is it an effective method of presenting more than one thought at a time, it also makes reading more understandable and memorable for the reader because of the almost rhythmic quality it produces. Within a sentence parallel structure can exist between words that are paired ("All work and no play made Jack a candidate for cardiac arrest"), items in a series ("His world revolved around debits, credits, cash flows, and profits"), phrases ("Reading books, preparing reports, and dictating interoffice memos—these were a few of his favorite things"), and clauses ("Most people work only to live; Jack lived only to work"). Parallelism can also be established between sentences in a paragraph and between paragraphs in a longer composition, often through the repetition of key words and phrases, as Lincoln does throughout the Gettysburg Address (494).

parallel structure (*see* **parallelism**)

paraphrase is putting someone else's ideas—usually the essential points or illustrations—into your own words, for your own purposes. Although a summary condenses the original material, a paraphrase is a restatement that may be short or as long as the original, even longer. Students writing research papers frequently find that paraphrasing information from their sources eliminates excessive lengthy quotations, and may clarify the originals. Be sure to acknowledge the source of either quoted or paraphrased material to avoid plagiarism.

parody exaggerates the subject matter, philosophy, characters, language, style, or other features of a given author or particular work. Such imitation calls attention to both versions; such scrutiny may show the original to be a masterpiece—or to be in need of improvement. Parody derives much of its humor from the double vision of the subject that writer and readers share, as in Jason Verge's double take on his love affair with the Montreal Canadiens in "The Habs" (119–23).

person is a grammatical distinction made between the speaker (first person—*I, we*), the one spoken to (second person—*you*), and the one spoken about (third person—*he, she, it, they*). In an essay or fictional work the point of view is often identified by person. Chang-rae Lee's "Coming Home Again" (156–64) is written in the first person, while Robert Reich's "The Global Elite" (459–66) is a third-person work (*see* **point of view**).

persona, literally a "mask," is a fictitious mouthpiece or an alter ego character devised by a writer for the purpose of telling a story or making comments that may or may not reflect the author's feelings and attitudes. The persona may be a narrator, as in Swift's "A Modest Proposal" (497–503), whose ostensibly humanitarian perspective advocates cannibalism and regards the poor as objects to be exploited. Swift as author emphatically rejects these views. In such cases the persona functions as a disguise for the highly critical author.

personification (*see* **figures of speech**)

plot is the cause-and-effect relationship among events that tell a story. Unlike narration, which is an ordering of events as they occur, a plot is a writer's plan for showing how the occurrence of these events actually brings about a certain effect. The plot lets the reader see how actions and events are integral parts of something much larger than themselves. See Tim O'Brien's "How to Tell a True War Story" (543–50).

poetry is a compact literary work of compressed meaning, held together by a dominant metrical and sound pattern, imagery, and sometimes rhyme. It is often sensual (Mary Oliver, 190), evocative (V. Penelope Pelizzon, 91–92), lyrical, and intended to provoke thought (Eliza Griswold, 591; Walt Whitman, 594), pleasure (Marilyn Nelson, 131–32), or other emotional reactions—including grief (Seamus Heaney, 541), laughter (Alexander Pope, 290), sympathy (Jenny Spinner, 333–34), anger, and social protest (Martín Espada, 493). *See* Chapter 1, 10–11.

imagery   may include symbols, similes, analogies, and metaphors—all aspects of figurative language whose meaning extends far beyond the literal language and requires the reader to supply many of its connotations. "Our flag," for instance, would mean different flags (or the countries they represent) with different connotations for citizens, friends, and foes of any given nation.

meter   is a rhythmic pattern of unaccented [‿] and accented ['] syllables. The number of feet in a line determines the meter.

foot   is the rhythmic unit within a line of poetry. Standard poetic feet in English are the: iamb (‿'), trochee ('‿), anapest, (‿‿'), dactyl ('‿‿), and spondee. ('').

line   The most common lines in English poetry are trimeter (three feet), tetrameter (four feet), pentameter (five feet), and hexameter (six feet). A sentence in poetry doesn't necessarily end at the end of a line; a sentence in poetry, as in prose, stops when the end punctuation—.,!,?— signals its end. Therefore, when you're reading poetry, let the punctuation—not the poem's shape—tell you where to pause.

point of view   refers to the position—physical, mental, numerical—a writer takes when presenting information (*point*), and his attitude toward the subject (*view*). A writer sometimes adopts a point of view described as "limited," which restricts the inclusion of thoughts other than the narrator's, as Scott Russell Sanders does in "Under the Influence" (249–59). Conversely, the "omniscient" point of view allows the writer to know, see, and tell everything, not only about himself, but about others as well, as Isaac Asimov does in "Those Crazy Ideas" (132–40).

prewriting   is a writer's term for thinking about and planning what to say before the pen hits the legal pad. Reading, observing, reminiscing, and fantasizing can all be prewriting activities if they lead to writing something down. The most flexible stage in the writing process, prewriting enables writers to mentally formulate, compose, edit, and discard before they begin the physical act of putting words on paper. Peter Elbow discusses this in *Writing Without Teachers.*

purpose   identifies the author's reasons for writing. The purposes of a writing are many and varied. One can write to *clarify an issue for oneself,* or to *obtain self-understanding* ("Why I Like to Eat"). One can write to *tell a story,* to *narrate* ("My 1000-Pound Weight Loss"), or to *analyze a process* ("How to Make Quadruple Chocolate Cake"). Writing can explain *cause and effect* ("Obesity and Heart Attacks: The Fatal Connection"); it can *describe* ("The Perfect Meal"), *define* ("Calories"), *divide and classify* ("Fast Food, Slow Food, and Food That Just Sits There"). Writing can *illustrate* through examples ("McDonald's as a Symbol of American Culture"), and it can *compare and contrast* people, things, or ideas. Writing can *argue, deductively* or *inductively*

("Processed Foods Are Packaged Problems"), sometimes appealing more to emotions than to reason ("Anorexia! Beware!"). Writing can also provide *entertainment,* sometimes through parody or satire.

revise to revise is to make changes in focus, accommodation of audience, structure or organization, emphasis, development, style, mechanics, and spelling in order to bring the written work closer to one's ideal. For most writers, revising is the essence of writing. Donald M. Murray discusses the revising process in "The Maker's Eye" (63–71); the chapter "Writing: Re-Vision and Revision" also includes original drafts and revisions of writing by Mary Ruffin for "Mama's Smoke" (76–84).

rhetoric, the art of using language effectively to serve the writer's purpose, originally referred to speech-making. Rhetoric now encompasses composition; its expanded definition includes a host of dynamic relationships between writer (or speaker), text (or message), and readers (or hearers). The information in this book is divided into rhetorical modes, such as exposition, narration, description, and argumentation.

rhetorical question (*see* **figures of speech**)

satire is humorous, witty criticism of people's foolish, thoughtless, or evil behavior. The satirist ridicules some aspect of human nature—or life in general—that should be changed. Depending on the subject and the severity of the author's attack, a satire can be mildly abrasive or ironic, as in Sherman Alexie's "What Sacagawea Means to Me" (93–95) and Evan Eisenberg's "Dialogue Boxes You Should Have Read More Carefully" (469), or viciously scathing, as is Swift in "A Modest Proposal" (497–503). Usually (although not always) the satirist seeks to bring about reform through criticism.

sentence, grammatically defined, is an independent clause containing a subject and verb, and may also include modifiers and related words. *Sentence structure* is another name for *syntax,* the arrangement of individual words in a sentence that shows their relationship to each other. Besides word choice (*diction*), writers pay special attention to the way their chosen words are arranged to form clauses, phrases, entire sentences. A *thesis sentence* (or *statement*) is the main idea in a written work that reflects the author's purpose. Some writings, notably parodies and satires, only imply a thesis; direct arguments frequently provide an explicitly stated thesis, usually near the beginning, and organize subsequent paragraphs around this central thought. A *topic sentence* clearly reflects the major idea and unifying thought of a given paragraph. When it is placed near the beginning of a paragraph, a topic sentence provides the basis for other sentences in the paragraph. When the topic sentence comes at the end of a paragraph or essay, it may function as the conclusion of a logical argument, or the climax of an escalating emotional progression.

short story is a fictional narrative, usually with a *plot* that has a beginning, middle and an end. A story may *emphasize character or character development, embody a theme* (Elizabeth Tallent's "No One's a Mystery," 388–90), *explore an idea* (Tim O'Brien's "How to Tell a True War Story," 543–50), or *express an abstract concept.* Readers accept the characters and events as fictional, even if they appear to be slightly changed versions of reality. *See* Chapter 1, 8–9.

simile (*see* **figures of speech**)

style, the manner in which a writer says what s/he wants to say, as the result of the author's *diction* (word choice) and *syntax* (sentence structure), *arrangement* *of ideas, emphasis,* and *focus.* It is also a reflection of the author's *voice* (personality). Although Ntozake Shange, "What Is It We Really Harvestin' Here? (166–71) and Matt Nocton, "Harvest of Gold, Harvest of Shame" (527–31) both describe farming, the writers' styles differ considerably.

symbol refers to a person, place, thing, idea, or action that represents something other than itself. A dove, for example, can be a symbol of peace, or a peaceable person, or—by extension—an antiwar proponent (even a militant opponent). In Maxine Hong Kingston's "On Discovery" (60–61), the man painfully transformed into a woman symbolizes the denigrated status of all Chinese women.

tone the author's attitude toward a subject being discussed can be serious (Tannen's "Technologically Enhanced Aggression" [297–304]), critical (Kozol's "The Human Cost of an Illiterate Society" [204–11]), or loving (Mary Ruffin's "Mama's Smoke" [76–84]), among many possibilities. Tone lets readers know how they are expected to react to what the writer is saying.

topic sentence (*see* **sentence**)

transition is the writer's ability to move the reader smoothly along the course of ideas. Abrupt changes in topics confuse the reader, but transitional words and phrases help tie ideas together. Stylistically, transition serves another purpose by adding fullness and body to otherwise short, choppy sentences and paragraphs. Writers use transition to show how ideas, things, and events are arranged chronologically (*first, next, after, finally*), spatially (*here, there, next to, behind*), comparatively (*like, just as, similar to*), causally (*thus, because, therefore*), and in opposition to each other (*unlike, but, contrary to*). Pronouns, connectives, repetition, and parallel sentence structure are other transitional vehicles that move the reader along.

understatement (*see* **figures of speech**)

voice refers to the extent to which the writer's personality is expressed in his or her work. In *personal voice,* the writer appears to be on fairly intimate terms with the audience, referring to herself as "I" and the readers as "you." In *impersonal voice,* the writer may refer to himself as "one" or "we," or try to eliminate personal pronouns when possible. Formal writings, such as speeches, research papers, and sermons, are more likely to use an impersonal voice than are more informal writings, such as personal essays. In grammar, *voice* refers to the form of a verb: *active* ("I *mastered* the computer") or *passive* ("The computer *was mastered* by me").

CREDITS

Texts and Graphic Essays

NATALIE ANGIER, "Why Men Don't Last: Self-Destruction as a Way of Life," *New York Times,* 2/17/99. Copyright © 1999 Natalie Angier. Reprinted by permission of the author.

KOFI ANNAN, "The United Nations in the 21st Century," from Nobel Prize Speech, 2001. Copyright © The Nobel Foundation. Reprinted with permission.

YASSER ARAFAT, "The Crescent Moon of Peace" from Nobel Prize Speech. Copyright © The Nobel Foundation. Reprinted with permission.

GELAREH ASAYESH, "Shrouded in Contradiction." Copyright © 2001 by Gelareh Asayesh. First appeared in the *New York Times Magazine,* 11/2/01. Reprinted by permission of the author.

ISAAC ASIMOV, "Those Crazy Ideas," copyright © 1959 by Mercury Press from *Fact and Fancy* by Isaac Asimov. Used by permission of Doubleday, a division of Random House, Inc.

AUNG SAN SUU KYI, "The Revolution of Spirit" from Nobel Prize Speech, 1991. Copyright © The Nobel Foundation. Reprinted with permission.

LYNDA BARRY, "Common Scents," copyright © 2002 by Lynda Barry from *One! Hundred! Demons!* Reprinted courtesy of Darhansoff Verrill Feldman Literary agents. All rights reserved.

WENDELL BERRY, "Thoughts in the Presence of Fear" originally appeared in OrionOnline .org's "Thoughts on America Series" and was published subsequently in the book, *In the Presence of Fear: Three Essays for a Changed World* (December, 2001). Reprinted by permission of the author.

SUZANNE BRITT, "That Lean and Hungry Look," *Newsweek* 1978. Reprinted by permission of the author.

AMANDA N. CAGLE, "On the Banks of the Bogue Chitto" from *The Ontario Review,* Spring 2005. Reprinted by permission of the author.

JIMMY CARTER, from Nobel Prize Speech, 2002. Copyright © The Nobel Foundation. Reprinted with permission.

STEPHANIE COONTZ, "Blaming the Family for Economic Decline" from *The Way We Really Are.* Copyright © 1997 Basic Books, A Division of HarperCollins Publishers Inc. Reprinted by permission of Basic Books, a member of Perseus Books, L.L.C.

THE 14TH DALAI LAMA, TENZIN GYATSO, "Inner Peace and Human Rights" from Nobel Prize Speech, 1989. Copyright © The Nobel Foundation. Reprinted with permission.

FREDERIK WILLEM DE KLERK, "Reformation and Reconciliation in South Africa" from Nobel Prize Speech, 1993. Copyright © The Nobel Foundation. Reprinted with permission.

EVAN EISENBERG, "Dialogue Boxes You Should Have Read More Carefully." This selection first appeared in the *New York Times.* Copyright © 2004 by Evan Eisenberg. Reprinted by permission of the author.

MARTÍN ESPADA, "The Community College Revises its Curriculum in Response to Changing Demographics," from *Alabanza* by Martín Espada. Copyright © 2003 by Martín Espada. Used by permission of W. W. Norton & Company, Inc.

ANNE FADIMAN, "Under Water" originally appeared in *The New Yorker.* Copyright © 1999 Anne Fadiman. Reprinted by permission of Lescher & Lescher, Ltd. All rights reserved.

LAURIE FENDRICH, "History Overcomes Stories" from *Chronicle of Higher Education,* Sept. 28, 2001. Copyright © 2001 Laurie Fendrich. Used by permission of the author.

HOWARD GARDNER, "Who Owns Intelligence?" Copyright © 1999 by Howard Gardner. Reprinted by permission of the author.

RIGOBERTA MENCHÚ TUM, "Five Hundred Years of Mayan Oppression" from Nobel Prize Speech, 1992. Copyright © The Nobel Foundation. Reprinted with permission.

SHERRY TURKLE, "How Computers Change the Way We Think," *Chronicle of Higher Education* 30, January 2004. Reprinted by permission of the author.

MARK TWAIN, "Uncle John's Farm" first appeared in *North American Review*, 1906–1907.

ABRAHAM VERGHESE, "Code Blue: The Story" is reprinted with the permission of Simon & Schuster Adult Publishing Group from *My Own Country* by Abraham Verghese. Copyright © 1994 by Abraham Verghese.

E. B. WHITE, "Once More to the Lake" from *One Man's Meat*, text copyright © 1941 by E. B. White. Copyright renewed. Reprinted by permission of Tilbury House, Publishers, Gardiner, Maine.

ELIE WIESEL, "Why I Write: Making No Become Yes." Copyright © 1985 by Elirion Associates. Reprinted by permission Georges Borchardt, Inc. Originally appeared in *The New York Times Book Review*, 4/14/85.

BETTY WILLIAMS, "The Movement of the Peace People," from Nobel Prize Speech, 1976. Copyright © The Nobel Foundation. Reprinted with permission.

W. B. YEATS, Four lines from "The Choice" are reprinted with the permission of Scribner, an imprint of Simon & Schuster Adult Publishing Group, from *The Collected Works Of W. B. Yeats, Volume 1: The Poems, Revised,* edited by Richard J. Finneran. Copyright © 1933 by The Macmillan Company; copyright renewed © 1961 by Bertha Georgie Yeats.

ZITKALA-SA, from *The School Days of an Indian Girl, Atlantic Monthly,* February, 1900. Copyright © 1900 Atlantic Monthly.

Photographs and Illustrations

p.1: © Royalty-Free/CORBIS. p. 24: © Brian Steidle. p. 30: © Bettmann/CORBIS. p. 49: © Peter Beavis/Taxi/Getty Images. p. 56: © Ed Bock. p. 70: Calvin and Hobbes © 1993 Watterson. Distributed by Universal Press Syndicate. Reprinted with permission. All Rights Reserved. p. 73: © George Shelley/CORBIS. p. 85: © J. Clarke/Taxi/Getty Images. p. 94: Courtesy Special Collections, American Museum of Natural History. p. 101: © Randy Wells/CORBIS. p. 105: © Don Seabrook, The Wenatchee World/AP Wide World Photos. p. 111: © Bettmann/CORBIS. p. 126: © Bojan Brecelj/CORBIS. p. 157: © Mark Leong/Redux Pictures. p. 176: © Stephanie Maze/CORBIS. p. 185: © David Turnley/CORBIS. p. 193: © David Muench/Stone/Getty Images. p. 199: © CORBIS. p. 214: © Walker Evans/CORBIS. p. 235: © Tee and Charles Addams Foundation. p. 255: © AP/Wide World Photos. p. 264: © Istvan Banyai. p. 285: © *The New Yorker* Collection 2000 Roz Chast from cartoonbank.com. All Rights Reserved. p. 300: © Larry Williams/CORBIS. p. 311: © Bob Daemmrich/The Image Works. p. 319: © Reuters Newsmedia/CORBIS. p. 328: © Michael Keller/CORBIS. p. 337: © Peter Johnson/CORBIS. p. 369: © ER Productions/CORBIS. p. 409: © Rudi Von Briel/PhotoEdit, Inc. p. 419: © Daniel Lee "Twins" 2004. p. 433: © Gordon Parks/CORBIS. p. 445: © Bettmann/CORBIS. p. 472: © Stan Honda/AFP/Getty Images. p. 488: © Tischler Fotografen./Peter Arnold, Inc. p. 495: © Bettmann/CORBIS. p. 506: © David Eulitt, Topeka Capital-Journal/AP Wide World Photos. p. 520: © Chris O'Meara/AP Wide World Photos. p. 535: © Alex Fuchs/AP Wide World Photos. p. 552: © Suzanne Plunkett/AP Wide World Photos. p. 584: © Al Grillo/AP Wide World Photos. p. 592: © Doug Kanter/AFP/Getty Images. p. 614: © NTB/AP Wide World Photos. p. 619: © David Van Der Veen/AFP/Getty Images.

Photo Essay

p. 2: © Joe Rosenthal/AP Wide World Photos. p. 3: © Thomas Franklin/Courtesy Ground Zero Spirit and North Jersey Media Group. p. 4: Fritz Scholder lithograph, "Bicentennial Indian" from "Spirit of Independence." Des Moines Art Center Permanent Collections; Gift of Lorillard, New York, 1975.40.12. p. 5: © Kevin Fleming/CORBIS. p. 6: © Scott Peterson/Getty Images. p. 7: © Gurinder Osan/AP Wide World Photos. p. 8: © Miguel de Casenave.

INDEX OF AUTHORS

❀ *Student writings.*